STANISLAVSKY
A LIFE IN LETTERS

Konstantin Stanislavsky transformed theatre in the West and was indisputably one of the twentieth century's greatest innovators. His life and work mark some of the most significant artistic and political milestones of a tumultuous age, from the emancipation of the serfs to the Russian Revolution. Little wonder, then, that his correspondence contains gripping exchanges with the famous and infamous of his day: men such as Tolstoy, Chekhov, Trotsky and Stalin, among others.

Laurence Senelick, one of the world's foremost scholars of Russian theatre, mines the Moscow archives and the definitive Russian edition of Stanislavsky's letters, to produce the fullest collection of the letters in any language other than Russian. He sheds new light on this fascinating field. Senelick takes us from the earliest extant letter of an eleven-year-old Konstantin in 1874, through his work as actor, director and actor trainer with the Moscow Art Theatre, to messages written just before his death in 1938 at the age of seventy-five.

We discover Stanislavsky as son, brother and father, as lover and husband, as businessman and 'internal émigré'. He is seen as a wealthy tourist and an impoverished touring actor, a privileged subject of the Tsar and a harried victim of the Bolsheviks.

Senelick shares key insights into Stanislavsky's work on such important productions as *The Seagull*, *The Cherry Orchard*, *Hamlet*, *Othello*, and *The Marriage of Figaro*. The letters also reveal the steps that led up to the publication of his writings *My Life in Art* and *An Actor's Work on Himself*. This handsome edition is also comprehensively annotated and fully illustrated.

Laurence Senelick is Fletcher Professor of Drama at Tufts University and a Fellow of the American Academy of Arts and Sciences. His many books include *Russian Dramatic Theory from Pushkin to the Symbolists*; *Gordon Craig's Moscow Hamlet*; *The Chekhov Theatre: A Century of the Plays in Performance*; and *A Historical Dictionary of Russian Theatre*. He has been awarded the St George medal of the Russian Ministry of Culture for contributions to Russian art and scholarship.

STANISLAVSKY
A LIFE IN LETTERS

Selected, translated and edited by

Laurence Senelick

Routledge
Taylor & Francis Group

LONDON AND NEW YORK

First published 2014
by Routledge
2 Park Square, Milton Park, Abingdon, Oxon OX14 4RN

and by Routledge
711 Third Avenue, New York, NY 10017

Routledge is an imprint of the Taylor & Francis Group, an informa
business

British Library Cataloguing in Publication Data
A catalogue record for this book is available from the British Library

Library of Congress Cataloguing in Publication Data
A catalog record for this title has been requested

ISBN: 978-0-415-51667-9 (hbk)
ISBN: 978-0-415-51668-6 (pbk)
ISBN: 978-0-203-12409-3 (ebk)

Typeset in Goudy
by Saxon Graphics Ltd, Derby

Printed and bound in Great Britain by
CPI Group (UK) Ltd, Croydon, CR0 4YY

CONTENTS

ILLUSTRATIONS

All illustrations come from the Moscow Art Theatre Museum or the collection of Laurence Senelick, and are used with their permission.

ACKNOWLEDGEMENTS

First and foremost, I should like to thank Anatoly Smeliansky, Rector of the Moscow Art Theatre School, who has, from its inception, supported this project with advice, suggestions, elucidations and introductions. He and his staff, along with the curators of the Moscow Art Theatre Museum, have been most helpful. The Art Theatre has granted me full permission to use any of its holdings, including all transcripts of Stanislavsky's writings, and to quote from any of its publications.

Trans/Script, The Mikhail Prokhorov Fund for Translation from the Russian, bestowed a generous subsidy on the project, which enabled me to complete it efficiently. A research grant from Tufts University was also useful in procuring materials.

The Routledge Stanislavsky edition, first mooted in the 1980s, brought together a number of experts who have remained friends and colleagues ever since. On the Russian side, it included Smeliansky and Inna Solovyova; the English-speaking world was represented by the late Jean Benedetti and the American Stanislavskian Sharon Carnicke. The American editors for Routledge John von Knorring and Bill Germano were highly supportive before the project was taken over by the British office. My editors there, Talia Rodgers, Sam Kinchin-Smith and Ben Piggott, welcomed the idea of this book as soon as it was suggested, and cheered it on to its conclusion.

LS

The publication was effected under the auspices of the Mikhail Prokhorov Foundation Trans/Script Programme to Support Translations of Russian Literature

Supporting the translation of Russian literature

transcript

PREFACE

The first biography in English of Konstantin Sergeevich Alekseev, David Magarshack's *Stanislavsky: A Life* (1951), devoted 346 pages to his life prior to the Revolution, and only sixty-eight to the remaining twenty years. This is understandable, since it was expected that a postwar English reader would be most interested in Stanislavsky's formative years and the foundation and development of the Moscow Art Theatre at the time when it counted Chekhov and Gorky as its collaborators. This has in fact remained the focus of most studies in English of the man and the theatre since Magarshack.

Magarshack's emphasis was also the natural result of his sources. These were, for the most part, the first English edition of Stanislavsky's *My Life in Art* (1923) and its Russian revision (1925), made with a Soviet reader in mind. Magarshack paraphrased at length the autobiography, whose coverage ends around the time of the Revolution, and supplemented it with excerpts from letters, speeches and memoirs from various Soviet anthologies. This was problematic. Publications on Stanislavsky issued in the USSR in the 1930s, 1940s and 1950s suppressed and airbrushed events, persons and ideas (Nikolay Gorchakov's book *Stanislavsky Directs* was largely fabricated). Stanislavsky's unfinished writings on acting were edited to support the Socialist Realist approach to his system taught in Soviet drama schools.

The death of Stalin in 1953 failed to loosen the censor's grip on historical documentation. The Soviet eight-volume edition of Stanislavsky's works which appeared between 1954 and 1961 was heavily expurgated; the letters, which appeared in the last two volumes, were filleted to create a Pollyannic picture of Stanislavsky's activities and attitudes. Materials expressing discontent or depression were deleted; the Socialist Realist nature of his system was affirmed; and the stormy course of his relationship with Nemirovich-Danchenko erased. As a result, Stanislavsky continued to emit the saintly glow cast on him by Communist hagiography.

The short-lived cultural 'Thaw' that followed had contradictory effects. Since the epistolary volumes of the Stanislavsky edition appeared in the years following Khrushchev's denunciation of Stalin, Stanislavsky's appeals to the General Secretary were either omitted or their addressee diminished to some lesser member of the *apparat*. The danger in correcting the iconic image of Stanislavsky was made clear in 1962 when S. S. Podolsky published in the scholarly journal *Istorichesky Arkhiv* (*Historical Archive*) eighteen letters passed between Stanislavsky and Nemirovich during a particularly turbulent period of their partnership. Although the letters appeared with the blessing of the Art Theatre Museum, their publication was denounced by leading critics and artists, Podolsky was demoted, and *Istorichesky Arkhiv* was immediately shut down.

Over time, however, as the archives yielded up more treasures, their circulation was met with little or no controversy. I. Vinogradskaya's four-volume chronicle of Stanislavsky's life (1971–76) quoted an abundance of unpublished documents, if only in excerpted form. She still had to be cautious; only in her second edition, issued in 2003, could the entries on the Soviet era be massively amplified.

When Jean Benedetti came to write his *Stanislavski* (1988), he was able to draw on Vinogradskaya, as well as a new Russian biography by Yelena Polyakova and a number of post-Thaw monographs on various aspects of Stanislavsky's career. Benedetti's emphases differed from Magarshack's: 222 pages lead up to the Revolution and 104 cover the remaining score of years. This is because Benedetti was particularly interested in the development of the System and its codification as it had evolved over the last two decades of Stanislavsky's life. Benedetti's Stanislavsky was almost exclusively a man of the theatre. His portrait was a close-up: there was minimal background detail to limn Stanislavsky's family, colleagues or cultural ambience. The social and political context played almost no part in his narrative.

Benedetti also had to rely on the fallacious *Selected Works*. The 887 letters represented in that edition were often excerpted to a few lines or paragraphs. When a new, less tendentious and more complete edition of Stanislavsky's writings was published in ten volumes between 1988 and 1991 under the editorship of a team headed by the Art Theatre's artistic director Oleg Yefremov and its literary manager Anatoly Smeliansky, the number of letters had grown to 1,460. These included messages to such previously unmentionable figures as Stalin, Trotsky and Yagoda, as well as those to his family circle, which had been in the possession of his granddaughter, resident in Paris. This wealth of fresh material, offered with almost no cuts, cast new light on the man and his achievements.

Although the Russian editors had made Herculean efforts to bring together as many letters as they could, a large number still exist in private hands or in repositories outside of Russia. Just as this book was going into production, a cache of fifty-five letters and notes to Elizabeth Reynolds Hapgood turned up in the possession of her family. With a correspondent as conscientious and diligent as Stanislavsky, the word 'complete' will always be relative. He was an assiduous correspondent and only in his later years relied on amanuenses to take dictation or transcribe his scribbling to a typewriter. Often he will apologize for torn paper, writing with a pencil or poor penmanship, for he regarded letter-writing as a bounden duty and the most exact way to convey his thoughts.

Editorial Principles

I have chosen a wide range of letters to illustrate the multi-dimensional nature of Stanislavsky's life. A great many of these letters are printed in their entirety; but in most cases I have been mindful to extract salient passages, those most revelatory of Stanislavsky's character, most informative about the cultural, theatrical and political life of his time, or most entertaining. Much of the omitted material deals with matters of health, which obsessed Stanislavsky and his family. Other excisions are of salutation and apologies, references to distant relatives or minor acquaintances. In every case I have preserved the salutation and the sign-off, because they are very revelatory of the correspondent's attitude towards his addressee. A whole gamut is run between 'Most esteemed' and 'Dearestdearie'. (Occasionally the signature is missing, probably sheared off for autograph hunters.)

At certain points, I have included passages from Stanislavsky's journals, diaries and drafts of letters. This is especially the case in the early years when there is a paucity of extant correspondence to reveal his artistic development. During the immediate post-Revolutionary period, when correspondence is scant owing to an irregular postal service and paper shortages, I have lifted passages from the Art Theatre daily reports, to which Stanislavsky frequently contributed.

Ellipses within brackets [...] indicate editorial deletions. Ellipses without brackets ... are Stanislavsky's.

The dates on the letters and in the commentary are old style, of the Julian calendar, prior to the Revolution, and new style, of the Gregorian calendar, after it. Often Stanislavsky, especially when abroad, used both. There is a twelve-day difference between the two styles of dating.

In my commentary and notes, I use abbreviations for the most frequent names: KS for Stanislavsky, ND for Nemirovich-Danchenko, and MAT for the Moscow Art Theatre. Other abbreviations and acronyms are listed separately.

Translation

Stanislavsky had great difficulty in devising a vocabulary for his evolving system of acting. He had recourse to psychologists and scientists for some of his technical language, but customarily tailored their terminology to his own needs. When Elizabeth Reynolds Hapgood made the first English translation of *An Actor Works on Himself*, she was inconsistent in her renderings and often made choices that were more euphonious than accurate. Since Stanislavsky could not read English, he could not pass judgment on terms such as 'superobjective' which became current in Anglophone acting training. In his retranslations, Jean Benedetti made other choices without effacing the traditional ones; and thoughtful commentators, such as Sharon Carnicke and Bella Merlin, have offered their own suggestions.

For the purposes of this work, I have sometimes adopted earlier usages and sometimes stuck to a closer rendition of the Russian original. So: for *sverkhzadacha* I have 'supertask', rather than 'superobjective', since *zadacha*, meaning task or problem, as in mathematics, is something to be carried out or solved, rather than achieved. *Yesli by* (literally, 'as if' or 'if only') becomes simply 'if'. For *voploshchenie*, which in Russian has the same religious overtones as 'incarnation', I prefer the more secular 'embodiment', since Stanislavsky's editors were sedulous in stripping his text of devotional terms. For *priposoblenie*, which is often translated as 'adaptation', I have chosen 'adjustment' because it refers to the way in which an actor adjusts to the given circumstances (*predlagaemye obstoyatelstva*) of a stage situation. *Samochuvstvie*, which appears in Russian-English dictionaries, as 'general attitude', is, for Stanislavsky, the attitude the actor must adopt when coming on stage and when inhabiting a character; although often Stanislavsky takes it to mean 'self-assurance' or even 'stage presence' I have gone for the very literal 'sense of self'. *Kusok*, transformed by Hapgood into 'unit', here is simply 'bit'. There is general agreement about how to translate subtext (*podtekst*) and through action (*skvoznoe deistvie*).

The trickiest of all these terms and the most frequent is *perezhivanie*. This is straightforward Russian for 'experience', although the word breaks down etymologically to suggest 'reliving' or 'living through' an experience. Stanislavsky infuses it with the special sense of recreating a feeling or an action, as if for the first time, in each performance. I at first adopted 'emotional experience', suggested by Maria Shevtsova, but, following a modification by Sharon Carnicke, expanded it to 'emotional experiencing'.

Transliteration

I have tried to use a system that is easily apprehended by an English-speaking reader, without introducing too many extra letters.

Initial E appears as Ye. Initial Э appears as E. Final э appears as é.

Final ий and ый appear as y. и or й within a word appears as i.

The soft and hard signs ь and ъ are suppressed. When a soft sign follows a consonant within a name (e.g., Vasil'ev, Leont'ev), it appears as an i (e.g., Vasiliev, Leontiev).

When a name is already familiar to the English-speaking reader through an accepted transliteration, such as Meyerhold, Tchaikovsky and Rachmaninov, I have retained that spelling.

Whenever Stanislavsky had occasion to sign his stage name in Roman letters, he signed it Stanislavsky. That is also the form in which it appears in all English-language publicity issued by the Moscow Art Theatre during and after his lifetime, and in the first edition of his autobiography. The Franco-Polish spelling 'Stanislavski' was, for some reason, preferred by Elizabeth Reynolds Hapgood and so was used by Theatre Arts Books when it issued his later writings in English. However, it has no authority.

The same holds true for the current British habit of referring to the Moskovsky Khudozhestvenny Teatr as the 'Moscow Arts Theatre', as if it were a playhouse in Hampstead. From 1920 to the present day the MAT has always called itself in English the Moscow Art Theatre.

ABBREVIATIONS AND ACRONYMS

AC	Alekseev Circle
AKTEO	Central Theatrical Division of the Chief Artistic Committee of the Academic Center of Narkompros (Tsentralnaya teatral'naya sektsiya Glavnogo khudozhestvennogo komiteta Akademicheskogo tsentra Narkomprosa)
GABT	Gosudarstvenny Akademichesky Bolshoy Teatr (State Academic Bolshoy Theatre)
Glavrepertkom	Chief Committee for the Inspection of the Repertoire of Narkompros (Glavny komitet po kontrolyu za repertuarom Narkomprosa)
K.O.	Kamernaya Opera, The Chamber Opera, alternative name for the MAT Musical Studio
KS	Konstantin Stanislavsky
MAT	Moscow Art Theatre (Moskovsky Khudozhestvenny Teatr)
MAAT	Moscow Art Academic Theatre (Moskovsky Khudozhestvenny Akademichesky Teatr)
MChK	Moskovskaya Chrezchainaya Komissiya (Moscow Emergency Commission) or Cheka, the secret police
MOUNI	Moskovskoe oblastnoe upravlenie nedvizhimosti (Moscow Regional Directorate of Housing and Real Estate)
Narkom	People's Commissar/iat (Narodny komissar)
Narkompros	People's Commissariat of Enlightenment (Narodny komissariat prosveshcheniya)
ND	Vladimir Nemirovich-Danchenko
n.s.	new style
OGPU	Unified State Political Directorate (Obedinyonnoe politicheskoe upravlenie)
o.s.	old style
Proletkult	All-Russian Central Committee of Proletarian Cultural-Enlightenment Organizations (Vserossiysky tsentralny komitet proletarskikh kulturno-prosvetitelnykh organizatsiy)

RAPP	Russian Proletarian Writers' Association (Rossiyskaya assotsiatsiya proletarskikh pisateley)
Repertkom	Repertoire Committee (Repetuarny komitet)
TEO	Theatrical Department of Narkompros (Teatralny otdel Narkomprosa)
TsEKUBU	Central Committee for the Improvement of Scholars' Daily Lives (Tsentralny Kommissiya po uluchshenemu byta uchyonykh)
TsIK	Central Executive Committee (Tsentralny ispolnitelny komitet)
VKhUTEMAS	Higher Artistic-Technical Workshops (Vysshie khudozhestvenno-tekhnicheskie masterskie)

Introduction

STANISLAVSKY

The missionary in the theatre

In a Man's Letters you know, Madam, his soul lies naked, his letters are only the mirrour of his breast, whatever passes within him is shown undisguised in its natural process.

Dr Johnson to Mrs Thrale, 1777

I

In 1940 at the Martinique nightclub in New York, the comedian Danny Kaye introduced a novelty song by his wife Sylvia Fine. It was called 'Stanislavsky'. Sung in the character of a Russian actor, it explained he had been taught by the illustrious director the 'mental pyrotechnics' which allowed him to 'suffer'. He was urged to

Be a tree, be a sled,
Be a purple spool of thread,
Be a storm, a piece of lace,
A subway car, an empty space.

Kaye's success with this number led to his hit the next year in the musical *Lady in the Dark* reciting the names of forty-six Russian composers in thirty-eight seconds. But how familiar could Stanislavsky and his ideas on acting have been in 1940, even to a sophisticated Broadway crowd? It would be another decade before the 'Method' of Lee Strasberg and the Actors Studio became common currency, owing to the notoriety of Marlon Brando and his epigones. That Stanislavsky's name already implied outré rehearsal-room exercises suggests its circulation in American popular culture, even if what he stood for is burlesqued for comic effect.

Until their tours of 1922–23, Stanislavsky and the Moscow Art Theatre were largely unknown in the English-speaking world, except for the occasional mention in professional journals. When Prof. Brander Matthews of Columbia University published a series of papers on acting in 1914, he included only luminaries from the Western European and Anglo-American orbit, such as Henry Irving, Constant Coquelin and William Gillette. Of course, Stanislavsky had not yet transcribed his ideas on acting in any organized way; he deplored the attempts of others to do so, groaning at what he saw as perversion of still inchoate concepts.

He had neither the will nor the time to frame his concepts for publication. Only his performances and those of his troupe could testify to their efficacy.

The tours made all the difference. The productions themselves, though often of work ten to fifteen years old, and the attendant publicity put Stanislavsky and his pronouncements on acting centre stage. Émigré Russian actors, displaced by the Revolution and unable to find work abroad, found that they could make a living by teaching their version of 'Stanislavsky'. The Group Theatre in New York devoted itself to his precepts, even as they wrangled over their details. Consequently, the US was Mecca for the Stanislavskian approach outside of the Soviet Union. England saw only the stagings of the breakaway Prague Group of the MAT and did not begin to respond to Stanislavsky's spell until an adaptation of his acting lessons appeared in English in the late 1930s. Still, he had by this time become sufficiently recognized to be commissioned to write the article on 'Acting' for the *Encyclopædia Britannica*. His name was now synonymous with a modern approach to acting. Just as those who had never read Freud could bandy about such terms as 'sublimation' and 'castration anxiety', so those who had scant acquaintance with Stanislavsky's life and work prattled of 'subtext', 'the superobjective' and 'the magic if'.

Prior to Stanislavsky, every famous actor who made pronouncements about his profession was, indeed, a professional. The celebrities whom Prof Matthews enlisted for his series had taken the usual route: either graduates of conservatories who entered a state-subsidized national theatre or case-hardened players who had learned their trade on the road and eventually in the commercial theatre. Stanislavsky was a glaring exception. He was essentially an amateur who despised dilettantism and what passed for 'professionalism' in equal measure. Largely self-taught through practice, imitation and observation, he chose not to rely on the tried-and-true conventions of the stage. At the same time, he loved the truly theatrical, the surprises and revelations that sprang from the creative imagination. 'Art' (*iskusstvo*) was the touchstone of his aspirations. He soon associated it with 'Truth'. It was the Holy Grail of all his experiments and achievements.

In this respect, Stanislavsky was firmly in the Russian cultural tradition. Throughout the nineteenth century, writers and thinkers extolled art as a means of national advancement. Poetry, music, painting, and, yes, theatre would elevate the benighted masses from their uncivilized state; the average individual would become refined and spiritually uplifted; and society would make rapid progress. Stanislavsky's theatrical ethics derived directly from Mikhail Shchepkin, for one of his few acting teachers was Shchepkin's last pupil, the actress Fedotova. An emancipated serf who had died the year Stanislavsky was born, Shchepkin extolled the theatre's progressive mission, for his acting career had been the agent of his manumission and eventual admission to a position of respect and responsibility. Therefore, the theatre was to be venerated as a Temple and its servants as votaries of enlightenment. The Russian actor had a civic duty to embody progressive ideals both in his private life and in his public persona. He had a social obligation to be a cultured human being. What he did on stage had to go beyond mere entertainment or cliché claptrap to serve a higher goal.

Stanislavsky, however, moved beyond a purely didactic or exemplary role for the theatre. He elevated Art and the truth to be found in art to a surrogate religion, even at times a surrogate life. By insisting on perfection, he tried to use the walls of the playhouse to insulate him from the compromises, vagaries and disappointments of the mundane. His constant search for an unfailing source of creative inspiration was motivated by this need to compensate for human failings. This was bound to meet with disappointment, for theatre is a synthetic art; its medium is human beings and its products result from collaboration. Hence the intense ups and downs of Stanislavsky's reactions to work in the theatre, and his gradual withdrawal to small-scale experimentation with limited groups of malleable actors.

Attentive to the fibrillations of his moods, Stanislavsky was sedulous in recording his own slow progress towards excellence as an actor. His earliest motives for appearing on stage were those common to all amateurs: the chance to show off to one's friends and relatives and receive an immediate (and favourable) response. He preferred roles that raised laughs or employed interesting costumes and makeup or allowed him to create an effect. At first he copied actors he had seen; but, without formal training, he soon discovered the need to teach himself the rudiments. Since his family background barred entry into the profession, despite invitations to do so, his experience had to be gained on the amateur stage before a coterie public. The opportunities offered by the Society for Art and Literature were a mixed blessing. The disadvantages of unpolished colleagues, uncritical audiences and primitive rehearsal conditions were offset by the ability to play a wide variety of leading roles and impose his own ideas without the pressures of box-office or managers. He could also avoid the perils of routine that might lead to rote performances.

With the foundation of the Moscow Art Theatre Stanislavsky was enabled to 'go pro' without actually doing so. In tune with the times, the enterprise professed a socially beneficial purpose, the introduction of carefully-staged classical drama to the underprivileged. When this turned out to be financially impossible, it became a joint stock company and it audiences were drawn from the educated classes; but its founders staunchly refused, at least in principle, to be guided by commercial concerns. From the first, the beacon was art with a capital A. Indeed, that word in the theatre's name – *khudozhestvenny*, 'artistic' – was a neologism of the 1880s and might more accurately be rendered 'aesthetic'.

Although Stanislavsky shared the duties of stage director with his co-founder Vladimir Nemirovich-Danchenko, he continued to play leading roles. He preferred character parts, in which he could lose himself in behavioural traits and heavy makeups. Cast in contemporary parts of ordinary men, he would protest that all he might do was play himself. Typically, when asked to take on Dr Dorn in *The Seagull*, he invented a caricatural old beau, which led to his being reassigned the role of Trigorin. Typically too, his interpretation of the commonplace writer as an elegant seducer struck Chekhov as an irritating misreading. Stanislavsky also tended to turn down parts of proletarians and peasants. The most famous example is his

3

refusal to create Lopakhin, the enriched muzhik in *The Cherry Orchard*, even though Chekhov had written it with him in mind. Instead, he chose the feckless aristocrat Gaev, thereby upsetting the dramatic balance of the comedy.

Poetic drama also seemed outside his range: he never managed to speak Pushkin's blank verse satisfactorily. His pre-MAT *Othello* had been an ethnological study of an Arab; he hated playing Brutus and relinquished Hamlet to Vasily Kachalov. With the entry of the velvety-voiced Kachalov into the troupe, Stanislavsky no longer needed to assume the romantic leads, visionary heroes or tormented intellectuals. Early on, they might share such a part (Kareno in *The Drama of Life*); but soon it was Kachalov as Ivanov, Brand, Chatsky, Rubek, Ivan Karamazov. Stanislavsky gravitated more and more towards comedy, making great successes of Ibsen's Dr Stockmann, Turgenev's Count Lubin, Ostrovsky's General Krutitsky, Molière's Argan and Goldoni's Cavaliere di Ripafratta.

When, at the Society of Art and Literature, the duties of a stage director first devolved upon Stanislavsky, that function was still ill-defined. Traditionally the responsibility of the stage manager or the prompter, it chiefly involved arranging entrances and exits, sorting out traffic patterns and composing stage pictures. Actors were left to their own devices, memorizing their lines at home or relying on prompts. Rehearsals were few, held in unheated, badly lit spaces. The more skilled or experienced the actors, the more could be entrusted to them; so that an 'ensemble' was often a pleiad of stars emitting individual lustre rather than an integrated company working towards a single end.

Stanislavsky's eyes were opened to a new concept in directing when he beheld the troupe of the Duke of Saxe-Meiningen, on tour to Russia in 1890. Under the tight control of its Intendant, Ludwig Cronegk, it presented a repertoire of classics in productions noteworthy for historical accuracy in scenery and costuming, well-drilled crowd scenes, picturesque groupings and atmospheric lighting. Even when directing light opera and contemporary plays, Stanislavsky adopted a similar approach. In the capacity of what he later described as the 'dictatorial' director, he took charge of every aspect of the staging and issued strict instructions for gesture, movement, and vocal intonation. He devised the ground-plan, organized the blocking and prescribed the lighting and special effects. The Meininger technique could produce impressive results when imposed on society players, whose crowd scenes were often recruited from unruly university students. At this period, these drill-like practices would have been strongly resisted by a professional troupe not under court supervision.

To avoid the ham acting and stereotypes of the professional stage, the first actors to be enlisted into the Art Theatre were either veteran amateurs or recent graduates of the Philharmonic's dramatic courses, with the reluctant admixture of a few provincial notables. What they lacked in star quality they made up for in freshness and pliability. Moreover, they were touted as being educated, well-bred and of impeccable private lives, unlike the bohemian rogues and vagabonds of common repute. The Meininger method served them well in the Art Theatre's first seasons, but only to a point. A blank-verse chronicle of early Muscovy, such as Aleksey Tolstoy's *Tsar Fyodor Ioannovich*, could only benefit from picturesque tableaux, often drawn from academic paintings, and painstaking attention to period detail. Faced with a modern play he did not understand, such as Chekhov's *The Seagull*, Stanislavsky applied similar methods, engrossing the audience in 'atmosphere' (*nastroenie*) created by dim lighting, asymmetrical ground-plans and restrained delivery.

Effective though this was for Chekhov, Hauptmann and, to some degree, Ibsen and Gorky, the 'one-style-fits-all' approach produced diminishing returns for Shakespeare, Sophocles and a great many contemporary innovators. By 1905, when a number of Russian theatres were dabbling in symbolism and other modernist fads, the Art Theatre felt itself straggling in the rear. Without abandoning his obsession with local colour, Stanislavsky believed that more of the production should emerge from the actors' organic development of their roles. In a play like Turgenev's *A Month in the Country*, in which the 'action' unfolds through lengthy duologues, the imposition of extraneous 'business' would be counter-productive. This led Stanislavsky to explore in greater depth the sources of the actor's creativity and the means to stimulate it. It is also significant that his role, the aging *cavaliere servante* Rakitin, was just the sort of 'average man' part he disliked. He had to find a way into the character that did not rely on false whiskers and romantic mannerisms.

Certain moves away from naturalism towards fantasy and a kind of proto-expressionism – *The Drama of Life, The Bluebird* – were well received by the public; others – the folkloric *Snow Maiden*, the allegorical *Life of Man*, a *Hamlet* based on Gordon Craig's ideas, Byron's *Cain* as a mystery play – were dead ends. Stanislavsky's directorial energies began to be channelled away from work on the main stage of the Art Theatre and to studios with younger, untried performers, more willing to serve as guinea pigs. As a director, he began to prefer to collaborate or even to come in at later stages in the process to correct and polish the work of others.

For nearly two decades, Stanislavsky the director was eclipsed by Nemirovich-Danchenko, Vakhtangov and others. Then, in the 1920s, with Nemirovich abroad and Vakhtangov dead, Stanislavsky enjoyed a resurgence of creativity in staging two high-spirited comedies. Significantly, they were both classics: Ostrovsky's *The Ardent Heart* was a romp for the 'old-timers' in the company; Beaumarchais's *The Marriage of Figaro* showed off many of the younger talents.

Thereafter, much of Stanislavsky's energy as a director was diverted to the Opera Studio, where he applied the principles and practices already developed to the musical drama. In the 1930s, his activities at the Art Theatre were usually billed 'under the guidance of', leaving the hands-on staging to colleagues. Occasionally, he could claim a success: *Armoured Train 14-69*, the first Soviet play to win approval at the Art Theatre, and an adaptation of Gogol's *Dead Souls* that was another showcase for veteran character actors. However, because he was at a remove from the theatre physically, Stanislavsky often found his intentions frustrated or thwarted; his letters are filled with complaints about the misinterpretation of his concepts or the abuse of his methods. He was particularly upset when his practice of slowly simmering plays for as long as needed was ignored. The rushed assembly line meant to fill government-issued quotas led to the botched productions of *Othello* and other works.

When Stanislavsky did participate directly in rehearsals, as with Mikhail Bulgakov's play about Molière *The Conspiracy of Bigots*, a power struggle between playwright and director made the experience hell for both of them. Stanislavsky tried to reconfirm his authority by mounting a play by Molière himself; long-dead, the author of *Tartuffe* could not protest the director's choices. In the event, it opened only after Stanislavsky's own demise. Bulgakov had the last laugh. In his posthumously published *Theatrical Novel* (known in English as *Black Snow*), he portrayed Stanislavsky as Ivan Vasilievich (the name and patronymic of the Terrible Tsar), a querulous, sycophant-surrounded valetudinarian, incapable of running a rehearsal without digressing into pointless 'études' and anecdotes.

II

Bulgakov's view, like that of all outside observers, is partial. A more fully-rounded portrait of Stanislavsky emerges from his letters. He referred in one of them (to General Stakhovich, 14 June 1911) to 'the Russian habit of wanting to cover everything with writing'. An inveterate diarist, annotator, correspondent, over the course of a long lifetime, he filled reams of papers that reveal him at every age and in every mood. In his correspondence, he tempers his style to his interlocutor: respectful and deferential to persons in authority and famous writers; jokey with close friends; affectionate, even passionate with his wife; stern but caring with his children; didactic with actresses; collegial but often unbending with colleagues.

As he becomes better acquainted with individuals, Stanislavsky's tone changes. Anton Chekhov, for instance had come in contact with the Art Theatre at the behest of his friend, fellow playwright and pedagogue Nemirovich-Danchenko. When he embarked on a directorial plan for *The Seagull* in 1898, Stanislavsky had met Chekhov only once, felt no particular sympathies with him, and was confused by the play. As Chekhov grew closer to the MAT and especially to the actress Olga Knipper, Stanislavsky began to understand him better and even tried, somewhat awkwardly, to adopt his deadpan facetious manner in his own letters. By the time of *The Cherry Orchard*, without losing his respect, Stanislavsky had no qualms about contradicting the author or offering his own alternative views.

This discrepancy between the social worlds and tastes of Stanislavsky and Nemirovich was only to increase. Over the course of forty years, the letters of the two partners read like a fever chart. To the outside world, they tried to present a solid front; behind the scenes, their relationship was often strained to the breaking point. Michael Chekhov in an American lecture of 1955 offered a lurid picture of this dissension: 'They were so necessary, so useful to one another – and between us – but they hated one another! Another problem! Why?! It's so strange. They were so necessary to one another, so loved one another as one artist loves another! And at the same time... I cannot explain it.' This is overstatement. Their relationship was more like a dysfunctional marriage, except that it did function. Though it teetered on the brink of divorce many times, it held together for the sake of the children, that is, the original vision of the Art Theatre. The honeymoon period lasted for the first few years: they were respectful to one another's ideas and co-directed a number of successful productions. Gradually, a rift began to be manifest: Nemirovich was devoted to producing modern plays with social messages in as efficient a way possible, whereas Stanislavsky began to be more interested in experimenting with styles of acting and producing, even if the experiments might be protracted or dead-end.

Nemirovich has received bad press outside of Russia, because most writers have accepted Stanislavsky's views. True, he failed to see the value of the Studios and Stanislavsky's experiments in staging and actor training, but, as Stanislavsky increasingly refrained from day-to-day management, most of the administrative burden fell upon Nemirovich. This was particularly the case in the early 1920s, when Stanislavsky was on tour abroad and Nemirovich had to ensure the theatre's survival while the Bolsheviks were reorganizing every aspect of Russian life. He was far more pragmatic and tactful in his negotiations than Stanislavsky would have been. And his own experiments in staging novels by Dostoevsky and Tolstoy were very fruitful, admired by critics and the public alike.

In the most disputatious phases of their correspondence, Nemirovich may come across as a nit-picking pragmatist set on thwarting his idealistic partner. But Stanislavsky can be exasperating in his stance as the more astute businessman, the more urbane socialite and the more sensitive artist. He often displays an unattractive passive/aggressive manner, implying 'I may have my faults, but I am right, and if I don't get my way, I shall take my ball and go home.' He washes his hands of the distasteful tasks of management. Cushioned by his fortune, he could afford an Achillean tactic: withdrawal. At regular intervals, he brandishes threats of resignation or reduced involvement. After the Revolution, what had been a histrionic tactic becomes reality: ill health and discomfort with the regime lead him to hole up in his home and conduct his rehearsals and classes there. By the late 1920s he rarely visits the Art Theatre.

Nemirovich rankled at being cast in Stanislavsky' shadow. His partner's public stature was greater, figuratively as a popular actor and wealthy celebrity, and literally, as a very tall man. Personally imposing, Stanislavsky towers over everyone in group photographs. He was the most handsome of his siblings, somewhat exotic in appearance with his almond eyes and thick lips. His hair turned grey and then white at an early age, which made a striking contrast with his black eyebrows and moustache. Late in life, he affected horn-rimmed pince-nez that gave him an owlish and scholarly aura. Not merely his looks but his staid, courtly manner, reminiscent of the *ancien régime* and inflected by his time on the boards, made him attractive. In public he cultivated a sedate deportment that was both affable and impermeable, and revealed his more mercurial side only to his intimates.

He was not an intellectual either in the Russian sense of *intelligent*, a well-informed, socially engaged citizen, or in the European sense of someone who trafficks in ideas. A poor student, whose reading was extensive but eclectic, Stanislavsky kept up with new ideas only when friends recommended a book to him or when he needed a technical vocabulary to express his concepts of acting. The opening pages of My Life in Art are at pains to stress the cataclysmic changes that took place over the course of Stanislavsky's lifetime. He describes the world of his youth as a quaint bygone era of the pony express and styrene candles. The fact is that he always remained rooted in that era. His deification of art is essentially of the nineteenth century, in line with the romantics, the Parnassians and William Morris. He clung to it steadfastly, even at the risk of becoming an 'internal émigré' under the Soviets. His artistic models were those of his youth. When he tried to accommodate his taste to new trends, exemplified by Meyerhold or Gordon Craig, he had considerable difficulty. He did not follow the avant-garde in art, except when it impinged on the theatre, and even then he usually found it unsympathetic. He resisted his daughter's desire to become a painter and looked askance at her alliance with the Futurists. The editor of the first version of My Life in Art, Aleksandr Koiransky, claimed that, as late as 1923, Stanislavsky had never heard of Degas.

An intelligent was supposed not only to keep up artistic matters; he was also expected to take an active part in social betterment. Stanislavsky, in common with his class, did so: he improved workers' conditions at his factory, dedicated performances as charitable benefits, and sat on the Board of Orphans, which looked after the interests of the children of defunct gentry. But he was not political. Until the Revolution, he was a loyal subject of the Tsar and his interest in affairs of state mattered only insofar as they affected his factory, his theatre and the lives of his nearest and dearest. His liberal views never exceeded those characteristic of his class. Although the Art Theatre provided the radical Maksim Gorky a platform at a time when he was still considered subversive, the writer himself found it too bourgeois and broke with it.

Outraged though he was by the pogroms carried out by the reactionary 'Black Hundreds', Stanislavsky, like many cultivated Russians, including Chekhov, preserved a kind of 'everyday anti-Semitism'. He was capable of friendship and collegiality with Jewish artists, musicians, playwrights and physicians, but regarded Jewish businessmen en bloc as crooks and swindlers. He and his wife commonly referred to Jews by the denigratory term zhid, 'Yid', not the more respectful yevrei, characterizing them as pushy and ignorant. In general, however, Stanislavsky tested traditional stereotypes against personal experience; as a result, he found the French to be unwitty, the Germans to be disorganized, and the Americans to be receptive to art.

The debacle of the World War dispelled Stanislavsky's waning loyalty to the Tsarist government, but he was caught off-guard by the suddenness of the Bolshevik take-over. Reduced living conditions were exacerbated by the demands made by an inflexible government and an uneducated audience. He hoped that his apolitical adherence to Art would be acknowledged by the new regime; he soon found that many regarded the Art Theatre as retrograde and even counter-revolutionary. As Stanislavsky explained in his letters from America, he found it well-nigh impossible to toe the Party Line and still maintain the artistic standards that were his credo. His life under the Soviets is a chronicle of evasions, compromises, panicky appeals, awkward accommodations, often sincere, occasionally calculated. By the 1930s, except when he was trotted out as a cultural totem for visiting celebrities, he conducted his work in private, within the safe confines of his home.

This was particularly functional for his experiments in opera production. For all his attraction to the circus and drama, Stanislavsky's first love was music. He rubbed shoulders with the great Russian composers of his generation and briefly trained to be an opera singer. His earliest ventures as an actor and a director were often in musical comedy and operetta. Although he deplored the 'Vampukicism' (shopworn and absurd clichés) of operatic convention and the obtuseness of their performers, he was constantly drawn to musical theatre. After the Revolution, circumstances led him to take over an opera studio, which he regarded as a haven and a respite from the frustrations of the Art Theatre. In the mid-1920s, when he was moved to new lodgings in Leontiev Lane, he found that a columned ballroom with a low stage was the perfect venue for chamber operas, and he used it as a laboratory for a more intimate, realistic style of performance.

The ability to work at home coincided with his growing reliance on ill health to excuse his absence from public activities. Concerns about health played a prominent role in Stanislavsky's life. How much of this was hypochondria is open to question, and there is a blatant irony of his enjoyment in playing *The Imaginary Invalid*. His concern had a genuine basis, however, since cardiac ailments were recurrent in his family and pulmonary weakness in his wife's (their son contracted tuberculosis at an early age). His letters spend a good deal of space monitoring the heart, lungs, bowels and diet of himself and his circle. In his youth, it was customary for the well-to-do to spend the summer months at a spa or health resort to correct the excesses of the social season. Stanislavsky got into the habit and, given the hectic triple life he led (commercial, theatrical and domestic), he needed the rest. Nevertheless, for all his anxieties, he and his closest kin enjoyed longevity, working to the end.

Sex and Stanislavsky is a subject neglected by biographers. He was no prude, but he loathed any sort of vulgarity. Although, when a highly eligible bachelor, he was fond of flirting with his feminine admirers, he claimed not to have seen an unclad woman's leg until he was twenty-five and then he was appalled. Aware of the facts of life, he preferred to idealize them. His affections had to be bound up with a spiritual element. He probably came to his marriage a virgin. He and Lilina clearly enjoyed the physical side of conjugal life; they longed to abandon the domestic jars that drove them apart and go for a dirty weekend in a hotel. On the whole, in his closest relations with women Stanislavsky preferred a tutelary role; when actresses such as Olga Gzovskaya or Alisa Koonen, in whose advancement he had invested much time and energy, left the Art Theatre for other opportunities, he behaved as if he had been jilted.

Opportunities to stray held no attraction for him. In 1907 he became infatuated with the American dancer Isadora Duncan; this may have been a symptom of a midlife crisis, for the passion arose at a time when he was disappointed on other fronts. For his part, he cast her as a muse whose bold reforms in movement stimulated his creative juices. She saw him as another celebrity trophy with useful connections and resources. He tactfully deflected her attempts to seduce him. And when he had the chance to observe her *in situ* as the mistress of the millionaire Paris Singer he wrote her off as a potential artistic inspiration.

Another face of Stanislavsky revealed in his letters is his attention to his commercial interests. Although, in his youth, he complained of the enforced hours at the office, his sense of responsibility prevented him from neglecting his administrative duties at the two merged family factories. He paid close attention to the well-being of his workers, found ways to convert the manufacture of gold thread to industrial cable during the war, and regularly attended board meetings. None of this was mercenary. Throughout his life, Stanislavsky's attitude to money was selfless: he and Lilina refused any salary from the Art Theatre and any profits from military materiel. After the Revolution, stripped of his assets and penniless, he pursued financial profit only to support his theatrical endeavours and his family and keep his tubercular son in a Swiss sanatorium. Except for his summer vacations, his pleasures lay in work.

III

Stanislavsky would not have turned up in Danny Kaye's nightclub act had he not inspired a generation of acting teachers. In a field noted for its ephemerality, even as his own performances faded from memory, his name was one to conjure with in the formation of new performers. The prevalence of Stanislavsky's tenets and terminology in acting classes and among a younger breed of player was conspicuous. The history of acting might indeed be divided into two eras: pre- and post-Stanislavsky. Even in adaptations that blurred his intentions and imbalanced his emphases, his writing stirred the imaginations of theatre practitioners.

Stanislavsky's reforms to the dramatic curriculum were revolutionary. In the past instruction in acting was hit-or-miss. An actor might study at a conservatory, where he would be taught a traditional style, so that he could be engaged by a national theatre that performed a fixed repertoire. Or he might take lessons from a superannuated barnstormer, who would pass on his own set of mannerisms. Or he might pick up the tricks of the trade empirically, working in fit-up troupes and provincial playhouses until the call came from a commercial manager. Stock companies classified actors in *emplois* or lines of business, requiring them to repeat their standard type until age moved them into another *emploi*. A performance was made up of a number of 'points', effective moments that could rivet the attention of a noisy audience in a fully-lit auditorium. How persuasive an actor was depended on the conveyance of emotion through gesture, stance, and vocal delivery. 'Realism' in appearance and deportment was less important than 'authenticity' at moments of passion or pathos. Even Stanislavsky's venerated Shchepkin always came across, in every role, as a tubby Ukrainian; it was the power and accuracy of his rendition of emotions that impressed the onlookers.

In Stanislavsky's writing two terms recur as the antitheses to Art: *remeslo* and *khaltura*. *Remeslo* is the neutral Russian word for a craft or handicraft, implying a trade or means of livelihood. In most languages what an actor does is traditionally referred to as a 'skill' or a 'craft', a learned profession that might be improved by talent, inspiration or intuition. Stanislavsky, however, rejected this definition; for him *remeslo* is a pejorative term connoting uninspired professionalism. It appears this way in his journal as early as 1889. After the Revolution, it frequently shows up in his notes on his system. He even published a lengthy essay on *remeslo* in 1922 in the magazine *Theatre Culture*, in hopes of warning the new Soviet actor away from that path. Stanislavsky would likely have endorsed Tom Stoppard's remark in *Artist Descending a Staircase* that craftsmanship is 'skill without imagination', and so I have chosen to translate *remeslo* as 'craftsmanship'.

Khalturnik is old Slavonic for a church lector who garbles his readings. It got a new lease on life immediately after the October Revolution as the topical coinage *khaltura*, a scornful calque of *kultura* (culture). Since government subsidies to theatres were too sparse and too irregular to provide a living wage, actors and other theatre staff had to seek outside employment. Touring to the provinces, special performances for audiences of peasants, workers and soldiers, appearances on the concert stage, in short freelance jobs outside the auspices of an official company, were all deemed *khaltura*, It might be translated as 'moonlighting', except that Stanislavsky and others equated it with the lowest form of slapdash day-labour. So, when *khaltura* is used simply to refer to commercial tours, I have translated it as 'moonlighting'; but in most cases it appears as 'hackwork'.

In other words, Stanislavsky repudiated the idea that the actor was a mere artisan, the instrument of another's genius. For him, the actor (and director) had to be an equal creator with the playwright, even if he professes to serve the playwright. This is why Stanislavsky's directorial 'scores' teem with novelistic descriptions and amplifications to the text and why he rarely inquires into the overarching intentions of an author. This is also why his research into the actor's ways and means goes beyond expressiveness to fathom the very wellsprings of creativity. The actor was to rely not merely on the text, but devise a past and future for his character as specifically as possible.

Before Stanislavsky, ideas about acting were deduced from specific performances. General principles were usually formulated not by actors but by spectators or dramatists, the likes of Aaron Hill or Denis Diderot. In the eighteenth century, with sensibility as a touchstone, the leading question was how exalted an actor ought to be on stage. Was it was better to keep a cool head or allow oneself to be carried away? By the next century, debates over the preference for inspiration or preparation had become critical commonplaces: the fulminous Kean or the statuesque Kemble, the erratic Mochalov or the invariable Karatygin, the intuitive Duse or the calculating Bernhardt? With the introduction of the box-set and more naturalistic stage furnishings, actors had to be more attentive to behavioural specifics without abandoning the masterful deployment of physical expression, vocal sonority and powerful emotions.

11

The actors who impressed the youthful Stanislavsky were the proficient technicians of the Moscow Maly Theatre and the tempestuous Italian tragedians Salvini and Rossi. Temperamentally alien to the latter, he copied the former. His earliest speculations about acting concern the need for originality and the maintenance of freshness from performance to performance. Why did the audience respond best when he was least effortful? Why could he not strike an even level without falling into routine? How could he prevent circumambient distractions (backstage noise, drafts, inattentive spectators) from disturbing his concentration? Professional actors had ready devices to achieve these results. Stanislavsky had to grope. He grew to distrust raw feeling and spontaneous outbursts. For all his love of circus acts, farce comedy and special effects, he cultivated a puritanical rejection of 'theatricality', by which he meant hackneyed and predictable standbys.

While insisting on the fullest incarnation of the role, Stanislavsky never expected an actor to 'identify' with the character to the extent of losing control. Muscular relaxation before coming on stage and intense concentration thereafter were not means for projecting one's own personality but for entering into the spirit of the role. Even the emphasis on 'affective memory' was intended to stimulate analogous feelings, relevant to the dramatic situation, not to express those identical to the actor's personal emotions. The actor was kept bound to the play by the 'supertask', the overarching meaning of his contribution to the production as a whole. Certain contradictions were inherent in the evolving system: the actor was to be 'natural' even in the most artificial situation on stage; yet the theatrical aesthetic was verisimilitude, not verity. The actor must seek in himself for authenticity but must not fail to incarnate the character. For all his own contradictions and tergiversations, Stanislavsky never lost sight of his principal objective· a 'truth' in acting that is difficult to define but an indispensable dynamic if the actor is to avoid stereotypes that impede creativity. 'Truth' is a more versatile and ungraspable term than 'realism', a word rarely found in Stanislavsky's writing. The quest for a quintessential 'Truth' will be more useful for an actor playing a water sprite in *The Sunken Bell* or Milk in *The Blue Bird* or Man's Wife in *The Life of Man* than will an effort to be 'realistic'.

Stanislavsky's letters and diaries map out his zigzag course in search of the source of the actor's ability to create. In his youth, he diagnosed each of his performances, trying to figure out what worked and why. Primarily self-taught, his conclusions were *a posteriori*. Then, with the founding of the Art Theatre, he applied what he had learned to the formation of other tyros, forging them into a seamless ensemble. (Incidentally, the MAT never lived up to its axiom 'Today Hamlet, tomorrow a walk-on'. Leading roles were always played by the same dozen actors, and walk-ons by students or hirelings.) As the 'old-timers' failed to live up to his expectations or refused to take part in his exercises, he put together groups of untried students who might be more responsive to his notions. From 1912 to the end of his life, he preferred working with such non-judgmental beginners; when they reached the point that they could leave the nest and fly off into their own directions (as was the case with Mikhail Chekhov), he was often bitterly disappointed. It is striking that Stanislavsky uses the word 'talent' sparingly; he seems to believe that even the greatest gifts must be subordinated to the discipline that his teachings prescribe. The actor must never rely wholly on his gift or mark time, but always be striving for improvement.

His principles remained constant, but his methods were always in flux. In his continual dissatisfaction with results, Stanislavsky could say, as Faust did to Mephisto, 'when I tell the moment "Stop", then am I damned'. Loath as he was to commit his fluctuant ideas to paper, he deplored the distortions others committed when pinning down his methods. He reluctantly took up the pen to pre-empt and correct them. The attempt to distil his practical experience into precepts and lessons took up much of his free time. His correspondence with Lyubov Gurevich, the astute critic who agreed to be his editor, reveals the difficulties in finding the proper words to encapsulate nebulous ideas. This was exacerbated by the fact that, as Gurevich kept reminding him, the Soviet authorities would not countenance such religiously-loaded terms as 'soul' and 'spirituality' or situations for exercises drawn from bourgeois life. Stanislavsky preferred to occlude reality in favour of a 'life in art'.

Aware of his educational shortcomings, Stanislavsky was deferential, often obsequious to writers and academics. This led him to seek support for his ideas from science and other arts. Trying for exact definitions of his concepts, he borrowed terminology from the Nancy school of behavioural psychology, from yoga and from Dalcroze eurhythmics: none of these lendings was explored in depth nor need they be taken too seriously. Stanislavsky's originality lay in his ability to draw general principles from a lifetime of experiential observation. He declared that mere theory was 'desiccating'; the most accurate findings came from 'the heat of the moment'. Direct action would enable the lessons to enter the actor's 'muscle memory'. Those of his disciples who had studied with him at the First Studio before the World War imparted that vintage of the System to their pupils abroad; but they were unaware of the interest in 'physical action' that dominated his later curriculum. The insistence on emotional memory in the earliest translations eclipsed Stanislavsky's emphasis on corporeal memory, the physical expression of a state of mind. Similarly, those directors who studied his detailed prompt-books for the Chekhov and Gorky productions at the *fin de siècle* had no sense of his more improvisational approach after the Revolution, his insistence that the actor should create independently of the director, though not of the playwright. The director's task would be to harmonize these individual discoveries. In an odd way, this had brought Stanislavsky full circle by the end of his life. His research was restoring the traditional pre-eminence of the actor and delimiting the director to a subsidiary function. Nevertheless, the Stanislavskian actor was a free agent only to a degree. In service to art, he would exercise an ethics and discipline that would prevent the abuses of stardom or self-indulgence.

Laurence Senelick
January 2013

Figure 1 Konstantin Alekseev at the age of 10.

1

A GILDED YOUTH

1863–1887

Blissful childhoods are the stuff of literary memoirs of the pre-Revolutionary period. Sergey Aksakov, Lev Tolstoy and Vladimir Nabokov are the most familiar writers to leave idyllic accounts of Edenic nests of gentry before the Fall. KS's recollections in My Life in Art *convey a similar nostalgia for a vanished way of life. By all accounts they are not inaccurate. Cosseted by wealth and encouraged in his artistic predilections, he comes across as a privileged but unspoiled participant in a world of moneyed leisure and informed dilettantism. Unlike Aksakov and Tolstoy, scions of landowning gentry and nobility, and unlike Nabokov, son of a highly-placed statesman, KS belonged to the highest circle of Russian industrialists who united patriarchal manners with commercial integrity and a love of art and culture. By blood and sympathies, the Alekseevs were related to the art collectors the Tretyakov brothers and Sergey Mamontov, the creator of a private Russian Opera.*

Yet the origins of the family were of the humblest. KS's great great grandfather was a Yaroslav peasant known only as Aleksey Petrov ('son of Pyotr', 1724-75); emancipated, he came to Moscow and, according to tradition, hawked dried peas from a tray. In 1746 he was enrolled in the merchantry and married another emancipated serf. Owing to his energy and that of his son Semyon (1751-1823), the family began to grow rich. Somehow Semyon perfected a procedure for weaving gold and silver thread, which was in demand for ecclesiastical altar cloths and liturgical garments. Having no family name was problematic, so he took on Serebrenikov (Silver-gilt), but it did not stick. Alekseev ('those of Aleksey') would become the proper name for both Semyon and his progeny. By 1812 he was a commercial magnate, capable of donating 50,000 rubles to the war effort against Napoleon. KS's grandfather Vladimir Semyonovich (1795-1867) founded the Vladimir Alekseev textile factory and occupied a prominent place in Moscow society. Fragrant with the aroma of Havana cigars, he lived like a king, but enjoyed a reputation for probity in business and close family ties. A cousin of KS, Nikolay, was honorary director of the Moscow Conservatory of Music and later mayor of Moscow (an appointment, not an elected office), who helped urbanize the capital.

The maternal side of KS's family was somewhat less reputable. The French actress Marie Varley (1800-85) came to St Petersburg in 1847 as a soubrette with the French troupe at the Grand Duke Michael Theatre. She left the stage to be kept as mistress of the marble contractor Vasily Abramovich Yakovlev and by him had two daughters whom she raised as Catholics; when he abandoned her, he acknowledged his bastards and had them brought up in his legitimate family. Varley, now known as Mariya Ivanovna Lapteva, was shunned by her children. One of them, Yelizaveta (actually Adèle) Vasilievna Yakovleva (1841-1904) was goddaughter of the famous actor Sosnitsky and a skilled pianist. When her sister got married, she ran away to Moscow where she met Sergey Vladimirovich Alekseev (1836-93). Bred up to the family business, he served as chairman of the board of the Alekseev Factory until his death. He enjoyed the rank of Hereditary Honorary Citizen, a distinction conferred only upon the most affluent, influential and respectable merchants. Sergey and Yelizaveta married in 1860 and had ten children, not all of whom survived to adulthood.

Since some of these siblings will appear regularly in KS's correspondence, usually under their nicknames, it is best to identify them now, in order of birth.

Volodya = Vladimir Sergeevich Alekseev (1861-1936), his mother's favourite; a member of the management of the VladimirAlekseev firm and a participant in the Alekseev Circle. Prone to stage fright, he left drama for music and became active in KS's Opera Studio.
Kokosya, Kotun = Konstantin Sergeevich Alekseev (1863-1938), known by his stage name Stanislavsky.
Zina = Zinaida Sergeevna Alekseeva (married name Sokolova, stage name Aleeva-Mirtova), 1865-1950); she acted in the family theatricals from 1879 and later taught her brother's System at the Opera Studio.
Nyusha = Anna Sergeevna (married names Shteker, Krasyuk, 1866-1936), member of the Alekseev Circle and the Society for Art and Literature, acting under the name Aleeva; at the MAT 1899-1903, when she left to have a baby.
Yura = Georgy Sergeevich Alekseev (1869-1929), amateur actor, a participant in the Alekseev Circle.
Lyuba = Lyubov Sergeevna Alekseeva (married names Struve, Bostanzhoglo, Korganova, 1871-1941).
Borya = Boris Sergeevich Alekseev (1871-1906), participant in all of KS's theatrical undertakings.
Pasha = Pavel Sergeevich Alekseev (1875-88), who died in childhood.

KS was born in Moscow on 5 January 1863. Shortly thereafter the family moved to a palatial mansion at Red Gates (Krasnye Vorota). He made his theatrical debut at age three or four, when he came on as Jack Frost in a domestic Christmas play and his costume caught fire. He noted that from an early age he felt 'pleasure in success', 'joy in sensing an action on stage' and the 'painful feeling of inaction on the boards'.

In 1869 Sergey Alekseev bought an estate in Lyubimovka, about an hour's ride from Moscow, on the banks of the Klyazma River. There the summer months were spent and a free clinic set up. The diversions were continuous: the boys were excellent riders and sailed the river. In 1870 their governess introduced them to living pictures, and they indulged in cross-dressed farces, amateur theatricals involving the whole family, St John's Eve skirmishes presided over by 'the Shah of Persia', and an amateur circus that played a huge role in their lives. A never-ending cavalcade of guests took part in picnics and musicales. Back in the city the children were taught at home, and attended the Italian opera and the ballet. Open house was kept for artists and writers.

When KS was eleven, his parents travelled to St Petersburg with three of his siblings to have their daughter Nyusha examined by the eminent physician Dr S. P. Botkin. The account of the other children's activities, in KS's first preserved letter, confirms that the account of an idyllic childhood depicted in his later memoirs was no fabrication.

To **his parents**. 24 June 1874, Lyubimovka.

Dear Papa and Mama!

I hope that you arrived safely in Petersburg and that Lyuba and Borya didn't cry a lot. We got your letter and added to the special little circle.[1] After you left Zina stopped missing you and we all went to swing in the hammock; after we'd swung a bit, we went to the gym, where we cut out paper soldiers and pasted them on cardboard. But we soon got tired of that, and we went to our room where, for the first time, I accompanied Volodya, who was playing a little pipe. Soon it was time for a swim. As you ordered, we sat in the water exactly five minutes and not once ducked our heads under. After the swim we had lunch. During lunch Anna Ivanovna visited us in a hired troika. After lunch we visited Auntie Vera[2] and arrived just when everyone was gathering for a concert at Viktor Nikolaevich's.[3] In their company we went home, because it was time for Yura and Zina to take a nap. We went to swing in Volodya's hammock. Then Volodya went into the study to compose a telegram. While Volodya was composing the telegram, we took naps. Volodya, Zina and Yura and I had splendid naps. Only Avdotya Aleksandrovna[4]

Figure 2 The Alekseev family, 1881. Left–right, standing: Boris, Vladimir, the nanny Fyokla Obukhova, Anna, Georgy. Left–right, seated: Lyubov, Sergey Vladimirovich, Pavel, Mariya, Yelizaveta Vasilievna, Konstantin, Zinaida

couldn't fall asleep until four o'clock. On Wednesday Volodya and I got up at eight and went for a swim. The water was very warm, so it was not very refreshing. After the swim we went to take tea. During tea-time we got your letter, Mama, the bouquets and the toys for Yura. Yura thanks you for the steamboat. After tea we went to sew flags and sewed them until dinner. After dinner a Punch-and-Judy show came by. After it left, there was a mighty downpour. During that time we wrote you letters, which we will send tomorrow morning [...]

Konstantin Alekseev

In 1875 KS entered the second form of the fourth boys' classical gymnasium at Pokrovka as a day-scholar. Although well-behaved, he was a poor student, inattentive and uninterested in the curriculum. The Alekseev brothers had a crammer in the person of Ivan Nikolavich Lvov, (1857-1922), a poor mathematician. A graduate of Moscow University (1879) he later studied in the artillery school and the General Staff Academy, but had a reputation for being something of a 'Red'. He would direct and take part in the first dramatic productions at Lyubimovka. He had a great influence on young KS and was the model for his interpretation of Vershinin in Three Sisters.

To **his mother**. 1875, Moscow.
Mama dearest!
    [...] At the high school everything is fine, I haven't had any tests. I was often called on for answers this week and I think I gave the proper answers. I play the piano before dinner. Ivan Nikolaevich Lvov drops in at 6 o'clock and stays until we have done our homework. [...]

Yours Kostya

Figure 3 The courtyard of the Alekseev Red Gates house

KS considered that his encounters with the art patrons of the merchant class, the Tretyakovs, Mamontov, the Sabashnikovs, the Shchukins, Aleksey Bakhrushin and Savva Morozov were among the most influential of his artistic impressions. These acquaintances and the prevalent spirit in his home gave him more of an education than the gymnasium and Lazarev Institute. He paid his first visits to Kiev and Petersburg and took a prominent place in the family circus but was already beginning to deplore amateurism, both of skill and attitude.

In adolescence KS transferred his interest to the dramatic theatre and attended the Maly Theatre with regularity. He especially admired Aleksandr Pavlovich Lensky (Vervitsiotti, 1847-1908), character actor, director, and master of makeup, and Glikeriya Nikolaevna Fedotova (Pozdnyakova, 1846-1925), an actress of wide range who played twenty-nine Ostrovsky roles as well as Shakespearean characters. He adored the Maly's grande dame Mariya Nikolaevna Yermolova (1853-1928), who stirred hearts with her tragic heroines. Rossi's[5] King Lear struck him as a bolt from the blue.

To indulge his son's interests, in summer 1877 Sergey Alekseev had an annex built at Lyubimovka with an auditorium and stage, dressing-rooms, costume shop and props storage. On 5 September of that year it was inaugurated with a performance of the short farces The Old Mathematician *and* A Cup of Tea. *KS played in both, imitating the Maly comedian Nikolay Ignatievich Muzil (1839-1906) in the latter. In summer 1878 he performed in French but condemned his own acting as 'cold, limp, untalented'. He feared he could have an effect on an audience only when he had someone to copy.*

In 1877 KS began to keep a diary. The Russo-Turkish War was noted in it only for Sergey Alekseev's donation of 70,000 rubles to the Volunteer Fleet. The hostilities in no way hindered the round of amusements.

For the fall term, Sergey Alekseev enrolled his older sons in the Lazarev Institute of Eastern Languages, which provided a six-year liberal arts curriculum. KS continued to be a conscientious but mediocre student.

KS was cautious about acting outside the family circle. That same summer he was asked to take part in another amateur staging of A Cup of Tea, *'but because there were few rehearsals, I refused'. He did participate in an amateur show in the Red Gates home of his cousin Vladimir Grigorievich Sapozhnikov (1843-1916), factory-owner, treasurer and member of the council of the Practical Academy of Commercial Sciences; KS played Zhilkin in Viktor Krylov's farce* A Dainty Morsel *and the lackey Semyonych in N. Frolov's comedy* The Flibbertigibbet.

Diary, *18 March 1879.*

At 6 o'clock, as had already been appointed, I showed up at the Sapozhnikovs'. None of the performers was there yet. Ivan Semyonovich[6] was fussing with the stage, Liza[7] and Volodya with the housekeeping side.

The scenery was set up for *The Flibbertigibbet.* A red room, on the left a sofa – a little table with silver knives, forks and other domestic utensils.

Little by little the performers started to arrive, whose first duty was to inquire about one's health, and almost everyone replied that they weren't quite well. We figured it would be a performance by invalids. I kept running down to the stage or up to the makeup room, as if I were on important business. They sent me to get dressed.

When I got into the little dark [room], because no one had lit the lamps yet, I saw Aleksey Sergeevich Ushakov, who was rooting about in his things.

'Kokosya, Kokosya, hurry and get dressed.'

'Right away,' I replied. 'How will we tell who's who?'

'What difference does it make; it'll come out all right.'

And so we bandied words in this way as we put on our costumes. And you could hear this sort of talk not only in this room, but all through the Sapozhnikov home.

I put on my Semyonych costume, consisting of dirty boots full of holes, patched grey trousers, an old grey overcoat, too short for me; my neck was bound with a coloured kerchief of poor quality, and in general a very unprepossessing costume in appearance, for this Semyonych was a drunken footman, coming back from town.

The makeup room was packed with actors, noisily laughing and conversing. The makeup man (Nekrasov) who has come alone this time, was making up Aleksey Sergeevich as an old man. When he was done with him he began to apply slap to me. He put a shaggy red wig on me, glued on a red military moustache sticking up in front, and smeared my nose, cheeks and whole face all over with red greasepaint. I was made up as a very typical drunken ex-soldier. Having tried on the footman's tailcoat, too tight for me, which they had decided I was to wear on my last appearance, I got down to going over my lines. And then for the first time I suffered real stage fright.

Figure 4 The auditorium and stage of the theatre at Lyubimovka

Finally everyone who was made up went downstairs. Having opened the curtain, I gazed on the audience, which had barely entered the drawing-room. Mrs Ladyzhenskaya had pretentiously sat next to some lady I didn't know and was conversing rather loudly. In the hall I noticed Mlle Bindou, chatting with handsome old Ladyzhensky.[8]

On stage everyone was quietly whispering, conveying their fear to each other. Natasha[9] was more frightened than anyone.

'Splondeed, splondeed', we heard the voice of Pyotr Viktorovich (Ladyzhensky), who, evidently, had no fear of what was to come. On the other side Tretyakov[10] was teasing Natasha.

'All righty, I'm ringing the last bell; Natalya Vasilievna, get in place; those who are acting – on stage, the others get out.'

At this time Nikolay Semyonovich[11] came up to him and asked him to leave the stage and get made up. He left, but soon came back holding a glass of wine, asked if he might drink it for courage. I was a bit scared and in my excitement walked around the stage. Finally everyone was in place. Mariya Matveevna Yezhova, who was playing the role of Matryona Markovna [the housekeeper], was in place, preparing to polish the silver.

'Mariya Matveevna, ready? The curtain is going up.'

'Ready, ready.'

The curtain went up, the stage was lighted. The faces of everyone offstage took on awfully odd expressions. I stood near the door, waiting out the time till my entrance. Finally I heard the words, 'What a pity that their poor mother didn't live to see it…' after which I was to enter. Nikolay Semyonovich gave me a shove, and I went on stage, hands in my pockets, pursing my lips and trying to give my face a somewhat drunken look.

On my appearance I heard the faint buzz of a laughing audience.

'Ah, is that you, Semyonych?'

'Yes'm, Matryona Markovna.'

Then I looked at the audience and saw right off the bat the laughing face of Polenov, Savva Ivanovich,[12] our Volodya and Sapozhnikov, then Repin, Papa and Mama, Zina Yak.[13] and the two Misses Krestovnikova.[14] When I saw the last two, I was delighted, first because it would be pleasant to be praised by young ladies, and second, I imagined that if I acted well (which I hoped was the case), I would rise a bit in their estimation. All this flashed through my mind in a moment. In a rather long monologue, in which I relate how I was asked why I had bought so many almonds, I left out a lot and got confused and two or three times stared at the prompter, but, apparently, nobody noticed. The audience laughed at my lines very often, which bucked me up. Finally, I embraced Matryona Markovna and made my exit, smoothing the back of my head. The audience burst out laughing and applauded me, I came back on pleased with myself, took a bow in the doorway, and went off stage again. The applause did not subside for quite some time; I was already encouraged and thought that I ought to go on again, but no, Matryona Markovna had started talking, and the applause died down. Then

Natasha ran on, and all the rest went as it was supposed to. When Natasha came off stage, they started to applaud her, I was annoyed, because at the dress rehearsal they had applauded me alone in the middle of the play; in the performance it turned out that the audience applauded every time a character made an exit.

On stage the centre door was open, so that you could not cross without being seen by the audience. Aleksey Sergeevich, not having considered this, sent one of the carpenters, who were standing in the doorway, to bring him some sherry, he went, but Nikolay Semyonovich had the time to stop him, but even so the audience had seen him (the carpenter). Aleksey Sergeevich was not pleased by this; he sent him a second time. So he crawled under the stage and, stamping loudly, crept to the other side. Nikolay Semyonovich got dreadfully angry with him and in his excess of rage broke a pencil over the carpenter's head. *Tableau!*

My second appearance involved my having to inform them of the arrival of Ivan Ivanovich Maleev. I came on.

'Ivan Ivanovich is here.'

At these words I shook my head, the way drunken, uncouth footmen do. This gesture was evidently successful, because it raised a laugh. Ivan Ivanovich came on, Ladyzhensky played him, and started to talk about Annypolka. I hastily went up the spiral staircase, which curved mightily, to the makeup room, to make my kisser even drunker, because Semyonych had drunk another bottle.

There Tretyakov had already started to make up and Savva Ivanovich, come to apply slap to me, began to congratulate me. I reminded him that I had to go on again soon. They put makeup on my nose and cheeks and adjusted my wig.

My third entrance was the most effective, and I had put my hopes on it most of all. Best of all I heard the words: 'There, you see, you make all sorts of preparations, but...'

KS remained a less than mediocre student, relying on cribs and notes scrawled on his paper cuffs. He failed his exams, but as consolation his father bought him a 600-ruble English horse, on which he took long morning rides. He also began performing with the Mamontov circle. Like many well-born youths, he would haunt the green-rooms of the Imperial theatres and flirt with actresses and ballerinas. He soon became a real balletomane.

KS's diary increasingly served to record analyses of his acting. He would glue in playbills and programmes, first handwritten, then printed. On 8 July 1880 he noted that he played a bombastic general to acclamation, because he smashed crockery, tore his jacket and broke up the furniture. He decided he had the disposition for a character actor, even though he revelled in the parts of young lovers.

On 1 March 1881 while the Alekseevs were performing a musical evening to sixty-four guests, Nikolay rushed in to announce that Tsar Alexander II had been assassinated. The outrage inaugurated the reign of Alexander III, the repressive and politically inert 1880s, so familiar from Chekhov's plays. Social reform was relegated to the margins, and progressive thinkers had to find other outlets for their projects. However, the government monopoly on theatre in Moscow and St Petersburg was rescinded; with one or two exceptions, those few entrepreneurs who rushed to open private theatres foundered on the lack of a cohesive audience.

In the summer of 1881, while in the seventh form, KS pleaded with his father to let him drop out before graduation. He began to work in the family firm under the supervision of his uncle Sasha (Aleksandr Vladimirovich Alekseev, 1821-82). At the office he showed great diligence and skill, but as a businessman could no longer use the family name when performing in outside theatricals. On 25 November 1881 he made his first appearance under the Polish-sounding nom de théâtre Stanislavsky. It was borrowed from Aleksey Fyodorovich Markov, the doctor at the Alekseev factory and amateur actor, who in turn had taken it in honour of the Bolshoy ballerina Mariya Stanislavskaya.

When the Italian tragedian Tommaso Salvini (1829-1915) came to Moscow in 1882, KS saw him as Othello and, in his words, underwent a coup de foudre. He set about forming a permanent amateur troupe, the Alekseev Circle, seriously devoted to artistic refinement, taste and discipline in the performances. Its stock in trade was light comedy and farce, with KS in character roles with plenty of quick-change. On 24 July 1882 his fellow actors presented him with a garland inscribed 'The amateur actors to their comrade director'.

That winter a theatre was constructed on the second storey of the Alekseev compound at Red Gates with a 300-seat auditorium, two dressing-rooms, and a refreshment room, where KS and siblings Volodya and Zina staged shows. The first on 28 April 1883 was an evening of three vaudevilles (with KS copying Lensky), one act from the operetta Javotte by Jonas and a scene from Verdi's opera Aida with KS as the high priest Ramphis.

The Coronation of Alexander III was scheduled to take place in the Kremlin on 15 May 1883; KS's father was invited to the festivities and KS was appointed one of the masters of ceremonies of chorus and orchestra on the triumphal day of the emperor's arrival in Moscow. He described it in a letter to 'Sis', the university student and civil servant Sergey Alekseevich Kashkadamanov, friend of the older Alekseev brothers, son of their tutor in literature, and brother of KS's closest boyhood friend Fyodor (Fif).

To **Sergey Kashkadamanov**. Friday, 13 May 1883, Moscow.
Dear friend Sis!

Bored and languishing in loneliness without you, I recall at every minute your *resplendent beauty* and do not cease to hear your *velvety voice*, which, unfortunately, have lost my [sic] upper notes from *do* to *fa*. I am sorry that in the very first missive I have to apologize for the prolonged silence and persuade you that it does not testify to obliviousness of your existence or coolness on my part; it has occurred in consequence of *manque de temps*, which I have suffered all this time. With absolutely no wish to boast, I must remind you that my activities at the factory have increased remarkably since Uncle Sasha's death [in December], and also due to the approaching coronation, so that during working hours it is extremely difficult to find time to chat with you; in the evenings I have been no less busy in the soon-to-be-completed, thank God, performance [in the new home theatre], of which I shall tell you everything in detail. Now I shall begin to describe that great mystery which is to be enacted within the walls of our town.

Figure 5 Kostya Alekseev, at right, in drag in the operetta *Javotte*

Last Saturday the sovereign came to Moscow with the whole imperial family and stopped at the Petrov Palace, where he stayed till Tuesday morning, that is until the entry into the city down Tver Boulevard.

No! I've changed my mind!

I shall merely remind you that this solemnity was the acme of splendour and magnificence, and shall not start describing it in detail, because before you receive this letter you will have learned it all from the papers. I would rather tell you the manner in which I beheld the imperial entry. On Red Square an enormous music platform had been erected for 10,000 persons, who were under the jurisdiction of Nikolay Aleksandrovich,[15] therefore, naturally, among the number of the managers even I wound up on the platform. Lord, what agonies I suffered that day! Lord, how even now my disgustingly stinky feet ache after eight hours of running up and down the steps of that platform! At eight o'clock all the managers assembled, myself among them. Aleksandr Petrovich[16] and I were assigned to mark out lines on the floor for places for various educational institutions, choral societies and other singers, who were supposed to take part in the anthem. Naturally, the best place was marked out for the Moscow and St Petersburg theatre schools and the ballet company. Veretennikov went completely off his head from this toil in the brickyards of Egypt and gleefully danced a mazurka before all of Red Square, when our map-making came to an end. The work actually was grim: we had to ascertain how many persons were included in each educational institution, and, figuring from that, mark out square yards on the floor, not forgetting to leave a passageway for each one.

Aleksandr Petrovich barely had time to dance a mazurka when S. M. Tretyakov arrives cursing blue blazes because we had idiotically drawn the lines without any preplanning.

He brings us back and Lord! What do we see: all our lines have been re-measured and in their stead an inaccurate plan has been drawn up by the former Moscow mayor in question – Tretyanini.[17] Aleksandr Petrovich was beside himself and said to me under his breath, 'They aren't managers, they're manglers.'

At 12 o'clock they started to let people on to the platform. Of course, I was sitting among the theatrical young ladies, and because there were none of the famous Moscow bits of fluff, I sat down among the Petersburgers, with whom I had time to strike up an acquaintance and one of whom, namely Loganson, has already had time to pilfer a little piece of my heart.

'Tis a joy for a lover to call to mind the object of his love, and so for a few minutes I shall talk about her. *I remember how I met her* at Manokhin's, [18] I flattered myself that, despite the horse guards, she showed me a meed of well-disposed attention; furthermore, *I also* remember how she invited me to sit down next to her at supper and, flirting extra-sweetly, lovingly conversed with me. *Never shall I forget how she, wishing to smear my whole physiognomy with ice cream*, dug her handkerchief into it and how she asked me to stand up, so as to sponge away the spot on my knee with white bread. I stood up like one possessed, but I had, wonder of wonders,[19] etc., etc., in short, I almost fell in love with her.

Betrayal! Pro-fidious betrayal! -- you will exclaim in indignation. Not true! I reply coolly: I love *her* just as *passionately*, just as *tenderly* and in the case in point I only advance an axiom well known to you: I can love one, but pay court to many. Furthermore, if a perfidious betrayal has occurred, it is not on my part, but on yours. Soon after your departure I was with my sisters at *L'Africaine* and was inexpressibly bored during the first two acts. In the intermission, strolling to the smoking-room, I suddenly see Sofiya Vitalievna[20] arm in arm with Vasilievsky.[21] She poor thing was eating her heart out *nec plus ultra*, blushed and pulled away her arm, in the process pushing Vasilievsky in front of her. 'Good evening, K. S., it's been a while since we've seen one another.' 'A long time, S. V., so much water under the bridge since then, so many betrayals, that is, changes have taken place, I meant to say.' I answered drily and, not allowing her to express what I think was

25

on her mind, I bowed, adding: 'But goodbye, someone is waiting for you.' And we parted. You should have seen how after that scene she couldn't take her opera glasses off me; I sat in the dress circle with a ferocious look on my face and aimed my opera glasses only when Vasilievsky turned to her with some question. Markovskaya,[22] who was sitting behind me, shook her head more than once and made signs for me to stop, but *no*! I would not stop. In the intermission Yevgeniya Konstantinovna came up to me; conversing with her I did not notice how I wound up in the stalls. She suggested that I sit beside her and at once seated me in Vasilievsky's place, but once I noticed, I did not wish to have a super-stupid explanation with S. V., so when she appeared I hastened to withdraw.

After that for a long time, that is until yesterday I have not visited the Bolshoy Theatre, because we have begun active rehearsals for the performance.

The performance that took place on 24 August 1883 at Lyubimovka consisted of the comedy A Practical Gentleman *and the operetta* The Cobbler Should Stick to His Last, *written by KS with his friend Sergey Kashkadamanov. He also began to stage the plays.*

Diary, 24 August 1883.
Today I demonstrated administrative aptitude which earned me the nickname 'impresario'.

Diary, 24 January 1884. Moscow. *Mischief. The Countess de la Frontière*, operetta adapted from Lecocq's *La Camargo.*
I brazenly copied Lensky in the role of Botov, delighting in the role of *jeune premier*. I handled the love scene in the second act passionately, so that thanks to the electric lighting and beautiful staging we achieved a poetic effect and were given many curtain calls. [..] During the second act the scenery fell down.
I've been waiting for the role of *jeune premier*, and a robber in a gorgeous costume to boot. Given my dramatic aspirations, it is no surprise that I forgot I was playing an operetta, and performed a drama. The chorus was made up of acquaintances to the number of thirteen. If you count the supernumeraries, there were some fifty persons on stage in all. The staging was wonderful. A rumour ran in the audience that the sets had been ordered from Paris. In fact the only things ordered from there were the spurs and two sabres. I was so happy that I did not know whom to copy. I copied everyone who came to mind. In the dramatic scenes, which I wrote into my role on purpose, I copied Lensky, in the singing Chernov. In general, the role came off, I was pleased that they thought me handsome. The trouble I took with my toilette! The finale of the first act was very effective, created a furore in the audience, and when it was over they brought me a silver wreath on a cushion.

In January 1885 KS played again under the name Stanislavsky at Sekretarev's theatre and despised his fellow actors as card-sharps and cocottes. Nevertheless, the following September, unbeknownst to his family but with Fedotova's blessing, he passed the entrance examination for the new dramatic courses at the Imperial Theatre School. He could not reconcile the time he had to spend at the office with the academic calendar. Also, at twenty-two, he felt too old among his classmates, who, in turn, resented the teachers' indulgence for this wealthy amateur. And he found the instruction too cut-and-dried. Used to the lax supervision of domestic tutors, he left after three weeks. He had been equally impatient in high school and would be again at the Paris Conservatoire.

Instead, he became more involved in the musical world, and in 1886 was appointed a member of the administration and treasurer of the Moscow division of the Russian Musical Society and its conservatory. There he befriended Tchaikovsky, Anton Rubinstein and a pleiad of composers and performers. The fresh attraction to opera led him to study voice with Fyodor Petrovich Komissarzhevsky (1838-1905), a distinguished tenor at the Bolshoy Theatre. KS now preferred to play romantic tenor roles or picturesque peasants and bandits in operetta. For his operatic debut as a bass he prepared a scene from Dargomyzhsky's Rusalka *and Gounod's* Faust *(with Komissarzhevsky playing the Prince and Faust).*

To **Ivan Lvov**. 8 April 1886, Moscow.

Young fella me lad!

I sent you a congratulatory telegram,[23] assuming that you would stick to your intention and, agreeable to your letter, soon be in Moscow, but, alas, a week has gone by, and you are still not here. Can it be you are waiting for the sovereign in St P. and will not come to the City of White Stones for Easter. That would be the greatest obscenity, especially since at the end of the holidays my first debut in opera is to take place. Komissarzhevsky's students are producing a show in our hall, in which I portray the Miller and Mephistopheles.

Young fella me lad! Come and have a look! Enough of your wooing the Petersburg ladies! We've got plenty of that kind of goods in Moscow! Write when you think you'll come.

Yours Kostya

The last rehearsal took place on 23 April; at first the debut was put off owing to a catarrh in KS's throat, then it was cancelled. This was the start and finish of his career as an opera singer, although Tchaikovsky had promised to write an opera based on the youth of Peter the Great for him. Nevertheless KS continued to take lessons from Komissarzhevsky, and opera remained a first love to which he would return later in life. With renewed interest in dramatic acting, KS instituted his own course of study, doing exercises at home from seven at night to two or three in the morning.

KS's youngest brother Pasha had been diagnosed with tuberculosis of the brain and taken to drink koumiss (fermented mare's milk) in Samara, in the company of his mother and two other siblings.

To **his mother.** Before 16 June 1886, Moscow.

Dear little Mama!

Nearly three weeks have gone by since you left Moscow, but it still hasn't got over it and goes on grieving, as it were, for the departed native Muscovites; at any

27

rate it has taken on such an inexpressibly languid appearance since that time with no desire to staunch the flow of tears of the pouring rain. It was so cold that everyone, I am sure, would have eagerly donned a warm overcoat, but the young folks were afraid to be considered mollycoddles and the old folk were afraid of frightening away summer. To tell the truth, we enviously thought about how the torrid rays of the Samarian sun are warming you, how the cool breezes wafting from the steppe are blowing on you. However, let us not entertain too bad an opinion of the Moscow climate, which has recently provided us with good weather. It's a pity that it won't last. [...] To give indescribable pleasure to Yelizaveta Ivanovna,[24] I take up cards and start to lay out her favourite game of solitaire, predicting thereby whatever can happen in life, then, if the outcome looks favourable, she is sincerely and heartily delighted and if, on the contrary, the solitaire reveals something unhappy, she stops the disgusting cards and makes me start all over again.

Ordinarily the prediction is decided by various card tricks in my repertoire, which not infrequently are achieved by extreme simplicity: so, for instance, I recently produced a single card, convincing her that it was the whole deck. She believed it and was awfully amazed, when after the word 'passez' the same card remained in my hands. I am dead serious about performing these tricks, so that, with nothing else to do, I arrange the cards and various objects in corners of the dining-room in advance, so that during evening tea I can profit by the naïvety of the old ladies. 'And such is my domestic idyll!!!' No sooner has 12 o'clock struck when everyone disperses and a sinister silence reigns over the house, broken by a terrible quaking of the floors overhead. The mysterious silence of an empty house involuntarily evokes a somewhat uncanny feeling, even trepidation, so that the slightest sound makes your heart beat faster – this is really not hyperbole. Just recently I happened to become the victim of an unfounded fear. The incident took place on Whitsunday, when Papa was at Lyubimovka. Coming home at one in the morning, I headed for my study, after turning off the gas in the vestibule and not closing the door to the stairs tightly. After I lit a match, the first thing that leapt to my eyes was that the shutters in my room were not closed, nevertheless I paid it no great heed and sank into thought: what should I do? Should I go to bed or settle into reading a book for an hour or two? I positively did not want to go to sleep and I felt quite in the mood to study the role of Anany from [Pisemsky's] drama *Bitter Fate*, which I will be performing next winter.[25] Everything was arranged for my chosen occupation: quiet, not a soul around to hear... I began to recite aloud the scene in which Anany takes up a cudgel to beat his wife to death. Soon I was carried away by the speech and, leaping up, I began to prowl around the chair that represented my better half. I got carried away and probably was roaring loudly and gesticulating in a frenzy, brandishing over the back of the chair the stub of a pencil that stood in for the hefty cudgel.

My imagination reached such a pitch that I forgot about the open shutters, nor did I think that the porter had probably applied himself to the window pane more than once to figure out: *has the master gone out of his mind?*

Figure 6 Kostya Alekseev as Anany in *Bitter Fate* when he got to play it in 1888.

Meanwhile I kept on with my monologue and had reached the dreadful moment when I wielded the pencil for the last time before dealing the fatal blow to my spouse; but I seemed to waver, hesitant about committing the dreadful murder and froze for an instant with my arm upraised... The silence of the grave... Suddenly I hear: in the room a sound like somebody yawning... Then I froze in truth. Can it be, thought I, that my shouting has awakened Leon or Stepan Vasilievich[26]; I became a bit embarrassed... Again someone yawned, and very loudly. Then I was convinced that I was not alone, and sank (not knowing what to do) on to my spouse, that is the chair. Again the quiet was deathly, but then a kind of whisper, tremulous, voices in the distance. I could not figure out whether these voices were coming from the street or from upstairs! Good heavens! Someone is snoring! He is tossing and turning! But where? In the bedroom or in my sisters' school-room? I cannot figure it out because the rain is beating so hard on the window pane… Has something fallen down?. . . Farewell, poor fellow! I am done in in the flower of my youth! Not rising from the spot, I glanced at the vestibule door, which was lit by a ray of light from my candle… What is that – a shadow or a man coming up the stairs? Another, a third… What a predicament, I think. There are three of them… a couple of men are snoring in the school-room or the bedroom – five men, and I am alone: it's no great matter to snuff out miserable me! Then, as if to prove my point, steps on the stairs… Yes, they're coming, and that's that. In short, my imagination was overworking to such a degree that I would have believed anything at that moment! I make a desperate movement and grab the Persian dagger. I lock the double-doors to the school-room and go into the bedroom with the candle – nobody; the billiard room, Yura's bedroom – nobody there either. Probably all five are in the school-room, preparing their ambush. I open the doors halfway… I listen… not a sound… But, go ahead and keep silent, you blackguards! I had the impression that the felons in ambush were standing on either side, impatiently waiting for me to come in, so they could leap on me from behind the doors. No! – I think to myself. I'm no fool! I fling open both doors at once, so that one of them smashed against something hollow – no doubt the head of our of the villains – wonderful! Dashing into the room in two bounds, I stare around like a wild chamois, expecting them to fall on me from every side. Total silence! Who is that rolled up in a ball on the sofa? No, it's a lap rug. Looking around the whole room, I found no one, and yet the yawning and wheezing had not ceased. This mystery baffled me and at the same time I was overcome by an irresistible desire to solve it as quickly as possible. Come what may! All or nothing!. . . I decided to go through all the rooms, upstairs, in short, everywhere and began to prepare myself to repeat my bold deed. Because I was particularly concerned about the doors, from behind which they could easily fall on me, I prudently decided to defend myself with a shield; I took it, conjuring up in my mind a hauberk. Again something started moving, dropped… and fell silent on the instant! No, enough is enough! I realize what's going on! It is clear that the noises are coming from above. I open the door to the vestibule, take two or three decisive steps. Ay!.. Oy! oy! oy! Well, I'll be damned! Who was hiding between the tables and the sofa and peering out from there? But what a weird face! Where is his nose? Eyes? You can't even make out a mouth. He is covered up somehow. Never mind, I will expose him! Where are the others? Can they be watching out for me from upstairs, with paving-stones in their hands? Never mind, what will be, will be! I take a firm step, lift up the lap rug covering the intruder. Before me lay a tall, bald man. Who is this? 'Ah!. . . Oh!. . . Konstantin Sergeevich?' -- 'Ah, Savely Ivanovich!' Damn it! I'll swear by whatever you like that it would have been more pleasant for me to encounter the most savage bandit Churkin[27] than him! Where do I put the shield and dagger! But Savely Ivanovich, as if to spite me, rubs his eyes and gets off the sofa, explaining that he missed his train and was spending the night in Moscow. – 'Really? Delighted! How are you? Lie down, please! Don't let me disturb you!' I murmured, completely crushed by this encounter. But he goes on staring in perplexity at the shield, dagger... Do I have to explain what's going on, otherwise he will make surmises! But what yarn shall I spin? Anyway I began to say: 'Well, I was just coming back from there! You know, there!. . . And look what I bought... these things here. Look, how magnificent! This is a dagger from the era of *Philippe of Anjou*, and this is... a *Philistine objet de vertu*, I paid a lot for it! Well, anyway, good night, sleep tight!' – 'No!' he exclaims. 'Somehow I can't sleep in a strange bed.' -- Is that so, I think, then who was snoring for five? We took leave of one another, and it all became clear to me: he was the snorer, the shadows running on the stairs were thrown by the porter, who was walking in the street past my window. That's how the trouble started![28]

Anyhow, worn out by the excitement, I fell into a sound sleep, with the sweet prospect that the next day was a holiday and I could sleep at least until 12. I was not mistaken in that and awoke right on the dot. Slush, muck, thanks to which Daddy couldn't stay in Lyubimovka and came to Moscow. From that day the house got a bit livelier, and I wasn't alone any more. [...]

Goodbye, dear little Mama. Kisses.

K. Alekseev [...]

To **his mother.** 10 October 1886, Moscow.
Mummy dearest!

It's winter here today, any day now we'll be travelling in sleighs. The snow has settled along the roofs, the trees, crunches underfoot, while the winter wind knocks over pedestrians. The horses stumble and fall on the icy thoroughfare, resulting in tumult, shouting, noise, cursing and no forward movement on every street. In short, it all assiduously reminds Muscovites that warm weather has gone and the time of crackling frosts has come, that now is the time when it is good to be somewhere south, as you are now, for example. [...] I am planning to write separately to Nanny [Fyokla Maksimovna Obukhova (1839-1909), his father's former wetnurse] and hope that I'll manage to do it, meanwhile give her a big kiss from me with all my heart, express to her my profound and affectionate gratitude for those sleepless nights, tears, privations, and finally, the premature old age, which, since she raised all of us, is indissolubly bound up with our years of growing up. Tell her how hard it is to put into words that feeling of gratitude that dwells within me and that awareness of her hard-won achievement that wells up in me when I think of her. Pushkin, for all his brilliance, took a long time before he could figure out how to depict the type of the Russian nanny, finding it too difficult and complicated. Only after many difficulties and many failed attempts did he succeed in delineating those extraordinary women, who are able to neglect their own kith and kin in order to bond with their charges, who are sustained by their blood, milk and health. Pushkin has taught me the kind of respect that should be paid to the honourable labour of our first instructresses, and therefore I will be eternally and profoundly grateful to our dear

31

Nanny. If before now I have not expressed in deeds what I am expressing in words, this has come about because there have not been enough occasions for it, but, perhaps, sooner or later Nanny will like a rest from her duties, and then the turn will come for us, her charges, who will not delay to respond with our sympathy. [...]

To **his mother**. 14 October 1886, Moscow.
Dearest Mummy!

[...] Point A, the most sinful of slaves, I as before frittered away my time at the factory, I am now worried about the Russian Musical Society, whose affairs are in a disgusting state. We are seriously at risk of going bust this current year. Despite the fact that the first meeting was this Saturday, we sold half as many tickets as last year. No matter how much I think, I cannot conceive how to improve the situation. I entered into an agreement with S. I. Mamontov, struck up an acquaintance with all his Italians,[29] having invited a few to take part in concerts, hoping that at least the vocal element might interest the public, but no, it was no go.

I drove over to A. G. Rubenstein to ask his advice, but even he cannot explain the coolness of the audience to the Russian Musical Society. By the way, I shall tell you about this encounter of celebrities.

I have to admit I was a coward, when I entered his hotel room, hoping to find a coarse and impudent fellow, who from the very first word is used to cursing out new acquaintances. However, I was mistaken; Rubenstein was in spirits at that time and welcomed me very cordially. He had not forgotten my participation at his brother's funeral[30] and therefore from the very first word dubbed me 'knight of the rueful countenance'.

I sat with him rather a long time. He told me about the Saint Petersburg Conservatory, the new operas that he wanted to write. For my part, I was so bold as to propose a wonderful subject for an opera – Turgenev's 'Songs of Love Triumphant', by asking his advice: could a good libretto be made on that theme. He fully approved and, it would seem, took an interest. [...]

Your son Kokosya

In November and December KS helped his brother Vladimir direct The Mikado, looking for 'a new tone and style'. Costumes arrived from Paris, including fans and silks picked out by his sisters. The scenery was designed by the easel-painter Konstantin Korovin.

In January 1887 KS was invited to take part in a club performance for a charity, staged by Aleksandr Filippovich Fedotov (1841-95), the actress's estranged husband and former Maly actor. Fedotov was a leader in the People's Theatre movement and had run such a theatre in 1872, until the government forbade it. For the first time, KS claimed, he had encountered a true stage director. Fedotov, for his part, was less attracted by KS's talent than by his seemingly unlimited funds. The idea was broached of creating an artistic club without card-playing but with a good-sized company performing plays.

The Mikado, with KS as Nanki-Poo, opened in April and met with gleeful approval from its invited audiences. It impressed both the Maly actor and playwright Yuzhin and the millionaire art patron Sergey Mamontov.

To **Ivan Lvov.** 13 June 1887, Moscow.

Young fella me lad!

[...] Aren't you ashamed not to have come at Easter? I suppose you simply decided to avoid our shows at all costs; but this time you did it in vain, because, without boasting, I will say that the show was remarkably successful. The best proof of that is that we had to repeat *The Mikado* four times, to an auditorium packed to the rafters with an audience of total strangers. What's more: after the show most of them asked permission to come and see the show a second time; likewise there were a great many who didn't get in even once.

All the songs were encored two or three times, the ovations and floral tributes were unending. You will find my statements repeated in the papers (*The Moscow Blade* 19 or 26 April [actually 3 May]), where some crackpot without our leave printed a whole article of praise.

Figure 7 Stanislavsky as Nanki-Poo and his sister Anna Shteker as Yum-Yum in *The Mikado*, 1887

What's more: there were inquiries after the first performance from *The Russian News* and German papers, whose editors wanted to insert their own reviews, but Pater did not deign to permit it. Nevertheless, however jolly the period of performances, it exhausted everyone and me in particular. My nerves are at the end of their tether, and I am glad that now I can rest in the evenings and lead the most proper way of life. These are my occupations: 1) a morning walk after a swim, 2) travel to Moscow and the office, 3) 1 hour of singing, 4) the rest of the time avid reading with exceptional pleasure. By 12 I am already asleep. Young fella me lad, come! We all miss you! Write when you plan to be in Moscow.

Kokosya [...]

Notes

1 Lyuba and Borya would fill these circles with kisses, written by themselves.
2 Vera Vladimirovich Sapozhnikova (1823-77), KS's paternal aunt, whose dacha was divided from the Alekseevs' by a park.
3 Viktor Nikolaevich Mamontov (1839-1903), first cousin of the opera patron Savva Mamontov, married to Vera Sapozhnikova's daughter. Assistant conductor and choir master at the Bolshoy Theatre, he financed symphony concerts at the Nobility's Assembly Hall, which he conducted himself.
4 Yevdokiya Aleksandrovna Snopova, nicknamed Papusha, had taught the Alekseev children to read and write; she was staying with the Alekseevs the last days before her marriage; KS always got her name wrong.
5 Ernesto Fortunato Giovanni Maria Rossi (1827-96), Italian tragedian, who regularly toured to Russia; he was acclaimed for Othello, though later eclipsed by Salvini; his King Lear was not to the taste of the English-speaking world.
6 Ivan Semyonovich Kukin, cashier of the Sapozhnikov firm.
7 Yelizaveta Vasilievna Yakunchikova (1856-1937), KS's cousin and wife of Vladimir Sapozhnikov.
8 Pyotr Viktorovich Ladyzhensky, man of letters, amateur actor.
9 Nataliya Vasilievna Yakunchikova (1858-1931), KS's cousin, wife of the artist Vasily Polenov.
10 Sergey Mikhailovich Tretyakov (1834-92), art collector and chairman of the Moscow Society of Art Lovers, brother of the founder of the Tretyakov Gallery.
11 Nikolay Semyonovich Kukin, worked in the Sapozhnikov firm, participant in the Alekseev Circle.
12 Savva Ivanovich Mamontov (1841-1918), prominent industrialist, philanthropist, impresario of his own private opera company; relative of KS.
13 Zinaida Vasilievna Yakunchikova (Morits, 1864-1929), KS's cousin, sister of the artist Mariya Yakunchikova.
14 Relatives of the Alekseevs, daughters of Grigory Aleksandrovich Krestovnikov (1855-1918), a prominent industrialist.
15 Nikolay Aleksandrovich Alekseev (1852-93), KS's cousin, at this time was one of the managers of the Moscow branch of the Russian Musical Society.
16 A. P. Veretennikov, cashier of the 'Vladimir Alekseev' firm.
17 Sergey Tretyakov, one of the managers of the Russian Musical Society, was briefly Mayor of Moscow.
18 Nikolay Fyodorovich Manokhin (1855-1915), ballet dancer at the Bolshoy Theatre.
19 A piece of the text is torn here.

20 Sofiya Vitalievna Cherepova (Obolonskaya), ballerina at the Ballet Theatre.
21 Romuald Viktorovich Vasilievsky (1853-1919), singer and stage director.
22 Yevgeniya Konstantinovna Markovskaya, ballerina at the Bolshoy Theatre.
23 Lvov had been promoted to staff-captain.
24 Yelizaveta Ivanovna Leontieva (d.1900), KS's mother's governess; participant in the AC.
25 KS first played the role of Anany, a peasant whose wife has committed adultery with his master, on 11 December 1888.
26 Stepan Vasilievich Tarakanov, butler of the Alekseev house at Red Gates.
27 A bloodthirsty brigand, the hero of a sensation novel by N. I. Pastukhov.
28 His mother wrote back, 'We laughed out loud an awful lot at your story...'
29 In its first seasons the Private Russian Opera had basically an Italian repertoire for which Italian singers had been invited.
30 In spring 1881 KS had been an usher at the funeral of Nikolay Rubenstein.

Figure 8 Stanislavsky in 1888

2

THE SOCIETY FOR ART AND LITERATURE

1888–1897

In January 1888 KS left the Russian Musical Society and the AC's performances at Red Gates came to an end: life had supervened and marriage was a chief reason for the departure of its members. KS's sisters Nyusha and Zina married the cotton broker Andrey Shteker and Doctor Konstantin Sokolov, respectively. KS himself was dissatisfied with the level of work in the domestic sphere; his father bowed to the inevitable and allowed his son to create an amateur group outside the family. KS's cousin Nikolay, the mayor of Moscow, expressed his displeasure that KS was spending more time on theatre than at the factory and called him daft.

KS founded the Society for Art and Literature, 'a club with no card-playing', in league with Fedotov, his former singing teacher Komissarzhevsky and the artist and costume designer Count Fyodor Lvovich Sollogub (stage name Burinsky, 1848-90). The Society proposed to 'dispense to its members artistic and literary knowledge, to contribute to the development of good taste and to allow stage, musical, literary and artistic talents to be revealed and develop'. There would be a school, with the dramatic division run by Fedotov and an operatic section run by Komissarzhevsky (this twinning would remain KS's ideal of a theatrical entreprise). Fedotov would be the stage director and the sets would be designed by Sollogub and Korovin. Backstage discipline and rehearsals conducted as lessons were to be the order of the day. The plan was approved by the Ministry of Internal Affairs and the Ministry of Enlightenment.

As she later recalled, Mariya Petrovna Perevoshchikova (1866-1943) had first met KS in the winter of 1886 when he invited her to play the leading role in a comedy by V. Aleksandrov (Viktor Krylov). This failed to take place and they first appeared together on 29 February 1888 in Aleksandrov's The Spoilt Child. Small, delicate, with glistening eyes and auburn hair, this daughter of a notary had to adopt the name Lilina whenever she appeared on stage, because she served as a junior teacher at the Catherine Institute for Young Gentlewomen. When news of her stage activities reached the ears of her superiors, she took refuge with an aunt in Petersburg. It was also in this show that KS met Aleksandr Akimovich Sanin (1869-1955), a Jew whose actual name was Shenberg and who would become his closest associate in staging plays.

In April KS rented the former site of the semi-professional Pushkin Theatre, the Gintsburg Building at 37 Tver Street, and had it converted into a luxurious clubhouse for the Society of Art and Literature. He was in Samara on 10 June, when his brother Pavel (Pasha) died of *tuberculosis of the brain at the age of thirteen. On 3 July KS and his brothers Boris and Yury left for a long trip abroad accompanied by their younger brothers' tutor Sergey Gennadievich Dudyshkin (1853-1903), a 'very cultured' literary critic and journalist, although, according to their sister Zina, 'he only made a repugnant impression on my brothers'.*

To **his parents**. 13/25 July 1888, Vichy. [Old style and new style]
Dear Papa and Mama mine!

Long weeks and not a single letter, don't you agree that is unloving! I swear that in future I will try to expiate my guilt. However, let me remind you: where could I find the time to write to you? Certainly not on the train, which rattles so badly, nor at the stations, where long before the train has come to a full stop, the conductor is shouting: '*En voitures, messieurs! En voitures!*' – a whistle, and '*maintenant, c'est trop tard!...*' Where then --- in Berlin, among those dear Germans, or in Paris, amid that maelstrom, hubbub, racket, fireworks --!!! *Oh, non, par exemple* -- ! you can't get two words out there. What's more, going completely demented, to the hotel *portier's* question I could not remember my name for a long time, or to the question whether I was Polish or Russian, I answered Polish, I am so good at passing for Polish. In Vichy, here I can and must write, gather my thoughts at last, and flicking through and refreshing my memory about everything I've seen and been through in the course of the past weeks, provide a conspectus of our travels, or, more accurately, a brief diary. In fact, let this letter to you take the place of my diary in remembrance of our really pleasant travels. This period is one of the brightest points in my life, and it would be a sin not to leave some notes in memory of it. Therefore, please do not tear up and lose these letters, I will copy them when I get back. [...]

Yours Kokosya

To **his parents**. [4] 16 August new style 1888, Biarritz.
My dear Dad and Mum!

[...] Leaving our things at the Hotel 'Continental' and having a quick wash, we hurried to the shore. Standing near the frothing waves, it was terrible to think that tomorrow we shall have to lie down there and plunge into those dreadful billows. Waiting for the next day to come, we usually end the evening in a café, but this time on the seashore The next day, barely having rubbed our eyes, we hastened to see the sea and, to our surprise, it did not make a great impression, that is, more accurately, the terrible impression that it had had on us the day before. The choppy waves seemed placid, the breakers unremarkable. Little toddlers were running along the beach, paying no attention to the ocean waves. This gave us courage, and we decided to start swimming today. The question of swimsuits arose. But before buying them, we had to learn the acceptable form, and so we went to the Grande Plage to see what sort of bathing suits the smart young men were wearing. The costumes seemed awful, hideous, so that I burst out laughing, imagining my lanky figure in the knee-length, roomy pantaloons and a little blouse *à l'enfant*. But more about this later, because I see in the distance Spanish women swimming... We head over there and lie on the sand, right at the spot where they walk out of the sea. And what do you know, total disappointment. No sooner does a pretty little Spanish lady or Frenchwoman put on a bathing costume when she stops being graceful, walking clumsily through the sand. And their legs, goods heavens, -- huge, fat! Do all ladies have such legs! Why does Pushkin hymn the beauty of women's legs? If I were a woman, I would never agree to show myself in such a hideous guise.

To tell the truth, it even angered me, I won't hide it, that I should be interested in French women's naked legs. I cursed myself, wheeled around and left. All of a sudden I am accosted by a fat frump in a sheet. I hear Russian spoken. I look more closely. Mme Kharitonenko.[1] Even in a frock she's unattractive, but now… what's going on! And you can't figure it out, you know!! I even got embarrassed for her and didn't bow. You can't possibly exchange greetings with a woman like that. I hadn't gone another 10 paces, in pursuit of my companions, lo and behold! Another acquaintance – the sculptor Antokolsky[2] and his little daughter. Eh! Well, that's all right, I think, we won't be bored here. However it's time to get back to the bathing suits. All four of us go to find a shop. We walk down one street, then another, and we keep running into one, a second, a third beautiful Spanish woman. I cast glances, but no, in my mind they're getting inflated, all those crinolines and corsets, and if you put a bathing costume on them – you don't fall in love. Try and get married after that. They keep slowing us down, they keep us from finding a shop! We decided to buy ourselves more human outfits. I picked out a black one, *collant*, with a red sash and a round Spanish cap, flat as a pancake. Yury and Boris fitted themselves out with a sort of circus costume, and Sergey Gennadievich something very ordinary, inexpensive, that is plain and simple – a soft Moscow travelling blouse and striped short pants. We killed time in this way right up to lunch. We go to the hotel, eat with an appetite; our stomach digests it, what's more. After lunch, to a café, in the shade, because you can't possibly be out in the sun. The café is packed with people, and our appearances create a certain sensation. First, because we are newcomers, second, Russians, most in Spanish hats, and Yasha's even wearing a white one, which, to be honest, suits him very well. Moreover, Sergey Gennadievich showed up in a black top hat and a three-piece shantung summer suit. This is quite a novelty for the French. They stared at us inquisitively, especially, I repeat, when they heard Russian spoken. You ought to know that at the moment anything Russian is considered especially chic; they're madly in love with us in France.[3]

Back in Moscow, he set about assembling a company for the Society. The amateurs engaged were all members of good society, including Fedotov's son Aleksandr.

To **his sister Zinaida**. End of October-beginning of November 1888, Moscow. Zinavikha!

I write to you in utter candour, as to why I want you to take part in our performances.

1. Of all the amateur actresses I have observed, you are the only one I know who is very talented, knows how to act not trivially but grandly, is capable of

handling a responsible role, knows how to sustain the tone and apply it to the characters you are playing. No other actresses with these qualities exist here or anywhere else. I would say the same about Kostenka.

2. Your involvement in the first performance is important for me (besides the fact that you are a good performer) in terms of publicity. You have no idea how popular our domestic theatricals are. People who were not in our shows have heard about us and know us all by name. For instance, the critic Vasiliev[4], Goltsev who asked about *The Mikado*,[5] Kotov [illeg.]. Our staging and brilliance are so universally known that my name as the stage manager makes them expect something miraculous. Now imagine that our troupe, so popular (especially with the actors of the Maly Theatre, who are members) will join our Society in almost its entire strength for the first performance and will be composed of serious and handpicked actors. The whole portion of the public that used to attend our shows will come to the Society, plus those persons who have heard about us but could not force their way into our building. Aleks. Vlad.[6] will be our perennial guest, and she will pull in the Mamontovs, Yakunchikovs, Tretyakovs, Sapozhnikovs, Kukins, Tsenkers, Shtekers, etc., etc.

3. Our productions at Red Gates are to be discontinued – wouldn't it be a pity to discard such a good, useful and beloved concern, in which we were able to achieve brilliant results? We can set up our own little troupe, and I promise that I will act only with it and nowhere else. A few unknowns will enter this troupe. But after all even Kostenka was unknown to us once, and we were shy of him. [...] The troupe is all right. The people are respectable, with serious attitudes and not superficial amateurs. I will finish telling you the rest when we meet.

Yours Kostya [...]

I forgot something else: if you act in the second production, that won't answer. One has to begin one's career at the right point. There will be lots of talk about the first production, but not about the second. Besides, our concern is so organized that if we are able to demonstrate to the public all our strengths the first time – it will come off, if not – the first performance will spoil the whole business.

In the event, almost no one from the AC took part in the new Society's productions, except for Nyusha under the nom de théâtre of Aleeva. Work and family matters drew them away. The Society opened on 3 November 1888 with a gala to celebrate the centennial of the great actor Mikhail Shchepkin, whose maxims about acting forecast KS's by half a century. Anton Chekhov was there in evening dress because Lensky was to read from his stories. An important by-blow of the premiere performance of the Society was that KS came to the attention of two of the Maly Theatre's leading actresses. Fedotova had already attended performances of the Alekseev circle. She would later take an active part in the life of the Society, especially when it was first abandoned by Fedotov and then by Komissarzhevsky. Nadezhda Mikhailovna Medvedeva (married name Gaidukova, 1832-99), who played grande dame roles and leads in Ostrovsky, became KS's confidante about his personal life and aspirations.

The first real performance came at the year's end with a short blank-verse tragedy by Pushkin and a two-act comedy by Molière. In the former, KS had the title role as an elderly German baron; in the latter a secondary role as a supercilious French aristocrat.

Diary, Thursday, 8 December 1888. Moscow Society for Art and Literature. Title role in *The Miserly Knight*. Sotenville in *George Dandin*.

A terrible and solemn day. A large audience assembled. Actors, artists, professors, princes, counts. It's no small matter to go on in such a responsible role! I was very worried about *The Miser*, but sure of *Dandin*. The result was the reverse. *The Miser* was better liked and worked better. Although the first act was a flop. The audience did not even applaud. Telegin[7] was the reason for this, he was very bad. Before I came on stage, I was overcome with apathy, the most unpleasant condition for an actor. At first, I did not manage to get inside my role, was tentative in tone and dragged out the pauses. Towards the end of the soliloquy, I flew into a frenzy, and I think I succeeded in the powerful passage. The actress Medvedeva praised me for *The Miser*, only said that I did drag out the pauses a bit. The actress Potekhina[8] assured me that it was very good. And the following remarks were made by members of the audience: 'Stanislavsky has fine gifts, he is very talented, but he did not present his own concept of the role, obviously, but what he had been taught.' [...] After the second act the audience very amiably gave me three curtain calls and as many after the third act.

a)   b)

Figure 9 Stanislavsky as a) the Baron in *The Miserly Knight* and b) Sotenville in *George Dandin*, 1888

It's a strange thing: when you are actually feeling --- the audience reaction is worse; when you have self-control and haven't quite given yourself to the role – it comes out better. I am beginning to understand the progressive development of a role. I have tested in practice the effect of acting without gestures (there are only two of them in the last act). I wear costumes well, I can feel that. My *plastique* is developing; I'm beginning to understand pauses. The mime work is progressing. They say that I died well – with physical grace and truth to life. The next day there was a good deal of talk about me at the Maly Theatre; of course, only the most flattering comments reached me. Medvedeva, as she said goodbye, remarked: 'You are a serious actor and love the work. I idolize you. It is rare for a young man to sacrifice money for a good deed and act well besides.' Then she kissed me, stating that our performances will catch on, because they are much better than Korsh's.[9]

I can say only one thing about *Dandin*: we were much more certain of it, all the more since that heavy stone, that is *The Miser*, had fallen from our shoulders, we were no longer so anxious and acted haphazardly. Medvedeva and Fedotova said that *Dandin* went insufficiently well. Yuzhin[10] praised me. Shidlovsky, a master of costume and makeup, said that he saw in my role of Sotenville a real Molière character for the first time.

A certain Ustromskaya[11] told me that she was annoyed watching *The Miser*. The technique was excellent, but there was no truth. She concluded that I should not play old men and dramatic roles. Fedotova said that, when I went into the cellar and began to speak in low notes beneath the vaults of the cellar, the result was a complete illusion– exactly what she was looking for. The critic Filippov[12] said that I played *Dandin* inimitably – I can compete with anyone at all. I recited the *Miser* well, but it was not acting. In his opinion, I am an actor of everyday life, and not a tragedian.

Diary, second half of January 1888.

[*Preparing the role of Don Juan in Pushkin's verse drama* The Stone Guest.] Memorizing and trying to grasp the meaning of the role in an undertone, I was temporarily delighted by the idea that it was coming along; I soon felt it, I understood the brilliance of the work. I felt all the variety of tones and experienced the pauses. I understood the subtlety, the refinement of all the lines which demand a special technical treatment, and these nuances were definitely emerging from me, but, I repeat, only so long as I recited under my breath. After ponderous prior roles, a few awkward ones, it was hard for me to go on stage as Don Juan. How I dislike the first rehearsals, especially with Fedotov directing. [...]

To top it all, one of the onlookers, I think Pogozhev,[13] explained that there wasn't much passion. Can that be true? After all I sweated blood trying for it, my heart was beating so that I had a hard time reckoning the beats, yet people say there much wasn't much passion. Even Donna Anna, played by Mar. Fyod. Ustromskaya who cherishes a tender feeling for those roles of mine she's seen before and considering it an honour to act with me, even she didn't praise me. I learned from her by chance another unpleasant piece of news. She had talked about me to Komissarzhevsky and, with his characteristic eloquence, he explained that I am cold by nature, ignorant of the passions, that I don't love women, and had never been in love. I was actually offended by this. Pogozhev taunts me, urges me to fall in love with Donna Anna, and invites her to take an interest in me. She doesn't refuse and sits with me a whole evening. I have to confess frankly that she started to interest me, and I stopped being inhibited around her. Perhaps I ought to ascribe this to the fact that at the second rehearsal I acted with great passion. I have begun in fact to be attracted to Donna Anna. The three times the two of us got together to go over the lines, that did not happen, because we preferred to discuss tender subjects, she even told me a few secrets.

What was my horror when the dress rehearsal didn't take place! No one was made up or in costume. I was the only one properly dressed. We rehearsed without scenery and lighting, to the noise of the chairs being set up in the hall, and indeed are to act tomorrow, and nothing is ready, not even scenery. [...]

The production opened on 29 January 1889 as part of a mixed bill on behalf of poor, homeless children.

Straight out of bed I arrayed myself in Don Juan's costume and performed the whole role before the mirror, paying special attention to *plastique*. I certainly cut a dash, and the Parisian boots were eye-catchingly elegant. The costumes were marvellous. I must confess to my shame that the wretched thought, unworthy of a serious actor, flashed across my mind, to wit: well now, thought I, even if I'm no good in the part, then at least I will parade my good looks, please the ladies, who knows, someone may fall for me, at least it will pleasantly tickle my self-esteem. It is not nice when such ideas get into my head; it shows that I have not yet achieved a love of pure art. [...]

[*After the successful performance he spoke with Fedotova:*] She chided me for superfluous passion and dramatic effects, she said that the last two acts should be taken more lightly, I should depict sham, not real passion, -- in short, adopt the same tone in which I had played the scene of waiting for Donna Anna in the graveyard. That scene, in her words, I had performed perfectly, just like the scene with the Commendatore. [...]

Perevoshchikova [Lilina] personally informed me that I was so handsome with a beard and even better without it (at the dress rehearsal) that there was no way to avoid falling in love with me, graceful as I was as well, as any young lady would. For the first time following a performance I was completely satisfied, but – alas! – it was not the pure satisfaction obtained from art! It was the satisfaction of a pleasant boost to my self-esteem. What pleased me most of all was that people were admiring me and falling in love with my looks. What I found pleasant was getting curtain calls and praise, ladies ogling me, etc.

Diary, 2 February 1889.
[*Played Sotenville in* George Dandin *and the Student Megriot in* A Woman's Secret. *Actors of the Imperial theatres were present at the show.*]

Figure 10 Stanislavsky as Don Juan and Aleksandr Fedotov as Leoporello in Pushkin's *The Stone Guest*, 1889

I am beginning to understand the specifically difficult thing in the practice of acting: to know how to get into a role whatever the auxiliary obstacles, to know how to get animated, not to let the role pall.

5 February 1889. Anany in *Bitter Fate*.
Brilliant show. Never have I felt so much pleasure in acting. […] Am I beginning to make progress in dramatic art? […] (I was constantly aware of what

I was doing, and at the same time I was living on stage, I was speaking with facility, the very words flew forth naturally one after another; I was wonderfully calm and at ease on stage. At the moments when I raised the tone, I voluntarily forgot myself momentarily, then I took myself in hand again and played with the same self-control.) […]

The next day at the hairdresser's I ran into the actor Yuzhin, whose wife had been at the theatre; he said, 'My wife told me that you play the role of Anany beautifully, and she is a very harsh critic. Tell me, why don't you come to the Maly stage? Family circumstances, I suppose?' I replied that I had no wish to be a minor actor, and dared not compete with Yuzhin and Lensky. 'What competition? The more good actors the better.' […]

6 February 1889. *The Baron in the vaudeville* A Cup of Tea *in a charity performance with amateurs.*

Disgraceful show, I will never again act with mere amateurs. Besides I was a fine one myself. To be frank, I took the role of the Baron in *A Cup of Tea* on account of the makeup. I thought the grizzled dundrearies and tailcoat would suit me well; in other words, I wanted to show off in my makeup like any trollop! It's disgusting, and I am well punished […] I was given a curtain call but I did not come out. I was furious and nervous to the point – what a disgrace! – of striking a stagehand.

16 February 1889 [*Don Juan*].

[…] Before I left the house for the theatre I recited the role and unexpectedly fell into a completely different tone: Don Juan came out of it not as a fiery, amorous page-boy, as at the first performance, but as an alluring man, who plays games with women. I decided to perform in the new tone, without a rehearsal, off the top of my head. I decided to discard theatrical effect, so that, speaking for myself, I was performing a completely new role. […]

Before 11 March 1889. [*During Fedotov's absence, KS made his debut at the Society as a stage director while playing a sailor in* Burning Letters *by Pyotr Gnedich.*]

[…] To give myself more weight in my new functions, I declared to the cast that I would stage the play not according to my own imagination but as I had seen the French perform it. Of course, I had never seen it at all, but in view of the innovations I had thought up for the staging, I needed to lean on authority, even an imaginary one. I picked the most docile and least mistrustful performers, specifically Ustromskaya, an obvious admirer of my talent […] Everything in the play should be simple, natural, refined and, most important, artistic.

11 March 1889.

[…] If I'm not mistaken, it was a real eye-opener to everyone: we brought a new, never-before-seen style of acting to the Russian stage, not our own, of course, but borrowed from the French. The cultured, sophisticated audience felt it and raved with excitement, the *routinières* protested. […]

13 April 1889. *Bitter Fate* and *The Bear as Matchmaker*. [...]

A few words from Perevoshchikova, who after the role of Luise in *Love and Intrigue* is starting to interest me again. I expected a lot from her this evening; I thought that having rehearsed a difficult dramatic role, it would be easier and more relaxed for her to play roles in farce. I was mistaken, for this time she played worse than ever, and the whole farce went rather amateurishly, was missing something. [...] After the show, on the pretext of choosing costumes, I had tea and stayed a long time at the Perevoshchikovs.

Before 20 April 1889. Baron Hubert von Aldringen in *A Debt of Honour* by Paul Heyse.

[...] It seems to me that I have definitely passed the elementary grammar of dramatic art, I feel at home in it, and only now is my creative work beginning, my mental and spiritual work is only now beginning to open up the broad path to the true road. The whole task is to find this true road. Of course, the truest path is the one that comes closest to truth and life. To achieve it one has to know what truth and life are. This then is my task: to study both from scratch. In other words, one must educate oneself, one must think, one must develop morally and cudgel one's brains.

23 April 1889. Ferdinand in *Love and Intrigue*.

Miss Lilina in my view possesses two rare and valuable qualities as an actress. The first is sensitivity, the second is artistic simplicity. With a certain temperament which the actress undoubtedly possesses, with her intelligence and taste these two qualities of hers offer great hope that an idiosyncratic, very original actress can be made out of Miss Lilina, capable of occupying an honourable place on the boards [...]

I would gladly show the actress her true path, were I not afraid of confusing her even more. I repeat that the delicacy of her talent makes one fear to jolt it in the least way. Nevertheless, I do not think it would be risky to help a young actress explain to herself the meaning of the solemn phrase 'self-analysis'. To simplify this expression, one might say 'know oneself'. It is not quite the same thing, but expresses the same idea to some degree. [...]

An artist, actor or writer can deserve those honourable names only when he becomes a creator. The task of a landscape artist is not limited to the accurate transcription of a landscape, but demands something great from him that distinguishes artistry from the craftsmanship of a photograph. This something is the individuality of the artist's talent, the prism that through his eyes refines its ambient realism. [...] This prism is artistic talent. [...]

Here I break off this scrawl, because a certain doubt has crept into my soul. All unproductive work becomes comic, reminding me of Don Quixote himself. Being no admirer of that negative hero, I would avoid comparison with him and although perhaps too late I will not ask myself: to what end am I writing this endless screed? [...] By no means wishing to impose my opinions, I shall ask

Figure 11 Mariya Lilina as Luise Miller, Fedotov as old Miller and Stanislavsky as Ferdinand in Schiller's *Love and Intrigue*, 1889

Miss Lilina to heed these lines, and, if they make sense, she will not delay to make use of them, and I shall see their fruits, which will inspire me to further co-operative work. If they do not signify, Miss Lilina will help me tear up this thick wad of paper, and I shall stop making efforts to no avail, something that has always been antipathetic to me.

To you I dedicate my humble scrawl, on you depends its continuation or annihilation.

To **Mariya Lilina**. 10 May 1889, Moscow.
Fufinka!

I am waiting for your ladyship's telegram, but your ladyship forgot even to give me a thought. My heart is ten times bigger than yesterday. It's wonderful what's going on in me. I fell asleep yesterday at 5 o'clock with your ladyship's card photo in my hand and a lit candle. I woke up at 9 and laughed out loud, when I remember how your ladyship laughed yesterday when I told you about something I can't remember what. I was awfully pleased when your ladyship laughed. I huffed and puffed, but could not go back to sleep, all on account of your ladyship. (I cannot go on writing to 'your ladyship', you do not reciprocate.) I was imagining how nice it would be to fly in a hot-air balloon with a hammock underneath it. What piffle my head is filled with, but I'm not ashamed to tell it to you.

At 10:30 I got up and went to my parents. A moving scene. This time Daddy was evidently not in a loquacious frame of mind, nevertheless he considered it not superfluous to point out the dark side of marriage. This is a father's obligation, he said, with horrible smugness. The news delighted him awfully, but it started to annoy me that everything is going so smoothly. All the same I would love to elope with you. I'd like to pick a fight over something, and get into a quarrel.

In conclusion Daddy commissioned me to kiss you on his behalf, but having remembered that etiquette holds that it is too early to exchange kisses, he asked me to kiss your hand. What do you think, should I kiss your hand or your Cupid's bow lips… (to my mind, you have Cupid's bow lips). I don't think I ever told you this!

I waited for Mummy a long time. Finally my wait was over and I shed tears of emotion. The scene was moving. I did not hold back and showed all your card photos. They found that you are a beauty in the photos and a bit touched-up. Probably in real life you are only pretty, but, to my mind, you simply have a silly little kisser.

At the factory, just fancy, it's not as boring as I thought. But for some reason I'm ashamed and I blush, thinking that everyone is guessing what's going on. One doesn't lift a finger, even though there's plenty of business. The old book-keeper is foul-tempered, and I tease him on purpose. For instance, in the draft ledger I drew a tree with a bench – in red pencil. Then I wrote that I received 100,000 rubles from a certain retailer and scratched it all out with a blue pencil. He is awfully fussy and wants to recopy the whole ledger from scratch. More power to him, if he wants to do it.

Things have got so bad that we have to bawl out the foreman for drunkenness. They asked me to call him in and play out the tragic scene. I was sure that I would fall about laughing, but for that reason I decided not to summon him, putting it off to tomorrow. If you ask me very kindly – I will forgive him, otherwise – I will flay him alive. Let's see if your heart is kindly or not.

Right! Another curiosity. Old Akulina, the housemaid, has become quite sneaky, peeping through keyholes at what I do when I get up. I crept up on her, quickly opened the door and landed flat on my face.* Then I opened a drawer of the bedside table. I put three card photos of Don Juan under a piece of paper, noting which order they are in, and went out. When I got back, -- the photos appear to have been reshuffled.

I am afraid to reread this, it all so silly.

I will try to be there at 3:30.

Yours Kostya

*Because I'm a barefaced liar!

To **his brother-in-law Konstantin Sokolov and his sister Zinaida**. Before 12 May 1889, Moscow.

Kostenka and Zinavikha!

It is a pity that I cannot convey my joyful news to you in person, but, confident that you will take it as a joke if you hear no confirmation from me, I hasten to assure you that I am in love and will marry Perevoshchikova, mainly, of course, in order to secure an actress for our troupe.

Yours Kokosya

To **Mariya Lilina**, 12 May 1889, Moscow.

Musya!

How boring, my God, how boring it is to sit in a stuffy office. I have lost any ability to be active. The work drops from my hands and seems a tiresome obstacle to attaining the evening's bliss.

Today, as you see, I am in a depressed state of mind, but even this depressed state is sweet and evocative. This is what I feel. First of all, physical fatigue and a headache. (I am as green as death, so that I keep walking over to a mirror and wondering at your taste.) The upsurge of schoolboy behaviour has abated, and I am at peace and the main thing that delights me is I am confident. That is a wonderful mood. I have begun to believe deeply in you and in myself. Our heavenly evening yesterday has left an artistic impression on my memory. You know that what I liked most of all was our mutual, unspoken glance, worth any of last night's ravings. The moment I looked at you, when you laid your head on the cushion, I was Romeo, you were Juliet, capable of anything, at least, I felt that way. My memory is suffused with sorrow, when I recall your words: 'Make believe that we are meeting for the last time', and then too there are your heart murmurs. They are beginning to torment me seriously. Reassure me, speak to the doctor and let me know me verbatim everything he says. Will you do this if I implore you?

Yes, Daddy and Mummy will call on you, probably on Saturday, to invite you to our place on Monday (my father's birthday). You wanted to have a grey frock, I would like that very much. Perhaps I will have time to be there on Monday. With no doubt that you are mine and we are so close to one another that we can speak openly, without mincing words, I can fearlessly propose to you the following. Order the frock and pay extra for a rush job, so it will be finished in time and whatever you need – accept from me. You know, I find it pleasant just to write to you. Pleasant, because I am doing this easily and uninhibitedly I can easily touch the most sensitive chords, which up to now have caused me to live as an orphan.

There is no doubt that you have cured me. That is why it has become intolerable for me to be alone, and I have reached the point that I kiss your portraits, morning and night I bid them hello and goodbye, just like a schoolgirl. I will probably be like that all my life long. When you are away I am as apathetic as I used to be. In your presence I am the schoolboy I was the last few days.

People in town are beginning to talk about our wedding. Today I informed my Leporello, Pyotr the footman, about it. I will tell you the details in person. Meanwhile I send a letter from Shteker.[14] I am afraid that I won't get out of the office before 4:30. If I am late, pull my ears as forcefully as you can, but do not worry and do not misinterpret it.

Be as I am, confident. That is good, and be sure to forget about Doctor Lavrov and his wife. It is too soon to torment me.

Your Romeo Kokosya

To **Mariya Lilina**. Before 5 July 1889, Moscow.
Maruska!

I have never loved so much as today. Such a wonderful impression of yesterday has lingered that I am ready to idolize you. Now I have no doubt that we were meant for one another. Before I only hoped for it, but yesterday I felt it in my heart and confirmed it in my mind. It seems, you said nothing especially clever to me, but a few of your remarks so clarified for me both your intuition and the simplicity of your views on life, the naturalness of your intelligence, inherent in only good and sincere women. Such women are my ideal, and no one but they can have a moral effect on me with such power as they do. I am ready to believe that, on your own, you will hold me in your arms and I will stop being Don Quixote. The memories of yesterday's ecstasies after a heartfelt conversation are also entrancing. It is womanly and even beautiful. In addition, yesterday, to my mind, you were a beauty. All I have to do is close my eyes, and you stand before me such as you were yesterday in your attractive blouse.

In short, despite the fact that I had ridiculously little sleep, around five o'clock, I am fresh, but chiefly, youthful and in love with you as only Romeo can be in love. I would have written a lot more, but the office is full of people. I will set to work, otherwise I will be late. [...]

Your friend, slave and gentleman Kostya

They married on 5 July 1889 in Lyubimovka, with an express train laid on specially for the guests. The honeymoon in Paris, Biarritz and Vienna lasted until the end of September. During it KS studied the role of despotic Prince Imshin in Laws unto Themselves *by Aleksey Pisemsky.*

The censorship on 29 January 1890 banned KS's one-act play Monaco *as 'Unsuitable for the stage'.*

Instead, he worked on a dramatization of Dostoevsky's novella The Village of Stepanchikovo and its Residents; *his widow had given her permission for the adaptation as far back as March 1888.*

To **Anna Dostoevskaya**.[15] 26 February 1890.

Gracious madam,

During my stay in St P., I had the honour of receiving your decision regarding the stage adaptation of your late husband's immortal novella *The Village of Stepanchikovo and its Residents*. After many attempts I managed to adapt the aforesaid novella for the stage, preserving as much as possible everything that could be contained within the narrow framework of the stage. I entertain the hope that the aforesaid adaptation has not misrepresented the work of your late husband, because not only did I not permit myself any additions, but tried as much as possible to select even the connecting words of two scenes, taken from early parts of the story, from your husband's work itself, thereby avoiding mixed colours and an uneven style.

The play had been sent to the censor with the following title: *The Village of Stepanchikovo and its Residents scenes from the novella of Mr Dostoevsky in 3 acts*. The censor imposed his unconditional ban on the play's performance. After some months, on the advice of a certain Moscow man of letters, I undertook a second attempt to have the play licensed, and with this aim I sent it under another name, specifically *Foma*; I changed the names of the characters and with an impertinence uncharacteristic of me I signed my name as author. As a result – total success and unconditional permission to perform the play. However, before such an event can

Figure 12 The wedding of Konstantin Alekseev and Mariya Perevoshchikova at Lyubimovka

51

take place, I feel it my duty to write the present letter to you and send you the play (which will be posted in a few days) in the hope that you will not refuse to give me your frank opinion of it. [...]

Do not refuse to accept my assurances of profound and sincere respects from your most humble servant

K. Alekseev [...]

No author's name was on the title page of the censor's copy, but both author and adaptor appeared on the playbill.

Lilina had been impregnated during the honeymoon and was expecting their first child, but her brother Dmitry Petrovich Perevoshchikov and his wife Yekaterina Vladimirovna Moshnina were the first of their generation to become parents.

To his parents [in Nice]. 19 March 1890, Moscow.

Dear Daddy and Mummy!

[...] On 8 March God gave Mitya and Katya Perevoshchikov a son. The wait was extremely prolonged, because Katya did not take care of herself as she should have (make a note!). Every cloud has a silver lining, Marusya is behaving herself in an even more exemplary fashion. Because I am much more agitated than when I confront a new role, I hastened to collect all the stage properties appertaining to the coming catastrophe. Vladimir Akimovich[16] made an inspection of all these things, and Anna Karlovna[17] came over a few days ago to wash them in carbolic. So far Marusya is not intimidated and behaves well, touch wood. She and I went to hear Masini (only now in the second subscription) and, strange as it seems, were disappointed by him. We heard how hoarse the poor 'dear' was, but singing, at least the sort he had done before, he did not favour us with. He got lots of tributes, but his reception was paltry. At the end of *Favorita* he was hissed, which was repeated at the second performance.[18] Neither we nor Zina managed to go on our subscription; it happened that we hadn't bought tickets in time (the subscription for a performance is advertised the same day) [...] At the moment Masini has been engaged by Savva Ivanovich and has left Moscow. They returned the subscription fees. He had arrived at the theatre, put on his costume, come on stage, tried out his voice with the curtain down, went back to the dressing-room – changed his clothes and left. So, Figner has triumphed.[19] [...]

Yours Kokosya

Diary, 21 March 1890.

The little old man [the factory book-keeper Roman Ivanovich Ebertè] marvels at the indifference with which I glance, and that after his insistent request, at the annual accounts. 'What's this?' he reasons with himself. 'I work all year long and he doesn't cast a glance, I put down these remarkable numbers in red ink and with special satisfaction, and it's no skin off my nose, I don't get anything out of it. His money comes easy!'

'If God takes away his capital, he'll sing a different tune and so on and so forth.' The little old man doesn't know how right he is, I put little value on the gifts God has given me, but in all sincerity I am not afraid to be deprived of funds. If there were no money, I could go on the stage. I would go hungry – that's true, but on the other hand I could act to my heart's content. And so, my work at the factory is pointless and hence uninteresting. Let the book-keeper judge me by his lights, but I am not ashamed to confess to myself and those who are fated to read this diary, that I am slothful, because I have found no interest and purpose to my work. As children are born, perhaps a purpose will appear with them.

To **his parents.** 24 March 1890, Moscow.
My dear Daddy and Mummy!
[…] Here is how our catastrophe came to pass.
The night before, that is Thursday,[20] Marusya came home on foot from Salaev's shop. It was easy for her, and as usual she strode the sidewalk with big steps. However near the general post office the baby gave her a reminder, and that is why all at once her stomach got so heavy that it forced Marusya to hail a cab and get home at a pedestrian pace. Anna Karlovna and Olga Timofeevna[21] were waiting for her, having come to inspect and wash out the phials and basins brought from the pharmacy. Marusya, despite the heaviness in her stomach, which soon departed, however, took part in this work and spent her time in this way until dinner. Then she rested and wanted without fail to go to the theatre to see *Gioconda*, to which we had been kindly invited by Medea Ivanovna and Nikolay Nikolaevich Figner.[22] The performance was long and stuffy, but, to my surprise, even in the intermissions Marusya did not want to leave her seat. After the performance Savva Ivanovich dragged me on stage for discussions. I thought I'd take advantage of the occasion to avoid a visit to Figner's home and give him his money now. To that end I headed for the dressing-room, but did not manage to hand over the money right away. Medea and other persons came in, and I did not manage to draw him aside. In this way a decent amount of time went by, and they chased Marusya, who was with Olga Timofeevna, downstairs and made her wait below on the staircase. We got home after midnight. We went to bed late. The next day Marusya was more cheerful and high-spirited than usual. All day long she dealt with guests, who showed up one after another and helped keep her amused. Snezhkova stayed for dinner and was here till 9 o'clock. When Marusya got up to accompany her […] new guests – Tretyakov and Aleksandra Gustavovna[23] kept her busy. After sitting in the drawing-room for about two hours during a lively conversation, we gathered in the study around 11 to take tea. Soon Marusya came in, followed by Aleksandra Gustavovna. Deep in conversation with Nikolay Sergeevich, I paid this no heed and was so distracted by our debate that I did not notice the signs made by the ladies on their return, nor did I notice that the noise of a carriage drawing up had caught the special attention of our female conversationalists. I even let past my ears the quickly uttered phrases, expressive of awaiting some mysterious guest. However by this time our ladies had risen,

leaving Nikolay Sergeevich and me in heated debate. Around 12 he prepared to go home. His wife appeared and before the departure revealed to me the secret that I had overlooked. 'Don't get excited,' she said to me, 'the cock will not have time to crow before you are a daddy.' I am such an ass! Nothing is ready! There's no baby linen! The rugs haven't been taken up! I myself am still not used to this idea! Then I made no effort to detain the guests, who withdrew in haste.

I flew like a bomb into the bedroom, and, oh horrors, Anna Karlovna is here! She is that mysterious guest, whom the female conversationalists had summoned. [...] A swift inspection led to the conclusion that it was safe to send for Granny. Anna Karlovna stated that the birthing had begun. This dreadful phrase was enough for me to put on my fur coat, take my hat in hand and run to my saviour – Akimych [Dr Yakubovsky].

What I endured during that journey! Will Yakubovsky be at home, if not, where should I go! Where I am to get linen! The easiest thing would be – to turn to Vovo and Panechka [*his brother and sister-in-law*], but I didn't figure that out until the next day, but at the time I wasn't thinking straight and prodded the back of the sleepy cabman. Vladimir Akimovich was at home and quickly scampered in excitement to Red Gates, while I fly to Olga Timofeevna [*Lilina's mother*] – to get linen and let her know. How to do this so as not to frighten a sleeping sick woman? It all turned out well, and in a quarter of an hour I had returned home, sitting on an enormous pile of baby linen, glancing in alarm at the constables, who followed me with a wondering gaze bespeaking a certain curiosity: haven't you done your laundry yet?

At home everything was quiet. The contractions had not yet begun, and Anna Karlovna had postponed the performance to the next day, disbanded her assistants in the person of Dunyasha[24] and the nanny and with great good nature disposed herself to sleep, saying that the matter could be dealt with calmly. However we were not fated to have a quiet night, and I had no sooner closed my eyes, when Marusya began to cry out [...]. But, despite this, Karlovna dropped into bed and prepared for a good kip, asking us to wake her in an hour. Between three and four I ran for her again, because the contractions had intensified each time. The hullabaloo began. The bedstead had to be re-arranged. Furniture had to be carried out, the rug wiped with a wet rag. We three worked, in haste, so we had no time to send for help and alert the nanny. Nevertheless we hastened to send for Yakubovsky, who, after hanging around for an hour, left, not expecting a speedy outcome. We had no sooner set up the bed and carefully laid Marusya in it, when the contractions arrived in quick succession, non-stop and very intense. At that moment I showed myself to be a hero and stood the whole time over Marusya, despite the fact that I would with great pleasure have run into a distant room. Marusya hugged me, prayed, pinched me, bit my shoulder, but did not cry out, and only wheezed. It was a horrible wheezing. To my mind, a cry would have been better! Anna Karlovna began to fuss, because nothing was ready. There was no one to send for the nanny, because at that moment every one of us three was needed. After a brief glance, Anna Karlovna began to yell, 'Lordy, it's started already.' What happened then I do not remember, all my attention was focused on Marusya. Finally the baby's first cry. Hooray! Victory. I looked – it's a boy. They tossed him somehow on to a chair and continued to busy themselves with Marusya. Around then the nanny showed up, Olga Timofeevna appeared, and behind her the doctor. [...] They washed the baby, swaddled it and, o horrors, -- it's a girl. What's going on, what am I going to do with her! However when I learned that it is easier to give birth to a girl, I was reconciled, despite the fact that her face is unprepossessing. She was able to inherit everything that is vile in me. Eyes – not my best feature, mouth possibly even bigger, long arms and absurd build. Thank God, everything is whole, complete. Her voice is stentorian.

[...] The next morning was devoted to finding a wet-nurse. Bogdanov had scheduled one for us for 15 April and was very chagrined that he could not give us the one he wanted. However he found a peasant woman with good, plentiful milk. Not beautiful, not attractive, pock-marked, twenty-six years old, had her third child on 10 March. Lived with strict Germans (known to Yakubovsky). Healthy enough, but with homely looks. We took her, sent her to Yakubovsky to be examined, then to the Society of Physicians. They washed her, dressed her in a nanny's uniform, by evening the baby had taken the breast and now, touch wood!, sucks well.

The christening is set for Friday. This was not because the baby might be weak, we did it to avoid people and having to invite boring guests. Because Daddy promised Marusya he'd be the godfather, we registered him without asking leave. [...]

Kostya

To **Anna Dostoevskaya.** 10 April 1890, Moscow.
Gracious madam!

[...] I am ill acquainted with the troupe of the St Petersburg theatre, but I suppose that Davydov and Varlamov would be the likeliest performer for the roles of Foma and Yegor Ilyich.[25] However I foresee that a production of the play at the imperial theatre will entail great difficulties. I happened to read the play to a few of the actors. The latter, accustomed to the modern repertoire, will look for action in the play first of all, by which they mean not character development but the unfolding of the mere plot of the play. By the way, our actors, specially of the private theatres, take a play's plot to mean action or, more accurately, running around on stage. Naturally, given those requirements of the actors, when they heard the play, they found it unstageworthy. Who knows, maybe even the management will regard the play the same way and either will reject it or pay no special heed to it, casting the roles with second-rate actors or cutting a good half of the play. If that were to happen, I would prefer, with your permission, to see the play in a sensible and careful amateur production, especially since this play would be excellently cast from members of our Moscow Society for Art and Literature. They are talented interpreters, who would treat your husband's work with due attention. Once they've seen this play on stage, I am sure that both the press and the actors will value it more highly than they can do by reading it, and then, God willing, the play will reach the imperial boards. To leave it to the distortions of a private theatre I would regard as a great pity. An amateur performance can serve as a benefit for the extremely needy family of the late S. A. Yuriev.[26] This charitable purpose will attract all the Moscow intelligentsia and bring it to the attention of lovers of theatre. […]

With sincere respect and deep devotion
K. Alekseev […]

In late March the Italian tragedian Rossi arrived in Moscow, but it was the advent of the Meiningen Troupe that most impressed KS. He attended eight of its performances, The Merchant of Venice, The Winter's Tale, Julius Caesar *and* Twelfth Night, Schiller's The Conspiracy of Fiesco in Genoa, The Death of Wallenstein *and* The Maid of Orleans *and Linder's* Blood Wedding, *and created an album of sketches and notes on their stagings, sets, props. He was influenced by the director Ludwig Cronegk's sedulous reconstruction of historical periods and his manipulation of crowds as well as by the sophisticated lighting plots.*

To **his parents**. 12 April 1890, Moscow.
Dear Daddy and Mummy!

[…] Many and manifold thanks for remembering us, for the bonnets and jackets for Marusya and Asya's[27] dowry (we have settled on that nickname). Ah, as far as we are concerned, it's not the gifts but the love that is dear to us, and remembering us at the other end of the world has moved us all the more. Meanwhile, Marusya has been forbidden reading and writing and all work in general, as liable to weary her eyes, which are weak, and so she hasn't written to you, but today she wanted to take up her pen. God has been gracious to us and all is going splendidly. Marusya is patient and gentle and behaves in exemplary fashion. All this time, touch wood, she has not once been feverish. The little girl is healthy, thank God, and behaves well, grows, but gets no prettier. Marusya is now up and about and even has her dinner upstairs, whither she is solicitously carried by the considerate arms of her exemplary spouse. She is even beginning to talk about the theatre, whither the Meiningers are drawing her, but, alas, she is not to see them, and it is up to me to see them for her. She is kind and sometimes lets me go to the theatre. […]

I was invited to act in a performance in Tula and in a new play by Tolstoy,[28] but I had to refuse so as not to abandon Marusya for two days. For this I received her permission to see two productions of the Meiningers. […]

Yours Kokosya

His first daughter Kseniya (Asya) died of pneumonia on 1 May 1890.

KS was forced to reorganize the Society's activities on more modest principles, because the first two seasons of the Society had entailed huge losses for him. Owing to the Society's debts, which he took on, KS held discussions about renting out the Hunt Club building or moving to a more modest building on Povarsky. The Hunt Club demanded that the performances be renamed 'Family Soirees' and re-established card games. KS set out to stage a play a week like other theatres and cut out the galas, bazaars and raffles that had enlivened and helped support the season.

To his mother-in-law Olga Perevoshchikova. 30 July 1890, Moscow.
Most kind Mama!

[...] In fact, is there any point in describing how I get up in the mornings, go for a swim, travel to Moscow, plug away at the factory, return at 5 p.m. to my wife's embrace, cast myself once more into the Klyazma's waves, dine, dicker with my spouse about the postprandial constitutional and, usually, insist that we end the evening sitting on the terrace, reading, and doing poker-work. Is it possible to describe in words the marvellously stylish chair I am working on now? It would probably be better to leave it in peace until your return. At least there will be something to show you, and to tell you about too. If I tell you in this letter about the changes that have taken place in our Society alone, about the fact that the Pushkin Theatre has been transferred on favourable terms to the Hunt Club, that we have moved to new and splendid premises and so forth, your return to Moscow will surely lose part of its interest for you. [...]

One of the Society's founders Count Sollogub died in October and Fedotov departed. An actor and stage manager from the Maly Theatre Pavel Yakovlevich Ryabov (1837-1906) was invited to direct Laws Unto Themselves.

On 10-11 January 1891 the Hunt Club burned down, but KS, who took on the duties of both producer and director, managed to find another home for the Society at the German Club. He staged Tolstoy's Fruits of Enlightenment *in February, and got around the censor's ban by posting no publicity and assembling an audience by invitation. KS regarded it as his first serious staging.*

Diary.

I did the casting with extreme care, thought and success, because I was well aware of the flaws of our performers. Of course, I selected no one from Prokofiev's, not even in small roles. I carried on rehearsals according to my constant system, that is the endless repetition of scenes that aren't working, with a ground-plan drawn up in advance and a set and with specific rehearsals with the individuals who are not playing leading roles.

Tolstoy's Fruits of Enlightenment *opened on 8 February. Its author was not present, despite an invitation, but the playwright Vladimir Nemirovich-Danchenko was in the audience and was impressed by the exemplary nature of an amateur production staged with intelligence and an ensemble. He was particularly taken with the detail of KS's acting as the landowner Zvezdintsev, addicted to spiritualism. When the Maly production opened at the end of the year, it was compared unfavourably with the Society's version.*

57

In April 1891 Fyodor Komissarzhevsky left the Society. To fill the gap, KS reorganized the management and invited Fedotova to preside over it. She accepted.

Lilina was pregnant again.

To **Nikolay Shlezinger**.[29] 22 July 1891, Moscow.

Dear Nikolasha,

I meant to write to you yesterday but a daddy's duties have proved much more burdensome than I supposed, and today is the first free moment I have had to share our joy with you.

Yesterday, Sunday, God sent us a daughter. Her name is Kira[30] Konstantinovna. The originality of this name has already given rise to much hilarity all round, so that people have started to call me Darius Hystaspes and her Cyrusia Dariusevna. I am not responsible for the cream of the joke, since it's not mine. Despite the fact that Marusya suffered long and hard, today she feels all right, although, of course, worn out. For the last ten days we let no one see her, but now we will be heartily glad to see you. [...]

Marusya sends regards and I send a hearty smack.

Yours, Kokosya

This letter was lying unsealed on the desk, when they brought us your splendid gift. Marusya is utterly delighted and finds your little basket very practical (the housewife in her). I found it very elegant and pretty (the artist in me). One way or another, the point is not the basket but the thought. [...]

Foma opened on 14 November 1891, and KS was praised as the self-effacing Colonel Rostanev (renamed Kostenev), for bringing a bland character to life. His methods of staging were beginning to gel: he would make preliminary sketches of the sets and occasionally costumes and makeup, often based on elaborate field and archival research, and then lay down every move of every character. His notes expatiated on atmosphere and lighting.

In April KS and Lilina went abroad: Warsaw, then the Purkersdorf Sanatorium near Vienna (to recover from the effects of the previous winter's 'flu), followed by the factory town of Müllhausen, the textile centre Lyon (for business reasons) and finally Paris.

To **his parents.** 8 May 1892, Paris.

Dear Daddy and Mummy!

[...] Besides foremen and engineers I have seen nothing but theatres in the evenings. Unfortunately, the repertoire is the most uninteresting. Except for the Comédie there is nowhere worth going to. All the plays are the Korsh Theatre variety [*light comedies and bedroom farces*]. Yesterday, for example, I saw a man get undressed on stage: that is he took off his trousers, his shirt. He got into bed. A lady came in and did the same. The curtain was let down at the most interesting moment. And all this went on in front of the most refined, that is most elegantly dressed, audience in Paris.

Last night I was at the ball at the 'Casino'. I will not attempt to describe the disgraceful goings-on, the chaos. Ladies uninhibitedly lift up their skirts and do the cancan with all their might. Squealing, shrieking, shouting, a commotion.

Fighting, rolling around the floor. They fall down and run around the hall like lunatics. I will tell you all about it when I see you. [...]

Yours Kostya

On 14 May, KS went on tour with Maly actors to replace an ailing Yuzhin.

His father died on 17 January 1893 and two months later his censorious uncle Nikolai shot himself. These intimations of mortality led KS to draw up his will before going abroad with Lilina again.

Will, 17 April 1893, Moscow.
To be opened after my death. [*on envelope*]

I am writing this letter before our departure abroad in the event of the death of myself and Marusya.

My wife and I leave to our daughter Kira all the money, shares, interest-bearing securities and portable property, with the interest from the capital to go to the costs of her education. Out of the interest received from the capital a monthly allowance of 100-150 rubles is to be made over to Olga Timofeevna Perevoshchikova.

I ask that Kira's guardian be my brother Vladimir Sergeevich, who will, perhaps, agree to take on the upbringing of my daughter and see to it even though it is an onerous but kindly task.

Knowing Volodya's and Panechka's fondness and love for children, we very much count on them and thank them in advance for being the educators and protectors of our Kira.

In the event of her death we bequeath the monies she leaves behind to the following individuals:

50,000 rb. To Olga Timofeevna.
50,000 rb. To Boris Sergeevich.
50,000 rb. To Dmitry Petrovich Perevoshchikov.

The remainder to my brother Vladimir Sergeevich Alekseev or the person who has taken on Kira's education. If Vladimir Sergeevich and Praskovya Alekseeevna find it impossible to grant our request, we ask Olga Timofeevna to take on herself the education of our daughter, using the interest from the capital for this. To my Mama Yelizaveta Vasilievna, who has seen so much toil and trouble in her life, we would like to relieve her of any new burden and give her the possibility of living out at least the rest of her life peacefully and independently. We ask her to love Kira and not spoil her too much.

Send Kira to a high school when she is fourteen. Up to that point educate Kira at home. Hire a good, strict governess. Employ no expensive teachers. If possible, teach her languages, but more importantly inculcate in her a fondness for reading, develop her [character] and drive out all precocious thoughts of a rich fiancé. Teach her, without fail, those arts for which she shows an attraction, and also from her earlier years impress on her that life is not a sugar-plum but a bitter pill and that the goal of life lies not in hedonism, wealth and pleasures, but in serious work and the beauty that elevates the soul.

Until she is of age, conceal from her the amount of her fortune.

Try to marry her to a good, intelligent and honest man, not an idler, whatever his calling: merchant, actor, scholar, doctor or teacher. Do not let this fiancé know of the existence of a dowry. If Kira chooses according to her own preference, do not stand in her way so long as that way is good and honest.

From her early years try to keep her away from the scions of nobility and potential layabouts of her own age who are mostly to be encountered in wealthy families. Teach her to sew and do not let her become someone who shirks work. Allow her no excessive luxury or toilettes until she has developed her own carefully considered and established view of life and her intellect. Ensure that she respects her grandmothers, her teachers and her relations. Have her frequent the Sokolovs as often as possible. Don't forget Petya and Uncle Mitya and Auntie Katya.[31] Bend every effort to make her religious, since only in that manner can one preserve the poetry in life and a sense of higher things.

When she is three, dismiss her nanny, assigning her without fail a pension of 60 rubles a year. Pension off the wet-nurse as well. When she is three employ a French nursemaid (not flighty) or, even better, an English one (like Sholard).

Teach her to help the poor and enter into the needs of others.

K. Alekseev

I endorse the above.

M. Alekseeva

This itinerary took in Vienna, Berne, Lyon, and Paris. On his return KS had to reorganize the Russian metallic-thread industry, in order to allow him more time for his theatrical activity. Two factories were merged, new manufacturing methods introduced and the buildings reconstructed for greater efficiency. The merger was approved by the Ministry of Finance in January 1894 with a capital of one million rubles, divided into 100 shares of 10,000 rubles each. When the new building was opened it was considered a model, especially in its accommodations for workers.

In March KS played in Ostrovsky's The Dowerless Bride with Mariya Yermolova on tour in Nizhny Novgorod. His own group the Society of Art and Literature was finding the newly refurbished Hunt Club, which wanted it to return, neglectful of the conditions for a well-regulated theatrical production.

To **Vladimir Korolev** and **Fyodor Shcherbachev**.[32] 5 August 1894, Moscow.

Most esteemed Vladimir Vasilievich and Fyodor Nikolaevich!

As a supplement to the letter [of 27 July to the council of senior members of the Hunt Club] from the Board of the Moscow Society of Art and Literature, where the terms were laid out by which we can take on the organization of family evenings at the Hunt Club for 1894/95,[33] I consider it essential, to avoid any misunderstandings in future, to acquaint you in this private letter with the answer which I gave our Board, which assigned me the leading roles and the function of director in the projected repertoire. Some familiarity with scenic requirements and my extremely serious attitude to this business, which I sincerely love, compels me to stipulate the part I am to take in your productions, and I venture to hope that you will not attribute the demands of a director to his personal whims and likewise grant me the possibility to state whatever I would consider essential for the successful stagings of the productions you have entrusted to our Society. In addition, if my requests, enumerated on a separate page, cannot be fulfilled, I will assume that you will explain why I have refused to participate in your productions (however you may express it) as well as my attitude to the matter, from which I would prefer to refrain completely rather than do it badly.

If you are familiar with theatrical matters, you will know that desirable results derive only from good management, only from strict discipline. If it is not always possible to demand such an attitude to the matter from amateurs, that is the performers in the production, then it is all the more proper that the labour be lightened by maintaining theatrical discipline in those who serve the stage management. You will agree that in the opposite case I will have neither the patience nor the strength to be everywhere at once in both the director's and manager's capacities. On the one hand, I will refuse the lion's share of the duties which fall to my lot, but after all one swallow does not a summer make, and therefore without your help or the help of other veterans of the club we will produce nothing good, and the whole undertaking will be limited to the same paltry results that were achieved in earlier seasons, when I took on myself alone the arduous labour, beyond my strength, of director, actor, designer, assistant producer, house manager etc., etc.

All these duties, no easy task on their own, became more complicated since the rights or assistance on the part of the veterans of the club not having been stipulated at the outset of the season, I had to give orders to people who had no reason to obey me unquestioningly; they were to shirk the tasks I foisted on them with flimsy excuses and at the moment the curtain went up we were to lack the necessary furniture, props and scenery on which the performers and director counted so much. What was the result of terms so disadvantageous to me and the enterprise?.. The most miserable: frayed nerves, agony instead of delight, and instead of the audience's approval – its well-deserved grumbling. To avoid everything I just described in the coming season, I have decided to write you this letter and give you fair warning of the following:

a) I am ready to take on all responsibilities, but *only* in the sphere assigned to me. I am ready to be a performer and a director, but no more. Whoever is to carry out the duties of scene designers, stage managers etc., this time is no concern of mine.

b) I will pledge myself for a week, two, three, if necessary, to organize a detailed list of everything required for a technical rehearsal; I will take part in it only when everything, down to the smallest nail, has been provided. If this is not dealt with in time and the start of the technical rehearsal is delayed, either call off the performance or replace me, but I will not take part in it and, to my deepest regret, will be forced to refrain from any further participation in your productions, refrain even *in the middle of the season.*

You will agree that I must warn both you and your administration about this well in advance.

c) It is likewise essential to eliminate some other difficulties and inconveniences, which prevent the success of the productions. From the appended list of these requests you will see how easy it is to carry them out. Lest they seem trivial to you, I forewarn you that my requests are precisely of a whole series of details, which produce results only when they are carried out in full, not in part. In the eyes of those who do not understand the business, I may seem picayune in my demands, those who do understand will understand that these are elementary, the most vital demands of the stage. And as a matter of fact: how can one perform any serious role whatever, when a few metres away from the actor who is working himself up a door is continually creaking, and the shuffling feet of latecomers drown out his voice? Can one yield to the mood, when barely a yard away from those acting on stage there are unruly and sometimes drunken scene-painters stamping, whispering or cursing? If under such conditions the actor cannot believe in his own feelings, what can you expect of the audience, who see nothing of what is going on on stage from behind a row of people going in and out, hear nothing because of the shuffling feet and creaking doors. If actors of the greatest talent will not be in a state to appear in public under such conditions, what can be expected of us amateurs who have even greater need that the audience at least to be not prevented by such things from starting to take a bit of an interest and even without that is prejudiced against us. Precisely because I have been more than once in the situation of the Hunt Club audience, I shall try to deliver myself and my colleagues from the situation of Demosthenes, trying to outshout the roar of the ocean, and those who attend our production from the situation of the spectator who has come to see a serious play and instead winds up at a folk festival. To put it more succinctly, I would like to deliver our audience from the idiotic situation I was in more than once as a spectator of shows at the Hunt Club. [...]

Always ready to serve and esteem you

K. Alekseev [...]

1) Add to the existing overhead and side lights on the stage two upstage side and overhead lights.

2) Make electric shutters for lighting the flats and backcloth from above.

3) Make two portable electric panels for lighting the back flats.

4) *It would be desirable* to increase the intensity of the down-front footlights.

5) Eliminate the creak in the door in the auditorium.

6) In the auditorium, in the aisles between the seats, lay down soft carpets.

7) To the doors of the auditorium affix locks and fit keys to them.

8) Once the stage manager has received in good time from the director a list of scenery, props etc., he must prepare for the day of the scenery inspection (see §) everything that the director finds it necessary to inspect. On the day of the scenery inspection the accoutrements for the play must be conclusively set up, a

list made, the stage ground-plans drawn up. On the day of the technical rehearsal (see § 9, 6) all the scenery, props and other things must be ready. On the day of the technical rehearsal, all persons officially connected with the stage must be in place, so that the director can make all the necessary instructions for the forthcoming performance at the same time.

9) For every production the club will reserve for the Society, beside days for scenery inspections:

a) For ordinary rehearsals -- the Sunday nearest the performance from 12 to 6.

Performance-level preparation of scenery and properties at ordinary rehearsals is not obligatory. The stage will be set up only approximately with whatever scenery, furniture, props etc. are on hand. With this is mind during these rehearsals a few workmen must be assigned to look after the stage for set changes. The stage must be ready at the hour set for the rehearsal; at the same time the stagehands must *without fail* be in their places.

b) The *technical* rehearsals must run from 7 p.m. to 2 a.m.; without makeup and costumes, but with full stage dressing and lighting (the scenery, furniture, props and other things); as in the performance itself, in the presence of the stage manager or his assistant and other stage workers (besides the evening staff). The stage must be ready, and all the workers must be in their places without fail at the appointed hour, that is 7 o'clock, irrespective of whether the characters enter at that time or not. §§ similarly repeat for the technical rehearsals.

c) *Dress* rehearsals must take place from 5 p.m. to 2 a.m., with *full lighting and stage furniture*, in the presence of the stage manager or his assistant and other stage workers (except the evening staff), that is the same as in the performance itself. Dress rehearsals may be scheduled by the director with both makeup and costumes, first, for the production of plays which the Society has not performed for a long time or never performed at all, and second, in case there are cast changes of new performers in more or less responsible roles. The dress rehearsals, and with it the performance, will be cancelled in these cases:

1. If the dressing-rooms and passage-ways leading to them are not ready by 5 o'clock;

2. If the stage and auditorium are not ready by 8 o'clock, that is, if by the appointed hour all the stage workers are not in their places, if the scenery, furniture, props and the other things are not ready according to the director's list *in even the slightest details*, and the stage is not set up and lit for the first act by the appointed hour;

3. If the auditorium is not prepared, as indicated in §

Even if, owing to the fault or tardiness of a performer, the start of the dress rehearsal does not begin at the appointed hour, the stage, dressing-rooms and auditorium must without fail be ready on time.

4. During the technical and dress rehearsals and performances one or two footmen should be assigned, who are responsible for:

a) seeing to it that during the time of the rehearsal no tea or snack tables are laid;

b) seeing to it that no one except the performers enters the auditorium without tickets;

c) seeing to it that after the action begins (during the rehearsals) the doors to the hall are locked with a key until the end of the act;

d) seeing to it that during the performance, before each act, when the music ends the door to the auditorium *nearest the stage* be locked with a key. In that way, the audience will enter during the action through the doors at the rear;

e) at the beginning of the technical and general rehearsals arrange 5 rows of seats in the auditorium and light a few small lamps in it.

5. Print admission tickets to the dress rehearsals with the following inscription: 'After the rise of the curtain the doors to the auditorium will be locked until the end of the act.'

6. On days of dress rehearsals and performances the actors' dressing-rooms must be ready and lighted by 5 o'clock.

7. In the actor's dressing-rooms pier-glasses will be set up and *lights fitted* to them.

8. It would be *desirable* to have a room with a good lock for the properties and furniture of the Society of Art and Literature.

9. It would be *desirable*, to keep down the noise backstage, to have the stagehands on duty during the performance change into felt slippers.

With the Hunt Club organized on a more professional basis, KS took on more ambitious productions. First came Uriel Acosta *by Karl Gutzkow, about a seventeenth-century Jewish dissenter in Amsterdam, which involved period costume, elaborate crowd scenes and multiple settings. KS decided to apply the Meiningen principles to it and designed the scenery himself.*

On 14 September his son Igor was born. Initially his name was going to be Svyatoslav.

To **Vladimir Korolev**. 7 January 1895, Moscow.
Much esteemed Vladimir Vasilievich!

On behalf of those taking part, and pre-eminently the ladies, I turn to you with a great request; might you give an order to have the building of the Hunt Club heated by tomorrow's rehearsal (8 January 1895), because in their medieval costumes our Dutchmen have caught terrible colds, as have those members of the audience sitting in the house. After the rehearsals of 2 January Mariya Fyodorovna Zhelyabuzhskaya[34] and two of the supernumeraries fell ill.

You will greatly oblige me by granting this request.

Forgive me for disturbing you again at the behest of others.

Respectfully K. Alekseev

On 12 January we could perform *Acosta*. I think two days in a row is enough for me, but I am worried about the students; they responded to our admonition submissively,[35] and the greater part of them didn't show up. The most awful thing is that those who do come show up at the performance after student parties and can turn a tragedy into a farce.

Uriel Acosta was played on 9, 11, 16 and 19 January, and proved to be a controversial success, because KS knocked Acosta off his customary pedestal and tried to play him as unheroic, with the philosopher effacing the lover. The crowd scenes were outstanding in their variety and fluidity, the voices polyphonic, the makeups varied. The costumes were rented, however, and some of the stage furniture came from the Alekseev household.

Fedotova, moving to a transition to a new line of business as older women and wishing to prepare herself and the Moscow spectator for this change, went on tour in the provinces in spring 1895, returning to the Maly stage only in autumn 1897. KS and Lilina saw her in Nemirovich-Danchenko's problem play of modern life Gold *in which she played a woman of around 60.*

In April KS played his first Chekhov role, the boorish Smirnov in The Bear, *and a few months later directed his first* Government Inspector *with professional actors at a summer theatre. In June KS embarked on an ethnographic* Othello, *with emphasis on the local colour of Venice and Cyprus, which he conceived as a Turkish protectorate. In August he and Lilina returned to Paris, where he saw at an outdoor restaurant a slim young Arab in national costume; he borrowed his clothes and copied his mannerisms for the Moor.*

To **his daughter Kira**. September 1895, Biarritz.

My dear, darling and dutiful little girl!

If only you knew how much your Papa and Mama miss you. At such times I think I ought to fly to my little daughter and hug and smother her with kisses, of course, if she is a good girl and obeys the grannies and Auntie Sonya.[36] I am writing you on a sheet of paper with a little picture on it. It depicts the sea, in which your Papa and Mama swim every day. Lots and lots of people swim with us in it, all in special little costumes. Even little kiddies, just like you and littler, float on the waves. What a pity that you have not studied French, otherwise you could come to us and swim in the sea. Try as soon as you can to learn French and then, next year, we shall come here and swim. Just think how jolly it will be. From early morning to night lots of little kids play in the sunshine and on the soft sand near the sea. They all have bare feet so they can run through the pools and sail little boats in the water. Along with the little kids, little doggies, poodles, leap and run along the shore. They are so cute and frisky. The little kids run around with them in the sand, throw little sticks and pieces of wood into the sea, and the doggies run like a shot into the water and bring back whatever the children have thrown. Then the kids gather in a big group and head out along the shore to look for little red crayfish, which here are called crevettes. They also look along the shore for pebbles and shells, here there are lots of very nice, very round and very smooth ones. We will ask some little girl or boy to gather you some pebbles like that. It is very jolly to watch the children swimming in the sea. 5 or 6 little girls get together, link arms and run into the water. A big wave washes over them, and they all fall into the shallows and the sand. There is so much shouting, squealing and laughing that even the grown-ups feel jolly, and they start to gambol in the water along with the children. But the favourite game here is this one. A big group of kiddies gets together and by main force dig a big, big hole. Around this hole they make an embankment of sand. They prepare lots of little boats and ships and sit on the shore, waiting for a big wave to come and fill their hole. How excited they get at every wave: will it or won't it reach the hole. Some are sure that it will, other kiddies argue that it won't, -- more laughing, shouting, squealing. But finally a big wave has swept in, filled the hole, and they all jump and dance for joy. Now the greatest fun begins – this launching of the little ships and boats. A whole crowd of kiddies gathers to watch this performance, and we sit on the shore and remember our darling little girl Kirenka and think what a pity that she doesn't speak French and we could not take her with us. How much fun she would have here. How many new kiddies and friends she would meet here, but, you know, they all speak nothing but French, German or Inghelish. No one knows how to talk Russian. Well goodbye, my good little girl. Kiss the grannies, Uncle Volodya, and all the aunties for Papa and Mamma. On my behalf kiss Auntie Sonya's hand, kiss Nanny too, Dunyasha, Varya, the wet-nurse and see you don't forget to smother with kisses our darling little angel Igorechek, see you kiss him nicely, all his hands and feet, We'll come back soon now. Take care, be a clever girl. Goodbye.

Your Papa Kostya

In October KS went to Venice to do research and began Othello *rehearsals as soon as he returned to Moscow.*

To **Vladimir Korolev**. Between 5 and 19 January 1896, Moscow.
Much esteemed Vladimir Vasilievich!

I address you with the most tremendous request, on which depends not only the success of the crowd scenes in *Othello*, but even the production itself.

The dimensions of the stage and especially the wings are so small for the crowd of 70 persons who figure on stage that it seemed impossible to position them and project a distant rumble until today the reception room was opened not only for props storage, but also for the offstage crowd scenes. All at once everything that had not worked before turned out impeccably. I entreat you to arrange things so that at all performances and *rehearsals* we are allowed to blare and make noise in this reception room, otherwise I can do nothing with the crowd, which not only cannot perform offstage under the aforesaid conditions, but there is no way to move there so that the soloists can be in their places on time. I know that my request will disrupt club life, but I assure you that *dire* necessity has made up my mind for me. Without this condition it is *unthinkable* to stage *Othello* according to the rehearsed plan. Once more I entreat that on rehearsal evenings of all performances the gaming rooms be moved upstairs. I am not a god to make a miracle, but even a slightly tolerable production given the cramped conditions that are messing everything up backstage would be a miracle. [...]

With utter respect K. Alekseev

Othello *was performed five times: 19, 22, 25, 31 January and 2 February 1896. The performance scheduled for 18 January had been cancelled due to KS's illness and much of the cast replaced at the last minute. The critics believed that, despite the exotic local colour, KS's Othello was a modern man with all his neuroses and frustrations, a big simple-minded baby. A young Meyerhold was, however, very impressed and preferred him to Rossi in the role.*

KS began to feel that he and Lilina, as actors, were outgrowing the limitations of the Society and its coterie audiences. He also began rehearsals of Hannele's Assumption *by Gerhard Hauptmann, a sortie into the mystical with professional actors, at Lentovsky's Solodovnikov Theatre, the largest private playhouse in Moscow (2000 seats).*

To **his wife Mariya Lilina.** 3-4 May 1896, Moscow.
My dear and dainty little darling!

I am sitting in the Hermitage, at 10 p.m. Straight from the Board of Guardians. While waiting for dinner I have decided to have a little chat and unburden my heart. Magnificence all round, cavalry officers and their ladies, I suppose, professional dancers, everyone in couples. The champagne flows, merriment, but I am lonely, missing my little dove.

Today wore me to a frazzle. At the Board of Guardians every day I have to hand out up to 300 tickets for free dinners for the poor. You can't protect yourself against the difficulties and confusions. And to top it all Yavorskaya[37] has paid for the *Othello* scenery. I thought that Dobrovolsky[38] would dig it out of storage and move it to the theatre and back. It turned out that Dobrovolsky had left Moscow and there was no one to look for the scenery in the sheds. The performance is scheduled for Sunday, and I do not know what I am to do. All this is irritating me even more.

Since yesterday was a public holiday I got up about 12. The house was empty. Where should I go? I thought and thought, went to mass, attended prayers at the Three Joys. What next… and I couldn't help it – sorry! I went to see Medvedeva. I stayed from two to eight, had dinner, drank tea and talked for the whole six hours, about theatre, of course. Medvedeva was in remarkable spirits. She tried to worm out of me why you are ill. Is it because you are jealous of my love for the theatre? I wondered how could she know?

Forgive me, my little dear, I may have made a blunder, but I did confess that part of your illness comes from the fact that you never see anything of me. Medvedeva does understand my situation as an actor and a husband and realizes how hard it is to reconcile these two responsibilities. She understands this duality that dwells in an actor. Love of one's wife is one thing, love of the theatre another. They are two completely different feelings, one does not exclude the other.

To my mind, she spoke very well, and I decided that, on your return, to ask her advice. It occurs to me that, as a woman, she will understand you and, as an actress, will understand me.

The whole time, for some reason she kept speaking on the theme that *I have a duty* to do something for the theatre, that *my name must go down in history.* For a long time she has been repeating this at the Maly Theatre and after *Hannele* Lensky began to support her. I don't know why she was saying this, but it seemed to me that she somehow suspected my intentions or my growing coolness to the theatre.

(Dmitry Filatych [Vosnyatsky] has come by, and so I interrupt the letter.)

67

Edition
„Richard"
St.Pétersbourg
330

A. PASETTI.

Яворская

Figure 13 Lidiya Yavorskaya. Photo: Vezenberg, St Petersburg

I am writing the next day (Saturday) over morning tea.

Yesterday I sat with Filatych until 11:30 and, of course, discussed the theatre some more. Before writing you this letter, I sent a messenger with a letter to Kupernik[39] that the scenery hadn't been found and I asked her in any event to take measures in case Dobrovolsky can't be found. Around 11:30 a note came from Kupernik, in which she implores me to take emergency measures.

I go to the Chernevskys,[40] it turns out she isn't living with them, but they with her. I encounter the damsel in distress [Yavorskaya] (a head shorter than Shchepkina from the Maly Theatre) in a terrible state. She had gone into management, because she considers herself a progressive woman, and now she has been torn to shreds. She pleaded with me with tears in her eyes to help her, otherwise she would go all to pieces. The conversation was interspersed with hysterics. Finally, her plea was reduced to my coming to at least one rehearsal. At that point I did not so much recall my intention to retire from the theatre, which, as if for spite, haunts me, as I did your advice – not to get involved in theatrical matters with such ladies who in the eyes of the public can involve me in scandal. Among such ladies, of course, Yavorskaya takes pride of place. After the most unsuccessful ploys, after all kinds of lies with dreadful efforts I somehow managed to give her the slip. But this all worked out dreadfully absurdly, and of course I have now made a new enemy in the theatre. It's amazing, this always happens to me when I have to refuse someone. At the most decisive moment, whenever I have to say 'no' as quickly as possible, I let the moment pass, pause, while I try to figure out some delicate motive for refusal, my face expresses dreadful embarrassment. The person doing the asking takes advantage of that moment, starts thanking me for agreeing, and I can come up with nothing and I start to get even more confused; finally a mist comes over me, I start to talk drivel, and as a result the impression comes across that I am falling ill, collapsing, in short, the most repugnant impression. One way or another, but the third time I do say no. Now they'll probably let me alone.

This morning Dobrovolsky finally showed up. I consigned to him the delivery of the scenery and now thoroughly wash my hands of the whole matter. [...]

Kotik

Lilina replied, 'Dovie, I also understand you perfectly as an actress, the proof being that I would be the first to be horribly upset if you gave up the theatre, but because I am perfectly aware that that is impossible, I sometimes grumble. I grumble, true, not at the theatre, but at the fact that you neglect me...I agree with Medvedeva that you can do something serious for the theatre, but then you will have to give up the factory, otherwise the one is bound to interfere with the other.'

To **his wife, Mariya Lilina**. No. 6, Monday, 6 May 1896, Moscow.
Darling angel!

My need to love you and live with you soul to soul has turned out to be so great that I would like to devote every free moment to you. Imagine, just this morning I sent you a letter, in which I hoped that when I arrived at the factory I would find a telegram from you – and there is nothing. Right now I am sitting at the factory and sent for a horse-cab to go to [my mother-in-law] for lunch. I want to drop in on Red Gates to ask about the telegram, otherwise I won't know anything until this evening. I shall probably spend all evening at [your mother's] and am even glad of it, because if she is not in a querulous mood she will ramble on about you, and that is now my favourite theme.

I keep sketching a picture for myself: if you have to go abroad – how are we to live apart.

And I start to become very gloomy. During everyday endeavours, having you at hand, I ungratefully trade you for the theatre, but when we are apart I cannot even think about the theatre. I have to confess to you that this time I somehow have even forgotten my intention to give up the theatre. However, that's not quite right, I didn't forget, but the theatre itself haunts me, which is only natural, because the few acquaintances I have left are all theatrical. For instance, Vosnyatsky suggests I take advantage of my solitude and get together with him every evening to prepare work on the project for a new theatre. I procrastinate – and I have no energy to start discussions, because, perhaps, I recognize in my heart that they will all remain only projects, and then, somehow... I have no energy. Yesterday at the [Maly] Theatre Preobrazhensky[41] makes the same suggestion, because he's free all this month, -- I temporize again. If you were nearby, I would take on this work enthusiastically and with an untroubled mind, if only to have occasion to talk about the theatre. You see how vile I am – I want you to sit beside me, you would miss me while I pay you no attention and am involved in business which interests me alone. To be fair, I ought to add that I behave this way, of course, because there are other secondary matters; and of course you are right that we would both be happy if my business were only with you and the theatre – only how is this to be done. I will think furiously about this during this time. I miss the Board of Guardians because, apart from theatrical matters, you and I could get together only in the cause of charity; you have the gifts for this: good sense, a certain broad view. You do not go off on tangents, for instance, snivelling over a single case to the detriment of the whole. You similarly do not easily let yourself be taken in by deception and exploitation. If this domestic-theatrical or in the extreme case domestic-charitable-works life were to appeal to you – I would be utterly happy.

Now about you. What you need, my lovie-dovie, I am a bit confused about, and however much I thought about it last night, I cannot paint a sharply delineated picture. All I can imagine is an imbalance. In domestic life I take a wider view than you do. You are narrower and more detailed in family matters, and have never tired these last few years in perfecting all of it. Give some thought to whether I am speaking the truth. Meanwhile all this is as alienating and confused for me as this letter, but allow me sometimes to bore you with this philosophy, because with pencil in hand it is easier for me to follow my thoughts logically. You and I do not agree on one thing: that I have started loving you less in recent days. No, this is not true – now I understand this well and clearly. Alas, I understood no worse that you have become colder to me and, of course, through my own fault or, more accurately, the fault of circumstances. Can Medvedeva be right and is it impossible to combine theatre and family. If, alas, it is so, I will all the same choose family, but only in the broadest sense: a life which is all-consuming for one another both spiritually and physically. Can it be that it is impossible to idealize family life. To challenge one another with the demand to share ideas on a daily basis. This demand is the only way to create affection and all the other manifestations of love, which, I understand, are not sufficient for you. And indeed not only are they not sufficient for you, even our inner life has not been sufficient for you so far. Let us strive for it to flourish, to the detriment of stomach and comforts. Accept this little sacrifice of mine and leave me at least for a little while without lunch, I shall be grateful for this spiritual sustenance. On your return allow me to simplify for you the housekeeping part of our home. Truly, I am capable of doing that, and then our lives will be splendid.[42] However, goodbye, my darling little beauty, my earthly little angel, my soul, my body, my 'all' – I have to go to [your mother], otherwise I'll be late, especially since I want to drop by our house. If I get back home early, I'll write you more, you write only when you want to, or write tiny little notelets.

Try to write in pencil, it's quicker.

All yours Kontunchik

Scold Kiryulka depending on how she behaves.

The references to housekeeping had to do with Lilina's thrifty approach to domestic economy – she had been brought up in a family of limited means – in contrast to KS's lavish expenditures and lordly generosity.

To **his wife Mariya Lilina**. No. 7, 7-8 May 1896, Moscow
My dearly beloved little angel!

I had no sooner rejoiced over your telegram: 'Health and weather wonderful', in which I connected the word 'wonderful' to your health, when I got your letter of 3 or 4 May, in which you speak of feverish chills. Again I was down in the dumps and want to come to you. Write or even telegraph: will it help you if I come? I cannot just up and leave, but, of course, the factory will credit me with time for a summer vacation. This is ridiculous, but I am afraid that what with the overcrowding and discomfort at home you and I will not get a chance to see one another, and that's why at night we will make up for what we neglected during the day. Give it some thought and consider it all prettily, do not think you will offend me by a negative answer. If you like and it will be useful for your nerves for me to come, telegraph: 'Come Kharkov' (this will mean that the house is so crowded and uncomfortable that it would be better for me to stop in Kharkov, at a hotel, where you can come to spend the night after packing off baby Kirinka) or telegraph: 'Come Bavaria.'[43] In a negative case telegraph: 'Don't come.' I might be able to get away on the 10th and stay till the 17th, because on the 18th I definitely have to be in Moscow for business. Your shivery shakes don't alarm me. After all the doctor warned us that they will recur less and less. I am afraid that you are down in the dumps and retarding your recovery. Please, weigh yourself and write how much weight you have lost. If so, you will have to make an appointment with Korsakov.[44]

Yesterday I dined with [your mother], with a headache and a murderous mood, at the end of the evening I talked with Mama and managed somehow. Of course, we spoke about you and the theatre. I get awfully aggrieved and insulted when people sneer at the theatre. Give up the theatre, they say, as if it meant nothing at all. Somehow without meaning to I would like my doing so to be taken to be a heroic feat. [She] and I quarrelled a bit on that theme. [...]

Yesterday I went to buy a hat. Yes, just before I left there was a new incident with Yavorskaya; she showed up to ask for more scenery. I refused point-blank for lack of it (I am beginning to learn to say no).

After I bought the hat I went to the factory. The factory is closed until Friday. Today is a holiday, so is tomorrow. What will I do? [...] I went to see [Maeterlinck's] *The Dream Princess* [*La Princesse Lointaine*]. I have seen a lot in this world, but such nasty stuff I never did see. Yavorskaya, probably for publicity purposes, lured me into her dressing-room. Thereupon she loosed all her hangers-on on me, who after every act with the utmost impertinence drag me backstage, but I recalled your advice and dodged them with the utmost audacity.

After the show I ran into Suvorin[45] on the stairs. He dragged me into the refreshment room, and spoke a while about the theatre, of course. They had turned off the lights in the theatre, -- locked it up, but we went on talking. When she heard that Suvorin was in the theatre, Yavorskaya and company ran in with candle-ends and started to drag us to her apartment (she lives near the theatre). At which point I arose and with a coldness uncharacteristic of me said no, but they dragged off the old man. Praise me for my success!

I got home around 12. Nyusha was at home, trading insults with Mama about the trip abroad. I fell asleep between two and three. [...]

Goodbye, my darling little dove, I love you terribly and feel dissatisfaction because I do not know how to express my love, where to send it. I think I would even get satisfaction or content by making you a sacrifice, possibly even by missing you; of course, this is only nagging. In fact I want awfully to caress you, fondle you, not to make up for bad feelings, but to express or vent an over-abundance of love. To do that getting together is indispensable. Letter-writing, day-dreams, philosophy – this is not enough. The demand to withdraw from everyone with you to some forest, cottage, so that we can see and love one another, but, alas, it is a dream. [...]

All yours, your adoring and tenderly sympathizing and pitying

Kotik

To **his wife Mariya Lilina**. 21 May 1896, Moscow

My dearest, darling treasure, my bright and dazzling little diamond!

You all-understanding and all-forgiving clever little person! [...]

Our little world is the cosiest corner on earth. Perhaps the edifice isn't quite finished yet, but my soul is at rest whenever I merely speak or dream about it. You are the empress of this little world, and I its emperor, and all its splendour consists in the fact that you and I are the only ones in it. There are no laws in this spot. These will arise by themselves through the good promptings of feelings and heart. When it is cold in the sick world – a warm little fire will be kindled in us, and we will heat up one another. When the outside world is too clamorous and fussy, we will embrace one another and rest, for at least one little hour, but in warmth and surrounded by caring and love. When the people out there get frenzied and brutal and nip at us, we will come together and lick and treat our wounds, and when we ourselves make mistakes and follies, we will not abuse one another as all the others do, but with kisses will crave one another's penitence and promises not to make the same mistakes. Everyone will seem powerless against the might of our love, and no enemies and opponents will terrify us, because we fear only our own consciences and one another and at the same time we will love God and one other most of all, that is our quiet, blissful little world. Let others think that we are insane idealists, but if we forget traditions and laws written by people not God and behave only at His behest, truly, an attractive blessed and poetical little world will be created and strengthened in us. To say everything to one another, to confess everything – and forgive everything. To learn to do the last is the most difficult thing of all, but somehow, together, with both our strengths let us learn this Christian feeling, if only in relation to one another. When it becomes insufferable in this atmosphere, you and I shall scamper off to Troitsa,[46] Petersburg or simply take a room at a hotel and lock ourselves in for a day or two. For the sake of this relaxation I sacrifice a certain disorder in housekeeping, a few tears from Kiryulka. Such trips, especially in wintertime, are essential for us to make at this critical moment, when our nerves are frayed, if only to confirm to one another all the ideas and communicate all the feelings that we have had no time to communicate to one another during the concerns of everyday life. We shall live off these few days for the following several weeks. Over the course of the winter they will be the oases in the desert that will quench our thirst for love and return us burned-out cases to the daily chores of life, refresh our weary brains and renew our strained nerves. This may be eccentric, silly, new to others, especially since we shall keep secret the building of our little world and shape it out of ordinary life. These, my one and only and invaluable friend, are the dreams in which I find my rest nowadays. To you in quiet Kharkov all the splendour of this little world and its relaxations may seem unclear, but at the moment for me, immersed in Moscow life, hemmed in by pretentious and cold Petersburg gentlemen and *raisonnable* and benevolent Moscow merchants, -- the minutes I write about (and live them at the same time) seem oases. Strain your clever little brains and your responsive and kindly little heart so that in our absence you put yourself in tune with such a life. Fortify your wasted, splendid, wonderful little body so that amid this life resonant final chords, full of lives and passions, will ring out. There is no way to rely on others, let's put our hopes in ourselves. Get accustomed to my quirks and try either to come to love them, or, at least, treat them like a little boy's pranks, and I will try to come to love and admire you at those moments when you are darning stockings, love you for whatever quirk, childish innocent mischief you may get up to. It seems (right now at least) that I have loved you for it and at the given moment I would like to see you specially for the chance to admire and love you with all my heart when you are black, because I always admire and worship you when you're white. Come to love me even when I am burrowing into a role and barely answer your questions. Love me, as you fell in love with Kirinka, with all the childish passion of playing with dolls. Do not prevent my playing and, when it is over, say that you understood my mood and did not resent it because you loved me at that moment, loved me like a child, like an actor. O! How grateful I will be and worship you, when I regain consciousness. I will smother you for those moments – all-forgiving and all-remembering – with the passion of a tragedian, with the tenderness of a romantic lead (it appears to me then, that passion) and with the love and respect of your husband – who worships you and is true to the grave.

Kotunchik

To **his wife Mariya Lilina.** No. 14, 27 May 1896, Lyubimovka.
My precious flesh and blood, meaning of my life and aspirations!
   [...] I am awfully glad that you are beginning to understand that actors must be a bit odd, in both their splendour and their misery.[47] If I were a mere bourgeois, we could not have been married for 7 years and have had such a wonderful little week. But these are still the buds. People expect berries from us, if you will forgive and understand my peculiarities and love them. Remember, I always repeated this, and now I admit and feel what you will become for me under these conditions. I will not be in a state to live without you and I will eternally hold on to your apron-strings as Kirinka does. [...]

Your adoring Kotunchik

To **his wife Mariya Lilina**. No. 18, Saturday, 1 June 1896. Lyubimovka.
My desired bride, madly beloved Kharkov lover Anelka!
   [...] I have already written you that I was invited to Tsarskoe Selo. At the time of the coronation [of Nicholas II] Yevgeniya Yakolevna [Poiré] made the acquaintance or was earlier acquainted with Colonel Krylov, an intimate of Grand Duke Vladimir Aleksandrovich,[48] and manager of the Tsarskoe Selo performances for the tsar. Seeing that the tsar loves theatre, they have fitted it up with everything: whatever he might find of interest. He has been to all the Moscow theatres and concluded that, except for Yermolova – it's null and void, as well as stale and of no interest. However Yermolova very much wants to get into those performances and is pestering Krylov about this, but, before asking her, he has apparently decided (I am quoting Yevgeniya Yakovlevna) to try his luck with me or, more accurately, with our Society: might we take *Acosta* to Tsarkoe. They promise a train almost free of charge, the Alexandra Theatre to rehearse in and the entire receipts from all the performances to cover the rest of the expenses. Ostensibly Krylov is waiting in Petersburg, eager for this visit. You know how colourfully Yevgeniya Yakovlevna talks (dearest, if I didn't lay on the colours so thick myself, I wouldn't like it). I don't know how much of this is to be believed and whether Poiré herself has had a hand in setting this up. She is terribly excited by this and has decided that after this tour the sovereign will immediately appoint me a minister. As soon as she learned of this, she was at Red Gates (a week ago now) and left the longest of letters. I paid it no attention and decided to plead

that I had not received it, because I didn't want to visit her – she has begun to get on my nerves. Today at Red Gates I am handed another letter with the request to meet as soon as possible about an urgent matter. So I had to go to her. She told me all the details, how all Petersburg and especially Krylov are mad about me (although he has never set eyes on me), that he had heard about me before, and, now, on his arrival in Moscow, hears nothing but my name and therefore charged her with persuading me. At any other time I would jump at this proposition, because, having acted before the tsar (and he is inviting us specifically for 20-30 July, that is just when all the actors of the imperial theatres are desperately swamped, because for some reason that is the imperial summer theatre season), we will assume quite a different significance in Moscow. Then we will cease to be amateurs. But now I can think of nothing but you, seeing that they expect an answer by 1 July, I stated that in the summer all my time belongs to you and therefore I can say nothing without your decision. [...]

Only, my little dearie, this is under the seal of greatest secrecy. [...]

You say that I do not know how to love, but you will never find such another lover. Set a date and you yourself, my dreadfully silly creature, will learn how fleshly love is the fruit of spiritual love. [...]

Your adoring Kotunchik

On 17 October the first performance of The Seagull *took place at the Alexandra Theatre in St Petersburg and was a dismal flop. Chekhov swore that the play would never be staged in Moscow nor would he ever write another play.*

KS's first performance as Mathias in The Polish Jew *by Erckmann-Chatrian (the play that as* The Bells *made Henry Irving's reputation) was on 19 November at the Hunt Club. The following year a charity performance of a scene from* The Miserly Knight *on behalf of needy students of Moscow University took place at Korsh's Theatre.*

Diary, 15 February 1897.

For me, an amateur, this was a remarkable evening. To perform in a real theatre, in a purely professional theatrical set-up... I was understandably excited, although this was not the first time I had played the scene. [...] Uncomfortable dressing-rooms with thin partitions, the conversation of some persons unknown to me while getting into costume – all this was unpleasant and spoiled the mood.

I performed badly, felt it and was embarrassed.

A. P. [Chekhov] stepped up to me and thanked me, but, alas, not for *The Miserly Knight*, but for a role... in his play *The Bear*, which I had played not long ago at the Society for Art and Literature. 'Listen, I'm told you perform my play wonderfully. I didn't see it, you understand? I'm just the author... the one who writes the flops.'

Work had begun on Much Ado about Nothing, *with KS in the role of Benedick whom he conceived as a coarse military man and true misogynist, an interpretation he would later transfer to the Cavaliere di Rippafratta in* The Mistress of the Inn. *It opened on*

6 February 1897 and was acclaimed as 'life itself'. His dinner scene in Act II was especially praised.

The First All-Russian Congress of Stage Workers was convened by the Russian Theatre Society in Moscow, 9-23 March 1897 to bring together theatrical practitioners from all parts of Russia. Their deliberations considered such matters as qualifications, pay, pensions and insurance, labour-management relations, bringing theatre to the lower classes, and (less nobly) limiting Jews on the stage. The conclusion was that a sound theatrical education was indispensable if the theatre was to make progress. Both KS and ND attended.

Meanwhile KS made his first stab at staging opera with Conservatory students at the Maly with scenes from Tchaikovsky's Queen of Hearts *and* Cherevichki, Glinka's Ruslan and Lyudmila, Rubinstein's *The Maccabees and G.* Cipolini's *Young Haydn. He thought it went better than expected but was inconsequential.*

Then KS and Lilina took another trip abroad, passing through Berlin 17-21 April 1897 on the way to Paris.

To **his mother-in-law Olga Perevoshchikova**. Before 8 May 1897, Paris.
Most kind Olga Timofeevna!

[...] What have we been doing all this time? Almost nothing. Unbelievable! Soon it will be two weeks we've been in Paris, and, judging by earlier excursions, I must have been to the theatres more than 25 times, that is twice a day, and this time I've been only, only 7 times. This is astonishing! The most interesting of all that I have happened to see here is *La Samaritaine* with Sarah Bernhardt. It is a completely new and wonderful genre, which, alas, we will not see any more than we will our own ears. The play is called 'Evangile en 3 parties'. This kind of performance is organized for those who wish to pray and cleanse their souls. Despite the fact that the play is performed God knows how and by whom, despite the fact that the characters, except for Sarah and Christ, are not very reminiscent of Biblical times, despite the fact that, finally, I do not agree with the image and characteristics of Christ as presented in this mystery play – I wept at all three acts and left the theatre completely refreshed.

Tell Sofiya Aleksandrovna [Kosheleva, a friend of Lilina's] that I am very sorry she hasn't had a chance to pray in a theatre; it's a pity that she could not be persuaded that a mystery play, performed in the slightest degree by talented people, has much more right to sympathy and existence than the mindless simpering and hoarse bawling of drunken and raggedy deacons and parish priests who in their old age have outlived their brains. Tell her that she would prefer the wonderful sets, painted by the inspired brush of the best French designers, to the hideous icons daubed by house-painters, and that 'Our Father', set to the wonderful verses of Rostand and uttered in a whisper by Sarah amid a sobbing audience, -- this is artistic in the highest degree, it moves one to tears. My dream now is to stage this play... if only in a private home. Let those people who have lost the ability to pray in churches come to us and be inspired in the theatre. In short, going to the theatre, I feared, that the play and especially Christ on stage would come across as offensive as depicted by a Frenchman, but to my surprise, it turned out that even a Christ, somewhat affected and devoid of simplicity, forced me to pray as I have not prayed for a long time in churches, despite their harmonious singing, despite the bawling of the deacons, the brilliance of the iconostases, the incense, genuflections, bows to the earth and such-like Phariseeism. In contrast to this wonderful mood it doesn't hurt to relate an evening in Montmartre. Shaikevich took me there… there are three cabarets: 'Le ciel', 'Le cabaret du néant' and 'Cabaret du diable'.

Imagine that you are entering the second establishment: black funereal drapes, skeletons, tombs instead of tables, requiem candles instead of electric lights, you are served by grave-diggers. Semi-darkness. You are greeted with the exclamation: 'Reçevez les cadavres O! que ça pue!' They serve you beer with the following line: 'Empoisonez-vous, c'est le crachat de phtisiques' etc. You move over to 'Ciel': walls painted like showbooths in blue and white circles; an assortment of horrible snouts – men dressed as angels with wings; a caricatural pastor in a skull-cap and a little brush around his neck (a brush for a water-closet). When you ask him what that is around his neck, he replies that on earth 'cette machine se trouvait un peu plus bas, mais ici, vous comprenez…' The apostle Peter, in a fairground costume, reads a sermon and confesses anyone who likes, angelic music and heavenly sounds, chosen from the raciest operettas, two gods set up in two corners of the room – le dieu Porcus (dieu de la cochonnerie) and the dieu Pognon (the golden calf) etc., etc. Finally, the 'Cabaret du diable' (we didn't go there), where, they say, there is another new way of desecrating the church, religiosity and rituals. This is the product of that respect for religion, which the Jesuits have achieved with the clergy in the lead. These are the spectacles which made the greatest impression on me. […]

Loving and grateful Kostya.

Before I seal the envelope, I remembered that you would be upset: had Marusya gone to the 'Cabaret du néant'. Don't worry: of course, she didn't. I went there alone.

Lucien Besnard (1872-1955), French theatre critic and dramatist, had seen both Uriel Acosta *and* Othello *in Moscow; he wrote to KS about the latter (22-23 January 1896), complaining that KS had betrayed tradition by 'modernizing' the play.*

To **Lucien Besnard**, Moscow, 20 July 1897
Dear Sir, Mr Besnard!

Allow me to address you in Russian, which will enable me to speak at greater length and more freely. […]

Better late than never… Allow me now to redress my oversight and fulfil my longstanding obligation to you for your longstanding letter sent before I left Moscow. At that time, the theatrical season was in full fling, and I could not reply at once, then at the end of the season, alas, I could not find your address which you sent on the letter. I am heartily grateful to you for having frankly and candidly expressed your impressions of *Othello*. It is impossible not to agree with you that the performance was very, very bad, because the play flopped and barely ran for four performances. Now we have stricken *Othello* entirely from our repertoire. But what was I to do? The week before the performance four leading roles had been replaced by second-rate performers, namely: Iago, Brabantio, Cassio and Emilia.[49] There was no way to replace the play, because we were afraid of grumbling among the cast.

I agree with you that I failed as Othello, but I will take issue with one of your remarks, namely: that we played and produced the play at variance with Shakespearean tradition. I adore him and therefore consider it my duty to stand up for him. My opinion is this: Shakespeare states his traditions in Hamlet's speech to the players. These traditions should be sacred for every actor. I revere the French for their tradition, which, by the way, has now become a simple

Figure 14 Stanislavsky as Othello and Khristofor Petrosyan as Iago, 1896

uninteresting routine in the realm of light comedy and drama. But their tradition in tragedy – what can be more dreadful, what has it in common with Hamlet's words? The French call their style of acting a tradition, and that is precisely in those outmoded conventions that Mounet-Sully[50] plays Hamlet. Where does this tradition come from? People say that Talma[51] played that way... But does any one of us remember him? I do not doubt that, perhaps, he did shout, but his shouting was the consequence of a vast artistic temperament. He shouted because the power of his expressiveness was so great that his voice too, on its own, so to speak, grew and expanded in proportion to his temperament. I did not hear Tommaso Salvini shout, because his voice is the truthful and natural consequence of his temperament. But when the diminutive Mounet-Sully puffs himself up and shouts at the top of his lungs to heighten his own nerves and the nerves of his audience, I cannot help remembering the fable about the frog and the ox, and say, 'What a pity that this tremendous talent is perverted by phony traditions created not by geniuses, but by untalented people', and this is really so: a genius is inspired by truth, by beauty, by life itself, while no-talents need a screen to conceal the poverty of their talent and imagination, and for this reason invent tradition. By now they have concocted so many traditions and different rules that Shakespeare is not understood by the ordinary public, and Molière has ceased to be funny. Whom does he owe that to? I assert, to tradition.

Judge for yourself: could Shakespeare be satisfied with Mounet-Sully's performance of Hamlet, after the author had inserted the following lines:

1. 'But if you mouth it, as many of our players do, I had as lief the town-crier spoke my lines.' (Act III, scene 2.)

2. 'O, it offends me to the soul to hear a robustious periwig-pated fellow tear a passion to tatters, to very rags, to split the ears of the groundlings, who, for the most part, are capable of nothing but inexplicable dumbshows and noise.' (Act III, scene 2.)

3. 'With this special observation that you o'erstep not the modesty of nature; for anything so overdone is from the purpose of playing, whose end, both at the first and now, was and is, to hold, as 'twere, the mirror up to nature.'

4. 'O, there be players that...neither having th'accent of Christians, nor the gait of Christian, pagan, nor man, have so strutted and bellowed that I have thought some of Nature's journeymen had made men, and not made them well, they imitated humanity so abominably.' (Ditto.)

Compare the above with what Mounet-Sully does and you will admit that he errs in his false tradition, just as all contemporary interpreters of Shakespeare do. A huge mistake, an inexplicable misunderstanding has arisen with respect to Shakespeare. Remember: Shakespeare's contemporary, Ben Jonson (Uncle John) [sic], also a writer for the theatre, preached word for word what is now imputed to Shakespeare. Yet the latter never agreed with him. It was Ben Jonson, not Shakespeare, who loved high-flown emotion, preciosity, pasteboard and pseudo-theatrical effects, or, more accurately, heroics. He ridiculed Shakespeare for having a penchant for everyday characters. Shakespeare, on the other hand, was carried away by the characteristics of the role, but thanks to his supernatural talent he delineated his heroes so vividly that they acquired significance for all mankind. If in our time Ostrovsky is described as the writer of everyday life, Shakespeare was such for his own time. Of course, I am not comparing these two talents, and all I say is that they are somewhat alike in their views on art. For does not Hamlet say in Act II, in the scene with the players: 'They are the abstracts and brief chronicles of the time'?

Finally, the adaptation of *Hamlet* as it is played by Mounet-Sully, is it not eloquent proof that Shakespeare's spirit has been misunderstood?

Those Gervinuses[52] and other learned critics are Shakespeare's greatest foes. They approach the living, artistic and inspired work from a dry, scholarly standpoint, suck the life out of it and make it uninteresting. If this vast scholarly library about Shakespeare's heroes and plays did not exist, everybody would regard them more simply and would understand them perfectly, because Shakespeare is life itself, he is simple and hence understandable by all. But if you pick away at his every word and search out the various sagacious meanings, Shakespeare will lose his brilliance, passion, beauty... and remain a boring philosopher and raisonneur, of interest only to scholarly specialists.

In short, the more simply we treat a genius, the more accessible and intelligible he will be. Genius must be simple, it is one of its principal qualities. So, on the one hand, we have traditions that someone anonymous has invented, and, on the other, we have the brilliant lines of Shakespeare himself about dramatic art. Whom are we to believe: the learned Gervinuses and company or William himself? Do as you please, but I believe the latter and say with conviction: all traditions that diverge from the words of the genius are nonsense, and should be forgotten as quickly as possible.

Now a few words about Molière. I was just in Paris last spring and saw *The Miser* and *The Misanthrope* at the Comédie (I didn't visit you, because again I didn't have your address. The concierge looked you up and brought me the address, but it turned out to be incorrect and I didn't find you.) The greatest foes of Molière are the actors at the Comédie. This is not tradition, but simply idiotic obstinacy – to desiccate such a great author the way they do. Remember, you write in your letter to me 'Traditions are great because they assist a lesser actor to perform Molière respectably.' With those words you harshly condemn the Molière tradition. For instance, I saw Coquelin cadet[53] in Moscow in *The Miser* (*L'Avare*) in a very bad production with a very bad troupe, and I only just saw the same play at the Comédie with Leloire[54] (I think that's his name) in the leading role. Lo and behold – there was no difference. Anyone who performs in the Molière tradition is boring in the same way. Whether Tartuffe is played by Coquelin aîné or Febvre[55] – there is no difference. Yes, you are right; an untalented actor will not spoil the role if he plays it in the Molière tradition. However do not forget that thanks to those same traditions a brilliant actor will never be outstanding in the role. Why? Because the existence of tradition means there is nothing for him to create, since everything has already been foreseen by tradition, all that is left is for him to copy his untalented predecessors. A genius cannot play to order, by a measurement set once and for all, he has to create, and to do this he needs room for his imagination and creativity. The actors of the Comédie in the roles of Molière are not living people, but mannequins. That is why the very best Tartuffe I have ever seen was our Russian actor Lensky, he did not act according to tradition but created the role and was interesting.[56] The Meiningen troupe, which played Molière in Moscow,[57] had a great success in those plays, whereas all the French troupes flopped in those plays, beginning with Coquelin aïné and ending with Coquelin cadet. The latter eloquently proved this this year. The public found him to be disgusting in his writhings, but isn't he acting in the Molière tradition? He provoked almost no laughs, and the public did not come to the theatre for Molière. The Meiningers had the audience dying with laughter and filled the theatre on the days when it played Molière. And the Germans are certainly no experts at comedy. What does this explain? The French played according to tradition, obsolete, outmoded traditions, and Molière struck us as boring and monotonous. The Germans could have done so, but created – and the result was life and laughter. I laughed heartily at the Germans and smiled not once at Coquelin.

I follow your example and say frankly what I think. Do not condemn me. My motives are good ones. Art has no nationality, and I love the Russian and French and German stages all the same. I am profoundly depressed that for some three years now the theatres in Paris have declined so badly. This may not be evident to you, but I, as a travelling man, noticed that routine prevails in your theatres and they have stopped making progress. The French theatre has ceased to speak a new word in art, and for the three weeks of my stay with you I saw nothing new, nothing original that I could take an interest in. The same effects, the same devices. Even in light comedy the French have forgotten how to laugh. They have started to take trousers on and off, climb into other people's beds with women etc. etc. But this is neither funny nor witty. We are reconciled to this, because the French themselves are by nature charming, refined, attractive, their language is delightful. Take away that quality from you, and even Berliners will outstrip you. The people, the language there are the most unattractive, but they work, they aspire to something, create something. During the four days of my stay in Berlin I saw: 1) *The Sunken Bell*, 2) *Hannele*, 3) *Coriolanus*, 4) *Much Ado about Nothing*. Each of these plays made me think. I carried around a stack of notes, filled a whole notebook, sketched a whole album, whereas in Paris I could not write a single line, sketch a simple production; everything seemed to me so stale and familiar. I am sincerely grieved by this, because we Russians are accustomed to wait upon what you say and do. Free yourselves from tradition and routine as soon as possible, and we shall follow your example. This will come in handy for me, because I am waging a desperate struggle against routine here in our humble Moscow. Believe me, the task of our generation is to drive obsolete tradition and routine out of art, and give greater scope to imagination and creativity. That is the only way we will save art. That is why it pained me to hear you defend what I consider to be the bane of living art, which is why I have now written you so much.

Wishing you success in your affairs.

Yours respectfully K. Alekseev

KS's ambitions continued to grow. He turned to another Hauptmann fantasy, The Sunken Bell. He was less attracted by its salvational message than the various technical problems it presented. For the first time he got in touch with the realist painter Viktor Andreevich Simov (1858-1935) to do the scenery. The play's premiere was on the small stage of the Hunt Club, 27 January 1898. KS lacked the necessary mystical aura for the bell-founder Heinrich, but again he excelled at crowd scenes, special effects, soundscapes, and a host of tricks that smacked of Christmas pantomime.

Twelfth Night with KS as Malvolio went into rehearsal, with for the first time on the Russian stage Viola and Sebastian played by one actor (Ye. V. Shidlovskaya). It opened on 17 December at the Hunt Club, its high spirits appropriate to the season.

Notes

1 Vera Andreevna Kharitonenko, trustee of the Society for the Protection of Impoverished and Needy Children.

2 Mark Matveevich Antokolsky (1843-1902), sculptor, famous for his statue of the devil.

3 The result of Germany's aggressive foreign policy.

4 Pen-name of Sergey Vasilievich Flerov (1841-1901), journalist and critic.

5 Viktor Aleksandrovich Goltsev (1850-1906), editor of *Russian Thought*.

6 Aleksandra Vladimirovna Alekseeva (Konshina, 1852-1903), wife of KS's cousin Nikolay.

7 Dmitry Vladimirovich Telegin (stage name Dolin), deputy from the Volokolam district to the Moscow Assembly of Nobles; participant in the first avatar of the Society.

8 Raisa Alekseevna Potekhina (1862-90), actress, daughter of the playwright Aleksey Potekhin.

9 A private Moscow theatre, opened in 1882, became a favourite with the middle-class public by alternating boulevard dramas and European innovators (Ibsen, Rostand).

10 Aleksandr Ivanovich Yuzhin (Prince Sumbatov, 1857-1927), actor, playwright, at the Maly Theatre from 1882.

11 Mariya Fyodorovna Ustromskaya, a dark-eyed beauty who acted under the name Mareva, became a member of the Society, often partnered with KS.

12 Sergey Nikitich Filippov (1863-1910), theatrical reviewer.

13 Pyotr Vasilievich Pogozhev, who played at the Society under the pseudonym Molchanov, was an employee in the office of the Imperial Theatres.

14 German Lyubimovich Shteker (1857-1903), father of Andrey Shteker and KS's sister Anna's father-in-law; member of the board of the Discount Bank, director of the Moscow Society of Fire Insurance; he was congratulating KS on his engagement on 11 May.

15 Anna Grigorievna Dostoevskaya (Snitkina, 1846-1918), widow of Fyodor Mikhailovich Dostoevsky.

16 Vladimir Akimovich Yakubovsky, family physician and friend to the Alekseevs.

17 The midwife who usually carried out that function in the Alekseev family.

18 Angelo Masini (1844-1926), Italian tenor, was part of the Italian opera company that visited St Petersburg 1879-1903; he was invited by Mamontov during Lent when the imperial theatres were closed to sing the role of Ferdinando at his private opera.

19 The soloist of the Mariinsky Theatre Nikolay Nikolaevich Figner (1857-1919) was also invited by Mamontov to appear in his opera in Lent.

20 Actually Wednesday.

21 Olga Timofeevna Perevoshchikova (Gorskaya, 1840-1920), Lilina's mother.

22 At her benefit on 21 March Mariya Ivanovna Mey-Figner (1859-1952) sang La Gioconda and her husband Nikolay Figner sang Enzo in Ponchielli's opera.

23 Nikolay Sergeevich Tretyakov (1857-96), son of Sergey Tretyakov, artist and participant in the society shows; and his wife Avgusta Gustavovna.

24 Avdotya Nazarovna Kopylova, the Alekseevs' housekeeper.

25 Vladimir Ivanovich Davydov (Ivan Nikolaevich Gorelov, 1849-1915) and Konstantin Aleksandrovich Varlamov (1848-1915) were the leading character actors at the Alexandra Theatre.

26 Sergey Andreevich Yuriev (1821-88), theatre critic and translator.

27 The baby's Christian name was Kseniya.

28 *Fruits of Enlightenment* was staged by amateurs on 15 April in the hall of the Tula Assembly of Nobility.

29 Nikolay Karlovich Shlezinger (1857-1929), employee at the 'Vladimir Alekseev' firm, participant in the Alekseev Circle; friend of KS's youth.

30 Kira is the feminine of Kir, the Russian form of Cyrus.

31 Pyotr Dmitrievich (Lilina's cousin), Dmitry Petrovich (Lilina's brother) and Yekaterina Vladimirovna, Dmitry's wife.

32 Vladimir Vasilievich Korolev, managing director of the Hunt Club; Fyodor Nikolaevich Shcherbachev, senior member of the Hunt club.

33 The coming season was to open with Prokofiev's staging of Ostrovsky's *It's Our Affair – We'll Deal with It!*

34 Mariya Fyodorovna Andreeva (Yurkovskaya, married name Zhelyabuzhskaya, 1868 or 1873-1953), met KS in summer 1894 when he persuaded her to join the Society; she made her debut at the Society 15 December 1894 as Vasilkova in *Light, Not Heat*, opposite KS as Rabachev.

35 Students invited to take part in crowd scenes were celebrating the traditional academic saturnalia Tatyana's Day.

36 Sofiya Aleksandrovna Kosheleva, not a relative, but a friend of Lilina's.

37 Lidiya Borisovna Yavorskaya (Hübbenet, married name Princess Baratinskaya, 1871-1921), an actress of sensational roles and a dubious reputation, eager to run her own troupe; Chekhov had a brief affair with her and modelled Arkadina in *The Seagull* on her.

38 Vladimir Nikolaevich Dobrovolsky (1876-1930), Society colleague; supernumerary at the MAT 1898-1930.

39 Tatyana Lvovna Shchepkina-Kupernik (1874-1952), writer, translator, great granddaughter of Mikhail Shchepkin.

40 Director of the Maly Theatre Sergey Antipovich Chernevsky (1839-1901) was married to the granddaughter of Mikhail Shchepkin Aleksandra Petrovna Shchepkina (1856-1930), the aunt of Tatyana Shchepkina-Kupernik.

41 Vladimir Petrovich Preobrazhensky, lawyer of the Moscow Palace of Justice.

42 Lilina attributed her seeming coolness to her illness and nervous condition.

43 The New Bavaria Station, close to Georgy Alekseev's home.

44 Sergey Sergeevich Korsakov (1854-1900), neuro-psychiatrist, founder of the Moscow school of psychiatry, who introduced a nosological approach to the study of psychoses.

45 Aleksey Sergeevich Suvorin (1834-1912), millionaire publisher of the monarchist newspaper *New Times*; playwright, friend of Chekhov and owner of the Theatre of the Art and Literature Society in St Petersburg. Yavorskaya was a member of its company until 1900. KS probably first met Suvorin in 1895 in Biarritz.

46 The Trinity-St Sergius Monastery, near Chernigov, maintained a hostelry for the laity.

47 A loose quotation from Larisa Karandyshev in *The Dowerless Bride* by Ostrovsky (Act 1, Sc. 4).
48 Vladimir Aleksandrovich, Grand Duke (1847-1909), commander-in-chief of the guard battalions and the Petersburg military district (1884-1905).
49 Iago – Fedotov; Brabantio – Prokofiev; Cassio – Lenin; Emilia – Mikhailova-Poiré.
50 Jean Mounet-Sully (1841-1916), leading tragedian at the Comédie Française.
51 François-Joseph Talma (1763-1826), Napoleon's favourite tragedian, who introduced classical drapery to the French neoclassic stage.
52 Georg-Gottfried Gervinus (1805-71), German literary historian, author of a four-volume study of Shakespeare, translated into Russian 1877-78.
53 Ernest-Alexandre-Honoré Coquelin (1848-1909), French actor, younger brother of Constant Coquelin.
54 Louis-Pierre Leloir (1860-1909), French actor, who wrote a play about Molière.
55 Constant-Benoît Coquelin (1841-1909), and Frédéric Alexandre Febvre (1833-1916) were the leading character actors at the Comédie Française.
56 Lensky first played Tartuffe at a benefit 6 December 1884.
57 The Meiningen repertoire included *The Imaginary Invalid*.

Figure 15 Stanislavsky, in bowler, addressing the troupe of the Artistic-Accessible Theatre in the courtyard of the Hermitage theatre 1898

3

THE MOSCOW
ART THEATRE EMERGES
1897–1900

The foundation of the MAT can be seen as the culmination of the reforming tendencies present in the Russian theatre from the beginning of the nineteenth century. Its principles had been enunciated sixty years earlier by Mikhail Shchepkin. There was the same emphasis on the stage as a rostrum from which to educate the public; the insistence on discipline, devotion and intelligence in the actor's work; dedication to high ideals of art and literature, especially Russian art and literature; and unity of ensemble, directing and design in the mise-en-scène. The concerns evident at the Congress of Stage Workers were also contributing factors. Theatrical reform was in the air. At the Imperial Maly Theatre in Moscow, Aleksandr Lensky created the New (Novy) Theatre in 1898 to allow the younger members of the troupe a chance to gain experience in major roles and to produce plays unlikely to be taken into the standard repertoire. In St Petersburg, the World of Art movement was founded by the critic Sergey Diaghilev and the artist Aleksandr Benois.

On 7 June 1897 KS received a letter from the prize-winning playwright Vladimir Ivanovich Nemirovich-Danchenko (1858-1943). The son of a Serbo-Ukrainian military officer and an illiterate Armenian mother, husband of a baroness, ND had become dissatisfied with the production of his plays at the Maly Theatre and had been teaching at the Moscow Philharmonic to improve the technique of young actors. He wrote: 'I prepared a long, long letter to you, but because I will soon be in Moscow, I did not send it.' This was followed on 17 June by a proposal to meet at the Slavonic Bazaar Hotel in central Moscow: 'We have been seeking one another for a long time, although it would seem there was no reason for the search, since we have known one another for a long time and have often met, but without fathoming one another.'

On 22 June there took place the famous meeting of KS and ND at a private room off the restaurant of the Slavonic Bazaar, eighteen hours of uninterrupted conversation continued at Lyubimovka until eight the following morning. The theatre they projected was meant to be Obshchedostupny_(literally, 'acccessible', but implying 'at popular prices for working-class audiences'); it was aimed at low-income groups, students, professionals of modest means, and workers with aspirations to culture. The repertoire planned was highly ambitious, from Greek tragedy to the latest European problem play, but with an emphasis on classics. A correspondence with ND in Yalta ensued.

To **Nemirovich-Danchenko**. 19 July 1897, Moscow.

Most esteemed Vladimir Ivanovich!

[...] Of course, I am heartily delighted that our project has met with general approval, but I am trying not to be carried away by individual opinions, although I sincerely believe in them. When I recall that all-round approval, those expressions of hope for our success and prosperity, which encouraged me when I founded our Society, I now can't help but regard this well-wishing for our new concern with distrust. As to Kosheverov's letter, that really is joyful and gratifying news; it leads me to believe that this man is both serious and eager to work. All that remains is to wish that he put his plan into action and settle in Moscow.[1] If he is talented, it is impossible not to agree that we ought to take advantage of his proposal and try in every way we can to bind him closer to us. How are we to relieve his financial situation? I could wring something out of the Society – take him on for this season at a salary of 100 r. or a fee per performance of 25 rubles. This would seem to offer him some sort of support. Taking part in the Society's performances he could obtain good experience and might prepare a few roles thoroughly and unhurriedly (with a more than sufficient number of rehearsals). I do not doubt that for such work, which is not complex for a real actor, he will have enough time left to assist you. However, I return to this question only below, meanwhile I clarify only that I set the sum of 100 r. on the following conditions: 1) at this fee in spring the Society will look for a romantic lead from among the novices, so that this expense will appear in the estimated budget of our Society for the previous season; 2) you write that Kosheverov would join our enterprise at 1200 r. a year. Of course, a salary like that would definitely entail a contract for a year's work, which I could not offer at the moment, but once he has got ready for Moscow and involvement with you and turned down all sorts of work and making a fee, and perhaps, even proposed that he is to get payment for teaching at the Philharmonic Society, then my proposal, in accord with that picture he sketched of himself, may appear to him as interesting and alluring. I could promise him two roles, interesting for Moscow, namely: Christ in *Hannele* and Heinrich in *The Sunken Bell* (the last in alternation with me). The following roles also come to mind: Glumov, Rykov (*Laws Unto Themselves*), Count Orsino (*Twelfth Night – maybe*), Claudio (*Much Ado – maybe*), a few roles in new plays in the coming season.[2] Usually in winter we stage about 10 plays. [...]

I ardently believe that with a month's exploitation of a provincial town in the summer one can earn about 450 r., but with the organization of a careful estimate one can forget about that and draw up a budget at a more modest figure. [...]

You write further that, in case of delay in distributing shares we could run the business at our own personal risk. Recalling our agreement to speak our opinions candidly, I have to linger over this passage in your letter and express myself concisely and clearly.[3] Bitter experience has taught me to swear: never to run a theatrical enterprise at my own risk, because I do not have the right to do so, partly because I am not rich enough (my capital amounts to 300,000, all of which is entirely invested in my business), and second, because I am a family man and I do not

Figure 16 The restaurant at the Slavonic Bazaar Hotel

believe that the money belongs to me alone, but to all the members of my family. How can I risk other people's money? Of course, I shall take about 5 thousand rubles' worth of shares, maybe 10 thousand, and in that case, I will risk that much and if worse comes to worst I can afford to lose it. Losses of a private speculator or entrepreneur are unpredictable. Besides, any private undertaking is looked on by the public as a kind of speculation, and that will bestow quite another character on the whole business. A joint-stock company is a social, cultural concern, an enterprise is mere profit-taking. That, I believe, is how the public will regard it.[4]

To the question: can those of our ladies with social standing take part in the concern as actresses[5] – I am almost prepared to say with conviction: 'Yes.' However, I will ask around and discuss this in greater detail.

I spoke with one lady, namely Poiré. Her reply: 'I will go wherever and whenever you like, I will do whatever is in my power. Just enough salary to enable me to lead a modest existence.' […]

[Vladimir Nikolaevich] Schultz, Barnay's impresario for the Lessing Theatre of Berlin, etc., came to see me today. He's renting the Paradis Theatre for the coming winter and refurbishing it, i.e., renovating it, cleaning it up and putting in electric lighting. Réjane will be playing for him from 14 to 22 October, from the 22 October to 15 November the theatre is free, from 15 November to 1 December Coquelin is playing, from 1 December to 12 December the theatre is free, from the 1 to the 22 the Lessing Theatre company is playing. From the 22 onwards and on all holidays the theatre is free. Later, also with gaps, Matkowsky, Sonnenthal, etc. are playing. He offers the theatre to our Society during the periods indicated above when the theatre is free from guest artists; the conditions are very favourable to the Society: he agrees to take it on either at his own risk or grant the initiative to the Society. It might seem at first glance that some kind of German trick [*Schwindel*] is lurking here, he's being too considerate, the conditions are too favourable, surely he's putting one over on us… But he gave me a perfectly reasonable explanation, namely: 'putting on one touring company after another without a break is bad for business. You can wear down the public. So I asked myself whom I should invite to fill the gaps -- Cherepanov's company[6] or the Little Russians, or a second-rate operetta company that's just been thrown together. – There is no other choice. But these jerry-built enterprises show no profit and damage the theatre's reputation, as touring companies are of interest only to the better class of audiences. That's why I prefer to offer you the theatre with no advantage to myself, because you will attract to my theatre the kind of audience I want to acquire, and with the help of your Society I can confer on the whole affair a respectable profile.' That is Schultz's reasoning, and I think we can accept his words as the truth. He is eager, among other things, for us to put on *The Sunken Bell* and *Hannele*. Our Society wanted to produce those plays and had to refrain only because the Hunt Club stage is so miniscule. It might make sense if, simultaneously with the productions at the Hunt Club, we were to perform Hauptmann at the Paradis (or 'International Theatre' as it is to be called this year). Think it over: isn't this where the concern should start? Shouldn't we engage such actors as Petrovskaya and Kosheverov to join the pre-existing core company of our Society? Shouldn't we take advantage of being given the use of a decent theatre without the obligation to put on a play every day, to show a few splendidly rehearsed and directed plays for one winter only and at the same time kill three birds with one stone: 1) augment the core company with two very important members, namely, a romantic lead and a dramatic actress who, perhaps, given the capacity of the theatre, can be decently paid; 2) prepare a repertoire of fully-staged plays on the Hunt Club stage -- for summer touring, and 3) demonstrate to the whole of Moscow how well we can produce and perform plays. I do think that Moscow will be more impressed by this means than by our successes in the sticks, about which the public will only see brief reports in the press and which, since they have not seen the productions, will probably find difficult to credit. They had some success in the provinces, Moscow will say, but here is quite another matter… I await your most speedy reply to this question, because in 10 days' time I have to give Schultz[7] a definite answer. If possible, send a wire – if necessary I can hold him off a bit to give me time to write back to you. If Petrovskaya is all that talented, it would be better to keep her here and not give her a chance of being spoiled in the provinces. A dramatic actress is nothing to sneeze at!

The rules are written and in a few days will go to the printer's. I am sending you a few copies. Because there is a limited number of them, I would like that those three or four copies that I can send you become known to the widest number of people. […][8]

Respectfully K. Alekseev […]

On 8 August, ND received a scheme from KS for the creation of a share-holding theatrical society, which was followed up by a letter of persuasion.

To **Nemirovich-Danchenko**, 19 August 1897, Moscow
Most esteemed Vladimir Ivanovich!
[...] A few more words about Schultz. I turned to you, when I received this proposal, first of all to hear your opinion: is this not the very beginning of our concern. I have now learned your opinion, to some degree. The benefit of these performances is that we, creators of a new concern, will show the public some interesting productions, and the general public, not a handful of fans of the Hunt Club, will say (if this is not over-enthusiasm on my part, of course) the same thing that the audience of the Hunt Club is now saying, namely: 'You ought to start a real theatrical concern.' If I and our Society deserve the attention of the public, if this is not mere enthusiasm on our part, it behooves us to show ourselves to the public so that it knows who the individuals are who will shortly turn to them for financial support. The general public knows you, I am known only to the small handful of fans of our performances. To make the Society acquainted with the general public is an expensive amusement and fraught with risk. In such a case it makes sense for us to show ourselves to the public without any risk to ourselves... It seems to me attractive and beneficial for the future concern. Add to this the inclusion in the troupe of a dramatic actress [Roksanova][9] and a romantic lead [Kosheverov], wouldn't this be a great enrichment of the troupe.

The great misunderstanding between us is, to my mind, the following: you are just embarking on something new and beginning at the point where I began 10 years ago. You want to assemble a company and have it perform plays; perhaps I have been carried away up to now, but it seems to me that I already have a small, but seasoned troupe. Confident of this, I am carrying forward something that is already begun and am trying to develop it here, within the confines of Moscow. If I am on the wrong track, I repeat, and all my calculations are wrong, then, of course, your plan stands, that is, the formation of a troupe in the provinces. It would be impossible not to concur that your plan is more than likely right, but, as I have already told you, I could participate only indirectly. At present, unless I have a solidly established concern, I cannot possibly neglect my business and spend the whole winter in the provinces. I might for a joint-stock company, but not for a provincial enterprise – no, because I will be arming against myself precisely those persons on whom I am relying to create a fund for the great concern.

What's more: speak your conscience, can you resolve to turn over to a joint-stock company a private undertaking like this once it has already earned the trust of the public as an artistic entity, and make do financially in the early days without the help of shareholders? Do you have the self-confidence to hand over such a concern to the shareholders at the very moment when, having sown the seed, you are ready to reap the ripe fruit? At that moment will you calculate the same way you do now? To hand over your children to other people's care, to hand over such a concern where the shareholders will exploit our artistic creativity for the sake

Figure 17 Vladimir Nemirovich-Danchenko in 1898

of financial profit? To hand over those profits that we garnered after great risk to our personal situations? I confess to you frankly I do not have the civic courage for that heroic feat. We need a joint-stock company at the very outset, at the moment of greatest risk, as a financial support; such a stock company is indispensable even after our death, to carry on the business along the lines we have established. That is why, it seems to me, it is unpropitious to begin the concern as a private enterprise.

Moreover, it seems to me, Moscow will not put its trust in a private concern, it will not even pay it attention, or, if it does, it will be too late, when our pockets are empty and the doors of the theatre have been boarded up. Moscow will deem my participation in a private enterprise, as was the case with Mamontov, a merchant's homegrown despotism, whereas the creation of a joint-stock company and, what is more, a theatre at popular prices, will invest me with the merit – that is what they will say – of being a reformer, of serving an artistic and educational concern. I am well acquainted with the merchantry of Moscow – they all reason the same way. In the first instance they will stay away from the theatre *on principle* and in the second case, solely *on principle* they will fork out a pile of money and attend the theatre to support '*our own concern*'.

A few days ago I learned that Mamontov has drawn up statutes for a popular-priced opera-dramatic theatre and wants to submit them to the ministry. Of course, I lost no time in meeting with him, ostensibly by chance. He promised to send me the statutes in the next few days. It would appear that joint-stock companies are the latest thing. [...]

Respectfully yours K. Alekseev

When the theatrical season opened again in the fall, ND attended the Society's performances assiduously and KS sat in on Philharmonic recitals to appraise the talent of prospective members of the new theatre. In November 1897 costs were estimated and at another meeting at the Slavonic Bazaar on 26 December ND and KS drew up a memorandum to submit to the Moscow City Council for a subsidy. On 31 December KS called on Prince Vasily Golitsyn, chairman of the Council, to apply for the subsidy. The matter was referred to the Commission for Social Benefits and Needs. It lay there for a year after the theatre was in operation, and then its answer was negative. This was in part due to an anti-theatrical prejudice that deplored the involvement of a scion of the respectable Alekseev clan in such a disreputable affair.

January 1898 saw the last production of the Society for Art and Literature: The Sunken Bell. *For the first time KS admitted to supplementing the author with his own inventiveness. On 15 January ND submitted to the Permanent Commission on Technical Education and the sanitary division of the Moscow Department of the Russian Technical Society a report which spelled out the theatre's rationale and budget. It stressed the educational and reformative aims of the enterprise.*

By May it was clear that, without a municipal subsidy, the theatre could not be commercially viable if it were Obshchedostupny although the word was not immediately dropped from its name. It had to be run by a Syndicate so that the founders were forced to issue shares. A stock company supported by a few patrons and public subscriptions led to the accusation that the MAT was 'bourgeois' although the initial capital was only 28,000 rubles. The financier and industrialist Savva Timofeevich Morozov (1862-1908) and KS contributed the lion's share: 10,000 rubles each. (The expenses for the opening years were predicted to be 98,000 rubles, with the hoped-for receipts at 88,3000 rubles.) To prospective investors, the directors insisted on total freedom of action.

They also petitioned the Governor General of Moscow to be allowed to stage the blank-verse drama Tsar Fyodor Ioannovich *by Aleksey Konstantinovich Tolstoy, censored for decades because it depicted Russian royalty and higher clergy. Since the theatre would not be easily accessible to the common people and had already rented a playhouse in Carriage Row, the novelty would be attractive to a literate public. Permission had already been granted to Suvorin's Literary-Artistic Circle in Petersburg. Hoping for a favourable response, KS began visiting cathedrals and museums to research the material culture of the period.*

KS put together the best elements of the Society (fourteen in all) and ND twelve of his best students. A few provincial actors were added though it was feared their bad habits might infect the others. Viktor Andreevich Simov (1858-1935), who had worked at Mamontov's Private Opera, was taken on as designer; essentially a painter, he would design most of the MAT productions until 1913, devising platforms and verticals to expand the action. As makeup artists and wigmakers, they hired Yakov Ivanovich Gremislavsky (1864-1941) and his wife Mariya Alekseevna (1870-1950), who had worked with the Alekseev circle from 1882; they were to reform the practice of stage makeup. The troupe comprised 39 (23 men, 16 women), the youngest aged 20. There were 78 workers, with enough additional musicians and choristers to number 313. Permanent supers were recruited from the students at the Philharmonic.

The company was installed at Pushkino, an estate a short ride from Lyubimovka, that belonged to Nikolay Nikolaevich Arkhipov (1869-1926), a lawyer who had acted with the Society under the name Arbatov. A wooden fit-up was constructed for rehearsals which began on 14 June, with Aleksandr Sanin as co-director. KS's opening speech to the actors emphasized the social-betterment aspect of the enterprise and urged them to 'common work, collaborative work'. 'We are trying to create the first rational, moral, publicly accessible theatre, and to this lofty goal we devote our life.'

To **Nemirovich-Danchenko.** 12 or 13 June 1898, Lyubimovka.
Most esteemed Vladimir Ivanovich!

[...] Here is my report on what has been happening with us.

1) The theatre is ready and has turned out splendidly, but cost more than we anticipated. The sudden cold spell gave us a fright. The inside of the building had to be lined with cardboard and hessian, and then to hide the unsightliness, -- with both. Outside, the heat had caused the boards to split and crack, so that we had to paint the building. We hadn't taken house-painters into consideration, and they turn out to be very expensive. We did it the cheapest way with our own materials. Burdzhalov[10] supervised the plastering. Arkhipov bought the materials. This came to about 200 rubles. In planning costs we had forgotten the upholsterer: the material for the box-set (a draw-curtain, like at the Philharmonic). Curtains for the terrace, otherwise you can't use it on sunny days. Curtains for the theatre windows (otherwise you bake in the sun). And this was done very economically. We bought scenic canvas that could perhaps be used for the sets. Kuznetsov the theatre's props-storage man is in charge of the sewing and hanging. The material cost 40 rubles (I bought it myself). The stage pieces – furniture, tables, sofas,

Figure 18 Viktor Simov (on stairs) supervising the scene-painting in the shed at Pushkino

cupboards -- proved to be very expensive (up to 200 rubles), I preferred to rent them from Gennert[11] for 75 rubles (20 for the transport alone). We had to buy brushes, combs, a samovar, tablecloths, etc. I still haven't seen Manasevich's[12] bill, I suppose it will come to 50 to 75 rubles. We have gone over budget without wanting to -- This amount will have to be covered by our performances in Pushkino.[13]

2) The scene-shop caused us a lot of trouble. Everything turned out to be dismantled. We had to take Kupchinskaya's dacha (for 300 rubles). However you can barely lay our canvas flat in it. We have to construct a sleeping-bench on the second floor. We've set to work on it (nearly 200 rubles). Simov will set to work after 17 June.

3) Materials on Russian history cost an insane amount of money, for example, a complete edition of Solntsev is 550 rubles.[14] I preferred to take on a sketch artist for 35 rubles, who has already sketched all the motifs we need. He is also relieving me of the job of sketching the costumes and props for the props-men and costumiers which is beyond my ability.

4) On calculating it seems more advantageous to take on a props man here rather than to order things from outside. We have found and taken on the best props man in Russia (a very business-like fellow) who will make many beautiful

things for us for 50 rubles a month. I consider this type of expense a saving and not an increase in the estimates.[15]

5) *The Merchant of Venice* is completely ready. It should turn out to be very effective. Simov's models are ideal: just what I had in mind.

6) Almost all the models for *Tsar Fyodor* are ready. I've never seen anything more original or more beautiful. Now I am calm and can guarantee that such an authentic Rus of yore has never yet been seen in Russia. This is the *real* olden times and not what they have concocted at the Maly Theatre.

7) Shenberg and I have read and re-examined everything we could. We have organized expeditions to the ancient cities. The whole company will travel for a few days to Rostov, Yaroslavl, Troitsa. We inspected everything of note in Moscow. We sketched everything and the result, to my mind, is brilliant.

8) I note with delight that Shenberg is a hard worker and Simov is a talented fellow.

9) Everyone will travel here at his own expense.

10) We have found a way to produce genuine Russian cloth (with oil paints, through a stencil). Gennert's wife has undertaken to carry out this work.

11) The production of *Fyodor* is beginning to take shape, and I think will be both interesting and, most important, far from stereotypical.

12) I read the role of Antigone with Savitskaya.[16] I went into ecstasy over her voice and temperament. If I succeed in turning her into a Greek woman – it will be very good.

13) I read Fyodor with Krasovsky[17] – no hope. He has absolutely no interest in anything but eating. Alas, he's a desperate character.

14) Shidlovsky[18] is unsatisfactory as well – he continues to dig in his heels, but it seems that this is the result of domestic disturbances.

15) I read Shylock with Darsky. Wonderful voice and temperament, but no sort of artist. He is a Russian version of Possart[19] with an admixture of Yuzhin. Pity that he's a coward with a limited imagination. He tries to make characters grandiose through bombast. If we manage to deflect him from this idea, then he will be a splendid actor; if not it will be trashy... he won't come near our tone. I'm comforted that he seems keen and takes direction quickly. Meanwhile he has little self-confidence. Something is holding him back. He has difficulty in submitting to new influences.

16) Reactions to your ideas: *Tartuffe*?... I hate that play. I don't see a Tartuffe in our company. Wouldn't it be better to replace it with *The Learned Ladies*? Without very great preparation I would be afraid to stage Molière. I got involved with him when I was in Paris... He is very difficult, although interesting Given the clichés about him, to my mind he isn't worth staging, even at the club.[20] [...]

23) The time after 16 June is very precious, and it is annoying that it is impossible at the moment to rehearse the assigned plays with a full cast: *Merchant* is missing Kosheverov [as Lorenzo] (he arrives no earlier than 1 July), *Hannele* is missing Roksanova [in the title role] (she is ill, and has to spend time in the Crimea. I agreed to it). She will return on 1 July.

Along with *The Merchant of Venice* and *Antigone* we are starting to read for roles in *Fyodor*. That's essential for everyone: the stage directors (to establish the blocking and test it), the designers (to establish the set designs and test them), the costumiers (to know which costume to build for which actor) and the props-men. You are right: you can't cast the roles until you have tried out the actors. So we must get started on *Fyodor* as soon as possible.

24) I would be happy if, not only in *Tsar Fyodor* but in the other plays you would start to go through the roles with individual actors. I don't like it and can't do it. But you are a master at it. However, there is something I would like: let me mould, sketch out the play as it takes shape independently You can correct things later if I have done something stupid, I am always afraid of falling under any kind of influence; then my work becomes uninteresting and cliché-ridden. I wind up unable for a long time to sketch out the thing that is dimly haunting me. It has often happened that these passages turn out to be the best of all. If I obstinately let them incubate in the unconscious, instinctively, then be patient, give me time to clarify my thoughts and let them achieve a more comprehensible form. After all, it's these details, prompted by instinct, which give a play its colouration. I feel there will be many of them in *Fyodor*, because we will manage to avoid the routine that we are so accustomed to in the interpretation of so-called Russian plays. This style of performing them I find intolerable... we must get as far away from it as possible... But that takes time. Until you arrive, we will have time only to unpack *Fyodor* and get an idea of the play's general colouration. Since I haven't tried out the actors, I'll wait to cast the roles. Who is to play Fyodor?... That is the main question. At the moment the only one I think will be successful is Meyerhold.[21] The others are too stupid for it. I have thought and talked a great deal about Irina. There is no doubt you are right. Irina is not what I would have liked to see in her. Involuntarily the role takes on – via history – a stereotypical character... We have no actresses to perform her. Least suitable of all (in this interpretation) are my wife and Shidlovskaya. Zhelyabuzhskaya [Andreeva], to my mind, is quite unsuitable – she is unsympathetic, has no soul at all. Savitskaya? – No, I'd sooner have her play Boris or Ivan the Terrible. She's an amazon, with little of the woman about her. To my mind, don't be surprised, best of all is Knipper.[22] According to history, Irina was a great fashion-plate – of the oriental (not Russian) type (a Tatar woman). There was something alluring about her that so pleased foreigners that they lavish praise on her in their chronicles. There was in her a great deal of femininity, queenliness. To my mind, she was an aristocrat among the peasant-boyars. Knipper has all of this. Let me know as soon as possible whether you agree with my opinion? I will read over the role with Knipper and will hold off on giving it to her.[23] [...]

28) I beg you awfully to save the role in *Laws Unto Themselves* for Zhelyabuzhskaya. It doesn't require great ability. The princess is a nasty little slut and ought not arouse any particular sympathy. If we take this role away from Zhelyabuzhskaya, which she dreams of and knows by heart, which was handed over to her twice, she will be done out of roles and make a big scene.[24]

Write me your opinion as soon as possible. We have to rehearse the play, because Zhelyabuzhskaya is leaving in August. [...]

Yours K. Alekseev

Rehearsals ran from noon to 4 p.m. and again after supper, often lasting to midnight. (Decades later, ND complained of KS's schedules and longed to begin work in the morning.) Chekhov attended a rehearsal and was very struck by the 'intelligent level of the acting', even though there were no great talents. Nevertheless he was deaf to ND's importunate pleas to stage The Seagull.

To **Nemirovich-Danchenko.** 26 June 1898, Moscow

Most esteemed Vladimir Ivanovich,

Following your example, in view of the heat, I am writing in pencil. Here is what we've been doing.

We are rehearsing *Antigone, The Merchant of Venice, Laws Unto Themselves* and *The Tutor* (for Pushkino) with all our might. Since yesterday I have begun reading *Fyodor* with Knipper and Meyerhold. The next reading will be with Moskvin, Platonov and Lanskoy (I expect nothing from him but don't want to dampen his ardour, although I felt cool towards his urgent request).[25]

Here is my opinion of the troupe.

1) *Darsky.* At the first read-through he recited the role [Shylock] in his own (so-called) interpretation and laid low me and everyone else. You know what kind of actor Darsky is in the provinces: he's a progenitor of Petrov,[26] he's the model the latter is trying to emulate. I know of nothing more absurd, more anti-artistic. Even in this kind of reading there is no way to judge an actor's abilities when he replaces his voice with whistles and hisses, and temperament with hideous grimaces and a diction in which the consonants rrrr... khkhkh... shch...ts...ch... etc. crackle in your ears. I didn't sleep for two nights. He put me in such a rage that my nerves got the better of me at the read-through, and, running to the opposite extreme, I began to read the role in a realistic manner (far more than was necessary). The result was rewarding. The other actors, Darsky among them, felt the rightness of my interpretation. I know that after this reading (his downfall) Darsky suffered in his morale. At first he argued, more with the others than with me. He insisted that this was an oversimplification of the role, that you couldn't take age-old figures off their pedestals... He tormented Shenberg in particular, defending all his caterwauling in rehearsal, but on the sly he was probably working strenuously in the direction I had indicated... Poor fellow, he lost weight, turned yellow, began to despair, but... one successful phrase, uttered simply, pulled him in another direction, and now he is no longer the former Darsky. Now he is a schoolboy afraid to take a single step on stage without me or Aleksandr Akimovich [Sanin]. A more industrious, attentive, hard-working actor I do not know. He turns up at every rehearsal (even when he is not called). He heeds every note given to others and, despite the internal wound to his self-esteem in the presence of the youngsters, learns his abc. He has already recovered the self-confidence he lost in the eyes of the other actors, attaboy! I am very pleased with him. Whether he has time to acquire a style of acting which is new to him is hard to say: whether he has time to master it enough to become a creator and not a mere imitator?... It's hard to say. But I guarantee that anyone who had seen Darsky in the provinces would not recognize his Shylock. I have succeeded

in so dismantling, so distorting his former Shylock that he will never revive it. One concern is that he should show off how clever he is less and study his role at home. He has an unusual and damaging habit of underlining everything, planning out every detail. Intelligence is in the foreground and feelings get smothered. I think I am using the right method with him. I am making him act almost over-realistically... so that he will forget his idealized images. Then we'll find a middle way. There is no doubt that he has temperament (if he doesn't let it wither). Can he play anything else besides Shylock? -- Yes... He will be an outstanding character actor. He has a feeling for character. We just have to develop his mimicry (his face has two or three fixed expressions). Cut down the gestures... He will never play Acosta, but he will play De Silva, Akiba splendidly. In *Othello* he is Iago, in *Hamlet* Polonius, in *Laws Unto Themselves* the fool, in *The Dowerless Bride* Karandyshev. I think (unless I am mistaken) that we will find more work for him in our concern than we imagine. [27]

2) *Sudbinin* is a dear, good-natured Volga barge-hauler with lisping, guttural diction, a vulgar voice and the temperament of a muzhik. Perhaps, because of the heat he dresses with insufficient refinement and therefore shows up on stage looking almost ridiculous. He tries to be bon ton, but you know what an actor's bon ton is like! Until he is replaced – he cannot be in *Merchant*, because a noble, regal merchant like Antonio has nothing in common with a Volga barge-hauler. It's laughable even to think of him as Boris. Neshchastlivtsev [in *The Forest*] is unthinkable! In *Hannele* it is impossible to assign him the wood goblin. He is so hopeless in these roles that the presence of his figure and tone in a good ensemble destroys the whole. Until we come up with another actor, I keep silence and regard him as a mannequin, temporarily replacing another performer. I don't even try to give him notes, because to achieve anything you would have to chop off his arms, legs, tongue, forbid him to speak with his diction...

He's a good chap, dim-witted, and a splendid draughtsman. More about that later. As an actor he is hopeless for me (he reads even the police officer in *Laws Unto Themselves* repulsively). Perhaps you will take a look and figure out which way to go. I cannot understand why he was paid money in the provinces. I suppose there's something there, if only in everyday roles, or is there? – I don't understand. [28]

3) *Andreev* -- I don't know what he's like as a dunce, but as a Venetian nobleman he is appalling: he's an amateur (from an ecclesiastical family) but not an actor. The voice of a sexton, the conversation of a hairdresser. [29]

4) *Nedobrova* (Aleeva) – a charming, well-behaved, impassive (so far) dicky-bird. Jessica's lyricism is expressed in rapping out the verses. Temperament in over-abundance. But there is nothing trivial in her (this is of immense value). Everything is bland, awkward. She is Sheremetevskaya without her beauty. There is no way she can play Jessica (we'll have to replace her), but she'll do in some musical farce or comedietta, where she can twitter away and stamp her little foot. Perhaps she won't come undone. (At the last rehearsal Aleksandr Akimovich so lit into her that she started to howl and then acted much better.) Perhaps she will end up fainting and then turn into an actress. I will hold off on expressing a definitive opinion about her. [30]

Книпперъ.

Figure 19 Olga Knipper

Those are three black blotches on our horizon; now I'll move to the light. [...]

Knipper. She was given a good lesson in Kuntsev, and she cannot wait to have her turn, that is rehearsals. Gave an unspecific reading as Irina but the part will be all right. [...]

Zhelyabuzhskaya [Andreeva] -- at the moment I can say nothing but good things, a very serious and heartfelt relation to the work, without affectation, caprices and conceit. [...]

Meyerhold is my favourite. He read the Prince of Aragon -- exquisitely – as kind of Don Quixote, swaggering, stupid, supercilious, with long, spindly legs, an enormous mouth and a way of chewing his words; Fyodor... surprised me. The good-natured passages were bad, routine, unimaginative. The strong passages were very good. I don't think I can avoid giving him Fyodor, although in alternation.

Moskvin. What a dear... He works his guts out to get it right. Only in places he's too common for a nobleman, but that will be ironed out (Salarino). (He read the scrivener in *Laws Unto Themselves* wonderfully).

Chuprov (Chirikov) is an excellent find. Awfully funny and even varied. Whether Chuprov can sustain a major role I don't know, but the centenarian Old Gobbo (in the read-through) created a furore (in Artyom's absence[31] I happened to cast him, and so far have no reason to repent of it).[32] I really liked his Mitrich (in *Laws Unto Themselves*) because of the everyday tone (which is not in Gobbo). Mishka in *The Tutor* will also be funny; a blissful expression never leaves his face (the kind you encounter in ancient icons) --- he is very surprised that he's been let into a decent house. I observe strenuously that we haven't snapped him up.

Tikhomirov. Very attractive and a serious actor. He is prone to great moral suffering, and therefore I am especially delicate and cautious with him. He is talented and has temperament, but on account of phony traditions or subtlety in acting everything is flabby, evened out and he is afraid to go beyond clichés. He lingers over details, but doesn't recognize the general mood. He strives to express a certain refinement, explains everything: the way he understands a role, why he does this or that nuance, and shirks the slightest audacity. Here is his impression of our rehearsals: 'I am completely confused,' he says, 'it seems to me that everyone is acting so sharply, so coarsely...' And along with that he is the first to laugh, if I succeed in making a successful remark to the actors. He has exhibited himself in four roles: the guard (*Antigone*), the Doge (cast temporarily), Devochkin in *Laws Unto Themselves* (ditto) and Ivan Petrovich in *The Tutor*.[33] In all four roles I had to disagree (with pain in my soul) with his interpretations. Aleksandr Akimovich asserts that in *Antigone* he has already acquired some audacity. In my plays I cannot say this was the case. This is not what troubles me so much. On the contrary, I expect that he will get carried away and go to extremes but specifically: he will start to speak so simply that everything will become boring, and for the sake of audacity will turn his back to the audience. In my experience such degeneration often occurs. I am sure that we will soon refashion him, but now, poor fellow, he is going through difficult moments. Ugh, this is all the fault of the provinces and a literary circle! Everything is nice and clean, nice and sleek. These aren't actors, but varieties of Molchalins in their staidness and punctilio! [34]

Lanskoy. Stupid, but a splendid fellow. Quite a neat little Petersburg article. If he turns Muscovite it will be a pity, then he will remind me of a cute little Jap in a modern suit, for a Moscow 'casual jacket' will fit him like a sack. He flung away his money along the road like crazy, but girded his loins and on the first day appeared in all his glory, dressed to the nines. He showed off his wardrobe, preened and posed. Now he dresses down a bit. I noticed, for instance, that he hasn't changed his wonderful blouse for quite some time, but nevertheless, he has rented a good room, travels by horse-cab. If he doesn't remain with us, it is because there's no one for him to woo – they're all faithful wives or strictly moral young ladies. But I am enamoured of his tone, manners and I set store by him as one sets store by a Negro in a fashionable restaurant... for the chic of it! I repeat, he's a splendid fellow...

101

kind-hearted… not once have I heard that he praised himself in any role. On stage he is a desperate coward… But I will sort him out… he lets himself be putty in my hands… he venerates me and fears me like the plague. When you shake him up, he laughs contagiously. He fears dramas like the plague and curses Apollonsky, who thrust on him a kind of dreadful sickly-sweet and phony tone.[35] He is playing Gratiano (he will be a real nobleman), Volodya (*The Tutor* – not bad), Rykov (a guardsman like this has never been seen on the Russian stage). In dramatic scenes the Petersburg style comes a bit to the fore, and I am awfully pleased with that and, can you imagine, this is very much to the benefit of the play, for it diminishes his romance with the princess and justifies Platon's behaviour.

Kaluzhsky. Very cheerful, energetic, despite the heavy workload and the heat. They say he acts Creon splendidly. He reads and practices Prince Sergey (*Laws Unto Themselves*) excellently. Today, just now, he is rehearsing *The Tutor* without me (I am waiting for my wife to find out if he has disgraced himself). (My wife is playing her old role in lieu of Roksanova.) He will be very fine as the Prince of Morocco (he plays a young tiger, impetuous, passionate and stupid in an oriental way). I am satisfied with him.

Shenberg [Sanin]. He works with all his might and never tires. Very satisfied with him… What will he come up with next?

Burdzhalov. Enthusiastic. Lies on the floor all day, searching for the tone for Launcelot.

Krasovsky. Licks my boots… When opportunity arises, flatters… I think he's embarrassed but afraid to show it. As punishment he was cast as the court clerk in *Merchant* and the bailiff in *Laws Unto Themselves*. Since he is not vulgar, but a king – in comparison with Andreev, in a few days I will have to give him the latter's role.[36]

Platonov. I find him very appealing as an actor, except for a certain melodramatic note in his voice (according to him, he employs it because the provincial young ladies love it so much). A bit dull, but can be influenced. Totally submissive. Opinions vary about him. Some like him a lot, others not so much (and this surprises me). I do not compare him with Ryzhov, for instance. He has charm, which the latter does not. [37] He Russifies a bit, but as Bassanio he does not grate on the ears. I think his melodramatic note will embarrass a lot of people. In any case, he is a find, and especially for 900 rubles.

Prompter [Valentin Frantsevich Valentinov] – is outstanding, but, it seems, prompts unobtrusively (this is even better, so they learn their lines).

Manasevich. Devil knows what he is! He says of himself that he is *subdued*, but actually he's lethargic. Our housekeeping is in total disarray. He doesn't have the energy, for instance, to select keys to the lock on the cupboard or the trunk of purchases, to put up the drapes and hang them in place. I would have parted with him a long time ago, if I hadn't been afraid of intruding on your realm; however he is such a decent fellow that he himself admitted to his incompetence and resigned, after explaining that he agreed to stay on until your arrival. Having learned of his resignation, Ryndzyunsky expressed the desire to take his place.

Now I am in great turmoil: how am I to proceed. I am a very bad manager and am afraid in undertake anything definite in this direction. For instance, I think it is a pity to let go of Ryndzyunsky. To my mind, he is efficient, intelligent, very devoted to business and has a great personality, but after all it is you, not I, who has to deal with him, this time. On the other hand, if Sudbinin does not suit as an actor -- couldn't he be made your assistant, for he has displayed great aptitude for management. Besides, he draws well... God knows, perhaps all this could be combined, because to break a contract with him (on a word of honour) would give the actors grounds to do the same with us. But we don't want to pay money for nothing... Here is what I've decided, forgive me if I've made a mistake, but I'm a little worried that it seemed irremediable: have Ryndzyunsky replace Manasevich here until you arrive. We will try him out at the business. I warned him that I can tell him nothing definite in your absence. He agreed to the test. If teaming him with Sudbinin succeeds, then I will turn out to be right, because I warned him... [38]

The *overall* mood is highly exalted. It is all so strange for the actor. Their communal quarters (a dacha, which Shenberg and Burdzhalov rented for the company at their own risk. A wonderful dacha, a very attractive dwelling), and the rather fetching, spruce little theatre building. The tone is good. Serious rehearsals, and, most important -- acting and working habits hitherto unknown to them. Here, for example, is Moskvin's opinion: 'When I was cast in the role of Salarino and read the lines I found it boring but now it is my favourite but also my most difficult role.' The first rehearsals roused much discussion back at the house. It was decided that this is not a theatre, but a university. Lanskoy exclaimed that he had heard and taken in less in three years at school than in one rehearsal (of course, that doesn't say much for the Petersburg school). In a word, the youngsters are astonished... and all a bit scared and wary of this new method of work. Discipline during rehearsals has been exemplary (and it's good that it happened without extra schoolmarmishness or strong-arm tactics), in a comradely way. If it hadn't been for the duty roster -- we would have been in utter chaos, since, at first we even lived without servants (Kuznetsov who had been taken on disappeared the day we opened). Those on duty have swept the floors, lit the samovars, set the tables -- and all most conscientiously, perhaps because I was the first on the job and I did it all very carefully. In a word, the overall tone is good. Rehearsals, since they are all new faces, are going very well (although we've had about 22 already). *Antigone* has been read as cast. The staging-plan is finished and will be rehearsed complete on stage. [...]

I move to the last and most important item. [...]

Vishnevsky.[39] Alas! – We need him desperately, and more than anyone as a stage director and actor. Without him *Merchant* won't go on (unless we enslave Kaluzhsky). Without him all my forces and time will go to *Fyodor*.[40] I say ALAS, because he has been treated in a very unfriendly way in the troupe and in the Society. I am at fault in regard to you. This question tormented me. I thought about him after my first acquaintance with Sudbinin. I am even ready (I have built myself up) to certify the good side of Vishnevsky's character, but, other than that, will not underestimate the seriousness and difficulty of this question. He already has a bad reputation. Half is tattle, and no one has given me any facts besmirching him. They simply don't like him – and regard his admittance into the troupe as a disgrace. I can judge of such opinions from last spring (remember, when we made inquiries about him). I do not say all of this in order to dissuade us from inviting him. On the contrary, the matter was settled. He was to join, because there was no way to do without him. I say this to justify myself. The chief obstacle and source of perturbation will be our ladies, chiefly Zhelyabuzhskaya and Shidlovskaya. In one of their conversations they began to express the fear that I will not last the season. They tenderly told me to look after my health etc... I pretended to be a hard-luck case and alluded to Sudbinin (about whom, even without that, everyone was dinning it into my ears). What is to be done? 'There's only one way out, but it is unthinkable, and you would be the first to discount it.' – What is it? – Promise on oath to keep mum and not gossip... -- 'Vishnevsky.'

To sum up: it is dreadful, they will not forgive us, but what are we to do if it is so necessary for the concern that we enlist him --- only... draw out the invitation... not right away... Right now it will raise a mutiny, but once everyone has suffered from Sudbinin, they themselves will ask for Vishnevsky.

So I agree to this feminine cunning. To my mind, we will have to settle things with Vishnevsky now, but be silent until 20 July. We have to send him all the roles. In view of such tactics, if you approve, it is appropriate for you, not me, to send a telegram and ask Vishnevsky to be silent so as (ostensibly) not to put you in an awkward position with me and give you time to inform me and have a personal discussion with me.[41] [...]

Your devoted and respectful K. Alekseev [...]

To **Nemirovich-Danchenko**. End June-beginning July, 1898, Lyubimovka. Much esteemed Vladimir Ivanovich!

I confess that we barely have time before 25 July for:[42]

1) *Merchant, Antigone, Tutor, Laws Unto Themselves, Hannele, Fyodor* (one more play for Pushkino: which one? *The Dowerless Bride* is the easiest of all.)

Much Ado, Uriel (a few roles),[43] *Magda, Malvolio*[44] – we will hardly be able to rehearse. We will go over these roles at odd moments.

2) So, as far as rehearsals are concerned we make do without you. What can go awry is the managerial side because nothing has been set up: not only is Manasevich doing *absolutely nothing* – he [hands over] even minor purchases to other people and doesn't check the accounts and even gets muddled in the book-keeping (which could turn out to be disastrous). We must *get rid of him as soon as possible*. Meanwhile in your absence my hands are tied, there's nothing I can undertake. Give me a definite answer about discussions with Sudbinin as soon as possible (I have settled nothing with Ryndzyunsky) – the consensus is that he will suit the business, even if temporarily, until your return. With the best will in the

world I don't have the time to take on the managerial side, because, on the one hand, I have rehearsals, and on the other the scenery, tailors, props-men, the selection of materials, the purchase of minor items for *Fyodor* and *Merchant*, -- it is all down to me and I have to do it quickly. […]

6) Misunderstandings and delays have arisen owing to our letter-writing. You would have refused much of the casting if you had a closer acquaintance with the actors, therefore do not bear a grudge because, without your agreement, I have made a few changes. It is fully necessary so that we don't hold up matters. […]

8) The role of the mother in *Hannele* I am giving to Zhelyabuzhskaya, [Andreeva] because, not knowing Knipper (whose voice is too low), I fear that she will not be able to cope with the tricks of the wings, transformations etc. Zhelyabuzhskaya (she was supposed to play the role in the first production) is made for all sorts of tricks and sentimental beauty.

9) Alas, Meyerhold has to play Death in *Hannele*. There is no one with a more appropriate figure. Sudbinin can play *absolutely* nothing and least of all a role with expressive gestures. He is the cab-driver, or else the house goblin (but a splendid fellow).

10) Meyerhold also wound up in *Laws Unto Themselves*, because there was no way to rehearse the play without him, because we don't have enough actors.[45]

11) For the hundredth time Sudbinin is not to act!!!.. I am afraid that, once you've seen him and Andreev, you will never let them on stage (at least in costume roles). I have never heard anything more repulsive than Andreev's voice (and you lay such importance – and for good reason – on voice). […]

15) If we have to talk things over with Vishnevsky, this is what I would say:

a) it may be your fault or sheer chance, but you have acquired a bad reputation, and you will not welcomed into the troupe with open arms;

b) we are closely acquainted with you and trust the sincerity of your sympathy with our concern;

c) it is based on friendly relationships, therefore for your own sake and to secure you to the concern, our first obligation is to make you a welcome member of the family;

d) for this at first, until the others are better acquainted with you, you must be stiller than water, lowlier than grass;

e) do not speak familiarly, as you are accustomed to doing;

f) do not hobnob with the actors (at first), until they approach you;

g) do your work, in your free time stay at home, until your comrades offer you an invitation;

h) speak your opinions and suggestions into our ears, but not aloud;

i) do not pay court to the ladies, because your mere amiability will be taken at first for smarmy flirtation;

j) do not proffer opinions on the acting of the other actors;

k) when the actors are used to you – do not abuse their confidence, lest they say that you are a wily Greek, deftly worming his way into their hearts;

l) if you have to employ your energy in helping Shenberg – rehearse the crowds;

Figure 20 Aleksandr Vishnevsky

m) when we tour the provinces help in this with your practical knowledge;

n) allow us, your well-wishers, the right to meddle and direct you in the private life of our theatrical family, that is, to give advice, criticize your actions, modulate your temperament.

Of course, I would soften the words but preserve the sense of the whole.[46]

I am very, very worried that the censorship problem is dragging on. The censor has still not passed *Hannele, Fyodor, Antigone, At Odd Moments*,[47] but we are rehearsing them and spending money on them. What if there's suddenly a misunderstanding? What if suddenly (as often happens) Litvinov[48] says in August, 'Why... It's a theatre at popular prices... ah!.. That had slipped my mind.' Then

106

we are ruined. What if the translator won't let us have *At Odd Moments?*.. We are setting to work with an awful lot of uncertainty. What if Korsh or Pogozhev play us a dirty trick concerning *Fyodor?*..[49] They are capable of anything. It's much safer to keep the authorized, censored copy of *Fyodor* in your briefcase. There are other problems with *Fyodor* too. How has it been cut? Are the ecclesiastical characters still in? There's a whole regiment of them. If they stay, -- then there's one cast-list, if not, -- the whole distribution has to be changed.

By the way: Meyerhold is afraid of an everyday (but not general) tone as Kuryukov. I want to try out Chuprov (he's a big young fellow).[50]

We have picked out three Fyodors: Meyerhold (he inspires the thought that Fyodor is the son of Ivan the Terrible), Moskvin (his Fyodor has no more than a year to live), Platonov (kind-hearted and fussy). [...]

Yours K. Alekseev

The censor passed Tsar Fyodor *for an 'accessible' theatre with the stipulation that the actor playing the lead be respectable (the actor who played the tsar in St Petersburg had a reputation as an alcoholic and a womanizer); all the ecclesiastical characters were omitted, however. Neither the Alexandra nor Korsh chose to stage the play, and ND wrote that Pogozhev was afraid of them. To fit out* Tsar Fyodor, *KS bought a large number of antiques at the Nizhegorod Fair, from household implements to boots.*

Antigone was also passed. In early August KS and ND discussed The Seagull, *with KS doing most of the listening and note-taking. ND had had to exercise all his powers of persuasion to get Chekhov to allow the revival, and KS, for his part, was also reluctant.*

Diary, 10 or 11 August.

I went to [my brother's estate Andreevka] in the Kharkov district to write the mise-en-scene. This was a difficult task, because, to my shame, I did not understand the play. And only during the work, almost imperceptibly, I began to get a feel for the play and unconsciously fell in love with it. Such is the characteristic of a Chekhov play. Once you give in to their charm, you want to breathe in their fragrance.

Rehearsals in Pushkino ended on 23 August. On 3 September they resumed at the Hunt Club and the Philharmonic School in Moscow.

To **Nemirovich-Danchenko**. 30 August 1898, Andreevka.
Much esteemed Vladimir Ivanovich!

Yes, now I understand what it means to sit in the sticks without letters. The horse comes back from the station, they bring a letter, and it... isn't for me. I felt such perturbation only in high school, when they read out the list of pupils promoted to the next class. Today at last I felt a pleasant perturbation, like the pupil who passed the exam... I got your letter, have read it over five times. It brought me back to a life recently lived, and again I felt I was with you all. I am very, very grateful to you for every line you wrote. They say tomorrow there will be a free moment, I will answer every point in your letter at once. By the way: free moments here are unique, at most twice a week.

So, Pushkino has emptied out!.. I am rather glad... let the actors scatter throughout Moscow. There will be fewer quarrels and tittle-tattle... Convey to Moskvin that I am heartily delighted for him and grateful to your instinct, which divined the real interpreter of this role, and your work, having created for us, God willing, a future star of our theatre.[51] How good it would be if you took Moskvin in hand as soon as possible for the last act, I am afraid that on my return (the hottest time) he will not identify with the part, and then it will be hard to find a time to work with him. [...]

Vishnevsky... isn't he an actor full of surprises... Time after time things don't work out! This is indeed a dangerous way of acting... by inspiration. Take a close look and see if he has the same problem as Darsky. The latter, when he's in the mood and tries to act – things come out vilely, and vice-versa. Maybe Vishnevsky is trying too hard – I noticed that characteristic in him in *Merchant*... With no news, I have begun to study [Antonio in] *Merchant*. Now I toss it aside... As an actor I am very sorry about it, as the father of a numerous family I rejoice. I even rejoice for Darsky. I sincerely pity him, but what was he thinking of before? I warned him after the first read-through that he shouldn't expect ovations the first season. He swore to me that he wasn't looking for them. How is one to comfort him?.. It is difficult, if he is simply a career actor and very easy if he is an artiste. For fourteen years he's been building a career. It is well renowned, but wrong-headed! For fourteen years he's being running amok and ruining his talent... It is high time he was called to account. He has now reached the Pillars of Hercules, there is no farther he can go. All his histrionics and fourteen years of technique have taken the form of rolling his 'r's and hissing and whistling all the consonants. There are no new letters to be created for his future progress. I don't consider myself a brilliant director, of course, but, if he has even the slightest degree of faith in me, tell him that his *salvation* lies in our concern. His salvation lies in the fact that he play Andrey Shuisky badly forty times, that thirty times he submit to a human tone and leave off his bestial sounds. Convince him that the Rubicon we want him to cross on our backs is not so terrible. So long as he does not resist. Remind him of my words: Moscow is a strange city; whoever gains a victory here quickly (if I am not mistaken, you told me this) will not keep it long. In Moscow you have to start small and win over the public gradually. Let Darsky break himself of some of his bad habits, and a series of roles will open up to him. He is energetic and knows how to work. He will make speedy progress once he admits this necessity. Once more I declare without any hesitation: three, five seasons in the provinces... and Darsky will be more insufferable and ridiculous than Petrov. In three years they will start to hiss him, and in five years he will be forced to leave the stage. Then he will be incorrigible, but now, perhaps, he can be set on the right track. Can one more thing be pointed out to him: a director can benefit an actor only when he is sure that his work will not go for naught? If Darsky behaves with us so that at every step we expect him to walk out, we will hardly have the energy and enthusiasm to cast him in good roles and strain our nerves with him in rehearsals. So long as he doesn't make us cool to him as Shidlovskaya did, who is influencing him, I believe. However, enough about him. I digressed at such length about Darsky because I can put myself in his shoes and sincerely pity him. I think that everything we are doing is to his advantage.

I have read about *The Seagull* with great interest. I rejoice for Meyerhold.[52] But what about Platonov?[53] You have nothing to say about him? I am beginning to read Dorn, but so far I don't understand him at all and am very sorry that I wasn't at the *Seagull* discussions; not prepared for, or, more accurately, not steeped in Chekhov, I cannot work in the direction I should. The role interests me, if only because I have not played character roles for a long time, but imagine, I do not understand or, rather, do not feel: why should Dorn be me, and not Kaluzhsky, for instance. Why do many people, you among them, say that I am very like this role. It upsets me that I do not understand what you expect from me in this role. I am afraid that I will play it only decently. I am afraid that I am not looking at the role in the right light. I can see myself, for instance, as Shamraev, Sorin, even Trigorin, that is, I feel how I can be reincarnated in those characters, but I can play Dorn consistently, evenly, and that's all. However, as always when the work begins, it seems that one can play well all the roles except those for which one was cast. This is how it always begins with me. I will do some reading... You have no time, but cannot somebody, even Meyerhold, who, as you say, is steeped in *Seagull*, fill me in on what was said about Dorn in the discussions and how he imagines him, what he looks like. He would greatly oblige me, and then I would be prepared for the tone you have laid down. For that same reason, that is, that I am not steeped in Chekhov, the staging notes I sent may seem of no use. I blocked it at random... I am stalled at the last act... So far nothing has come into my head, but I wouldn't want to squeeze it out by force. I will read the play again in the hope that the three acts I sent (registered) will be enough to keep you busy for a long time.[54]

I grieve over some unexpected cuts in *Fyodor*, but even more over the dreadful insertions. Would it be possible to improve the brilliant inventions of the censor?... [...] To my mind, it is better to let Tolstoy's verse be spoiled than that it be improved by the censor. [...]

To preserve the comedy of the scene with the bear (even by making it much coarser) and replace Varlaam and Dionysius in some degree, I would stick in two boyars (councillors), each about 150 years old (like the members of the State Council). Because of their age they are led by the hand, they are purblind. When Fyodor, speaking about the bear, leans on ruins of that sort, perhaps something will remain; if we have to do this scene with walk-on boyars, the whole thing will fail.[55] [...]

Your respectful and devoted K. Alekseev [...]

To Nemirovich-Danchenko. 10 September 1898, Andreevka, Kharkov gubernia. Most esteemed Vladimir Ivanovich!

I gulped down your letters with great avidity and hasten to thank you for them a thousand times. So, you are in winter quarters. Congratulations to you and all the actors for the temporary new home in the Hunt Club. The Huntsmen, however empty the place may be, will not welcome us very hospitably. Speak whatever sweet nothings you can: there must be no card-playing. That's a pretext for them to ban all plays with crowd scenes.[56]

I repeat: I do not understand myself whether the blocking for *The Seagull* is good or worthless. I only recognize that the play is talented, interesting, but I do not know which way to tackle it. I tackled it haphazard, so do with the blocking what you will. I enclose the fourth act with this letter. Your remark that in the first act, during the performance of Treplyov's play, the secondary roles should not eclipse the leads, I fully understand and agree with it.[57] The question is how to achieve this… As is my wont I sketched out a broad overview of the role for each character. Once the actors have mastered it, I begin to pare away what is superfluous to highlight what is more important. I proceed in this way because I have always been afraid that the actors will settle on a cheap, uninteresting outline, and indeed the result of such a canvas is always puppet-like, banal figures.

Take into account that I put in frogs during the play-within-the-play to give the impression of total silence.[58] After all on stage silence is expressed by sounds, and not by their absence. If you don't fill the silence with sounds, it is impossible to achieve the illusion. Why? Because backstage (the stagehands, uninvited visitors behind the scenes, etc.), the audience itself in the hall are making noise and destroying the mood on stage. Remember, for instance, the end of the first act of *Bell*. I believe that we managed to convey the silence of nature…but with all those sounds!.. A good five men placed all around the stage – whistling, puffing and blowing into all sorts of bird-calls. I chose frogs partly because I have a little machine that successfully imitates this sound, and also because I think that the soliloquy, which treats of animals, would produce a great effect against the background of living creatures making noise. I may be mistaken. If you adapted your own plan out of tact to keep from changing mine, it would be a pity. We would have to compare which one is better?[59] At least I hope that you don't attribute to me the presence of petty director's or even worse actor's vanity. In this particular play – you hold all the cards. Of course, you know better and have a more intense feeling for it than I do. […]

Once again Simon[60] has failed to understand me, and he seems to have dashed off music (a symphony) for the orchestra in *Merchant*. I was hoping for the smallest yid orchestra (primarily string instruments, a harp, a flute, a clarinet) with six musicians, no more – only then will the scene with Bassanio be sentimental, ingenuous and charming, like a true Carpaccio– charming and ingenuous.

It occurs to me that *Hannele* will have to be staged sooner than we proposed, and, of course, it will proceed more quickly than, say, *Antigone*. It would be good if the pupils at the Philharmonic set to learning the choruses as quickly as possible. I don't know, somehow I feel I can't count on the accuracy of schoolboys – could we stock up on scores (second vocal copies) and hand them over to [Leonid Sergeevich] Vasiliev (the choir director) to check – whatever happens?

Thanks a lot for sending the repertoire (rehearsal schedule) and the cast of *Fyodor*. I don't understand who Zagarov (Starkov) is? Is he a new actor?[61]

Thanks a lot too for the character sketch of Dorn... Oh, how I fear him! After your letter even more. Already the demands are very great and responsible for this, at first glance, insignificant role. Serenity... I could probably achieve... but intelligence, mildness, kindness, good looks, elegance – that's a lot of qualities and traits, given the small quantity of words and actions... It scares me. Most of all I fear remaining myself in this role, with my own individual characteristics, I am afraid of playing this role in my own, generalized tones... I have come up with a certain tone, original it may be... [*text damaged*] of an obese, provincial, aging Don Juan, speaking in a tenor voice and at times a local amateur singer, but this gentleman has lost whatever elegance he had; except for Treplyov and Nina he treats everyone flippantly and a bit sarcastically. This one can swing on a swing, but your Dorn, of course, cannot do so... So I'll abandon this tone and look for a new one... But I'm afraid of what will turn out!..

[...] As to the boys' choir in *Hannele*, we can do with them what we did in Solodovnikov's theatre. The chorale was sung by a female choir, backstage, and the little boys on stage were chosen from the usual supernumeraries (at 20 k. per phiz). Of course, Aleksandr Akimovich has gone overboard: 90 people [for *Antigone*] on the Shchukin stage, and what's more with the stage shrunk to the amphitheatre, and what's more in a classic... Remind him that at Solodovnikov's Theatre in *Othello* the crowd scenes with soldiers came to 60 or 70 people, and it was very constricted.

I am not getting much better, but at least I am not getting fat. According to the scales (perhaps they lie) I put on 2 pounds here. Why... I don't know... When I get a good night's sleep, I feel all right, but I don't always manage it, thanks to the impossible noise made by children from early morning. The weather is bad and cold all the time... My wife doesn't feel very well either. [...]

Respectfully yours K. Alekseev [...]

Although Lilina was a member of the acting company, she spent much of her time with the children in Lyubimovka, and when she was in Moscow, KS was at the factory, the theatre or travelling. It put a strain on their marriage.

To **his wife Mariya Lilina.** Friday, 7 o'clock, 18 September 1898, Kharkov. Splendid little dovie! [...]

Your coming here is worthwhile, my reassurance that you are here, that at any time I can pour out my grief or joy to you is worthwhile, and then the need for talk will somehow cease. But in the meantime there is a need to say everything, but imperceptibly. Why? Now imagine that we can see one another only one hour a day (we are lovers). Lord, how much one would say in that short interim! Let's assume we have uttered 10,000 words. Spread these 10,000 out over 18 hours – it no longer has the same effect. In theatrical slang it's called: shuffling along. Add to this that the words are spoken between business matters, in fits and starts – not

111

at all the same thing. We would have said as much, but with no satisfaction. That's why I write. At least, when I can – I don't have to stop myself.

Today I went and thought: you are my poor little darlingest dear, after all I'm making you unhappy, and you patiently put up with it all. I put myself in your place. No, I wouldn't put up with it. At times I tried to imagine another life for me: I am a businessman, I work till 5 o'clock, and all night long I'm yours. It was so clear to me that then I would be quite a different man – repulsive not only to my own, but to your taste –, and you know who I would remind myself of – Vasya Bostanzhoglo. I would be exactly like him. Sleepy, thoughtless, dozing off every minute, not just at home but with strangers, and back to sleep. In order to be different – I would have to do some other work. Which? The only one that would suit me – charity work. Again the same story, only with the difference that rehearsals would be replaced by meetings, and nervous excitation and learning lines replaced by preparations for speeches and debates at meetings. The only comfort is that everybody lives like that, at least all respectable people.

Furthermore, I thought, isn't there some way to organize one's life so that at least once a week we can belong to one another. This can and must be done. How?.. Leave Moscow or even more simply, leave the Slavonic Bazaar. This idea is beginning to attract me. Am I right, could we put it into practice?

At least, I will work at it and reassure myself that at least I will manage one night or day a week to belong to you alone. And I have become so ashamed and offended for you, my dear darlingest, the one and only one dear to my heart. [...] I love and respect you awfully much.

Furthermore, I thought I ought to reassure you about an idea that sometimes creeps into your mind – jealousy. For instance, do not worry your head about Zhelyabuzhskaya [Andreeva] or Knipper. There can be nothing to it, particularly because youthful frivolity has flown. Today, for instance Klavdiya Yakovlena Bazhyonova[62] travelled with me on the train. I said good day and spent a moment. She was very attractive and affectionate. But I had difficulty speaking to her. It was irksome or, more accurately, offensive to talk to her, because I had just left my darling dear, because this silly darling dear, if she knew about this meeting, would have turned sad in a second. I left and, of course, was glad, because I could take a nap. Only it turned out awkwardly, because at the station in Kharkov I didn't meet her to say goodbye. As if on purpose her husband ran into me on the way, he probably had come to meet his wife. He had time to shout at me – we'll be expecting you.

Now I don't know: should I go or not... I think I won't go and let them be offended, and besides I don't know the address. [...]

I did nothing along the way but read the role of Trigorin – it is more to my taste than Dorn. At least there's something in it, but nothing in the other, and they're expecting God knows what. I don't like it. Right now I'm about to go to see two or three acts at the theatre. They're playing [K. A. Folomeev's comedy] *The Evil Pit*. It's an interesting play. [...]

Your adoring Kotunchik

To **his wife Mariya Lilina**. Saturday, 19 September 1898, Kharkov.

My darling angel!

There's no time to write much. It's 2 o'clock now, I only just had lunch, in half an hour I'll be travelling to Moscow, I still have to pack my things, settle up. But I would write a lot concerning the philosophy of good, tender and friendly love. Till another time, if only we have a success in Moscow.

I'll tell you what I've been doing. The devil tempted me to go to the theatre – *The Evil Pit* prompts a staggeringly repulsive reaction due to the author's complete lack of talent. The troupe isn't bad. [Evelina Fyodorovna] Dneprova (you remember, a pretty little brunette, who doesn't know her?) isn't bad. Petipa[63] played in the farce – enchanting. And all the same I left the theatre (I hadn't seen a show for a long time) feeling depressed. None of it is serious – it's not worth devoting one's life to it. Can I be doing the very same thing and ruining my life for the sake of such a chimera? This torments me a great deal. Can you go on living and be unaware of what you're doing? I thought it was all serious business and it turns out to be trivia. And my whole life is not only mine, but to waste another's on this --? -- The thoughts come again: how am I to organize things differently. [...]

Goodbye, my darling life. Write or wire about yourself, otherwise I will worry about you and the dear little girl. Is she scared at night? I said my prayers – I made the sign of cross over you more than once.

Kiss the kids. I love you awfully and am tormented about you.

All yours – awfully loving and respectful

Kotunchik

On 20 September KS returned to Moscow and went to see how the troupe was getting on. They had been able to rent the cramped Hermitage Theatre of 815 seats in a public garden. KS plunged into collecting and sorting museum pieces and antiques to renovate the 'boyar style' which had itself become antiquated in the theatre.

To **his wife Mariya Lilina.** 21 September 1898, Moscow.

My dazzling little angel!

Today is Wednesday and I have no rehearsals. I'm spending my time on costumes, and so (you see, I am not wearing myself out) I even picked out a free little hour to talk to you. Thanks, my little beauty, my dearest little heart, for your kind but sad letter. So I hasten to answer you as quickly as possible, so I can inform you of lots of pleasant things.

[...] I got home – and there I found a whole display of boots for *Fyodor*. I was delighted: I hadn't expected that they would already be finished. It was announced in all (or some) of the newspapers that I was returning today so that I had scarcely arrived when a telegram came from the theatre, inviting me to a full rehearsal of *Fyodor* which they were putting on specially for me.

At first I didn't want to go, but then I felt it would be much worse and more nerve-racking to sit at home with my Mum. It's simpler to go and find out what's happening and calm down. I said a prayer and left.

«ЦАРЬ ѲЕОДОРЪ ІОАННОВИЧЪ», гр. А. К. ТОЛСТОГО М. Х. Т.
Царь Ѳеодоръ—И. М. Москвинъ.
Право собств. заявл. № 1866.

Figure 21 Ivan Moskvin as Tsar Fyodor. Photo: K. A. Fischer, Moscow

The first impression of the theatre was not encouraging: total chaos, rebuilding, cleaning up and so on. I was giving birth to, I was taking part in a disaster. The first scene did not please me, and I was beginning to get depressed (I arrived in time for the reconciliation scene between Boris and Shuisky). The second was better and the rest quite good. Moskvin's acting (although I was told he was not on form) made me blub. I even had to blow my nose loudly. Everyone else in the house, even those taking part, were blowing their noses too. Splendid fellow! The crowd scenes (of course, still in a rough state) are all ready. Shenberg is worn out, but I think he is purposely exaggerating his ill health so we will feel sorry for him

114

and relieve him of his actually difficult scut work. I egged him on and he became very pleased and brightened up. The 'Yauza' scene is ready, in rough shape, of course. I think with a few more rehearsals *Fyodor* will be ready.

I left the theatre very cheerful, especially when I was told of Suvorin's and Chekhov's enthusiasm.[64] I came home, fell asleep and in the evening (sorry) couldn't resist – I went to see the sets for *Fyodor* which have been set up for the last time, because the electricity is to be switched off for a week or so for repairs. Not all the sets are equally magnificent, but they are all interesting and good. With the exception of two scenes, all of *Fyodor* is ready with furniture, props, etc. So now I don't think we'll have the usual agonies at the dress rehearsal as in the past. The costumes have been ordered. I'm told they're ready too. Dress parade will be tomorrow. A number of conversations and the hopes of the actors and the fact that two performances are sold out greatly relieved me and I came home in a cheerful mood. I was in bed by twelve, deliberately read some book (about art – by Tolstoy[65]) till twelve forty-five and went instantly to sleep. I woke up about ten today feeling good. Close to the work, I think I shall feel calmer here than in Andreevka. At night I was worried about poor little you. I thought that now you are alone in the whole house, you'll get frightened and so on. Today I received your angelic letter and hasten to reassure you. This is how I think things will go. Until the first play is on, there will be nothing but consternation. There will be blow-ups but appreciably fewer than at the Hunt Club. When we have surmounted the vast peaks – *Fyodor*, *Merchant* and *Hannele* – then everything will go smoothly. That's how it looks to me.

Goodbye, my precious, good, dazzling one. I miss you very much, but know that nothing bothers me so much as your worry and ill health. Let the world fall to rack and ruin, so long as you and the kids are healthy and beside me.

All yours Kotunchik

Say the most loving things to the kids so that they know that I remember them. Regards and kisses to everyone.

The premiere took place on 14 (26) October 1898 to an audience made up of old friends, skeptics and antagonists, who regarded the Art Theatre as an affront to the Maly. The wealthy middle-class who had known Kostya Alekseev from his cradle could not take him seriously as a professional mummer. There were no 'names' in the company. The papers had been sent only one ticket each and through the post, not by personal solicitation. Despite all these drawbacks, it was a smash, owing less to the individual performances than to the stage pictures and ingenious groupings. It was played for 920 performances until it disappeared from the repertoire in the mid-1920s.

The Sunken Bell opened on 19 October; as a revival its reception was respectful but not enthusiastic (seventeen performances). The Merchant of Venice followed on 21 October and, despite a skillful staging and attractive sets, proved to be a total flop. KS had imposed a Yiddish accent on Darsky and it was unacceptable to the audience. Ten performances were as much as could be eked out. At the dress rehearsal of Hannele, a telegram from the Chief of Police banned the play. The financial situation of the MAT was at risk. If the rent on the theatre wasn't paid by 1 December, the landlord would cancel the lease and demand damages.

The rest of the season was equally disappointing. The staging of Laws Unto Themselves (4 *November, directed by KS, Luzhsky and Sanin*) *seemed like reheated leftovers and audiences expected the character Prince Platon (KS) to be a savage beast, whereas KS humanized him.* Audiences found Greta's Happiness (*opened 2 December, directed by ND*) *dismal, but they enjoyed Goldoni's* Mistress of the Inn *with KS as the misogynist Cavaliere di Ripafratta. Houses for both were far from full. The first ran only nine performances, the second three, and the last seven. Everything was staked on* The Seagull, *which opened on 18 December 1898, after three dress rehearsals. The audience was sparse, the cast was sedated by valerian drops, and KS's leg developed a nervous twitch during the play-within-a-play scene. To everyone's surprise, the audience became drawn into the action and gave the actors an ovation.*

To **Anton Chekhov.**17 December 1898. *Telegram.*

Just played *Seagull*, colossal success. From first act play so enthralled that series of triumphs followed. Endless curtain calls. My explanation after act three that author not in theatre, audience demanded we send you telegram on its behalf. We are crazy with delight. All kiss you warmly.

Vl. I. Nemirovich-Danchenko, Stanislavsky, Knipper, etc.

Figure 22 A studio photograph of the last act of *The Seagull*, 1898. Left–right: Nikolay Tikhomirov as Medvedenko; Vasily Luzhsky as Sorin; Vsevolod Meyerhold as Treplyov; Olga Knipper as Arkadina; Konstantin Stanislavsky as Trigorin; Mariya Lilina as Masha; Aleksandr Artyom as Shamraev; Aleksandr Vishnevsky as Dorn; and Yevgeniya Raevskaya as Polina

The Seagull *played to packed houses, despite the fact that no one liked Roksanova as Nina and KS was thought to have misinterpreted Trigorin.*

Hedda Gabler, *with KS as sole director and Løvborg and Andreeva as Hedda, opened on 18 February. He was acclaimed for a brilliant performance, but Ibsen did not enthuse the public and closed after eleven performances. The MAT's first season ended on 28 February. It had managed to create an audience of its own, but was still on shaky ground. KS and Lilina drew no salaries, and KS requested that the factory reduce his wages there from 5000 rubles a year to 4000. The couple again took a vacation at the Chernigov Hostel near Troitsa-Sergievsky.*

KS then set about writing the staging plans for the second season: Hauptmann's Drayman Henschel, *Ostrovsky's* The Dowerless Bride, *Chekhov's* Uncle Vanya *(in which KS wanted to play the title role but was cast as Astrov) and Aleksey Tolstoy's* The Death of Ioann the Terrible, *all of which went into rehearsal simultaneously. On 1 May a special performance of* Seagull *was shown to Chekhov in the Paradis theatre. He approved of the whole, but did not care for KS or Roksanova.*

Sanin's production of Antigone *had had thirty-six rehearsals but never achieved tragic stature. It opened on 1 January 1899 and ran for fourteen performances.*

To **his wife Mariya Lilina**. 17 May 1899, Moscow.
My dearest darlingest, my little Snow Maiden! [66]
I didn't write to you the day before yesterday, because I had fallen ill, the letter would have turned out to be depressing. Yesterday morning and night there were rehearsals, and after them, having sat at a table all day, I came home on foot (from Nikitsky St!!) and then returned at one. I feel all right, although… something isn't right. You and I have not lived well recently and said our farewells not quite the way we should have. Now, I feel that you are enjoying living at Lyubimovka without me, and I am heartily delighted on the one hand, but on the other I am annoyed, why can't you live happily with me, why it is necessary for us to part to relax. It means, we are bound to one another. That's the way things are now – why I am writing all this, after all I am disturbing your peace, and yet I cannot not write to you. So these kinds of ideas torment and irritate me. Therefore, I swear, my mood is turning from fair to foul. Well, I think, if Marusya needs to rest away from me, let her rest, I will not go to Lyubimovka in the near future, and then nothing will drag me away from Moscow.

As to the theatre, it ought to have cheered me up.

Yesterday were the trial rehearsals. *Terrible* produced an effect and *Henschel* will be all right, if Roksanova finally takes charge of her role [Hanna Schell]. Today I inspected *Uncle Vanya*, and I think that the play will be excellent. Norova[67] cannot act, but, it turns out they are appealing to Komissarzhevskaya ⁓ !?[68] I will be annoyed if you don't wind up in the play, and I want to discuss this matter with Nemirovich.

On Saturday I realized: here I am with no family, no theatre (we assume). I am a businessman and actually spent the day that way: a day at the factory in company with Shamshin, Vishnyakov and Buchheim[69] – until 5 o'clock (then a massage –

the best hour of the day). I dined at the Hermitage with Buchheim and spoke till my throat was raw about Chetverikov.[70] My head began to spin, and I had to go home on foot in order to sober up. If a year like this is in the offing, I will shoot myself... With what avidity and satisfaction I fell upon on the staging-plan for the last scene in *Terrible* (it is finished) – you can judge by the fact the staging-plan was ready by 2 o'clock. In the evening I got your note and was delighted by it. I collect your little notes and I immediately lost this one and couldn't find where I had mislaid it.

I feel all right. The massage stirs up in me a need for walking and movement, and Lindström [the Swedish masseur] said that this is how it's supposed to be. Yesterday I walked home with Baratov from the theatre and had no ill results, wasn't tired. On my return I saw the little cold fowl and gulped it down with great appetite and felt that I was not alone, that there is a little person to whom I am dear... Merci for the little fowl.

I slept well last night, about nine hours, but not much tonight, I awoke at 8 and didn't drop off again. At least that's how it feels. Now I'm sitting in the Prague, before tonight's rehearsal of *Uncle Vanya*. Tomorrow morning we plan out *Terrible*, at night *Henschel*, day after tomorrow I plan the last scene in *Terrible*, at night, probably, or I write *Uncle Vanya* (if I can think up a set), or rehearse.[71]

On Thursday, if my little dearie misses me very much, I may go to Lyubimovka, and perhaps it would be better if you came here – ah!..

Somehow Lyubimovka with its intrigues and mouldiness has become dreadfully distasteful to me. The queen of the place[72]... poisons my whole life.

Well goodbye, my dear little dove. Kiss the kiddies. Have they forgotten me or do they remember? [...]

The letter turned out sickly, but, in truth, I am not ill, but only philosophizing and thinking.

Yours Kontunchik

To **Olga Knipper.** 24 June 1899, Moscow.

Most respected Olga Leonardovna!

[...] I take this opportunity to share a few of my thoughts concerning the role of Yelena in *Uncle Vanya*. The polished manners of Arkadina and Yelena, their temperament offers the actress playing them the temptation to repeat herself to some degree. That is undesirable... To create the greatest difference between the two characters I would present Yelena – naturally, in moments of calm – with great immobility, languor, indolence, reserve and refinement and at the same time shade the nuances of her temperament more sharply... I throw out this thought, which came to me after the last rehearsal, for you to try. I am doggedly looking out for a role for you. If only you knew how difficult it is! There is a wonderful role in Ibsen's *Pillars of Society*[73] but like Arkadina it's not young. And it is undesirable, -- before the time is right, two years running, for you to play roles which are unsuitable for your age. I will keep looking when I have the time. [...]

Deeply and respectfully yours K. Alekseev

Chekhov suggested to his publisher Marks that he publish his plays with KS's staging plans and the idea was met with encouragement. Meanwhile KS was on his way to Vichy.

To **his wife Mariya Lilina.** 30 June 1899. Train compartment.
Greetings, my bright, dove-grey-winged, tender, kind, clever, wonderful little angel!
[…] Throw open to me my own dear little heart and warm me in my loneliness. Yet, no, I am not quite lonely yet and here is why. The train pulled away. I could hardly make out your little phiz with my already brimming eyes. Then the pitiless crowd pushed you into the background. All that could be seen was a blue hat and a slender dear little white hand, but even that soon disappeared. I felt totally alone. The tears had waited for this moment to relieve my depressed state, -- and I burst out sobbing. I stood a long time at the window – I gazed into the distance and watered my jacket, while the wind buffeted my face… As soon as the tears begin to abate, I recall your dear little phiz, and again the tears gush forth in even greater force. But here comes some station or other, the train has slowed down. Crowds on the platform. I have to hide my puffy face – I break my pose, up to that time motionless. I sat on the divan, pulling out a handkerchief. Something fell – it was your parasol. I burst out sobbing again and began to kiss it. And after that try and insist that there is no sentimentality in me. This parasol is my guardian angel, my mascot, I will not part from you until we meet again and I return it with thanks. At night I lay it down and make the sign of the cross over it, in the morning I greet it. Like Narcissus I shall converse with it, and it will seem to me that I am not entirely lonely. Comforted by the parasol and fearful of falling back into a tearful mood, I went as soon as I could to the dining-car and there ordered coffee. I also took with me a book about Ivan the Terrible. For a long time I didn't understand what was written in it, but finally I began to distinguish sentences, words and finally made out a bit of it. For a long time I forced myself to read and only by nightfall did I understand that the book is interesting and useful to me.[74] I will have to read it thoroughly from the beginning, because reading in the evening doesn't count. […]

All yours Kotunchik

To **Mariya Lilina.** 3/15 July 1899, Paris.
My white snow maiden, my poor dear little orphan!
Here, in licentious Paris, you must imagine me as white as snow and purest of the pure. […] You are more beautiful than all the powdered Parisiennes. Either I am growing old or Paris is no good any more. All these words, my snow maiden, you will understand from this cursory story. I travelled through Germany all right and comfortably, all the time alone in a separate compartment (there were few people). In Kelno, as is traditional, I had supper, sent my bee-ootiful one a telegram so she wouldn't worry. I got back into the French carriage (alone again in a four-seat compartment). I decided to take a nap hurray, because the French did not want to lose face with the Germans and sent a carriage there, as I have already said, that was luxurious. Electricity, wonderful upholstery, luxury everywhere.

We set off. Good heavens, what rattling! First disappointment. I lay down – a narrow divan, the arms (elbow-rests) rise up. The iron staples on these arm-rests serve as two cold compresses. One immediately falls where the kidneys are located, the other on the calves. One mighty shake, and I fall on the floor. I try to pull out the divan so it's wider – it doesn't pull out. The electricity goes out. I flounder about in the dark and end up dozing off sitting up. At six in the morning, in torment, I figure it out: I take the mattress off the divan, put it on the floor, and, knocked about on all sides, fall asleep. There's your illustrious nation; everything for show.

Paris, customs. They take 21 francs from me for cigarettes! It turns out that I showed up right on 14 July, the national holiday. [...]

I woke up about seven o'clock. I walked to 'Félicien' (that, I believe, is that restaurant in the Champs Elysées). I ate turbot, very tasty, and Spanish-style chicken (disgusting). It was so muggy that I decided not to go to the theatre. Besides there was nothing interesting. The Comédie had a matinee of *The Marriage of Figaro*. I didn't go, to keep my promise to you, I thought there might be a demonstration. In the evening the Comédie is closed. The rest of the theatres are playing melodramas. There's nothing to do with oneself. I had dinner, strolled along the Champs Elysées – nobody there. I dropped in at the Ambassadeurs. I wanted to hear Guilbert,[75] but she was ill and didn't sing. [...] A Russian turned up next to me, rather charming. He took me to a low-class dance hall in the Quartier Latin. Again that revolting cancan, dressed by horrible mugs. Belle Fatma is a very beautiful stupid woman performing living pictures. Ghastly costume. Completely decent. Boring. Again the *danse du ventre*. [...] At midnight no one was in the garden. I looked back at the city. At the Café Américain I drank coffee. More acrobats, indecent tableaux. Two rather fat women invited me upstairs to show me *des belles choses* and some new ways of doing things. They assured me that they adored Russians, made a few vulgar remarks, not very clever ones concerning the *alliance franco-russe*. I gave them five francs to be rid of them and ran away, because I was afraid they would tear me apart. No gaiety nor the one-time wit, not even a vestige of this. They say that the French love women. No. They stare at them cold-bloodedly. They don't even want to pay court to them, be gallant, they're too lazy. They demand that they lift their skirts for them right away. And after that you dare chide me for my gallantry... I am now more French than all of Paris put together. Paris is not racy, but simply – Silenus. I remember the Volga... [...] you, my bee-ootiful one, my wee cocotte, my woman, my goddessette, my everything... everything in the world. I lie in a soft bed that is very uncomfortable and short, and fall asleep in sorrow. After making the sign of the cross over my parasol. Bless the kids.

What I live for now is the poetry of homecoming.

All yours Kontuchik [...]

To his wife Mariya Lilina. 4/16 July 1899, Vichy.

My angelic, pure Russian darling soul!

[In Paris I went] to the Comédie. Last year I resolved never to go there again, but yesterday I was ready to swear an oath not to. What routine! What monotony!

What paucity of imagination reigns there! I cannot understand what's going on, since the French are a talented people. Yes... we can teach them a good deal right now.

Admittedly, they were acting some...hm... pretty... little plays. For instance, a wife is dying, her husband and daughter are at sea (why they couldn't have picked another time to go on their travels I do not know). The least little excitement and the wife will turn up her toes, the doctor warns. Suddenly the husband (Silvain[76]) arrives – the daughter has gone for a swim and drowned (my little dove, watch out, be careful in Feodosia!!!) The husband wants to tell his wife everything, even though he knows that it will kill her.

You think that he loves her – he adores her (a special, French kind of love). The doctor is persuasive, the husband tries to keep mum. The doctor leaves, the couple is left alone. He says nothing for a long time, then up and tells it all, and with such shouting that it would make a healthy person ill. Then he falls into a faint, and the sick wife starts to look after him. Obviously, this news has improved her health. She puts on a fashionable black mourning coat (provident lady!) and drags her husband to the seashore to say farewell to their child... I suppose she has recovered.

In another play a certain scholar has studied and studied and suddenly got to the point that in the open theatre he starts to curse the Virgin Mary in uncensored (by Russian law) words because fifteen years earlier she had taken the wife whom he loved more than she. The Virgin is a woman, which means, she must be jealous of him, so she took his wife and thereby had her revenge. He has found some document, a vicious one that debunks the Virgin, and with its help he wants to have his revenge on her. He is on the verge of doing so, but a little girl tells him a truth which he, unfortunately, for all his scholarship, does not know: without faith people find life hard. Isn't that interesting. In short, the devil knows what.

In the theatre I ran into the St P. actress Pototskaya[77] – I unbosomed myself a bit in Russian and cursed out the actors with her. Early to bed, because today I had to get up early, at 6:30. [...]

Yours Kotunchik

To **his mother.** 20 July 1899. Vichy.
Dear Mum,

[...] Here in Vichy I am beginning a serious treatment; to tell the truth, there is no way not to have a serious treatment here, because nobody thinks of anything else. The boredom is unimaginable, the heat...All day long music and outdoor amusements, but not the kind of amusements you might expect from the French, animated, joyful... no... Everyone walks around downcast, pompous, prim and sleepy... You might think you were in Nemetchin... What has become of the French, where has their liveliness gone, I don't know. Even on 14 July, the national holiday, I didn't see a single cheerful face or a single witty joke, not a single impassioned patriotic outburst.

The French themselves shrug their shoulders and say: things are no longer what they were.

[…] To say that I have nothing to do here would be untrue. I am frightfully busy, from morning to night, but with the most frightfully boring business. You have to get up at 7 (scandalous!). At 8 a shower. They put me, one of God's creatures, on a soft table, pour on stinking water, and two scrawny little Frenchmen pummel my whole body with their fists. I cannot say that this was interesting and entertaining. After the shower you perspire and go to change your shirt. Then you walk for a quarter of an hour, run a distance to the spring ('Hôpital') to drink the waters, then walk for half an hour, then back to the same spring, then walk for half an hour, finally go to another spring (source 'Chomel' – for catarrh of the nose and throat). A long corridor, adorned with spittoons, and a crowd of people spitting, coughing, blowing their noses. Having blown your nose and spat, you run off to lunch, because so far you haven't had a bite to eat. Of course, having worn your legs to stumps, you eat with an appetite. They feed you very well, in truth. After lunch, coffee in the café, and you can barely drag yourself into bed. I just have time to rest and get busy with something when it's time again to go twice to drink the waters, sit and so on, then dinner, an hour or two of idle chat, and sleep. That's my life. I can't wait for it to be over and done with. […]

Yours Kostya

To **Aleksandr Sanin.**[78] 23 July 1899, Vichy
Most kind Aleksandr Akimovich!

[…] While the troupe was vacationing in June, I was busy with costumes, sets, money matters (in Vl. Iv's absence), of course, and with the factories until 29 June, including 10 days travel along the Volga.

There the doctor demanded my rapid departure abroad and I could complete the treatment only by 20 August. Without this treatment, the doctor says, I would not get through half the season. Therefore, it appears to be indispensable. In fact, counting the 20 days I worked through in June, I will catch up in August, so that my vacation will not exceed two months. I absolutely need this period to gain the strength to work the way I work. In the present year, thanks to *Terrible*, even greater strength is required of me.

All this, dear Aleksandr Akimovich, is intended for your talks with the actors. […] To avoid loose talk, let a few persons, on whom you can rely, know the real inside story. […]

Do not spend everything all at once. Do not repeat last year's mistakes. That would be unforgiveable. Do not expect results all at once. Good heavens, how much progress we have made in the theatre compared with the French. This trip aided me in realizing once more the negative side of the theatre. I am returning now with the firm intention of achieving truth to life and the most realistic action both in tragedy and the most vapid farce. Only then will the theatre be a serious institution, otherwise it is a plaything (as in France), and a very boring plaything at that. […]

Yours K. Alekseev

KS made proposals to ND about staging various plays: Strindberg's Miss Julie *(no) and Hauptmann's* Lonely Lives *(yes). Sergey Mamontov wrote to KS professing fellow feeling and suggesting that the theatre may become a religion in the new age; he offered his help whenever needed.*

The new season began with three productions directed by KS in collaboration with Sanin and Luzhsky. The Death of Ioann the Terrible opened on 29 September with an ailing KS playing a dying tsar. The Chief of Police insisted that the scene of Ioann's coming from prayers and the reading of the bill of mortality be excised. The consensus was that KS was weak as Ioann, too naturalistically senile and petty, but, as usual, the carefully observed detail of the staging evoked admiration and it achieved 50 performances.

Twelfth Night *followed on 3 October, and barely made it to eight performances.*

Drayman Henschel *opened two days later and was praised more for the staging than the acting (it had already been played by the Maly and Korsh's). Its sedulous recreation of German proletarian life failed to attract audiences.*

On 17 October Vera Vasilievna Kotlyarevskaya (Pushkareva, 1875-1942), an actress of the Alexandra theatre, attended a performance of The Seagull. *She wrote to KS that she had thought she had understood the character of Trigorin when she had read the play and at first could not figure out what Stanislavsky was getting at, but gradually accepted the clarity of his interpretation. She would become one of his favourite correspondents for discussing the finer points of acting.*

To **Vera Kotlyarevskaya**. 21 October 1899, Moscow.

Gracious madam!

I sincerely thank you for the little card you sent me with the pleasant and encouraging postscript. This is almost the first encouragement I've had for the role of Trigorin, whose image as I present it is appreciated neither by the press nor the public. The latter wishes to see him not as a character part, but a banal *jeune premier*, performed in generalized tones. In view of the stated reasons you will understand that your opinion has cheered and encouraged me considerably, because I cannot change the image of Trigorin, whom I love so much. [...]

K. Alekseev (Stanislavsky)

The joint staging of Uncle Vanya *by KS and ND opened on 26 October. (It was not a premiere since the play had already had a number of provincial productions.) Over the course of rehearsals KS had managed to adapt Astrov from his original concept of a fiery lover to a dispassionate materialist. Maksim Gorky, who had already enthused to Chekhov over a provincial production of the play, beheld the MAT treatment in January 1900 and was impressed. Tolstoy was not, and considered Vanya and Astrov to be trashy men. (The production would achieve 323 productions prior to KS's death.)*

Lonely Lives, *directed by KS and ND, opened on the previous 16 December and had an unexpectedly brilliant success except for Meyerhold in the leading role of Johannes Vockerat. He was judged to be too neurasthenic, even though the character is a weak-willed young husband who commits suicide. (He was later replaced by the more charismatic Vasily Kachalov, enabling the production to reach seventy-three performances.)*

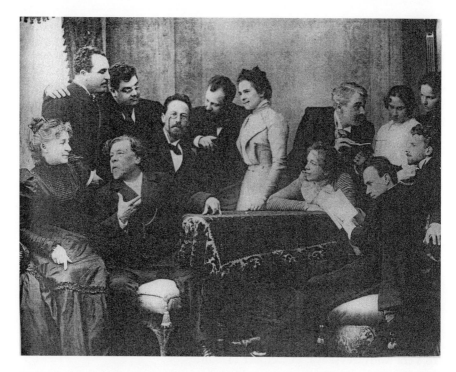

Figure 23 A joke photo taken after the formal picture of Chekhov reading *The Seagull* to the MAT company, May 1899. Left–right, standing: Vishnevsky, Luzhsky, Anton Chekhov, Nemirovich-Danchenko, Knipper, Stanislavsky, Mariya Roksanova, Mariya Andreeva. Left–right, seated: Raevskaya, Artyom, Lilina, Iosaf Tikhomirov, Vsevolod Meyerhold

In mid-February ND sent KS a long letter, complaining of the growing influence of the millionaire Morozov in the MAT's affairs; he resented what he saw as a power grab on KS's part and his own treatment as 'a secretary'.

To **Nemirovich-Danchenko.** Before 20 February 1900, Moscow.
Dear Vladimir Ivanovich!

I give you my word that this is a peaceable letter, but I am so shattered and I feel so abominable that I'm on the verge of beginning to fear for my mental health; during the day I am over-excited, at night I am an *absolute* insomniac with a breakdown in my strength and energy. I live on bromide and laurel water. So, put yourself in my place and do not be cruel. Such letters as your last I am *very* familiar with. I got exactly that kind of letter 12 years ago and that was the beginning of the end of the Society for Art and Literature. Two months ago just such a letter from the Board of Guardians was put into my hands. I hastened to distance myself from it, and now of the 50 active members there remain only 6. I think that you have convinced yourself that I can make all sorts of sacrifices for my beloved concern. For its sake I strive as best I can to suppress my own ego. For its sake I put myself into very strange, sometimes ridiculous positions. I am prepared to share my labour and success with anyone you like, I tack between personal vanities, I try unobtrusively to stitch up all the seams; not only do I turn down money, but for the right to busy myself with a concern I love I cross 10,000 rubles out of my own budget, I put my last bit of money into the concern, I deprive my family and myself of the greatest necessities and, taking a bit of evasive action financially, I patiently await the time when the debts will be covered so that I can recover what belongs to me by right. When the vanities and ambitions of the shareholders flare up and everyone starts talking about wounded honour, their rights and so on, I keep silent and take on myself the upshot of these disputes, that is financial losses. Prokofiev[79] is ruined – I pick up the pieces without complaining. I am reconciled to the fact that I have to act and (frequently) stage things that do not appeal to me, I act whatever I have to, and not what I would like to. In short, I am ruining myself both morally and financially and do not complain so long as my nerves are not stretched beyond endurance. I suppose that's the point we have reached now and, as you see, I am beginning to complain… Yes, I am very distressed and offended that everyone else has the right to talk about himself, but I am deprived of this right… it is not fair!

So, I am ready for any kind of sacrifice, but one thing I will not agree to *under any circumstances*. I cannot play the role of the fall-guy. But I am now close to doing just that. You and Morozov cannot or will not see eye to eye. It looks as if quarrels and misunderstandings are about to begin, and I am to stand between you and take the beating. No, that is out of the question, nor will my nerves stand it. Without you, I won't stay in this concern, because we began it together and ought to go on leading it. Having recognized in you, as in any human being, failings, at the same time I *greatly value* you and many good aspects, I also warmly value in you your good relationship with me and my work. Without Morozov (especially with Osipov[80] and Co.) I can't stay in this concern – *under any circumstances*. Why? Because I value Morozov's good features. I have no doubt that fate sends such an aide and man of affairs once in a lifetime. Finally because I have been waiting for just such a man since I began my theatrical activity (as I was waiting for you). We are fortune's favourites, and if we cannot or do not know how to make use of her favours, then, no matter what, absolutely nothing will come of our concern. Do not forget that I have no money, that I am a family man and that I have *no more right* to risk this portion of my assets. With the Osipovs I risk a great deal (You don't, I do). I have no faith in their probity, I have blind faith in Morozov's probity. I have so much faith in him that I do not want to conclude any signed contract with him, for I consider it superfluous, I do not advise you to do so, because I know from experience that such a contract only leads to quarrels. If two individuals, moved by the same common goal, cannot come to an agreement orally, then what good is a piece of paper. Nor will I likewise in future play a double game: on the sly reconciling Morozov with Nemirovich on your behalf and vice-versa. If a quarrel is unavoidable, let it break out as soon as possible, let our concern collapse while people will still regret it, let us Russians show once again that we are a vile nation, that we let egos and petty vanity destroy all our good efforts. This will be demonstrated all the more persuasively by our concern because in the history of the worldwide theatre there will be found no more brilliant page than the one we have written in the last two years. If this should happen, I will spit on the theatre and art and will go and spin gold thread in my factory. To hell with that kind of art!

I will make the ultimate sacrifice for our concern, which I am beginning to hate today. If you find it necessary that I be present when a contract is concluded with Morozov, -- very well, I shall be there, but in my present situation I cannot deal with two pieces of business at once. If you find, as chief of the repertoire, that *The Heart Is Not a Stone* ought to be staged in the current season, put off discussions with Morozov until the play has been produced. Otherwise *Heart Is Not a Stone* will have to replaced. I will stiffen up my nerves and summon up all my energy so as to bring the season to its close and stage *Heart Is Not a Stone*, but to do this it behooves me to marshal my forces as economically as I can, because, I repeat, I am *very, very* weak both *physically* and *morally*.

Recently I have been over-generous in the employment of my mind, and it refuses to serve, and I still have to compose the 3rd act, the most difficult in the play. I will refrain from *Motley Stories* (which I came to believe in more than once) and not stage them.[81] They are a deliberate obstacle and no one cares about them. One would need much too much energy to make them work, I don't have it, and from the financial standpoint – we don't need the stories. We can finish the season without them. It would be unfair if you attribute this refusal to vanity or something else. I give you my word that I am acting for the welfare of the concern so that I will have the strength to finish out the season. I conclude this portion of my letter with a hasty exclamation... Your letter...is the beginning of the end. Another request: until the play *The Heart Is Not a Stone* is put on, let there be little talk of this lamentable matter, because one worrisome phrase will deprive me of sleep all night long, and I very much need my sleep, especially now. [...]

Figure 24 A joke photo of Stanislavsky and Nemirovich reviewing the "second rank"

In conclusion I wish with all my heart that we all value as it deserves that rare treasure bestowed on us by fate, so that we realize in time what riches this treasure promises us, and forget all those petty things for the sake of which we risk losing our hold on the treasure. For my part, despite my enfeebled energy, I am ready to make whatever sacrifices the concern requires and which I have the right to make. The idiotic position in which I may stand in relation to you and Morozov I consider no sacrifice at all, because it will not save but only destroy the concern and will heap all the consequences, which I do not deserve, on my shoulders (exclusively).

Your devoted K. Alekseev [...]

The Moscow season ended on 20 February and KS and Lilina returned to the monastery hostelry, followed by an expedition to the Arkhangel district, where he began work on Ostrovsky's fairy-tale play The Snow Maiden.

In March KS held a private audition of Vasily Ivanovich Kachalov (Shverubovich, 1875-1948), who had been working at Suvorin's Literary-Artistic Society in St Petersburg. KS considered that, in terms of acting, they spoke different languages; he did not hire him but intended to keep an eye on him. Unable to find an actor for King Berendey in Snow Maiden, *they tried out Kachalov again – successfully. Kachalov would become in time, with KS and Moskvin, the inevitable lead in the MAT's productions.*

In April the MAT went on its first tour, to the Crimea, where everyone had a very good time. They performed for Chekhov, now an invalid in Yalta, and KS met Gorky for the first time. Aleksey Maksimovich Peshkov (1868-1936), who wrote under the name Maksim Gorky (Bitter), was a celebrity among the literate proletariat and the progressive youth. He supported the Social-Democratic cause and preached a tolerance for all humanity. Urged on by Chekhov, Gorky promised the MAT a play and attended rehearsals throughout September, but was unable to keep his promise.

Ibsen continued to attract them. In June, off on another rest cure in the Caucasus, KS began sketching out Act IV of Enemy of the People, *while ND worked on* When We Dead Awaken.

To **his wife Maria Lilina.** 8 July 1900, Essentuki.

[...] Where have I wound up? In Asia, Persia or China?... I am sure that people live there no worse and, of course, more merrily. If I survive in this hole for a week, I will ask for a medal for endurance.

Picture Pushkino, only inhabited by ailing shopkeepers, merchants, Armenian officers. Picture the Pushkino streets unpaved, and the dust not dark, as with us, but white. Another difference: the dachas there are somewhat dirty, whereas here they are dreadfully dirty. There you sometimes see smiling faces, here absolutely none, there sometimes you hear human voices, but here an oppressive silence. I daresay that in all of Essentuki today only one man smiled, and that was me. You know when I burst out laughing? When I opened my trunk and saw in it white trousers and a jacket from Duchard's. Nothing is funnier than a man in white trousers, walking down the streets of Essentuki. What shall I wear from my stock of big-city wardrobe? That is the question...

Travelling pants, slippers, a night-shirt without a waistcoat and an old overcoat thrown over one's shoulders, on one's head a fez or some kind of knotted yashmak – that's the most suitable costume for these parts. Imagine the whole outfit in this spirit, then you will get an accurate picture of where I am now. I have to tell the truth, the baths are well organized, the park would be all right, if it weren't spoiled by the public.

'You seen a chicken?'

'Yes, I have.'

'You're a chicken.'

'How is that?'

''Cause you wear fedders.'

That is a sample of a conversation I overheard of a cavalier and a lady in a very smart dress with a bunch of feathers on her hat. The cavalier was a Georgian officer, probably a prince because they're all princes here, even the guide who came with us. The lady is probably one of the local lionesses. […]

Loving you tightly Kontunchik. […]

To **Sergey Flerov**. 12 July 1900, Essentuki.

Deeply esteemed Sergey Vasilievich!

[…] the rehearsals [for *Snow Maiden*] are over. In a single day the actors scattered to various ends of Russia. I remained in Moscow alone in the company of property men, costumiers, scene-painters and other backstage workers. All sorts of numbers on paper swam before my eyes. Estimates, square yards of canvas sets, materials, pounds, tons of size and paint, calculations, explanations, models, sketches. Pouring with sweat, lumbered with these papers, I suffered amid the Moscow dust awaiting evening in order to return to my family and breathe fresh air, converse with my wife, with whom during the season and work hours I had not exchanged two words. But I had only the strength to get home. There I collapsed on a sofa, and my poor wife could only feast her eyes on my sleeping figure. A whole month went by like that. […]

Respectfully K. Alekseev […]

To **his daughter Kira**. 22 July 1900, Essentuki.

My dear, sweet little daughter, my good, kind and clever little girl.

Yesterday I was racking my brains: when did you come into the world -- the 21st or the 22nd?[82] I decided it must be today. If I am mistaken, forgive your absent-minded Papa, who cannot remember even his own birthday.

I bless that day – 21 or 22 July, when God sent you to me, my glorious little daughter. We were particularly overjoyed after the death of our poor firstborn. And you grew, you tiny thing, and comforted us and now, thank the Lord, you bring us joy to this very day; of course, you can be a bit naughty sometimes, but what's to be done, there are spots even on the sun and still it shines and warms us.

You too must try to live so that in every way you will shine on everyone around you and warm others with the goodness of your little heart.

Do you know what my Papa, your Grandpapa, used to tell me? Live and let live. So you too must try to make everyone around you happy and merry, then your life will be fine too. Am I right? Life is much more fun when everyone is smiling and loving each other. But when everyone goes around dull and cross and doesn't want to talk to each other, then you start to feel dull inside too. Right? And do you know what has to be done in that case? Whenever you can forgive others their mistakes and bad behaviour.

We'll talk this over with you some time, and I will recall for you lots of interesting stories from my life, who knows, maybe they will do you some good, but meanwhile I cordially wish you to be merry and bright, so that you will gambol, leap, dance, in short do whatever you like.

Give Mama a big kiss from me. Be sure to make your kiss as big as my love for her, and you know that I love her very, very much. Kiss our kind Granny Liza [KS's mother] too, and our good Granny Olya [Lilina's mother], if she is still staying with you. Rumple Igorechek with your hugs. Don't forget to convey my regards to *Mademoiselle*, Nanny, Dunyasha, Polya, Yegor, in short, each and every one. In my thoughts I hug and kiss you.

Your warmly loving Papa.

Before returning to Moscow, KS visited Chekhov at Yalta on 8 August. At the start of the season the Hermitage stage was enlarged and the auditorium increased to 400 seats.

To **Nemirovich-Danchenko**. 9 August 1900, Alupka.
Dear Vladimir Ivanovich!

[…] *I am writing to you under the seal of utmost secrecy.* Yesterday I wormed out of Chekhov: tomorrow he is going to Gurzuf to write, and in a week plans to be back in Alupka to read what he has written. [83] He hopes to deliver the play on 1 September, with the proviso that it turns out well, slips out quickly and so on. He is writing a play about everyday military life with 4 roles for young women and about 12 for men. I know that there will be good roles for Meyerhold, Knipper, Zhelyabuzhskaya, Vishnevsky and Kaluzhsky.[84] *I repeat* that for the moment all this is under seal of utmost secrecy, I promised. But you need to know. I think it will be easier to release you at the beginning of the season rather than before its opening. We will have to think and give you an opportunity to rest and finish your play.[85] […]

Yours K. Alekseev

What if we could stage [Gogol's] *Dead Souls* with a new approach!!! – superb.

Ostrovsky's folkloric play The Snow Maiden, *staged by KS and Sanin, opened on 24 September 1900. Gorky travelled on purpose from Nizhny Novgorod to see it and found it enchanting. The press was mixed but for the most part complimentary, as usual praising the highly-coloured staging and fairy-tale quality, even though the acting struck critics as too realistic. Kachalov came in for especially harsh treatment. Writing to Chekhov (1 October 1900) Meyerhold, growing increasingly disenchanted with the MAT, deemed it*

129

a failure because the actors lacked spirit. Audiences rapidly dropped off and it barely made it through twenty-one performances. The public's indifference in turn affected the cast, and to stimulate the troupe's enthusiasm, KS began rehearsals for Enemy of the People, *grounding it in the minutiae of Norwegian life. Under the less incendiary title,* Doctor Stockmann, *it opened on 24 October, now considered a red-letter day in the history of the MAT. The play's message of standing up to authority in the cause of right coincided with a turbulent political mood among the intelligentsia and the common people. KS's slow-moving, slow-speaking medical man, his physical appearance based on Rimsky-Korsakov, was regarded as one of his best roles. It enjoyed eighty-one performances.*

26 November saw the premiere of ND's production of When We Dead Awaken *but the splashes of local colour failed to bring it to life and it was laid to rest after eighteen performances.*

Sometime during the year KS began work on a book about the actor's creativity. He made notes, but insisted that without talent no one could be made into even a mediocre actor. He took a stand against type-casting and declared that every role should be a character role. He also promoted the actor's lofty civic mission and the theatre as 'an arena of social activism'.

Notes

1 Aleksandr Sergeevich Kosheverov (1874-1921) had studied at the Philharmonic under ND and had acted in the provinces for three years. He had expressed to ND his desire to continue his professional training and was invited to play romantic leads. He remained at the MAT until his death.

2 Kosheverov did not take part in the Society's productions.

3 ND believed that investors were not needed until the third year, and suggested that he and KS take the risk on themselves.

4 ND agreed, doubting that the dividend shareholders would require could be provided by an 'educational' enterprise.

5 Mariya Fyodorovna Andreeva (Yurkovskaya, 1868-1953, wife of the highly-placed official Andrey Andreevich Zhelyabuzhsky, chief comptroller of the Kursk and Nizhegorod railway); Yevgeniya Mikhailovna (1854-1932, widow of the senior civil servant General Ierusalimsky); Mariya Aleksandrovna Samarova (1852-1919, widow of the senior civil servant Koposov); Yevgeniya Yakovlevna Mikhailova-Poiré ('the general's lady'). All, except the last, joined the MAT.

6 Andrey Alekseevich Cherepanov (d.1919), a provincial actor-manager, worked for a few years at the Skomorokh (Mountebank) Theatre in Moscow, whose repertoire consisted of carefully selected censored plays performed in a primitive 'folk spirit.'

7 This plan fell through.

8 For the rules for 'the normal running of rehearsals and productions' at the MAT, see *National Theatre in Northern and Eastern Europe, 1746-1900*, ed. Laurence Senelick (Cambridge: Cambridge University Press, 1991), pp.418-20.

9 Mariya Lyudmilovna Roksanova (Petrovskaya, 1874-1958) had just graduated from the Philharmonic and was playing suffering ingénues in Vilna and Odessa. She was at the MAT until 1902.

10 Georgy Sergeevich Burdzhalov (1891-1948) was highly valued by KS both for his character acting and his ability to deal with technical matters; he was to play 38 roles at the MAT.

11 Ivan Ivanovich Gennert was the stage manager and later ran the prop shop.

12 Albert Fyodorovich Manasevich (1869-?), administrator in the Society; employee of the MAT office 1898-1901.

13 No performances took place in Pushkino.

14 F. G. Solntsev's albums *The Antiquities of the Russian State, Published at the Supreme Behest of the Sovereign Emperor Nicholas I* (1849-53) and *Antiquities of the Russian State* (1871-87).

15 ND was unconcerned, convinced that all the expenses would be repaid by the successes due to KS's 'taste and love for this concern.'

16 Margarita Georgievna Savitskaya (1868-1911), one of ND's recent graduates, whom he appreciated for her voice and temperament.

17 Ivan Fyodorovich Krasovsky (1870-1938) acted at the MAT only in its first year.

18 Eduard Yulianovich Shidlovsky, classmate of Vladimir Alekseev at the Lazarev Institute.

19 Mikhail Yegorovich Darsky (Shavrov, 1865-1930), a gifted amateur, had been invited because of his reputation as a cultured player of Shakespeare and Schiller in the provinces. Ernst Possart (1841-1921), German actor, outstanding in Shakespearean roles.

20 ND loved the play, and suggested testing it with a single intermission at the club. This did not happen.

21 Vsevolod Emilievich Meyerhold (1874-1940), a student of ND, would eventually become the leading director of the pre-Soviet and Soviet periods. ND wrote: 'Fyodor is *Moskvin and no one* is better than he, if not Platonov. He is a clever fellow and has heart, which is so important… Meyerhold is too dry for Fyodor.' Moskvin did wind up playing Fyodor. Aleksandr Ivanovich Platonov (stage name Adashev, 1871-1934) alternated for him a few times.

22 Olga Leonardovna Knipper (1868-1959) had begun by studying music; she graduated from ND's class at the Philharmonic in 1898.

23 Eventually, ND agreed with KS that Knipper should play Irina, alternating with another of his students Savitskaya, whom he appreciated for her voice and temperament.

24 Zhelyabuzhskaya (Andreeva) played the Princess in *Laws Unto Themselves*.

25 Vladimir Aleksandrovich Lanskoy (Solyanikov, 1871-?) did not play Fyodor.

26 Yevgeny Alekseevich Petrov, a student of ND at the Philharmonic school.

27 Darsky was in the MAT only one season and played none of these roles. He left in 1902 to join the Alexandra Theatre.

28 Serafim Nikolaevich Subdinin (1867-1944) stayed in the troupe to 1904, but played small roles. He became a sculptor who made many busts of KS; emigrated to the US.

29 Aleksandr Ivanovich Andreev (d.1940), cast as Solanio, wound up playing a scribe and subsequently appeared only in minor roles to 1906.

30 Lyudmila Vladimirovna Nedobrova (stage name Aleeva, a student of Lensky) played Jessica, and stayed two seasons.

31 Aleksandr Rodionovich Artyom (Artemiev, 1842-1914), a former painter and writing-master, the oldest member of the troupe. Despite his narrow range, he was admired by Chekhov.

32 Sergey Vladimirovnich Chuprov (Chirikov, d.1904) was in the MAT only for the first season.

33 Iosaf Aleksandrovich Tikhomirov (1872-1908), another student of ND, was the only actor cast as the Duke, and did not play Devochkin.

34 After graduating from the Philharmonic, he worked in the provinces a few seasons. Molchalin is the sneaky and ambitious secretary in *Woe from Wit*.

35 Vladimir Alekandrovich Lanskoy (Solyannikov, 1871-?), like Roman Borisovich Apollonsky (1865-1928), had first graduated from the ballet programme of the Theatre School, and only then the dramatic.

36 Krasovsky wound up playing Solanio.

37 KS was comparing Platonov, playing Bassanio, with Ivan Andreevich Ryzhov (1866-1932) of the Maly Theatre as a type.

38 The secretarial duties were soon transferred from Manasevich to Sudbinin, who also worked as an actor, and to Grigory Davidovich Ryndzyunsky (1873-1937), a Society member, who prepared reports for the shareholders and eventually became secretary to MAT administration in 1902.

39 Aleksandr Leonidovich Vishnevsky (Vishnevetsky, 1861-1943), a former schoolmate of Anton Chekhov in Taganrog, played romantic leads in the provinces; owing to his beautiful voice and good looks, he partnered Fedotova on her tours.

40 ND had seen him at the Yekaterinovslav Theatre. He was first invited to play Antonio and Boris Godunov to free KS, cast in those parts, for directorial work.

41 Rumours had arisen that ND was against Vishnevsky's joining the troupe, chiefly because he had been so prominent in the provinces.

42 They were waiting for ND's return from the Crimea.

43 *The Dowerless Bride, Uriel Acosta* and *Much Ado* did not enter the MAT's repertoire.

44 Magda is a character in *The Sunken Bell.*

45 Meyerhold played the major-domo in *Laws Unto Themselves.*

46 ND considered these precepts to be wise, but that they would make it hard for Vishnevsky to act.

47 A play by the Italian writer Gerolamo Rovetta.

48 Ivan Mikhailovich Litvinov, censor, member of the Council of the Chief Directorate for Press Matters. The Moscow Metropolitan Vladimir was to forbid the opening of *Hannele* on grounds of sacrilege.

49 Fyodor Abramovich Korsh (1852-1923), a former lawyer, managed the most popular private theatre in Moscow. Vladimir Petrovich Pogozhev (1851-1935), head of the Petersburg office of the Imperial Theatres. ND feared they might pre-empt the MAT premiere of *Tsar Fyodor.*

50 Meyerhold did not play Kryukov; Chuprov alternated it with Artyom.

51 ND: 'Moskvin delights me with each rehearsal and is now so identified with the role that he can start being a virtuoso."

52 ND: 'Everyone is gradually falling in love with *The Seagull.* Vishnevsky plays Shamraev excellently. Meyerhold is very good as Treplyov. Knipper as Arkadina in style. Petrovskaya as the Seagull is all right, but distracted by Hannele.'

53 Platonov rehearsed Trigorin, but KS played the role.

54 ND found it 'bold and interesting and it brings the play to life.'

55 The scene 'The Tsar's Chamber' (Act II) when Fyodor draws the Metropolitan Dionysius into his parable of how Krasilnikov flogged a bear to death.

56 ND had written that the Club would not allow crowd scenes to be rehearsed in the evening because it prevented card-playing.

57 ND had written that Treplyov's audience should act in half-tones so as not to disturb the 'neurotic, decadent gloomy mood' of Treplyov's play. This was also to avoid the hilarious reaction the scene had evoked in Petersburg.

58 ND preferred 'complete mysterious silence' during Treplyov's play. So did Chekhov, who later told KS he was going to write a play which will begin with the speech 'You can't hear a bird or a dog or an owl or a nightingale or sleigh-bells or a clock or even a single cricket.'

59 ND accepted KS's plan.

60 Anton Yulievich Simon (1850-1916), composer and conductor.

61 KS didn't know that Aleksandr Leonidovich von Fessing, a student of ND, acted under the name Zagarov. His father, a retired colonel, became the inspector of the MAT.

62 Wife of the psychiatrist N. N. Bazhyonov.

63 Marius Mariusovich Petipa (1850-1919), a popular character actor in such roles as Khlestakov and Tartuffe.

64 Chekhov and Suvorin attended rehearsals of *Tsar Fyodor* and *The Seagull* and were impressed by the intelligence of the enterprise.

65 KS owned a paperback copy of Tolstoy's *What Is Art?*, first published in 1898.

66 The theatre was planning to stage Ostrovsky's play, but put it off for financial reasons.

67 Olga Petrovna Norova acted at the MAT 1898-1903.

68 Nadezhda Fyodorovna Komissarzhevskaya (stage name Skarskaya, 1869-1938), sister of the star Vera Komissarzhevskaya, was invited from Petersburg and cast as Sonya; in the first run, only Lilina played the role.

69 Aleksandr Ivanovich Shamshin (1852-1924), one of the managers of the combined 'Vladimir Alekseev' and 'Aleksandr Shamshin and Pyotr Vishnyakov' factories; Eduard Karlovich Buchheim (d.1903), member of the board of the Alekseev factory; Vinyakov, unidentified, is clearly another employee of the factory.

70 Sergey Ivanovich Chetverikov (1850-1929), manager of the 'Vladimir Alekseev' factory, Mariya Alekseeva's husband.

71 Rehearsals for *Uncle Vanya* began before KS had finished the staging plan.

72 Praskovya Alekseevna Alekseeva (Zakharova, 1862-1922), his brother Volodya's wife.

73 When *Pillars* was produced in 1903, Knipper played Lona Hessel.

74 KS was preparing the title role in Aleksey Tolstoy's *Death of Ioann the Terrible*, which was to open the MAT's second season.

75 Yvette Guilbert (1867-1944), French *diseuse* and singer, a star of the Parisian *café-chantant*, immortalized in the drawings of Toulouse-Lautrec.

76 Eugène-Charles-Joseph Silvain (1851-1930), French character actor, outstanding as Louis XI and Tartuffe.

77 Mariya Aleksandrovna Pototskaya (1861-1940) was known to KS from her time at Korsh's Theatre 1889-1892; at the Alexandra from 1892. Her Nora in *Doll's House* was well regarded.

78 Sanin worked at the MAT 1898-1902, left to direct at the Alexandra Theatre (1902-07), the Antique Theatre (1911), Free Theatre (1913) and returned to the MAT 1917-19. After the Revolution he was at the Maly Theatre (1919-23) and in the 1930s-1950s staged operas in America and Europe.

79 Ivan Aleksandrovich Prokofiev, an industrialist and shareholder in the MAT.

80 Konstantin Viktorovich Osipov, a businessman, supporter of 'People's Theatre' and shareholder in the MAT.

81 KS was working on dramatizations of Chekhov's short stories and finishing a staging plan for Ostrovsky's *The Heart is Not a Stone*, which went into rehearsal but never opened.

82 It was the 21st.

83 KS visited Chekhov in Yalta on 8 August.

84 Eventually, Meyerhold played Tuzenbakh, Knipper Masha, Zhelyabuzhskaya [Andreeva] Irina, Vishnevsky Kulygin and Kaluzhsky [Luzhsky] Andrey in *Three Sisters*.

85 *In Dreams* was produced the following season.

Figure 25 Stanislavsky and Lilina in the Crimea 1900

4

CHEKHOV AND GORKY

1901–1904

With its adoption of Chekhov and Gorky as house playwrights, the Moscow Art Theatre begun to develop a clear profile. ND, a good friend of Chekhov, had to persuade his partner to stage The Seagull; *with its success and that of* Uncle Vanya, *KS became personally acquainted with the author. He was attracted to Chekhov's personality, but never overcame his awkwardness in the presence of a writer he admired; his letters veer from forced facetiousness to hyperbolic praise. The theatre, however, felt an affinity to Chekhov and solicited him to write for them. Chekhov in turn, attracted by the actress Olga Knipper whom he eventually married, followed the MAT's fortunes closely. Three* Sisters *and* The Cherry Orchard *were written with specific actors in mind.*

Gorky was a less likely ally. Whereas Chekhov was a darling of the educated middle-class, Gorky was the idol of the radical youth. He and his colleagues, clustered around the Znanie (Banner) publishing house, had been inspired by the MAT's production of Hauptmann's Lonely Lives *to try their hands at drama. ND, eager for plays that might advance social progress, welcomed these authors, and Chekhov persuaded Gorky that the MAT was the likeliest host for his maiden efforts.*

Five days after the opening of The Snow Maiden *in late September 1900 came the read-through of* Three Sisters *in its first version, with even the stagehands listening in. The actors were somewhat bemused by the tone and Chekhov was asked to do some rewriting to clarify his concept. Rehearsals for* Three Sisters *were agonizing and de-energized at first.*

To **Anton Chekhov**. Between 19 and 22 December 1900, Moscow.
Most esteemed Anton Pavlovich!

Countess Sofya Andreevna Tolstaya , with her husband's encouragement, is organizing a charity concert,[1] and I have been asked to read a newly completed novella by L. N. Tolstoy, 'Who Is in the Right?' Since they are not including readings from any contemporary writers other than yourself, the Countess is, of course, hoping for some scenes from *Three Sisters*.

I confess that I was so overawed in the presence of Lev Nikolaevich that I could not bring myself to say no to this request. I only said that without your permission I had no right to allow a reading of extracts from a work as yet unperformed on stage.

Now you are my only hope: don't agree to it!.. Or provide something in place of *Three Sisters*. Your play, which I love more and more with every rehearsal, is so integral that I could not extract individual scenes to be read on a concert platform at a charity event. Imagine two or three readers, in evening dress, carrying on an ordinary, everyday conversation, in the middle of an enormous hall in front of a high-society audience in low-cut gowns. The first impression of the play in that kind of set-up will be unfavourable, and, of course, such a reading should not be allowed until the play has been appreciated by the public and the press. So, for heaven's sake, don't agree and find some other way out. Forgive me for having acted so clumsily... I was overawed! The Countess expects a speedy answer or even a telegram.

On 23 December we are running a very sketchy dress rehearsal of the first two acts. It seems, God willing, that the play is in pretty good shape. I think Luzhsky, Vishnevsky, Artyom, Gribunin, Moskvin, my wife, and Mariya Fyodorovna will be good. Savitskaya has still not left off whining. Olga Leonardovna has found a beautiful tone. If she works on it she will play beautifully, if she puts her hopes in inspiration -- ? Meyerhold has still not found the proper tone but is working with all his might. Needless to say Gromov[2] and Sudbinin are not getting anywhere (even as alternates). Shenberg [Sanin] is fussing and finally realizes that he has overlooked a treasure, for the role of Solyony is a real treasure for an actor. He'll probably play it. If you agree I'd like to try out Kachalov as an alternate instead of Sudbinin. He will be pleasant and aristocratic, but Sudbinin won't do even as Vershinin's orderly.[3]

The actors are attracted by the play, because only now, as they come on stage, do they understand it. Today they got Act 3, and I am getting down to the staging-plan. We impatiently await Act 4. I do not lose hope that the play will go on around 15 January, if it isn't delayed by the influenza epidemic, which has put the brakes on our business horribly.

The first act set is ready and, to my mind, successful. A few days ago Simov finished the fourth act; I think it will be successful. All we know about you is that you are in Nice and, thank heaven, healthy. Whether you miss us or not – we don't know. We often think about you and wonder at your flair for and knowledge of the stage (that new stage that we dream about).

When Natasha started to speak French, Kaluzhsky rolled all over the floor laughing for a few minutes (don't worry, my wife did not caricature those lines). During her walk round the house, Natasha puts out the lights and looks for burglars under the furniture – right?

Respectfully, affectionately and devotedly yours,

K. Alekseev [...]

Chekhov refused the charity reading in no uncertain terms and then addressed the play: 'it would be better, in my opinion, if she walks across the stage in a straight line, looking neither right nor left, à la Lady Macbeth, with a candle – that's quicker and more terrible.' This was entered into the promptbook. Lilina worked on Natasha exclusively with KS. Meyerhold hated working with KS on Tuzenbakh, because the director constantly interrupted him; later on, he came to understand what KS was getting at.

To **Anton Chekhov.** 9 January 1901, Moscow.
Most esteemed Anton Pavlovich!

Of course, I got confused. Natasha doesn't look for burglars in the third but in the second act. The Tolstoy concert did not take place. You were disturbed for no good reason, because I wrote a letter in which I found the most graceful way to turn down the Countess's request. Rehearsals for *Three Sisters* would be quite successful, were it not for influenza and my considerable fatigue, or, more accurately, my total exhaustion. I can say with absolute certainty that the play works very well on stage and if we don't turn it into a great success, we ought to be horse-whipped. Today we introduced and read through the staging-plan for the last, 4th act and I started on the role of Vershinin. If, God willing, Olga Leonardovna brings off the last act it will be powerful. The set for it is ready and works well. Sudbinin has finally been removed, even as an alternate, as Kachalov is much more gifted. Shenberg is playing Solyony. Up till today he has been very obstinate and tried to give him the tone of some Calabrian bandit. I have now talked him out of it and he is on the right path. What can I say about the performers? Kaluzhsky moves slowly, as ever, but correctly. Meyerhold is working, but his qualities are sharp-edged. Artyom moves a bit woodenly but will find the tone, it's almost there, Samarova ditto, Gribunin ideal, Rodé cheery but is playing himself, Tikhomirov ditto, Shenberg -- too soon to tell, Kachalov very nice, Vishnevsky ideal and doesn't fade out, Marusya will act well, Marya Fyodorovna very good, Savitskaya good, plays herself, Olga Leonardovna was under the weather, have not seen her since her illness.

A dress rehearsal of the 2nd act took place and was a delight. At all events, the play is wonderful and very stageworthy. The tempi are apportioned, or more accurately come across like this:

Act 1 – merry, lively.

Act 2 – Chekhovian mood.

Act 3 – terribly nervous, rapid, moves by tempi and nerves. Towards the end their strength is overtaxed and the tempo slackens.

Act 4 is not clear enough yet.

Olga Leonardovna promised to write to you in detail about the ending. I'll tell you in a couple of words. The final speeches of the sisters, after all that has preceded this, focus attention and have a calming effect. If, after this, the body is carried across the stage, there will be no calm at the end. You have written: 'The body is carried across in the distance', -- only in our theatre we don't have any distance and the sisters would have to see the corpse. What are they to do? Much as I like this crossing the stage, during rehearsals I'm starting to think whether it might be to the play's advantage to end the act with just the speeches. Perhaps you are afraid that will be too reminiscent of the end of *Uncle Vanya*? Settle this question: how are we to proceed?

Yours K. Alekseev

Chekhov agreed that Tuzenbakh's body should not be shown; he was unconcerned by similarities to Uncle Vanya. Returning from abroad, ND found KS's staging brilliant but overloaded with details and business; he slowed it down and edited the clutter. KS did not join the cast as Vershinin until 23 January, a mere week before the opening.

Three Sisters, *directed by KS and Luzhsky, assisted by ND, opened on 31 January. It was immediately declared the MAT's best production, particularly in regard to the transmission of 'mood'. KS was successful in his part but did not feel the necessary 'sense of self'. 'Visiting the Prozorovs', as attending* Three Sisters *became known, turned it into a flagship production for the company and enjoyed 297 performances prior to KS's death.*

The troupe left for St Petersburg on 14 February, opening with Uncle Vanya, *followed by.*

Enemy of the People *opened on 23 February to great enthusiasm. At the second performance the audience kept interrupting Act IV, the scene of the town meeting, with applause. Censors were present at every performance to make sure sensitive cuts had not been restored. On 4 March, when* Three Sisters *was billed, explosive student demonstrations took place around Kazan Cathedral in St Petersburg to protest the 'provisional regulations' of 25 July 1899, whereby recalcitrant university students could be expelled and enlisted in the army. It was bloodily put down by the Cossacks and mounted police. The arrested students were released on their own recognizances on 13 March. That night the nervous audience of Ibsen's play interpreted everything from the stage as political and interrupted with frenetic applause. In the last act they began a call, 'Students, students!' Police began to run through the aisles, but the performance was not stopped.*

Aleksandr Dmitrievich Borodulin, a sixteen-year old high-school student in the Rybinsky gymnasium, wrote KS three letters asking to be let into the troupe.

To **Aleksandr Borodulin**. 11 March 1901, St Petersburg,
Dear sir, Aleksandr Dmitrievich!

I have not written you before now, because I was very busy – rehearsals from 12 to 5 and at the makeup table at 6:30, and then the performance until midnight. That is how I spend every day (don't think stage accolades are obtained without real work).

I liked your first letter for its youthful sincerity, and, despite my sizeable correspondence, I decided that I should reply, because I, too, have experienced and undergone everything that you are feeling now. I know that I can give you good and sensible advice. I shall not conceal from you the fact that I did not like your second letter. It was shot through with a kind of provincial resentment. Such sentences as, 'if I am not wanted, I won't impose'...'I'll try and manage on my own somehow', etc. I would rather I had not read those words! They indicated that you, still a very young man, possess somewhat touchy chords of self-esteem. If that is so, it is *very* dangerous ground for a would-be actor. I should like to forget those words, which prevent me from speaking to you as a companion-in-arms.

Do you know why I gave up my personal concerns and took up the theatre? Because the theatre is the most powerful pulpit there is, far more potent in its influence than books and the press. This pulpit has fallen into the hands of the dregs of humanity, and they have made it a resort of depravity. My task, insofar as I am able, is to purge the family of actors of ignoramuses, semi-literates and exploiters. My task, so far as I am able, is to explain to the modern generation that the actor is a preacher of beauty and truth. For this reason the actor should stand above the crowd, either through talent, education, or some other merit. Above all, the actor should be cultured, and understand and know how to raise himself to the level of the geniuses of literature.

This is why, in my view, there are no actors. Out of a thousand no-talents, drunkards and semi-literates – so-called actors – 999 should be discarded, and one worthy of the calling picked out. My troupe consists of university people, specialists who have graduated secondary schools and higher institutions of learning -- therein lies the power of our theatre.

Love of the theatre is inherent in you. Start by making sacrifices to it, because serving art consists in making selfless sacrifices. Study... When you are a literate and well-rounded person, come to me, if my work will be to your liking then. Along with me and all my comrades, prepare to tread a thorny, toilsome and arduous path, heedless of fame and loving your work. All this, of course, is feasible, provided you have talent... But talent alone is not enough, especially in the 20th-century theatre. The Ibsens squared, in philosophical and social significance, will occupy the repertoire of the new theatre, and only cultured people will be able to play such authors. Provincial ranters and poseurs have come to an end, and soon, God willing, a time will come when illiterate people will be forbidden by law to serve on the stage, which is something the actors' congress is concerned with at present. To verify what I have said, read Ibsen's plays *The Master Builder* and *Hedda Gabler*, and decide for yourself how much you still have to learn to understand this universal genius. Those are just the buds, the berries are still to come. Therefore: go on studying -- I will then readily accept you as an assistant. If you remain untutored, -- I will consider you an enemy of the stage and will aim all my shafts at you.

Your well-wisher,

K. Stanislavsky

Forgive me my poor handwriting and the slips of the pen, there's no time to reread the letter. I am writing it between the acts.

To **his son Igor**. Before 23 March 1901, St Petersburg.
My dear, glorious, affectionate and dutiful little son Igorechek!

You are little, and so this letter to you has to be little... I miss you very much in Petersburg. How happy I would be to sit beside your little bed and tell you some anecdote. I can't wait until we get back to Moscow. It's much better to be with you than in Petersburg, although the streets here are good and the houses big and rich, and the people all dressed nattily, but you know the proverb: clothes don't beautify a man, the man beautifies the clothes... That's what it's like here. The town is a good one, while the people, even though well-dressed, are far from good ones... So, for instance, a hussar just sped past me on Nevsky (that's a street). He was all in gold, in sables, moustache above, beard below, handsome, rich, and I cannot stand him, even though I don't know him. You ask: why don't you like him? Why, because he does nothing, but all day long eats, drinks, smokes good cigars, drives down Nevsky and that's all... Only his looks are handsome, but his soul is not handsome. In Moscow the people are better, because they have beautiful souls, and not only bodies and clothes. I remember, I was introduced to a certain gentleman, and I almost threw up when I looked in his face. What a monster, what a monster!.. I spoke with him for half an hour, and he told me such good things, such kind, affectionate, clever things. I looked into his eyes and liked him very, very much indeed. But try and strike up an acquaintance with a Petersburg hussar. You will like him at once for his good looks, his uniform, but try and talk with him for half an hour, he will tell you such idiocies, such nasty things, that you will spit and leave him and forget his uniform and his face. So now you see why I want to be in Moscow – because there the people are good and, mainly, because you, my dear kiddies, are there. Be kind and good so that everyone will love you as I love you. Give Kiryulya a big smacking kiss. [...]

Your Papa

Ibsen and Hauptmann remained touchstones of modernity, so that in April KS began work on The Wild Duck *and* Michael Kramer.

To Vera Kotlyarevskaya. 18 April 1901, Moscow.
Most esteemed Vera Vasilievna!

[...] What am I to say to console and encourage you? Perhaps it will comfort you a bit to learn that, but for a few periods of my stage career, I *constantly* experienced the same feelings of dissatisfaction, anxiety and concern. Of course, all the various expressions of sympathy we get from the public do encourage us, but not for long. For instance, now, when I have to create a new repertoire for next season, I feel bad. Fear of repeating myself, fear of marking time, make me worried and upset. You may ask the question: why are you getting so upset?.. Because the audience won't appreciate your hard work? Not at all, in truth. Such ideas in a man who is well provided for, who works in the field of art only for art's sake, would be criminal... You get upset for your own sake, for fear of losing faith in your own abilities and becoming impotent in your own eyes. Haven't you experienced the very same feeling? One is bound to recognize, however, that it's an ill wind that blows nobody good. In these worries of the performer there is much that is pleasant, interesting, that fills our humdrum life. Take those worries, that struggle, away from the performer, and he will stagnate in his greatness and become 'venerated'. What could be more absurd than a venerated actor, especially a fat Russian one... I prefer to remain pale, thin and nervous.

The search for new horizons, new paths, new ways and means to express complex human emotions, and the fretting that goes with them, -- that is indeed the true atmosphere for the performer. You should not lay it on too thick, otherwise you will suffocate and lose your mind, but God forbid that you should encase your imagination in an academic framework and lay down for yourself, once and for all, laws of eternal (read banal) beauty and the rules for its reproduction. That is the kind of atmosphere in which one stagnates, and… of course, gets fat.

You must firmly believe that your fretting is not in vain, but meant to expand the horizon narrowed by conventions. To force the breach through which a human being with an as yet underdeveloped imagination select from *life* materials for his creations takes a lot of time, a whole lifetime, and the widening of this breach requires even greater intensity, labour and energy… What is to be done! If you lack the strength of Samson, you have to be like the prisoner who digs day after day to undermine the strong, age-old bars of the prison that shut him away from living people and God's light, without which he cannot exist. And what prospect awaits this prisoner? New attempts, new shackles, new prison bars. No matter! He will always aspire towards people and towards life…

So, walk with a clubfoot, walk with the hunchbacked gait of a decrepit old woman, the majestic gait of a queen, but never in buskins, those senseless concoctions of human convention. May your feet tread real earth: damp, humid, alive. If you step into mud, don't be afraid of it, for there too you will find a stone, perhaps a beautiful one, which you may use as a stepping-stone without fear of dirtying your feet. And the main thing… *don't show this letter to my enemies, or else they will come to hate you, and will start calling me a symbolist, a decadent, etc.*

I seem to have lost sight of the time and started to ramble, and that is permissible only so far, therefore I close with the following wishes: God grant that you find a way to convey all the truthfulness and beauty from life to the stage. God grant that in the search for this beauty you do not fear the mud with which people have sullied it; bring to the stage, if necessary, beauty smeared with mud, and cleanse it of this mud for everyone to see. […]

Respectfully, K. Alekseev […]

On 25 May Chekhov married the actress Olga Knipper and went on a honeymoon straight from the church to Samara to take a koumiss cure. KS was off on his habitual vacation in the Caucasus.

To **his wife Mariya Lilina.** 20 July 1901, No. 9, Essentuki.
My dazzling darling light of my life!
[…] Although curious things have happened to me here, I can't wait to leave and am very bored. At the end of my short stay here I am beginning to have insane success with the ladies. On the train people I don't know come up to me and give me flowers, saying, 'From your admirers'. Their escorts come up and give me flowers from ladies I don't know. From passing trains fly more flowers from ladies with the same declarations. And last night a little romance occurred.

Ессентуки. Гора Бештау видъ отъ Санаторій Др. Зернова.

Figure 26 Essentuki. The mountains as seen from the sanatorium

For a long time now I had noticed a far-from-bad-looking little brunette in Kislovodsk, who would stare at me brazenly. With an excited, somewhat imploring face she dogged my footsteps, and had with her some male escort. I saw that more than once she told the escort to scrape up an acquaintance with me. He tried to do it, but got embarrassed and couldn't make up his mind to it. Last night their efforts assumed threatening proportions. In the Kursaal during dinner they sat next to me at table, and she didn't take her eyes off me and kept smiling, making some sort of signs. You were not at hand, and I didn't know what I was supposed to do. I went to the station to go to Kislovodsk. Before the third bell she shows up at the station, bashful, and keeps circling me. I begin to lose my composure and get embarrassed. The carriage has left the platform. She is following me. I think, she won't possibly be able to get back to Essentuki at night. Finally I turn to her: 'I see by your eyes that you would like to ask me something'. – 'Oh yes, I would like to make your acquaintance'. She extended her hand and I shook it. 'When will you be in Kislovodsk tomorrow?' – 'As always', I reply, 'around five o'clock'. – 'We shall meet, shall we not?'

The third bell, and she jumped off.

Who is this young damsel or brazen lady? All I know is she is a minor little actress from the Maly Theatre.

My lovie-dovie! Be assured that I do not like pushy ladies, and do not think to be jealous. There is only one danger for you. Under the influence of Narzan [a brand of mineral water] and the Kislovodsk ladies I can come home in such a condition that I will smother you in my embraces. My whole dream now is to

142

arrange a week's trip with you, if only to the Volga, and there… watch out!!! The more other people make advances to me, the more terribly I am starting to love you. The more my chastity is imperilled, the dearer and more loving 'the poetry of faithfulness' becomes to me. […]

Adoring Kontuchik

The Wild Duck, staged by KS and Sanin, opened the new season on 19 September 1901; it ran no more than sixteen performances.

To **Vera Kotlyarevskaya**. Sunday, 23 September 1901, Moscow.
Deeply esteemed Vera Vasilievna!

[…] I began the season badly. After [a stay in the Finnish spa at] Sestroretsk our factory burned down, then I caught a malignant quinsy and am still not recovered from it. The health I recovered in the summer is already entirely spent, and this greatly distresses me. I have to take action, but my hands are tied. A couple of days ago I acted in *Three Sisters* and that trifling role brought on a collapse. Weakness, flabbiness, a temperature of 37, a gloomy, Chekhovian mood, etc. *The Wild Duck*, despite the exclusive participation of young actors, was a success. The audience was willing to take an interest in the play, but the newspapers were in a hurry to spoil the affair. They had recourse to inadmissible devices to undermine confidence. As a result, the play will not be a financial success, and our three-months' work will have been wasted in this respect. We have to hurry and prepare a new play, and I am chained to the spot and I am vexed… I am vexed… I think that in Petersburg, where they pay no attention to the gutter press, the play will please and arouse interest, despite its ponderousness and prolixity.

Nemirovich has written a wonderful play, which will go on after *Kramer*.

I sincerely wish you success in the productions on new principles.[4] Is the choice of *The Intruder* a good one? I personally don't care for Maeterlinck.[5] I have seen the play in amateur performances under bad conditions.[6] It was boring and it seemed as if the author were striving to come across as original. Perhaps this was the result of a bad performance?… Isn't there something in Hauptmann: *Before Sunrise, The Peace Festival*, the Schnitzler trilogy… If something comes to mind I will write. We couldn't do *Hannele*, because of – a ton of reasons!! What's more, there is a Metropolitan named Khannéle[7] If we are attacked for not letting Yavorskaya do *The Seagull* – stand up for us. We had no intention of putting on the play, but Chekhov was offended when we were willing to cede it to Yavorskaya. He is afraid of this play in Petersburg. […]

Yours respectfully K. Alekseev

Michael Kramer opened on 27 October, staged by KS and Luzhky. The basis of Hauptmann's play is a creative-philosophic conflict between two artists, father and son, Michael and Arnold. KS played the father as a 'super-artist', a preacher pronouncing high-flown statements on aesthetics. It managed twenty-six performances.

143

KS's production of ND's In Dreams *opened on 21 December 1901 with KS as Kostromsky. The reviews were negative and KS was criticized for not fully incarnating his dream-preacher character; nevertheless as a contemporary Russian play it managed to achieve thirty-eight performances.*

There had been ongoing discussions about providing the MAT a building of its own, renovated to its specifications. Morozov played an important role since he provided the funding for the complete reconstruction of the Lianozov Theatre in Kammerherr Lane. KS was very grateful. When the company moved into the new theatre in 1902, the curtain bore an emblem of an art-nouveau seagull in honour of the play that had saved their first season.

In October Gorky had submitted his play Petty Bourgeoisie *to KS for comment and proceeded to be 'knitting a four-act dramatic stocking'* The Lower Depths. *The former play was read to the troupe by ND on 28 December and rehearsals began in January 1902. Chekhov recommended to Stanislavsky that he play the heroic role of Nil, the rabble-rousing engine driver.*

Gorky's election to the Imperial Academy of Literature was cancelled by an outraged Nicholas II and a number of writers, including Chekhov, quit the academy in protest. It made the production of Gorky's first play all the more significant.

To **Anton Chekhov**. 14 January 1902, Moscow.
Most kind and deeply esteemed Anton Pavlovich!

I thank you for your wonderful, simple and heartfelt letter. It deeply moved me and made my wife burst into tears. She will write to you herself as soon as her nerves improve, which have recently been shattered. What a shame and what a pity that you have been out of sorts... News of this reached us, and we were all very upset but kept it quiet so as not to disturb Olga Leonardovna even more. I suppose spring will be early, and we shall soon see you among us... That will be a great holiday for us, you may be sure; somehow our spirit is more serene when *himself* is nearby.

I am embarrassed and gratified, flattered that the Taganrog Library wants a photograph of me. Don't think me naïve, but I simply don't know how to respond in these circumstances. Suppose I send a simple cabinet photograph unframed. People will say: 'Look, what a pinchpenny, he couldn't run to a frame and a big portrait'. You send a big framed photo... They will say: 'He's pretty pleased to get into a museum!' What should I do? Don't refuse to advise me in one of your letters to Olga Leonardovna: what kind of a picture should I send – cabinet-sized or somewhat bigger? Framed or un-? Don't refuse to thank whoever needs thanking for the honour bestowed on me. On receiving your answer through Olga Leonardovna – I won't delay in sending it on.

Your comment that I ought to play Nil has been giving me no peace for some time. Now, when rehearsals are beginning and I am busy with the staging-plan, I am paying special attention to this role. I realize that Nil is important for the play, I realize it is difficult to play a positive character, but I do not see how I, without a physical reincarnation, without a clear-cut outline, without distinct characteristics,

Figure 27 Maksim Gorky. Photo: M. Landeberg, New York

almost with my own face and talents, can be transformed into a run-of-the-mill character. That is not my style. True, I have played various muzhiks in the plays of Shpazhinsky,[8] but that was presentational, not realistic. There must be no presentation in Gorky, you have to live... While retaining minor details of his everyday life, Nil is at the same time intelligent, knows a good deal, has read a lot,

145

he is strong and confident. I am afraid I will come across as Konstantin Sergeevich in disguise and not Nil. It is much easier for me to play the chorister Teteryov, because his character drawing is more distinct, coarser; it would be easier for me to get away from myself. Meanwhile I will keep myself in reserve and act only in case the roles of Nil and Teteryov don't work out with one of their current interpreters and, of course, if one of these roles does prove right for me.

On the whole there is a good deal of excitement over Aleksey Maksimovich's play. Everybody wants to act in it, and the public is waiting and demanding that we cast it with our strongest talents. Even so not all the actors whom the public is used to and trusts can act in this play. It may turn out that Baranov[9] in the role of the chorister, for instance, will knock all of us for a loop. That is why we are putting together a second team of performers. Both teams will rehearse the same staging-plan. One team works under the guidance of Kaluzhsky, the other with Tikhomirov. In a few days we will take a look at both teams, pick the best one and then draw up the definitive cast-list. And there may be changes in individual roles. My wife is eager to play Polya, but I am afraid she is not old enough for her, and besides, she is busy in all the plays, and hasn't the strength for rehearsals. The same is true of me. [10] If the business cannot do without old performers, I will urge that the play be put off to next year and not be shown to the public with any flaws in the performance. To my mind, that would be a crime against Aleksey Maksimovich, who has confided his maiden experiment to us.

Meanwhile everyone is rehearsing with great enthusiasm and nervousness. One team tries to outdo the other. What will come of it?

You probably already know that the doctors brought us your portrait (a photograph of the portrait in the Tretyakov gallery, not a good likeness) with an inscription on a golden plaque: 'To the actors from the physicians attending the Pirogov Congress'.[11] The production was interesting and, it seems, made a great impression. We had hoped to encounter the most cultured of audiences, but, evidently, there was a lot of the kind of people who rarely if ever go to the theatre. I recall, for instance, one shaggy old fellow who sat the whole time on the edge of his seat with an expression of wonderment on his face. In the first act, during the curtain calls, he got up, grinned from ear to ear and bowed to the actors. In the second intermission he smiled and waved his hat. In the third intermission he began to try and applaud, but couldn't extract a sound from his clapping. Only at the conclusion of the performance something began to emerge from him, and he got so carried away that he was the last one to leave the theatre.

After the performance everyone who had taken part in *Uncle Vanya* whooped it up at the Hermitage and Aumont's.[12] We got very merry in our box, but what was on stage was very boring, because it wasn't indecent enough. Most interesting of all was to see how Papa Aumont would walk down the corridor of the women's dressing-rooms and call out to the actresses: '*Mesdames, ne vous décolletez pas trop*'. It was most touching... But you probably know the details of that evening.

However, you must be fed up with me! Once more thanks for your letter. My wife sends you regards, respects and thanks, and my sonny-boy asks me to send his respects to the man who wrote Chebutykin. He's his favourite.

I warmly shake your hand. I wish for your speedy return to Moscow.

Respectfully and devotedly yours K. Alekseev

Meyerhold had sent KS a sarcastic letter on 26 January, complaining that he had been waiting three weeks for a meeting and could not wait any longer. He felt that he was being accused of intriguing and planting people to hiss ND's play, and wanted to know if KS was among the slanderers.

To **Vsevolod Meyerhold**. 26 or 27 January 1902, Moscow.

I must request you in future to spare me letters written in the tone of your last, as well as your monitoring the people whom I choose to receive at home. I likewise request you in future to spare me the threats which frighten me very little, as my conscience, as far as *you* are concerned, is completely clear. I will not answer this type of letter. Perhaps you might find it more logical, before resorting to threats, to acquaint me with the matter that has called forth such extreme measures on your part. As for meetings on 28, 29 or 30 January, which you schedule in such a high-handed fashion, please understand that I must decline them, lest I seem a coward, and also to allow you liberty to act. If you really do need to meet with me, then you will have to write a more appropriate letter and take cognizance of the fact that at the moment my time is not my own but is at the disposal of the concern which you serve and of whose circumstances you cannot be ignorant.

Despite KS's pleas that banning Gorky's play would spell the end of the MAT, the Bureau Chief of the Moscow Imperial Theatre Pavel Pchelnikov found his pleading to be 'crocodile tears' and the play 'weak' and unsatisfactory. He believed the censor's interventions to be well advised.

To **Mariya Andreeva**. After 24 February 1902, Moscow.

This is my third attempt at a letter. Perhaps it will be more successful. My letter is turning out to be cruel, I don't know why. Meanwhile I would like at this exact moment to be gentle, so that you will sense my real relation to you as both a human being and an actress. Help me and give me your word that you will grasp the general idea, and not the individual expressions which, I know, will be unsuccessful for me – and untypical.

Let's begin at the beginning, with Adam, and we will skim over the history of how we met. So, we met. You were talented and beautiful. We needed an actress, and I was attracted by your gifts and was not mistaken and do not repent of it now. However you, like everyone else, have not only qualities. There were faults as well. As an actress you were spoiled by praise and admirers and avidly listened to compliments, but not criticism.[13] This was only natural. For a long time you

Figure 28 Mariya Andreeva as Hedda Gabler

did not accept my criticism, and this had a chilling effect on me. Finally you gained some self-control and became an actress and not a starlet, and began to grow in an artistic sense. I very much valued, do value and will go on valuing that triumph over vanity and I love you for it. Whenever I sensed the gleam of an idea in your work, when the amateur in you disappeared, giving way to the serious worker, I became attached to you as to an actress and I began to regard her exclusive gifts as my own, began to protect them. Only then did I perceive the human being in you, because the actor and the artist make one whole. I loved the expansiveness in you, a typical feature of your 'ego'. Just what is this 'expansiveness'? An exaggerated relation to all the events and phenomena of life. Not always to the good and natural ones, sometimes even to the bad ones. I am expansive too and I know how I exaggerate both my good and bad feelings. An expansive person is always a bit of a coquette with himself; even when everything is going well, his nerves are coming up with new problems to solve. When an expansive person is sincere – he is even more to be pitied than someone else, when he errs in his sincerity – he mustn't be indulged. I tell you all this from personal experience and some general affinities I feel in you as well. I think that an actor cannot be expansive. When you are sincere in your expansiveness (for instance, when children are ill, when actors are in doubt), I pity you and sympathize more with you than anyone else. When you are insincere in your expansiveness, I do not always like you and seldom sympathize. This is the question: when are you sincere and when are you not. This distinction does not yield to words, but only to feeling and a person's knowledge and learning. You say that I do not know you. Perhaps my feelings are deceiving me, and that is disgraceful, because you are right: I should have known you well. I *very much* cherish our beautiful relations and I wish to clarify them as much as possible. So point out to me my mistakes, and I will take your pointing-out very seriously.

However, I have strayed from the narrative. I love your mind, your views, which with age are becoming both more profound and more interesting. I love your kind responsive heart. (But this heart is expansive and not always true to its nature.) I love in you a real feminine purity, so long as it does not cross over into coquetry, affectation, lapses of good taste. In short, I love you when you are simple, in a little hood, simply chattering away, I love you in that same little hood striving sincerely, expansively. I love you in a ball gown too, sincerely, sometimes merry-making, flirting uninhibitedly, but I do not love you at all as the General's lady, either in a hood or a ball gown, and I do not love you at all as a starlet in life, on stage and behind the scenes. That starlet (do not find fault with the word) is your chief enemy, the sharp dissonance in your general harmony. This starlet in you (do not be angry) I hate. True, she shows up in you less and less frequently, but, alas, she has not disappeared entirely. When this starlet shows up, she kills everything that is best in you. You begin to tell lies. You stop being kind and intelligent, you become abrupt, tactless, insincere both on stage and in life. I try to fight down the unkind feeling in me at such moments – and I cannot. To keep from being abrupt with you, I avoid you in life and I do not attend to your acting on stage. If I am mistaken (God willing), then I am not alone, for the whole troupe is too, because none of them love this starlet in you, but they do not tell you about this. At such moments I cannot stand up for you and tactlessly, before others, in your absence, I castigate in you what I do not love. Believe me, dear Mariya Fydorovna, it is that starlet who is at fault for this fluctuation in our relations. She is keeping me from blindly investing my confidence in you. Having passed through all the stages of youthful emotions, we could stop at good, friendly relations. In relation to you I am ready and purified for that, but I cannot love the starlet... Ask yourself the question – should one love and come to terms with her? I do not like people who indulge you at such moments. They do you harm, and I do not want to be of their number. I will go farther and keep silent. Perhaps I should speak up? Yes, it's pusillanimous. The starlet surfaces in you whenever your nerves are over-stimulated, that is, during the season, but at that time I am not my own man and therefore I postpone the discussion. But now allow me to have my say to the end and not be pusillanimous.

Savva Timofeevich [Morozov's] relationships with you are exceptional.[14] Relationships of that sort are the kind that lead people to wreck their lives and become victims, and you know this and treat him carefully, respectfully. But do you know the sacrilege you are heading for at such moments, when the starlet is at the controls? It is so contrary to your nature that, I am sure, you do not notice it yourself. You publicly boast to persons who are almost unknown to you that Zinaida Grigorievna[15] is painfully jealous of you and soliciting your influence over her husband. To pamper your actor's vanity, you tell the world at large that Savva Timofeevich, at your urging is investing his whole capital in Vannovsky – to rescue him.[16] If you had seen yourself from the sidelines at those moments, you would agree with me. [...]

I adore it when you come backstage to act and take matters seriously, respectfully, but I do not love you at the twentieth performance of a play, when, untrue to yourself, you begin to utter actor's comments and wise cracks and engage in actors' conversations with Mundt.[17] At such moments you are convinced that a Grand Duke turned around on Tver Street and kissed his hand to you. He actually shouted: 'Good morning, Mariya Fyodorovna!' He is the very same Grand Duke whom you in another mood so properly criticize.

At such moments you are dissembling with me. You insist that you have business with me, and very awkwardly, without hiding the seamy side, -- I recognize that you are simply jealous of some actress with me, the director. At such moments you are afraid of Vladimir Ivanovich and seek protection. But after all in your situation, one which you created, do you need this protection? Or do you have cause to allege that I am treating you unfairly as an actress and leading player in our concern?

If you had simply come to me and said that the success of some actress was upsetting you, -- would I not have believed that this was natural, that this was as it should be, that without this jealousy you would not be an actress? That this jealousy is equivalent to an agonizing distrust of one's own personal abilities, that without these doubts an actor will not make progress. Then I could calm you down, but you are insincere, and I avoid you and do not believe you, assuming your feeling to be a starlet's petty vanity. [...]

They decided to take the bull by the horns and hold the premiere of The Petty Bourgeoisie *in St Petersburg during the tour. Besides the censor's cuts, there was a special showing to hear the text from the stage and the MAT itself went over the lines with a fine-tooth comb. One more line 'in the shop of the merchant Romanov' was cut later, lest audiences think it a reference to the Imperial family.*

To **his daughter Kira.** 21 March 1902, Petersburg.

My dear, precious, priceless little girl Kiryulechka!

I am writing to you first and the next letter is for Igorechek. If you only knew how much I miss the two of you, how sick and tired I am of Petersburg and how I would like to smother you both with kisses as soon as I can. But there has been so much business up to now that I could not only not write but even get to the telephone to talk to you. Although there's no great pleasure in talking over the phone. In three minutes you can't say much, you can't even recognize your voices. For instance, when you talk on the telephone, your little voice reminds me of Mama [as Natasha] in *Three Sisters*. You drawl your words so much. Igorechek's voice reminds me of Punch. [...]

Granny Liza is interested in knowing whether the performance for the tsar came off all right. Tell her that it did and he asked through Countess Orlova-Davydova[18] to let us know that he would like to see yet another play. When the tsar asks, it is just the same as a command. That is why they granted us the tsar's theatre again and we will perform another show, probably *Dreams*. It is dangerous to perform *Enemy of the People* and *The Petty Bourgeoisie* before the tsar. *Uncle Vanya* is impossible, because Mama is afraid. *The Wild Duck* is boring. There is nothing for it but to perform *Dreams*. It is very flattering, but also tiresome, because it involves a lot of trouble.[19]

Tell Granny that the day before yesterday we were scheduled for a dress rehearsal of *Petty Bourgeoisie* by the order of Minister Sipyagin.[20] All the authorities came to see the play and decide whether it should be put on or not. Of course, we cut all the dangerous lines.

Minister of Finance Witte was at the rehearsal with his wife and family, his colleague Minister Svyatopolk-Mirsky and family, ex-Minister Voronotsov-Dashkov, Grand Duke Vladimir Aleksandrovich, the entire censorship committee and lots of different princesses and countesses. They like the play a lot, and did not find anything subversive in it, however, whether they permit us to perform it I don't know, because they are afraid the name Gorky will foment demonstrations.

Baranov created a furore, and all the princesses and ministers fell in love with him. He, not a whit embarrassed, chatted with them, as if they were his best friends, and kissed all the ladies' hands. It was a magnificent tableau. We roared with laughter. [...]

Your fondly loving Papa

The premiere took place on 26 March and had a great success, less on account of the play than as a demonstration on behalf of Gorky. The casting of secondary members of the troupe who were personally of the same class as the characters and the careful attention to the minutiae of a philistine household overshadowed the revolutionary message and turned the play into a domestic drama. (It eventually achieved twenty-seven performances.)

While these public events were occurring, a private drama was also taking place. On 30 March Olga Knipper-Chekhova, who believed she was pregnant, bled profusely and passed, in her words, 'something strange'. While KS and other actors paced the corridor in her home, the doctors determined it was an embryo of one and a half months. Scholars have argued whether it was a miscarriage followed by curettage and peritonitis or an ectopic pregnancy. Whatever the case, she was rendered hors de combat *for the stage for many months, owing to a long and troubled convalescence.*

At the end of the season several actors left the troupe for various reasons, chiefly dissatisfaction with their position in the theatre and failure to be made shareholders: Meyerhold, Mundt, Kosheverov, Roksanova, Sanin et al. Sanin went to the Alexandra, the others joined Meyerhold's Fellowship of Russian Theatre to tour the provinces with a mixed repertory of MAT standards and new drama.

KS began work on Tolstoy's The Power of Darkness. *Rehearsals for Ibsen's* Pillars of Society *began at the same time.*

To **Olga Knipper-Chekhova**. Between 3-11 May 1902, Moscow.
Most kind Olga Leonardovna!
My dear Olga Leonardovna,
I have cast all business aside and sat down to write to you, because without that energetic measure I would never manage to carry out my longstanding wish.

Savva Timofeevich is on fire over the building of the theatre, and you know what he's like at such moments.[21] He doesn't let one pause for breath. I am so touched by his energy and effort, already so in love with our future theatre and stage that I am all a-flutter and barely have time to answer all of Morozov's questions. God willing – the theatre will be a wonder. Plain, austere and serious. There will be a room for literary men.[22] The foyer opens into a gallery of Russian writers, which will be a more attractive feature than wainscotting above the oak panelling. On one of the walls in the foyer there will be a big glass showcase with all the gifts and testimonials to the theatre. The corridors will be laid with soft carpets (as at the [Vienna] Burgtheater) and very brightly lit. The walls of the corridor will be fabricated of big white stone slabs. The bottom of the stage in the auditorium will be finished in the same way. The auditorium is very simple, in the grey shades of our curtain, with a wide art-nouveau border along the top and at floor-level. A tier of wooden boxes (water-seasoned oak) with chandeliers of a recherché style in dull bronze. No portieres. In front of the proscenium, in the audience, running the whole width of the stage is a large number of stalks with flowers of antique bronze. In these flowers are hidden a few dozen electric bulbs, which will light the actors from the audience and from overhead. This contrivance allows us to eliminate the footlights. Instead of chandeliers some sort of electric lamps are installed along the ceiling. Rows of oaken arm-chairs (as abroad, with seats that go up and down). A reading-room and a library for the audience. A complicated ventilation system, allowing us to keep the theatre at a temperature up to 14 degrees. Under the whole auditorium are store-rooms for props, furniture and costumes. Next to the dressing-rooms is a separate little stage for school exercises and rehearsals during performances. Two green-rooms. Each of the actors and actresses has a separate dressing-room. A big washroom with running water for the performers. A three-tiered stage (instead of a single tier, as at Shchukin's). A revolving stage with enormous traps that go up and

Figure 29 Sergey Morozov at the construction site of the new theatre

down. A photographic studio, a museum of rarities and a museum of set models. A separate entrance for actors and a lobby for them, etc., etc. With our minds on such a theatre, our acting is starting to suffer, especially in *The Power of Darkness*, which is making our lives a misery at the moment. Incredibly difficult. The first act has been gone through, but we're still all French *paysans*, not Russian peasants. Somehow we'll get there!!! [...]

A small request of Anton Pavlovich. Could someone ask Lev Nikolaevich Tolstoy the following: the 4th act (the infanticide) is awkward because it is broken into two separate scenes. As soon as the nerves of the spectators have been screwed to a high pitch (the scene in the yard) – the curtain comes down and the variant begins again in a muted tone. This means the audience has to turn back mentally, because the two variants, which take place simultaneously, force them to make imaginative leaps in time as they watch the play. However it is easy to merge both scenes into a single consecutive act (without lowering the curtain). It is possible through a special construction of the set. Here it is.

[*Sketch showing the yard taking up all of stage left, and the hut and its room all of stage right.*]

The interior of the yard and the hut are both on stage. When the dialogue in the yard is cut short and Nikita, Matryona and Anisya go down to the cellar, the Mitrich-Anyutka scene begins – in the hut. To do this without changing the text, we need only restage the scenes. Would Lev Nikolaevich allow such a restaging? I have no doubt that the effect this will have will be redoubled, if only because it will not be broken up by lowering the curtain and a long intermission.[23]

I have re-entered the life of the theatre so very much. I cannot talk about anything else any more. True, I intentionally have indulged in such talk, because I know that it will chase away a bit of your morbid spleen. I sense it in your dear letter. Thank you for that, thank you for noticing my absence. As to us, -- we very much miss you and Anton Pavlovich. God willing, he is better. As to you, -- unfortunately, you will have to be a bit bored. If you now develop the desire to take the air, run about, then, the result will probably not be brilliant. Nature does not delight you? Is that not because you are a real artist. I would not exchange any landscape in nature for a good scene painting. On stage both life and nature are more beautiful… Keep cheerful, get well quickly and, most important, do not be in a hurry to get on your feet, otherwise everything will be worse.

Deepest respects to Anton Pavlovich, from my wife too. She will write you in a few days, meanwhile she sends you a kiss.

I kiss your hand.

Respectfully yours K. Alekseev

In 1902, the symbolist poet Valery Bryusov's essay 'Superfluous Truth' appeared in the World of Art *journal. As a manifesto, it deplored the MAT's materialist naturalism and propagandized for deliberate stylization. 'The theatre's sole obligation', wrote Bryusov, 'is to assist the actor in revealing his soul to the audience'. KS took in the message, but interpreted it in his own way.*

Diary. Late May 1902.

Many people think that the Art Theatre has launched its experiments for the sake of dead mundane staging material, but we are much more interested in living human material, the life of the human soul in the milieux which we have depicted. For its sake we have gone back to the village for the production of *The Power of Darkness*.

Lilina and the children went abroad on 26 May. KS joined them in mid-July.

To **his wife Mariya Lilina.** 2 June 1902, Moscow.

My priceless dearestdearie, my priceless little diamond!

[…] On Thursday they ran *The Power of Darkness* and very successfully. […] Stakhovich (Mikhail)[24] and Sergey LvovichTolstoy ([1863-1947] the son of Lev Nikolaevich) were at the rehearsal. He admired my adaptation of Act 4. A peasant biddy arrived from Stakhovich's estate. She is such a talent that I gave occasional thought to assigning her the role of Matryona. She performed it with all its lines, took cues from the actresses. At moments of swearing and assertion she wept real tears. Matryona is right for Pomyalova.[25] The actresses are inviting the biddy to their homes and there she gives performances free of charge.

Chekhov and Olga Leonardovna arrived. She has a temperature of 37.5. Of course she rode off to rehearsal the day they arrived, and as a result last night she almost gave up the ghost; she was in torment, they say, in desperation. This morning they sent for me, and I sat there all day. I feel very sorry for her and Chekhov. He is also poorly. […]

I was just at Komissarzhevskaya's performance and went into foolish raptures. She is the Russian Réjane in femininity and refinement. I liked the whole troupe. Vera Fyodorovna is very sweet and kind to me and asked me to drop by tomorrow (it's a holiday [Whitsunday or Holy Trinity], all the same it's impossible to do anything on going out). I think she will bring the talk around to a move to our theatre. That wouldn't be so bad… Especially now, when hopes for Knipper next season are bad. […]

All yours Kontunchik

The weather's hot.

KS originally tried out the 'biddy', a professional mourner from Tula, in the role of the evil Matryona, then in crowd scenes, then recorded her songs on the gramophone and had them played in the production.

There were parleys with Vera Komissarzhevskaya, but the Theatre would not meet her conditions.

To **Vera Kotlyarevskaya**, Thursday, 21 June 1902, Villa Windsor, 24, Franzensbad. Dear Vera Vasilievna! […]

I have written a good deal and at length about all the details of the complicated construction of the future theatre. There is no need to wait, because it is built, and what may be said quickly takes a good deal of time to write. Besides, this whole time was topsy-turvy owing to the illness of O. L. Chekhova. Imagine, she is still lying in agony, and just a few days ago I heard from Chekhov the news that she has peritonitis and ruptured intestines. We were worn out here with waiting, wrote letters to everyone who could reassure us, and finally reassurance arrived. O. L. had a turn for the better, and she and Chekhov are coming to rest in our dacha outside Moscow; housekeeping letters and instructions have gone out. […] But, I daresay absolute rest is not my lot. I would like to get down to my book, which is advancing at a snail's pace in the absence of any literary ability on my part. Meanwhile I cannot say that I am bored in Franzensbad. There is no time to be. The waters, then the mud baths, and, to speak frankly, after Ibsen and all sorts of lofty sentiments a Russian man enjoys wallowing in a muddy bog. Once I wash myself off, I go for a walk… in the mountains… to the very top. Isn't that the correct thing to do? A fine theme for a symbolist play of ideas! The latter part of the day is passed among a whole nosegay of ladies and young ladies, and, probably, at those moments I experience the same feeling a billy-goat feels, let loose in a vegetable patch. Alas, all my youthful impulses are shackled by the presence of my family and the absence of a stock of German words in my vocabulary. I have only enough to slake thirst, hunger and other bourgeois needs, but barely has my speech touched on anything high-minded, when I become a tongue-tied idiot and suffer the torments of Tantalus. At the most critical moment I have to shrug my shoulders and say: 'Ich verstehe nicht!' And that is very stupid and tiresome. I would so like to translate the object of my attraction into Russian, but it is impossible. I tried to pay court to the local Russian ladies, but they are all anæmic and talk about nothing but their stomachs, not their hearts. No… Essentuki it isn't!!… I don't recognize myself here. The food, the domestic conversations and concerns are also prosaic. They all centre around the waters of this or that spring and its potency, while outside the rain and cold never let up, and sometimes, for fun, they stoke the stoves. Under this dispensation I have worked a miracle. I lie in bed for 10 hours, and get up at 7, I think about what I might enjoy eating and that I won't be allowed to eat with impunity, and having barely noticed the shadows cast by the setting sun, I stretch and say, 'Is it bedtime yet?' That's how the day goes by. But, I repeat, I am not made for such a life and intend to change it radically. Soon I shall reform and set to work.

I would like to try and establish something in the nature of a manual for beginning actors. I have a vague inkling of a kind of grammar of dramatic art, a sort of workbook of ready-made practical exercises. I will try it out in practice in the school. Of course, all this will be rather abstract, like life itself, and therefore the more interesting and more difficult the task. I fear that I will not be able to cope with it.

It's good that you are acting for yourself and not for the audience. You will find this a great artistic pleasure, I would say: freedom in art is the most precious thing there is. I'm very sorry that I will not see you in *Zaza*.[26] I would have liked to have seen the outer limits of your brazenness. […]

Your sincerely devoted K. Alekseev

To Olga Knipper. 12/25 July 1902, Franzensbad.

If you only knew, dear Olga Leonardovna, how glad my wife and I are that you, Anton Pavlovich and Aleksandr Leonidovich [her brother] are at Lyubimovka and feel at home there. Only on condition that you will consider yourself at home, you can expect that Lyubimovka will do you good. All our hopes rest on you and Aleksandr Leonidovich. Be mistress of the house and take charge of things. For instance: you need beer. Every day my brother is in Moscow, you have only to write a little note and give it to Yegor. The first chance he gets he will send it to Moscow, to our house at Red Gates. From there they will send you whatever you need. What's more: Anton Pavlovich has got to go fishing. I suppose that Yegor has neglected the boat. It still exists, although, no doubt, in a pitiful state. Tell him to launch and repair it. Have they decorated the balcony with flowers? If not, my mother will be appalled. It's a tradition in our house!! And traditions are sacred!!!

I am peering into the future and am concerned not only for you but for Anton Pavlovich. In about two weeks my mother will show up. You don't know her, and therefore her presence may disturb your peace and destroy the cosiness. I hasten to warn you and draw a character sketch of her. My mother is a small child with grey hair. She is half French and half Russian. Her verve and high spirits come from the French, but many of her quirks are purely Russian. She goes to bed at 6 in the morning. She eats when she feels like it. Her greatest pleasure is to make a fuss over something, fret and fume about it. But you mustn't prevent her experiencing this pleasure and draw attention to it. Right now she's proud and happy that you and Anton Pavlovich are living at Lyubimovka. 'Look', she says, 'the people my son hangs out with!' The great blow for her would be if she feels that you are uncomfortable to have her around. The first day she will be all smiles and make an effort to be affectionate, but will soon be offended, and suddenly you will perceive a frenetic acceleration. The old lady will give vent to her temper and start to yell at anyone in reach. And how!.. The way people used to yell at serfs!... An hour later she will go and apologize or pamper the one she just yelled at. Then she will find some poor creature and fuss over her day and night and give her the last shirt off her back, until, finally, this poor creature robs her blind. Then she will start to curse her.

There is one other danger: her passion is to minister to invalids. If she could play the role of chambermaid to you, she would be happy. But, alas, this dream is unrealizable, she knows it, -- so don't be alarmed, she's won't stick to it. She will be terribly afraid to converse with an author and will make an effort to talk about intellectual things. Every second word she will mix up *The Seagull* with *Three Sisters*, Ostrovsky with Gogol, Shakespeare with Molière. And despite all this – she is a very talented and intuitive person. For heaven's sake, don't be afraid of her or inhibit her. Believe me, she is an exceptionally kind-hearted person and sincerely happy whenever she can be of use. She will not pester you, but will send you fruit and candy every day. Go ahead and eat them, but not too much, or you will get ill. In general it won't prevent Anton Pavlovich from staying at Lyubimovka. We have lots of characters. I direct your special attention to my old nanny Fyokla Maksimovna. She's a piece of work!... The farm manager is not a bad sort (he never managed anything anyhow). Everyone is waiting for the time when he can be retired on a pension, and for some reason is afraid to do it... so he lives on. Everything will suddenly fall to pieces, and he lives pleased with himself, he never troubles about managing the farm, because he has incredible corns (so he says), which keep him from walking. My brother's sons are wonderfully splendid kids. I will sketch their portrait, since Anton Pavlovich will have a talk with Mikey. He is a presentable, talented little boy. He plays the role of a sloven, and therefore his trousers are always falling down. His brother Koka, on the contrary, is an English gentleman. They despise one another, but are amusing... If Anton Pavlovich would care for some music and singing, he will find my brother at the conservatory. Have Vishnevsky take him to Volodya. On his own, out of morbid shyness, he would refuse to go. And it will be awkward to have sent greetings from a distance for a long time and then snort with embarrassment on meeting. Volodya is a wonderful man, a great musician, who is ruining his career. However! Why am I writing all of this. No, this isn't right... I love them all very much and am afraid that you, when you see their quirks, will be alarmed by them and be deprived of the cosiness which is so dear to us. Of course, everything I write is to remain among us. People don't like when you notice their peculiarities, even if they are attractive ones.

I have just returned from Bayreuth and will describe my experiences in a letter to my brother. I will add a postscript that he should send the letter to you. Read it if you are interested in an artistic pilgrimage.[27]

The weather here is super-disgusting. Rain and cold. Hence we will leave on Wednesday or Thursday next week. Meanwhile here is our next address: Lucerne, Poste restante. [...]

I am very worried about *Bourgeoisie* in view of the strictness of the censorship. Stakhovich writes that the censor Zverev is a little Nero. What will we do without that play?[28]

The first months will be difficult. Abroad there is not a single play on the horizon. Potapenko is writing for us, but... Why the silence from Andreev, Naidyonov?[29]

My profound regards and I shake the hand of Anton Pavlovich. God willing, in August in the past we had a superb number of striped perch. Near the church by the Smirnov swimming-hole in the past people caught hundreds of them.[30] [...]

Your sincerely devoted K. Alekseev [...]

In late July ND wrote a long letter to KS, worried that the Gorky plays and The Power of Darkness *constituted a trend in the repertoire towards grubby naturalism. He called for greater audacity in repertoire and casting. He also deplored KS's habit as a director of absenting himself from early rehearsals, praising the work of the assistant directors and then changing everything. At a board meeting in August the concern was expressed that the repertoire, glutted with Hauptmann and Ibsen, was getting monotonous.*

In preparation to incarnate the underbelly of society, some of the male members of the troupe were taken slumming in the Khitrov Market and visited a dosshouse for copyists of playscripts. One of the urban tourists was the designer Simov, to whom KS gave the instruction: 'Don't stint on the colours'. Even so, the scenery turned out grey. Gorky read The Lower Depths *to the company on 6 September to great effect. Chekhov saw KS in the role of the Actor, but Gorky wanted him for the eloquent gambler Satin.*

On 25 October the new Art Theatre building on Kammerherr Lane opened with a celebratory matinee and in the evening the Moscow premiere of The Petty Bourgeoisie *was performed. Critics considered that the production was frittered away on detail and skirted the play's political message. Sudbinin as Nil made a free-and-easy proletarian, but not a stalwart paragon of the working class.*

Diary.

I love this serious, somewhat gloomy and pensive auditorium with its dark oak furniture and similar railings on the boxes. Dim lighting suits it, as twilight does our northern nature. They provoke thoughts and evoke dreams.

The Power of Darkness opened on 5 November. Again, despite or perhaps because of the sedulous attention to ethnographic detail, the tragic quality was thought to be lacking; the realism overwhelmed the inner life of the characters. As the workman Mitrich, KS scratched, spat and slurped soup to no avail and dropped the role after the third of the twenty-four performances.

A week before it opened, the censor passed The Lower Depths with excisions. It opened on 18 December with KS as Satin (more picturesque than necessary, thought some. Following advice from ND, he had given the role a picaresque comic tinge). The actors' nervous state replicated that of the opening night of Seagull, but the play was rapturously received. This time the naturalistic detail was overlaid with a patina of flamboyance. The audience howled and roared with laughter and gasped to see the refined Art Theatre actors squashing lice. The conservatives disdained the work as a peasant rebellion from the stage, but for most it was a new word in the theatre, a contemporary variant of romanticism. By the fourth performance, KS found the key to the 'What is man?' speech by not trying to make an effect but going through it logically in word and action. The play was to enjoy the second greatest number of performances of any MAT creation, outdone only by The Blue Bird: 1788.

To **Anton Chekhov.** Between 24-27 December 1902, Moscow.
Dear Anton Pavlovich!

I haven't written to you for such a long time as I (like all my colleagues) have been very busy and overwhelmed by the imminent production [of *The Lower Depths*]. We thought that if a Gorky play were to flop a second time the whole business would be ruined.[31] Now, as you already know, victory is ours and, most important, Gorky is pleased. The first performance was sheer agony for the actors and, if it hadn't been for the tumultuous reception of the first act, I don't know if our nerves would have held out to the end.

Vladimir Ivanovich has found the right style for performing Gorky's plays. It turns out that one must declare the lines lightly and simply. It is difficult to characterize under such conditions and everyone just stayed himself, trying to convey the splendid lines of his part distinctly to the audience. All the more honour to Olga Leonardovna [as the prostitute Nastya] who alone transformed herself. Of course the Efroses of this world will not appreciate it,[32] but among the actors she had a very great success and, as we say in the troupe: 'She put it over!' I am not satisfied with myself, although I am being praised.

Figure 30 Joke photo of Stanislavsky and Nemirovich as tramps during rehearsals of *The Lower Depths*

Gorky was present at two performances and had a very great success. He was charming and merry all that time, the way he was when I first met him two years ago in Yalta.[33] He has gone away pleased and intends to write for the theatre. I repeat: that's the most important part of our success.

I have just ordered Yegor to buy all the newspapers and I will send them to you or, at any rate, the cuttings (but I won't read them myself). Gorky's presence at the performance led to thunderous ovations for him, so it is hard to figure out how much of the success is attributed to the play and the actors. The press, it appears, is favourable.

Now comes an oppressive time: instead of the great pleasure of starting to rehearse a Chekhov play we have to take on an onerous task: learning Ibsen's lines. Pity two artists: Knipper and Stanislavsky. They have the most arduous work to do…

[…] After the performance Gorky threw a banquet for the actors. The celebration ended with a very painful scene made by Baranov. I don't want to write about it. Olga Leonardovna will fill you in in detail.[34]

Your loving and devoted K. Alekseev. […]

To **Anton Chekhov**. 21 February 1903, Moscow.
Dear and much esteemed Anton Pavlovich!

I am writing you a brief note only lest you think that I am silent because I have forgotten about you… My wife and I and Olga Leonardovna often think and daily speak of you. There is little time now. The dress rehearsals for [Ibsen's] *Pillars of Society* are going on. My God, if a quarter of the forces spent on that repulsive play were devoted to your *Cherry Orchard*, the theatre would collapse from the applause and a pleasing prospect would lie before us: to perform your play a few years in a row.* Now, thinking about the shakiness of *The Pillars of Society*, we repeat that phrase of yours we've come to love: 'Nobody needs it!!!'

I play a foreigner [Consul Bernick] in an English frock-coat, and play him rather repulsively. For a long time Olga Leonardovna's role [Lona Hessel] would not come right, and suddenly at the first dress rehearsal she amazed us. Her talent made itself known. She found an interesting tone and… calmed down. Now the role has stalled a bit, nevertheless we do not lose hope that she will act well. We are afraid to believe our luck that on 20 March your play will be in our hands… If not, we will have to rehearse *The Lady from the Sea*, although we know that 'nobody needs it'.[35] […]

Devotedly and respectfully yours K. Alekseev

Thanks a lot for your letter.
*Of course we would have to perform in the ruins!

Pillars of Society, *primarily the work of ND who was not enamoured of the play, opened on 24 February and played fifteen performances, ending on 6 January 1904. Like the previous Ibsen production, it seemed colourless and subdued in contrast with the Gorky and Chekhov repertoire. Chekhov himself regarded Ibsen as undramatic because there was no 'vulgarity' in him.*

Gorky wanted the Petersburg premiere of Lower Depths *to take place at the Alexandra Theatre, where clandestine rehearsals for the play were being held, but they were soon interrupted by government agents. Minister of Internal Affairs Plehve decided that the play could not be performed at an Imperial theatre, because he regarded Gorky a revolutionary who deserved exile to Siberia. So the MAT had to appeal to the magnate Suvorin to lend his Literary and Artistic Society Theatre. The appearance on 7 February 1903 of Sergey Lvovich Tolstoy's protest letter in Suvorin's conservative newspaper* New Times *against the 'cynicism and nakedness' of current literature and especially*

Leonid Andreev, could only fuel Gorky's hostility to Suvorin and his theatre with its often sensational productions.

To **Vera Kotlyarevskaya**. 25 February 1903, Moscow.
Much esteemed Vera Vasilievna!

Thanks for your letter, but no thanks for the incredible suspicion. We could not forget you. You are perfectly aware of that. I provided you with no information as cheerleader of the Petersburg successes, because a police constable himself couldn't figure out whether we're going to Petersburg or not. All this happened because we were dealing with Suvorin. We had to deal with him because it is too hard to set up the scenery for *Lower Depths* at Panaev's and cover the cost of the trip. He is asking an insane price per performance or guarantees us 50,000 for 17 performances. The last proposal is connected with the rights [for him] to perform *Lower Depths* next season. Gorky, having made an effort to show Petersburg his play for the first time in our production, agreed to this combination. We did not try to dissuade him, because we didn't want to be monopolists. After Tolstoy's letter about Andreev Gorky doesn't want to have anything to do with Suvorin, and the whole combination broke down.[36] Tomorrow Nemirovich is going to Petersburg, and how the matter will be decided is unknown. If we do go, it'll be at Easter and the following week (15-17 performances). We'll take *The Lower Depths* and *Uncle Vanya* (only). Thanks to Petersburg for its good relations with us. You do know that we appreciate it. For the first time I am hearing that Satin is a successful role.[37] Here they abuse me, and how, no matter what role I may play. The press gives me a very hard time. Yesterday I played the most difficult and ungratifying role of Bernick (*Pillars of Society*). My friends praise it, but the press, of course, insults me.[38] I have become very indifferent to this, because I never read newspapers, and at the end of the season, with the powerful play *The Lower Depths*, I don't have to worry about the financial success of the theatre. This year was a prosperous one, and, despite the short season and the belated beginning, the business will offer a dividend of around 50-60 thousand to cover all expenses and the newly made costumes and sets. What's even better is that we aren't chasing after profits and only want to stand on our feet. Come to Moscow as soon as you can and see *The Pillars of Society*. [...]

Respectfully and devoted K. Alekseev

The season ended on 28 March and the Petersburg tour began on 7 April at Suvorin's Theatre. The hostile attitude to Gorky in the seat of government led to insulting reviews of Lower Depths, *whereas* Uncle Vanya *was a big hit.*

ND proposed Julius Caesar *and* Rosmersholm *for the next season, but KS admitted that the latter did not excite him. With great reluctance, he agreed to play Brutus.*

While KS was in Essentuki, Lilina had written, 'Why is it that as soon as we are apart, we start to understand and feel sorry for one another, but when we are together, we torment one another. You go on wanting to help me with the housekeeping, but I think that if we can keep from ever talking about it, much more poetry would be preserved. What will the winter hold for us?'

To **his wife Mariya Lilina**. Monday, 21 July 1903, Essentuki.
My precious little beauty!

I love you very much, I miss you very much and I am desperate to break out of here. I'm not a canting hypocrite, but this year it is uncomfortable here and the society is uninteresting. Today from morning to night it poured with rain, and then Essentuki becomes unbearable.

I have not had any letters from you for a long time and do not know what's going on with you. Tight hugs, congratulations on today's dear birthday girl. Thank you for our sweet daughter. I remember that day 12 years ago. How you, my poor little dear, were going through agonies. Then you were pleased with me for my concern and were still in love. Now I do not know how to preserve that feeling in you. If only it would return, and together with poetry beautify my life. A question: how to remake myself, how to become easier to get on with at home – torments me. You and I have everything, inclusive of the most trifling thing, but we are both very dear and necessary to one another. You need affection. I give it… and I get a reward which is sometimes not enough for me. It seems something simpler… But even now I am not sure that the season will go on… willy-nilly my brain is directed at one point, and then it is not in my power to change its direction. I need a kind of jolt, which only you can provide. But I understand that you don't want to. You want me to remember on my own and come to you. Only then will your feminine nature be satisfied. Hence the enchanted circle from which you will not be drawn. I am looking for a way out and am coming to the conclusion that one needs to inure one's organism to the point that at certain hours of the day one can learn how to do nothing and be in no way occupied. This is very difficult even here, in Essentuki, where nothing important ever happens. Then there will be time for you and I to adopt new interests and relations and in this way draw you closer to me once again.

[…] I have decided not to meddle in the housekeeping at all. I do not help but hinder you in that. I will wait until you require my help, and I will provide it with complete enthusiasm and a desire to lighten your load. But I am not capable of specific, occasional help. It is easier for me to make a radical change all at once and help you organize it somehow from scratch and thereby ease your situation. […]

Kotik

To **Olga Knipper**. Wednesday, 20 August 1903, Moscow.
Dear Olga Leonardovna!

[…] There is nothing for it, our theatre is Chekhov's, and without him things go badly for us. If there will be a play, the theatre and the season are saved, if not – I don't know what we shall do. You won't get far with *Julius Caesar*, but with Chekhov as far as you like… God grant before all else health and good spirits to both of you. […]

Devotedly K. Stanislavsky

«ТРИ СЕСТРЫ» А. П. ЧЕХОВА.　Моск. Худож. Театръ.
Вершининъ—К. С. Станиславскій.
Собств. изд. К. А. Фишеръ, Москва.

Figure 31 Stanislavsky as Vershinin in *Three Sisters*, 1901. Photo: K. A. Fischer, Moscow

On 27 September KS shaved off his moustache. He had had difficulties with it in certain earlier roles, partly covering it with nose putty. He had proposed to do the same as Brutus, but the makeup designer Gremislavsky vetoed that and insisted on a clean-shaven upper lip. He promised to make a prosthetic moustache to replace it. The new face made KS self-conscious and it is noteworthy that no photographs exist of him in the role of Brutus.

Caesar opened the season on 2 October with to an audience responsive only for the Forum scene. Kachalov as Caesar bore away the acting laurels, everyone else was swamped by the archaeological staging. The connoisseurs, such as Sergey Diaghilev and

164

Mariya Yermolova, appreciated KS's Brutus for its humanity, but the critics and the general public found him too unheroic, too contemplative, too arid. Nevertheless, school audiences prolonged the run to 84 performances.

The divided opinion about Brutus also brought into KS's sphere two individuals who would become his closest collaborators. A letter of praise from Leopold Sulerzhitsky initiated their friendship and a laudatory and insightful critical article by Lyubov Gurevich made her acquaintance. Because of his own doubts, he deeply appreciated their support. 'Suler' and Gurevich would be his staunchest allies in the rehearsal room and the publishing world.

On 11 October KS's family moved from their lordly residence at Red Gates to a new apartment in Carriage Row, the Markov Building, across from the Hermitage Theatre. The rest of the Alekseev family remained in their former home.

To **Anton Chekhov**. Monday, 13 October 1903, Moscow
Dear Anton Pavlovich!

I angry with you? What right would I have? I see no cause for it. Obviously, you do not know how much I respect you. If I heard that you had committed a crime, I would not for a second doubt your innocence.

Am I incapable of understanding why you can't write a play to a deadline and to order? For that you have to be an untalented Krylov,[39] and not the brilliant Chekhov. I cannot contain my impatience to read the play and start rehearsing it... That's the truth.

I am haunted by the fear that your play will appear at the end of the season and will not have time to create enough of a stir for the public to form a more accurate conception, after it has absorbed all the idiocy that will be written about it ... The truth is that since yesterday we have all started longing for your

Figure 32 The building in Carriage Row where the Stanislavsky apartment was located

play. Yesterday was a joyful day. We all started to live after *Caesar*... After a long break we performed *Three Sisters*. Last year's history was repeated at rehearsals. We gathered together to talk through the play, got carried away and performed it for ourselves with the full tone. Yesterday we performed it a second time for the audience.

It's been a long time since I performed with such satisfaction.

The reception was enthusiastic, and by the end of the play there was an ovation at the stage door. It would seem that we played well yesterday. [...]

I confess to you that it took me a long time to get over my dismal failure as Brutus. It dumbfounded and confused me to the point that I could no longer tell good from bad on stage. On the day of the performance, at night, I wrote you an account of the premiere, but I had to tear it up, it was written in such gloomy tones. Now my mood has altered, although I still cannot figure out where I went wrong in playing Brutus. Mine had become a convict's life, because 5 times a week I had to act an ungratifying and exhausting role – in nothing but a shirt and tights. It was depressing, cold and you feel 'nobody needs this!' I am awaiting your play with great impatience.

Your devoted and loving K. Alekseev

Knipper received the manuscript of The Cherry Orchard *on 18 October; KS read it the following day.*

To **Anton Chekhov**. 20 October 1903, Moscow. *Telegram.*

Have just read play. Deeply moved, can't get a grip on myself. In unaccustomed raptures. Consider play best of all your beautiful writings. Cordial congratulations to brilliant author. I feel, appreciate every word. Thanks for great pleasure already received and also in store. Keep well.

Alekseev

ND read it to the troupe the same day. Gorky was unimpressed and thought it pedestrian, with nothing new in it. 'Everything -- mood, ideas if you can call them that, the characters – it's all been in his plays already. Of course, it's beautiful, and – naturally – elements of nostalgia will speak to the audience from the stage. But nostalgia for what – I don't know.' He convinced Andreeva to turn down the role of Varya.

To **Anton Chekhov**. 21 October 1903, Moscow. *Telegram.*

Play read to troupe. Exceptionally brilliant success. Listened enraptured from first act. Each subtlety appreciated. Weeping in last act. My wife in raptures, as are we all. No play ever greeted with such unanimous enthusiasm.

Alekseev

Chekhov wrote to Olga Knipper on 21 October. 'Today I got a telegram from Alekseev, in which he calls my play a work of genius; which means he's overpraising it and removing from it a good half of the success it might have under optimal conditions.'

To **Anton Chekhov**. 22 October 1903, Moscow.

Dear Anton Pavlovich,

To my mind, *The Cherry Orchard* is your best play. I am fonder of it even than of dear *Seagull*. It is not a comedy nor a farce, as you wrote,[40] -- it's a tragedy, whatever outlet to a better life you may reveal in the last act. The effect it makes is colossal, achieved by half-tones and delicate pastels. It has more poetry and lyricism, it is more stageworthy; all the roles, the passer-by included, are brilliant. If I were offered to pick the role most to my taste, I would be perplexed, so great is the appeal of every one of them. I am afraid all this is too subtle for the public. It will not soon appreciate all the finer points. Alas, we shall have to read and hear so much stupidity about the play. Nevertheless the success will be enormous, because the play is a captivating one. It is so integrated that not a single word can be cut. Perhaps I am biased, but I found no flaws in the play. Just one: it calls for very great and subtle actors to reveal all its beauties. We won't be able to do it. At my first reading I was struck by the fact that I was at once enthralled and began to live in the play. This was not the case with *The Seagull* or *Three Sisters*. I am used to the vague impressions I get from the first readings of your plays. That is why I was afraid that the play would not enthrall me in the second reading. Not a bit of it! I wept like a woman, I wanted to get a grip on myself, but could not. I can hear you say: 'Excuse me, but it is a farce'... No, for the average man it is a tragedy. I cherish a special affection and love for it. I have heard almost no criticism, although actors love to criticize. This time all of them seemed to submit to it at once. And if a critical voice is raised, I smile and do not take the trouble to argue. I feel sorry for the critic. Someone said: Act 4 is the best, and Act 2 is the least successful. That is laughable, but I do not argue. I only begin to go over Act 2 scene by scene, and the person is at once confounded. Act 4 is good precisely because Act 2 is magnificent, and vice-versa. I proclaim this play a nonpareil and not subject to criticism. Anyone who fails to understand it is a fool. That is my sincere conviction. I shall play all of it with delight, and if it were possible I would really like to play all the parts, darling Charlotta included. Thank you, dear Anton Pavlovich, for this great pleasure, the pleasure I have had and the pleasure still to come. How I would like to throw everything aside, shake off the yoke of Brutus and live and work on *The Cherry Orchard* the livelong day. This repulsive Brutus oppresses me and drains my vital juices. I hate him even more now I have my dear *Cherry Orchard*. I firmly shake your hand and beg you not to take me for a lady psychopath.

Your fondly
devoted K. Alekseev

On 28 October at the Hermitage restaurant there was a meeting of the leadership of the MAT, devoted to casting Cherry Orchard, at which KS made some snide remarks about the state of art in the theatre. ND took it personally and wrote a letter complaining that his creative work went unappreciated. He was especially annoyed that KS had criticized Julius Caesar in the presence of Morozov, with whom ND had strained relations. Before sending it, ND had read it to Luzhsky, Vishnevsky and Knipper, who informed Chekhov about the incident.

To **Nemirovich-Danchenko**. 28 or 29 October 1903, Moscow.
Dear Vladimir Ivanovich!

What a bolt from the blue! May Christ be with you, what are you accusing me of? Being underhanded, conspiratorial or simply stupid? Could you draw such conclusions, if you were not prone to find fault with my every word?.. One would think that the very fact that I spoke in Morozov's presence, knowing something of his plans,[41] might have convinced you that I said nothing wrong. Otherwise, you must have a very low opinion of me.

Calm down and recall the meaning of my words. They were most innocent. If I criticized anyone, it was myself. You were staging the play, and I foisted my advice on you. That prevented your independence, I could not carry out my suggestions myself, because I was not staging the play. This dual responsibility for productions has always troubled me and goes on troubling me. I do not believe that we have found the right path when it comes to directing plays together, and I go on searching in that direction.[42] When *Caesar* was being staged, didn't I say at the very beginning that we would have to make concessions and stage the play without artistic realism in the sense that I conceive of it? Not wavering in my beliefs, I never pressed you to rumple and dirty the costumes, to put patches on them. We decided together that *on this occasion* it would be superfluous. [...]

I give you my word I do not share your distress for a second, just as I can't at the moment conceive what I said that offended you. I was criticizing myself, not you. If I spoke so directly it was precisely because your role as a stage director is so explicit and well established, so prominent and acknowledged by everyone, that it isn't you but *I* who stays in the background, not I but *you* who appears by right to be chief director (I don't mind that in the least). Were you really satisfied with the performance of *Lower Depths*? Did you really consider it to be exemplary? How many times have I heard you give a negative answer to that very question. Whose fault is it: the actors' or the directors'? Isn't it our *obligation* to raise that question? Remember how we rehearsed the play over and over, sometimes at top speed (at my suggestion), and other times at your suggestion at the opposite speed. Perhaps our dual responsibility is distracting the actors? Are such questions and doubts criminal on my part? Neither as far as *Caesar* is concerned nor *Depths*, have I ever uttered any verdicts that might insult you. On the contrary I told everyone that it was you who found the tone for Gorky's play. Meanwhile, you have never missed an opportunity to remind me of the failure of *Snow Maiden* and *The Power of Darkness*, but, as you see, I have not taken offense.[43]

As for *Pillars*, as you well know, I have always blamed myself more than anyone for a bad setting in which no one could act anything. The only reproach that can be made against you is that you accepted that bad set.

As for my capriciousness while rehearsing the role of Bernick, I repented of it, and as Brutus tried to behave differently. [....]

So I saddled you with the responsibilities of chief director? That very chief director whose title has been diminished in the theatre and removed from the playbills.[44] I thought otherwise. After our conversation about how you were dissatisfied with your position in the theatre, how you were sacrificing everything for the theatre and getting nothing from it, I considered it my obligation to transfer to you whatever you considered you needed to take from me to consolidate your position and benefit the concern itself. I dealt with that question very honestly. I did not give up but simply gave over everything that was yours by right. If you have the heart to tell me now that you are the only one working, and I do nothing, if you do not understand what I have sacrificed for the theatre – business, family, health, which is in a much worse condition than you can imagine, -- then it is not worth living, working or believing in people. You do work a great deal, and I respect you for it. It might seem that I deserve the same from you. You can and must know what it costs me to bear the thankless work as an actor that depends on me.

In conclusion I leave you with a single thought: for 15 years I was used to being independent. For the past 5 years I have reined in my well-developed self-esteem and submitted. I now reconcile myself to many things which I would not have agreed to under any circumstances in the past. I have taught myself to turn a blind eye to outrageous abuses going on under my very nose. I get on with Baranov and Gromov, whereas I cannot, any more than before, endure Shidlovskaya, with whom I was on good terms for a very long time.[45] I see everything that is going on backstage, I see how with every passing day manners get worse -- and I am silent. You think that I am not aware of how far my significance in the theatre has declined? You think I cannot foresee how it will be reduced to zero in a very short time? However, I reconcile myself to the present and even to the future without malice and envy. I will even be reconciled to suffering the same fate as Sanin.[46]

One thing I do very much cherish. The right to express loudly my artistic 'credo'. I am beginning to be deprived of that right. Haven't you noticed how emphatically this has been demonstrated recently. If I speak to Tikhomirov, as *a private individual*, about his new business (Tikhomirov knows my position in the school –precisely zero) -- people claim that I have messed everything up and students are leaving the school on my account.[47] If I give any kind of advice or instructions, they all shout 'He's made a mess of things', and no one takes the trouble to explore my ideas in any depth. If I ask for someone to be fined – for blatant outrageousness about which I would have raised a ruckus 5 years ago so that the whole theatre would be goaded to action – now, my objection is passed over quietly and without consequences. If I give any kind of artistic advice, -- 'crackpot' is written on everyone's face. My idea yields a sparse crop, the actors are praised for it, I suffer, as I see the desecration of everything I hold sacred and dear. I keep silent. First, because I am exhausted and lack the energy, the strength to carry on, stand up for what is mine, and second, because I shall never again insist on anything in this concern of ours. I believe that if I am right, -- a just cause will pull me through, if I am wrong -- then it's time to admit it and for me to devote the rest of my life to something really useful, even it's from quite another opera.

Now, on principle, I will not a lift a finger to create any kind of new position for myself in the theatre. If I have started to slide down a slippery slope -- then the sooner I hit bottom the better. I am a very introverted person and say much less than I know. I hand over the theatre without any struggle. If it needs me -- then let it use me carefully and cautiously. If not -- then let them kick me out and the sooner this happens ((if it is inevitable), the better. In the opposite case -- I shall no longer speak so frankly. I shall confide my secrets to you, and as for the theatre itself, let it deal with me and my energy -- as it thinks fit.

I reserve one right: if I become convinced that my family needs me more than the theatre does, I will come and say so. Of course, without prejudice to the concern. Then you must release me of your own free will, and not ask new sacrifices of me that are beyond my power. It is time you alter your opinion of me. I understand and feel more greatly and more delicately than I can say.

Affectionately and devotedly, K. Alekseev

If I have offended you in any way – I apologize, because it was entirely unintentional.

ND replied on 29 October: 'I am pained to tears that I made you express so much [...] Well, what's to be done! In the theatre vanity is so touchy!... And everything you write about your situation is in the highest degree *exaggerated.'*

By this time most of the roles were cast, not entirely to the taste of the author, especially the role of Lopakhin, written with KS in mind. Chekhov told him as much on 30 October: 'When I wrote Lopakhin, I conceived that it was your role. If for some reason it doesn't appeal to you, then please take Gaev. Lopakhin, it's true, is a merchant, but a decent man in every respect, etc. etc.'

In the upshot it would be played by Leonid Mironovich Leonidov (Volfenzon, 1873-1941), scion of a Jewish doctor. Having made his name in the modern problem play Vanyushin's Children *at Korsh's Theatre (1901), he was invited with no particular line of business specified. He possessed a resonant voice and bright eyes, and, prone to monumentality, would become one of the pillars of the troupe.*

To **Anton Chekhov.** 31 October 1903, Moscow.
Dear Anton Pavlovich.

It is now 1:30 in the morning, and I just returned home after the eighteenth performance of the detested *Caesar*. I wanted to write to you, but found only this little piece of paper. Forgive me, I'll write on it rather than wake my wife to look for paper. Finally, yesterday, we got around to your play. And so we have unforgivably lost a whole week. So far they've been muddled about the casting. This is what I've decided for myself: to study and prepare two roles: Lopakhin and Gaev. I cannot say which role I want more. Both roles are marvellous and to my liking. It's true, I am afraid of Lopakhin. People say that I'm not good at merchants or, more accurately, they come out stagey and contrived. Lopakhin is a decent fellow, isn't he – good-natured but forceful. He even buys the cherry orchard somehow by accident and then is thoroughly embarrassed. That's probably why he gets drunk. Gaev, to my mind, should be flighty, like his sister. He doesn't even notice what he is saying. He understands after he has said it. I think I have found the tone for Gaev. He comes out, as I do it, as an aristocrat but a bit of a crackpot.

We are living in the new apartment; it's wonderful, even too nice and luxurious. I feel very sorry for my mother, who has to stay at Red Gates with my sister [Anna]. We, and she herself, thought she would be more comfortable there, but it has turned out not to be the case. Twice a week there are mobs of children – once for dancing (Manokhin) and the other time lectures on natural history, also for the children.[48] They find it very entertaining. I shake your hand and go to sleep.

Yours K. Alekseev

To **Anton Chekhov.** 1 November 1903, Moscow.
Dear Anton Pavlovich!

Olga Leonardovna just said that you haven't had any letters from us! Meanwhile I sent you two big letters (in one of them I set out my insane excitement over *Cherry Orchard*.) I consider this play to be the best of them all. I love every word, every stage direction, every comma in it. Besides, last night I sent you a little note. Can you still doubt that you are a genius? Besides this is excusable in us – humble worker-bees. I have been experiencing and still experience moments of depression.

I sat down to write you about the play after I first made its acquaintance. I wanted to sort out my impressions and ended by praising everything indiscriminately. And this was the upshot: if anyone doesn't understand the play, it means he's an idiot. I become more and more deeply rooted in this opinion.

Today at last Simov put aside *Lonely Lives* (they need us to free certain persons, including myself, for rehearsals of *Cherry Orchard*). Today we got down to the set-model. The 1st act is difficult. Olga Leonardovna says there should be traces of the former lavish and baronial way of life.[49] But shouldn't the house be somewhat or even very dilapidated? Lopakhin says he will pull it down. That means it's actually no use at all. Otherwise he would have turned it into a vacation cottage and rented it out the following summer. Or repaired it and sold it.

Is the house wood or stone? Perhaps, the centre part is stone and the wings are wooden? Perhaps the lower part stone and the upper wooden? Another puzzle. In the third act a hall is visible but in the fourth act there is talk of a hall on the ground floor. So, are there two of them?[50]

This summer I recorded a shepherd's horn on my phonograph. The same shepherd you liked so much at Lyubimovka. It turned out splendidly and now this cylinder will come in useful.[51]

Tomorrow I hope to write again, but goodbye for now. We are starting Act 3 of *Three Sisters*. They are ringing the bell. We are acting well today and with gusto.

Fondly K. Alekseev

To **Anton Chekhov.** 2 November 1903, Moscow.
Dear Anton Pavlovich!

I seem just now to have found the set for the first act. It's been very difficult. The windows have to be somewhat downstage so that the cherry orchard is visible from both the upper and lower parts of the auditorium; three doors, we need to see just the tiniest corner of Anya's room, bright and virginal. The room communicates between two others but one should feel that here (that is, in the nursery) it is cosy, warm and bright; the room has been neglected and one can sense a slight emptiness. Above all the set must be comfortable with lots of spaces for blocking movements. We seem to have managed to accomplish all that now. Do you remember last year Simov showed you a model he had designed for Turgenev's *The Weakest Link?*[52] At the time we decided, and you agreed, to save the set for the last act of your play. I am looking at the model now and I find that with a few small changes it will be very suitable (for the 4th act). If you remember the model, have you any objections? Right now we're beginning the third act of *Uncle Vanya.* The response is enthusiastic; it's the 89th performance, and we took in 1400 rubles despite the fact that yesterday we played *Three Sisters.* So you have earned 140 rubles today. That's not important. But do you know what is important? It's that this year as never before the audience is listening to you. A death-like stillness. Not a cough, despite the dreadful weather. Poor Vasily Vasilievich Kaluzhsky buried his father today and has to act tonight [as Prof. Serebryakov]. Meanwhile he's cheerful and holds fast.

I shake your hand. Tomorrow I will try to write, if I'm not too knackered after *Caesar.* Today I act for the 7th day running. 'I am weary, Fyodor Ilyich!'[53]

Your loving and devoted K. Alekseev [...]

To **Anton Chekhov**. 3 November 1903, Moscow.
Dear Anton Pavlovich!

[...] I swear to you that I love all the roles in the play and will keep only one thing in view as I cast the roles: what will be best for the play, how can we show the audience the splendour of each role. I very much like Lopakhin, I will play him with delight, but I can't yet find the right tone in myself. Still I'm searching for it stubbornly and with great interest. The trouble is that Lopakhin is not a simple merchant, with the sharp characteristics typical of one. I see him exactly as you characterize him in your letter. It needs great control over the tone so as to colour in the everyday tone of the character. All I'm managing to produce so far is Konstantin Sergeevich trying to be good-natured. I feel from your letter that you want me to play this role. I am very proud of that and will search in myself for Lopakhin with redoubled energy. I will not countenance Vishnevsky as Lopakhin in any event. Such as he is, he is unsuitable in every way. Nothing Russian about him.

4 November 1903. Monday.

When Vishnevsky tries to be a character, he becomes dreadfully affected. I feel that he will exploit not Lopakhin's gentler traits, but the coarse one, more effective on an audience. He will come up with a ruffian of indeterminate nationality. There was talk of Vishnevsky before, but so far I cannot imagine such a Lopakhin. I can imagine Leonidov: he himself is gentle and delicate by nature, a strong figure, a good temperament. It would seem he has the attributes. One alarming thing: he is not always simple on stage. Sometimes his tone evinces an actorish quality. Although there is no doubt that he is a Jew, on stage he comes across as more Russian than Aleksandr Leonidovich. There's another factor that tells against Vishnevsky. He has to work a great deal on a role, but, poor fellow, he gets very worn out. Every morning he is busy with business matters, and every night he has to act. Since the season began, he has not had a single night off. Now he's a nervous wreck, falling ill and again getting to be womanish. […]

Your loving and devoted K. Alekseev

To **Anton Chekhov**. Wednesday, 5 November 1903, Moscow.
Dear Anton Pavlovich.

[…] One more piece of business concerning the directing. I don't know why, but I would like to see the 3rd and 4th acts in the same set. In the last act stripped bare and ready for the departure. This is not, really, a case of foolish sentimentality. I have the feeling that it will make the play tighter, because the audience has got intimate with the house. A second hall brings in a kind of messiness. Perhaps you need it so as to highlight past splendour even more. But that can be expressed this way too, I should think. One set for two acts won't be monotonous, because vacating the house completely changes the mood of the 4th act. We will go on working out the model, and perhaps in the meantime you will write a couple of words. One more question: can Yepikhodov and Dunya sit in Lopakhin's presence? To my mind, yes. [54] […]

Devoted and loving K. Alekseev

To **Anton Chekhov**. Thursday, 13 November 1903, Moscow.
Dear Anton Pavlovich!

Outrageous!.. 5 days have gone by and I haven't written to you. Saturday was the first performance of the renovated *Lonely Lives*. The participation of Kachalov (in place of Meyerhold [as Johann Vokerath]) enlivened the whole production. Besides, the old actors and actresses have grown as performers. Perhaps, who knows, the audience has begun to understand it better. Whatever the reason, it had a very great success, both artistic and financial. So the excitement of the first performance deprived me of the possibility of writing. Sunday was the first discussion of *Cherry Orchard*, and at 4 o'clock the wedding of the daughter of the manager who replaced me at the factory. I had to be there and stay to the end, so as not to offend them. Monday and Tuesday morning was spiking the model on stage and setting up new models, try-outs etc. on stage. This is very tedious work, when you have to speed up and strain your imagination. The nights are for *Caesar*, and afterwards – I'm almost a lifeless corpse.[55] All day yesterday I was free of the theatre. In the course of one day I had to write the stage-plan for the first act. I was in the mood, and therefore I succeeded. I wrote non-stop, and, from being unused to it, my arm got so tired that I could hardly finish writing at speed. This morning the staging-plan was read to the actors, but they sent me home to carry on with the second act. No sooner had I settled in, when I was called into the vestibule. It turns out that the children's Russian mistress, come to give them a lesson, had fallen on the floor and had a stroke. The result was bedlam. Guests were expected for dinner. People began to gather, doctors, guests… Of course, everyone was ordered out, except the close family, including Olga Leonardovna and Mariya Pavlovna. The patient lies in a sorry state at our house, and I had to leave for *Caesar*. [56] I'm writing to you in the intermission. That is my diary for these last few days. The rehearsals have begun, and in a very genial way. *For the time being* I am playing Gaev. Leonidov is trying out Lopakhin. This has happened in part because I am afraid to play merchants, in part because with Gaev I have a chance to have a hand in the staging. With Lopakhin (who would take up a great deal of time) it is difficult. Olga Leonardovna and Mariya Pavlovna are well. We miss you a lot. Be well. My wife sends her regards for your efforts.

Yours K. Alekseev

To **Anton Chekhov**. 15 November 1903, Moscow.
Dear Anton Pavlovich!

[…] I treasure and will make use of every one of your remarks even about the sets. The model for the 3rd act has turned out successfully. I am beginning to waver, because in this set the view of the distance is more interesting. The trickiest model of all was the first act. It is quite simple on the ground-plan. It is designed to provide a better view of the orchard. The set depends on the scene painting. If Simov manages it -- it will be splendid, if not, it will be bad. Nothing really definite is coming from the actors yet. Actually Kachalov [as Petya Trofimov] is offering something interesting. Artyom [as Firs], as usual, started with Kuryukov (from *Fyodor*). That means epic tones… I am worried about Muratova as Charlotta. Big, in men's clothes, -- it could be crude… You write that your arrival depends on Olga Leonardovna. Unfortunately she is right not to send for you. The weather is dreadful. Sometimes the snow falls, sometimes it melts. The roads are full of potholes. Mud, stench. Very soon there will be frost.

Goodbye, dear Anton Pavlovich. I have to go play a scene in a tent.

You asked: why don't I like *Caesar*. Very simple: because I am bad in it and it is hard to act.

Loving and devoted K. Alekseev

Today is the 25th performance of *Caesar*.

To **Anton Chekhov**. 17 November 1903, Moscow.
Dear Anton Pavlovich!

[..] Rehearsals go on every day. They are working energetically. Some are finding interesting tones. Olga Leonardovna has interesting glimmers. I believe I have found something suitable for Gaev. My wife is playing Anya, and has found a beautiful tone for Charlotta. We have to transplant it to Muratova. Every day I mentally thank you for the play: it is such a pleasure to work on it. The only woe is *Caesar*. I want to cast everything aside and think only abut *Cherry Orchard*. I've just gotten up to full speed, just submerged in the mood, and then along comes Brutus with a heavy, hot cloak, bare legs, cold armour and interminable monologues. You act and you feel nobody needs it. [...]

Loving and devoted K. Alekseev

To **Anton Chekhov.** Wednesday, 19 November 1903, Moscow.
Dear Anton Pavlovich,

Again yesterday there was no time to write. I was busy with the second act and finally finished it. To my mind, it will turn out to be an enchanting act. God willing, the scenery will manage to be effective. A little chapel, a small gully, a neglected graveyard amid a small wooded oasis of trees on the steppe. The left side of the stage and the centre without flats – just the horizon and beyond. This is done with one continuous semi-circular backdrop and extensions to the flats to deepen the perspective. In the distance in one place a rivulet is glistening, the manor house can be seen on a hillock. Telegraph poles and a railway bridge. Allow us, during one of the pauses, to run across a train with little puffs of smoke. That might have a splendid effect. Before sundown the town is briefly visible. Towards the end of the act mist; it will rise especially densely from the ditch downstage. A concert of frogs and a corncrake at the very end of the act. Downstage left, a hayfield and a small haystack, on which the scene will take place with the whole group out for a walk. This is for the actors' sake, it will help them live their roles. The general tone of the set is like a Levitan.[57] Countryside – like the Orlov region but no farther south than the Kursk regions.[58]

The work is now going on as follows: Vladimir Ivanovich ran the first act rehearsals yesterday and today, and I wrote the subsequent acts. I haven't rehearsed my own role yet. I am still wavering as to the sets for acts three and four. The model is made and came out very successfully: full of mood and besides, the hall is set up so that it is visible to the whole theatre. Down front there is something like a topiary near the hall. Farther upstage are the stairs and billiard room. Windows are painted on the walls. This set is more commodious for the ball. Still, a small voice keeps whispering in my ear that if we have a single set, which we change in the 4th act, it would be easier, tidier.[59] This will have to be decided in a few days.

The weather, alas, is murderous. Everything is melting again and it rains frequently.

Yours, K. Alekseev

To **Anton Chekhov.** 23 November 1903, Moscow.
Dear Anton Pavlovich!

[...] What am I to say about rehearsals? We have not found the tone, although we've been going in circles in Act 2. Finding tones and images, of course, slows down the general rehearsing. With every production it becomes more and more difficult for us to reincarnate ourselves and be more variegated. I suspect that the whole play will come out in quite a different tone from its precursors. Everything will be lighter, more cheerful… In short, we want to use water-colours. […]

Devoted and loving K. Alekseev

Luzhsky took over as Brutus on 4 January.

To **Nemirovich-Danchenko.** Saturday, 10 January 1904, Moscow.
Dear Vladimir Ivanovich!

I very much regret that I must trouble you with this letter.

My request that the matinee of *Caesar* be cancelled you answered with a categorical refusal.[60]

Meanwhile my appeal implies the resolution of a major question of no small importance to me, in which we used to be united.

This is what it is all about: Kachalov is confronting the prospect of acting 11 times in 8 days, Leonidov 10 times in 8 days.

Of these 10 or 11 times 3 are dress rehearsals and 1 is an opening night. Everyone knows that a single dress is equal to several performances, and a single opening night even more. Ask yourself the question: can human nerves support such work given that the first performances of a new play have to go brilliantly in order to meet captious demands.

My categorical answer is no. Under such conditions an artistic concern turns into a commercial enterprise and the actors are correct when they say that the shareholders care too much about their dividends. The fact that Aleksandr Leonidovich [Vishnevsky] pays great attention to the financial side is fine; but why you are not worried by this pursuit of dividends at the expense of artistic quality of a performance is something I did not have the time to clarify during our last conversation.

I think that you have not given adequate thought to my request, and therefore I am writing this letter. I swear to you, if a refusal ensues, I will be very dismayed and will give furious thought to the future, but I do not think it will come to that.

Now let us pass to a purely commercial question. The first rule here is: 'do not be distracted by immediate gain, -- look to the future'. Bad is the businessman who thinks about the morrow's profit, without thinking about the future. It is more profitable to take a loss today in order to earn in the future. It is more profitable therefore to lose 1200 r. on a matinee performance and protect the actor who by his illness will bring about a loss of 10,000 in future.

The cancellation of this performance will kill two birds with one stone for us: 1) the future financial risk and 2) the preservation of the principle, the most lucrative and forceful in our theatre; artistic and humanitarian interests first and foremost, and financial ones second.

All this is written to you by the man who, perhaps, more than most bears the burden that our theatre still does not stand on a firm and independent financial footing.

Respectfully K. Alekseev

In reply on 14 January 1904 ND suggested tactlessly that as a rich man KS could not understand his partner's position. 'That is our tragedy.' However, after consulting with Vishnevsky and Luzhsky, ND agreed to cancel the matinee on the 18th. Some of ND's pique came from KS's restless behaviour at the dress rehearsals. The actors were complaining that constant requests to repeat a phrase or an action were driving them crazy.

To **Nemirovich-Danchenko**. Between 10 and 14 January 1904, Moscow. [Unfinished and possibly not sent.]

Dear Vladimir Ivanovich!

I shall answer point for point and, believe me, in the most pacific tone.

I swear, I do not love the tone that you took yesterday with me, but I understand and excuse it. There is such a tone in me as well, and I contend with it, I hate it. It occurs to me that you sometimes have recourse to it deliberately, as a governess does with a child, to have a stronger influence over me. I keep silent so as not to give rise to a quarrel, but an after-taste, and a very bitter one, stays with me.

Unfortunately, I cannot deny that I am being intolerable, that the form of my demands are repugnant, perhaps indecent. At such moments I am mentally ill and suffer by it. This is the result of overstrain, the result of a disparity with my wholesome work. I think that this fault of mine is justifiable. Just give it some thought: am I always in the wrong at such moments. Was I so wrong yesterday and the day before that – that is still the question. I am not talking about the manner, which I do not seek to justify. Yesterday a *complete* rehearsal was needed, it was impossible to discuss the play at the table at least because half the participants had refused to do so, but...[61] It was impossible to do the rehearsals on stage and Simov and you were at fault for this.

I will speak frankly, since you yourself were good enough to admit that you wanted to prove something by the production of *The Cherry Orchard*.[62] That's where your fault lay, first of all to Chekhov.

A man more dead than alive has written with his last strength, perhaps, his swansong, and we pick this song to show off to one another our personal dissensions. This is a crime against art and cruel to the man. I was tormented by this the whole time while working on *The Cherry Orchard*, but I had a millstone around my neck – Brutus. This millstone was lifted from me not when *The Cherry Orchard* was in need of it, but only when I had lost my voice and there was a risk of the performances coming to a halt.[63] Any little thing made me touchy– and I believed in the existence of some intrigue or other. If that state of mind had gone on much longer, I would have asked Morozov to release me, and I would have explained to you my utter incompetence at working under such conditions. Everything that you did to prove something upset me agonizingly and proved nothing, but merely estranged me from you. That was my view regarding the impossibility of running a full rehearsal yesterday and for this I blame you, this is my view regarding the matinee. Before *Caesar* the actors were taken care of, and now this has become impossible. My vanity as a director plays no part in all this, I am upset on behalf of Chekhov and *The Cherry Orchard*. The proof is at hand. Chekhov gave me quite a slap for

«ВИШНЕВЫЙ САДЪ» А. П. ЧЕХОВА.   Моск. Худож. Театръ
Гаевъ   и   Аня
К. С. Станиславскій и М. П. Лилина.
Собств. изд. К. А. Фишеръ, Москва.

Figure 33 Stanislavsky as Gaev and the 37-year-old Lilina as his 18-year-old niece Anya
in *The Cherry Orchard*, 1903. Photo: K. A. Fischer, Moscow

my directing,[64] but I soon swallowed my vanity and am guiltless in relation to
Cherry Orchard. If you were completely guiltless as well, I swear to you now –
forgive me. It will give me sincere pleasure and joy to ask your forgiveness. I will
be glad if you overcome the petty passions unworthy of you, which so easily and
quickly spring up backstage. Why then, you will ask me, was it for you to goad
Simov, when I was considered the stage director of *Cherry Orchard*?

Of course, not because I am trying to assign you a role subservient to myself.
God forbid, but because at the given moment you were freer than I was and the
case demanded this service on your part.

A question for the future: can I remain a stage director, while an actor in major roles… can I remain an actor, while being a stage director? These questions are still waiting for answers, and the time for *The Cherry Orchard* to blossom will not wait. We have had to take action for the benefit of the concern, for its financial good. You, as it now seems, deliberately sought to prove something… and this is your mistake, because there is another means of proof: persuasion.[65] Your verbal persuasions have always had a powerful effect on me, but the persuasions to which I refer embroil relationships, cause division and undermine trust and love.

Can you not be convinced enough of this after *Snow Maiden*? Why repeat that unsuccessful method again. What did you manage to persuade of me this time? For heaven's sake, I don't know. That if we stick spanners in one another's spokes, our concern will come crashing down? I have no doubt of that. Or, perhaps, that we should bolster one another for the welfare of the concern? I have no doubt of that either.

I will say more. The disagreement between us began at a time when we had obliterated our primary principle: you had the veto in the literary realm, I in the artistic. Both vetos were transferred to you, and the equilibrium collapsed.

Meanwhile in my realm I am self-sufficient and consider myself stronger than you; in literary matters I do not butt in and contend with you, but only learn. Our theatre, having lost its original equipoise, is becoming literary. The artistic side of it is making poor progress, and this circumstance angers me, leaves me unsatisfied and chills me.

Our theatre pleases the Efroses[66] more and more and is beginning to inspire the audience with a different attitude more tenuous in the artistic sense.

We are moving forward in the literary sense, but in the artistic one we have almost stopped looking for anything new.

The 17 January premiere of Cherry Orchard *was combined with a tribute to Chekhov. Seriously ill, Chekhov chose not to attend until summoned by a note from ND during the third intermission. Both directors' names appeared in the programme until 1928. The premiere had a so-so success. Nevertheless it became the perennial favourite with audiences and chalked up 1,209 performances.*

Russia broke off diplomatic relations with Japan on 26 January. Two days later Japan fired on Port Arthur, a pre-emptive strike against Russian forces.

KS's diary for February 1904 recorded his attraction to the idea of reviving and reforming the theatre in Russia. He proposed to create an affiliate of the Moscow Art Theatre for the regular service of provincial towns and the dissemination among the general public of the culture and 'artistic principles' of the MAT. The affiliate was also to provide for further 'practical development' of pupils at the MAT school and serve as a source for supplementing the parent troupe.

To **Ioasaf Tikhomirov**. 16 February 1904.
Dear Ioasaf Aleksandrovich!

[…] Something interesting is under way with us. The final plan is conceived along very broad lines, but to be specific:

The organization of a stock company of provincial theatres. The directorate would be located in Moscow. Rehearsals in the spring, part of the summer and fall would take place in Moscow. The *Art Theatre* will provide the concern all the help in its power.

3 troupes will be assembled. Each of them will prepare around 15 plays. Hence 3 troupes, 45 plays – *of all sorts.*

A single director will not be capable of staging so many plays in an exemplary manner. That is where the Art Theatre will provide its help. Its whole repertoire, models, plans, wardrobe can be copied. To assist the director of a troupe one of our actors or unemployed directors who knows the play well will be released. After all, such an actor, even if he is not a real director, can copy a play he is familiar with better than a real director who is badly acquainted with the play.

Each director of a troupe will be assigned the autonomous staging of 5 plays.

The company will rent 3 provincial playhouses, fit them up for the whole repertoire of 45 plays, and the troupes will travel around their sector. After performing their repertoires, the towns will swap troupes and each troupe will repeat its own repertoire. Thus, each town will see 3 troupes and 45 plays, very well staged. During the rehearsal period everyone will gather in Moscow – close to the Art Theatre, so that they can again be infected by its spirit. This, roughly, is the task of the new concern. It may not be possible to attain this goal straightway, if only because it is impossible to assemble three troupes all at once. Meanwhile one might put together a single troupe with a very good female contingent and an average male one. We are even now assembling one. If you turn out to be free – we are thinking of putting you at its head. Next year the troupe will perform as a team and function in Moscow. Acting a repertoire other than ours, of course. We have in mind a few plays – new ones. The repertoire will probably consist of 5 plays. Performances at the Hunt Club (amateur, charity and club performances). Travel on tour to nearby towns. Touring the provinces in Lent with the season's novelties. Acting in factories. If some theatre happens to come free – to lease it and tour there for a month, playing the whole repertoire. […]

There is money for this new concern.

The chief stumbling-block is the male troupe. Can one be put together?

I await your answer as soon as possible. The matter must be decided within the next few days.

Regards.

Affectionately and devotedly K. Alekseev

To **Mariya Andreeva**. Before 26 February 1904, Moscow.
Dear Mariya Fyodorovna!

A long acquaintance bordering on friendship in the past, striving for a particular good purpose – all this, perhaps, gives me the right to abandon the central role I accepted by force of circumstances.

Figure 34 Mariya Andreeva as Natasha in *The Lower Depths*. Photo: Nabholz & Scherer, Moscow, 1903

Of course, I understand that your latest behaviour – breaking with the past without warning or explaining why – clearly shows me the place you assign me in the origin of the sad event. Nevertheless I have decided to be importunate; I am forcing myself to set aside my self-respect and very pained feeling of offense.

Who knows, perhaps, I shall succeed in saying something that will make you think things over and avert a great misfortune.

I will say nothing about health. Specialists and people close to you know better than I how they ought to behave. I will talk only about art. Our role in it was exceptional. We had taken it upon ourselves to ennoble it, to snatch it out of the

181

hands of tradesmen and present it to its rightful owners. Our activities were endowed with social significance, society acknowledged them and rewarded us with a position that no single actor had ever achieved.

Now – you renounce this honourable position, which the best provincial actors envy above all, and voluntarily enter their ranks. How can you stop worshipping your former god and renounce his ideals?

Are you giving any thought to what you are exchanging your current service to society for?

To perform the best works of literature with ten rehearsals or vulgar and untalented works with three rehearsals? To perform some ten new roles a season? Is this not the profanation of art. To devote one's life to the profanation of good works of literature or show the public works of vulgarity – is that really a worthy activity for you?

Your success will be great, but can it satisfy you if you are aware of this? Don't let the money tempt you! True, the compromises with which a performer's life is fraught are compensated with more money in the provinces. All the less reason for her to deserve respect!

It is no coincidence that the best part of society spurned actors and neglected the theatre. That is why performers are forced to create for themselves the glory of publicity, tributes at benefits, portraits in shop windows and on chocolate bars and the whole artillery of a wretched celebrity. That is how names and ranks are created in the provinces. When people choose for themselves this base, irrelevant and unjust craftsmanship out of necessity – it is sad but forgivable, but you cannot by your own wish serve something you do not respect.

Perhaps you would like to improve the provinces. An honourable task, but you are not going about it the right way.

Or perhaps you have come to the conclusion that our concern has gone bad? Devote half the energy to it that you will pointlessly devote to the provinces… You will do more good than by any attempt to cleanse and drain a vile swamp. Save yourself! Stay and serve society by those means with which nature endowed you. I give you my word that so long as you serve this honourable goal, you will find no one more devoted than I.

Otherwise we shall go off in different directions, and with a breaking heart I shall bid you farewell, preserving the very best memories of the past and prematurely grieving for your future.

Your sincere well-wisher K. Alekseev

This letter repeats KS's earlier reference to 'craftsmanship' as the antithesis to art. Andreeva replied that it was not a desire for notoriety but poverty that drove her. Although she respected KS's originality, she found the MAT banal and no longer believed it was driven by ideas. On leaving the MAT, she signed a contract with Konstantin Nezlobin's theatre in Riga.

The Petersburg tour opened on 29 March with KS playing an improved version of Brutus.

To **Anton Chekhov**. 2 April 1904, St Petersburg *Telegram*.

Cherry Orchard success very great, incomparably greater than in Moscow. After third act insistent calls for author. Connoisseurs rapturous over play. Newspapers don't get it. Troupe in high spirits. I am triumphant. Congratulations. Alekseev.

On 18 April Gorky read to the MAT his new play Vacationers. *KS judged it to be 'dreadful and naïve', and ND accused Gorky of caricaturing the intelligentsia. He recommended that its raw material be reworked. Offended, Gorky withdrew the play.*

Chekhov was a great admirer of the Belgian symbolist Maurice Maeterlinck, who was enjoying a surge of popularity in Western Europe; he had advised Suvorin to put on Maeterlinck's plays in his St Petersburg theatre. KS thought it might be a way out of the realist impasse.

To **Vera Kotlyarevskaya**. 10 May 1904, Moscow.
Dear Vera Vasilievna!

[…] The very day of my arrival, almost straight from the station, I went to a reading of Balmont's[67] translations of Maeterlinck. The translation is good, but the reading… well, God forgive him. On the other hand your chum spoke splendidly, was almost inspired. With his help I sank into the gloom of death and tried to glimpse the threshold of eternity. So far I have not come across either pink or light-blue feelings in my soul. Obviously, one needs a certain degree of intoxication. I just don't know which medium to employ: a woman or wine… By Balmont's lights, obviously, the first method is the most efficacious. At least I was a witness of the following. In the first part of the lecture Balmont was surrounded by ladies and was intoxicated and inspired. Afterwards I took a seat on one side of him, and Nemirovich on the other. From both sides we puffed the fragrance of our cigarettes around him. Surrounded by smoke, he himself seemed to turn into a cloud and came detached from the earth. Alas, this means of intoxication was no help, on the contrary… he only began to sneeze, blow his nose, and soon left with a headache, having said not a word in the language of eternity… So, I am giving up smoking, will drink vodka and take up with women and only after that will I set to the mise-en-scène and rehearsals. I think that this will be the most pleasant of my productions. I will hang out with Misha Gromov and Aumont… and only then will I understand Maeterlinck. […]

Cordially devoted K. Alekseev

On 7 May Chirikov read the troupe his short play Ivan Mironych, *which made KS roar with laughter and ND grin broadly.*

KS began to draw up plans for three Maeterlinck one-acts, trying somehow to overcome their pessimism and hopelessness. Maeterlinck himself proved to be useless in making suggestions for staging, but Chekhov took a real interest.

To **Anton Chekhov** in Badenweiler. 20 June 1904, Lyubimovka.
Dear Anton Pavlovich!

Neither we nor the Muscovites have heard from you, and we are worried. From Olga Leonardovna's open letter to my wife we know that you reached Berlin safely, but beyond that… we know nothing. God grant that you are well settled and that your weather is not like ours. It is cold in Moscow, every day rain and thunderstorms, cold nights and, as you probably know from the papers there was a dreadful cyclone that caused a good deal of damage. It moved from Podolsk to Yaroslavl. It touched down at Lyublino (near Tsaritsyn), Lefort district, Sokolniki, Mytishchi (near us) etc. In a hundred-year-old park in Lyublino not a tree remains. The roofs were torn off of almost all the dachas, and some were destroyed. Many villages were razed to the ground. Horses, cows, carriages, logs, roofs flew through the air. In Mytishchi the hurricane got a hold of an 8-year-old boy. They found him alive in Sokolniki (nearly 10-15 versts away). There were also some comical occurrences. The wind burst into the apartment of a notary or judge. There the hurricane busted up all the furniture, tore open all the cupboards and blew all the official papers and protest petitions throughout the neighbourhood. It overturned a carriage in Iverskaya, and conveyed the icon to the nearest police station.[68] Luckily, there are relatively few killed and wounded. The killed number about 100, and the wounded many fewer. I was not in Moscow that day. I was in Old Rus.[69] […]

I am reading from morning to night. Right now I'm rereading all of Chekhov and enjoying myself immensely.

Your devoted and affectionate K. Alekseev

Chekhov and Olga Knipper had departed for Germany on 3 June; on 2 July, the writer died in Badenweiler. Sulerzhitsky rode to Lyubimovka to inform KS, who was leaving for a spa in France. On the train, he wrote letters to Chekhov's sister and his wife, crossing out lines and starting afresh. He also began to compile notes for a memoir of Chekhov.

To **Mariya Chekhova**.[70] 3 July 1904.
Much esteemed and dear Mariya Pavlovna!

I am taking my mother abroad and with heavy heart have departed Moscow. I can write in the railway carriage only with a pencil. Forgive the paper, there is no other. I am writing to you not only to express my condolences: they are inadequate, because the grief is too great.

Alone in the carriage, with my thoughts and memories about dear, good Anton Pavlovich, an understandable need has arisen in me to speak with those who at present are more despondent at the loss than I am myself. If this is egotistical, forgive my weakness, but I have an irrepressible desire to squeeze your hand so that you feel that I am not a stranger to your grief, that in my mind I am experiencing everything that is going on in Moscow. I am distressed for your dear mother and respectfully kiss her hand, and in my mind I press the hand of Ivan Pavlovich and your other brothers.

I am comforted by the thought that those kindly relations which were established between your family and ours will strengthen even more the memory of dear Anton Pavlovich.

My mother asks me to convey her respects to you.

Devoted, respectful and spiritually affectionate
K. Alekseev

To **his wife Mariya Lilina**. Sunday, 11 July 1904, Contrexeville.
My precious, poor little invalid!

[…] Last year, it's true, I was unbearable, but this year I cut back as much as I could, and all the same nothing came of it. The fact of the matter is, I suppose, that I do not have that affection so essential to you, or sentimentality, and where I am to get it I don't know. That is why everyone respects me, but does not love me. […]

Poor Anton Pavlovich never leaves my mind. I am rereading his stories and love and treasure him all the more.

Yesterday Pravdin,[71] who is here, upset me. He had read in the papers that Goltsev ('Russian Thought')[72] has taken the funeral on himself, which means we have again been caught yawning and have no part in the funeral. This is offensive and unforgiveable. We have to give a thought to erecting a monument to Anton Pavlovich on the theatre's account, otherwise we'll be caught yawning here too.

From your telegram I understood that you, my bee-ootiful one, were at the funeral. I admit I was upset – how could you go there and with whom? It was probably an enormous crowd. Did Kaluzhsky arrange for a requiem mass? Oy… this isn't good!

[…] I am having sad thoughts about our theatre. He didn't have long to live. I cannot imagine life without him. Perhaps the war will toughen up society a bit and lend us support for our ruined strength. It is disgusting that everything good perishes or fades so soon. […]

The troupe's farewell to Chekhov's corpse took place at the MAT building, where the catafalque stopped on the way to the cemetery.

To **Olga Knipper-Chekhova**. 13/26 July 1904, Contrexeville.
Dear, kind Olga Leonardovna!

Instead of paraphrasing my sister's message to you, I attach her letter to this one. I know that it was written with tears, and therefore the feelings of an outsider at a real, bitter moment of your suffering will not offend it. Who knows, perhaps, you will weep at the letter, and those tears will bring you some momentary relief.

I have been wanting to write to you every day, but have held back, because it is difficult to know at a distance what you are undergoing, and how you are bearing up under your grief, and how appropriate my letters might be. Furthermore, I know nothing of what has happened and is now happening in Moscow, since I have no news and look in vain for Russian newspapers here. I am in a great hurry to leave these French backwoods, because here, in isolation, it is harder to inure oneself to our grief. I want to speak and be with those who have experienced it first hand, but here you meet with no one except spa-haunting dolls. Fortunately, I took along two volumes of dear Anton Pavlovich's stories, and at present his books are my best friends. I am rereading them a second time and between the lines I divine what only someone who has seen this man, the best of all people, close up can understand. Where are you now, and when will I see you? Will you head for Yalta, or, on the contrary, would that be too hard for you? Will you change your Moscow apartment, or, on the contrary, will you want to live there?

My mother, thank God, has begun to calm down and get better. Perhaps I shall soon be able to leave her here and hurry back to Moscow. There, I will get the answer to all my questions. God grant that I shall meet you as I expect to see you. Strong, assured that you have graced the last days of a man who needed beauty more than anyone else. Having selflessly given him a little portion of your life, you have kept him among us a few years longer, and for this we should be grateful to you.

Cordially devoted and affectionately yours,

K. Alekseev

Notes

1 The Countess headed the Society for the Care of Poor and Homeless Children.
2 Mikhail Apollinarievich Gromov (1871-1918) acted at the MAT 1899-1906 in twenty-four roles.
3 Artyom was cast as Chebutykin, Gribunin as Ferapont, Moskvin as Rodé, Lilina as Natasha, Andreeva as Irina, Savitskaya as Olga, Gromov as Solyony; Kachalov was KS's alternate as Vershinin (and later took over Tuzenbakh). Meyerhold was Tuzenbakh.
4 In autumn 1901 Nikolay Popov founded in Petersburg a club of amateurs and professionals to stage 'idiosyncratic productions'.
5 Maurice Maeterlinck (1862-1949), Belgian playwright, one of the spearheads of European symbolism. Chekhov had suggested that the MAT take a look at him. The business relation between the MAT and Maeterlinck was forged by the journalist and translator V. L. Binshtok. This play was produced at the MAT in October 1904 under the title *The Uninvited*.
6 At the Hunt Club on 3 May 1894.
7 A reference to the ecclesiastical censorship which forbade *Hannele* in 1898.
8 He played in only one Shpazhinsky play, *The Major's Lady*, as the miller Karyagin.
9 Nikolay Aleksandrovich Baranov, an uneducated former church chorister, was at the MAT 1899-1903; his eventual success in the role of Teteryov proved to be his undoing.
10 Neither of them appeared in *The Petty Bourgeoisie*.
11 In the intermission of *Uncle Vanya* O. E. Braz's portrait of Chekhov was brought on stage with the inscription 'The physicians to the artists. In memory of the performance for physicians, who came to the Eighth Pirogov Congress. 11.1.1902.'
12 Charles Aumont, French impresario whose theatre offered variety shows and bedroom farces.
13 Before she entered the Society for Art and Literature Andreeva had great success at the Tiflis Artistic Circle.
14 Andreeva had become Gorky's mistress and had got money from Morozov to support a Bolshevik newspaper *Iskra* (*The Spark*) and other party activities.
15 Zinaida Grigorievna Morozova (d.1942), wife of Savva Morozov.
16 Morozov bought a great lot of fur jackets and by means of the Minister of Enlightenment P. S. Vannovsky donated them to students who had been exiled for political activities, among them Dmitry Ivanovich Lukyanov, tutor to Andreeva's sons.
17 Yekaterina Mikhailovna Mundt (Golubeva, 1875-1954) acted with the MAT until 1902.
18 Mariya Mikhailovna Orlova-Davydova, chairwoman of the Society of the Red Cross.

19 Nicholas II saw *Three Sisters* on 13 March, at a performance on behalf of the Red Cross. It took place at the Grand Duke Michael (Mikhailovsky) 'royal' Theatre. A second charity performance *In Dreams* was performed on 3 April.

20 Dmitry Sergeevich Sipyagin (1852-1902), Minister of the Interior from 1900.

21 Morozov was in charge of the rebuilding of the theatre building, in which he had invested over a million.

22 Chekhov had seen such a room in a dream.

23 Tolstoy allowed it.

24 Mikhail Aleksandrovich Stakhovich (1861-1923), president of the nobility of Orlov gubernia and journalist; brother of the MAT shareholder Aleksey Stakhovich.

25 Aleksandra Ivanovna Pomyalova (Valts, 1863-1930s), acted at the MAT 1898-1905 and 1908-09.

26 *Zaza*, a play by Pierre Berton, deals with the private life of a music-hall singer.

27 KS was at the Bayreuth Festival on 9 and 11 July when he heard *Parsifal* and *The Flying Dutchman*. That letter does not survive.

28 KS's fears proved to be groundless.

29 Leonid Nikolaevich Andreev (1871-1919) and Sergey Aleksandrovich Naidyonov (Alekseev, 1868-1922) were popular writers, members of Gorky's *Znanie* group.

30 The swimming-hole on the banks of the Klyazma belonged to Yelena Fyodorovna and Sergey Nikolaevich. Smirnov, relatives and neighbours of KS near Lyubimovka.

31 Reference to the cool reception of *Bourgeoisie*.

32 Nikolay Efros, writing in *Theatre and Art*, praised her for transforming herself almost to be unrecognizable.

33 They met during the autumn tours in Yalta in 1900.

34 Olga Knipper to Chekhov, 20 December 1902: 'Baranov began to howl, smash glasses and plates and howl. This was more disgusting, nasty, than I can describe. I started to tremble, and ran out of the hall into the lobby. Vlad. Iv. took me home. It ended, as you can see, in a scandal. I'm told that the ladies who stayed fainted and went into hysterics. Morozov tussled with Skitalets and Baranov. The whole troupe is upset by Baranov's crudeness.'

35 It never happened.

36 Ultimately, the censorship permitted *The Lower Depths* to be performed only at the MAT.

37 Kotlyarevskaya: 'I've heard that your Satin is as brilliant a creation as your Stockmann.'

38 KS, as usual, exaggerates the press reactions to him.

39 Viktor Aleksandrovich Krylov (pseud. V. Aleksandrov, 1838-1906), dramatic hack, who provided much of the modern repertoire for the Alexandra Theatre and Mariya Savina. On seeing Chekhov's first play *Ivanov* in 1888, he offered to give the young writer tips to make it stageworthy.

40 Chekhov to Lilina, 15 September: 'It issued from me not as a drama, but as a comedy, in places even a farce.'

41 A reference to Morozov's plans to found a new theatre with Gorky and Andreeva.

42 At the reorganization of MAT in 1902 the obligations of the chief stage director (KS) included writing the mise-en-scène and staging four plays a season. The rules governing members of the Board of the Fellowship of the MAT made the independent staging of one play the obligation of the artistic administrator, that is ND, in addition to literary, administrative and artistic work. This was never observed in practice and each of them went beyond his official duties.

43 ND had written: 'A wonderful phenomenon is taking place. Before *Depths* the theatre was hurtling to hell in a hand-basket. *The Power of Darkness* for all its brilliant directorial talent was staged in such a way that if I hadn't taken a hand in the staging,

it would have been the same story as *Snow Maiden* all over again, that is Stanislavsky is brilliant, but the play is a flop.'

44 With the reorganization of the MAT in 1902/03 the chief director was named on the playbill; ND's title was 'head of the repertoire'.

45 Baranov let his success as Teteryov in *The Petty Bourgeoisie* go to his head and took to drink; after he was dismissed, he would declaim in the streets. Gromov, an adherent of Gorky, left because of lack of discipline and education. Shidlovskaya, whom KS had known from his youth, had for the same reasons been asked to leave the troupe even before the theatre opened.

46 Dissatisfied with the MAT's artistic and fiscal policies, Sanin had left the theatre in 1902.

47 A few students left the MAT school to go the Theatre of the People's House in Nizhny Novgorod, organized by Gorky. Tikhomirov had proved to be a limited actor, most useful in collecting research materials for productions. When he was invited to be director of the theatre in Nizhny Novgorod, he took a year's leave from the MAT, having informed KS of his plans in advance, he stayed away till 17 May 1904.

48 Nikolay Fyodorovich Manokhin (1855-1915), a ballet dancer from the Bolshoy, taught dance. The lectures were delivered by a high school teacher, Prof. Sergey Grigorievich Grigoriev, who taught aesthetics to KS's children.

49 In a letter to Knipper, on 14 October, Chekhov explained: 'The house is old, baronial: the life in it was once lavish, and this should be felt in the furnishings. Lavish and comfortable.'

50 In a letter to KS, on 5 November, Chekhov replied that 'the house should be large and solid: wood [...] or stone, it doesn't matter which'.

51 Chekhov wrote to KS on 5 November: 'Your shepherd played nicely. It fits the bill.'

52 In the 1903/04 season they proposed a Turgenev season, consisting of *The Parasite*, *The Lady from the Provinces* and *The Weakest Link*. KS was still writing the plan in March, but it was only a few years later that it was realized.

53 Kulygin's line in Act I of *Three Sisters*.

54 Chekhov wrote to KS on 10 November: '...of course, there can be a single set for Acts III and IV, specifically with the hallway and staircase. [...] Whatever you do will be beautiful, a hundred times better than anything I could come up with. [...] Dunya and Yepikhodov stand in Lopakhin's presence, and do not sit. Lopakhin after all conducts himself freely, like a master, says "thou" to the maid, while she addresses him as "you".'

55 By 13 November KS had played Brutus six times that month.

56 Olga Yakovlevna Suslova died in hospital two days later at the age of 42.

57 Isaak Ilyich Levitan (1860-1900), painter, a close friend of Chekhov, noted for his evocative landscapes; he also designed scenery for Mamantov's Private Opera.

58 Chekhov to KS, 23 November:' 'Haymowing is usually from the 20 to the 22 of June; by that time the corncrakes have stopped cawing, I believe, and the frogs have fallen silent as well. Only the oriole cries. There is no graveyard; that was very long ago. Two or three slabs lying helter-skelter – that's all that's left. A bridge – that's very good. If the train can be presented without noise, without any sound at all, then go ahead.'

59 Eventually: Act III had its own set and that for Act IV was the same as Act I.

60 KS was aware that the day after the premiere of *Orchard* there were to be both a matinee and evening performance of *Caesar*, where the leading roles would have to be played by Kachalov and Leonidov who had no alternates.

61 ND had accused KS of wasting time and gilding the lily.

62 ND preferred the way they had worked together in rehearsals before 'Morozov and the shareholders' came along.

63 KS did not get an alternate as Brutus until 4 January 1904, when Luzhsky took over the role.

64 The specific instance is unknown. Chekhov disagreed with KS about missing the comedy, made some remarks in rehearsals, and in his dissatisfaction soon stopped coming.

65 ND had written: 'The problem is that you judge everyone by yourself, forgetting that *in all* relationships you are exclusively an actor. In your artistic gifts and your methods and your personal habits. Hence the bulk of your mistakes. For the most part *The Cherry Orchard* rehearsals brilliantly disclosed the virtues and vices of the regimen of our stage direction, and we have to revise them, if we so choose, so that our theatre be stabilized. And my behaviour at those rehearsals was *deliberate* so that everything would be clear to both of us.'

66 I.e., the critics, Nikolay Efros at their head.

67 Konstantin Dmitrievich Balmont (1867-1942), poet, translator; Chekhov made fun of his symbolist verse.

68 The reference is to the wonder-working Iver icon of the Holy Virgin.

69 At Savina's request KS was rehearsing her in the role of Ranevskaya, performed in Old Rus 17 June in Nezlobin's summer company.

70 Mariya Pavlovna Chekhova (1863-1957), Chekhov's sister and (until his marriage) housekeeper.

71 Osip Andreevich Pravdin (Treyleben, 1849-1921), Maly Theatre actor 1878-1921.

72 Viktor Aleksandrovich Goltsev (1850-1906), man of letters and journalist, from 1885 editor of *Russian Thought*. Chekhov was a friend and the newspaper, which had published many of his works, took on the arrangements for his funeral.

Figure 35 Stanislavsky and Nemirovich in Berlin, 1906

5

FLIRTING WITH SYMBOLISM
1904–1908

The reactionary policies of Minister of the Interior Plehve, suppressing liberals, co-opting factory workers and instigating pogroms, did not end with his assassination in July 1904. A conference of rural councils calling for freedom of conscience, speech, assembly, press and association, intensified the demand for a Duma or Parliament. The first Duma was convened in 1905, but dissolved the following year. The tug of war between the tsarist government and the proponents of reform perpetuated social instability. Meanwhile, the war in the Far East against the Japanese had gone badly from the beginning.

The unsettled political situation fostered an idiosyncratically Russian form of symbolism in literature. The classical scholar Vyacheslav Ivanov promoted the playwright as the keeper of the flame, who would introduce the nation to the sublime through a shared experience of communality (sobornost). The old 'civic goals' of progressive literature were replaced by a religious vocabulary. This idealism, more evident in theory than practice in the theatre, was affected by the failure of the 1905 Revolution. Reflecting a more fatalistic view, such writers as Nikolay Yevreinov and Fyodor Sologub promoted 'monodrama' (the action viewed from the standpoint of one protagonist) and 'theatre of a single will,' in which actors would become mannequins manipulated at the behest of the dramatist.

In the light of all these debates about the nature of the theatre and its relevance to the contemporary situation, the MAT began to feel itself out of touch with current trends. Bryusov's criticism of the MAT for leaching the theatrical out of theatre and obscuring drama behind a screen of trivial and pointless naturalistic detail, his plea that it stop imitating life because stage art is essentially unrealistic, did not go unheeded. As the symbolists began to make inroads in the public consciousness, the MAT felt under pressure to adapt to the fashion and expand its spectrum of authors and styles. ND increasingly disdained KS's eagerness to experiment with staging and acting techniques, however, while KS chafed at the organizational and managerial tasks that fell to his lot.

Angered over the cool reception of Vacationers and what he saw as ND's condescension, Gorky turned his back on the MAT. He decided to open his own theatre, borrowing money from Morozov and taking Andreeva with him. Ultimately the couple decided that building a theatre was irrelevant in a time of barricades.

To **Nemirovich-Danchenko**. After 25 July 1904, Lyubimovka.

Dear Vladimir Ivanovich,

Troubles come not single spies -- and on us as on poor Makar the blows are raining down.[1]

1) We have lost two dramatists,[2]

2) Savvushka [Morozov],[3]

3) a useful actress [Andreeva],[4]

4) for the time being, apparently an urgently needed actress (I mean Olga Leonardovna [Knipper] who will need a lot of time to recover).[5]

5) No repertoire.

6) You have no time to finish writing your play.[6]

7) My wife has fallen ill and is not getting any better.

8) Kachalov is looking for greener fields.[7]

9) Vishnevsky is winning laurels in Essentuki and has quite outstripped us when it comes to art.

10) The war and its influence on the coming season.[8]

11) All our plays (Yartsev, Chirikov) are being done by Komissarzhevskaya in Saint Petersburg,[9] and we have nothing to take on tour.

12) We must expect our actors to be called up for the war at any minute.[10]

13) I have lost faith in myself as an actor and my wretched health has convinced me of the need to take up my position in the second rank of my own free will...

To all these minuses there is only one plus. The friendly work of those who love and understand our concern. There are few of us. So we must do even more to forget everything personal, the vying for first place, and the petty passions that degrade us, and do the impossible to save the season and the concern.[11]

If that is not done – this is our last year of existence.

The picture I paint of the season is this:

Maeterlinck (might have a certain artistic success, financially so-so) --

    15 performances @ 1300 rubles   20,000

Naidyonov and Yartsev[12] (as I am very doubtful whether the Chirikov will be permitted) –

    15 performances @ 1300 rubles   20,000

One-acts, I have a feeling, won't work again and if they do, only at matinees and school performances --[13]

    15 matinees @ 900 rubles   14,000

I won't believe in the Chirikov until there is a script that has been passed by the censor.

The Cherry Orchard (perhaps, owing to Chekhov's death the play will finally be understood) –

    15 performances @ 1300 rubles   20,000

Uncle Vanya (ditto, because of Anton Pavlovich's death) –

    10 performances @ 1500 rubles   15,000

Three Sisters (for the same reason) –

    5 performances @ 1300 rubles   7,000

Seagull (revived, with magnificent new sets) –[14]

15 performances @ 1500 rubles	23,000

The Lower Depths –

5 performances @ 1300 rubles	7,000

Pillars –[15]

5 performances @ 1200 rubles	6,000

Fyodor they say will be banned.[16]

The Sunken Bell – no actors.[17]

The rest have either been sold off or are out of the repertoire.[18]

So, at a rough estimate

100 performances at	132,000

Total performances (say) 180, with a budget of 210, 220,000…

We need 80 performances – at 78,000, i.e., three plays, or, if the Chirikov is permitted, *two*.

The Chirikov is trivial artistically but could prove profitable –

20 performances @ 1300 rubles	26,000

Ivanov – must be staged, or we lose it forever. I don't consider it profitable but with a good production, something might be made of it

25 performances @ 1300 rubles	33,000

? some play or other of great interest.

If it's yours –- then the season would be complete (I have no faith in the Gorky however he rewrites it).[19]

One cannot come up with a play that would reach 35 performances.

Let's suppose a play with 15 performances @ 1,300 – 20,000.

Then the season will be covered financially.

So which play?

In the first place I propose *Beyond Human Power* (Bjørnson) if we can get it past the censor.

Second place – Ibsen's *Ghosts*.

Third place – Strindberg's *The Father* as there is much talk about the boldness and audacity of this writer.

Fourth place – *A Month in the Country*, because we do not have the strength to come up with motifs and put it on as we would wish.

I will say nothing about *Rosmersholm*, because so far I don't understand the play.[20]

The amount of work is appalling – and almost impossible. Nevertheless it will have to be done by three or four pairs of hands.

Maeterlinck is a new little note in the literary sense.

One-acts are also a novelty in the formal sense.

Naidyonov and Yartsev are a slight compromise, which will be submerged in the rest of the repertoire. The Chirikov (?) as well.

Ivanov
Seagull } our debt to Chekhov.

Bjørnson, Ibsen, Strindberg – the old but honourable note. Something substantial.

I have spent a very nasty summer as usual, and the death of Chekhov has shattered me, travel polished off the rest. I hear you had an unsatisfactory vacation too.

I am troubled by something which is nobody's fault… and which no one can in any way correct. At the funeral and other initiatives to immortalize the memory of Chekhov our theatre has stood on the sidelines. Nevertheless we must think of something for the future. Aside from some series of Chekhov performances (I call them a Chekhov week), aside from a special Chekhov production (I forgot to mention this most important matter above) put together out of his one-acts and vaudevilles, e.g., *Calchas* (never performed), *The Celebration*, *The Wedding*, *The Dangers of Tobacco*… etc. Aside from all that we must come up with something; either a prize for the best play, or a grant of some kind… […]

1904-05 became known as 'the ill-starred season.' An evening of Maeterlinck one-acts, Ibsen's Ghosts *and the launching of a studio, against the background of an unsettled political situation, failed to stimulate the theatre's creative juices.*

To **his wife Mariya Lilina.** 15 August 1904, Moscow.
Darlingest!

I do not know why you think I am angry with you. I am simply out of sorts. I have not dragged myself to work, I get worried about you when we are apart, I feel lonely, I want to help you, I cannot or do not know how, I feel I have lost my influence over you.

I am working alone in the theatre these days (Kaluzhsky's still here, the rest do nothing, and you can't shift them in any way), I still get upset as an artist, because I cannot find the right tone for Maeterlinck, the war, but most important, I cannot wait for the time when you yourself are ready to go again and become a healthy little darling.

At such moments, it's true, I lose my temper when impatient with someone. Whether it's the doctors who do not to know how to help you, myself for being impatient, and you for being illogical in your way of life. All this is nerves as the season is about to start. I will not go to Lyubimovka because I have to organize the work, explain it, otherwise the whole season will fail. I also won't go because I am afraid to be unbearable again and spoil the life you have organized. […]

Your friend and husband Kotun

On 2 October the evening of Maeterlinck one-acts 'The Blind,' 'The Intruder' and 'Interior' opened and was savaged by both critics and audience. The MAT's upbeat approach ran counter to Maeterlinck's symbolist emphasis on Death. A public, its nerves on edge from current events, was unsympathetic to the musical cadences of the dialogue and the passivity of the characters. ('The Blind' and 'Interior' had twenty-two performances, 'The Intruder' only seventeen.)

On 21 December 1904 Morozov sent the shareholders of the MAT a letter to explain why he had broken with the theatre. Without naming names, he blamed ND for preventing the theatre from achieving its potential, and praised KS as 'its talented creator'. That same day saw the first performance of the Chekhov miniatures 'The Schemer', 'The Surgery,' 'Non-Com Prishibeev.' They were afterpieces to Yartsev's At the Monastery (directed by ND; sixteen performances); critics thought the miniature a return to the theatre's strength (twenty-five performances.)

The new year began with the humiliating fall of Port Arthur which further discredited the government. An epidemic of strikes of almost every trade and profession ensued.

To **Vera Kotlyarevskaya**. 3 January 1905, Moscow.

Dear Vera Vasilievna!

[…] You know of our loss.[21] Thank you for your sympathetic letter.

It was very hard to perform during our late mother's illness and to communicate by telegraph before her death. The situation with the theatre was such that even on the day of the funeral cortege I had to play a comic role [Count Shabelsky in *Ivanov*]. Concerns before and after the funeral, daily acting (I have already acted more than 80 times),[22] daily rehearsals, want of plays... but chiefly – the war, hopes and disappointments in internal politics, all this has exhausted us dreadfully.

To top it all a new competitor – a theatre – forces us to exert our last bit of strength. Someone has been circulating rumours throughout Moscow and the newspapers that there is dissension in our ranks, that our business is falling off, that I am leaving the Art Theatre and moving to a Petersburg ladies' theatre, the actors are being bashed.[23] They are a gullible tribe and succumb easily to slander and gossip. The literary world has begun to despise us, because they are starting to be won over by Zhelyabuzhskaya [Andreeva] and the Petersburg theatre. Gorky has inflicted every possible insult on us – and this is all happening at the moment when there is talk of constitutional self-government, and this is done by people who consider themselves to be heading the liberals or leading the mob. This is no good!.. It is even destructive!..

Do not fear for the theatre. Our folks are good lads. They have shown once again that they know how to look after their own business. Those it needs will not leave it; those who do not understand will leave, and good riddance... A good spirit of camaraderie prevails in the troupe, as never before. The exit of a few individuals cleansed the atmosphere; nevertheless the season is boring, without interesting novelties, although we have succeeded in presenting two new little notes: Maeterlinck and the [Chekhov] one-acts. The public reacted to them either hostilely or coldly, but at the present time one needs bold statements, liberal emotion and other non-serious attractions of this kind for the general public. Most of all we were afraid we would be thrown out of the theatre.[24] We have managed to hold on to it for a year. […]

Your devoted and affectionate K. Alekseev […]

On 9 (22) January, 'bloody Sunday', an unarmed assembly of petitioning workers marching on the Winter Palace was cut down by Cossacks. Believing that the Revolution had begun, Gorky abandoned any vestige of pacifism and called for an equally sanguinary reaction. He was arrested and imprisoned.

Rehearsals for Ghosts *('a Norwegian Uncle Vanya') began by plunging into Scandinavian local colour. KS and ND were both beginning to feel dissatisfied at the thought that the theatre was marking time, capitalizing on its past successes, and not moving forward by taking chances.*

On the evening of 24 January for the first time KS saw the American dancer Isadora Duncan (1878-1927) perform. She had been working in Europe from 1903 and was considered by some ground-breaking in her choreography. KS was enchanted by her 'art and taste' and attended every one of her concerts.

On 28 January a double bill of Naidyonov's The Prodigal Son, *directed by Luzhsky under KS's supervision, and Chirikov's sub-Chekhovian comedy* Ivan Mironych *opened and managed to reach thirty-one performances. Naidyonov, despite Gorky's persuasion, was never again to submit a play to the MAT.*

The Tsar's uncle, Grand Duke Sergey, the detested Governor General of Moscow, was assassinated by a bomb thrown by the Socialist Revolutionary I. Kalyaev in broad daylight. The immediate result was the Tsar's manifesto that he intended to maintain the autocracy.

Diary, 4 February 1905.

Learned of the murder of Sergey Aleksandrovich (Grand Duke) – work stopped, people scattered... In the evening the performance was cancelled on account of mourning. What an accident-prone theatre. It is suffering from the total violence and lawlessness. Losses – 2000. In the evening we gathered for this occasion.

Gorky remained under police surveillance. After the rejection of Vacationers, *he forbade the MAT to dramatize and stage his story 'Chums'.*

Ghosts *opened on 31 March, directed by KS assisted by ND. Again the complaint ran that the production missed the author's pessimism and determinism, and was merely a snapshot of a stuffy Norwegian family. KS attributed the failure to a cerebral, rather than an emotional approach to the play. At the end of the season it was dropped after thirteen performances.*

The MAT toured to St Petersburg; their annual appearances were now so anticipated that tickets were scalped and few members of the lower classes could get into the theatre.

To **his children.** Between 14 and 18 April 1905, Petersburg.
My precious Kiryulya and my dear little boy Igorechek!
Christ has arisen!..
Here it is lonely, boring and empty without Mama and you.
I even thought of writing you to come here, but there is no room in the lodgings. It is a pity to be away from you, poor little things, during all the holidays, but what am I to do.
It is so boring to rehearse all these old plays all day long... and set up the scenery...
The weather here is good, how are things with you?

Figure 36 Stanislavsky with Lilina, Igor and Kira

I read that the butchers have gone on strike in Moscow, which means, you are stuck without beef. This is very beneficial, especially for Kirlyulya and Igorechka. You and I shouldn't eat this sort of thing on account of our stomachs. The most interesting thing here in Petersburg is the exhibition of portraits. In the enormous Tauride palace they have brought together from all over Russia portraits of our great great grandmothers and grandfathers, and what not! This is very a propos for me, especially now, when we want to stage *Woe from Wit*. In the exhibition we can find Famusov and Sofiya and Skalozub. I will go there every day and sketch it all. There are also pictures that depict rooms. I might be able to pick up all sorts of sets for *Woe from Wit*.

One picture is very good and naïve. A stern husband with a lash is going out the door, while his wife and grown-up daughter are on their knees, in the middle of the room. Obviously, they committed some offense and were punished. So you see how strict they were in those days! 'You types nowadays! Fancy that!'[25]

I am very glad that they have put us up in lodgings. Here it's peaceful and quiet, no one gets on your nerves, the noisy Nevsky is some distance away. The landlady seemed to be nice and doesn't hang around. Although today when I brought her the rent money, she took it and suddenly pulls out five enormous copybooks... It turns out she writes plays. Now I'm quaking with fear... what if she knocks on my door, sits herself down and starts reading? Then I'll have to kill her with a paperweight, as in Chekhov [his story 'A Drama'], and instead of Moscow I'll end up in the Peter and Paul fortress. [...]

Your dearest Papa

KS feared that the theatre was veering back and forth in its style and decided to create a laboratory studio to experiment with new techniques of stage art and actor training. It would attract young talent to rejuvenate the parent company. To this end he turned to Meyerhold. Since leaving the MAT, Meyerhold had toured as an actor and director in his Fellowship of New Drama, with a repertoire combining MAT hits with more daring modernist plays. KS took the entire expense of the Studio on himself and rented the former Nemtchinov Theatre on Povarsky Street. He invited to it Ilya Aleksandrovich Sats (1875-1912), composer and conductor. A manic-depressive Tolstoyan, who had done time in Siberia for anti-government agitation, he had been introduced to the MAT by Sulerzhitsky. He helped KS realize the importance of music to a production.

This move began to widen the schism in the theatre between conservatives and innovators. Although Meyerhold swore allegiance to the MAT, his aims – to be unique and 'to ignite the imagination in a search for the poetry and mysticism of the new drama'– were at variance with the parent company's principles. 'The theatre must be a cloister', he argued. 'The actor must always be a dissenter.' This was diametrically opposed to ND's ideas of social progress. ND, who resented his former student's turn away from him and towards KS, was to characterize the Studio as 'a pesthouse'.

The Studio repertoire was made up of modern European playwrights with a poetic bent: Hauptmann, Hofmannsthal, Przybyszewski and Maeterlinck. As KS began to work with Meyerhold in May two blows fell, one private, one public. Sergey Morozov shot himself in Nice on 13 May. The second Pacific squadron was defeated by the Japanese at Tsushima the following day. The good news was that KS and some of his actors convinced Gorky to give the MAT his new play Children of the Sun. *Consequently, Mariya Andreeva deigned to return to the troupe.*

To **Mariya Andreeva.** 19 May 1905, Moscow.
Much esteemed Mariya Fyodorovna!

[...] The death of dear Savva Timofeevich and the destruction of the squadron have brought my nerves to the breaking point. Only today have I recovered and can carry out the commissions of the board.

Will you please assent to these matters concerning the productions.

1. Your service to the theatre will begin from the moment the annual vacation ends, that is from 15 June 1905.

2. On returning to the troupe, you will accept the salary that had been assigned you at the time you left on vacation, that is 3600 r. in wages plus 300 r. due you as a raise. To wit 3900 r. a year.

3. The rehearsals will begin, as always, around 1 August; we will expect you at that time.

If you wish to become familiar with all the work on *Woe from Wit*, in which we ask you to assume the role of Sofiya, you will have to arrive now, before the troupe goes on leave, that is before 1 June, or ask some friend to acquaint you with the general details of our preparatory work. Unfortunately, I am not capable of taking this on, because I am mighty busy right now.

4. Please offer some way to indemnify the theatre in case of your leaving Moscow, which you admitted was possible. Will you agree to have alternates for your new roles and if so, what is to be the system of alternation? The board considers this to be a ticklish question and asks you to resolve it yourself.

5. An even more ticklish question has to do with the old roles. The board has categorically refused to resolve it. You yourself can settle it simply and in a comradely fashion… Your good relations with Kachalova can resolve this question favourably.[26] Arrange with her the disposal of old roles by a comradely mutual agreement.

6. Looking over the new repertoire of four plays at the moment (*Woe from Wit*, *The Drama of Life*, *Children of the Sun*, *Rosmersholm*), we see work for you: Sofiya in *Woe from Wit* and one of the roles in *Children of the Sun*. What will happen beyond that is for the moment unknown. It is impossible to dismiss actresses whom we have had to take on. To leave them without work is also impossible. Do not be exigent and unjust to the board, if it has not managed to satisfy you entirely with artistic work.

I await your confirmation of all these matters.

Aleksey Maksimovich's decision to assign us his wonderful play was greeted with excitement. We are all delighted and send him our sincere and friendly greetings.

I kiss your hand, rejoice in your return, if it will not be temporary, and secure your connection with the theatre forever.

Respectfully and devotedly yours K. Alekseev.

Andreeva agreed to these conditions, though doubting if she was young enough to play Sofiya. She rehearsed it but never played it because she left the theatre again before Woe from Wit *opened.*

Stanislavsky decided to direct the four-act Livets spil *(1896) by the Norwegian Knut Hamsun; the title,* The Game of Life, *was misleadingly translated into Russian as* Drama zhizni *or* The Drama of Life. *After KS read it to the company, he and Meyerhold prepared a new style of rehearsal, whereby, without preliminary discussions or a directorial plan, the actors would get on their feet and conduct their 'own experiments.' ND objected strongly to this improvisational approach as leading to confusion and waste of time. He found it an abnegation of the director's responsibility and a repudiation of the sedulous preparation and 'table rehearsals' the MAT had perfected. He sent KS a twenty-eight-page letter spelling out their differences, maligning Meyerhold and raking up past failures, while insisting on the need to preserve good relations.*[27]

To **Nemirovich-Danchenko**. Between 10 and 28 June 1905, Moscow.
Dear Vladimir Ivanovich!

I admire some of your qualities too, your talent, intelligence and so on… and I am distressed that our relationship has deteriorated… I rack my brains over how to improve it.

I expected rather different words from you and therefore your letter, for all the good intentions for which I thank you, has not achieved its desired effect. I don't think that our relations can be improved by explanations. That is too painful for my (perhaps very bad) character and dangerous for your touchy self-esteem. Shouldn't we look for some other means? Let's replace talk with deeds. That is the most powerful weapon you hold -- against me. Believe me, no one admires you more than I, in periods of your great work. Unfortunately, my wretched character prevents me from speaking frankly and revealing my feelings.

That is one of the reasons that even now will not let me answer your letter point for point. I assure you, it would not do any good. But the main thing is I am not in a fit state to do so now because of the state of my nerves.

I absolutely have to forget last season as quickly as possible, forget the Art Theatre for a time. Otherwise I can't get started on *The Drama of Life*.

Things may be as you describe them. It's all my fault: my homegrown despotism, my whims, my willfulness and the vestiges of my amateurism. Even if everything in the theatre is going well.

I ask only one thing of you. Make a life in the theatre possible for me. Allow me at least some satisfaction, for without it I cannot go on working. Don't advance the time when I shall lose even my love for and faith in our theatre *forever*. Understand that at present, like all of us, I am far too concerned about what is happening in Rus. Let us not talk about professional jealousies and vanities. For heaven's sake, I have done with them forever, if only because I have aged a great deal. There was never any jealousy in my directing. *I do not like this* activity and I do it out of necessity.

When it comes to acting I have subdued my vanity, I constantly step aside for everyone and have made the sign of the cross over myself. From now on I shall act only lest I forget how to show others.

Demonstrate *at least some* appreciation of my internal struggle and victory over myself and don't remind me of my successes as a director, on which I spit.

I would never before have let anyone else have a role I was right for, -- even now I do it with great distress -- but how easily I have *always* done it in the field of directing. It costs me nothing to hand over to someone else a play that is to my taste, once I believe that he can bring it off.

Isn't that clear proof that I am an actor by nature and not a director at all. I cannot keep from smirking with delight when I am praised for my acting and I laugh when I am praised for directing.

My success as a director is needed by the theatre, not me, and I rejoice in those circumstances *only* for its sake. Never settle any accounts with me on that score. Take me off the playbills once and for all. In this -- I am not your rival. Think rather what it cost me to give up pride of place as an actor -- to Kachalov and others. I did it for the concern and my family and from now on I have no personal vanity. On the contrary, I have become stricter and more jealous in regard to the concern itself, from which I demand even more, to compensate for all I have crushed in myself. I now have the right to demand widespread, public theatrical activity throughout the whole of Russia even if... and in that respect it will be impossible to restrain my homegrown despotism. I may end up beating out my brains, but ...it may be that I shall die in peace.

Therefore I cannot go into detail about: what kind of person Meyerhold is, great or small, shrewd or simple... I need him... because he is a great worker. I am delighted when he talks intelligently and it pains me when he offers up a bland staging-plan. If you broaden the scope of your concerns to such activities as the social and the civic...I shall be grateful to you, but if you reduce their scope to the dimensions of a mere business deal -- I shall suffocate and put up a fight, as befits a homegrown despot. Judge for yourself: can you achieve anything with such a homegrown despot – by means of explanations? I doubt it. What is needed is superhuman work. If you are summoning me to that, -- I shall be the most submissive of slaves.

Let us work as every *decent* man is *now obliged* to do.

Do as I do. Humble your vanity.

Defeat me with deeds and work. Then you will find no one more devoted than I. Explanations will not stand in for deeds... Let us take a breather and apply ourselves to *real* work.

Affectionately yours, K. Alekseev

ND deferred to these demands, but remained hostile to the Studio. He conceded that if it provided good new designers in the persons of Yegorov and Denisov to lighten Simov's load, there might be a benefit. Vladimir Yevgenievich Yegorov (1878-1960) had met KS in 1904. His approach to design was experimental, influenced by art nouveau and other modernist trends, with flat colours and straight lines.

To **Vera Kotlyarevskya.** 1 July 1905, Essentuki, Voynova's house, to 1 August, then in Moscow.

Dear and much esteemed Vera Vasilievna!

[...] I am more tired than ever before. In Moscow I worked with my last bit of strength at both theatres. Millions of all kinds of difficulties and aggravations. As you work you think that nobody needs it in these ghastly times. [...]

What am I to tell you about Charlotta. [28] It is a wonderful role for anyone who knows how to create characters. If you have emerged from the period when you want to be cute or charming on stage, of course, grab onto this role with both hands.

First of all you must live the character, without touching or flattening out the lines. Lock yourself in and play whatever comes into your head. Imagine this sort of scene: Pishchik is proposing to Charlotta, and she is his fiancée How will she behave. Or Charlotta has been dismissed, and she has joined a circus or a *café chantant*. How does she do gymnastics, or sing music-hall ditties. Do your hair in various styles and search within yourself for things that remind you of Charlotta. You will be reduced to despair 20 times, but don't give up your search. You will find it!.. Make this German woman you are so fond of speak Russian and observe: how does she pronounce words and what are the characteristics of her pronunciation. Don't forget to play Charlotta at a dramatic point in her life. Make sure to have her weep sincerely for herself. Through such an image you will find the whole gamut of notes you need.

This letter was broken off by a fever that I caught here. For 4 days I was bed-ridden. We definitely have to get out of here. Where to? Russia at the moment is so restless and agitated that to find a congenial place for a rest is almost impossible.

You say nothing about my notes. I understand perfectly that you find them totally useless... But... I need your criticism, not your praise... For heaven's sake, write your opinion in the *harshest* terms. I want to make one more ultimate effort at finding the right form. It would be a great pity if my material dies with me. So, don't stand on ceremony and bawl me out. I need it... [...]

Your devoted and loving K. Alekseev

The Drama of Life *is the second play in a trilogy revolving around the hedonistic Lapp thinker Ivar Kareno, who insists that a genius owes no obligations to anyone or anything; he is the sexual object of his employer's nymphomaniac daughter Teresita. She sinks the ship carrying Kareno's wife and then rejects him for an engineer. As is often the case in Scandinavian drama, a culminating fire is set that burns up Kareno's manuscripts and Teresita's little brothers. This sensational piece, which also features an epidemic fever infecting an open market, may have appealed to KS, because of its portrait of a beleaguered intellectual. In any case, he was determined to use it as a test case for a more stylized form of acting, free of psychological realism and mundane behaviourism. When Olga Knipper travelled to Norway, he solicited her for local colour. KS hoped Knipper could meet Hamsun, but the Norwegian dramatist was on his travels.*

To **Olga Knipper**. July 1905, Essentuki.
Dear Olga Leonardovna!

[...] After receiving your first letter, I rushed to set up a series of figures for the crowd, which I will send through this letter.

So here we are in the Caucasus, imagining a Norwegian crowd!

Test according to nature. Make changes and additions to everything that strikes you as characteristic in life. Sketch, as best you can, and a little bit more. Subscribe at the theatre's expense to the illustrated newspapers. In short, collect more, take things down.

Let us in corpore kiss your hands, but as directors – even your feet, if you will let us.

But these are the most essential points.

1) How is the telegrapher Jens Spira dressed?

2) How is the engineer Brede dressed (would you like him to be in a characteristic uniform or simply in a hat)?

3) How are the children Gustav and Elias dressed?

4) Shouldn't there be an interesting style for Kareno?

5) How do landowners such as Oterman dress?

Answer all these questions in great detail. For heaven's sake, make sketches, as best you can, not only in outline, but in colour. Make notes about fabrics (cloth, leather, felt, etc.). In short, everything in great detail. As to the common people, you know about that a hundred times better than I do.

Trace the drawings and put in everything that strikes you as characteristic. Make changes, additions. Everything that is unlike the Russian will serve our purposes. Everything that gives a sense of the unusual, decadent, impressionistic in costumes, objects or landscapes will also serve our purpose. In picking out postcards don't forget about *Lady from the Sea* and *Rosmersholm*; the interiors in *Lady from the Sea*... [...]

To **Maksim Gorky**. 20 July 1905, Essentuki.
Deeply esteemed Aleksey Maksimovich!

[...] How are things with my favourite *Children of the Sun*? Have you finished the play and when will you cheer us up by sending it? Perhaps you will read it aloud yourself? Sincerely trusting that our theatre's interests are not foreign to you, I make so bold as to acquaint you with our plans and hopes.

We dream of setting the date for the opening of the rehearsal season, 7 August, by reading your wonderful play and rapidly embarking on its staging. This would at once both inspirit the actors and ignite their energy. Here's what would be wonderful: to take up your play with renewed strength and imagination and work on it without the usual season's haste!

How can I convince you that this work will bear the very best fruit! To make this dream come true, we absolutely have to have the play by 1 August, because before rehearsals begin (7 August) we have to copy out six copies of the play and all the sides.

This work takes a great deal of time, especially if you bear in mind that copying your plays cannot be entrusted to a mere copyist. It has to be done in the theatre under a certain scrutiny. It takes more than a little time to get play passed – by the censorship.[29]

If any delay occurs in sending the play, we will have to change the plan of work completely and waste fresh forces on less interesting work. That would be a shame and would sharply alter the profile of the repertoire and the coming season for the worse.

It is not enough to pick good plays, one has to know how to open them at the right time, one must clinch the season from the very start, otherwise, it will be stillborn.

This would be a splendid repertoire for opening and clinching the season:

1. *The Seagull* (revival).[30]

The first play is rarely successful. *The Seagull's* reputation is already established. The audience expects it and asks for it, since it has been out of the repertoire for 4 years.

2. *The Drama of Life* by Knut Hamsun.

The play will not be a success, but there will be plenty of discussions and arguments about it.[31] That is the best way to shake up the public.

3. *Children of the Sun*.

Your play will show up at the very best moment of the season for new plays, that is the end of October and the beginning of November. So as not to spoil this order, *The Drama of Life* and your play have to be finished before the end of the season.

If there is a delay, the picture is altered.

First of all, we will have to rehearse your play over the course of the season, when evening performances will weary and distract the actors.

Second, your play will be ready no sooner than December. At that time the public's attention is worn down and coarsened. Besides, there will be no time for the play to be performed the desired number of times during the season.

In terms of the theatre's interests this is our reasoning: the most difficult and dangerous season stands before us.

On one hand, the public has been distracted from the theatre by political events. On the other hand, the terms of the theatre's lease and budget have increased to such an elevated figure that we have to tremble for the future of the institution.

It is imperative to win the season at once.

The most powerful and interesting play is, of course, *Children of the Sun*.

These, dear Aleksey Maksimovich, are our plans and calculations. I wanted you to know them and take them into account.

Forgive me if I have wearied you with my letter. [...]

Cordially devoted and respectfully yours

K. Alekseev [...]

By mid-summer the Russian Empire was seething with unrest. Defeats in the war with Japan, the shut-down of basic industries, mutinies within the army and navy (among them, the famous Battleship Potyomkin *revolt in Odessa), pogroms against the Jews in Southern Russia, and uprisings among the ethnic minorities created the background against which KS, characteristically, concentrated on his theatrical experiments. The work at the Studio was finally ready to be shown to the 'family'.*

To **his wife Mariya Lilina**. 12 August 1905, Moscow
[*Throughout the letter, KS gets the dates wrong by one day: Gorky read on 7 August and they travelled to Pushkino on the 11th.*]
My priceless dearest darling!

[...] I have returned here with great energy and pleased with the work. At 8 a.m. Gorky read the play... The troupe liked it and accepted it. Mariya Fyodorovna was modest and sat apart from everyone else... out of modesty. Gorky was enchanting and charming. He is obviously glad to return to the Art Theatre and is trying to visit us as usual when he can, to establish the best and simplest relations with everyone. At 8 p.m. there was a meeting, and Vladimir Ivanovich was energetic.

9 a.m. the costumes for *Woe from Wit* were gone over. We did a lot. 9 p.m. I was on stage blocking the first act of *The Drama of Life*. At 10 a.m. I was at the Studio Theatre put-in with Popov.[32] Everything there was ready in rough shape, and Popov is working splendidly. For now I'm calm and don't have to think about it.

At 10 I staged the first act of *The Drama of Life*. At 11 a.m. I was in the office of the 'Vladimir Alekseev' company. At 11 p.m. – staged Act 2. On the 12th (I got the dates confused), in short, yesterday was a wonderful day. It was devoted to a review of the studio's summer work.

At the Art Theatre the rehearsals were cancelled and many members of the troupe left for Pushkino: Vishnevsky, Knipper, the Kachalovs, Muratova, Mariya Fyodorovna, Gorky, Kosminskaya, Gribunin, Zvantsev et al. The day was superb. They brought along a picnic. At Mamontovka the whole troupe came to meet us. General greetings, animation, trepidation. Mamontov came too, and all the youngsters: artists, sculptors et al. At noon [Hauptmann's comedy] *Schluck and Jau* began. Fresh, young, inexperienced, original and charming. Of the youngsters Baranov acts magnificently [as Jau]. A success, animation and a wonderful impression.

An improvised lunch, a game of tennis, skittles, dinner, set up by Meyerhold in an ancient alley. Heated debates, youthful dreams.

At 6 [Ibsen's] *Love's Comedy* – it is weak, childish, but one still had to admit that there is good raw material in the troupe. [Maeterlinck's] *The Death of Tintagiles* created a furore. It is so beautiful, novel, sensational. Meyerhold got an ovation. Well done. The whole troupe accompanied us to the station. Gorky was in good form and spoke in a fascinating way. At the Moscow station supper – very animated. Today the factory and at night casting the roles in the Gorky play. [...]

Ever yours Kontunchik [...]

To **his wife Mariya Lilina**. 14 August 1905, Moscow.

Beautifulest-darlingest!

[...] Something super-stupid has occurred to me. The fact is that, with all the publicity, it is imperative that Gorky's play go first. Otherwise there will be a disastrous flop – a financial one. So far I have perfidiously dodged taking part in the play, even though the role [of the scientist Protasov] is appropriate and interesting. I foisted it on Kachalov, despite Gorky's request. I absolutely have to lay out the play, that is two acts, write the director's plan, make the models and help find the images of the characters. After that I might leave if only for two weeks. [...]

Bless you and the children tenderly and lovingly.

Tenderly loving Kotik

To **Nemirovich-Danchenko**. Friday, 9 September 1905, Sevastopol.

Dear Vladimir Ivanovich!

The third act is defective in that it can take place in the morning, at night, in the evening. It is outside of time and space. Anything you please... Personally -- I get the sense of an overcast rainy day.[33]

I am firmly convinced that no better ending could be contrived than yours. Psychology has nothing to do with it. There are millions of ways to go mad. The important thing is that this ending should close the act well and in an original manner.

Figure 37 The Studio troupe, 1905. Meyerhold is standing second from the left, in the shadows

I will stand up for it with might and main!

I'm afraid Aleksey Maksimovich is confusing and intimidating Mariya Fyodorovna, but how I am to deal with it – I still don't know. He stitched together the part for her, and the character is full of holes. [34] I'm afraid I'll have to get closely involved, or else later on I'll be accused of God knows what.

I have written half the 4th act.

It is difficult. There is little space on the ground-plan.

Don't forget that the gates in Act 3 are to be broken down by the mob [in Act 4].

And what about the [censor's] license? Oy – this is awful. [35] One more thing we forgot to discuss before we left.

I am quite alarmed that Meyerhold has no alternate as Treplyov [in *The Seagull*]. [36]

In the Studio everything depends on him and he is already overtaxed. Just now Repman's [37] wife is about to give birth, and he will drop out just at the hottest time for the theatre. We need Meyerhold especially now. He is needed at every *Seagull* rehearsal. There is no one to alternate with him. He would hardly require many rehearsals. [...]

If work comes to a halt in the Studio -- we have to postpone the opening, and then I am in trouble. That will affect me financially, because I have put aside no more than 20,000 to cover losses. An alternate is indispensable, particularly in the early period. Later on, when the studio business has got going, Meyerhold will have much more free time. I have nothing against his taking part in *Seagull*. On the contrary. I am very glad for the Art Theatre, which does not have a Treplyov, but I am afraid that in the early period Meyerhold might start cutting corners at either the Art Theatre or the Studio [...]

Yours K. Alekseev

Intrigues and discontent were roiling the Studio company. The actors felt they had reached an impasse and wrote to KS asking for work that would invigorate their energy and spirits. An attempt to recreate the commedia dell'arte *thwarted by the Ministry for Internal Affairs's ban of S. Razumovsky's play* Pulcinella, *though KS protested that it had no political* sous-entendus.

The date set for opening of the Studio was 21 October. That month, however, saw the arrest of the leaders of the powerful railway union and the railways went on strike, leading most of the factories to down tools. On 14 October work at the Studio was halted because of ongoing events; the next day an announcement was posted: 'In view of the outage of electrical lighting rehearsals are cancelled, and the start of the season is put off to an unspecified time.' After seven months of work KS closed the Studio. Its actors demanded the six month's remainder of their salaries and so he paid off all the contracted salaries for the year up to 1 May 1906. He told the participants that the Studio had eaten up half his fortune (18,000 rubles), but the chief motive for its closure was artistic: KS considered Meyerhold's highly conventionalized approach to staging to be wrong-headed. The last rehearsals were, in his opinion, masterpieces of ineptitude.

Diary.

I am the party who suffers most in this failed undertaking, but I have no right to have bad memories of it. The Art Theatre must preserve an even better memory of its stillborn offspring, because it alone can take reasonable advantage of the results of its youthful fermentations. With their help the Art Theatre will be rejuvenated, renewed.

The political unrest in Moscow culminated in armed uprisings. The strikers demanded a constituent assembly based on universal suffrage. The MAT decided to cancel the 14-19 October week of performances in sympathy with the strikers. Houses had been sparse in any case, except on subscription nights. The Tsar's proclamation of 17 October 1905 guaranteed civil rights; the following day the Social-Democratic politician Baumann was murdered by the secret police. On 20 October workers gathered for his funeral were shot down by Cossacks. A petition, which KS signed, was presented to the newly created Duma demanding a Committee of Public Safety and a municipal militia.

Children of the Sun had its premiere on 24 October, ran for 21 performances and closed on 4 December.

To **Vera Kotlyarevskaya**. 3 November 1905, Moscow.
Dear Vera Vasilievna!

I am a scoundrel and an ignoramus, but do not stop loving me! I carried out your commission as badly as a member of the Black Hundreds[38]... I remitted the money to Mariya Vasilievna [Pushkareva], wore myself out, and, when I happened by chance to have a free hour, -- just my luck... I lost the address and could not remember your sister's last name.

There is an excuse. You know how it always goes. Life is flowing along quietly, peacefully... Then all of a sudden!.. It is as if everything goes crazy. I am required simultaneously at 3 factories, the office, the Art Theatre, the studio and at home to protect my family. Just then I catch a cold and fever and just then miss a whole week of the repertoire and shut the door on my finger. Add to that business was bad at the Art Theatre, because the audience is staying home behind closed doors, and there was no way even to think about opening a studio in these troubled times. We had to close it and bury it, after bringing it as far as ringing up the curtain for the first time. I informed the actors just at the moment of liquidation! Well, the nation!.. I've been gutted!.. I will remember!

[...] I am tired at the moment. At such times you curse the actor's lot. Things are so oppressive and sorrowful for poor, ridiculous Russia. We have been through hard times that, in the course of events, we shall be chewing over for years. And then I feel as if since last we met I have aged 95 years. I feel as if I am an old man, and you are an old, old granny... Yes! It is impossible to consider that such freedom is rejuvenating. On sleepless nights I lie and wonder who I am, to what party I belong. It is hard to figure out! All the deviants, all the perverts are infecting each other. What a horror in such a time to have to act and rehearse that no-talent hodgepodge *Children of the Sun*. But it is even more horrible to behold what went on at the first performance. I have to tell you that Gorky and I were at one another's throats and I cannot see him anymore. He is the paragon of smugness and bad taste. He smashed up the whole production we had devised, and now the play is going as if it had been staged in Hayseed Centre. It's appalling!.. in its banality. Alas, that is precisely why it is having a success with the public. We got to Act 4. In rehearsals we rolled on the floor laughing hysterically when the Black Hundreds broke in and the janitor bashed the mob on their heads with a cardboard plank. Of course, when I was away they went and asked Gorky to delete that Punch-and-Judy detail – the gentleman lost his temper and refused to allow it.

We expected Homeric hilarity and the failure of the whole play. But... it created a panic – 30 separate swoons. The ladies' male escorts grabbed their pistols and were ready to shoot at the stage. The audience climbed on stage, shaking their fists. The devil knows what. It turns out that it took the mob for a real Black Hundred gang and thought that they had burst on to the stage. Professor [I. I.] Ivanov shouted that Kachalov had been killed, and they immediately went into hysterics.

It was a dreadful picture of barbarism and ignorance.

After that evening – I suddenly got tired and so far cannot relax. You see how obstinate I am. Not a word about politics. I gave myself my word and stick to it. Now there is no politics, but there is gossip, the worst old wives' tales, the most vulgar sort.

Now we are rehearsing *Woe from Wit* – and taking pleasure in it. The only comfort of my present existence.

Be well, do not be angry, do not curse and forget

Your devoted K. Alekseev [...]

The failure of a full-fledged revolution led by workers alienated the sympathies of the general public. Both reactionaries and revolutionaries were discredited. Kotlyarevskaya had heard rumours that the MAT had dissolved and that KS had joined a nationalized Maly Theatre.

To **Vera Kotlyarevskaya**. 29 November 1905, Moscow.
Dear Vera Vasilievna!

[...] The Art Theatre is intact for the moment. It is incurring enormous losses, and, probably, by the end of the season all its capital will be spent. (This between ourselves.)

Business is exceptionally bad. The entire audience has left Moscow. The budget is exceptionally large. We are under pressure from all sides.

Actually, there *has* been a proposal to merge with the Maly Theatre and found a state theatre. But... This business will have to be deferred until a State Duma is convoked. There is no way to benefit from a subsidy, especially a very big one, doled out by officials. To try for such a subsidy in a period of interregnum is no easy matter. I don't believe a merger with the Maly will produce a good result.

What we shall be doing next year is unknown. Probably we shall spend the whole year abroad, where we are in great demand. Perhaps we shall organize the tour during Lent.

The future is veiled in mist. Whether anyone needs art is a major question. Whether a theatre with high prices has a future is another.

I promised not to spread rumours about the Maly's proposition to us. I talk about it only to family and friends. Don't give me away! The mood is rather nasty... Everyone shirks work, no one has need of it at the moment. I feel like a buffoon... what a shame...

Woe from Wit could turn out to be original and not at all bad.

The factories go on strike at every turn. Something curious has occurred. Those factories that kept their skilled workers down by abusive treatment are able to make concessions. At places like that they are satisfied with very little. At our place for a long time concessions have gone as far as they can go, business brings in an insignificant percentage. There is no way to make fresh concessions, and our skilled workers' demands are 10 times greater than those made by men who were used to brutality. It gets you going in circles... The number of speeches I've made... and nothing comes of it.

At the moment we feel very put upon. [...]

Your devoted K. Alekseev

On 6 December, performances at the MAT were cancelled for two weeks. The Board of the MAT decided that guest appearances abroad for an indeterminate period of time was the only alternative to diminishing houses and malaise within the company. Their most loyal fans were upset by the decision, considering it an abnegation of responsibility to Russian culture at a time of crisis. The MAT left for its first international tour in early February 1906 and was away from Moscow until May, going into debt to do so. The 'Moskauer Künstlerisches Theater' opened in Berlin on 10 February.

To **his sister Zinaida**. 26 February 1906, Berlin.
Dear Zina!

[…] We are the heroes of the day. An extraordinary success. What the Russian papers report is only a fragment. The biggest success was had by *Uncle Vanya*… What reviews! We never had such reviews in Russia. What a sensitive appreciation of the Chekhov flavour! [...]

The most interesting and touching thing is the mutual affection that has sprung up between ourselves and the Hauptmanns. He is so captivated by us that the Germans no longer recognize him, whom they know to be a taciturn man. There have been a few amusing episodes. During the intermission, at a showing of *Uncle Vanya*, he went out into the lobby (to everybody's amazement), collected a crowd and declared for everybody to hear (sic):

'This is the most forceful theatrical impression I have ever had. Artistic gods, not humans are playing on that stage'.

After Act IV of *Uncle Vanya* he sat still in his seat a long time, biting a handkerchief. Then he stood up and wiped away his tears. Nemirovich-Danchenko came up to him, but all he said was:

'*Ich kann nicht sprechen.*'

Nemirovich told us he had the face of a Schiller or Goethe at that moment. After seeing *The Lower Depths* he said he had not slept all night, thinking about a play he intended to try and write specially for our theatre. In brief, Hauptmann has been conquered.

The next is Barnay. He is the director of the imperial theatres, but attends all our performances, presents us with flowers, and says for all to hear that he is learning from the Russians. Something quite unusual for Berlin occurred today. They have a critic here, by the name of Norden.[39] He writes reviews in exceptional cases (the local Stasov[40]), always fulminating. He has never praised anyone yet. Today, in a short article, he wrote roughly the following: 'A big event has occurred in Berlin. Russians have come here. Each generation is destined to encounter six to eight great artists. In this company all are artists, all in one place. That is brilliant. All criticism is silenced. Let not only actors, but also diplomats, politicians, and those who say Russia is a lost land, go to the theatre and make its acquaintance. A nation that has created such art and literature is a great nation. It has a culture, but we do not know it. It is unlike ours, but it will do us good to get to know it better.' […]

To **his brother Vladimir.** Before 6 March 1906, Berlin.
Dear Volodya!

I have never had to work the way I do now. Not only by day, but by night as well. I have to turn a pigsty into a respectable establishment. The punctuality of the Germans, their cleanliness, work ethic – all that is a myth. In no Russian province have I ever seen such a dissolute bunch as here: they not only pick us clean and rob us blind, but in addition make fun of us and insult us in every conceivable way. That's how things went until the first performance, and what it cost us!.. not only financially, but in terms of morale. That's how things went until the first performance. It was a triumph, the like of which we have never seen in Moscow or Petersburg. The whole of Berlin: men of letters (Hauptmann, Schnitzler, Sudermann, Halbe, etc., etc.), scientists (all the famous professors and medical men), financiers (Mendelsohn and all the other bankers), Barnay, Duse, all the theatre managers and the 80-year-old Haase, the famous actor, who never leaves the house, and the famous critic Kerr.[41] Those two callers particularly surprised the Berliners, because they had renounced theatre. The next day we were swamped with articles. There are more than 100 newspapers here, with evening editions as well. All, without exception, printed tremendous articles, transports of delight. I have never seen such reviews. As though we were a revelation to them. Almost all of them raised the cry and ended their articles: we know the Russians are a hundred years behind the times politically but, good Lord, how far they have outstripped us artistically. Recently they took a beating at Mukden and Tsushima. Today they have won their first significant victory. *Bravo, Russen!...*

Everywhere actors and directors are being recommended to come and learn from us. The apogee of the success (a refined one) was achieved with *Uncle Vanya*. Hauptmann bawled like a baby and sat in the last act with a handkerchief to his eyes. In the intermission he (notorious for his reclusiveness) ran out into the foyer demonstratively and shouted out loud to the whole hall: 'This is the most powerful theatrical experience I have ever had. These are actors are not people, but gods of art!' Hurray for us! Of course, we were introduced to him and his wife. He fell immediately in love with us and stayed in Berlin until the end of our tour. After *Depths*, which had a dreadfully clamorous success (not as refined as *Uncle Vanya*), Hauptmann told us that he hadn't slept all night but thought about the play he wanted to write for our theatre. A regular visitor to our performances is Barnay. He has already seen all the plays twice, brings us wreaths with inscriptions 'To the best of theatres' and so on. Fr. d'Andrade and Spielmann[42] are very taken with us.

In short, in terms of success, we have had, as [Morozov] used to say, more than our fill.

The financial side is brilliant by Berlin standards, and everyone expresses amazement that we are making around 2,500 marks a night. The most popular theatre here is the Deutsches Theater, and that makes the same amount. But, alas, it's not enough for us, we are barely covering costs, which, I repeat, are appalling. We had dreamt of coming back with a tidy little sum. Everyone is unanimous in saying that you can't make money in Berlin, that here is where you gain a reputation and then you take this reputation, go to other cities and make a fortune. That's probably true, because the very best impresarios of the whole world flock here in Berlin like mice to cookie crumbs. Of the gentlemen who have not even seen us, some are inviting us to Austria, others to America, etc. I don't know if we shall be able to make a profit from our successes, but it is abundantly clear that we cannot do without another city. All this is very difficult to organize with my Moscow activities and my children. It is impossible to drag them around the

211

world with me. I confess that these trips are uncommonly interesting, because you make the acquaintance of interesting people, whom you wouldn't meet any other time... but... all the same – there's no place like home. It's cold and hostile here. It's a good thing that our success exceeded all expectations, for if we had flopped! It's ghastly even to think of, they would have pecked us to bits and gobbled us up. Yesterday Berlin gave us definitive recognition. A crown princess came and the crown prince was supposed to have been there as well. All night long there were phone calls from Potsdam so that we had to drag out the intermissions, because he insisted on attending at least the last act after his meeting. The last intermission dragged out interminably and they even informed the audience of the reason for this hiatus; finally Her Highness had someone phone that there was no point in drawing things out any more. Permission to begin was forthcoming, because his meeting had not yet ended. So he wasn't there. They expect him next time. People say that even Wilhelm intends to come. That would be the first instance of his attendance at a privately owned theatre. Today we received a request from the court to inform them of this week's performance schedule... The greatest handicap is ignorance of the language. The Germans were sure that we would be acting in German. When it was explained to them that Muscovites speak Russian, they were genuinely amazed by this brazenness: to come to Berlin speaking Russian. Good Lord, how people hate the Russians, but on the other hand the intelligentsia here is superb. It has great faith in Russia and ordinary Russian talent is sincerely taken to be genius.

How hard it is to open the Russian newspapers here and read about everything that is happening at home. It is especially hard because all our adversities are at best heading us in the direction of western culture – that is appalling. That culture is worth exactly 5 kopeks... There is no heart here – and that is why the critics mostly praise the heart of Russian man, given their own lack of strong emotion. [...]

Love and kisses.

Yours Kostya

The Berlin appearances were followed by a triumphal progress through Dresden, Leipzig, and Prague, but things began to fall apart in Vienna. Financial disagreements with the French director Lugné-Poë prevented the tour from going on to Paris, where Diaghilev would make a stir the following year. Instead, the itinerary took them to Wiesbaden where no smoking was allowed backstage. The Kaiser applauded loudly and awarded KS and ND the order of the Red Eagle, fourth class (they would be pilloried for this in Soviet times). Then came Dresden, Leipizig, Prague and Frankfurt-am-Main, Hanover, and Warsaw.

In Warsaw the question had arisen of the independence of the experiments of the co-founders and drawing a 'line of demarcation' that would allow them to continue to work together in a single theatre space. Back in Moscow in May, KS shared his concerns with Aleksey Aleksandrovich Stakhovich (1856-1919). They had first met when Stakhovich was adjutant to Moscow's tyrannical Governor General Grand Duke Sergey Aleksandrovich and was one of the MAT's first shareholder-patrons. After his *retirement in 1907 he would become an influential member of the MAT Board, and eventually even went on stage there and at Second Studio, teaching classes in manners and social deportment.*

To **General Stakhovich**. May 1906, Moscow. *Draft.*

If the fate of the Art Theatre is dear to you, come as soon as you can, before it is too late. [...] The theatre finds itself in great danger for financial reasons. Nemirovich and I cannot take on the responsibility for its fate, and therefore come as soon as you can to share it with us.

Here is why the responsibility is so great. I remind you of the kind of responsibility I'm talking about.

1) The Art Theatre – this is no accidentally composed troupe. It has been put together with love, assembled over the course of 20 years. Actors for this theatre are cultivated, not hired. The troupe can be split up in a day, but to assemble it a second time is impossible at any cost.

2) Six months ago people would have regretted the closing of the theatre and quickly forgotten it. Now Europe has learned about it, and its rebukes and sneers would rain down on us.

3) If somewhere on the horizon some glimmer of a stage art about to be born could be glimpsed, I would care less passionately about the fate of our theatre. What is to be done: no renascence of our art is to be seen either here or anywhere else. And you cannot name me a single institution or a single individual in whom one might invest one's hopes in this specific case. Everything is grey and empty. Not a single insignificant hint. After all, art is not created by a single individual. You need a whole group. You need a decade to give birth to new people, and until then the theatres will propagate vulgarity. I speak with utter conviction: with the closing of the Art Theatre Russian art will come to a stop and expire over many years.

Can this happen to the most vital institution on account of some 30-50 thousands at the very moment when Russian society is awaking and on the eve of Russia's flowering.

I know that in a few years great sums of money will arrive and be offered to revive a moribund theatre, but we shall have to answer: 'Too late. One must begin all over again, and for that I am not young enough.'

So I alerting you and everyone I can. You must alert those who understand the significance of our theatre, believe in our theatre!

The situation was ameliorated with the help of two men about town, the rich playboy Nikolay Lazarevich Tarasov (1882?-1910) and the rotund Nikita Fyodorovich Baliev (Mkitrich Balyan, 1877-1936). They became enthusiastic investors and Baliev began acting in small roles at the MAT in 1906.

During his summer vacation in Finland, KS tried to figure out why he felt so lifeless in his recent performances. He commenced an investigation of the creative processes of the actor and attempted to formulate 'certain principles' common to all great performances. He also sought to pursue the Studio experiments: he enrolled into the

MAT the poet Valery Bryusov who had attacked the theatre's naturalism, the composer Ilya Sats as leader of the musical division, and Leopold Antonovich Sulerzhitsky (1872-1916), who was promoted from informal and occasional helper to KS's unofficial assistant in the directorial sector. Trained as an artist, but expelled for his loudly-proclaimed political opinions, he was conscripted, but as a conscientious objector was tried and imprisoned. Behind bars 'Suler', as he was known, studied Tolstoy, who helped to liberate him and chose him to accompany the persecuted sect the Dukhobors (wrestlers with the spirit) to Canada. The twists and turns of Suler's career first brought him to the MAT in 1900, when a letter to KS analysing his interpretation of Stockmann led to a meeting. KS would work with him on The Drama of Life, The Life of Man, The Blue Bird, *and* Hamlet, *but he had no official status in the troupe and was frequently subjected to snubs by ND and other company members.*

ND wanted to open the season with Ibsen's Brand. *He was also in charge of staging the classic verse comedy* Woe from Wit *as a period piece, though KS was bothered that, in the role of Famusov, he was not given a single note.*

To **Nemirovich-Danchenko**. 19 September 1906, Moscow.
Dear, good Vladimir Ivanovich!

There is no point in quarrelling at the present time. Forgive me.

I, more than anyone, hate that tone in myself, which I was not able to restrain yesterday. It insults and degrades me more than anyone.

I sincerely repent of it and once again I apologize.

I have two reasons that mitigate my guilt.

First. One must never demand explanations from an actor whose nerves are in tatters after performing in the most difficult of acts.

Second. I can never reconcile myself to any crude behaviour or unchivalrous conduct in the theatre. When people I don't know abuse the theatre to me and I know they are right and I cannot enforce their silence or expose them as liars, I suffer more than anyone, because it is especially important to me that our theatre be not only artistic, but cultivated and polite in the highest degree. Otherwise it loses half its value for me.

When it seems to me that you, in your capacity as administrator, are making a mistake, I suffer in the most real sense and cannot sleep the whole night through and am more upset with you than anyone else can be. What is that, a token of love or bad feelings?

I will answer you with an example: 'A mother who spanks her child because he has crawled under a trolley-car displays the highest degree of love, not hate.'

You are one of the very few people I love, and therefore I am often too demanding, because you and I meet only on business, when there are too many reasons for clashing.

Forgive me, but do not misinterpret the state of my nerves. I embrace you and ask forgiveness. I wish very much that all those who witnessed yesterday's ill-fated scene could read this letter.

Yours K. Alekseev

I am writing badly, but today too the second act of *Woe from Wit* is to blame.

Woe from Wit opened on 26 September. Reaction ran the gamut from ecstasy to antagonism, for it broke with the traditions that the imperial theatres had, over half a century, established for its staging. KS felt the public's indifference and even hatred, and thought about giving up acting. Thanks to several changes of cast and a revised staging just prior to the Revolution, it ran to 205 performances.

To **Vera Kotlyarevskaya**. *Early October 1906, Moscow.*
Dear Vera Vasilievna!
    […] Dumas said: 'When everyone abuses something, it doesn't mean that it is bad. When everyone praises something, it is probably banal. When some abuse and others praise something, it is a success.' The press universally abuses us [for *Woe from Wit*], the public comes to blows in its arguments. That means it's a success. There are full houses 5 times a week. We ourselves consider the production extremely successful, although, of course, it is impossible to expect that there be suitable performers in the troupe for all 30 roles. I act my role with satisfaction, although I am not fond of it, but come before the audience with loathing. You cannot imagine the attitude of Schadenfreude and hostility directed at us by the Moscow public after our tour and successes abroad. This surprising result is pure Moscow. A very small group is proud of us. The whole remaining mass of obese bodies and souls hates success and ironically refers to us as 'the foreigners.' The press devotes no reportage to us. It is impertinent, impudent and mendacious to the point of cynicism. In order to besmirch us even more, it almost intrudes into our private lives. We make a profit because everyone is flattered to be a critic and show off his familiarity with *Woe from Wit*. In short, I observe such an appalling change in the public that we are beginning to think about moving to another city. The best we can hope for in the Moscow hole is to get past ten performances and charge 20 rub. for the first row. Then they'll respect us. They drench me in spittle, of course, for my Famusov, but I have already begun to despise the public and the Russian know-it-alls. No one is stupider than this sort of person. […]

Devoted K. Alekseev

The strain in the relationship between the co-founders had reached the breaking point. Each rehearsed his own production, either on stage or in the foyer.

To **Olga Knipper**. Before 3 November 1906, Moscow.
Dear, good Olga Leonardovna!
    I am writing this letter with the best of intentions and I very much *pray that you not misinterpret my good intentions*.
    Here's what it's about.
    I have undertaken to stage *The Drama of Life* to explore new forms.
    The theatre had thought it might take a risk with this play. If it goes on – fine, if it doesn't – they will put on other plays.
    The case is altered.

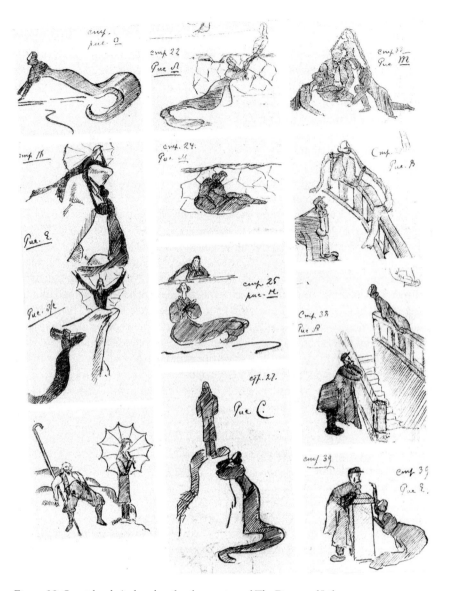

Figure 38 Stanislavsky's sketches for the staging of *The Drama of Life*

The repertoire has turned out so that a double responsibility falls on me.
The first is that the financial aspect of the concern might suffer from the play's failure.
The second is my responsibility for you. A leading actress, coming forward in a responsible role, may suffer on account of my, well, let's at least call it, -- obstinacy.
I willingly accept the first condition.

216

I cannot accept the second.

And therefore I consider it my duty, while it is still not too late, to refrain from my right as a director and allow you total freedom in the treatment of your role.

I do this *without any offense and wounded vanity.*

I have done everything I could, and was sincerely happy when I saw that genuine temperament, which I sought for the theatre: meanwhile I thought I am helping you gain a foothold in it, I was useful. Now though, having come to be convinced that you consciously despise this treasure, I am becoming harmful and therefore I fade into the background.

If you will allow me to give you some advice, -- turn to Vladimir Ivanovich and with him take the role into a tone which I cannot organically understand given the bent of my artistic nature. *I repeat, I wish this without any bad feelings.*

I have spoken with Vladimir Ivanovich on this subject and he amicably agreed.[43] God grant us success!

Yours affectionately K. Alekseev

The situation between ND and KS became more strained after a rough tech of Act 3 on 3 November. At a meeting of the shareholders, ND expressed a negative opinion of what he had seen. Nikolay Podgorny,[44] who was playing Kareno, was ill, and there were two candidates to take over the role: KS and Kachalov. ND feared the postponement of Brand *in which Kachalov was playing the lead, for he didn't think the alternate Leonidov suitable to open the season. Rather than accepting KS in the part, ND proposed that* The Drama of Life *be postponed to the following year, and* Brand *be opened, so that KS could begin work on Andreev's* The Life of Man. *At first the shareholders rejected the proposal, whereupon ND questioned his position in the MAT.*

To **Nemirovich-Danchenko**. Saturday, 4 November 1906, Moscow.
Dear Vladimir Ivanovich,

I cannot answer that part of your letter which concerns me personally.

Therefore I pass directly to the business part.

Here I have to repeat what I have already written to you today. I will play Kareno, if it is necessary; I will direct those plays that are assigned to me.

I can work energetically in an unsullied atmosphere, and if that expression is unclear, I am ready to explain it in the presence of all the shareholders. I have considered and still consider it my obligation to defer to all your demands relating to the literary aspect. As to the artistic one, I insist on what you arranged this spring in Warsaw.

I have publicly expressed my views on *Brand*. They are set out erroneously in your letter.

Personally I shall be very happy to let *Brand* go first, because I am mighty tired. Whether Kachalov can sustain it is a question I spoke to more than adequately at the meeting.

I shall be very happy for the theatre's sake to let *Brand* go first, with Kachalov, as our theatre will gain from it both artistically and financially.

Once more I emphasize that I am amenable to any arrangement.

I take no personal responsibility and will submit wholly to the joint decision of the shareholders.

It behooves you, as chairman, to convene them for a definite decision on the matter. I believe that my presence at that meeting is superfluous and even harmful.

In my capacity as a shareholder, I ask you to settle the matter as quickly as possible, so that we do not lose two days in which there are no performances.

I earnestly request you to acquaint the shareholders with the contents of this letter. As soon as I am notified -- I will show up at the theatre to work.

Yours K. Alekseev

ND asked KS only to make a token appearance at the shareholders' meeting and that he, ND, as chairman, would take full responsibility for the season. He also objected to the activities of Suler as an unrecognized employee of the MAT.

To **Nemirovich-Danchenko**. 4 November 1906, Moscow.

Dear Vladimir Ivanovich!

The chairman of the board is the speaker, leader and executive officer of the board of directors. The role you wish to have in our concern is called the managing director.

I agree to granting you these plenary powers, if the shareholders agree to it. Without a shareholders' meeting, I do not have the right to decide this matter.

I did not notify you *officially* about my invitation to and personal payment of Mr Sulerzhitsky. You had learned of it from private conversations, you had seen Sulerzhitsky directing on my responsibility and said nothing to me.

At that time our relations were simpler and it seemed strange to me to resort to bureaucratic procedures. On the official side and perhaps even the ethical side, -- I am in the wrong and I offer my apologies.

To rectify this mistake, I now address you officially with the application to acknowledge Mr Sulerzhitsky as my assistant. I assume responsibility both for his activities and for his financial remuneration. This question exclusively concerns the management that now exists. Therefore, in this matter, I give my vote, and also Stakhovich's vote, which I am able to certify by letters in my possession. I ask for a swift response to this request, because I cannot stage *The Drama of Life* without an assistant, given the daily performances and my obligations at the factory and the office.

So far I have tried to inform you of all the instructions I issued concerning the play I was directing. Rehearsals never began on stage without preliminary discussions with you. As for rehearsals in the foyer, they are always known from the book the actors sign.

In my capacity as an administrator and a stage director I am *obliged* to keep an eye on anything untoward that occurs in the theatre. I have the right to bring in any person I consider necessary for the theatre, and to answer letters addressed to my name, either by private members of the public, or by actors.

I don't think you wanted to deprive me of the right to talk to whom I please or write to whom I please.

As you are aware, I have shown you all the letters from authors.[45] If you know how to relieve me of the burden of talking to Naidyonov, Andreev, Kosorotov, Asch, Przybyszewski[46] and others who send me their plays, I shall be very grateful to you. This point in your letter is simply not clear to me.

I don't think you wanted to turn me into a silent partner. It's not a role for me. If the shareholders agree to release me from the onerous role of administrator in the middle of the season, -- I shall be glad to retire and thereafter shut my eyes to everything that goes on in the theatre, including things that threaten catastrophe.

In view of the confusion and danger our theatre finds itself in, as a shareholder and an administrator, I must protest that the question of the next play was resolved by a single individual. The ultimate decision of the shareholders concluded that *Brand* should be put on with Kachalov and *The Drama of Life* with me.[47]

I gave my consent and therefore will not take on any responsibility for altering the shareholders' decision.

Of course, you are free to act as you wish, on your own personal responsibility. One cannot be guided by the resolutions of absent shareholders. [...]

I can start on *The Drama of Life* at least tomorrow, but to do that first the question of Sulerzhitsky must be settled, because without him I cannot stage the play by myself. As to Hauptmann's play, -- I am very much in favour of approaching Efros. Have him translate it.[48] At least it will be successful.

Yours K. Alekseev

I earnestly request you to communicate this letter to the shareholders.

As to the school, I am ready to cease my involvement, but on condition that you authorize me to tell the pupils, whom I promised to work with, that the termination of my involvement is not my fault.

In addition, of course, I reserve the right to work at home with anyone I like as well as elsewhere and in another school, even Adashev's, if he invites me.

Aleksandr Ivanovich Adashev (Platonov, 1871-1934?), a founding member of the MAT, opened an acting school in 1906 that proved to be very popular. MAT actors taught there, as did Suler, and it is where Vakhtangov began his training. It took the overflow from the MAT school and became a kind of forcing-house for the parent company, its students recruited to play juveniles and extras in crowd scenes. KS hoped to work out in practice his embryonic system there. (In 1913, Adashev was accused of immorality, the faculty and student body walked out, the school was closed, and he moved to Kiev.)

To **Nemirovich-Danchenko**. Sunday, 5 November 1906, Moscow.
Dear Vladimir Ivanovich!

No doubt, you are the man to gather all the reins of the individual sectors in your hands, and so long as you hold them, all will go well in the theatre.

I have already apologized for Sulerzhitsky, acknowledging that I was wrong both in the official and ethical respects. I explained why all this happened. I eagerly apologize once more for my tactlessness.

I don't see any threat in my giving lessons either at home or at Adashev's. On the contrary, this is a request, because otherwise I would not have considered I had the right to talk to Adashev. These last few days I have read so many strange and surprising things that I have come to believe sincerely that my classes are not wanted. So much the better if this is not so.

I am sure that my participation in the school was wanted not so that I could do what other people were doing, but so that I could find something new, I took up musical farce. I could not run it myself, so I invited Aleksandrov[49] to do it on his own account (we still haven't discussed payment).

At that period, when you had fallen ill and couldn't work, I wanted to keep up their spirits by giving them all work. I think that Aleksandrov would take to drink without this new work, for which, to my mind, he is fully qualified. I wanted to combine the pleasant with the useful. If you pay attention to the fact that I especially stressed that musical farce should in no way interfere with the classwork, and, when I learned from Samarova that the female pupils were coming to class fatigued, I asked Aleksandrov to find another time for his rehearsals.

In a formal sense I was wrong there too and I beg your pardon, but I made this mistake without ill intentions.

In the future I will ask to be informed if I should discontinue these classes.

As to authors you are absolutely wrong.

It is ridiculous to suspect me because I like to read other people's plays and write comments on them. I have written to everyone without exception that I am passing on the plays to be read and will inform them of the results. [...]

I am probably happier than anyone for myself and for the theatre at those moments when you are working energetically. At those moments you do not complain.

When you are not working, against my will I have to strain my last bit of strength to maintain the troupe's drooping spirits.

If this protracted correspondence is a sign of your renewed energy, I am the first to rejoice and probably the first to support you and set an example by my obedience (with the exception of those indiscretions I commit in the heat of the work and for which I apologize in advance).

I thought and I continue to think that you yourself want our theatre to be on the side of neither the Revolution nor the Black Hundreds. So I have acted in that spirit. I would not like to stir up either the revolutionaries or the Black Hundreds. Does that mean that we are afraid of them or, on the contrary, that we are superior to all that? When we are nagged at, we must avoid nagging back, so as not to divert attention from the important thing, that is art. This is a question not of politics but of art.[50]

For your desire to support my artistic intentions I bow low and thank you sincerely.[51] I swear I did not understand that from your previous letters.

I wish with all my heart that our relations were not only respectful, but more expansive, especially since it is so easy to accomplish. Let me unburden my heart in just one play and I will do anything, otherwise I am stifling and, like a starving man, think only of food.

It is shameful in the times we are living through to be so caught up in the things we have been caught up in these last few days. [...]

Yours K. Alekseev

Rehearsals for The Drama of Life *were arduous, because KS was trying to work out both a different kind of pictorialism and a new approach to character creation. His sketches for the scenes of Kareno and Teresita show them, to quote the Mock Turtle, 'reeling and writhing and fainting in coils'. He wanted it to be barebones, so that the least movement would take on symbolic value. While the actors fell into art nouveau poses and tried to conjure up passion from within, the designers applied primary colours and Fauvist patterns as their contribution to simplicity.*

To **Leonid Leonidov**. 7 November 1906, Moscow.

Dear Leonid Mironovich,

We Russians love with one hand to make abundant sacrifices for something we love, and with the other to destroy it.

This is happening in our theatre.

It is impossible to number the sacrifices made by the actors to the concern, but thanks to a certain purely Russian nature these same actors are themselves dismantling it.

Even you have barely ever given serious thought to how many of their best spiritual ideas and feelings have been offered to the actors by the directors of our theatre.

And this energy is being expended not only in artistic affairs.

So, for instance, give a bit of serious thought to what it costs to keep up the far from ideal order that prevails in the theatre, at rehearsals and backstage.

This order is maintained not by the whole troupe serving in corpore, as it ought to be... It is kept up by a very small group of individuals.

If they were to leave or the reins slacken, our concern would turn to chaos.

Ask yourself a few questions, for instance, do these persons get proper support from the troupe?

Do not some find fault with every word and action of those who are fighting for order, and, after all, isn't order everything both for us and for all Russia at the present time?

We, Russian-style, make sacrifices with one hand, and destroy them with the other.

You will never know, unless you have experienced it yourself, how much blood and nerves and health and spiritual torment and disappointment it costs a director to sit on his chair in rehearsals.

Tell me honestly: are there many actors in the troupe who can or know how to work independently. Do they bring on stage many characterizations and creations independently, without the contribution of the directors' imaginations?

The supremely comic opinion has even become axiomatic with us: ' this is normal in our theatre: it's how things ought to be.' That is not true, it is abnormal for one man to work for dozens.

It is hard to come up with a unique characterization on one's own, although who knows his stage material and spiritual talents if not the actor himself.

It is even harder to come up with a characterization for someone else, whose talents the director cannot fathom.

How is one to create dozens of characterizations and convey them to dozens of variegated actors' talents.

But even there: can these characterizations, devised for others by the directors, be easily mastered or accepted by the actors?

Will not a great many try only to grasp the superficial details, or will the actors not simply behave capriciously, even those who simply do no work at home?

Directors, in doing the actors' work for them, are forced to plead and entreat that what they have done for the actors themselves be accepted graciously or merely looked at. Such cases are not rare in our theatre, and then, sitting at the directors' table, you are met with insults, malice and humiliation, which a mortal man cannot always withstand.

One might think that at such moments the earnest and highly-strung work of one man for dozens could expect to be indulged and if not assisted, at least not mocked. That is not the case.

Everything that can destroy the mood during a director's tense creativity (the director cannot take a step without this mood and nervous afflatus), everything that might humiliate him in terms of disrespect for his labour is constantly met with by the director at every turn as the reward for his labour. And all this is done unconsciously, because of the Russian habit: despise another man's labour.

One can create in silence, amid general sympathy. Every one of the actors knows this perfectly – and goes on talking.

One can create while undergoing great nervous tension, but the director's abnormal condition does not justify an outburst of cutting remarks on the part of the director in the eyes of capable actors. The director speaks indefatigably to the whole theatre, and this does not prevent those present from speaking even more loudly, forcing the director to strain all his vocal powers in order to outshout the crowd.

The most difficult moment for the director, whose intuition and imagination need to be screwed to the highest pitch, is when for the first time and the second he visualizes the stage picture. He must conceive this picture in order to bring the actors and the whole production to it. He has already lifted a bit of the edge of the curtain, he is ready to lift it all… but he is distracted by an untimely joke or people running to find an actor who isn't there, and everything collapses. Many rehearsals are needed, a new happy accident is needed for such a moment to be repeated. Give some thought to what the director undergoes at such moments.

And in our practice such examples are endless.

Everything said at rehearsals has a meaning for everyone. All the details of the production create the atmosphere in which the actor merges with the author and the other actors and all the parts of a complicated theatrical mechanism.

Can we support the actor in this atmosphere voluntarily? Don't you hear people say: 'It's inhuman to keep an actor at rehearsals who has a part in the play but isn't in this act'?

The director has to sit interminably, and this is supposed to be humane, but for the actor it is impossible.

And so the director must repeat a dozen times one and the same thing to everyone individually, and this is not considered inhumane, and the director has no right to get angry or chide the actor for his cold-blooded attitude to the business.

Do not forget the most important thing.

The director works with the most subtle and delicate parts of his organism, which are worn down very quickly.

There is the question of health and life. One cannot sacrifice one or the other for the sake of other people's caprice or thoughtlessness.

To return to my personal case, it needs to be recalled that up to now I assumed all the leading roles and was extremely busy as an actor, that I own a prominent business in which I have to take part, that I also have community activities, such as the school, a trusteeship, that I have a family and that I am a sick man.

I have borne such work now for 20 years – without complaint.

I did it as long as I could.

Now – I have to take care of myself.

Fortunately, I have found the means for this, which is to call off rehearsals in cases when they are unworthy of our theatre.

I am glad that I have made this discovery, and I will use it forever.

In one of the agonizing moments for a director I may be rude to you.

If that is so, I fervently ask forgiveness. If you have been rude to me, it is not for me to teach you what you have to do.

Respectfully K. Alekseev

Diary, 6 November 1906.

It's a mockery. I am paying Sulerzhitsky with my own money, he is working with might and main, and I still have to beg permission to have his assistance from Vladimir Ivanovich, who does nothing himself. When Suler heard about it he almost walked out of the theatre.

ND's production of Brand *opened on 20 December, with Kachalov in the lead. It proved to be the hit of the season and ran for eighty-seven performances.*

Diary, 24 December 1906.

The worst insult I have ever received. Today when I was very ill I went to the dress rehearsal of *The Drama of Life* after ten days in bed.

The play was announced in the papers last Saturday without my being asked (today is Tuesday).[52] On Tuesday and Thursday they postponed the performances because of dress rehearsals.

I am ill. Suler took charge of the play for the first time. Before it even began I learn that neither Vladimir Ivanovich nor Kaluzhsky would be present at the theatre. And they didn't even bother to inform us.

This is theatrical bitchiness and revenge. I cannot remain in such an atmosphere any longer. I have decided to quit the theatre.

Figure 39 Leopold Sulerzhitsky

To **Nemirovich-Danchenko**. 23 December 1906, Moscow.
Draft in Notebook

Dear Vl. Iv.

I am writing this letter sooner than I intended, because an unforeseen circumstance has arisen which compels me to make haste. I refer to Nelidov's proposals to enter our theatre.[53]

I refrain from any discussions of this matter, but put before you my statement which may influence a proper response to Nelidov's proposal.

I give you my word that I am writing this letter quite calmly, thoughtfully and conscientiously.

Pain, offense, humiliations, thwarted hopes and all the other elements of internal conflict are put behind me.

My statement is a friendly request to you. I hope you will enable me to carry it out, if only in memory of our prior good relations and our work in common.

By virtue of the innumerable circumstances well known to you, next season I shall have to leave off being an administrator and a shareholder and can remain an investor. Instruct me as to how to do this without adversely affecting the concern.

I repeat: I have no possibility and no right to remain an administrator and a shareholder any longer.

Practically speaking, the theatre will suffer in no way from my departure, because I am an administrator with no responsibilities and a shareholder with no influence.

The theatre needs me as a stage director and an actor.

These and other responsibilities I shall carry out no better and no worse than I have done heretofore.

Please try and accept this letter in the same simple, good spirit with which it is written. I am sending the letter sooner than I expected. The reason for this haste will be explained at the very end.

Dear, dear man, release me from the administrators and shareholders. I shall remain an investor and an actor. I shall execute anything entrusted to me, I shall work more than I do now, and shall feel myself free and happy.

Bear in mind that you can look forward to this as well. You will be free and independent. There is no need for more new rehearsals excruciating for both of us to be convinced that we are such different people that we shall never agree on any point.

Up to now the unique feature of our merger was the respect for the work we put into the concern. But this feature has collapsed. We are pulling the concern in different directions and are tearing it apart.

That is criminal.

Married couples have divorce, lovers, friends break off relationships so as not to poison one another's lives. Can't we find some *modus vivendi* so that we wouldn't have to take the greatest of sins on our souls, spoiling another man's very existence.

To establish these new relations the first thing we need to do is part.

I do not want to play at gratitude or humility. I should make the move, because I am an administrator without responsibilities and a shareholder without influence.

Once I have sloughed off these duties, the theatre will not change its course for a single day.

Once you leave, the theatre will cease to exist.

Furthermore – I cannot and do not have the right to remain in these offices. I cannot because official duties without any obligations and rights, without any possibility of realizing my ideals in life are insulting and insufferable. I do not have the right to be a shareholder or an administrator because my family, commercial situation and financial means do not permit me to remain in the false and dangerous position I find myself in at the moment.

I am one of the few actually solvent members of the association. Do I have the right to risk what I do not have. The risk is enormous. It threatens my whole family with total ruin, it also threatens my ability to deserve the trust of the stock exchange and compromises a commercial enterprise which has been renowned for its probity for 150 years. Please be fair and grant that I have no right to take such a risk. Do not assume that I wanted to avoid sharing the losses in case of bankruptcy. I am ready to give an undertaking to take part in losses to a specific amount, extremely great for me.

Therefore: under the present conditions I cannot and have no right to take on the aforesaid duties.

Can these conditions be changed so that I need not bear this risk? What is needed for that? First of all, a dictatorial power. That is understood. If I take the risk, then I should be in charge. Or, second, blind faith in whoever is running the concern. I cannot be a dictator, I do not want to be, do not know how to be one. I don't trust myself in that role. I would overdo it. Blind faith, despite mutual respect, cannot exist wherever people do not agree on a single point. There is no way out until such time as what is genuinely created by the concern itself is acknowledged. Set me up in those genuine conditions of the concern, and everything will go smoothly, no matter how you have regarded my new position.

1. The theatre needs me for certain roles as an actor.

2. The theatre needs me for one or two productions as a director.

3. Sometimes it needs my business tact and acumen. All this will still be with me in my new role.

After the opinion you expressed of me in one of your letters it is easy to profess doubt from your standpoint; will I show up at the necessary moment, when I am freed of obligations and responsibilities.

True, I am powerless to remove that doubt, if my whole life and activity are insufficient to convince you. In answer to this situation one can pose a single question: do you and the concern need a man who inspires such doubts?

As you see, I am not writing this letter in a fit of temper, but having thought things out for years, tested them and put them into practice myself.

As you see, I am making no demands, but amicably ask you to offer me help.

As you see, I accuse no one, but rather acknowledge my own guilt.

It is easy to conclude from this, it seems to me, that I am writing this letter with good feelings and await from you a similar attitude to me.

I am very much indebted to you and will be grateful; I love and value you very much.

Let these feelings bind us if not by the bonds of intimate friendship, then by the bonds of grateful remembrance and respect. Let us part as friends so that afterwards we shall never be separated by the participants of a general world concern. It is our civic duty to support it. To destroy it should be a barbaric crime.

Of course, until the end of the season no one will know about this letter (except for my and probably your wife). Until the end of the season everything will remain as before. [...]

KS tinkered with this letter and eventually withdrew it. He did not let his feeling of being misunderstood prevent experimenting during rehearsals of three non-naturalistic plays: Byron's Cain, *Maeterlinck's* The Blue Bird *and Andreev's* The Life of Man.

To **General Stakhovich.** 5 February 1907, Moscow.
Dear, good Aleksey Aleksandrovich!

The Drama of Life still hasn't flopped, because I have fallen ill and haven't acted for two weeks. I have been going out the last few days and working, but illness has sapped all my energy. I get weary very quickly, and so rehearsals are unproductive. We are terribly sick and tired of the play, and can't wait for the time when we can write it off. That, it seems, will be in three days' time, i.e., Thursday the day you get this letter.

For the rest it's the same old thing at the theatre. Nemirovich is behaving abominably. He demonstratively failed to come to a single dress rehearsal of *The Drama of Life*.[54] Luzhsky too. The troupe take a malevolent attitude to my experiments and whoever can be is sarcastic and obstructive.

Meanwhile they have quite worn Suler down to the nub. Yesterday there was a great blow-up. All barriers had to be knocked down, and today at last things have pulled together. Knipper seems to have somewhat reverted to her former tone. Moskvin [as Oterman] and Vishnevsky [as Ensa Spira] are working well. I do not expect a success, but there will be a sensation, lots of arguments and abuse. And I give thanks for that.

Brand is making money like crazy. The rest of the plays as well. But even so my illness will cost us dear. [...]

Affectionately yours K. Alekseev

To **General Stakhovich.** 6 February 1907, Moscow.
Dear Aleksey Aleksandrovich!

I write a couple of words about the dress rehearsal of *The Drama of Life*.

I fear invoking the evil eye, but it had a great success. It shouldn't be forgotten that the audience was very, very small, moreover all our own crowd: actors and their close acquaintances, an enthusiastic tribe.

The truth is that these individuals did include more than a few who were prejudiced and ill-disposed to the production. Apparently, we convinced them.

Apparently, we even convinced Nemirovich. At least he abandoned his frivolous tone. There were decadents there – writers and artists (Baltrushaitis, Polyakov, Sredin[55]).

They were extremely excited and certain that their long awaited discovery was accomplished.

There were no giggles. The first act was received well, the second act made a great impression on everyone, so did the fourth act which ended with applause (Nemirovich said of it that it was immeasurably better than the preceding ones). The third act – opinion was divided. Some are dismayed; others say that it was boring in spots.

Zinaida [Morozova] who had made such an effort to keep me calm) had the worst attitude of all. She abused everyone and everything and demonstratively left during an act.

It should not be forgotten that it is precisely her kind of audience that will be most prominent at the premiere, so don't be surprised if I write shortly that the

Figure 40 General Stakhovich

performance flopped. I think that it will stimulate a great many rumours, discussions and arguments. [...]

Affectionately K. Alekseev. [...]

After the dress rehearsal on 6 February ND wrote to KS a long letter of caution about the elevated tone of the play. It opened two days later, with KS, suffering from a fever, playing Kareno. Brysuov was ecstatic, feeling that the MAT had definitively turned its back on kitchen-sink realism. It would chalk up twenty-seven performances, a decent number but far from the popularity of Brand.

Diary, 15 February 1907.

Not a single one of Nemirovich's predictions about *The Drama of Life* has come to pass.

He said: Knipper cannot play Teresita. She is playing it and has shown exceptional temperament, which she has never shown before. K. S. A. cannot play Kareno. The audience will not accept him. The Chinese shadows and the whole third act he rejected – many people have found them successful. [...]

To **Vera Kotlyarevskaya.** 15 February 1907, Moscow.

Dear friend Vera Vasilievna!

[...] *The Drama of Life* had the success I had dreamt of. Half the people hiss, the other half rave in ecstasy. I am satisfied with the result of several trials and experiments.

They have revealed many interesting principles to us.

The decadents are pleased, the realists outraged, the bourgeoisie offended.

Many are agog and phone to ask if I am all right.

If a lot of people have it in for us, what more could one ask?

We worked well and, I think, achieved a lot.

It is settled that we are going to St Pb, to the Grand Duke Michael Theatre. [...]

Devotedly and affectionately yours K. Alekseev

Andreev's The Life of Man *was an allegorical drama peopled by lay figures rather than three-dimensional human beings. KS sought a solution by playing it to music by Sats and positioning silhouettes inspired by Aubrey Beardsley against black velvet. The play ran against the grain of KS's earlier principles, particularly in its fatalism, and the result fell between two stools.*

Nothing daunted, in April KS begins work on The Blue Bird, *calling for it to be 'naïve, simple, light, filled with the joy of life, merry and transparent as a child's dream, beautiful as a child's fancies, and yet magnificent as the idea of a brilliant poet and thinker'. At the same time the censorship was solicited to license Byron's* Cain *for production.*

2 April 1907 saw the opening of a play of Jewish content, Naidyonov's Walls, *directed by ND: they toppled after ten performances. The Petersburg tour took place from 23 April to 17 May. The production of* Woe from Wit, *a sharp break with the traditions of the Imperial theatres, aroused lively literary discussions and* The Drama of Life, *as KS had predicted, provoked extremely contradictory reviews.*

To **his son Igor.** Saturday, 27 April 1907, St Pb.

My dear and wonderful little boy – Igrushon, you, chum, are not only an historian but a poet. [...]

So, you and Volodya have gone crazy for history and are going to take a look at the Kremlin. Possibly, when you see the palace, this is what will happen: you will get carried away talking and absent-mindedly sit down on the Tsar's throne. They will arrest you, march you down the street, then in Red Square they will set up two gallows – they will hang you, and you will swing in the air as you go on talking and arguing about Assurbanipal. I see by your letter that you are interested most of all in history, poetry and the Hermitage. You are standing right at a crossroads and wavering about who you will be: Vipper, Balmont or Shchukin.[56] Taking into account the fact that you love *money*, probably when all is said and done, you will open a music hall and there you will put on historical plays in verse. Do not forget me. I can play the roles of old kings. Volodya will be a critic, and Mama the cashier, Fyodorova the leading actress, and Daisy your wife.[57] Twelve children, prosperity, lots of money. Some life, eh? Lucky boy! They abuse us here, poor impresarios, and the public packs the place. The weather is cold. Petersburg is excruciatingly boring. We have climbed so high that no one comes to visit us in our rooms, and so nobody gets on our nerves.

Yesterday a whole crowd of students broke into the theatre and insisted on being seated. They proclaimed that the theatre is for everyone. They shouted, banged on the locked boxes. They almost created a riot. Boorishness and lack of discipline prevail here even more than in Moscow. [...]

Your intensely loving Papa.

Back in Moscow, KS decided to direct another familiar classic, Gogol's The Government Inspector, *and started looking for antique furniture. ND, fearful that his Boris Godunov, would not be ready to open the season, indifferent to* The Blue Bird, *and doubtful that the Gogol would ever come to be, asked KS to concentrate on* Cain. *However, its production was prohibited by the Holy Synod, because figures from Scripture were not to appear on stage.*

Olga Vladimirovna Gzovskaya (1883-1962), a blond and buxom student of the great actor Aleksandr Lensky, entered the Maly Theatre troupe in 1906. She had acted with KS at a Caucasian spa, and, at her request, he began to go over with her the role of Psyche in Zhulavsky's Eros and Psyche, *which she was to play on the imperial stage. She was married to the bureaucrat Nelidov, and the negotiations for him to join the MAT had infected her. Her desire to enter the MAT soon became a cause for internal tension in both troupes.*

To **his wife Mariya Lilina**. 15 August 1907, Moscow.
My dear little angel!

[...] At 9 o'clock [Gzovskaya] came to the house.

Now here comes a *big secret*. She is so poisoned that she cannot bear what is being said and done in the Maly Theatre. She pleads to be admitted to our theatre now. She promises to deal with the ethical aspect of leaving the Maly Theatre with complete propriety; she is not asking for leading roles, is willing to be a supernumerary. One way or another, she is going to tear up her contract with the Maly, especially since she isn't needed there, because they banned *Psyche*, the way they did *Cain*, the way they ban everything. She was charming, but very overwrought and not in a mood to exhibit her *charme*. Stakhovich liked her, although he didn't go into ecstasies. Tomorrow this question is to be resolved at the meeting. Stakhovich and I escorted her home on foot, because I was tired of sitting. [...] Knipper came by yesterday and was already starting to get depressed without a new role. Kachalov came back and did not drink more vodka, intends to learn a language. [...]

Yours Kostya [...]

Maeterlinck had written The Blue Bird *to be acted by children; so far no European theatre had had the courage to produce it, so he was very open to KS's ideas.*

To **Maurice Maeterlinck**. 20 September/3 October 1907, Moscow.

[...] I am afraid my style may offend your musical ear. [...]

I shall try to expiate my guilt with a circumstantial report on our work on *The Blue Bird*.

The strictness of the censorship has crippled our entire repertoire. They have forbidden [*Cain*], which was to have begun our season.

The whole plan of work, along with the preliminary work and other conditions of our complicated concern, has been crippled.

We either had to stage *The Blue Bird* as first in line, to open the season, without a sufficient number of rehearsals – or move it to the third in line. I selected the latter way out and hope that you will not have cause to complain of me for that.

We have to do everything in our power to justify your trust. Hasty rehearsals would spoil all our preliminary work.

On the other hand – the first play of the season loses a good deal from the fact that the audience has a colder attitude to the theatre at the start of a still not warmed-up and established season. I proposed that we move the play to the end of November or the beginning of December, especially since one of the practice sessions gave us the following unexpected results. Our old and experienced actors do not manage to be sufficiently rejuvenated to provide that wonderful aroma of youth that the play is redolent of. Experience and art are not enough to do this – we need real young people.

We decided to cast the play, except for the few most important roles, from the younger component of the troupe. This casting will provide an unusual freshness and beauty.

Along with that young actors require intensive work to achieve that lightness and virtuosity which the interpretation of your works requires.

I think that you will approve of my plan.

The practice sessions are over, and I consider them successful. We managed to achieve unusually simple means for a complete illusion for all the transformations you indicate, with almost no deviation from the text. The scenery models are suffused with a child-like fantasy, and some of the musical numbers that I have heard are beautifully achieved. But the most important thing ahead of us is the actors and the acting. Meanwhile I can say with assurance that we are waiting impatiently for rehearsals to begin and we shall approach them with all the zeal to justify your trust and receive the right to ask you to do us the honour of attending the first performance of the play. For my part, we shall do all we can to facilitate your journey to Moscow. We shall send someone abroad to meet you,

231

you will encounter no difficulties from ignorance of the language, we shall protect you from the cold – with a real Russian fur coat and a warm stove. Our frosts are exaggerated. 10-15° Réamur is the normal temperature in the winter. It is not unlike Paris. As to the Revolution, don't believe the newspapers, everything will be quiet this year. We flatter ourselves with the hope that you and your wife will be our guests in Moscow for a rather long time. We will arrange for your arrival such a repertoire as will acquaint you with the platform and activity of our theatre. In the pleasant hope that our dreams will come true, I take advantage of this opportunity to express to you once more my excitement and admiration of your talent.[58]

Throughout the summer KS had been busy with Gzovskaya's roles in Lensky's productions of Eros and Psyche *and* Much Ado *and in November she was accepted into the MAT. He undertook to tutor her in the theatre's approach to acting. Maria Germanova[59] made a public objection, claiming to be surprised that a single individual was privileged to have private lessons and sorry for the female students in the school. This stirred up a flurry of letters between KS and ND over the course of a week, ending:*

To **Nemirovich-Danchenko**. *26 November 1907, Moscow.*
Dear Vladimir Ivanovich!

I rejoiced at the last part of your letter.

The most important thing is that we do not diverge in artistic principles and tendencies. Everything else is open to remedy and of secondary importance: whether we stage plays in tandem or separately, whether we agree on administrative matters, whether we resemble one another in temperament, -- all this is unimportant.

I do not agree with the first part of the letter.

The matter is not whether Baranovskaya or Gzovskaya will leave after the trumped-up incident thanks to my arbitrariness and despotism or the decision of the board (I do not pretend to autocracy and understand perfectly well that I have no right to discharge persons unilaterally). For my female student it is a matter of considerable importance if I stop being her teacher. Of course, I reject any student who does not carry out my legitimate demands. Such a student will never understand ethics and, consequently, will never be an actress. I was taught this by Nad. Mikh. Medvedeva and Fedotova, and it has been driven into me forever.

First of all students have to be taught ethics. [...]

It is not always ethically sound simply to confront an actor with his transgression. There are cases when the whole troupe expects a public statement of the incident in order to uphold the ethical standards.

There is no such thing as your actresses and my actresses nor should there be, but your students and mine will always be just that. Cover me in gold, but I will have nothing to do with Pomyalova or Raevskaya or Gorich etc. I cannot have anything to do with them, because their talents are incapable of attracting me. In general ethical questions I agree, no female students, and I will inform the students of this in every way. Your orders are law for Baranovskaya and everyone else. Your instructions as a director are law for her, and my obligation as teacher is not to change the mise-en-scène or the interpretation of roles, but to approximate it. I tried to do this with Gzovskaya, taking into consideration the absurdity of productions at the Maly Theatre. It costs me nothing to do this with Baranovskaya, and that's how I behaved when I went over the role in *Walls* with her, that's how I behaved with Baranovskaya when they scheduled her to go on, despite illness and the doctor's forbidding her to go on. Since she is an actress, she has to learn to have staying power and must not inject vanity into questions of big and walk-on roles. That's how I dealt with all my present comrades from the Society for Art and Literature.

I have no doubt that you conveyed this to Germanova, but it was in private, and not a business-like resolution of the incident, given a public hearing.

Of course, from the day she entered Gzovskaya was not subservient to me (she will not go for that), but to the administration, but it is extremely natural that in artistic matters she will come to me for corrections and explanations, so long as she has not lost faith in me. It is understood that Germanova will go to you, because you know her better than I and are more interested in her talent than I am. I do not know a single one of my good impulses towards Germanova that hasn't met with rudeness.

Let's assume that I am being unfair to her. Why is my wife, who responded so enthusiastically to work on the role of Marina [in *Boris Godunov*] with her, so reluctant to repeat her experiment a second time.

It means that there is something in Germanova herself that repels everyone. Until you as teacher eliminate this flaw in her, Germanova will be a stranger to the troupe and will suffer. Grant for a minute that I see this and appreciate her qualities and am afraid that, behaving this way, she will soon put herself in a completely hopeless situation. You stubbornly refuse to think about this. If Germanova were to benefit from this incident in order to maintain the prestige of the theatre – she would grow in the eyes of everyone. Now she has diminished herself.

Do I really claim to be the protector of Knipper, Lilina, Gzovskaya? God forbid I take on that role. I look after Knipper, Lilina – because their talent interests me. I made an effort on behalf of Gzovskaya, because she is talented. I am indifferent to Germanova, because her dramatic talent does not interest me in the least. I lit up, when during the auditions for *Life of Man*, she performed a doll.

I am ready to make peace with Gzovskaya and Baranovskaya and Germanova, but… My attempts as to Germanova have so far had no results, and even a series of her failures has not convinced you… That means one of us is in error. I have done all I can. I cannot force you to adopt my opinion. Time will tell. It will show which of us is right.

What's yours and what's mine – that is dangerous. I agree. I will try not to make anyone mine, even my own wife. Do not make Germanova yours either. That is the crux of the matter. You must understand that whatever I write is not out of animosity to Germanova, but perhaps quite the contrary.

Yours K. Alekseev

The Life of Man *opened on 12 December, directed by KS and Suler. It was highly praised, especially welcomed by the young, who regarded it as revolutionary. It seemed to answer the objections of Meyerhold (who was now on the staff of the Imperial Theatres and directed his own version of the play in St Petersburg). Andreev preferred the MAT performance. It ran for forty-eight performances, thanks in part to Sats' evocative music.*

In December 1907 KS renewed his acquaintance with Isadora Duncan during her tours in Moscow. Their relationship was fraught with cross purposes. Evidently undergoing a midlife crisis, KS became infatuated with her, but attributed this foible to the appeal of her dancing. Duncan, on the other hand, saw him as a powerful, influential and attractive man who could advance her ambitions and perhaps be bagged as a sexual trophy. Her response to his enthusiasm was: 'I am so glad that I am ready to leap up to the stars and dance around the moon.'

To **Isadora Duncan**. After 6 January 1908, Moscow. [*In French*]
Dear Friend!

How happy I am!!!

How proud I am!!!

I have helped a great performer to find the atmosphere she needed!!! And it all happened during a splendid pleasure excursion, in a cabaret, where vice prevails.

How strange life is! How beautiful it is at times. No! You are good, you are pure, you are noble, and within the great, exalted feeling and artistic admiration which I have experienced towards you so far, I sense the birth of a deep and genuine love as a friend.

Do you know what you did for me? -- I have not yet spoken of it to you.

In spite of the great success of our theatre and the innumerable admirers who surround it, I have always been alone (except for my wife who has supported me in my moments of doubt and artistic disappointments). You are the first to tell me in a few simple and convincing phrases what is important and fundamental about the art I wanted to create. That invigorated my energy at the very moment when I was planning to give up my artistic career.

I thank you, I truly thank you from the bottom of my heart.

Oh! I waited impatiently for your letter and danced when I got it and read it. I was afraid you had misinterpreted my reserve and would take pure feeling for indifference. I was afraid that your feeling of happiness, the energy and new creative strength with which you departed would abandon you before you got to Saint Petersburg.

Now you are dancing the Moon Dance, I am dancing my own dance, as yet unnamed.

I am content, I am fully rewarded.

Allow me in my next letter to describe the impression you made on all your admirers and its magic has not been dispelled even now.

Every free minute, in the midst of business, we talk of the divine nymph who came down from Olympus to make us happy

We kiss your beautiful hands and will never forget you.

I am happy if the new creation is inspired by my love for you. I would like to see this dance... When shall I see it? Alas. I don't know your itinerary?!

Figure 41 Isadora Duncan. Photo: PMR

On tour in Finland, Kiev, Warsaw and Odessa, Duncan regularly sent KS telegrams, suggesting a meeting. She wanted to move her studio of free dance to Russia.

To **Isadora Duncan**. Before 14 January 1908, Moscow. [*In French*]
Dear Friend and Colleague!

This time I am pestering you on business. It concerns your school. The administrator of all the imperial theatres, Mr Telyakovsky (excellency)[60], happens to be in Moscow. The administrator of the Moscow theatre, Mr Nelidov (the same one who was supposed to have been here, but didn't come because of illness), spoke to him about you today.

Mr Telyakovsky took an interest in the proposal, he wants to make your acquaintance and discuss your school.

Tomorrow Telyakovsky will be coming to our theatre, and I will try to inveigle him even more. The day after tomorrow, i.e., Tuesday evening, Mr Telyakovsky leaves for Saint Petersburg. Try to see him on Wednesday. I asked Mr Nelidov to draft a letter for me that I am to send to you. Unfortunately I haven't the time to rewrite it and so am sending it as it is, because I am in a hurry to get this letter off. Forgive me.

I am sending you the rough draft so that you can know Mr Nelidov's opinion, he knows Telyakovsky very well. It's not for me to teach you how to talk to people. Your talent will prompt you better than I.

Even so, I take the liberty of advising you:

1. At the start ask for about 15 thousand rubles a year. If you ask for more, you risk frightening Telyakovsky off.

2. Ask for some amount or other for the removal cost of the school, -- but it would be better to save it for the end of the meeting or the next discussion.

3. Tell Telyakovsky that you could refund part of the amount, if he would make the stage of the Imperial Theatre available to you for a few student recitals.

4. Above all try to describe the principles of your art to him with the talent, intelligence and charm characteristic of your artistic spirit. (Don't abuse old-fashioned ballet too much.) May the gods assist you...

Telyakovsky was uninterested. Duncan wired from Petersburg that she didn't know when she might travel to Moscow, but made the suggestion that her former lover, the English director, designer and theatrical ideologue Edward Gordon Craig (1872-1966) might be a valuable asset to the MAT.

To **Isadora Duncan**. After 20 January 1908, Moscow. [*In French*]

I took your telegram to be a refusal, a very delicate and gracious one, and decided not to bother you in Petersburg. Alas! For now we won't see one another anymore, and I hasten to write you this letter before your departure because soon I won't have an address for you.

Thank you for the moments of artistic ecstasy which your genius aroused in me. I will never forget those days, because I love your talent and your art too much, because I delight in you too much as a performer and love you as a friend.

Perhaps you will forget us in a short time, and I will not be cross with you for that. You have too many acquaintances and transitory meetings during your constant travels.

But... in moments of weakness, disappointment or ecstasy you will remember me. I know this, because my feelings are pure and disinterested. Such feelings, which become tiresome over time, are rarely encountered.

At that time – write to me or come yourself. I know that I could support you, that the atmosphere of our theatre could invigorate you.

I continue my endeavours for your school. They promised to introduce some interested parties to me. If something is to come of it, where should I write to you?

At the present time I cannot inform Mr Craig of anything definite, because the financial conditions of the theatre are in difficulties.

I acquired the promised works of Chekhov and will send them to you in Berlin.

My wife, who greatly admires you, sends you her best wishes.

Farewell or so long: thank you.

Your devoted friend. [...]

This letter was delivered to Duncan by General Stakhovich who wrote to KS: 'I was with Duncan. Your name is a magical passe-partout. [...] 'Pon my soul! Either I'm an idiot, or she is acting the fool, but it seems to me que vous ne vous entendez guère and that the two of you are of two entirely different minds, she is in love with you, is attracted to you as a man and – as a capricious and temperamental woman – desires you. To all the appeals about art she repeats: 'Je souffre, je suis amoureuse de loui [sic]...' And you are singing from quite another opera. [...] If you were less chaste, you might make her see reason about 2 weeks after the Fall. But, out of friendship, I do not advise this means of rescuing this emissary from Olympus.'

Duncan phoned to say she was off to Imatra and invited KS to come. He had originally written: 'What temptation! A fairy on the shores of the Imatra waterfall. A splendid picture, I am devoid of the possibility of seeing all this, I am a poor day-labourer.' He crossed out the lines.

To **Isadora Duncan.** 29 January 1908, Moscow. [*In French*]

Dear friend!

I am cheerful and happy. First, because you have not forgotten me, that you are not angry. Second, because I have had no news from you. They write me that you are working a lot. What joy! Is it true?

I must see your new creations!!

Around here they are saying that your charming children are coming to Saint Petersburg. Is that true?

That means... that the business with the school is settled? My dream will come true, and your great art will not vanish with you! You know I am much more enthusiastic about you than about the beautiful Duse.[61] Your dancing said more to me than the commonplace performance I saw last night.

You have shattered my principles. After you had departed I sought in my own art the things you created in yours. That simple beauty, like nature itself. Today the beautiful Duse repeated before my eyes something I have seen a hundred times. Duse didn't make me forget Duncan!

I entreat you: labour for the sake of art and believe me, your labour will bring you joy, the best joy in our life.

I love you, I am in raptures over you and I respect you (forgive me!) – a great and admirable performer. Write me at least one little word, just so I know about your plans.

Perhaps I will manage to go there to take delight in you.

I entreat you to inform me as soon as you can about the day when you and your school will give a recital. Not for anything in the world would I want to miss that peerless spectacle and must do what I can to be available.

A thousand times I kiss your classical hands, and till we meet again.

Your devoted friend K. Stanislavsky

The thorny issue of Nelidov's recruitment had called forth an open letter to KS from ND. KS spent a good deal of time drafting a lengthy reply, but discarded it for a more laconic answer, resigning from the Board of Directors of the MAT.

To **Nemirovich-Danchenko**. 7 February 1908, Moscow.

Dear Vladimir Ivanovich!

Now that our decade of activity has ended with the letter I read today, -- any conviction of my *infinite* devotion and love for you, the theatre and our colleagues is futile.

I ask you to bear in mind that at the end of this season -- I shall cease to be a shareholder and an administrator.

As to the future, I offer my services, -- gratis as an actor -- in my old roles -- and as a director – on the terms you are aware of.

The question of Nelidov I consider closed and do not wish to return to it.

Respectfully K. Alekseev

Maeterlinck had wondered whether, in their striving for beauty in The Blue Bird, *they might overlook the humour in the play. He did not want the mystical aspect to overshadow the warm, human side.*

To **Maurice Maeterlinck**. 12 February 1908, Moscow. [*In French*]

Cher maître!

I want to thank you for your two letters. One of them brought me the joyous news of your imminent arrival in Moscow. I hope that our climate joins with our hospitable and warm (in the proper sense of the word) reception. Often in late March it is as hot as in summer. But it may, alas, turn out that the March frosts will give you a hint of our winter. Your second letter assured me that our work had gone in the right direction the author desires. Such assurance is more than pleasant for us. Know, dear friend, that we highly esteem the elegance, lightness, 'humour' of the play and are striving to emphasize its child-like purity. We are doing all we can to avoid any theatrical machinery, capable only of making the work ponderous and reducing its value.

I admit that, although we have leavened our production as far as possible, on stage it all still looks rather awkward and rough, and at the present time we are concerned to make it all the lighter and more refined. If only we can manage to do it!

Thanks to the staging-plan, with over-sized furniture and objects, a choice of tall actors for the roles of the grown-ups, we were able to achieve the necessary effect: the actresses look like real children. 'The Azure Kingdom' no longer worries me, for we succeeded in creating successful scenery, following your stage directions. The same for the costumes; as much as possible, they approximate your wishes. The souls of inanimate objects and animals are presented humanly (I don't know whether this word expresses my idea), to avoid ballet and masquerade. Otherwise the actor would turn into a prop, and the role would lose some of its inner content.

Now only one thing concerns me – that the actors *perform well*, that the ensemble be at its best and that the performance go merrily, lightly, without longueurs.

If you could come to Moscow a week before the opening to confirm the results of our work and make the indispensable alterations, we would be delighted and our souls would find peace. But if this all seems impossible to you, all that is left for us is to follow your instructions after the first performance. There is one more question, causing us a good deal of concern. I have in mind the need for our actors to strive for the lightness and elegance of the French language and French temperament, while they are forced to use the Russian language, much too slow and more ponderous than your language. This will come, alas, only after numerous performances, after a complete merger with the play and its text.

On 1 March KS asked the shareholders to honour his wishes:
1) To be allowed one play a season for experimentation, with ND having the right to veto it;
2) To stage independently no more than two plays a season, though he might advise others;
3) An annual leave till 15 August.
ND's Rosmersholm opened on 3 March and crept through twenty performances.

To **SergeyAndreevsky**.[62] 9 March 1908, Moscow.
Much esteemed and dear Sergey Arkadievich!

[…] I have to produce Maeterlinck's *The Blue Bird* in a few weeks, in order to astonish Europe. Maeterlinck himself, managers and impresarios from America, England, Germany and Austria are coming to our opening. I am worried, I am alarmed by the long list of things to be staged, I am trying to do a dozen things at once and I am wracking my brain to deal with the difficulties and banalities that proliferate in Maeterlinck's new play. I have to turn a Christmas pantomime into a beautiful fairy tale, portray a dream with crude theatrical techniques. The work is difficult and uninteresting, because it is purely external, putting things on stage.

[…] The reviewers liked *The Life of Man*, but we didn't.

The problem with Pushkin's poetry is that our sort tend to sing it out at the top of our lungs. The ear of the contemporary spectator has become unaccustomed to this theatrical emoting. We have to find another style: to speak beautifully. We have not found it, and therefore the play, effectively staged (I haven't directed it), is played by the major roles in a mediocre way.

I agree with everything you write about *The Life of Man*. It is a bad play. […]

Spiritually devoted and respectfully

K. Alekseev

In Florence Duncan has given Craig KS's address, telling him that KS hoped to have him work at the MAT. Craig wrote that he had heard nothing for six months and so was importuning an answer.

To **Gordon Craig**. 26 April 1908, Moscow. *Telegram.*

Repertoire confirmed in few days. 10-13 June travel to Homburg near Frankfurt, stay month. Request meeting, to see you and discuss. Greetings. Stanislavsky.

To **Vera Kotlyarevskaya**. 30 April 1908, St Petersburg.
Poor, dear Vera Vasilievna!

[...] So, let yourself be carried away for a second to that world backstage, which is alien to you at the moment, but was dear to you not so long ago and will soon be again. A ferment of struggle and life is boiling in us here. The first upheaval of the revolution has died down, and we are counting up the pluses and minuses. Nevertheless after great efforts we have managed to move the troupe out of that dead zone in which they would all have liked to stay rooted and rest on their laurels. Now one can speak more freely about stylization, the rhythm of emotions and all the new things that are coming into being, though still in distorted form. This is a plus. The actors have understood that this is no time for napping, and are wide awake. I myself, sifting through all the residue of the dreams and quests of the past two years, see that nothing serious has been discovered. This is a minus.

We have succeeded in blazing the trail of new principles. These principles may turn the whole psychology of the actor's creativity upside-down. Every day I conduct experiments on myself and others and very often achieve the most interesting results. Most of all I am absorbed in the rhythm of feelings, the development of affective memory. With the help of such experiments I have succeeded in bringing myself to a remarkably greater simplicity and power in my old roles, and succeeded in bolstering my creative powers to such an extent that, even when feverish or under the weather, I forget about illness and get energized on stage. It seems that the troupe has got a taste for the new stuff and has stopped making fun of my researches and pays great heed to my words. When we meet we can talk about all this, because now this whole complicated theme would weary you in its details. Let's gossip instead.

First, a slight commission, which will also amuse you, and will do us a favour. One of our actors has to be in Gurzuf – Gorev (the son of [the Maly actor] Fyodor Petrovich).[63] He is competent, like his father, but silly, boastful, a bit of a braggart and very much in love with himself, but a charming and attractive boy. Without giving away that I whispered such a testimonial about him to you, take him in hand and, with your native intelligence and tact, tease him for his defects. Make him believe that only at the Art Theatre can he become an actor, that the sooner he stops playing big roles of romantic heroes the sooner he will become a real artist. Thanks in advance for this friendly service.

What can I say about us? It's all the same old stuff. They tear us to pieces – more than humanly possible, but the receipts are immense, despite the fact that we arrived without any sort of repertoire. *The Life of Man* is one long horror, muck, but not a play. *Rosmersholm*, although well staged by Nemirovich, is not very theatrical. The rest is old stuff. Invitations fly in from all sides, but I have no strength to answer them. This season I am very tired. Old friends move away, scatter, and the new ones are uninteresting. [...] How are we to keep from dying of a drought of repertoire. [...]

With cordial love and devotion K. Alekseev [...]

While KS was in Petersburg, his son was taking high-school examinations.

To **his son Igor**. 3 May 1908, St Petersburg.

My dear little boy!

[...] To make you laugh, I shall tell you about one of my sleepless nights. I had just about dozed off – suddenly a dreadful rustling. A mouse! I get up, look for how it can make so much noise. Obviously, the box of cookies. I slam down the lid and put it as high as possible on a shelf. I get in bed. The same thing. I get up again, move the box to the cupboard. I move it away from the wall. The same thing. I hide the box in the cupboard and lock it – the same thing. I put the box on the bedside table and get in bed with a slipper to bash the mouse. The same thing. Then I figure out that the mouse had been rammed into the box. I go to the toilet to drown it. Actually, the mouse jumps out and falls in the water.

Hugs and blessings.

Papa

Lyubov Yakovlevna Gurevich (1866-1940) was one of the perceptive and objective literary and dramatic critics in Russian journalism. Her encounter with the MAT completely reoriented her activities; beginning in 1904, she often found herself defending productions other reviewers had dismissed out of hand. In time she became the troupe's historian and KS's literary collaborator, editing his writings and framing his thoughts in appropriate language. She helped to introduce him to philosophers and theatrical ideologues otherwise outside his ken.

To **Lyubov Gurevich**. 9 May 1908, Petersburg.

Dear and deeply esteemed Lyubov Yakovlevna!

[...] At a time of arduous work a man gets self-involved. Especially an actor, on whom a whole repertoire depends. I hearken to every beat of my pulse and tremble for my health. I am waiting impatiently for the time when I can let myself fall ill. Till then I do not have the right. I must see out the season to the end for the sake of the concern and my comrades. But I have no strength at all. Illness has worn me out.

In addition, everything in the theatre is delayed. The repertoire is not set, material for *The Government Inspector* hasn't been selected, the roles aren't cast, the budget isn't done, nor the contracts with the actors (and on Tuesday the troupe disperses), the report isn't ready. The general shareholders' meeting hasn't been held yet, and there is no small amount of unfinished business. That's why my day goes like this: from 12 to 5 at meetings (amid cigarette smoke). At 5 dinner, at 6:30 the theatre, when I'm acting, or more meetings. I go to bed no earlier than three, and so it is every day, and even so there's no time to do it all, and I have to stay put in Moscow until 15 June, because I have no right to leave Moscow before I've ordered all the production elements for three plays for next season. So far I've set up only one. [...]

Heartily devoted K. Alekseev

To **his wife Mariya Lilina**. 12 June 1908, Paris.
My dear, good Marusya!

[...] I had dinner at Ledoyen's. *Sole vin blanc* and rotisserie chicken, strawberries, in short, the whole routine. I listened to a flea-bitten yid[64] and went to the Vaudeville to see an English troupe. According to the yid, it is performing a fairy tale like *The Blue Bird* with wonderful effects etc. This English rubbish is called *Peter Pan*. A magician flies into a nursery to the children (each of whom is about 60 years old), and they go on their travels, of course, to the Indies, the sea, -- to a nymph. Then pirates kidnap them. The first moment, when the magician suddenly flew up to the ceiling and sat on the mantelpiece, I was worried about my own inventiveness in *The Blue Bird*. But other than that effect, repeated individually and in groups all over the place and wherever possible – there is absolutely nothing. With the second flight everything became clear. The wires were visible and noisy. You could see how they were harnessed. It is so simple that for the flying the walls come apart like a double-leaved door, while at the back you can see the stagehands, the foremen and supers walking around the stage, all the flies, etc. There is no point in describing the lack of talent in the play and the actors. They don't believe in it. It's painful for the theatre! The actresses are all an assortment of beauties and quarry for sportsmen. They are even graceful in a circus sort of way. In this regard extraordinary leaps, spins and physical movements were executed. And this whole school has the circus and clowns for an ancestor. Diction, comicality, psychology are those of a clown. When it comes to drama, Veva and Kira during their childhood were more intelligent and closer to the truth. Their leading actors and touring stars of this company could not enter the troupes of our Solovyovtsevs or Zharovtsevs [provincial impresarios]. Judging by this troupe – there is no theatre in England. After the performance I sat in a café. In every respect the very same one that was there 15 years ago. The same words, the same jokes, the same faces. It is impossible to walk along the streets, the way people accost you.

Can it be I have got old, I wondered, -- but no. I have got young, the French have got old and obsolete. Everyone I dealt with – the cocher, garçon, cashier at the theatre, porter --- tried more or less to swindle me. Alas! The French never fail to disappoint me. [...]

Your tenderly loving Kostya [...]

ND, travelling back to Moscow by rail, noticed, as the train pulled out of the station at Malenkoe Sinelnikovo, shadowy figures get on. He locked and chained the door to his compartment, heard gunshots, and later discovered that the conductor had been murdered and his assistant seriously wounded. [65]

To **Nemirovich-Danchenko**. 16/29 July 1908, Homburg.
Dear Vladimir Ivanovich!

How horrible! Yekaterina Nikolaevna's letter informed us of the attempt to rob you and the murder of the railway guard, and before that that you had drowned.[66] I sympathize with all my heart and, as I turn it over in my mind, imagining all the details, I am very worried about you. What an abomination. It is impossible to live in Russia without a pistol. I embrace you and congratulate you for your lucky escape.

Yesterday I sent a letter. Today I go on with it. Today something in me wanted to revive *The Seagull* and made me miss *Ivanov*. Both plays may be needed for Petersburg. When we revive the old repertoire we cannot avoid thoughts of touring. [...]

1) There is no way we can take charming young ladies and students, teach them our art with all its subtleties, skim the cream from the school for our theatre, and eject the rest into the provinces, where all our skill will vanish without a trace, for what the provinces require are effrontery and impudence, hasty work, acting without learning the lines and other workmanlike devices.

2) Ejecting them from the school one at a time, we achieve no results either in the sense of propaganda for our art nor in the sense of the improvement of provincial art. On the contrary, our people will not improve the provinces nor will they be improved by the provinces. Consequently, we have to graduate them from the school not one at a time, but as whole troupes. The first success of such a troupe (not so much artistic, as financial) will spur imitation and provide a good example. But... while this question lies ahead, we still have to put a troupe together.

3) Three years of study in the school hones, but is far from educating a student. It needs another good three years of practical work under guidance to grow as an actor in the current atmosphere. In our theatre there is no work for them. What's more, there is nowhere to create such an atmosphere except in our theatre. Ergo, it is essential to enlarge our team and broaden the range of the theatre's activities, that is to open a theatre at popular prices, and in the meantime [offer] parallel performances.

4) The same artistic demands must be made of these performances as were made on us when the Art Theatre was founded.

5) Experienced amateurs and exceptionally gifted students had joined us before. Our troupe included Moskvin, Luzhsky, Burdzhalov, Lilina, Samarova, Artyom, Knipper, Vishnevsky and so on. It is essential that there be someone in the new troupe who will set the tone of the performance.

6) There is yet another goal in founding a popularly-priced branch of the Art Theatre. Not all of our actors are satisfied with the work. Savitskaya, Knipper, Germanova, Lilina, Leonidov, Vishnevsky frequently lie fallow for years at a time; not to take advantage of them is criminal and wasteful. You will say that this is impossible, that it will muddle the repertoire, but it is even more impossible to allow actresses to decay. To force them, when they are no longer young, to sit idly by, which they can do very well, and – for fear of a slight confusion in the repertoire – to cast aside what we have created, and to consecrate all the strengths of the new theatre to something that has not yet emerged. (I remind you of my

speeches in defence of youth and will passionately defend it as well; but I am unprejudiced and therefore now turn to the old-timers.)

I conclude from what has been said that a repertoire should be organized for a parallel division. [...]

K. Alekseev

To **Nemirovich-Danchenko**. 3/16 August 1908, Westende.
Dear Vladimir Ivanovich!

[...] We have to have *The Seagull* in the repertoire, when a real seagull shows up (Baranovskaya is not ready yet, besides it probably will not suit her). But not to exploit *The Seagull* for Petersburg is wasteful. [...]

Where I've been cruelly tasked is in creating the stage-plan for *Inspector*. My imagination as actor and director is so depleted, and *The Inspector* is so removed from this maritime locale in which we now find ourselves that I can come up with nothing except banality. [...]

Today I will ponder the first act. Something is coming into my mind.

As to *The Blue Bird*.

Maeterlinck had nothing of import to say. All he does is praise and admire. Whether he is flattering us or is serious I don't know. At his place I saw models and sketches. They are very bad and stagey, some of it is excellent. I'm ashamed to say I forgot the most important thing – to ask about the lighting. If I am able to express my doubts in French, I will write to him, but I don't think that he will give a sensible answer. I'm referring to The Azure Kingdom. To my surprise, he so liked the idea of the flying heads with wings that he decided to rewrite the act, but what he sent is not a rewrite, but a minor addition or pretext for the winged heads. He understands that grown women cannot speak the children's lines, and therefore he put in a dungeon (that is according to our last project), in which the ripening children will sit, with their bodies removed so that they cannot escape. The motif is uninteresting and, mainly, impractical. Hardest of all is to cope with the heads when they are sent to earth, because we would need to take them out of the dungeon, where they are set against black velvet. The way it works now the heads are sent to earth and their bodies remain. If worse comes to worst, it can be done like this: a long tail will drag behind Time, the tip of which can fade into a dense black shade, and the departing heads can be grouped against its background.

At first they are sitting in the dungeon, that is behind bars. That is easy to do. In this way all the childish dialogue is done by the heads, while those who portray machines, fruit and the rest are Duncan women.[67] [*Sketch of the set.*]

It might work if in distance we put non-speaking seated figures (that is picking their noses, sucking their thumbs etc.) – of real children. In this scene, of course, all the beauty will be in the beauty of the grouping. The lovers is another question, are these heads or women? Two lovers are women – that is something indecent. We will have to make them heads, but how are we to get them out of the dungeon? [...]

Heartily devoted and affectionate K. Alekseev [...]

To **his wife Mariya Lilina**. Wednesday, 13 August 1908, Berlin.
Dearestdarling!

[...] I had dinner at the 'Russ. Hof', an appallingly nasty feed, with margarine. Then I went to the Kammerspiele. I saw *Lysistrata*. A wonderful building, a nasty stage and everything on it as horrible as horrible can be, starting with the three-dimensional set down to the last costume and performance. It is a fairground show booth, and a very bad one into the bargain. The staging is Shenbergian (in its noise and mindless racket and shrillness) and Arkhipovian in its tasteless novelty.[68] It ended at 9:30. I slept all day – I didn't know what to do with myself. I took tea at Bayer's. At 10 I dropped into the Nachtasyl cabaret – they recognized me there. It turns out that this dump was the favoured spot for our actors to get drunk in. Especially famous in this regard were Gribunin and Moskvin. Lots of secrets were divulged there, and the Moscow cabaret The Bat was obviously built on impressions of this one. And it is a museum of stupidity, not witty, ponderous, irritating. They close at 11. I dropped into another cabaret on Unter den Linden. Men and women come on stage and sing Berlin 'witze' very decently. Bored, home by 12. Slept well. [...]

Kostya

To **his wife Mariya Lilina**. 22 August 1908, Moscow
My tender and precious one!

[...] In the evening I went to the theatre. On stage they were performing Acts 1 and 2 of *Government Inspector*. Nothing doing, although something was taking shape in Uralov, Gorev and Moskvin. They have not understood the serious relationship to the roles and my methods of conviction.[69] At 10 the rehearsals ended. [...] The next day [...] rehearsals from 11 to 3 and from 7 to 10. We went through the whole first act and at night did a complete run-through. A good deal is working, and I think the tone has been found. It may come out well, and the troupe felt this and got enthused. Between rehearsals I took the horse-tram to get a breath of air in the park and dropped in on the races. In the course of 10 minutes, I ran into all our gambling actors, with Moskvin in the lead. Suler spent the night again. On Monday at 11 a.m. Act 2 of *Government Inspector*, tighter, didn't work. Gorev can be very good. At night review of 'The Forest' [the fifth scene of *The Blue Bird*.] A slight scandal. Yegorov got worked up and demonstratively left the rehearsal. The next day he came by embarrassed. Tuesday – morning: Act 2 of *Inspector*; evening: inspect 'The Azure Kingdom' (bewitching set), 'Night' (good), the second scene of 'Night' (good). Wednesday morning – Act 2 *Inspector*. Evening meeting. Decided to open with *The Blue Bird*. Afterwards *Inspector*. Suler spent the night every day. Thursday morning – factory, evening – Act 1 *Blue Bird* in the foyer. They had forgotten everything. Germanova as the Fairy is nowhere. Today Friday – morning – run-through of Act I. It's going well. Germanova is all right.

In the evening 'Night' on stage – run-through. No one is late. Fines imposed. They tighten up. [...]

All yours Kostya

The weather is warm, but damp. All around influenza and grippe.

KS sketched out an opuscule called 'The Actor's Ethics'. It was a step towards putting on paper his evolving ideas about the actor's technique and its context.

To **his wife Mariya Lilina**. 26 August 1908, Moscow.
Dear and precious one!
[...] We worked well at the theatre, but the day before yesterday, when we started on the 2nd scene in *The Blue Bird*, it turned out that no one knew his lines or blocking, despite the fact that last year we had rehearsed the act ten times if we rehearsed it once. This plunged me into despair, and last year's mood came over me again. My evening was free. After the rehearsal I walked around the park and back. The mud, vileness, savagery of Moscow intensified my longing for order and discipline even more. It seemed to me that we are perishing in dissipation. Discipline is required. In the evening I stayed home and wrote what I think is not a bad chapter on ethics. Yesterday, Monday, I read it to the actors. They seem to have thought things over, and the rehearsal was a good one, the 2nd scene is well in hand. [...]

Ever yours Kotun

To **Leopold Sulerzhitsky**. 26 September 1908, Moscow.
Dear Suler!
I'm writing this while still at the director's table.
Forgive me if I offended you, but it wasn't my intention.
Whether I yelled or not -- I don't remember, but I had been shouting from 11 in the morning to 11 at night, and lacked both the voice and the nerves to maintain order.
To be fair, the board of directors does insist that I let the orchestra go as soon as possible.
Sats has changed the music, and now my imagination is working to fold in and connect the movement to the music.
After a year and a half the water -- doesn't work. People whisper to me that I must give up something I have been dreaming about for half a year.
Anyone who has sat at the director's table must forgive a man if, at such moments, in giving of himself unstintingly, behaves rudely. I am the only thinking person here and I impose my will on all the actors, I am living for all of those who sit at my table.
Forgive me – perhaps I was at fault, but I deserve indulgence.

Yours K. Alekseev

The Blue Bird opened on 30 September 1908. There had been nearly 150 rehearsals. Over time, it broke all records for MAT performances: 438 between 1908 and 1923, and 4,574 by the theatre's centennial in 1998. The production was copied for the play's premiere in Paris (supervised by Suler but somewhat vulgarized) and, without acknowledgement, for London.

The tenth anniversary of the MAT on 14 October was celebrated by fans as if it were a national holiday. The theatre had become the standard-bearer for the ideas, hopes and tastes of a certain segment of the intelligentsia.

Craig arrived in mid-October and original discussions suggested that he design an Ibsen history play.

To the **Board**. 28 November 1908. [*'I presented the letter "Help". They thought it unfair. The board advised me not to post it.' ND made several comments to make it seem less insulting. Four revisions were made.*]

LETTER TO SOME OF MY ACTOR COLLEAGUES
HELP!!!

1. The [tenth] jubilee honours, the success of our plays, full houses do not increase the theatre's energy, but sap its capacity for work.

2. In the first half of the season the theatre has staged *not one single new play*.

3. The play created after two years' work [*The Bluebird*] and which now feeds our theatre, no longer stirs up a feeling of affection.

4. It seems that it is not complicated production values that prevent us from staging plays, but apathy towards creative work within the troupe itself.

5. The staging of the best works of our national literature in the jubilee year no longer appears to be an event for our theatre.

6. At the critical moment the theatre is going through, when actors feel their pride has been offended, they are not only indulged but sympathized with.

7. People want to use the cancellation of two performances in a week for rest and recreation, and not more intensive rehearsal work.

8. People feel able to leave Moscow without official permission from the board.

9. Notification of illness or non-attendance is reported only after the performance has begun.

10. Neither requests nor reprimands, neither regulations nor a sense of collegial ethics are capable any more of eliminating tardiness or failure to turn up for rehearsals.

11. The behaviour of individual persons which impedes the work of the theatre is no longer capable of provoking general protest.

12. To speak out boldly against troublemakers in defence of the general concern is considered to be an act of denunciation, while concealment of the guilty parties is considered collegial ethics.

13. Fledglings in our art publicly plume themselves on their yet unproven talent and congratulate themselves in advance for successes to come, instead of earning them by work. This is considered amusing.

14. New theories in our art, which should be realized through dogged effort, are capable of interesting our theatre for no more than a couple of weeks.

15. New currents in our art that come from the West are not welcomed sympathetically.

16. The extreme efforts of a small group, which constitutes the soul of our whole concern, encounters less sympathy than the petty offenses of those among us who have in no way proved themselves.

17. The superhuman work of the directors, who give the actors the best elements of their souls as actors, is appreciated only in words and not in deeds.

18. The artistic, administrative, ethical and disciplinary facets of the theatre are kept up by a small group of self-sacrificing, hard-working individuals. Their strength and patience are being exhausted. The time will soon come when they will have to turn down work which is beyond human abilities.

Come to your senses while there is still time!

Your well-wisher
K. Stanislavsky

Diary for 1908.

Commandments.

1. Thou shalt bring to the theatre powerful feelings and great ideas, and leave the petty ones at the door.

2. At the threshold of the stage – thou shalt feel.

3. In costume thou shalt array thyself.

4. Thou shalt not mouth thy lines, but learn their feelings and ideas.

5. Thou shalt be cheerful and then create.

6. Thou shalt know what you want to create, and know how to want to create.

7. Thou shalt believe everything that happens on stage, and never pretend that thou art believing.

8. Thou shalt live on stage for thyself and think for others.

9. Thou shalt always live the given moment with all thy being.

10. Thou shalt be everything on stage and enjoy the creativity for thyself.

11. Thou shalt not strive to act well for others; thou shalt be wont to speak clearly and be visible, and thereby be on good terms with the spectator.

12. Thou shalt live on stage, and not pretend to be undergoing experiences.

13. Let not the words outstrip the ideas, and the ideas the feelings.

14. Thou shalt not think of the word, but of the feeling.

15. The first performance is the first public rehearsal.

The Government Inspector *opened on 18 December. It embodied a new principle of exaggeration which some critics read as caricature. As usual, the divergence from traditional interpretations provoked a wide spectrum of responses. It managed fifty-seven performances.*

Sloe-eyed Alisa Georgievna Koonen (1889-1974) became one of KS's favourites, though ND thought of her as primarily a comic actress. She began in third-rank roles; her leads were in symbolist drama or as exotic types, such as the gypsy Masha in The Living Corpse *and Anitra in* Peer Gynt. *Craig wanted her to play Ophelia, but he was overruled.*

To **Vera Kotlyarevskaya** LS. 24 December 1908, Moscow.

Dear friend Vera Vasilievna!

[…] Our season wasn't bad. *The Blue Bird* was a success, so was *The Government Inspector*, although, I'm told the papers abuse us obscenely. As a director I am overworked, as an actor I am quite removed from the stage, and this upsets me, because all I love is acting.

My summer work has borne good fruit. The new psycho-physiological method is giving good results and has begun to interest the troupe. The theatre has shone with another young actress – Koonen, in whom I invest great hopes. […]

Cordially devoted

K. Alekseev

Notes

1 A peasant proverb: 'All the pine-cones fall on poor Makar'.

2 ND had written: 'We had already lost Chekhov with *The Cherry Orchard*. He wouldn't have written anything more. As for Gorky, if he writes a play, it will be for us, I am sure of it.' In fact, Gorky withheld *Vacationers*, saying he wanted to publish it first.

3 Morozov had retired from the theatre, but had retained his shares in it.

4 ND: 'A useful actress, yes. But a great "troublemaker" in the whole concern.'

5 ND: 'Olga Leonardovna for the time being? No. Now she will devote herself entirely to the stage and very soon. She is already spoiling to act and will bend every effort to be in Moscow. She will return about halfway through August. And we have to give her work.'

6 ND: 'Not only have I not finished my play, I haven't even sketched it out yet.'

7 Andreeva and Gorky had discussed with Kachalov moving to their new theatre, but he remained at the MAT.

8 KS was afraid that the ongoing war would adversely affect the box-office, which had already happened in other theatres the previous season. ND: 'The war? Imagine, as I follow it very carefully, I am beginning to believe that at the very opening of our season we will be continual winners. And this will very much lift the spirits of society.' His prognosis was mistaken.

9 Komissarzhevskaya did not stage a play by Pyotr Mikhailovich Yartsev (1871-1930), and her production of Yevgeny Chirikov's *Ivan Mironych* did not prevent the MAT from putting it on successfully during its spring tour to Petersburg.

10 None of the actors was called up.

11 ND: 'The work will be friendly, there is no doubt. As to "first place", you and I have already become completely inured to this. We have already been through everything that can harm us in this sense. If we haven't chewed up one other by now, there is no further danger at this point.'

12 Sergey Aleksandrovich Naidyonov (Alekseev, 1868-1922) and Yartsev were both members of Gorky's Znanie group. Naidyonov was the better writer and the more popular playwright; *Vanyushin's Children*, a drama of intergenerational conflict, was one of the biggest hits of the pre-Revolutionary stage. Yartsev was primarily a critic and later a director.

13 A proposed evening of one-acts by Chekhov, Turgenev, and Gorky never happened.

14 It was revived the following season.

15 It was not put on in the new season.

16 It never happened.

17 Krasovsky, Tikhomirov (the Pastor), Andreeva (Rautendelein) and Sanin (the Water Sprite) had left the company.

18 *Julius Caesar*, whose sets, props and costumes were sold to the Solovtsov Theatre in Kiev.

19 *Vacationers*, which Gorky refused to rewrite and gave to Kommissarzhevskaya.

20 *Ghosts*, *Rosmersholm* and *Month in the Country* were the only ones staged.

21 KS's mother died on 12 October and was interred five days later with the cortege leaving from the church of the village of Spas.

22 From 2 October when the season opened to the date of the letter KS had acted 67 times.

23 The press had been reporting on the reorganization of Komissarzhevskaya's theatre into a stock company composed of Morozov, Gorky, Nezlobin, Komissarzhevskaya and Andreeva – hence 'ladies' theatre.' They proposed to invite KS for specific productions.

24 This fear arose from Morozov's leaving the board, since he rented the building from the merchant Georgy Liazonov and, having had the largest part in reconstructing it, sublet it to the MAT for 25,000 rubles a year.

25 A phrase from Famusov's monologue in Act II.

26 Nina Litovtseva had played many of Andreeva's roles after her departure and continued to be her alternate in a few of them.

27 A somewhat abridged translation can be found in *The Moscow Art Theatre Letters*, ed. Jean Benedetti (London: Routledge, 1991), pp.213-34.

28 Kotlyarevskaya was preparing the role of Charlotta Ivanovna in the Alexandra Theatre premiere of *The Cherry Orchard*, 23 September 1905.

29 The censorship passed the play on 17 September 1905 without any changes required.

30 It eventually opened on 30 September.

31 It was postponed to the following season.

32 Nikolay Aleksandrovich Popov (1871-1949) had collaborated with KS at the Society; director at Komissarzhevskaya's Theatre in the Passage (1904-06); ran the People's Theatre of the Vasileostrov Society for People's Amusements in Petersburg.

33 ND saw it taking place at night, lit by lamps. KS upheld the author's stage directions.

34 ND had written that Andreeva was getting nervous over her role and Gorky.

35 The play had gone into rehearsal before receiving the censor's license; it came on 17 September.

36 Meyerhold's alternate in the revival of *Seagull* (30 September) was Vladimir Vasilievich Maksimov (Samus, 1880-1937), who did not take on the role until 14 November.

37 Vladimir Emilievich Repman (stage name Vladimirov, 1871-1918), a director at the Studio on Povarsky.

38 The Black Hundreds, a monarchist, ultra-nationalist faction, supported by the tsarist regime, active 1905-07, fomented pogroms against the Jews and assassinated liberal politicians.

39 Jurgens Norden published a review of *Tsar Fyodor* and *Three Sisters* in the paper *Tagliche Rundschau*; KS's quotation is from another article.

40 Vladimir Vladimirovich Stasov (1824-1906), Russia's leading music critic.

41 Friedrich Haase (1825-1911), German actor, especially of roles in Schiller and Shakespeare. Alfred Kerr (Kempner, 1867-1948), Berlin's most influential theatre critic.

42 KS remembered the singer Francesco d'Andrade (1859-1921) from his appearances at the Russian Private Opera in Moscow. Julius Spielmann (1866-1920), Bohemian tenor, outstanding both in Wagner and operetta.

43 ND did not send her notes on Teresita until after the production opened.

44 Nikolay Afanasievich Podgorny (1879-1947), an MAT student on stage from 1903; he would eventually become one of the most prominent members of the MAT administration.

45 In summer and fall 1906 they had sent him plays and received personal answers. In a subsequent letter, ND explained that authors did not send him their plays because he had the veto or were his literary enemies, so they approached KS, who didn't send the works on to him.

46 Aleksandr Ivanovich Kosorotov (1868-1912), whose play, *Spring Torrent*, staged by Meyerhold, had been banned. Sholom Asch (1880-1957), Russian Jewish writer, popular with both Russian and Jewish readers. Stanisław Feliks Przybyszewski (1868-1927), Polish aesthete, novelist and playwright, espoused by both Vera Komissarzhevskaya and Meyerhold.

47 ND proposed taking on *The Drama of Life* work with Kachalov in the lead.

48 *Pippa tanzt*, an allegory on an aesthetic theme; it wasn't put on. The astute critic and translator Nikolay Yefimovich Efros (1886-1954), who had begun writing about KS back in the days of the Society, often did work for the MAT.

49 Nikolay Grigorievich Aleksandrov (1870-1930) was been one of the Society's actors absorbed into the MAT. Described as 'not much of an actor but an extraordinary assistant director', he was best in secondary roles.

50 ND considered the production of *Brand* essential for its philosophical and civic content. In the argument over the predominance of Ibsen or Hamsun, ND said his heart sank when Stakhovich asserted that their repertoire lay outside all contemporary movements, and KS referred to the Black Hundreds.

51 ND declared that he wanted power in order to support KS's artistic intentions.

52 The opening was put off until on 8 February 1907.

53 Vladimir Aleksandrovich Nelidov (1869-1926), official in the office of the Imperial Theatres, critic and translator; married to Olga Gzovskaya. The long adjourned question of Nelidov's admission to the MAT soon became a bone of contention.

54 ND, after the rehearsal of 30 January: 'If I thought that the play might still be taken off, I probably would not consider my presence yesterday harmful for the concern… However, all this can be dealt with later, whenever.'

55 Jurgis Baltrushaitis (Russian name Georgy Kazimirovich, 1873-1944), Latvian symbolist poet. Sergey Aleksandrovich Polyakov (1874-1942), poet and publisher, was the play's translator. Aleksandr Valentinovich Sredin (1872-1934), post-impressionist artist, brother of Leonid Sredin.

56 A historian like Robert Vipper, a poet like Balmont, or a collector like the Shchukin brothers.

57 N. I. Fyodorova, a student at the MAT school 1902-03. Daisy is Igor's friend M. Giziko.

58 Maeterlinck was not to attend the premiere.

59 Mariya Nikolaevna Germanova (1884-1940), a high-school classmate of Gzovskaya and one of the first students at the MAT school in 1903, was said to be reminiscent of Duse. ND favoured her and cast her in leading roles, including Andreev's nympho-maniac Yelizaveta Ivanova. In 1919-22 she acted outside Russia with the Kachalov Group and then headed the so-called Prague Troupe.

60 Vladimir Arkadievich Telyakovsky (1861-1924), conservative administrator of the imperial theatres.

61 Eleonora Duse (1858-1924), the great Italian actress, was admired by Chekhov for her emotional honesty, but KS was less impressed.

62 Sergey Arkadievich Andreevsky (1847-1918), lawyer, literary critic, author of the one of the first studies of the MAT ('The theatre of a young century', *Rossiya*, 2 December 1901.)

63 Apollon Fyodorovich Gorev (1887-1912) had partnered Yermolova; KS invited him to work on Schiller's Don Carlos. He died young of tuberculosis.

64 Vladimir Lvovich Binshtok (1868-1933), translator and journalist.

65 See ND, *My Life in the Russian Theatre*, tr. John Cournos (London: Geoffrey Bles, 1937), pp. 253-55.

66 He couldn't swim.

67 There was a special class at the MAT where young actresses practiced plastique in the Duncan style.

68 He's comparing Reinhardt's work with that of his former colleagues Sanin (Shenberg) and Arbatov (Arkhipov).

69 KS suggested building interaction by having one partner either convince the other or say: 'Convince me.' Uralov played the Mayor, Gorich the Superintendent of Schools, and Moskvin Dobchinsky.

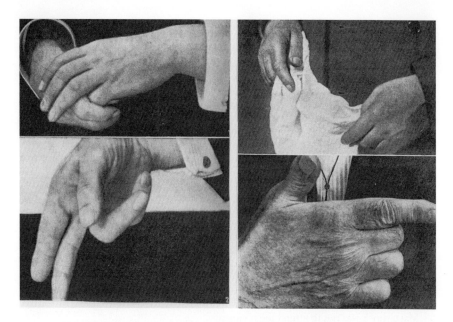

Figure 42 Stanislavsky's hands, photographs taken by A. P. Saveliev in 1933. Clockwise from upper right: in life; as Gaev in *The Cherry Orchard*; as General Krutitsky in *No Fool Like a Wise Fool*; and as Dr Stockmann in *Enemy of the People*

6

EXPERIMENTS
IN ALL DIRECTIONS
1909–1911

The existence of a Duma, no matter how unsatisfactory its powers in the absence of a constitution, lent stability to society, as it rallied the confidence and support of the public. The term of the Third Duma (1907-12) was one of remarkable economic prosperity. Education became universally accessible, and major reforms were instituted in land settlement and industry.

This was the period when KS first tried to put his ideas about acting down on paper. His forty-six page typescript was never published, but was circulated among the members of the MAT, many of whom regarded his 'system' with skepticism. With ND's grudging approval, KS tried out many of his ideas with the actors. The ten-year report had complained that the MAT needed to enlarge its repertoire and its methods to make it capable of staging poetic drama. It put out feelers to other artistic camps, especially the World of Art movement, based in St Petersburg.

Gurevich had written a critique of The Government Inspector *which appeared in the magazine* Slovo *(The Word) on 22 December 1908.*

To **Lyubov Gurevich**. Before 9 February 1909, Moscow.
Deeply esteemed Lyubov Yakovlevna!
[…] Thanks for your comments about *The Government Inspector*. […] There is no way to correct Gorev's youth, inexperience, inadequately developed temperament and voice. It is his second year on stage and, if you don't include Sugar [in *The Blue Bird*], he is playing the first big role in his life, and Khlestakov at that. Khlestakov is to comedy what Hamlet is to tragedy. This role is the acme of *technical* difficulty. When an experienced old-timer, such as Sadovsky, plays Khlestakov, he is old, although technically perfect. It is understandable that Gorev will be technically imperfect, but young. Which is better? To my mind, the latter. Time will improve Gorev. It is dangerous to force matters.

Details about the boots, the waiter's topknot can be fixed.[1] They are not important, but if you bear in mind that the action takes place in '35, and remember the attitude of a master's son to servants at that time, there can be no other attitude. Not long ago, with my own eyes, I saw a landowner's son, well-known about Moscow, in a moment of irritation dash a glass of wine in the face of a waiter, who had not informed him of something in time. And the waiter smiled in embarrassment.

РЕВИЗОРЪ н. в. гоголя.　　　　　Моск. Худож. Театръ.
Хлестаковъ—А. Ф, Горевъ.　　　47
Изд. «Искусство и Жизнь» И. И. Корнилова и Ко. Москва

Figure 43 Apollon Gorev as Khlestakov in *The Government Inspector*. Photo: K. A. Fischer, Moscow

A week ago in our theatre I saw this sort of scene: an exasperated and flashily dressed lady (from Siberia) wailed so loudly in the foyer that they had to take her into a distant room. She wailed just like the most authentic *cook*.

And this contrast with the dress and the outer luxury was especially typical for the provinces. She was wailing because she had been late for Act I and they had made her wait in the foyer.

I told you about the daughter of a provincial mayor, who in a low-cut pink satin dress went down to a steamboat in thirty-degree heat to meet *a Negro king from Negroland.*

All this happens in the 20th century the same as it did in the time of Gogol.

All these details create that atmosphere of naïvety, in which the story of the Inspector can be played.

But, of course, if the audience has not matured up to the level of audacious truth on stage, if its understanding of aesthetics goes no farther than the academic – it is not worth cluttering up its timorous imagination with details, because it will not descry the important thing behind them. Therefore thanks a lot for your remarks. [...]

Our actors' ten years of activity have involuntarily developed gimmicks, habits, damaging to an artist, owing to daily performances and exhausting involvement in acting. The troupe is aware of this and has decided to fight against it. The whole troupe and the school have been divided into groups, and now every day we get together and reform each other from what we consider to be undesirable. The actor's general attitude on stage is deceptive and does not produce the results he counts on. With such authenticating work one can regulate and verify one's general creative attitude. [...]

We've decided on the plays for next year: *Hamlet* (with Kachalov and Craig) to open the season; then [Andreev's] *Anathema* [to be directed by N-D], then *A Month in the Country*. [...]

Heartily devoted and grateful

K. Alekseev

Andreevsky had advised that they stage Byron's Cain, Manfred *and* Sardanapalus *instead of* Anathema, *because of their contemporary relevance and greater poetic power.*

To **Sergey Andreevsky**. 17 February 1909, Moscow.

Dear and deeply esteemed Sergey Arkadievich!

Between ourselves, I agree with you about *Anathema*. But...

Did I not dream of *Cain*?! The lines were learned, the scenery and costumes were ready, and the Synod forbade it, because it turned out that Abel was a saint, and Cain, Eve and Adam -- aren't they something like saints as well?! Sardanapalus – Manfred!!! Is there an actor for these roles? If only someone we may have overlooked. For Hamlet there may be one, perhaps, though far from ideal, but Manfred – Sardanapalus!.. None of us can play these roles.

But you have to go on living...

Against our will we have to settle for *Anathema*.

Pity us, starving ones.

Heartily devoted and respectful

K. Alekseev

After the seventy-eighth performance of The Blue Bird, *KS had written a note complaining of the actors' lack of discipline and inability to act on the notes they were given. Only foreign actors can be good technicians, he complained; a Russian actor's art has to excel at emotional experiencing.*

To **Leonid Leonidov.** After 22 February 1909, Moscow.

Dear Leonid Mironovich,

I consider your meeting today to be very important if the discussions are directed towards an area where a dangerous enemy of theatre and all art lurks.

That enemy is craftsmanship.

We must *combat* it.

We must *learn* to combat it.

In order to convince my colleagues of the danger threatening us and to influence the discussions in that direction, I want to tighten up the last report I wrote concerning Mr Sulerzhitsky's opinions, and supplement it with new and convincing facts.

I am referring to the last performance of *The Government Inspector*. More specifically, Acts 1 and 5.

Not only can I not rebuke anyone of the participants in the performance for a negligent and uncaring attitude to his role, -- I can do quite the opposite: regret that in these acts there was too much straining and therefore little art.

But…

The result is discomfiting.

Such performances have no place in the Art Theatre.

This is not art.

It is conscientious craftsmanship.

It is a perversion of Gogol.

People will say that I am too picayune, that my colleagues cannot keep me amused, because I am too demanding and know them too well.

This opinion would be mistaken.

Why in the same performance did I blush during Acts 1 and 5 and wanted to run from the theatre, but in 2 I was sincerely amused, I watched 3 with pleasure, and in 4 I was bored only occasionally? To the question, why are the same characters good in some acts and very bad in others, I venture to answer and substantiate my conclusions by examples.

For this I need:

1) the troupe to realize clearly the impending danger. To be disturbed by it and become alarmed in earnest. Then things will happen.

2) – that is, everyone will want to arm himself against the dangerous enemy.

Fortunately, I am firmly convinced that the weapon is at hand. It is honed by the long practice of the theatre and is in waiting for those in need of it to come and get it.

My next discussion is on Wednesday – at 1 p.m.

Yours respectfully, K. Alekseev

KS invited everyone interested in the art of emotional experiencing to renew their involvement; the first meeting took place 25 February. Many in the company disdained these seminars, and ND put his own tolerance to the test. He grew increasingly frustrated that rehearsals for what should be highly polished productions were being turned into lessons and études. He himself had taken on another play in the Knut Hamsun trilogy, At the

Gates of the Kingdom. *It opened on 9 March and played for 394 performances, not least because Kachalov was a more sympathetic and accessible Ivar Kareno than KS had been.*

The annual Petersburg tour opened with The Blue Bird.

To **his daughter Kira**. 31 March 1909, Petersburg.

My dear, precious Kiryulya!

I am sitting backstage, in this little red drawing-room of government-issue type. Remember?

The Blue Bird is on for the second time. Yesterday was the first performance and today a matinee performance of *Three Sisters*.

Grand Duke Konstantin Konstantinovich[2] is in the theatre with his own family from the littlest kids on up, who roar with laughter at every line. Another celebrity is there – Leonid Andreev.

Yesterday's premiere went like all premieres. They applauded the first act, then, after 'The Forest' they got weary. Some went out of their minds with ecstasy, others with indignation, a third – the intelligent ones – chided it as a childish play, the fourth slipped into childhood and were delighted. Backstage things were very uneasy, because the stage is disgusting, ill-adapted, and the cues, that is the signals for the music, were spoiled at the very beginning. The audience was rather lively, although they were talking more about Stolypin than Maeterlinck.[3] The performance was so-so. I was especially sorry for Koonen, who got cold feet and stagefright and leaned on the lines, laughed too much, yelped, overemphasized the childish tone too much. They didn't appreciate her at the first performance, and most of them preferred Khalyutina.[4] The external aspect of the production was very successful. Of course, the ruffian reviewers see nothing in the play except cinema. Others, on the contrary, see far too much, and, to show off their remarkable intelligence, get indignant that the theatre did not extract from the work what the intelligent brains of the reviewer had seen. In short, the same old story. […]

Your Papa

To **his son Igor.** 2 April 1909, Petersburg.

My dear boy,

I am writing Kira an account of *The Blue Bird*, and you about *The Government Inspector*. […] We were expecting *Inspector* to go like the Battle of Tsushima.[5] This is the perfect moment to fling mud at us. The battle was tough going and disgusting. Everyone was desperately upset. The first act went horribly. Uralov [as the Mayor] had no voice and did us in. We were tearing out our hair, especially when Gorev [as Khlestakov] got even colder feet. But even so he's a talented little fool and immediately captivated the audience, although he was acting worse than ever. The second act went well. In the third act, after the boasting scene, they applauded Gorev in the middle of the act. The fourth act also went decently. The fifth was worse, because Uralov was quite hoarse. The final scene made a great impression. Again some praised, others abused us, and hell reigns in my heart, because we have to admit in our hearts that the performance went badly.

In the morning we waited for them to fling the mud, and to our amazement the notices are better than we might expect. Gorev is already swanning down Nevsky Prospect like Khlestakov and a curious thing happened to him. This morning a letter is brought to him in everyone's presence. He makes a face and impatiently says, 'What! Again! It's started.' That is, he hints that he's beginning to be showered with love letters. He unseals the letter, everyone looks. It turns out that they sent him a bill from his tailor, whom he didn't pay in Moscow. [...]

Your Papa

To **his son Igor**. 21 April 1909, St Petersburg.
My dear, precious boy!

[...] here in Petersburg it is impossible to get any work done. People senselessly pay one another visits and if you let them in once, they think they have to do it every day. There is no peace.

Add to that – Duncan and Craig. [...] Yes, Duncan has grown as Iphigenia, she didn't finish the second programme – and Beethoven is beyond her abilities.[6] During this stint she was much more serious and talked more than she danced. We have seen her frequently; she has called on us and talked a lot about art. The last few days she told me in detail about her system, and I explained to her my circles and arrows.[7] I thought she would laugh at my theory, but it turned out that this theory seemed more interesting and useful to her and Craig than to any of our actors. This cheered me up a good deal.

One curious thing has happened, at which everyone is still laughing. On Thursday she was supposed to depart and invited Suler, Craig, Knipper and Maklakov[8] to a farewell dinner. At the last minute she arrives and says that there are 15 minutes till the train leaves. Panic broke out and everyone jumped up and started to sort out the packages. Duncan asks me to escort her. I get into a barouche and ask the doorman at the hotel – which way do we go? He confidently says – to Warsaw Station. This is round about Robin Hood's barn. We tear away as fast as we can go. We get there with 2 minutes to spare and there we learn that we should have gone to the Tsarkoeselo Station. It turns out that the maid and the baggage had left for Kiev, Duncan was too late, and all her friends had scattered all over the place with the hand baggage. We go back to the inn—Duncan's room is being cleaned up. Clouds of dust. Where is she to go? We go to our place. After the performance the actors show up and turn it into a perfect bedlam. Finally, everyone disperses, the baggage is found, and Duncan has been installed in place. [...]

Your tenderly loving
Papa

To **Ilya Sats**. 27 April 1909, Petersburg.
Dear, good Ilya Aleksandrovich!

I did not reply at once to your letter when I got it, because it came during a regular hurly-burly of a week. First, Duncan was in Petersburg – that should say it all. They danced every day till 6 o'clock in the morning. If you bear in mind that

Craig is also in Petersburg and that from 12 to 7 o'clock every day I have to talk to him about the twists and turns of Hamlet's soul in an Anglo-German language, you will begin to understand the head I've been walking around with all week long.

[…] At the moment we are strenuously engaged on *Hamlet*, and, as was obvious from the beginning, there will be rather a good deal of music. […] Craig is staging *Hamlet* as a monodrama. He regards everything through the eyes of Hamlet. Hamlet is the ghost; everything else around him is crude matter. Included in the latter are, for instance, the 2nd scene (the King's speech). The whole court and its pomp are imagined by Hamlet in the guise of monstrous gold courtiers. In the course of his musing he hears trumpets, the sound of bells, sometimes resounding and triumphant, sometimes cracked and dirge-like. Those sounds are mixed with echoes of a funereal motif. Hamlet hears the very same sounds of the trumpets and anthems, associated with the wailing of the wind, the sound of the sea and the funereal, sepulchral sounds in the scene with his father as well, that is in Act 1, scenes 4 and 5. What happens next I don't yet know.

Duncan as her first duty asked about you, then demanded the promised polka from *The Blue Bird*. She said, among other things, couldn't you write her something to dance to, because she despairs of finding appropriate music.

Don't worry about the financial aspect. We shall do everything in our power.

Craig is very fond of your music for *The Blue Bird*. Not long ago he sat backstage and listened to it. When they sang the mother's song – he jumped up and kept declaring: 'Very good' [*in English*].

Meanwhile, for heaven's sake, rest, and in May we'll talk.

Hugs. Be well.

Yours K. Alekseev

To **Lyubov Gurevich**. 14 May 1909, Moscow.
Dear and most esteemed Lyubov Yakovlevna!

[…] The figures I provided are accurate. We took in 160,000 r., that is 80,000 clear, and in Moscow 25,000 clear. But this split is not exact. Moscow earned so little because it incurred all the expenses of the productions, which are enumerated in [category] 1. These expenses include not only sets and costumes, but 2 months of rehearsals before the season began. Besides that, Moscow pays the annual salaries of the troupe, whereas the Petersburg accounts mention only the supplemental salaries for Petersburg.

As to Craig – it's all poppycock![9] People have already begun to peck at him because he is no slave to routine. Nemirovich, myself and the whole theatre not only are not disappointed in him, but, on the contrary, are persuaded that he is a genius. That's why he was not acknowledged in his own country. He created astonishing things, and the theatre is trying to carry out all his wishes to the best of our abilities. The whole directorial and stage personnel are put at his disposition, and I am his closest assistant, entirely devoted to him, and this role fills me with pride and joy. If we manage to demonstrate Craig's talent, we will be doing a great service to art. It will take a while, not many people will understand Craig all at once, because he is ahead of the whole world by half a century. He is a magnificent poet, an astonishing artist and a knowledgeable stage director of refined taste. I will not conceal the things I write about him from the public, so long as it does not take these lines to be publicity for Craig. [...]

K. S. Alekseev [...]

Isadora Duncan was now living in Paris, under the protection of the American sewing-machine heir Paris Singer, and had opened a dance studio.

To **Leopold Sulerzhitsky.** Between 7-22 June 1909, Paris.
Dear Suler!
[...] Yesterday my wife and children left for Vichy, but I am staying here exclusively on account of Duncan. I don't really understand what she needs from me, but she asked me to help her set up her school. Here's what it's about: Singer[10] has built her a magnificent and enormous studio near Paris. I went there during the children's lesson. Mysterious semi-darkness, quiet music, dancing children – it all stupefied me. She was sincerely glad to see me and asked a lot of questions about the Muscovites, you, Craig, etc.

When the dances were over, she took me around to show me her rooms – tiny little kennels. Then I got worried. These are not the rooms of a Greek goddess, but a French cocotte. Showing me the bedroom, she poked her fingers into the lace that veiled the sluttish red wallpaper. 'Mr Singer had this made for me,' – and... she got embarrassed.

Then for a long time she asked me questions: could she accept all this studio, house and land as a gift from Singer. Then came stories about the school. Her sister had fallen in love with some German, and they want to open a school together. Unbeknownst to Isadora they signed a contract with all the remaining children or their parents and now they are taking away all the children whom she's been feeding and raising for 8 years, and will exploit them. She has a studio, Singer is building a whole building for the children next door, but there are no children. At first she thought that Singer was building it all for the school, and she could accept such a gift for the school, but now, when there is no school, she has to accept the gift on her own behalf, in other words, sell herself. In addition Singer's jealousy is coming into play. 'I got huffy for a moment; he got angry and went off somewhere, without telling me.' She does not love him, he does not love her. That's clear. Duncan is in vogue and, obviously a rich man like Singer is living with her for fashion's sake. That's the consensus. Yesterday Duncan asked me to visit her at noon: 'There will be no spies, and we shall spend the day together.' Which means, there are spies! – thought I. At noon I arrive. In the studio I am met by a tall, very handsome gentleman and he greets me with unusual courtesy and formality. He led me to Isadora's room – she was finishing her toilette and powdering herself -- and I went straight downstairs. I waited in the dining-room for about ten minutes, while she was putting on her makeup next door. Neither of us said a word. Then she came in and said that the lunch wouldn't be at home, but that Mr Singer was taking her to a restaurant, and she invited me to go with her. We got in the motor-car, a very luxurious one, and drove off. Along the way they talked dreadful rubbish and vulgarities. He was dressed to the nines, I was in a travelling suit and a dirty Panama hat. We arrived at some restaurant in the Bois, packed with fancy-men and cocottes. We sat down. I felt as if I were playing the role of a parasite. Singer was unusually attentive. He tried to engage me. He smiled charmingly, while I got embarrassed and talked rubbish. They talked rubbish too. The luncheon ended. I wanted to make off, but Isadora asked me to go with her to the studio. I agreed. They spoke English, and we set off for town. I don't know why. There we drove past my hotel, and I thanked them and asked them to let me off. They stopped. We said our affectionate farewells. I got out, and, as the car was driving away, Duncan, somewhat bashfully, boldly blew me a kiss. I became so offended that I burst into tears. The Greek goddess in the golden cage of the factory-owner. Venus de Milo had ended up among the expensive knick-knacks on the desk of a rich man to serve as a paper weight. While she is so imprisoned there is no way I can talk to her, and I will no longer go to her home. In the evening she dances, I will call on her in her dressing-room to say farewell and slip her a note: 'You asked for my advice... now I have understood everything and can speak.

1) Run away from Paris.

2) Treasure freedom above all.

3) Reject the school, if it has to be paid for at such a high price.

4) Whatever may happen to you, I will understand it all and sympathize with you with all my heart.'

I watched the children dancing on stage, saw her class. Alas, nothing will come of this. She is no teacher. Our Yelena Nikolaevna[11] will achieve greater results in a single year than she will in eight years. She needs to dance, and let others open schools. Craig was right about that.

I am exhausted and tomorrow will try to escape this depraved Paris.

I went to the theatre – what a horror!!... I will probably even throw over Maeterlinck. Hugs.

Yours K. Alekseev [...]

To **Leopold Sulerzhitsky.** Between 7-22 June 1909, Paris.
Dear Suler!

I am definitely stuck with Singer. I'm ashamed and so I swear. Yesterday was Duncan's receiving day. A mob of people. The manager of the Comédie Française, famous writers, artists, politicians. The company was interesting, but to no purpose.

Singer played host. He was touching and reminded me of Morozov in his best moments. Like a nursemaid, he fusses over the school children, while she, posing very deftly as a great celebrity, sits in a white outfit amid her admirers and listens to compliments. This time the barometer of my sympathy completely altered, and I was friendly with him and helped him roll up the rugs and comb the children's hair before they were allowed to dance before the select society. Ultimately it turned out that the company began to take me for the host, and by the end of the reception stepped up to me to thank me for the pleasure. In short, we were all mixed up. Singer has stopped being jealous of me and trusts me to take Duncan away in the motor-car, and when we get in, she begins to kiss me, and I begin to persuade her that Singer is charming.

In short, we were all mixed up.

After the reception they took the whole school to Luna Park. It was a regular witch's kitchen, for instance: they climb up a mountain, get into a kind of car, it shoots down into some kind of tunnel, then bumps along potholes so that your soul goes into reverse, and ultimately drops headlong into a lake and by inertia floats so that the waves inundate the boat. In another place – we're walking along, and suddenly a gust of strong wind knocks everyone off his feet and blows their hats to hell and gone. In a third – suddenly you slip and slide down a slippery mountain, then you fall on to a kind of carpet that shakes and rocks incredibly. In a fourth place you go up a staircase, and when you reach the middle, the stairs begin to bump and slip out from under your feet. You can imagine the delight of the children and Duncan herself. Again she was as dear there as she been in Moscow. But he was charming in his concern for the children.

I saw Craig's and Duncan's little girl. An enchanting child. Craig's temperament and Duncan's grace.

I liked her so much, that Duncan has bequeathed her to me in case of her death. So here I am now in the new role of uncle and papa. If she bequeathes me her future children, I am sure that my old age will be spent amid a numerous brood.

Nevertheless it all made me sick, and I have spoken my firm farewell to Duncan. [...]

Yours affectionately K. Alekseev

To **Gordon Craig.** Before 9/22 July 1909, Vichy.
Dear Mr Craig!

I want to do everything I can to help you, but here, far from home, things are hard. I carry only as much money with me as I need for the trip, -- this is calculated to the penny. In Moscow my money sits in a bank. Cheques (these are pieces of paper that enable one to draw money from the bank) are locked in my desk, and the key is with me in Vichy. My brother is not in Moscow either. How much money is left in the theatre I do not know. The fat administrator Mr Rumyantsev[12] knows. That is why I wired you, so that you could discuss it with him. Did the two of you meet? I requested a certain famous Russian here to lend me money. He could give me only a thousand francs. But I do not know how to send them to you. I go to London, but you remain in Paris or are going somewhere else, like last winter. If I sent it from here and leave, it will be very hard to return them in Moscow.

Wire me whether you can remain in Paris and wait for the money. I will send it as soon as I get the telegram. Do not forget that I shall send the money in the name of Alekseev, because that is the name on my passport, and not Stanislavsky.

If I find someone else whom I can appeal to, I will send you more, but we are not staying here very long. From here we will probably go to Rouen. It's a pity that we cannot meet in Vichy. Some of your friends are here, for instance, Doctor Botkin, Mrs [I. G.] Kalina, Moskvin. Poor Suler is still ill. He had another misfortune, his son fell very ill (typhus), and now his legs are paralyzed. Suler and his wife and son are in the Crimea – in a town called Evpatoria (poste restante).

I didn't quite understand, did you improve Reinhardt's *Hamlet* or not. Should I take a look at it or not bother. If necessary, I will go, but... I do not really believe that Reinhardt can create anything artistic. [...]

K. Stanislavsky (here – Alekseev)

Can you tell that I express myself badly in German?

To **Nemirovich-Danchenko**. 15/28 July 1909, Saint-Lunaire.
Dear Vladimir Ivanovich!

[...] I don't understand what's wrong with you? Are you out of sorts – or awfully occupied with the theatre. Are there not enough plays? Are the Maly Theatre and Nezlobin[13] enjoying a renaissance (?!)? I don't know what's worrying you. When you're like this – I fear for the theatre. The season is very risky, especially since Yuzhin is not to be caught napping. He has gone to London with a native Greek (from *Libra*[14]) to look at a new play by Conan Doyle. They say it will be serious (not Sherlock Holmes).[15] Obviously *Hamlet* is on your mind. Suddenly there isn't enough time? Two things are on my mind – Kachalov and Craig. Not only when he's in Moscow under our control, but when he's far away. In Vichy I got a desperate telegram. The bank isn't giving him any money. 'Send 2000 francs.' I make a formal reply. He is silent. I risked sending 1000 francs. Again he doesn't wait for them in London and has gone to Florence. Now I'm carrying on a correspondence to get the money returned. When he is under surveillance, he is business-like, but, who knows – at liberty will he make all the designs? Did I make a mistake in helping him arrange for English workmen in Florence? [...]

To **Nemirovich-Danchenko**. 13 August 1909, Paris.
Dear Vladimir Ivanovich!

[...] I very much want some role for Koreneva.[16] I don't see her as Anya. Anya is the daughter of gentry, and Koreneva is vulgar. The quality of gentility is very important, because this is the older generation, which, like the orchard, is being chopped down. Anya is the future Russia. Energetic, striving forward. Lilina had none of that, and it is her shortcoming.

Who is an Anya? In terms of energy – Baranovskaya,[17] but she is no gentlewoman. Koonen might be, but she is already busy (if Koreneva doesn't act in *A Month in the Country*, where I do not see her). Is Koreneva Liza in *Woe from Wit*?! Marusya would very much like to give that role to Koonen, if it doesn't involve too much fuss. [...]

We shall soon need an actor, for Kachalov is growing old. [...]

Yours K. Alekseev

KS's daughter Kira had declared her intention to be a singer and a professional painter, which led to differences with her father.

To **his wife Mariya Lilina**. 15 August 1909, Paris.
Dear Marusya!

[…] All Paris is blazoning the name of Ida Roubinstein[18] [*in Roman characters in the original*]. I used to know her, as did Kira. She is only a high-school graduate. I invited her to study as a matter of form. She found the Art Theatre obsolescent. She was an amateur, studied everything in France and Germany and England. She wanted to be a German actress. Again she came to me. Again she didn't attend. She entered the Imperial Theatre, thinking she'd find something new there (in words, the old stuff which is ostensibly becoming new). Then plans with Meyerhold and Sanin, they would build a theatre on the Neva. Again she came to the Art Theatre. Again she didn't attend. She joined up with Duncan, and Duncan threw her out. And now this little rich girl Rubinstein, daughter of the same multimillionaire from Kharkov with whom we used to barter woollen goods, this Rubinstein, who considered everyone and everything beneath her, having squandered it all, breaks out at the 'Olympia'. Her famous name is printed next to a troupe of dogs and Maria la Bella. Today I'm going to see for my edification what pride, conceit and ignorance of art lead to. And so I'm sorry for Kira, so clearly do I understand and predict for her, of course in another form, an absurd life in art, which will make her much more disappointed and regret those deceptive first steps. Well, good luck to her. So long as she is wearing the same face which she made at my departing train, I will not talk to her. […]

Ever yours Kostya

Ida Rubinstein played 'The Dance of the Seven Veils' from Wilde's Salome *with music by Glazunov.*

To **his wife Mariya Lilina.** 16/29 August 1909, Paris.
My precious and dear one!

[…] Yesterday I went to the 'Olympia' and beheld Rubinstein. More nudity and untalented nudity I have never seen. What a disgrace! The music and staging of 'dance of the seven veils' (Fokine) was very good. But she is untalented and nude.

Can Kirlyulya have gone so astray in painting? I can't get her out of my head. Such an evil and malicious look of hers, aimed at me, I had never yet seen. It is a very malicious look.

After the show, in which the dogs, apes and marionettes were enchanting, I headed for home. […]

Yours Kostya

KS had long been dissatisfied with Simov's pedestrian design ideas which, at best, carried out the director's instructions, and decided to draw on the talent of the St Petersburg group of aesthetes The World of Art (Mir Iskusstva). Mstislav Valeriyanovich Dobuzhinsky (1875-1957), proficient in book design, had begun scenic work in 1907 at the reconstructive Antique Theatre. When KS invited him to the MAT, he proposed Turgenev's A Month in the Country *to create a confluence of atmosphere between the*

mood of the play and the style of the design. Dobuzhinsky moved into the Alekseevs'
apartment. Simov was assigned Andreev's parable-play Anathema.

To **his wife Mariya Lilina.** 21 August 1909, Moscow.
Dear and precious angel – Marusya!

I have begun. Yesterday I was at the rehearsal. The mood is rather drowsy. No
one is whetting his knife for the battle. They are working conscientiously. Secretly
they are grousing about Luzhsky. Luzhsky is a mass of nerves, believes he is well,
and is working mechanically but very diligently. Simov has done nothing over
the summer. He has definitely coarsened into a swine. Dobuzhinsky has sent three
acts, they are being copied.

They are being painted – judging by what I saw in the scene-shop, -- extra-
vilely, like theatrical stage-painting.[19] I cannot understand what went wrong. The
furniture that's been sent is beyond all praise. Who did it and decorated it?
Dobuzhinsky himself or the new props man – I don't know. [20] If it's the new props
man from Komissarzhevskaya's, he's got talent. But... despite all our efforts, we
haven't persuaded him to live in Moscow. The little bit that Simov sent is extra-
vile. Again the whole stage floor is cluttered. He's made a mess and all kinds of
unnecessary modelling. Simov ought to follow instructions – nothing of the kind,
he's not even in Moscow. In short, the swine of swines. [...]

Ever yours Kostya

To **Vera Kotlyarevskaya.** 4 September 1909, Moscow.
Dear friend Vera Vasilievna!

[...] Remember last year I told you about creative concentration, about the
circle of attention? I have so developed my circle of attention that I take it with
me day and night. I almost got run over by an electric tram, I would have robbed
you of the 25 r. I owe you. In our cabaret [the Bat] where they read joke telegrams,
the following tidings were recently received: 'Stanislavsky encircled. Send Kirillin
(the theatre locksmith) to set him free a.s.a.p. Lilina.' Another anecdote about
me is making the rounds. Someone comes up to me and says: 'K.S., here's 15
rubles for you.' I spin around quickly – where?.. and start moving backwards,
scanning the floor for the money.[21] [...]

Interesting experiments are going on in the theatre. My system is doing
wonders, and the whole troupe has taken it up. A whole new system for schools
is being elaborated. Everything's been turned topsy-turvy. I'll explain when we get
together. I kiss your hand and thank you for your friendship and favours.

Yours K. Alekseev [...]

To **Baron Nikolay Drizen.**[22] 12 September 1909, Moscow.
Deeply esteemed Nikolai Vasilievich!

Today Yushkevich[23] departed Petersburg. He submitted to the censorship his
new play with the wonderful title *Lord, Have Mercy on Us!* At this moment when
the theatres are beginning to experience a real famine from a total literary lean

year, Yushkevich's play shows up – I can see it on stage and infinitely rejoice that a writer has finally appeared who has observed life widely and poetically. Whatever the flaws in the play, it has one great quality --- it is poetic and youthful in feeling and temperament.

If you understand the impatience of the starving, you will forgive my appeal to you.

Allow me to take advantage of your kindness and affection and, without abusing them, ask you to expedite the quickest possible verdict on the play.

If this happens soon, you will relieve the theatre of the necessity of staging other projected plays which are performed out of expediency and not out of passion or enthusiasm. I will be eternally grateful to you for this favour; at this very moment, I confess, I am most ashamed to trouble you with my request and draw you away from your numerous obligations. [...]

K. Alekseev

ND had another success with Anathema *which opened on 2 October 1909, but the Holy Synod campaigned to have it closed, and it had to be removed from the bill after thirty-seven performances. A mood of depression set into the MAT.*

Rehearsals for A Month in the Country *were intended to test KS's ideas about the internal life of the characters, especially inner concentration and emotional experiencing (perezhivanie). He did not provide elaborate schemes for gesture and action, but allowed them to develop in rehearsal out of the actor's instincts. The actors were unaccustomed to this creative freedom and floundered. Knipper said she felt like a dilettante when trying to put KS's theories into practice.*

Diary, late October 1909.

When we transferred [*A Month in the Country*] to the stage it wasn't a rehearsal, it was hell.

Everything was lost. What had been all right at the table came out weak here. Everyone spoke quietly and could not project his voice. Knipper was exasperating in her obstinacy, Koreneva in her bad character and obtuseness. Boleslavsky out of inexperience turned into a blockhead. The enemies of my system croaked doom, and said it was boring and lowered the tone of the rehearsal.

It's been a long time since I have felt such torment, despair and a slump in energy (not since *The Drama of Life* and *The Life of Man*). [...]

To **Baron Nikolay Drizen.** 3 November 1909, Moscow.

Deeply esteemed Nikolay Vasilievich!

I am writing in the intermission between the acts. This is the only time when I can deal with my personal affairs. From 10 to 12 every day I'm at the factory – office business. From 12 to 4:30 rehearsal. From 4:30 to 5 receiving people at the theatre, from 5 to7 dinner and rest, from 7 to 11:30, an evening performance or a rehearsal. After the performance I work on my role until 2 a.m. On Sundays and holidays – two performances. When am I to write? When am I to concentrate and plunge into memories of Anton Chekhov so dear to me? For a long time I've been planning, if only roughly, to describe everything preserved in my memory, but, alas, I did not succeed even in the summer.

My correspondence with Anton Pavlovich is completely personal. Everything dealing with productions and plays he wrote to Nemirovich. This was agreed upon.

[...] Now about the directorial sector.

The right to photograph productions belongs exclusively to the Moscow photographer Fischer[24] (formerly Dyagochenko). By contract he alone possesses and disposes of the negatives and prints. What is to be done with the production material? The sketches for sets of A Month in the Country, as well as the costume sketches, belong to Dobuzhinsky. The theatre keeps only copies. There will be no mise-en-scène whatsoever. Benches or a sofa, to which people come, sit down and talk, -- no sound effects, no details, no minutiae. Everything is based on emotional experiencing and intonations. The whole play is interwoven of the sensations and feelings of the author and actors. How is one to describe them, how is one to convey the elusive means directors use to condition the performers? This is a special state of hypnosis, based on the actors' sense of self at the moment of work, on knowing their personalities, shortcomings, etc. As in this play, so in all others – this and *only this* work is essential and worthy of attention. Whatever is said about the details and realism of the production is fortuitous, last minute, after the first dress rehearsal.

Anathema has a more complicated mise-en-scène, but even there the grouping of the characters is interesting and necessary only in its relation to their inner emotional experiencing. How is one to bring across all these emotional experiences which enliven the aridity of the play? In order to convey this directorial work, the uniquely necessary and interpretative work, one would have to write a volume and burrow into the debris of the psychology of the actor's creativity.

That is why our attempts were unsuccessful. That is why even now I do not know how to approach this work.

A general outline of a production is very harmful and confusing. In our time we wrote such an outline of Chekhov's play Three Sisters. Some people staged the play according to those notes. I saw that production. You could not dream up anything more ghastly. All they understood was that there needed to be tedium and sorrow in the play. In our production this yearning is achieved by laughter, because three-quarters of the play is built on laughter. This laughter was missing in their production and the result was desperate tedium – on the part of the audience. [...]

Sincerely devoted and respectfully yours
K. Alekseev

Olga Knipper later recalled that work on the role of Natalya Petrovna caused her 'great suffering', fearful that she could not capture the subtlety of the psychology of Turgenev's women. At one rehearsal she burst into tears, relinquished the role and went home.

To **Olga Knipper**. 8 November 1909, Moscow.

Dear, good Olga Leonardovna!

I am staying away from you, rather than cause you unpleasantness. I have pestered you so much that I had better go into hiding for a while. In my stead -- I am sending flowers. I hope they will convey to you the tender feelings I cherish for your great talent. This enthusiasm compels me to be cruel to anything that might sully the beauty that nature has bestowed on you.

At the moment you are going through some serious moments of artistic doubt. Deep feelings of suffering on stage are born of such torment. Do not assume that I am indifferent to your pangs. I am in constant distress and at the same time know that these pangs will bear splendid fruit.

Let someone else, not I, perhaps Moskvin, explain to you what nature has bestowed on you. I am ready to admire patiently from a distance how your talent, once it has cast aside the superfluous, will feel free and manifest itself in all its power, which for the time being is inhibited by the actor's damnable professionalism.

Believe me, all the things that seem so difficult now are actually trivial. Have the patience to investigate, ponder and understand this trivia, and you will know the greatest joy in life possible to a human being in this world.

If you should need my help -- I will divide [your role] into sections and promise not to frighten you with technical terms. That was probably my mistake.

I beseech you to be staunch and courageous in the artistic struggle which you must master not only for the sake of your talent, which I love with all my heart, but also for the sake of our whole theatre, which constitutes the meaning of my whole life.

Figure 44 Stanislavsky as Rakitin and Olga Knipper as Nataliya Petrovna in *A Month in the Country*. Photo: K. A. Fischer, Moscow

Do not turn the theatre over to an untalented adventuress. [25] Do not abdicate your throne. I am ready to serve you, a genuine talent, but I do not have the strength to remain in a concern where vulgarity prevails.

You need to do so little to be the beautiful Nataliya Petrovna, whom I have already seen a dozen times. Take a look at the whole role and clearly define the units it can be broken down into.

At this point -- I want to conceal my excitement; at this point -- I want to impart my feelings to someone else; at this point -- I am amazed and frightened; at this point -- I am trying to convince him that nothing awful has happened and to do that I become now tender, now capricious, now I try to be persuasive. Then I once again try to concentrate. Verochka has arrived, I do not immediately stop concentrating. Finally I have understood – I assume the role of her mistress and try to persuade her that she must marry.

At every point in the role look for certain desires of your own, and banish all other vulgar desires that have to do with the audience. This mental work will easily enthuse you.

Once you find this attractive, you will abstract yourself from what is unworthy of a true actress – to serve and fawn upon the audience. The more illogical you are in this latter event, the more logical you will be in your attraction to real experiencing.

You are lucky, you have charm on stage, that makes people listen to you, and so it easy for you to do on stage whatever you want.

It is more difficult for us poor folk, because with every new role we have to think things out, think things up, simulate charm, without which an actor is like a rose without scent.

Take courage and claim once and for all your royal place in our theatre. I will admire from a distance or, if necessary, work for you like a navvy.

Forgive me for the torment I have caused you, but believe me -- it is unavoidable. Soon you will acquire the real joys of art.

> The cordially loving admirer of your great talent.
> K. Alekseev

On 9 December A Month in the Country *opened. The critics considered that the production captured Turgenev's pastel tones and 'pensive beauty'. As Rakitin KS used almost no gestures but his emotions were clear. Its popularity kept it running for 131 performances.*

To **Lyubov Gurevich.** 24 December 1909, Moscow.
Dear Lyubov Yakovlevna!

[...] You are such an oasis in our artistic life. Good Lord, how obtuse, narrow-minded and unthinking most critics are. This year any praise they send our way is completely unexpected. This has occurred because Yuzhin and Nezlobin ordered them to praise their theatres and clumsily abuse no one but us. They do praise us, but they probably would do better to abuse us... How difficult to prove the simplest truths.

The outer aspect of this season is revolting, because the audience, which, as you know, is cleverer than most of the critics, is confused, and we have to combat this by the most determined measures. Yuzhin [at the Maly] preaches freedom for the actor, which means: the production department provides any old kind of scenery and furniture; stages the play any old way; schedules as soon as possible 15 or 20 rehearsals (even for *Dmitry the Pretender, Caesar and Cleopatra*), then they cast 2 or 3 stars in the leading roles. They each have 5 to 7 rehearsals. Then they often rehearse without them, they perform with anybody. When the youngsters turn to Yuzhin for advice as how to feel a certain passage in a role, he replies: 'What do I care? Act well.' All the no-talent actors are in ecstasy, and so are the old-timers; the most talented of the youngsters apply to us… In 4 months they seem to have concocted 8 to 10 plays. The press tears itself to pieces in ecstasy, and the public flocks to them (this means instead of 700 r. on average they make 1200). And so, it's a business enterprise, the most provincial kind, and an impetus to an actor's craftsmanship. […]

What are we to do under these circumstances? We have decided to establish artistic standards for ourselves and discard anything that had become banal on stage. No mise-en-scène, no sound effects. Everything tends to simplicity, to the inner design of the role. You must understand what it costs to shift the whole troupe suddenly to what we had arrived at gradually and systematically. Still, it's an ill wind that blows nobody good. This forced everyone to pay heed to my system, which I had sufficiently elaborated these last few years. Hellish work, but interesting.

We are praised, but, of course, many do not even understand the new direction of the theatre. So, for instance, in *A Month in the Country* there is a bench centre stage, in another act a sofa, and in a third a little bench. Everyone enters in pairs, sits and, without any action, talks. The play is a great success, and the reason must be that the director did it all and the production, while the actors are mediocre. The audience sees the changes, writes me letters, asks me to elucidate. I make a formal reply. But there is no way to explain to the crowd individually the nonsense that goes on in all theatres. And there too, with the light hand of Baliev, these damnable cabarets have come in!..

Nevertheless our new tendency, which can move us forward, only skipping over all the phases of the 12th year of hard work and research, does its job. We stand as unique, and we are not mocked with that vulgarity which is nestling in next door. So our concern goes well for the time being, even very well. Before the production of *A Month in the Country* – with only *Anathema*, which could not be put on five times a week like *The Blue Bird*, because the actors would have died of exhaustion depicting devils and gods… with *Anathema* twice a week, and old plays on the other days, by 9 December with the matinees we had made on average 2175 r. From [the opening of *A Month in the Country*] 9 December up to now – continuous full and sold-out houses.

From the holidays to 7 January we are fully sold out. This, of course, is more than brilliant. Better than last year. So it would be wrong to complain about the audience. Or the work either. But… what will happen next?! Isn't our public, which we have been grooming for the last 12 years, getting confused? […]

Heartily devoted K. Alekseev

To **Mstislav Dobuzhinsky**. 28 December 1909, Moscow.
Dear and much esteemed Mstislav Valeriyanovich!

[…] The [Turgenev] production for next year has been settled, especially since if we do not put it on, the Maly Theatre will latch on to it.

To be precise it consists of the following plays:

1) *The Parasite.*
2) *The Weakest Link.*
3) *The Lady from the Provinces.*
4) *Evening in Sorrento.*[26]

I should like to know your opinion: how do you envisage the distribution of time-periods among these plays.

There is no doubt that *The Parasite* is the earliest play in terms of period, while *Evening in Sorrento* is the latest.

For some reason I would like the widest of crinolines in *The Lady from the Provinces.* […]

A Month in the Country gets full houses, but except for the subscribers the audience listens to the play rather poorly. There's a lot of coughing. Today Knipper tried to change her hair-do. She acted with her own hair. To my mind, it is incomparably better and even more typical for her face. We often remember you and are very sorry that Petersburg is not in Moscow, nor Moscow in Petersburg. […]

Cordially devoted and respectfully yours
K. Alekseev

Throughout all of this KS had not stinted on work at the factory, where the technical expertise at metallic threads was now extended to cables for telephone and telegraph communications.

Report to the **Art Theatre Board**, read to Nemirovich by Stakhovich in my absence after dinner, before the meeting (to cast *Miserere*[27]), 19 January 1910, Moscow.

1. Most of all I am angry with myself for being unable to explain my wishes.

2. My wishes are extremely natural, and I find it odd that sometimes they are taken to be capricious.

3. Above all, I want complete freedom for all those who love our theatre in a pure and disinterested way. Let whoever will come up with his own trials and experiments. I want the same right for myself.

4. Perhaps I have got carried away but therein lies my strength. Perhaps I am mistaken but that is the real way to make progress! I am now persuaded as never before that I have stumbled on to the right track. It is my belief that very soon I will discover the words that will make sense of it all and help the theatre to discover the most important thing, that will serve as a true compass for many years. Without that compass, I know that the theatre will lose its way at the precise moment when even one of its present pilots, who are steering it so tortuously between Scylla and Charybdis, lets go of the rudder.

5. My demands on myself are great and perhaps presumptuous. I want not only to discover the fundamental principle of creativity, I want not only to formulate a theory of it, I want to put it into practice.

6. Anyone who knows the difficult, ill-defined and backward nature of our art will understand the difficulty, scope and importance of this task. Perhaps it is insane and arrogant. So be it! Then it will prove to be beyond my strength and I shall crack my skull. And serve me right. But from my splinters there may arise someone else, or at all events, something without which there can be no theatre, without which it is destructive and depraved, without which it is a den of thieves and not the temple of the human spirit.

I may be a madman and a dreamer but I cannot and do not wish to be otherwise. At my age one cannot change root and branch.

7. The task is complicated and long-lasting, and I am not young in years. Especially if you bear in mind that in my family people die young. At the very most I have ten years' work left in me. Is that term great enough to carry out a project which is perhaps beyond my powers? Then it's time to think of one's last will and testament. One must hurry to work hard on one's legacy. What's one to do, every man wants to leave some small mark behind him. That's understandable.

8. I need material for my project. I need help. It's impossible to count on everyone, but there are a few persons whom I have trained with great difficulty or who believe in my dreams. Of course I prize their help in particular.

9. The paths of our art are pitted with ruts and potholes. They are deep and one can't get past them without stumbling. In moments like those you should come to one's aid and lift up those who have stumbled and not think of them as already dead. We, and I, perhaps, at first were too delighted by every embryonic talent and then too quickly grew disenchanted when the rising talent ceased to surprise us by doing the unexpected. I learned this not so long ago and have tried to be more patient and consistent. Otherwise you can't take a single pupil through to the end and I want not only to begin but to complete the education of those who have fallen into my clutches.

10. The theatre is right to accept those who apply afresh to be selected, but once that selection has taken place, once that student has been put in my care, I am responsible for her.

There was a time when we had not a single young person who showed any glimmer of ability. Now there are such young people, and we must be the first to express satisfaction in their work, until something miraculous occurs, for which there must always be a place in our theatre.

11. Without work there can be no progress. I should like to assert that principle and not make my pupils an exception to it.

12. I ask you to forget, at least for a while, many hurtful expressions used in respect of me – 'scatterbrain', 'capricious child' – because they are unjust. I don't always get into a muddle, sometimes I succeed in the given case, my caprices are not always frivolous.

13. If I am cleansed of these expressions, perhaps it will result in greater faith both in me and in the people I have trained as assistants.

Figure 45 A montage photograph of the audience for first Cabbage party at the MAT

14. For reasons that I do not understand anyone I have got close to has, from contact with me, been quite reborn in the eyes of my colleagues. Baranovskaya has become an arid and irrelevant no-talent. Koonen has arrested development and not lived up to expectations. Suler has stopped understanding the thing we have been working on together [illegible], and has become intolerable. I have begun to be cautious about getting close to individuals for fear of doing them an injury thereby.

15. Perhaps the people I have chosen are failures, perhaps I am damaging them, or perhaps I am a bad teacher. If this is the case, then it is better to tell me so straight out and not fight me with concealed weapons.

16. But perhaps there is another possibility. That path of pitfalls that I tread with tentative steps cannot be tamped down and paved by tried-and-true clichés. Under those conditions the stumbling and falling of my students is normal. A brief experiment convinces me that the true sense of self is defined by errors. Everyone who will come after me will expect to fall in this way. Once and for all they should recognize it as normal and be reconciled to the fact that youth should have the time to slip up.

17. For my research I need all kinds of material, not only what is suitable to an artist, but also the defective. It's more difficult to eradicate defects than to assay correctly the value of talent. I need both people who are artistically dull, inert in talent, somewhat anaemic, indolent, as well as those who are very zealous. I can

verify the things I am working on only with such an assortment of pupils. That is why in my research on the material I sometimes go for those people who have no connection with the theatre. So long as others are not denied the right to have private pupils, let me also be allowed that privilege.

Craig was back in Moscow to work on Hamlet *and was thus able to attend the MAT's first public cabbage party on 8 March. It collected nearly 20,000 rubles for charity. One of the liveliest instigators of the cabbage party was also one of the troupe's richest shareholders, Nikolay Tarasov. Prone to 'tædium vitæ', when his mistress abandoned him he shot himself. Later ND remarked that how curious it was that three of the MAT's biggest investors – Morozov, Tarasov and Stakhovich – each committed suicide.*

KS had a comic triumph as superannuated General Krutitsky in No Fool Like a Wise Fool. *Directed by ND and Luzhsky, it opened at 11 March 1910, and ran for 235 performances, not least because KS loved playing the part of the senile mossback.*

Notebook. I hate the Black Hundreds more than anything and therefore I know very well what is retrograde. It is pleasant and easy for me to mock them in the role of Krutitsky.

To **Isadora Duncan**. 20 March 1910, Moscow.
Your charming letter infinitely rejoiced your loyal friend and admirer. I received it on the day the new play opened, at the very moment when I was sitting down to be made up. My role was successful, and the production enjoyed a success, of course, you continue to be the good genius of our theatre, where your name is remembered continually.

Thanks for the memories and the joy of receiving news about you. It proves that you have not forgotten us. I hasten to obey your command and inform you of everything that has gone on here. Last week was especially wearying. We were preparing the new play, and simultaneously our theatre organized a grand soiree with a plethora of all sorts of actor's jokes, approximately fifty acts. We performed a parody of *La Belle Hélène*, where the leading role was played by Knipper; there were other parodies as well: of the *café chantant*, silly ballets, the circus, in which I portrayed the ringmaster and introduced Vishnevsky to the audience in the role of a trained horse. The performance went on all night long – till nine in the morning. We made a considerable sum on behalf of needy actors (nearly 20,000 rubles).

This soiree and the preparations for it so exhausted us that only today do I feel strong enough to answer your letter.

Today we began seriously to work on *Hamlet* under the leadership of Gordon Craig, who is now in Moscow. Everything he does is beautiful. We are trying to carry out his slightest wish, and he seems to be as pleased with us as we are with him.

Our theatre created two workshops especially for him. In one of them he works like a hermit. No one is allowed in. The other holds an enormous model of the stage with a whole detachment of young directors, who under Suler's command carry out all of Craig's imaginings; as soon as they are approved, they are transferred to the main stage. Yesterday Craig dressed all the participants in the performance in tights in order to study their bodies and movements. I am working with some of the actors separately on scenes from *Hamlet*, in order better to understand what Craig is getting at with this experiment. When we have fathomed his concept properly, he will go to Florence, and we will work on our own without him. We will prepare the play till August; he will come back to Moscow to correct our work and give final instructions. *Hamlet* must be ready by November of this year.

Let us remind you of your promise to come to the dress rehearsal of this interesting production. It was you who introduced us to Craig. You told us to trust him and create a second homeland for him in our theatre. Come and find out whether we have carried out your wishes.

What am I to tell you about your friends and myself? After I left you in Paris, two days later my family and I went to Vichy, and from there to Saint-Lunaire in Brittany. There I worked a lot on my theory and wrote part of the future book. All winter long I tested my researches in practice, and, I must admit, the results exceeded all my expectations. The whole troupe is enthused by the new system, and therefore, from the standpoint of work, the year was interesting and important. You yourself played a major role in this work, unawares. You inspired a great deal in me of what we have now found in our art. Thank you and your genius for this. [...]

I cannot send you [postcards of] beautiful landscapes, because our life goes on amid sets and props.

I do send you our latest work – Turgenev's play *A Month in the Country*,[28] in which Knipper plays the leading role, and I the aging lover, who has no success with his beloved. [...]

Moscow remembers and awaits you.

I kiss your hand, your enchanting daughters' hands and ask you to let Mr Singer know that I remember him with pleasure and would like to thank him again for the hospitality and affection shown me in Paris. I remind him of his promise to allow me to reciprocate it in Moscow. [...]

To **his daughter Kira**. 10 May 1910, Petersburg.
My dear friend Kiryulya!

[...] What can I tell you about our theatrical affairs? The same old thing: the press chews us out and the audience comes in droves. All the plays make a hit with the public, *Wise Fool* is no hit with the connoisseurs. Many aristocratic ladies come to the theatre to see Vishnevsky. During meals they don't bother serving him, as he roars into the telephone for the whole room to hear: 'Hello, Count, tell the princess that the prince and the baron will be with their graces after dinner at their highnesses' (one of the phrases transcribed). We sit and roar with laughter, and the moment the hilarity erupts he puts his hand over the receiver, so that the princes can't hear our disrespect over the telephone and makes a tragic face to bring us to reason. Those are moments of high comedy.

There was another comical evening. Baron Drizen, the censor, arranged a soiree with all the decadents, critics, writers etc. They quizzed me and tried to catch me out. I foresaw this and quite by chance at the beginning of the debate warned everyone that I am practical man and can talk only about practical matters, because theoretical disputes, to my mind, have no relationship to the activities of an actor and director. For this reason all the critics caved in. All evening long they could not think up a single practical question and time and again digressed into theory. Gornfeld[29], a local critic, was supposed to sum it up. He frankly admitted the complete bankruptcy of a literature incapable of representing the business of living. It made an impression. […]

Your Papa

To **his son Igor**. 14 May 1910, SP.
My dearest little boy!
[…] The present production always seems to be the most important and the most dangerous. Thank Nemirovich, he gave me wise practical advice, to wit: in such cases – he said to me – one must forget the past, which is already irremediable, and not think about the future, which is out of our hands. One must be concerned only about the *present*. Without exaggeration and sentimentality, but with great practical sense one must do everything that can be done. At the moment when an inner voice whispers that everything is done, -- one must lay down one's arms and wait quietly. […]

Your tenderly loving
Papa

To **Gordon Craig.** 21 June 1910, Essentuki. [In English]
Dear Sir!
I am in the Caucasus, where I have gone for a rest, which is why only now do I have time to write to you.
I will try to give an account of what has been done for *Hamlet* up to the present time, but also inform you of certain completely unforeseen circumstances.
First and most important. Hamlet must go on when the season opens; in other words, the play must be entirely ready by 1 October (old style, 14 October new style). It would take me too long to explain the reasons for this decision, as unexpected for you as it is for me. I can only say that I tried by every means to avoid this, but at the moment I have also come to the conclusion that if we do not begin with *Hamlet*, we shall not be able to stage it in the coming season, because it's impossible in practical terms to rehearse such a responsible and difficult play when other performances are going on every day. So, we have to begin the season with *Hamlet*.
The second surprise is an outcome of the first. I entreat you to come to Moscow before the date we contracted before your departure in the spring. In other words, we ask you to be in Moscow on 20 August (old style, 2 September new style). This is essential not for the scenery, not for the actors, but for the costumes. You will learn the details associated with this below.
That way you will not have to come from Florence to Moscow twice.

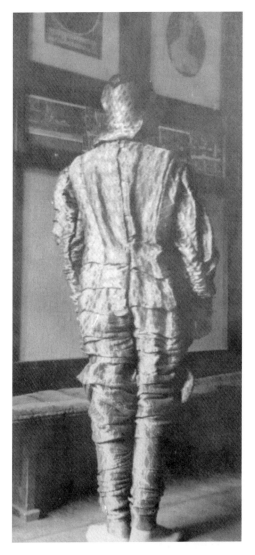

Figure 46 A model fitted with a trial soldier's costume for *Hamlet*, made of gold thread
from Stanislavsky's factory, in the MAT lobby, 1910

The third annoying surprise is that I overestimated my strength, and on my return
from Petersburg, where I had to act 29 times in 25 days, I felt completely knackered
and could not summon up enough energy in myself to finish the task I had taken
on in time. Everyone went on leave, and only Mardzhanov[30] and I tried for two
weeks from morning to night to sort out what you need and to translate into
reality those lines and folds that we saw in your sketches. But alas, we achieved

277

nothing. Perhaps, we did not understand you clearly; perhaps, we are not sophisticated enough; or, perhaps, our materials do not answer your purposes. The fact is that we ran into a lot of difficulties in our work. Unfortunately, we cannot find well-built individuals to model our costumes. All our own folks hastened to go out of town, and no one was willing to take on such an arduous task. And it really is rather arduous – to be constrained to stand up all day long, while the costumes are measured, to slip out of one to array oneself in another. It is impossible to force people to do such work, one can only ask them. We found two youths and two girls. They are very dear and patient young people, but they do not resemble Apollo and Venus in any way. I am sure that you will start tearing out your hair, if we show them to you in trial costumes. So prepare yourself in advance for such unforeseen disappointments.

The second difficulty is purely the pecuniary question. It would seem that the costume fittings, prepared from real and expensive materials, cost us very dear; for instance, the fittings last spring cost us nearly 200 pounds sterling. I cannot tell you how much all the later fittings would cost us, which we are make in the next two weeks in May. Therefore we have had to figure out the cut, lines, pleats on inexpensive materials, and we can only presuppose, and not see how the lines will look. So another disappointment awaits you, namely: the trial costumes shown to you will be constructed out of cheap materials.

There is yet another disappointment – we can show only a few costumes, and they are not very interesting.

Nevertheless I think that we have understood your concept. You wish a simple, natural cut, which gives a simple, natural sculptural line and good sculptural folds, which can be well lit on stage and will harmonize with the simplicity of the lines of the screens. But everything that is exquisitely simple is always hard to find. We have retested all the patterns and all the fashions that you gave us, as well as a lot of our own. But these subtle, beautiful store-bought materials are, for the most part, totally inexpressive. All the costumes hang like dressing-gowns or peasant blouses. There is almost no difference among them, they are all alike; not a single one of these patterns, when fitted on one of our mannequins, has that simple artistic 'cachet' that has to function in such a work of art. All these costumes, draped on supernumeraries, seem flimsy, uninteresting, the complete opposite of exquisite, although all the patterns and sketches were studied attentively and their essence fully understood. Sometimes we gave rein to our own imaginations and took advantage of whatever came into our heads. But, despite all this, the costumes are flimsy, uninteresting. I tried to rummage in my memory. I attentively reread everything connected to those costumes and periods when they were worn, and finally came to the conclusion that many of the patterns that you selected demand very dense and heavy materials, which provide the beautiful and profound folds you have sketched. Take, for example, no. 8c. It has no look if you construct it out of thin material, and can in no way be distinguished from any other style. But, constructed out of dense material, it has its own look, somewhat reminiscent for me of the costumes of Russian boyars in *Tsar Fyodor*. [...] In your book (Viollet

Le Duc)[31] I read that such gowns were usually trimmed with fur. So you can imagine their weight. Only with such conditions as using heavy fabrics can we achieve those beautiful folds that we see in the costume sketches. Replacing them with thin fabrics, we will only get rumpled towels or aprons.

[*There follows a list of 55 costumes with comments on cost and patterns.*]

We have not gone near the costumes for the King and Queen, because by and large we cannot figure them out.

I am writing these details about the costumes because they represent the greatest danger for us. They are far from clear to us and worry us a lot. Now, when you know that we are waiting for you to deal with the costumes, you can, obviously, prepare for all the difficulties listed above.

But there are also some pleasant surprises.

Mardzhanov, with his completely exceptional energy, has prepared all the screens, cubes, furniture and props for *Hamlet* over the course of two weeks. When we return to Moscow from Petersburg, everything will be quite, quite ready. So this aspect of the matter has been fully settled.

The second pleasant surprise is that Kachalov is beginning to show some interest in the role of Hamlet. I worked a bit with him in Petersburg and later in Moscow he, I and Mardzhanov analysed the entire role and made notes in accord with your remarks and my system, which you still do not like, but which fulfils your intentions better than anything else.

As to the lighting, we ordered a big new portable soffit (overhead, above the audience) and side lights. Two Fortuny-brand spotlights to light the stage were already on hand. We ordered a few other things. Mardzhanov has gone abroad, and we gave him letters of introduction to a few Berlin theatres and electric firms. Perhaps he will find something interesting there.

Now about the plans for our forthcoming work.

Suler and Mardzhanov will return to Moscow on 20 July (old style). They will set about the scenery and lighting. They will carry out a series of experiments and teach the stagehands how to deal with the screens. On 2 August (old style) you and I will come to Moscow and immediately began to deal with the costumes, till then no one will deal with them.

From that moment on you will for some time concentrate all your attention on the costumes, while I will deal with both costumes and rehearsals. When we have prepared a few acts in the rough, we will invite you to rehearsals and together we will polish this raw work. Then it will be obvious what needs to be done next.

One more surprise. Leonidov asked my permission to look over the role of Hamlet. He does not hope to play it, but the work very much interested him. I thought that this will be very useful for us from the practical point of view, because chances are that I will need to take Kachalov for a while and study Hamlet with him separately from the others. In such cases Leonidov could rehearse in his stead. In that way, Leonidov will be his own kind of whip to spur on Kachalov.

Similarly pay attention, if you please, to the following: I do not see and cannot understand how Knipper is to play the queen; the more so since I do not believe that she really yearns to play this role.[32] Anyway, she is actually having a pleasant time in Paris. Meanwhile Savitskaya is studying the role. I think and I am sure that she will play it well. True, she does work very slowly and ponderously – but I see no other actress for this role. Of course, if you insist, we can try out Knipper when you come, -- in any case, she will not touch her role during the summer.

How are you? We all miss you and are delighted that we will soon see you again. […]

Sincerely yours K. Stanislavsky

P.S. Please, write in English, only on the envelope to my Moscow address, add that the letter is to be sent to Mr Likiardopulo, who will translate it and deliver it to me.

To **Olga Knipper.** 13 July 1910, Essentuki.
Dear Olga Leonardovna!

[…] You are taking an interest in *Hamlet.* If that is so – I am truly delighted.

Craig still wants you to play the queen. I thought it didn't attract you, and, to tell the truth, I don't see any tender maternal feelings in you.

You want to work on the costumes – I would be pleased.

You want to know about psychology and circles?..

In short, choose what's on your mind.

If you want to work – believe me, I'll do everything in my power. […]

Heartily devoted K. Alekseev

Unfortunately, in the midst of all these preparations, Igor fell desperately ill and they were unable to find lodgings in Essentuki for any length of time.

Although Olga Gzovskaya had not entered the MAT in 1908, lest it be seen as a betrayal of her teacher Aleksandr Lensky, she was admitted in 1910. This triggered a fresh conflict with ND, because she was made a shareholder, had a higher salary than other actresses, and was exempt from appearing in crowd scenes. KS valued her taste and temperament, and used her as a guinea pig for his new system of actor training.

To **Olga Gzovskaya.** 27 July 1910, Kislovodsk.
Dear Olga Vladimirovna!

[…] My entire vacation went on treatments, doctors and minor domestic problems. I am a fatalist and believe that all this was necessary for some reason. […]

How are we to manage in future? By Vishnevsky I shall send a marked-up role of Ophelia (with Koonen), of course, it won't suit you, you will have a different characterization. Mardzhanov needs this copy for general guidance and for the notes on the sections (and parentheses).

Together with Mardzhanov break it down into sections on your own. Once that is done, turn away from my script and note and start to write down whatever you do not understand. Then, with Mardzhanov, start to mark out the sections however you wish. Mardzhanov seems to understand the uncomplicated secret of this work, and if there are things you do not understand, it won't be serious. I should have

Figure 47 Lilina cooking during Stanislavsky's convalescence in Kislovodsk, 1910

said that Suler can also help with this work. Of course, he can, a very great deal. But I am cautious here: I do not know how touchy Mardzhanov's vanity may be. And you must be cautious not to bruise a yet untried vanity. If things go smoothly – talk it over with Suler too.

Of course, there may be mistakes and differences of opinion, but how difficult could it be to correct them? When I arrive we will do so in a few rehearsals.

Before I come there will be rough preparatory work. Make notes and try to understand it all.

The most important thing is to try from the very first to find a good, calm sense of self on a new stage. It is important that it be there from the very first, not as over-excitement, but specifically as calm. Come to rehearsals early and enter the circle [of concentration] a few times on the stage itself. However, there is still plenty of time before the on-stage rehearsals.

Actors have a habit of paying close attention only to the notes on their own roles. You know this mistake better than I. It would be very important for you to get a sense of the production as a whole, Craig's whole concept in all the great fullness of *Hamlet* in its entirety. Then, on your own, you'll also start to understand the part you play in it all. This is hard work – to trace the whole play, because it takes a lot of time, but you will see how important it is and how it will help you identify with the totality, that is with the whole ensemble.

When you get to the theatre for the first time, do not create an illusion for yourself – many disappointments lie in store for you. There is only one good thing about our concern –we are still capable of struggle. Put on blinkers and direct your gaze to the point you would like to reach. Everything that goes on on the sidelines is of no concern of yours or mine. It seems unlikely, but you may get both hostile glances and wry smiles – pay them only as much attention as you would to animal's snouts. In a month's time wry snouts may break into a smile (I am beginning to speak Shakespeare-fashion).

Remember that in our theatre there are only four persons whose attitude to the work itself is pure: my wife, Moskvin, Stakhovich and myself (apart from Suler, but he brings it down to earth). There is one other competent person – Nemirovich. There are decent, honest people, who love the theatre, but don't understand its goals with much sophistication, among them, Knipper, Savitskaya, etc. There are plain ordinary good people – the journeymen of our concern. There are the dear, green youngsters, yet inchoate. (The rest – the crowd the background – are sheep.) There are 6-7 persons like that in the Art Theatre. You may come in contact with them, and you will have to fight with the rest. I call you to this fight. If you will strive for real, artistic goals – you will not find a livelier, more energetic assistant than I. If our goals part ways – then I will become powerless and unnecessary to you. Entering the theatre, from the first step do not try to be more modest than you are. Be what you are. Actors are instinctual folk. Do not try to deceive them, you can win them over only by genuine simplicity. If you're cheerful, then be cheerful, if you're bored, then be bored. When it comes to ethics and discipline – you are superb and will draw in the others, who often go very far astray. God willing. Be calm and do not fret for no good reason. [...]

Devoted K. Alekseev

To **Leopold Sulerzhitsky.** End of July 1910, Kislovodsk.
Dear Suler!

I am writing to Mardzhanov that if he has no time, to hand Gzovskaya over to you [for work on Ophelia]. I haven't been busy with her this summer, and therefore she is quite helpless.

Now that Mardzhanov is running the general rehearsals, you realize there's no point in wounding his vanity, so, in order to clear the way, I will write to him.

In addition, come up with something for the costumes. From Craig's letter you realize that he himself is up in the air. I feel that sooner or later the costumes will become our headache. When I get back, first order of business, we should all focus on the costumes. Be ready for this, especially since Mardzhanov who is up to date about the costumes will have to run the crowd scenes.

After costumes you and I ought to focus on Kachalov and Gzovskaya, while Mardzhanov organizes the general ensemble.

Husband your strength. Work systematically and rest. You will need all your strength for the days ahead. [...]

Yours K. Alekseev

A few days later KS himself fell ill with typhoid fever, began raving about his future plans for the theatre and lost a good deal of weight. Although his physical condition worsened throughout August, his head cleared and he talked constantly about the state of the theatre. Suler quit Moscow to look after him and take notes on the system; he did not return to the MAT until September.

To **Suler's wife Olga**.[33] August 1910, Kislovodsk

[...] This is my harvest season. For two months I have planted in my mind a whole series of ideas and questions concerning the system. They have ripened tortuously all summer, kept me from sleeping, and all of a sudden the first shoots have now appeared – I cannot jot down fast enough the things that are emerging, springing up and requiring an at least approximate verbal definition. If I don't hurry to jot down everything now, I shall have to start all over again in future, because everything is still so vague, so quickly forgotten and, on the other hand, in a year's time, just as here, in the Caucasus, I will not manage to jot down everything that has ripened. [...]

Meanwhile ND was rehearsing The Brothers Karamazov *as a series of scenes drawn directly from the novel. By October KS was well enough to work with others.*

To **Leopold Sulerzhitsky.** Wednesday, 6 October 1910, Kislovodsk
Dear Suler!

[...] You are under a delusion: one of the reasons for inviting Mardzhanov on my part was to organize parallel performances by the youngsters and actors for their exercise, because you know yourself, as a pedagogue, what it means for an actor not to see the glare of the footlights. Initiating such performances with somebody new, it would be crazy to hope that these performances will go according to all the rules of my system, even the Art Theatre hasn't managed to achieve that, and it would be even stranger to assume that Mardzhanov after a few talks with me has mastered my system. I was delighted that Mardzhanov wanted to explore my system and even became keen on it on his own as he learned about it.

You must agree that I can only love him for that, and have no cause to hate him; you must agree that even you, the champion of this system, should strive to assist him and me and not turn your back on him. Mardzhanov has understood it with his brain and has not mastered the system with his feelings – I agree. But after all this mastery can come without long practice. Is it not our obligation to provide him this practice and carefully watch that he does not go astray? Mardzhanov is self-sufficient – it may be that this is his failing, but it still does not mean that he is hopeless as a director. Why then, you ask, should we woo him. Because we love our theatre and we serve art.

The theatre needs stage directors, there are none except those employed in our theatre; not even a hint that they exist; on the margins there are only two directors: Mardzhanov and Sanin, we have to take them in and educate them, educate them for their own sake. Haven't you said that when Mardzhanov arrives, you will be relieved of a lot of boring stuff, and this is actually the case. We need Mardzhanov for the scut work, and he is industrious. Apparently none of this gives us the right to entrust him with parallel performances, when there are those in the theatre more worthy than he, but after all have I not over the course of many years delegated the same kind of work to you, Luzhsky, Moskvin, Aleksandrov? After all didn't Luzhsky show his incompetence the very first time he was tried? And the exploits of Rumyantsev and Moskvin – how did they end up? Does Aleksandrov's ineptitude have to be demonstrated? And does your health allow you to take on this business? To whom are we to delegate this matter if not Mardzhanov; he is looking for more work, he is energetic, he is a man of the theatre.

If you insist that *it is crucial in the nth degree for the theatre that this activity be artistic,* help him all the more in these first steps and, most important, be indulgent to him.

I am telling you all this with the warmest and most affectionate feelings; for me, for you, and it is extremely important for the concern that its participants walk hand in hand. If you quarrel with the directors, it will be very difficult for me, harmful to the concern and no good for you. Therefore we will finish discussing Mardzhanov next time, and now, to keep the letter from being dry and business-like, I will move to other matters. […]

I am very glad that our system is penetrating into the core of the Art Theatre; for heaven's sake, take an interest in pedagogy, you have a great capability for it. You cannot imagine what a benefit you will render the Art Theatre and how tightly it will bind you to it. […]

What can I tell you about our life here? It's turned cold, there are frequent storms, fog, the balcony is blocked off by a cupboard, the furnaces smell of carbon monoxide. I am told that I am getting better, but I do not feel it or, more accurately, I do not notice it. I long desperately for Moscow, but still haven't the strength to make the journey. […]The fearful secret of the *Karamazovs* is out at last, and I fail to see why they kept it secret: it's a brilliant way through the Theatre's difficult situation. […]

Yours K. Alekseev […]

The two evenings of The Brothers Karamazov *opened the season on 12 and 13 October 1910, and were immediately recognized as a major achievement on the part of ND and the older actors. (It reached eighty-four performances.) The staging was of the simplest, before black draperies, and the dialogue drawn directly from the novel. KS was not allowed to see letters, so he did not know that the Dostoevsky had superseded Yushkevich's* Miserere *in the schedule. When Karamazov opened, a telegram was sent to Kislovodsk. KS wired back.*

To **Nemirovich-Danchenko**. 14 October 1910, Kislovodsk. *Telegram.*

Today one of best days of my life. Just learned inscrutable news about transformation of *Miserere* into *Karamazov*. Delighted by tremendous work of theatre, read hidden letters, acquainted with past and moved to tears by everything you have undergone.

Praise for your administrative genius, Napoleonic resourcefulness, energy. Admire, take pride in and love you with all my heart.

Glory to all dear companions for their enormous talented labour. Hooray! Theatre still strong, its members talented, united, industrious. If only half tremendous work succeeds, I shall shout hooray and applaud like a psychopath and rejoice like a child. Congratulate and love you all. [...]

> With sincere devotion and fraternal affection
> Konstantin Alekseev-Stanislavsky

To avoid distressing the invalid, news of what was to replace Hamlet *was kept from KS, but Suler described* Karamazov *to him in detail on 18 October.*

ND wondered whether he should start working with Dobuzhinsky on the Turgenev evening, for which models had been made, before KS returned.

To **Nemirovich-Danchenko**. 22 October 1910, Kislovodsk.
Dear Vladimir Ivanovich!

[...] I'll get down to business. Of course, you have to get down to work with Dobuzhinsky, you can't let the theatre hang on my illness. I only advise you to be careful with Dobuzhinsky, because purely directorial matters and matters of stage mise-en-scène might easily wear him down. Once he moves away from his artistic plan, he begins to stray and get confused. My mise-en-scène is calculated on immobility, even during the most rapid tempi of Turgenev's semi-vaudevilles. I relied on this internal tempo of the vaudeville to achieve the rapidly changing mental adjustments. What happens if my protracted convalescence keeps me an invalid for many months more! I am overcome with despair by the slow progress of my convalescence. I feel frozen in place, I've got as far as patties in broth, getting out of bed for two hours a day, and my improvement does not progress beyond this point. My intention of returning to Moscow by 12 November now seems infeasible, while, according to the doctor, my organism is so overtaxed and exhausted by both the preceding work and the illness itself that he will not be surprised if I don't return to normal before January. Who then will play the nobleman in *The Lady from the Provinces?*[34] [...]

It will be ghastly for Gzovskaya if she fails so dismally in that role. Her little song in our theatre will be sung, because the role of Tina meanwhile is not her sort of thing. However, she is bold and courageous.[35]

Here's what comes next: don't forget that Benois has left up to us a definite commission for *George Dandin* and *The Imaginary Invalid*.[36] The latter has already been performed at the Maly Theatre.[37] Benois definitely has to design something, otherwise he will be offended, and his being offended is extremely dangerous, because his whole close circle, consisting of the finest artists, the ones we need most, will spurn us in turn. He has probably already done some work on *Imaginary Invalid*, and obviously will have to be paid. Benois' commission is to be the last production I prepare, because it is time to think about the future.

After looking over Dostoevsky, I am convinced that *The Insulted and the Injured* can be fitted into the stage frame in its entirety in the following way. On the first evening the romance of Natasha up to Alyosha's departure inclusively. On the second evening the romance of Nelly concluding with the reconciliation scene. [*There follows a breakdown by scenes.*]

Baliev writes me that Maeterlinck made a personal appearance, but my wife in her letter writes nothing about it. How are we to justify to him our deletion of 'The Forest' and 'The Graveyard'? This ploy occurs to me: *The Blue Bird* is performed at matinees for children. We can excuse ourselves that children are scared by the scene in the forest, and therefore we had to leave it out. As to 'The Graveyard', whose set was built and the act rehearsed and the music written, we had to leave it out because it prolonged the performance owing to the mechanical difficulties in staging this scene by a whole half hour. It comes on just at the moment at the end of the performance when the play has to proceed post-haste. How are we to put this so that we don't reveal our secrets to the French or offend Maeterlinck. Tell them that our shareholders, who are planning to send the play to Paris, have forbidden us to sell this production either in part or as a whole. [...]

With heartfelt affection yours K. Alekseev

To **Olga Gzovskaya**. 22 October 1910, Kislovodsk.

Dear Olga Vladimirovna!

Forgive me for writing on scraps of paper in my own blood. It is because the only surviving fountain pen has red ink, I have no other pens; secondly, because, lying in bed, it is much more comfortable to write on note-pads.

The fact that I am writing to you in my own hand, and not dictating, is a *great secret*, and here's why: I am strictly forbidden to write by myself, and if I do my wife cruelly punishes me by depriving me of my favourite foods and sweets (today she and the children have gone to the mountains to see the snow which fell last night and is lying all day on Saddle Mountain, they've found something to look at!)

If they knew at the theatre that *I am writing a letter by myself*, they will be offended at receiving dictated letters. Another time I may not manage to escape the vigilant gaze of my strict wife. Of course, I will confess to her today and for

Figure 48 Olga Gzovskaya as Ophelia, 1912. Photo: K. A. Fischer, Moscow

this will be deprived of apple sauce. It will be replaced with stewed fruit which I hate. Ugh! I can taste it. But my business with you is so important that it is worth a little sacrifice. Besides, it is essential that I write by myself and not dictate; you will hardly find it pleasant to feel that there is a third party who listens to all our intimate artistic secrets, which I must be concerned with now. The only person I could turn to is my wife, but I feel sorry for her, she is so busy and so tormented by us.

One more word of preface: I probably will not finish this letter today, because this is my first experiment, and I send it unfinished. But will you allow me some other time to dictate all these artistic secrets to Kira? Drop me a little line about this.

Therefore, having put success out of our minds for a while, let us turn to the work [in *Brothers Karamazov*]. What you made out of Yekaterina Ivanovna I do not know, because I believe absolutely no one. It is very likely that, since they abuse you, it is praiseworthy from a pedagogical point of view. So, for instance, if you strive in a dramatic scene for naturalness before all else, and not for volcanic power, forcibly evoked, we specialists will find it praiseworthy, and the profane, that is the critics, will not. At a remove all I can know is only from my earlier involvement with you and, second, all I can deduce from what critics and letters have noted. So, for instance, people write to me that at rehearsals you were surprising in your nerve and glimmers of real temperament. They also write that it was worse in performance. I understand. First, understandable agitation at the exceptionally untoward conditions of your debut, and second – the reaction of a warhorse, startled by a crowd of people, and hearkening to the call of battle.

This is the first question I must deal with, because I am sure that there was an awareness of the audience and a display of yourself and your feelings. It takes years to get rid of this and then only during conditions of a propitious production and atmosphere, which you have so far not enjoyed. Acting for the other side of the footlights, as it is written somewhere; a certain difference in tone from our actors (this is written about nowhere, it is my formulation) and, finally, many old habits – all this is the result of an awareness of the audience.

How one is to fight this off you now know as well as I do: the circle [of concentration], the development of naïvety, the sense of communion, a sense of the proximity of the object and adjustment. This is what makes one completely forget about the audience, because there is no time to think about it. There are too many mental tasks without that.

But look, you still do not sufficiently appreciate (although, of course, you understand) that it is the general sense of self on stage that is created out of all these auxiliary feelings – concentration, the feeling of communion (radiation and being irradiated), a feeling for the object and, as a natural consequence of such sense of self, -- a variety of adjustments.

It seems that you managed to achieve the proper creative feelings – at table rehearsals. No sooner did you get up and start to move – this feeling was destroyed or completely altered by the actor's sense of self. However, once, when I was in the house, you managed a bit to act with a correct sense of self ([as Cherubino in] one of the first rehearsals for *The Marriage of Figaro*). However I still did not manage to sense a similar proper creative sense of self on stage in you. It has to be achieved on the stage itself, at the very moment of being before an audience. It is precisely in such a stage situation that you will feel and learn everything that you have mastered in theory (that is the circle [of concentration], naïvety, communion, object. I do not mention affective feelings and adjustments, because even those and others will develop, as soon as the ground for them has been laid).

Therefore every performance is a valuable lesson for you. You can't convene an audience every day and organize the staging of a performance for such a lesson. So treasure these performances as lessons. I am writing all this because I know you have one special failing: 'I had to catch my train to Yaroslavl as quickly as possible', you once told me, 'I shrugged off *Caesar and Cleopatra*, it didn't matter, the audience was stupid and none of them understood any of it...'

This is a great evil, because a performance like that creates evils ten times over.

It is easy to contract a disease (for instance, typhus), and it spreads with remarkable speed, but health will return by degrees. I am experiencing this even now. The same thing happens in the given case I mention. Stereotypes, craftsman-like devices are the disease, they will take root like a rapid contagion: one, two performances and, all unawares, the stereotype has already infiltrated muscles, and nerves, and brains. To weed out this stereotype one needs no fewer than 20, 30 performances, and sometimes more. Simple arithmetic will illustrate to you the sum of the evil and the difficulty of correcting it: 2 as opposed to 30.

The role of Katya does not suit you in any respect. What kind of Dostoevsky woman are you! But you will feel even this role accurately, logically, simply and sincerely. You will create an image that is yours and not Dostoevsky's, perhaps, but it will be artistic, pleasant and, most important, it will bring you as an actress not harm, but benefit. You must not only achieve an accurate creative sense of self on the audience, but you have to adapt your whole being to it: muscles, nerves, thought processes and so on.

Only when an accurate *habit* is formed (a very important thing in many grace notes of technique and sense of self) can you consider yourself beyond the danger of stage contagions. In order to form and fortify this habit, you need *hundreds* of proper performances with a true sense of self. I will explain this by an example. Let's assume that you have played 30 performances with a correct sense of self and only one performance with an actorish one. What is the result? You have reverted to the original state and have not progressed one iota. Do not think that I am exaggerating. For you in particular, deeply infused with the stereotypes of the Maly Theatre, my words and figures are no exaggeration. Believe me that it is so.

I am tired, I shall close. [...]

Cordially devoted K. Alekseev [...]

To **Nemirovich-Danchenko**. 10 November 1910, Kislovodsk.
Dear Vladimir Ivanovich!

[...] I must begin with what is on my mind... We are alone here, and have undergone our grief over Tolstoy in solitude, for we got the news after a delay of two days. I did not think it would be so hard to bear. We learned of Tolstoy's death only on Tuesday and on Wednesday there were no papers from Moscow. So it was only today we learned of what has been going on, where and how the great event took place. I am overwhelmed by the greatness and spiritual grandeur of Tolstoy's soul and the way he died. The clergy, trying to creep in on the dying man, like a thief through the back door. His pathetic, too earth-bound family, not daring to enter the now historic house; the whole regiment of reporters, photographers and curiosity-seekers, wandering around in the dark and whispering while the naïve Sage imagines that he is quite alone, and, surprised by the arrival of his son

Sergey, says, 'How did you find me?' The authorities and the police, bending over backwards with affability, the attitude of the peasants and their singing, the absence of the clergy -- all this is so extraordinary, so noteworthy, so symbolic, that I can think of nothing but the Great Lev, who died like a king, in the presence of death waving away all that is vulgar, superfluous, and only offensive to death. What good fortune to have lived in the time of Tolstoy, and how terrifying it is to remain on earth without him. As terrifying as to lose one's own conscience and ideals.

I read about the Moscow Art Theatre's decision to open a school [in Pushkino in Tolstoy's memory]. A good deed, but it alarms me. I am not referring to the funding (not once, but annually). How is one to insure a school in case the theatre closes?

Not long ago a school was opened in Tarasovka in memory of my father and mother. Disaster! The Pushkino peasants are highway robbers one and all. They are the sort of people whom the late count was not overfond of. Of course, they have to be instructed and educated, but… where is the means to do it? Of course, not a school. What's more, a school has a lot to do right now, but does anyone consider a theatre for peasants, whereas such a theatre would have more effect on the Pushkino peasantry than a school with a modern curriculum and trends. If a depraved peasantry such as those of Pushkino were to be shown *The Power of Darkness*… perhaps it would stir their calloused souls more efficiently. Somebody is making great efforts for such a peasant theatre at the moment. I read it in the papers. Shouldn't we lend a hand to that enterprise, especially since we are more competent at that than at pedagogy. I think we could select from our supernumeraries a troupe of highly principled people – at least for the summer and fall. Perhaps everything I write is foolish and impractical, but do not judge me too harshly – I am accustomed to getting down to business and coming up with ideas; moreover, I have not heard all your arguments and reasons.

Peace to the ashes of this greatest of men!!!

Let me move to my second concern. The box-office returns for *Karamazov*. I am racking my brains and cannot understand it. Expensive? – two evenings?..[38] but after all it is *Karamazov*!! How can an educated or simply a curious person not go to such a show! This brings my pessimism to the surface and starts to whisper to me: they are jaded. The public is beginning to turn away from us! They're forgetting us! They do not appreciate all the subtleties which are dear only to us – the specialists! What about Yuzhin! What about Nezlobin! When they weren't around, we somehow guided the public with stubborn and longstanding work, but now they have been led astray. Nezlobin has pretty little sets, wonderful nooks, foreshortening, lots of rooms, the acting is all easy to understand or very incomprehensible (and that's good too). I'm told that the Maly and Nezlobin and Zimin[39] are doing tremendous business, and we have no audiences… It's appalling and incomprehensible. And to have to experience this at a distance is hard. [….]

Yours K. Alekseev

To Nemirovich-Danchenko. 16 November 1910, Kislovodsk,

Dear Vladimir Ivanovich,

Two of your letters are lying before me. One is moving, the other magnificent. One is somewhat shorter, the other immense.

In reply to the first I must and will express the best of my feelings for you, who is always in my heart (they are what makes me pout sometimes, and get angry – out of love).

I feel I am unable, at least at the present moment, to express the gratitude and excitement stirred up in me by your letter about our fraternal intimacy, written to my wife during my illness. Simply, I am not strong and vigorous enough yet to give free rein to my emotions. When we meet again I shall embrace you as firmly as I love you. I will not even assure you that I believe in and know and have always known of your kind and affectionate feelings for me and I have no doubt that you too believe and know of my feelings for you. I also believe that as the years go by they will grow stronger, because the former professional envy, vanity, impatience and so on must give way in old age to life experience and wisdom. Once you realize what constitutes success and popularity, you want to flee from men, as Tolstoy did.

And so, I am sending you brotherly thanks for your letter to my wife: I shall always treasure it -- in my heart. When we meet again, -- we shall embrace.

Passing to the monster letter – I am staggered by its size -- I ask myself: do I have the physical stamina to reply to all the important questions you raise, for they cannot be answered offhand and have to be answered circumstantially. After all, when we settle these questions, we will be defining the future fate of our theatre.

No, I feel too weak for such work. My mind is still not working properly, there's a good reason I am forbidden brainwork, along with excitement and writing and anything else I find attractive. I am prescribed only boredom and an animal existence. I think of returning around 6 December and dream a great deal of the day when we shall con your letter and discuss it point by point. You don't have to convince me about [dramatizing] novels or the Bible or even Plato.[40] (Was it so long ago that you and I laughed at Craig. Not so long ago I was reading about Komissarzhevskaya's dreams before she died – to go into the back of beyond and found a new school. That's Craig's idea too.)

Another new obstacle also arises: what to do about the box-office? After all if the public can't fork out for *Karamazov*, which has made such a stir, then it will be even more difficult with other works. You are wise – it's up to you.

I can't write anything about *Karamazov* and adapting novels for the stage in general. I have many plans, many drafts, many notes on one-acts and short stories and so on. All this is in theory. Now comes the practice. Therefore, first of all we have to see.

Let me touch lightly on what you say about my system. Of course, before starting to work on a role, it has to be evaluated in general from the literary, psychological, social and everyday points of view. Only then can one begin to break it down, first into physiological bits, and then, moving from them, into psychological bits or desires. I know a few practical techniques now (because it is my task to find a way of realizing every theory. Theory without realization is not my field, and I reject it) to help the actor in his psychological, physiological, living, and even everyday analysis, perhaps even the social appreciation of a literary work and a role. But the literary side awaits your word. You must respond to this not only as a man of letters, a critic, but as a practitioner. We want a theory fortified by a practical method thoroughly tested by experimentation.

All I know so far is that, before tackling my system, we must a) stimulate the process of the *will*; b) initiate a process of exploration – with some literary discussions (you have the floor), for I know how to sustain and develop the process of further exploration; c) I know how to stimulate the emotional process of re-experiencing; d) I do not yet know exactly how to promote the process of *embodiment*, but I have already felt out the ground and think I am about to find the true path; e) the processes of *synthesis* and *influence* are clear.

It is up to me now to find a practical way of stimulating the actors' imagination in all these procedures. This aspect is very poorly worked out in psychology – especially the creative imagination of actors and artists. As for the rest, I think all of it is not only worked out, but also rather thoroughly proven. A few odds and ends have been written down. I believe you will agree with me in all respects. At the moment much of this is conveyed to you by intermediaries, who have understood it cerebrally, but, perhaps, not emotionally. Therein lies the principal difficulty. It is not hard to understand and remember; it is hard to feel and to verify. And that is what I would like to talk about, but where is the time (for you, since I am idle at the moment), where is the energy? […]

I embrace you.
Affectionately, K. Alekseev

To **Nemirovich-Danchenko**. 25 November 1910, Kislovodsk.
Dear Vladimir Ivanovich!

[…] It's true – from afar the theatre seems awful, when you learn that it is not selling tickets. Then depressing and dreadful ideas come into one's head. It seems that there are full houses at Nezlobin's and the same at Korsh's and the same at the Maly, while we are forgotten. This malice of the critics strikes one as sinister. It's as if they have conspired to inflict the *coup de grâce* on a theatre they hate. And it seems that the antichrist in our field is come – it is Nezlobin. In terms of artistic depravity, we have never had a worse enemy. Everything is pretty-pretty, refined in a boudoir way, tasteless to the point of boorishness, but adapted to the taste of the public and the critics, whom they know how to pamper. Everything that the idiotic critics rebuke us for, not understanding our theatre at all, can be attributed wholly and by rights to Nezlobin. Neither the flashes of talent, luxuriousness (wretched to our taste, but genuine for the critics) nor the most provincial, easy understandable stereotypes. He is the antichrist. Next year Nezlobin will strengthen his troupe (of course, to the taste of his public), and then they will convince everyone that his actors are talented. As for us! Oy, how we always hang by a thread. The budget is padded, demands go sky-high, the prices of seats ditto, while all the same there are no solid troupes. Kachalov will very quickly falter. My constitution is stronger, and

I have endured only twelve years, while every year he toils in drudgery. Leonidov?! – he will never replace Kachalov. It seems as if, after the torment of this present season, Kachalov has got in his head: what's the point, says he, of being tormented… over there [at the Maly], it's peaceful, there's lots of money, little work, touring, a pension… Just take away Kachalov alone, who has barely a year to prepare many roles -- and there will be nothing left to perform. And when you think about Artyom, Samarova… and you see that the troupe is enormous, only Moskvin and Kachalov can play leads, and there are five or six persons good enough to understudy them, and the rest are taking cues from the directors.

We have to take a decisive step. We have to turn Art into Accessible. This is painful, because you cannot sustain art in such a theatre. On the other hand, when you think about it, to whom are we dedicating our lives — the rich men of Moscow. Is it really possible to enlighten them? Of course, they will be the first to throw us over for Nezlobin. You remember Tolstoy, the grey life of the poor intelligentsia, who had nowhere to go, -- ugh! Something has to be done or else, on the contrary – one has to squeeze the juice out of the Art Theatre, provide for everyone and dwindle into a little club. To tell the truth, I am repeating your words, but now, at a distance and at liberty, one experiences them more clearly. Lord, how crucial it is that next season be highbrow in regard to art!

You know I'm starting to get worried: will they recognize Craig's genius or will they take him simply as a crackpot? It seems to me that the Maly and Nezlobin have so worked on the public and the decadents have so glutted it with their novelties that the corrupted audience will want a production with good sets and when it sees *Hamlet* will say, 'What a pity they didn't stage it in the plain, old-fashioned way with Uralov as the King!' I'm starting to think that if the public attitude to *Karamazov* is so cold, what's the good of *Hamlet*?!.. Shouldn't we (seeing that the *Hamlet* sets are ready) along with *Hamlet* put on something stunning with scenery by Dobuzhinsky? We need to provide him with work, otherwise other theatres will snatch him away. What if it were possible to get permission to put on *Emperor and Galilean*.[41] *Hamlet*, followed by *Galilean*. Or – which is, of course, not so good – simply stage a great Russian play? Like, for instance, *Tsar Boris* by [Aleksey] Tolstoy.

A repertoire is a-borning once again… We have to talk lots and lots about the future, if I only have the strength! I know, I understand and seriously sympathize with the situations you've landed in. It is appalling. The rehearsals and the old plays and the administration. I am ashamed and I am distressed to have caused so much trouble. But all the same it is not normal that such a theatre should depend on only two individuals. Why haven't we developed independent agents both as administrators and as actors? Can we lay so much weight on them? It would be so awful that I am ready to shoot myself to keep from having such a bad influence on others. It seems to me that Mardzhanov has this independence and initiative. […]

Yours K. Alekseev

Stakhovich greatly praises the first four scenes of *Miserere*. And that play is not his sort of thing. […]

On 7 December KS moved back to Moscow, although his illness recurred sporadically and he did not leave the house.

The production of Miserere *opened on 17 December: opinion was divided between the liberals and the anti-Semites and it ran for only twenty-six performances.*

To **Vera Kotlyarevskaya**. Early January 1911, Moscow.
Dear friend Vera Vasilievna!

[...] This whole period was very turbulent for the theatre. Just think, the most unprecedented season had been scheduled: *Hamlet* (Craig), a Turgenev production (Dobuzhinsky), Molière (Benois). On 1 August I fell ill, and on the 2nd the troupe met. The reins for preparing the productions were in my hands. In two months' time we had not only to stage them, find the concepts, do all the try-outs, but also create the very play of *Karamazov*. We had to stage *Miserere*, which had been accepted as an opportunity for the younger portion of the troupe, we had to make up for lost time with Hamsun's play, etc. The whole season is ruined, to the delight of our enemies, who come out of hiding with Yuzhin at their head and use whatever comes to hand with the help of the whole press to beat down their enemy any way they can.

What is going on in the realm of art in Moscow at the moment beggars description. The Maly Theatre has turned into almost a farce and gone to the dogs in order to attract the public. Its almost full houses come from the battlefield.[42] The Maly Theatre has become a theatre of supreme vulgarity. Nezlobin has become a bit high falutin, he works well enough with *Les Misérables* and *L'Aiglon* (this in the XXth century, after 23 years of the cultivation of an artistic repertoire!!). Korsh performs everything that has a name effective on a poster. The public is confused by the press, which praises everything it is shown, because the scribblers are bought off by Nezlobin and bewitched by Yuzhin at his club (a literary one).[43] The decadence is total. And despite this, despite the defamation, insinuations, insults, the Art Theatre holds firm. The greatest thing our inveterate enemies can achieve is that instead of last year's pure profit of 117,000 the theatre will make only 40-50,000 r. Does this matter? [...]

Heartily devoted and affectionately yours K. Alekseev

On 12 January KS and his daughter Kira left for a European convalescence. He believed Kira had her Alekseev grandmother's temper and 'it will be hard for her to live and for others to live with her.'

To **his wife Mariya Lilina.** 15 January 1911, Berlin
Dear Marusya!

[...] In the evening at a circus we saw *Oedipus the King* (Reinhardt). This was so awful that I became quite ashamed of my profession as an actor. The heightened emotion, the racket made by the crowd, the props-man-costumier's luxuriousness. [...]

K. Alekseev

To **his wife Mariya Lilina.** 16 January 1911, Berlin.

Dear Marusya!

[…] Last night I was at Reinhardt's, saw *Hamlet*. Bassermann[44] plays very well. The rest are beneath any indulgent criticism. It is the most degraded and most shabby Nezlobin. […]

Yours Kostya

The International Fine Arts exhibition was being held in Rome and Russia had an extensive showing there, including the Diaghilev ballet. KS and his daughter Kira joined the Stakhovich family there.

To **his wife Mariya Lilina**. Sunday morning, 23 January 1911, Rome.

Dear, good and precious Marusya […].

[Rome] is a marvellous city, and not at all in the way I pictured it before. I imagined it as enormous, awfully lively, overcrowded. Quite the contrary. The town is small (400,000 inhabitants), half the size of Moscow. Similar to it in a certain provincialism and lack of bustle. On the Corso (the main street), true, at certain hours there is a crowd, but nothing in comparison to Paris. And the Corso itself is half as wide as our Kammerherr Lane, with extremely mediocre shops, selling pictures, engravings, statuettes and antiquities. There are no other shops, and that is wonderful. Rome is good in that at every turning, in every corner there is something unexpected. Such dead-ends, nooks, steps, niches, little old ruined columns built into houses, an obelisk unexpectedly crammed in, an ancient monument amid the modernity and so on – you do not meet with that in other cities. […]

Yours Kostya

To **Leopold Sulerzhitsky.** 24 January 1911, Rome, Italy, Trinita dei Monti, Hotel Hassler.

[…] Now, to get down to Craig. I hope you know that he is in Paris now. I want to and ought to meet with him. […] There is an enchanting expansive young girl here – Stakhovich's daughter Zhenichka (whom you know).

She (between you and me) is attracted to Craig, and Craig is attracted to her. Knowing Craig's lack of principles when it comes to women (which I beheld), I cannot resolve to invite Craig here, besides I won't be here much longer and I will go either to Capri or Cannes (near Nice) to Dr Botkin. I can't go to Florence, because there's no suitable diet there and that's the most important thing for me […]

So where can I meet Craig? Cannes, but it's the season there and very expensive. Berlin. That would be best and here's why. In Dresden there's a Dalcroze school of plastic movement and eurhythmics. I'll go there because they say it's marvellous. Craig should find it interesting too.[45] So here's what we'll do. We'll leave Cannes or wherever the same day Craig leaves Paris, we'll travel to Berlin and then on to Dresden. Meanwhile we'll talk over some of things we have to talk over, i.e.,

1) Whether he will permit us to find arrangements for the screens on the stage itself, looking for a general mood and not scrupulously reproducing his models.

2) Whether he will permit us, while preserving the general concept of King, court, Ophelia, Laertes, i.e., their caricatural aspect, to depict or present them to the audience in a somewhat different form, i.e., more subtly and therefore not so naïvely. You realize that to present *Hamlet* in the guise Craig wants is dangerous. It (i.e., not Hamlet himself who is superb à la Craig, but the treatment of the other roles) will not be accepted in Moscow in the form Craig presents it. We must do as Craig would, i.e., the King is a Herod, a barbarian, the court is mindless in its absurd protocol, and Ophelia and Laertes are offspring of its environment, yet we must show this not by those puppet-like devices that Craig has endowed them with. Personally, that's really all I have to talk to him about, the rest relates to a simple desire to see him and arrange for his trip to Moscow.

Here are my ideas on that score. I'll get back to Moscow around 25 February. There will be a cabbage party on the 28th. Then rehearsals for *Uncle Vanya* (new scenery) – and directly afterwards *Hamlet*. So that there will be no delay. I've sent my notes to Muratova (for the actors) and Gzovskaya (for the youngsters). They will read them before our arrival, and then will be able to go straight to work. The school and colleagues who need not only to read but have my notes explained are left to you; as soon as you arrive, take up this matter at once. You and I shall work with the main characters, Ophelia, Hamlet, King, Queen, Polonius and Laertes, while Mardzhanov takes charge of the rest. Beforehand we shall all explain things to one another together and come to an understanding on analysis, psychological moments, desires, etc.

Along with this we must adjust the general details of the staging, the lighting and rehearse the arrangement.

Finally costumes.

Have Craig clarify, with this time-table in hand, when it will be most convenient for him to come: now or May?

If he has to see the action on stage, we'll have to schedule him for the 4th, 5th and 6th weeks of Lent (Lent begins on 21 February). Let him bear in mind that before that time, perhaps, he may have to come to Moscow. If you decide on another date, write. Write me whether Craig wants or has to go to Berlin. Of course, his way there and back will be paid. Tell him, dear Suler, that I have tried to write him a letter in German. I cannot explain all the complicated intricacy of my proposals set forth in this letter. That's why I have been silent for so long.

Hugs to you and Craig. Regards to the Maeterlincks. Kira's regards to you.

K. Alekseev

To **his wife Mariya Lilina**. Monday? 31 January 1911, Rome.
Dear Marusya […]

[…] We visited the Zoological Gardens. Extremely scary and interesting. A thorough impression that the lions and tigers are at liberty. No cages, walls and cliffs along the side, a moat in front which the lions cannot leap over. At first sight you don't notice this moat, and the perspective brings the beasts closer. They seem to be quite near. They climb up the rock face. Five tigers were playing

– incredibly beautiful. Next door are the jaguars and pumas. A few days ago a jaguar ate another jaguar, leaving only the head. [...]

Tenderly loving K. Alekseev

Suler reported that Craig left all the decisions to KS 'who knows best', but also asked for another £300.

To **Leopold Sulerzhitsky**. 6 February 1911, Rome.
Dear Suler!

Thanks for your letter. Now that Craig relegates everything, I have no need to meet him. *Do not tell him of this.* I shall defer the question and leave ostensibly urgently, without having seen him. He is now in a Western European mood and thinks only of getting money out of the theatre for doing nothing. Help is at hand for him, if he would act not with bravado but discretion. As he is now I don't like him. *Do not tell him of this*, but say, offhand, on your own or explain that the theatre, not yet having seen any results, has already paid for *Hamlet* (plus experiments) nearly 25,000 rubles. Can he demand more of foreigners and strangers? Now you know how foreigners treat us Russians. If we were to find abroad such generous people as ourselves, the management of the Moscow Art Theatre, we would shout it from the rooftops and glorify their name. Craig should understand this. He had better.... Remind him: I arranged for him a guaranteed annual salary of 6000 rubles. He went on a spree and squandered it all. Now the devil himself doesn't know how much he gets. In autumn he was ill – he couldn't come; he brushed aside costumes and production. Naturally, the Board sends to me and asks for an explanation of what Craig's salary is being paid for. Now he's beginning to act uppity. What can I do? It'll end with the Board repudiating him. Talk as if on your own – don't embroil him and me.

Yours K. Alekseev
In short, things are at the breaking point, and one false move will do it.

To **Leopold Sulerzhitsky**. 6 February 1911, Rome.
Dear Suler!

I am not done with Craig. Ask him if we can adapt his sets, that is, the arrangement of screens, and, in devising costumes, eliminate the tone of the South and Italy? [...]

Once you get back to Moscow, find out from Nemirovich, Kachalov, Leonidov, Gzovskaya which translation they want to use? If the old one, the roles have to be copied out again, because they've been lost; if the new one, we have to buy texts of KR [Grand Duke Konstantin Romanov] This has absolutely got to be done before I arrive. Then set up the stage, screens and lighting. We have to find new arrangements for the screens.

To **his son Igor.** Wednesday? 11 February 1911, Rome.
My dear boy,

I wrote you a letter, tore it up and now I do not know how to answer you. Perhaps you have been reading a lot of Tolstoy and latched onto a philosophical theme and just happened to write that gloomy letter with its philosophizing about death. You did not want to rewrite it, -- so you sent it. If so, then everything is understandable and natural. It is only a little vexing that you are wasting your rosiest years on the gloomy side of life. But... if your letter really and truly expresses the present state of your pure soul, – then I am astounded, confused and depressed. Then we need to have a good long talk. We need to delve into the root causes and change them come what may, before it is too late, before your pure soul is poisoned by the putrescence which mercilessly rots young souls before they have any understanding of real life.

Your letter was that of a 50-year-old man, weary of life because he has seen everything and is fed up with it all. But you have seen nothing. So drive away the darkness and seek the light. It is shining all over the place. Learn to find it. When I come home, we'll talk for a long time, but till then I embrace you, bless you and love you tenderly.

Your Papa

Suler reported that Craig was penniless and advised the theatre not to turn its back on a great artist with no means of support.

To **Leopold Sulerzhitsky**. 12/25 February 1911, Rome.
Dear Suler!

[...] As to Craig, here's what we've decided. He is not right in any respect, and you should advise him not to take such a high-and-mighty tone with the theatre, or else he will spoil everything for me. It makes no difference if he gets paid a part rather than the whole. It would be best if he were to come to Moscow at the beginning of the third week in Lent. On his arrival, i.e., 16/29 February, Stakhovich will send Craig 300-500 rubles. This is what I'm asking the theatre and hope it will grant my request.

[...] Explain to Craig that I cannot send him money from here, because I hardly have enough for my own return trip. You can do nothing by telegram, because things are stretched to the breaking point, and one must be cautious with the Board of Directors. The quickest thing is to act through Stakhovich, who is leaving for Moscow today.

Explain to Craig that what I write is my plan of action and not a promise; he might latch on to it and assume it was a promise of mine. That shouldn't keep Craig from writing, because the question of costumes is very important. I don't understand Craig's concepts. In addition, have him bring the mise-en-scène for Act 5. [...]

Yours K. Alekseev

To **Olga Gzovskaya**. 14/27 February 1911, Rome
Dear Olga Vladimirovna!

[...] I am happy if I have managed to help you. Only please be very strict and demanding in your sense of self on stage. Most of all try out your muscles (especially your facial muscles), which are very tense. *Constantly* study to relax them *before the audience*.

Second – the object. (Please be insanely demanding in this.) The third is the *unexpectedness* of the adjustments. They surprise and thereby raise the tone in the audience.

Be very strict in selecting adjustments.

In addition, transmit and express the inner design of the role ever more clearly and sharply.

I am glad that the readings are going successfully. [...]

Let me reply to the questions you asked. 1) How does one develop naïvety? I've explained it in the notes, but, I suppose, not very clearly. You have to get rid of doubts, critical thinking and everything else that prevents naïvety. I will add you have to take on great trust all the other techniques of the system, that is, the circle, the object, the adjustments. The general combined action of all these techniques will also increase naïvety (please, make notes in the margins and remind me to develop this part about the general influence of the techniques in increasing naïvety.)

2) So far I know only one exercise for affective memory – writing down the history and nature of love, jealousy, fear etc., as well as the division of various roles into pieces and a definition of the desires. You will write that this is difficult. Do not complicate the work overmuch, do not be afraid of naïvety at first and writing something stupid. What matters is not the form, but the process of self-analysis and emotional memories. [...]

K. Alekseev

To **his wife Mariya Lilina.** 19 February 1911, Capri.

Dear, precious one!

The day before yesterday, on an early rainy morning, at 8 o'clock, I got on the steamer and rode to Capri. Surrounded by fog, I could see nothing, but the sea was calm.

I travelled alone, because I would not let Mashenka become acquainted with Gorky. [...] Kira would have to sit with grown-ups all day and listen to talk about politics. It was better to leave her with the young people and go to a museum.

Gorky and Maria Fyodorovna [Andreeva] met me at the landing dock in a boat. I got in with them and sailed away; it rained all the way.

They had only just moved into a new villa, and it was not all in order. They had prepared a wonderful, comfortable room there, but, because it had no heating, I preferred the hotel.

They are living well, neither richly nor poorly. They eat well. Two small, comfortable cottages. At first things didn't go well somehow, we couldn't find the right tone. We talked until nightfall. Gorky was fascinating again and conquered my soul. His looks have changed a great deal, he does scads of reading and scads of work, and has become much more modest. Here, even in Naples and throughout all Italy, they not only love him, but take pride in him. When he walks down the

Figure 49 Joke photograph of Stanislavsky and his daughter Kira in Rome 1911

streets, you would think he is the reigning duke. And the good thing is that he doesn't ingratiate himself, does not set much store by this role, and laughed charmingly when I told him that he had dwindled from socialism to feudalism.

I left the Gorkys early, because I was tired. But along the way, in a café, I saw something lively: they were dancing the tarantella; I went in. There I scraped up an acquaintance with the musician Noguès[46] (a friend of Volodya Alekseev, who wrote *Quo Vadis?* for Zimin). Tomorrow morning, back to the Gorkys. The weather is vile. There was even hail. Today the conversation went somewhat better.

At 12 o'clock I was handed a note from Kira. It turns out that she had arrived with a German woman (a Lieven). They brought her to the Gorkys. After lunch everyone went into the mountains. There they danced a tarantella and drank tea. Then the Noguèses showed up at the Gorkys'. He decided to write us a mimodrama.[47] In the evening Gorky spoke wonderfully. I recited to him Famusov (successfully) and Krutitsky (unsuccessfully). He liked the first, the second not so much. Gorky is very fond of Kira, Mariya Fyodorovna is not. She's not sincere, she says, and tries to be ingratiating. [...]

Kostya

ND kept excavating the Hamsun vein with In the Clutches of Life *which opened on 28 February 1911 and chalked up a remarkable 163 performances.*

Back in Moscow, KS formally stepped down from the Board of Directors, leaving the shareholders in charge. He played Astrov in Uncle Vanya *as his official return performance and checked on the progress of the* Hamlet *scenery. On 10 March Suler introduced him to Yevgeny Vakhtangov, one of Adashev's alumni. Because he knew the Pitman shorthand method, KS took him on as his amanuensis at the* Hamlet *rehearsals.*

To **Lyubov Gurevich.** 14 March 1911, Moscow.
Dear and much esteemed Lyubov Yakovlevna!

[…] I read your article about Reinhardt,* having just seen *Oedipus* and *Hamlet* in Berlin. Reinhardt has become unrecognizable. He is a Jewish impresario, not an artist, and with great sadness I admit this and turn my back on him. Alas, what a pity! Another one gone!!! […]

Cordially devoted K. Alekseev

*I like it and agree with you.

Craig had been complaining that he wasn't being paid and that his letters went unanswered.

To **Gordon Craig.** 7/20 April 1911, Moscow.
Dear Mister Craig!

[…] I am confused, I do not know which way to turn. I do not understand what you are after. You have done everything to spoil those good relations that I continued to establish between you and the administration of our theatre. The administration is offended and insulted and considers your demands as derision, insofar as you yourself set the conditions between yourself and the administration.

As you remember I declined to regulate the money matters because even then I did not understand your wishes. I arranged for you to receive an annual salary of six thousand rubles. You found these conditions unsuitable and arranged for a flat sum for each visit. I remember how surprised I was, as was the Board, when your conditions were explained to them. Your conditions were favourable to the administration and unfavourable to you; I was surprised, shrugged and spoke to you about this. And that is all that I know at the present time about the conditions between you and the administration. Now a misunderstanding has arisen. I know that in money matters you can never reconcile people unless they themselves effect such a reconciliation, and you always behaved rather offensively and in most of your letters you have quite destroyed the good relations of the administration to you. To dispel this misunderstanding, I will ask the Board to comply with your demand and send you 1500 rubles. But I am afraid that after that the administration will put an end to our further collaboration. I will be your ardent solicitor, but I have great doubts as to the success of my mission.

One way or another, I ask you to keep me informed of your whereabouts, so that I know where to send you the money, if the administration decides to break things off with you and send a conclusive severance payment. […]

My situation is awful: I had just begun to understand your concepts in staging *Hamlet*, and I foresee an enormous lot of doubts and questions, which will be very difficult for me to resolve even with Suler.

The question of costumes remains quite undecided and quite obscure for me. We have not received from you any final versions of the sketches, and I am obliged to stage *Hamlet*, with such incomplete materials, being able only to surmise your intentions. I feel that such work is difficult and my strength is not up to it. I thought of returning to Yegorov's project,[48] but I cannot do that now as I am too much infected with your wonderful plan of staging *Hamlet* and because the administration demands that I justify those considerable sums, already expended on *Hamlet*, -- an expenditure made on my personal request and my responsibility. And now I suffer doubly: both for you and for myself.

I am suffering greatly from all that has occurred, because I know: you will never again find any institution that, in spite of all its defects, would so ardently answer your call and your artistic aspirations and so sincerely want to work with you.

Personally I always remain your unchanging admirer and friend and will be sincerely grieved, if I shall not manage to finish the work begun with you. […]

Sincerely yours K. Stanislavsky

To **Olga Gzovskaya**. 21 May 1911, Moscow.
Dear Olga Vladimirovna!

[…] Yesterday Suler demonstrated the set-up of the screens and the lighting.
Magnificent, triumphant and grandiose.

If I manage to figure out Craig's concept for the costumes too – something *great* will come of it.

At the moment the whole thing is up to the actors. I wish with all my heart I could rest, because the coming season promises to be interesting and difficult.

Cordially devoted K. Alekseev

To **Gordon Craig**. Before 3 June 1911.

Accept the most sincere congratulations from your Russian friends and admirers, who are destined to be the intimate witnesses of your artistic researches, joys and sufferings, experienced at a distance from your native land. At all those moments you kept your native theatre in mind and your thoughts turned to its doors, closed to you.

Now those doors have opened, and today the best representatives of your artistic world have recognized you as a prophet in your own land. Now we – your friends – turn our thoughts to you, to be present at your long-deserved triumph. We wish with all our hearts the same acknowledgement and success for you in your homeland as you have gained in foreign parts. We wish you the patience and energy to carry out the beautiful things that you create. They are too subtle and innovative to be understood immediately by the crowd of ordinary people, whom genius overtops. [...]

K. Stanislavsky,
Administrator of the Moscow Art Theatre

To **his wife Mariya Lilina**. 2 August 1911, Moscow.
Precious one!

[...] I got to Berlin early in the morning, at 8 o'clock. [...] I read in a restaurant that that night Reinhardt was putting on *Faust Part 2*. What was I to do, no matter how indolent I felt, I had to go. It started at 6:30, with a long intermission between 10 and 11, and the end was from 11 to 12. Our train was at 11:25. That means, I had time to see the first part of the show. Vasily Ivanovich [Kachalov] refused to go. He went shopping. I went home, lay down and at 6:30 headed for the theatre. I was very put out with Reinhardt for his *Oedipus* and went reluctantly, thinking that *Faust Part 2* is a bore. But... without understanding a word, I watched it with gripping interest. Say what you will, good for Reinhardt. The performance gave me great pleasure, although it was performed trivially, it was staged with imagination, although the concept was carried out in a mediocre way. [...]

Your loving Kostya. [...]

On 4 August 1911 KS asked Vakhtangov to form a group to be taught 'the system'. There was much cynicism and doubt, but even ND gave it a try. Work on Tolstoy's The Living Corpse *was officially declared to be a test of the system.*

To **his wife Mariya Lilina**. 6 August 1911, Moscow.
Dear Maruysa, my darling little angel!

[...] The work is interesting. Everyone is studying the system with great enthusiasm and conscientiousness and sincerely wants to act in accordance with it. Vladimir Ivanovich [ND] is first and foremost and like a schoolboy doing all the exercises. Right now Vasily Ivanovich [Kachalov] is sitting in Igor's room and looking for 'desires' for the second scene of *Hamlet*.[49] He has already understood the main thing and, I think, is starting to love the work. [...]

Tenderly loving K. Alekseev [...]

To **his wife Mariya Lilina.** 11 August 1911, Moscow.
Dear, tenderly beloved!

[...] Nemirovich-Danchenko and I are living on friendly terms; it's a pity we see one another infrequently, both very busy. How is the work going?.. As to what has been done – not much. As to what has been instilled in the actors in terms of my system, -- something has been done. Things go the way they always have. Nemirovich has taken on himself the so-called instruction of the system very well and very enthusiastically. I talked for 2 days and 2 nights -- just to the principals in *Hamlet*. Nemirovich is convinced that it is not possible to explain things to the majority of characters all at once. When all is said and done Nemirovich did all the exercises, and not at all badly. On the 3rd day the whole company was called and Nemirovich himself, in my presence, explained my system. He spoke lucidly but in generalities. I think he has understood only five out of ten points. Nevertheless it was decided that everyone learn the system. Then we marked the 1st scene in *Hamlet* (2nd part) and the actors even performed it while I was there. Of course, it was all shallow, but the important thing is that they all suddenly came to life. Moreover, all of them suddenly, according to the tasks I assigned, performed various external images. The Hamletics seemed to be convinced by the system, and, from Vasily Ivanovich and Luzhsky down to the newcomer Nelidov, they all do the exercises.[50] But since then it's been a long time between *Hamlet* rehearsals, because meanwhile I have to be at the office and the factory and help on *The Living Corpse*. There matters get on in the old way. Vladimir Ivanovich lectured. Everyone (especially Moskvin) ostensibly understood. But it only stopped at ostensibly. For a whole hour Nemirovich stated that he had been talking about this for a long time now and was far from agreeing with it. You know his system of stealing up on someone else's work and over the years, piecemeal – appropriating it. Then, in a raised voice, that is in a general's tone, he began to say that we would not finish analysing my system this or next year. I showed him that each person had to learn to make this analysis at home for himself, that it is very simple. After this I had to withstand another cannonade. Everyone was persuading me that I am a credulous child, that everyone lies to me, but I believe that the system is at least good, if far from elaborated. That it takes years and years of daily practice and reading to understand all its complexity, and I'm the only one who finds it simple. In short, there poured forth the stereotypes and clichés that have poisoned my life in the theatre. In a single day I got so tired of these beliefs and these struggles with obtuse minds that I spat on it, kept my mouth shut and stopped going to *The Living Corpse*.[51] During that time I reviewed the scenery for *Corpse* and *Hamlet*.

The sets for *Corpse* [by Simov], with a few exceptions, don't work, that is they are uninteresting and stale. I don't exempt myself from blame, because last spring they showed me the models and I wasn't energetic enough to insist on revisions. What is wonderful and worthy of all kinds of praise is that all the scenery down the least detail is ready, fitted and on display. Everything is ready for *Hamlet* too – sets and costumes. This is down to Mardzhanov, Tretyakov, Sapunov and chiefly Nemirovich – beyond all praise. Sapunov and Mardzhanov – good for them. They have made beautiful costumes. Perhaps more variegated in colour than Craig would like, but nevertheless according to Craig and beautiful. Scene 2, that is the king on the throne and all a solid mass of gold is beyond all praise. For the first time our troupe understood the genius of Craig. [...]

Yours Kostya. [...]

The MAT Council advised the directors to put all their energy into getting The Living Corpse *ready for opening and postpone* Hamlet. *The Tolstoy drama opened on 23 September with KS as Prince Abrezkov. He and Lilina walked off with the reviews. It achieved eighty-two performances.*

In a notebook for 1911 KS wrote a memo to read Sigmund Freud's Psychopathology of Everyday Life *(1895, translated into Russian in 1910), Daniel Hack Tuke's* Illustrations of the Influence of the Mind on the Body *(on the logic of emotions, 1872)),* Experimental Psychology *by the Danish scientist Hovting, and the highly recommended* Theory of Creativity *by Pyotr Engelmeier (1910).*

To **Nemirovich-Danchenko**. November-December 1911, Moscow.
Dear Vladimir Ivanovich!

My role is a strange one. I would like least of all to insult anyone and I think that I, more than anyone, am concerned with the fate of those with whom I have studied life.

I am personally well enough provided for to live out my life... There is no need to work any more than I am working... And what do you think... Except for insults, distrust and being called a fifth wheel on the carriage -- I get nothing. No encouragement from anyone, or else it comes too late. I do not want to accuse others... Obviously, I cannot do anything by myself and I do not know how to...

But why don't they say to me straight out: give it over, your efforts are pointless, they aren't needed and aren't appreciated. I would torment no one and would live for my own satisfaction. Just now my role is an idiotic one. I work for those who don't even have need of it.

I am very, very tired. I have turned my back on a personal life. My life goes on at rehearsals, in performances, and, like today, on a free evening, -- I lie in bed, as if after hard labour, almost an invalid.

To live like this is oppressive.

To make unnecessary sacrifices is stupid, and to poison someone else's life is a sin. I have to undertake something decisive, but what – I do not know.

Let them teach me...

I have worked out my whole life according to a plan – a clear, sharply defined one. Obviously, it is unsuitable. I have no other. Let them offer another one. No one will.

I hear contradictory, fortuitous, unsystematic, flimsy offers.

Let them offer something integral, firm, clear, well-defined, but don't mark time, wishing everything go on as of old.

Everyone says no to everything and no one offers anything, no one undertakes anything in order to relieve our burden, and we act and act, grow old, burn out... And they all have a presentiment of catastrophe, and no one tries to avert it.

I hope I am wrong... I will eagerly step aside with my own plans, and let others take action...

Only let them *take action* and not make plans to do so, not get angry, not envy each other and not hold such long meetings. I am ready for anything, and most of all to clear the way for those who want to take action. I will be angry with no one and do not wish to offend anyone. Just get on with it, get on with it.

Yours K. Alekseev

At a technical rehearsal of Hamlet, *the screens fell over and it was decided that they would have to be grounded and thus changed behind the curtain, not before the audience's eye. Craig returned to Moscow to attend the dress rehearsals of* Hamlet. *He objected to a number of details and KS argued with him to brighten the lighting. On 19 December he walked out of the auditorium during a rehearsal of 'The Mousetrap' because it wasn't staged as he had conceived it. Suler's name was left off the playbill at Craig's insistence and the assistant director was offended in turn.*

To **Leopold Sulerzhitsky.** 22 December 1911, Moscow.
Dear Lev Antonovich!

Today you were not in the theatre, yesterday you didn't come by...

Either you have fallen ill, in which case write a little note about the state of your health, or you are demonstratively protesting and getting angry, and so I begin to get depressed that the work, begun joyously, is ending so sadly.

When I entertain such conjectures, I feel stupid and don't understand. I feel I need to do something, to understand something, and I don't know and don't understand what's going on. You got angry with Craig for changing the lighting? I don't believe it and I don't understand it. After all, the design and concept were created by Craig... Don't you think he's the best one to know what he had in mind... It would be as absurd for Hansen [the Ibsen translator] to consider *Brand* his own work as for me to take the screens and the idea of *Hamlet* for my own creation. Nobody criticizes a winner, and indeed 'The Mousetrap' did have an enormous success yesterday.

That's not all. Didn't you really feel the day before yesterday, when Kachalov was rehearsing acting in the darkness Craig had just arranged, that it (the darkness) is the salvation of the whole show. For actually, yesterday the darkness hid all the unfinished bits. And Lord, how Boleslavsky's [Laertes] shortcomings came to the fore when he was lit by light from all the reflectors! And the last tableau worked precisely because the lighting concealed all the operatic garishness of the costumes.

It has been suggested that you are offended on the account of the playbill.[52] But what have I to do with that?

Craig started to be capricious, rejecting all suggestions. The theatre requires that Craig's name be on it, because the scandal he created became notorious throughout the city. Craig demands my name on the playbill, because he's afraid of responsibility and hides behind me as a scapegoat. Amid all these cunning schemes I have to reconcile Craig with you or you with Craig, because I cannot stand alone on the playbill. I can never figure out what to do at such moments. I go to you for advice, and you start talking about *The Blue Bird.* And then I stop understanding anything. Is this to be the end of work so well, so amicably begun? If so, -- then one would have to cast aside the best thing in life – art, -- and run from its temple, which has become suffocating.

You cannot go on living – and suddenly take offense, without explaining why.

That Craig has offended you I understand, and for that I'm sorry. But...

Figure 50 Vasily Kachalov as Hamlet, 1912. Photo: K. A. Fischer, Moscow

Craig is a great artist, our guest, and Europe is now watching how we handle his creativity. I don't want to be embarrassed, and as for schooling Craig – I really don't care to. Isn't it best to finish what is begun, especially with only one day to go.

Exchange your anger for graciousness and do not spoil a good beginning by a bad ending.[53]

Tomorrow at 2 we shall arrange the apparition of the Ghost in the closet scene. Hugs.

K. Alekseev

Hamlet *opened on 23 December to very mixed reviews, acknowledged at best as a* succès d'estime. *Despite plans to tighten it up and change some of the casting, it ran for only forty-seven performances.*

Notes

1 In Act 2 Khlestakov pulled the hair of the inn waiter and threw his boots at Osip.
2 Grand Duke Konstantin Konstantinovich (1858-1915) was an ardent theatre buff who translated and acted *Hamlet*; he wrote plays under the pseudonym K. R.
3 Pyotr Arkadievich Stolypin (1862-1911), Minister of the Interior, had petitioned to be retired from the post of Chairman of the Council of Ministers.
4 Sofiya Vasilievna Khalyutina (1875-1960), a former Philharmonic student, was cast mainly as very young women or children. In *The Blue Bird* she played Tyltyl. She opened her own school in 1909.
5 The Japanese had annihilated the Russian fleet at Tsushima, signalling the ultimate defeat of the Russians.
6 Duncan had inserted into her repertoire Gluck's *Iphigenia* and dances to the music of the first movement of Beethoven's seventh symphony.
7 Terms of the system.
8 Vasily Alekseevich Maklakov (1869-1957), lawyer, one of the leaders of the liberal Cadet Party.
9 Certain newspapers had reported that there was dissension with Craig.
10 Paris Singer (1868-1932) was the third son of the American sewing-machine inventor and millionaire Isaac Singer; he was a married man at this time.
11 Yelena (Ella) Ivanovna Rabenek (Bartels, married name Knipper, 1875-?), dancer, teacher of stage movement.
12 Nikolay Aleksandrovich Rumyantsev (1874-1948), a young and simpatico doctor, had joined the MAT as an actor in 1902 and moved to the administrative-financial division. He left in 1925.
13 Konstantin Nikolaevich Nezlobin (Alyabev, 1857-1930) had managed theatres in Riga and Kiev before opening one in Moscow in 1909: with an ambitious and eclectic repertoire, it was the MAT's leading competitor among private theatres.
14 Naples-born Mikhail Fyodorovich Likiardopulo (1883-1925) came to Russia in 1894; translator of Oscar Wilde, Maeterlinck, Jack London, H. G. Wells into Russian, secretary to the MAT administration 1907-17; contributor to the symbolist journal *Libra* (*Vesy*). He cobbled together the translation of *Hamlet* from various existing versions.
15 The rumour did not pan out.
16 Lidiya Mikhailovna Koreneva (1885-1982), at the MAT school in 1904, began as one of KS's favourite actresses, who saw her as a born Irina in *Three Sisters*. A lady-like ingénue, she played Verochka in *Month in the Country* and Lise in *Brothers Karamazov*. Characterized as 'the most capricious actress in the history of the MAT', after the Revolution she would prove to be a bane of KS's existence.
17 Vera Vsevolodovna Baranovskaya (1885-1933) entered the MAT in 1903. KS considered her one of his students and believed she carried the 1908/9 season. Her desire to play tragic roles led her to leave the MAT and create her own studio. She is remembered in the title role of Pudovkin's film *Mother* (1926).

18 Ida Lvovna Rubinshtein (1885-1960) took part in the first 'Russian seasons' in Paris, dancing an exotic Salome.

19 Dobuzhinsky was very concerned about the work being done in his absence.

20 The property man I. I. Zablotsky, who had been taken on in April 1909 and who was charged with preparing *A Month in the Country*.

21 One of KS's favourite exercises was having the actors improvise looking for lost money or jewellery.

22 Nikolai Vasilievich Drizen (von Driesen, 1868-1935), theatre historian and censor of the Chief Administration for Press Matters.

23 Semyon Solomonovich Yushkevich (1868-1927), Jewish novelist and playwright.

24 Karl Andreevich Fischer, proprietor of a Moscow studio, was the MAT's official photographer until just before the Revolution, and recorded the individual characters and full-stage pictures of most of their productions, issuing them as postcards.

25 KS was afraid that Knipper's failure as Nataliya Petrovna would lead to the role being assigned to Germanova. ND did not think she was up to it and said that casting her would 'kill' Knipper.

26 The Turgenev evening with sets by Dobuzhinsky was staged in the 1911/12 season. *Evening in Sorrento* was not part of it.

27 *Miserere*, a play about the suicide epidemic among Jewish youth by Semyon Yushkevich, was originally entitled *Lord, Have Mercy on Us*. When the censorship forbade that title, the Latin word was substituted, after failed attempts to find a Russian equivalent.

28 A series of photographs of the production taken by the K. Fischer company.

29 Arkady Georgievich Gornfeld (1867-1941), literary scholar and translator.

30 Konstantin Aleksandrovich Mardzhanov (Koté Mardzhanishvili, 1872-1933), Georgian director, who, after a start in Tiflis, worked in Riga with defectors from the MAT, such as Andreeva and Roksanova, in an MAT repertoire. This greatly annoyed KS, and when Mardzhanov began to direct in Moscow at Nezlobin's Theatre, he referred to him as 'the antichrist'. Still, he welcomed him to the MAT in 1910 'to do the heavy lifting'. Despite considerable work on *Hamlet*, Mardzhanov's name was left off the poster. His only sole finished productions at the MAT were *In the Clutches of Life*, which was a success, though KS disliked it, and *Peer Gynt*, deliberately in the MAT style. Conceived to be played over two evenings, it was compressed to one and its failure led to his departure from the troupe.

31 Evidently Craig had given KS Viollet Le Duc's illustrated encyclopedia of the material world of the Carolingians.

32 Mariya Savitskaya was originally cast in the role. KS was at odds over this with Craig who preferred Knipper and got his way.

33 Olga Ivanovna Sulerzhitskaya (Pol, 1878-1944), pianist and concert mistress of the MAT and the First Studio.

34 The production of *The Lady from the Provinces* was postponed. KS remained cast as Count Lubin.

35 Gzovskaya had been disliked as Katerina Ivanovna in *Brothers Karamazov*, and KS feared that Mardzhanov's casting her as Tina in *Miserere* was a mistake.

36 Aleksandr Nikolaevich Benois (Benua, 1870-1960), prominent member of the World of Art movement, was an expert on the eighteenth century. Benois was commissioned to design and direct *The Imaginary Invalid* and *Tartuffe*.

37 The Maly production went unnoticed.

38 ND suggested that the modern public was afraid of Dostoevsky.

39 Sergey Ivanovich Zimin (1875-1942), impresario of a private opera in Moscow that often employed innovative easel painters as designers.

40 ND saw the benefit of *Karamazov* in changing the nature of the contact between theatre and literature.

41 KS was afraid that the ecclesiastical censorship would ban Ibsen's two-part play, whose characters include canonized saints.

42 A reference to I. I. Kolyshko's play *The Battlefield*.

43 Yuzhin had founded and chaired the influential Literary-Artistic Circle for many years. He retired from it in 1905. His ill-will towards the MAT was exaggerated by KS under the influence of Nelidov, a personal enemy of Yuzhin.

44 This was Reinhardt's third version at the Deutsches Theater. Albert Bassermann (1867-1952) was one of the stalwarts of the classical German stage.

45 Craig told Suler he had no interest in eurhythmics and doubted that KS would.

46 Jean Nougès (1875-1932), French composer.

47 Gorky spoke to KS about a studio where young people, while learning the theatrical arts, would simultaneously try to create a collective and act in the tradition of strolling players. He also proposed to create subjects for studio improvisations.

48 Yegorov had travelled to Denmark and provided a production design prior to Craig.

49 Until his family returned, Kachalov was living in KS's apartment.

50 Luzhsky played Polonius; Anatoly Pavlovich Nelidov (1879-1949, not to be confused with the bureaucrat Vladimir Nelidov) did not act in the show, having moved to Nezlobin's Theatre in September.

51 ND began to feel that the attraction to KS's ideas was drawing him away from the original plan.

52 The first playbills for *Hamlet* read: 'Production by G. Craig and K. S. Stanislavsky. Direction by L. A. Sulerzhitsky. Design by Gordon Craig.' Later they read: 'Production by Gordon Craig. Direction by K. S. Stanislavsky, L. A. Sulerzhitsky.'

53 Suler's lengthy response the following day was heart-rending. Although he protested that he was not offended, he accused KS of regularly betraying him for the benefit of other friends. A translation of the whole letter appears in Laurence Senelick, *Gordon Craig's Moscow* Hamlet: *A Reconstruction* (Westport, Conn., US: Greenwood,1982).

Figure 51 Stanislavsky as Argan in *The Imaginary Invalid*, 1913. Photo: K. A. Fischer, Moscow

7

THE STUDIO AND STEPANCHIKOVO

1912–1916

The domestic stability prevalent under the Third Duma did not prevail in foreign relations. France and England were staunch allies of the tsarist government, but this was closely connected with the championship of the Balkan Slavs, who were politically liberal. Austria was regarded as an enemy, not least because of its annexation of the Balkan principality of Bosnia-Herzogovina. Still, the balance of power was shakily maintained and the Russian populace was more concerned about the situation at home.

The fact that the younger members of the company were more welcoming to the System than the resistant 'old-timers' led KS to propose a studio once more. It would explore the System and prepare actors and even productions for the parent company but without permanent deadlines. KS would continue to provide three productions a year for the MAT. As an actor he would continue to create small roles, but no more leads. In that regard, he started to rehearse the evening of Turgenev one-acts, with himself in the comic role of Count Lubin in The Lady from the Provinces. *He reversed his process with Dobuzhinsky, now insisting that the actors' needs must dictate the design of the setting and costumes.*

On 22 January Jaques-Dalcroze demonstrated his rhythmic gymnastics at the MAT.

Meyerhold and Golovin wrote to KS that they were concerned about news that he alone was bearing the burden of the conflict between old naturalistic ways and new practices at the MAT.

To **Vsevolod Meyerhold**. *10 February 1912, Moscow.*
My dear Vsevolod Emilievich,

I am deeply touched by your good letter, which was prompted by fine sentiments, and I am very grateful to you and Mr. A. Golovin. Wherever there is working and questing, there is struggle. We struggle, but I do not dare complain about our adversaries. On the contrary, I respect them. The greatest pain is caused by 'theatre' itself.

Goodness, what a crude institution and art it is! I have lost faith in everything that serves the eye and ear on the stage. All I believe in is emotion and, chiefly, nature itself. It is cleverer and subtler than all of us, but…!!?

Yours, until we meet again,
K. Stanislavsky

On 5 March the Turgenev evening opened: the first act of The Parasite, The Weakest Link, and The Lady from the Provinces. He played Count Lubin in the last as broad farce and it worked for most, though some complained of caricature. Since laughter was rare at the MAT, it was a welcome respite, but KS felt embarrassed. KS improved his performance, sensing that it was wrong to proceed from externals, but to 'find oneself in every role'. The trio proved popular and ran for 165 performances.

To **his son Igor.** After 6 April 1912, St Petersburg.
My dear boy, my unhappy crammer!
   [...] They have lit into our Hamlet, I am told. I myself have read nothing and therefore I do not send the reviews either to Craig or to Kira. 'Who'd enjoy it!!' I cannot recall when we've been so insulted as this year. To cap the climax, Benois abused us and Craig and Turgenev.[1] And Benois was our most fervent adherent.

„ПРОВИНЦІАЛКА" И. С. Тургенева. Моск. Худож. Театръ
Графъ Любинъ—К. С. Станиславскій.
Изд. А. А. Горожанкина. Худож. фот. К. А. Фишеръ Москва. 1912 г.

Figure 52 Stanislavsky as Count Lubin in *The Lady from the Provinces*, 1912. Photo: K. A. Fischer, Moscow

On top of this, *Oedipus*, that dreadful Berlin *Oedipus* [directed by Reinhardt] creates a furore in the very Moscow that we have educating for 30 years. So I don't know whether to go into a monastery or open a circus.

[…] This year you and Kira have done everything that could be asked of you. Your conscience should be clear, and an awareness of your good behaviour should give you confidence. May God bless you all.

Your sincerely loving and friendly Papa

To his daughter Kira. 12 April 1912, Petersburg.

My dear clever-dick Kiryulya!

[…] Mama has fallen ill. We brought her back in a motor-car because her temperature was around 39. From that time she hasn't left her room and hasn't acted. We had to put Knipper into *The Living Corpse*, Kosminskaya into *The Cherry Orchard* [as Varya], and had to perform *A Month in the Country* instead of *The Lady from the Provinces*. Mama is better now and can act, but yesterday Gribunin fell ill and went to Moscow without asking leave. Again we had to put Moskvin into *Month in the Country* instead of him and Aleksandrov in *Hamlet*.[2] No sooner had this been settled, when we hear from Moscow that Zhdanova, who had been given leave to go to Moscow for a few days, had fallen dangerously ill.[3] A new mess, and we had to put Koreneva into *Cherry Orchard*. So, what with all this illness and turmoil, we are dragging out this damned Petersburg season and think with horror about Warsaw and Kiev, where we are almost sold out. […] What will make you laugh and entertain you? Nemirovich's mishaps. The poor fellow has no luck. Not long ago in a restaurant he fell through the crack of a revolving door (like the one at the 'Russischer Hof') and got squeezed in it. Then he was at Bilbasova's looking at a big stereoscope. As he turned the handle somehow his beard got caught in a cleft, and he was pulling it along with the turn-table inside the stereoscope. He sat for a long time without moving, afraid to admit the accident. People came up to him, but he pretended that he was attentively looking into the stereoscope. Finally he had to admit it, and everyone rushed up to rescue him. Fortunately, Kachalov was not present at this.[4] The third time, the day before yesterday, he gave a dinner for our designers (Benois, Dobuzhinsky, Roerich) and began by breaking a stool and falling down. Then he dropped a big piece of salmon between a window and a steam radiator and poked a fork into the space between – and burned himself. Whichever way they tried to retrieve the fallen fish, even the waiter didn't manage to do it. 'This could only happen to me', poor Nemirovich whispered to Moskvin sitting next to him (one Yepikhodov to another).[5] They had barely sat down at the table, when Nemirovich's finger slipped into a groove in the table. Just at that moment Benois, sitting across from him, leaned his elbows on the table. This movement, it turned out afterwards, pinched Nemirovich's finger, and he started to groan in pain. They rushed to pull out his hand, but could not do it until Benois got up from his seat to rescue the agonized man. His rising freed the finger from the vice all by itself. […]

Your tenderly loving Papa

Mikhail Aleksandrovich Chekhov (1891-1955), Anton's nephew, who had been acting in other companies, was accepted into the MAT. After the season ended, Nikita Baliev left the troupe and, building on the public success of the annual cabbage parties, founded the cabaret The Bat. Many MAT actors moonlighted in it and parodies of MAT productions were often staged.

KS began his summer vacation in a euphoric mood. The Studio was approved and granted a rented space, a floor above the Cinematograph (later the Luxe) cinema at the corner of Tver street and Gnezdnikov lane.

To **Nemirovich-Danchenko**. July 1912, Mineral Springs.
Dear Vladimir Ivanovich!

I am very touched and grateful to you and the theatre for having faith in me at this time and for helping me to do something without which, I am profoundly convinced, the theatre would freeze in place and come to a dead end. Do any of us know what ought to be done now, in which direction one must take the actors, which plays to perform? These are hard and difficult times. We must experiment and experiment... On what? I don't know, or, more accurately, have just a presentiment of it. If nothing comes of these experiments, it means that I am too old, it's time to retire, time to make way for someone else.

In appearance the rooms are splendid. I didn't expect such luxury, in terms of dimensions. How shall we settle in? What do we need, what should be going on in these rooms:

1) First of all -- the Molière rehearsals, which take place initially at the table (i.e., they are also possible in the small room), and then can move onto the main stage.[6]

2) Daily exercises with those who know the theory (actors, students). Sometimes with me, sometimes with Suler.

3) Theory for actors and students, who are not familiar with it (again the beginners – Chekhov, Vyrubov,[7] pupils who have just been admitted, and those of the old-timers who trust me and want to get acquainted with what they've missed). Sometimes me, sometimes Suler.

4) Old and new collaborators – Vakhtangov and, perhaps, someone else who will show off what he knows. All this should be carried out and put in action in the first instance.

5) When all this has been undertaken, we must think about how the person who has thoroughly understood the SYSTEM and mastered it is to apply it. At first in performances for himself (not for the audience). For that we must employ two methods: 1st -- extracts or one-acts, to test out what has been learned in practice (i.e., under the supervision of me or Suler). Independent work on other extracts or one-acts.

Of course, it is desirable to provide training and show an audience (our own) what has been done not once but several times. It would be good, therefore, to select extracts to a particular purpose. I have my own plan for that, but for the moment I will wait before I talk about it.

6) We must set up a workshop for stage directors, to discover new possibilities for staging, lighting, popular shows for touring companies, hand puppets, marionettes, new theatrical architecture, shows in large halls, circuses, itinerant theatres, etc., etc. Often this research in the most varied fields is needed not so that we get actively engaged in puppet shows or folk theatres, but in order for us to put out feelers in various directions so as to find new paths for our theatre.

7) Experiments in new ways of playwriting and a new view of art...[8] I will keep mum for the moment about other dreams.

How can we adapt the rooms to these ends?

So we need: a) A room with a stage and lighting, where performances can be given. Raised platforms are not necessary. I have explained to Bazilevsky[9] how to fix the ceiling and the movable curtain. In the same room we need a folding table for discussions, two easy chairs and bentwood chairs. Lighting for those parts of the room where the audience sits (that is, for the moment the wiring). Stage lighting – hanging, portable lamps. (I have explained it to Bazilevsky.)

b) We need a room for Suler's or my activities –at the table.

c) Ditto for Vakhtangov's activities.

d) For the directors' work.

e) Assembly room.

f) Reception room.

g) Smoking room.

h) A table for the housekeeping department.

i) Offices for me and Suler.

I would divide it this way:

[Diagram]

Without having seen the rooms, I may be in error. But meanwhile the most important thing is to provide three rehearsal spaces and install lighting. Then without loss of time we can start work on 1 September.

What do we need for that?

1) To take action so that the three rooms can be used simultaneously. If the walls are thin and let in sound, they must be upholstered with something. If the doors are thin, then make felt curtains for one or both sides. [...] I am afraid that the rooms may be small and one of them will have no windows.

There's still the question of where to put the watchman and the charwoman, both of whom we shall probably have to have. The latter may perhaps come and go, but we shall need to find a place for the former (perhaps a folding cot).

To **Olga Gzovskaya.** 15 July 1912. Essentuki.

Dear Olga Vladimirovna!

[...] I've been recalling a story about a congratulatory telegram sent to Chekhov. Tikhomirov, who used to be an actor, now deceased, had sent it. They woke up Chekhov, he got alarmed, they charged him a ruble, and when he saw the rain-soaked bearer who had brought the pointless telegram, Chekhov added another ruble as a tip. They opened it – 'Heartfelt congratulations'. Anton

Pavlovich threw away the telegram and announced: 'Write to him that I have cut his role and we shall give him another role – a messenger who brings a telegram and exits immediately'. [...]

Cordially and affectionately yours K. Alekseev [...]

To **his wife Mariya Lilina.** 2 September 1912, Moscow.

Dear and beloved!

[...] Yesterday, Saturday, I was at the theatre at noon. All the doors were locked. People were loitering in the corridor. Feelings of boredom and dejection, although they were working wholeheartedly. I felt quite alien and unneeded. Nemirovich invited me to a rehearsal upstairs. We had a chilly meeting (Vladimir Ivanovich himself tried to be charming). I sat half an hour in the tearoom. [...]

I went home, slept. In the evening Vladimir Ivanovich came by. In a good mood. He tried to smooth things over and explain the chilliness that prevails in the theatre in relation to me. He made a few advances concerning the studio. He was very charming, but my heart turned cold, empty and forlorn. [...]

Yours Kostya

The Studio was subsidized by KS, and headed by Suler. The first group of fourteen included Vakhtangov, Mikhail Chekhov, Aleksey Diky, Sofiya Giatsintova, Serafima Birman, Olga Baklanova and Maria Uspenskaya. KS began systematic work with the Studio folk, first in his apartment, then in the new quarters above the cinema. There they worked with yoga and concentration exercises. From Capri Gorky offered support and suggestions for improvisations.

ND was annoyed that KS was 'enjoying himself' with his hobby instead of helping combat the indolence, capriciousness and dissipation at the MAT.

From the beginning of the year, KS had begun confabulations with Aleksandr Benois about the Molière productions.

To **Vasily Luzhsky.** After 24 September 1912, Moscow.

Dear Vasily Vasilievich,

[...] Benois turned out to be enchanting. He listens, enthusiastically attends every try-out, adaptations and, obviously, wants to understand the secrets of the stage. He is a wonderful director-psychologist and splendidly grasped all our techniques at once and was attracted by them. Very hard-working. In short – he is a man of the theatre.

Work at the studio has stopped temporarily, because the boiler for heating has broken down. [...]

Yours K. Alekseev

Rehearsals began for Tartuffe *and* The Imaginary Invalid. *On 9 October* Peer Gynt, *directed by Mardzhanov under ND's supervision, with designs by Nikolay Roerich and Leonidov as Peer opened, and attained 42 performances.*

318

To **Aleksandr Benois.** 30 November 1912, Moscow.

Dear and much esteemed Aleksandr Nikolaevich!

[…] The most absurd thing of all is that I am busy, but the Molière, that is my principal work in the theatre, makes no progress.

Rehearsals have stopped short.

Why? Lots of reasons. Beginning with the fact that the sick and dying dismay and grieve us and force us to turn away from business to save them, sometimes to bury the dead, sometimes to make arrangements for orphaned families, sometimes to come up with a grand project to provide for them.

The other problem is that *Peer Gynt* has in no way lived up to our hopes, and instead of sustaining five performances a week, it is played once a week. All the rest of the time the theatre lives off of the old stuff and, especially, the Turgenev show and *Hamlet*. During this time I have had to renovate and overhaul almost the entire repertoire – 12 plays. But even there there's a problem! Gzovskaya fell ill on two separate occasions, and I had to remove *Hamlet* and the Turgenevs from the repertoire temporarily, that is our best bread-and-butter plays.[10] Along with that I had to cut short the just begun rehearsals of *Imaginary Invalid*. They are going on somehow, without many of the characters. Koonen is busy in *Peer Gynt* and rehearsals of *Yekaterina Ivanovna*, so is Bazilevsky, so are Baksheev and Pavlov.[11] However one can only just manage to rehearse. But when Gzovskaya fell ill, there was definitely nothing to be done.

Then I turned to *Tartuffe*, but Stakhovich wasn't around (he arrived not long ago). At the same time Luzhsky is busy with *Yekaterina Ivanovna*, so are Damis and Elmire. Bravich got sick and died.[12] We held a few rehearsals with Knipper, Koreneva and Valère.[13] Now they have stopped, because there's nothing more I can do with this trio. I wanted to rehearse the interlude, but there was no music. Now it (the clavier) is in our possession. The orchestration was sent over from the Odéon.[14] I have to meet with you, because we are starting rehearsals. Your next visit is necessary for: a) costumes and fabrics; b) props (to explain and procure), c) plan out *Tartuffe* and hold a general discussion, d) to take up the interlude.

At this time there's no point in showing you actors, because nothing's been done. Nevertheless I would like to show you some *commedia dell'arte*.[15] There might be certain misunderstandings.

All this work demands four or five days (morning and evening) and the release of some of the actors (Kachalov, Germanova, Luzhsky, Koonen, Bersenev[16]). In addition, release of the costumiers, hair-dressers and props men. They will all be free once the dreadful *Yekaterina Ivanovna* goes on – that purulent abscess in our repertoire. This will happen soon – around 10 December. We will expect you at that time, only be in possession of a fur coat – it's cold. It would be good if you stayed with us, in the room vacated by the traitor Dobuzhinsky. […]

We have received all the sketches for costumes, makeups and objects. Thanks for the precision and clarity. It is pleasure to work under such conditions. […]

K. Alekseev […]

Andreev's drama of jealousy and nymphomania Yekaterina Ivanovna, *directed by ND, opened on 17 December; its sensationalism allowed it to run for thirty-six performances. KS considered it unworthy of the MAT. Tartuffe was replaced by Molière's short comedy* The Marriage Perforce *to be staged as a curtain-raiser to* The Imaginary Invalid.

To **Aleksandr Benois**. 19 February 1913, Moscow.
Dear Aleksandr Nikolaevich!

[…] 1) The *Bonnet de nuit* is delightful. It's been ordered and will be donned at the point you have indicated.[17]

2) Wouldn't it be better to make some kind of outdoor wrap for Béline. After all between Acts 1 and 2 (very short ones) there will be no intermission. Will the actress, having finished Act 1, have time to change her costume in the middle of Act 2? It is undesirable to slow down the actress for this.

3) To my mind, also, the olive colour is unsuitable for the street and Sganarelle's costume. Nobody knows that Molière wore a costume of that colour. Isn't that a detail for the Antique Theatre?[18]

4) The instructions about the cupids are wonderful and will be carried out to the last detail.[19]

5) The red portable curtain is quite un-*compliqué*.[20]

Mordkin[21] was very attracted by it, and it will be rung up very quickly, easily and beautifully. I think that the coat of arms, rising in the fold, will be less imposing and more troublesome and expensive, and here's why. It cannot be done by means of scene-painting, that is on primed canvas, which wouldn't allow for folds. It cannot be made out of ordinary canvas, because after the first try-outs it got so crumpled that it will look like ugly crumpled canvas. It has to be made out of cloth, but this is expensive and cumbersome. Besides, as the bars are raised, it is very difficult to strengthen the various cords for gathers and hoists. It will make the bars shake.

I do not much regret the chamber-pots. What if this joke seemed coarse on stage.

6) I am very worried about Zamirailo. [22] I spoke with him today.

He casually asserts that he is making haste, and not without irritation asserts that he is hurrying to do *Marriage Perforce*.

I am afraid to make him cross – then he won't finish the apotheosis. It's Shrovetide now. Nevertheless, a lot won't get done for the two productions, if we transfer work to someone else. Zamirailo assured us that he will lay out the invalid's room this week and make the arch for the apotheosis. We shall see. Then the first week we will be able with your instructions to transfer the work to our own people. They said that they could carry it out in about two weeks. […]

The little blackamoor is wonderful (it's not a problem that Meyerhold has used them a lot).[23]

We are rehearsing whole-heartedly and daily, and I think that on Monday we can present you *in rough form* two and a half acts. I myself am afraid of getting preoccupied with the role. If it soaks into me, then it has to be happen unconsciously, involuntarily. I still haven't found the tone, because I am distracted by directing (Stakhovich has left, Moskvin is busy with *Fyodor*, Nemirovich with *Fyodor* and *Marriage*).[24] [...]

With heartfelt devotion and respect
K. Alekseev

To **Lyubov Gurevich**. 14 March 1913, Moscow.
Dear Lyubov Yakovlevna!
[ ] The most excruciating work is going on with Molière. This is where we have to find a genuine (not Meyerholdian) – emotionally experienced, succulent grotesque. I am mortally afraid of a flop. [...]

K. Alekseev

To **Nemirovich-Danchenko**. Between 16-19 March 1913, Moscow.
Dear Vladimir Ivanovich!
The problem, of course, is not the main and small stages. So long as a play is rehearsed properly and systematically, does it matter where it is rehearsed? The main stage is needed only when the actors have to be coached quickly.
The problem is the actors themselves, whom I have been unable to assemble all year long, unless you count the two weeks before Shrovetide. While they've been rehearsing *Peer Gynt*, I've had to wait for Pavlov and Baksheev. When they were free, Bazilevsky left; when he was free, Koonen left.
Then I had to stop all the work and deal with old stuff all month. Then they started rehearsing *Yekaterina Ivanovna*. We stopped to wait or replace Koonen, then Massalitinov left etc. Before the last two weeks there was no way to assemble the cast of characters.
While they were rehearsing *Peer Gynt* and *Yekaterina Ivanovna*, the whole theatre, that is the whole troupe, relied on the plays that were already running. The Molière production does not have this indispensable advantage. At matinees, yes, but there are too few matinees, and 15 rehearsals for a Molière production is not enough.[25]
Let me add another list:
from the time rehearsals for *Imaginary Invalid* began there have passed through my hands three Bélines (Knipper, Sokolova, Lilina)
4 Angéliques (Koonen, Solovyova, Krestovozdvizhenskaya[26] and Baranovskaya)
2 Béraldes (Massalitinov[27] and Duvan) [There was a third performer, P. A. Baksheev]
3 Cléantes [V. P. Bazilevsky, N.A. Podgorny,[28] Stakhovich also worked on it]
2 Thomases (Massalitinov and Baksheev)
2 Fleurants [A. P. Artyom and N. F. Kolin][29]
2 notaries [I. E. Duvan, P. A. Pavlov and B. M.Sushkevich[30]]
2 Toinettes. [Gzovskaya and Lilina]
Ask yourself: am I am patient enough, or are new try-outs necessary? To top it all – the Molière production I've been dreaming of for three years will be staged with 15 rehearsals, Diaghilev-style.
Yet one more mutilated dream, yet one more Nezlobin-like production. The wounds of *Hamlet* and the Turgenev production have not yet healed – and now this new humiliation.

That is the reason for my nervous tic. I am very sorry and regret that I cannot control myself.

Yours Alekseev

I accuse no one, I point no fingers; I only regret that I have no luck in our theatre.

27 March saw the opening night of double bill of The Marriage Perforce *and* The Imaginary Invalid, *directed and designed by Aleksandr Benois. The music was drawn from Lully, Charpentier and Couperin. KS as Argan was praised for his brilliant acting, right out of Molière, and his wide range was remarked on. It led to a decision to put on Goldoni's* Mistress of the Inn *next season for Gzovskaya.*

To **Aleksandr Benois.** 6 April 1913, Moscow.
Dear and much esteemed Aleksandr Nikolaevich!

Until today I could not write to you, because a great fuss had been made about my person. I had to do this, because I hardly had the strength for the evening and it was impossible to fall ill. Yesterday, an immense weight fell, like a mountain, from my shoulders: we presented the 8th subscription series and ended the Moscow season. Only today can I give you an account of the current performances. But they have all merged into one, and I have a somewhat polychromatic impression of them. It is clear that the role [of Argan] has not yet been refreshed and there are still sickly bits in it; it is clear that the tempo still hasn't gathered momentum to its fullest extent. Why is this happening? Either from the hackneyed nature of the role and the play, or else unbearable nervous and physical exhaustion. They acted on pills and valerian drops! I expect no more from the first Petersburg performance. Obviously, I didn't manage to rehearse the play fully on stage to remind myself of the theatre's acoustics. The first performance will proceed while it adapts to the conditions of the theatre. The play has gathered momentum to a certain degree. What comes across the footlights is well-made, and this provides precision and confidence. When one is in a good mood one becomes naïve, and then everything seems funny, but with the obligatory daily acting, when art turns into craftsmanship, the good mood evaporates. There were good performances, when the audience roared with laughter, but there were also less successful performances, when one's mind turned to cardboard. Mstislav Valeriyanovich will provide you a more circumstantial account, for he was at the evening performance (5 April), the last this season. [...]

Heartily devoted K. Alekseev [...]

To **Olga Gzovskaya.** 6 and 7 April 1913, Moscow.
Dear Olga Vladimirovna!

Christ has arisen! [...]

Yesterday we performed the eighth performance of Molière for the eighth subscription series. Somehow, it came out very well indeed. What am I to say? It's a success, and a very big one. The mood in the theatre is a kind of renewal. The audience laughs a lot, even applauds. (Yesterday even Kolya Larionov made his exit to applause.)[31] Thanks to you he acts very well and has great success. He is beginning to realize it, and therefore do not write anything to him about yesterday's applause. I cannot say that the production and the success have satisfied me. My role, which is praised, delights me not. It is too cramped (in *Invalid* I have had to interact and swap dialogue with eighteen performers). Very few of them are good actors. [...]They praise my wife [as Toinette]. [...] Everyone likes the 'Ceremony', but I don't much. The staging was agonizing. Everything was left to the last minute. It was staged quickly and the fourth week, rehearsing day and night, till four o'clock in the morning.[32] There were moments of utter despair. It even got to the point that at one rehearsal (they had met at my house) I forced myself to rehearse, but the role became so odious and desperately nerve-wracking that I burst into tears during my first soliloquy (oh shame!) and ran upstairs, I could not rehearse. I collected all the reviews for you, but now (oh horrors!) I see that only the mortal remains are left of them. Who threw them away – I do not understand. [...]

The studio performed ten times. The eleventh is still to come, but a delegation from the fire department arrived and forbade public performances [in this building]. Therefore the last performance which was for charity has to be moved to the Hunt Club. On 4 April there took place the public dress rehearsal of *The Peace Festival* by Hauptmann, under the direction of Vakhtangov. The performance went well, but the play itself is ponderous and tedious and this tedium wore one out. All the same the youngsters – despite *Fyodor* and the Molière (daily rehearsals and performances) -- and colleagues were able to prepare two well-rehearsed and well-staged productions. Both productions will go to Petersburg and Odessa,[33] and at the end of the season the studio will pay for itself. It's a brilliant result for the first year. Now we are looking for a building. We found a wonderful one on Little Dmitrovka. The auditorium is as wide as the current one, that is 12 square yards, but its length is not 18, as now, but 35 square yards, moreover the arrangement of rooms is exactly to order: two foyers, four dressing-rooms, a beautiful entry-way and three hundred seats for the audience. Now the whole matter is up to the fire-department committee. If they agree, we shall triumph.[34] The price is relatively cheap, five or six thousand, and with this not a hundred, but three hundred rubles in box-office receipts. If you take into consideration that we already have two plays which, at the price of a ruble a seat, will go on about a score of times, -- twelve performances could pay off the building. The studio has been recognized, and they are scared to death of this. Nemirovich demonstratively repeated to me more than once that he had been waiting three years for results, but that now the results were beyond his expectations. Now, in Petersburg, we will work out the repertoire for next year. Will you write that you want to act in the studio, that is take part in next year's repertoire?

I have announced that next year I shall stage *The Mistress of the Inn*, and Benois is thinking about a second playlet to supplement the performance. Today Nemirovich comes up to me and says, 'What do you think, wouldn't it be best to engage Olga Vladimirovna for Susanna in *The Marriage of Figaro*? The performance would be capital.' I replied, 'In this production I want to present the theatre not with a play, but an actress. In our present situation that will be more important than a play. We need a role that will show off the actress. I think that *Mistress of the Inn* is more suitable for that. It is showier, and the showiness will make a more powerful impression. That is why, any favouritism aside, I prefer *Mistress of the Inn*, although I realize that the performance of Beaumarchais' play would be more significant.' Am I right or not? In any case I prefer Beaumarchais, but give it some thought. [...]

Sincerely loving and devoted

K. Alekseev [...]

Gzovskaya objected to The Marriage of Figaro, *protesting against the complexity of the staging (crowd scenes, songs, an orchestra, etc.) and was worried lest everyone remember the Maly Theatre production. Also ND wanted Germanova for the Countess. Gzovskaya preferred the role of Mirandolina, and so it fell out.*

The matter of Andreeva's return was deliberated at a meeting of the MAT board on 12 March and was left open. Her arrival in Petersburg was not without danger for her, because the criminal persecution of her as publisher of the radical journal New Life *did not officially end until 17 July 1913. KS had twice lent large sums to Gorky at Andreeva's behest, when the writer was in dire straits as the result of the failure of the Znanie publishing house. To clear part of the debt Andreeva offered KS a bit of land near Toinse.*

To **Mariya Andreeva**. 9 April 1913, Moscow.

Dear Mariya Fyodorovna!

[...] You should be in no doubt about my complete willingness to come to your aid. It will not be difficult for me to do this in the studio, where I enjoy some authority, and so I am entirely at your service there, so far as my time and current work will allow. I will do everything for you that I can and am able to.

The theatre is another story. A great deal has changed for me there. I no longer enjoy any authority, although I take shelter behind my name, I have no legal rights nor a vote, which I myself chose to abnegate for purely external and fortuitous reasons.

I can take part in the theatre, but not make a decision. And I do take part, but – so far to no purpose. I have not noticed any hostile attitude towards you and I don't think there is one. There are no roles, there is no money to spare; a certain incredulity that you will give up the leading line of business and be content with a more modest role in the theatre; those are the remarks that I have happened to hear in talk about your return to our stage. I need to be fair and state that all these objections were made out of a kind of misunderstanding, a kind of passivity and somewhat apologetically.

What will things be like and how is one to behave in future? We shall have to meet and discuss this. And I hope we can – in Petersburg or Odessa. [...]

I owe an apology to Aleksey Maksimovich for not keeping him informed of our experiments with *commedia dell'arte*.

Suler, who has been busy preparing the work for these experiments, has already written in detail to Aleksey Maksimovich [Gorky, about young actors' improvising from scratch]. But no one yet knows the secret, the very essence of the idea of Aleks. Maks., that is what he expressed so beautifully in his article, which Rumyantsev gave me. I have shown this article to no one, fearing that it will get into the papers. Meanwhile practice sessions are going on, and the preparation of students in the first course (because the old-timers are no use for that work; they are too infected with stereotypes and actor's tricks to devote themselves to the spontaneity of affective emotional experiencing).

What Al. Maks. wants is not so simple. Now, after a year of work, we are starting to arrive at the requisite end. But here's the problem. It is impossible to keep what is going on in the studio secret, and our experiments will get into the papers. Efros came to me and declared that one of these days articles about those practice sessions we are doing are going to appear. It would be best if he were to write about this delicately, rather than let others do it any old way, in haste. I asked him to write about this to Aleks. Maks. But Efros was afraid that this would take too much time. I confess he convinced me, and I gave him a few details, reminding him at every third word that the idea is not mine but belongs to Al. Maks.

The eventual article was not very successful and not very precise.[35] To object or write an addendum would lend the whole matter a tinge of publicity. It is best to keep silent in the meantime, especially since no one, other than our students, can do this difficult work – collective creativity. [...]

Sincerely loving and heartily devoted
Yours K. Alekseev

Isadora Duncan had two children, both born out of wedlock: a daughter, Deirdre (b.1906) by Gordon Craig and a son Patrick (b. 1910) by Paris Singer. Both children and their nanny died in an accident, when the motor-car they were sitting in rolled into the Seine on 19 April 1913.

To **Isadora Duncan**. After 10 April 1913 (o.s.), Moscow. *Telegram.*

If expression of grief by distant friend will not wound your immeasurable suffering, let me express my despair at the unimaginable catastrophe that has befallen you. My whole family joins me in this.

Alisa Koonen left the MAT for the Free Theatre founded by Mardzhanov.

To **Olga Gzovskaya**. *16 April 1913, Petersburg.*
Dear, good Olga Vladimirovna!

Verily he has risen!

[...] Thank you for your dear, warm, heartfelt letters. Believe me, they are very precious to me, and I value them highly, especially now when I am having a hard time digesting the insult visited upon me by Koonen. After four years of work (even if unsuccessful, but nevertheless heartfelt) she came in and rather frivolously and cruelly announced to me: I am leaving the Art Theatre. I confess, I started howling and left the room. We have not met since. [...]

Yesterday *Peer Gynt* went on. So-so. People will abuse it, but not much. The first acts went with great success, the last flabbily. Today *Yekaterina Ivanovna*. The first two acts went with success. After the second they called out the author [Andreev] without any protest, he was presented with a wreath from the 'Shipovnik' Almanac. After the third applause mixed with hissing. After the last friends called him out. There was hissing there too.

Poor Duncan. It's terrible to think of. [...]

Cordially devoted and loving
K. Alekseev [...]

To **Olga Gzovskaya**. 18 April 1913, Petersburg.
Dear Olga Vladimirovna!

Yesterday, the 17th, the Molière was performed. *Marriage Perforce* (I saw bits of it on stage from the wings) went inconsequentially, but the audience laughed. Sparse applause. *The Imaginary Invalid* began with an ovation at the rise of the curtain. One can't figure out whether it was directed at Benois or me. Lots of laughs. After the first act there was sparse applause. In the second act they laughed at everything and especially at Massalitinov, who performed beautifully. On Kolya Larionov's exit a storm of applause. The kid is proud, and I have already explained to him that they are not applauding him but you, because you really taught him in a wholesome way. With a firm hand. He is growing in the role and has an excellent understanding of what he is doing. (Thanks to you.)

At the end of the second act stormy applause. In act three they laughed even more loudly. In places we even had to hold for a long time. In the 'Ceremony' bursts of laughter. At the end an outburst, shouting, they sent out Benois a few times, then I had to go on. The result is a great success. [...]

Your loving K. Alekseev [...]

On 25 April the Studio gave its first performance of The Wreck of the 'Hope' *in Petersburg.*

To **Aleksandr Benois**. 14/26 June 1913. Essentuki (Hotel Azau). Kislovodsk, Ganeshin House (from 25 July).
Dear Aleksandr Nikolaevich!

[...] You know what? When we in the theatre move too carefully, things go all right, but they're boring. When we take bold steps and even take a tumble – things always come out all right. Let's do it – let's shake things up! Let's agree to do a pantomime with improvised *commedia dell'arte*. Let's decide and *basta*, what will be shall be. But the plot? That's what's needed. Here's where we need your help and the help of your friends. Let you, the Italians, so learned, versatile and experienced, decide what scenario is most typical for Italy and for its theatre. Bring in music too. If you will be so kind, write the scenario and characters in their most general features, with their rough characteristics. I will give it some thought.

To perform *commedia dell'arte* is easier than it seems and I do not fear at all for our actors, if only we ourselves do not deprive them of joy and freedom by excessive demands (I am throwing stones at my own house). I will even make this proposal. Let's prepare a few themes and perform them for the audience to choose. After all, rehearsing one scenario or three is nearly the same thing. Only we have to find the characterizations and the tasks.[36] [...]

I have information that the Free Theatre is working very hard. The mood is cheerful and spirited. In short, they are repeating what has been repeated scores of times. They are beginning pretentiously, like Nezlobin, and the second year they will fold, unless they shift definitively to operetta and comic opera. All the more reason why we need something extraordinary for this year. Let's offer pantomime and *commedia dell'arte*. A building for the studio is still not sorted out, but, God willing, it will get built. I am living here the life of Argan and often remember *The Imaginary Invalid*, because all day long I am busy with my stomach. [...]

Yours K. Alekseev [...]

Igor was staying in Kanev, with the Sulerzhitskys.

To **his son Igor**. 20 July 1913, Friday, Essentuki.
Greetings, my darling, my dear friend Igorechek!

Thanks for your enchanting letters, which I can put to use. They are interesting, sincere, heartfelt and accurate. You wrote them with a trusting, open mind, and this, you know, most of all rejoices your Papa and Mama who especially value and take pride in their children's friendship and frankness. I do not conceal from you that, being out of the habit – I am constantly feeling worry and concern over your absence. I am literally sitting on the edge of my seat and waiting: when will the real vacation begin, with all of us together... But this real vacation is already over. I am heartily glad if an independent life will make you hale and hearty and teach you to control your nature. I heartily wish for this and am sincerely grateful to dear Lev Antonovich for his kind feelings for both of us. I realize that we ourselves would never have agreed to what seems so simple and clear to a less interested person. Do try and thank those who have given you a piece of their heart and provided for that rest which it would be impossible to ensure here in the Caucasus. But how can you thank them? First of all by declaring your feelings and not, out of inordinate shyness and delicacy, hiding and concealing what you must learn to show and pay back through the proper channels.

There is no more bitter humiliation than for good feelings to fall on the cold, stony ground of the human heart. Moreover: if you can, then you try and do a good turn for those who have done one for you.

So, do not leave having repaid everyone only with money and not feelings. By the way, on the subject of money. Do you need any? It would be scandalous if you had to borrow from Suler who has hardly enough to make ends meet. Keep exact accounts. And do not be ashamed to settle scores in plain language. It bothers me that we were not able to instill in you and Kira greater care about money, especially other people's. Meanwhile, what can be more vulgar, coarse, indelicate and boorish than to treat other people's money as if it were one's own. Young people usually do not understand this. They are incapable of worshipping money, and that, of course, is very good, but they rush from one extreme to another, by despising money and not only their own, but other people's. Despising other people's money is tantamount to loving it, to avarice and lack of scruples. It is catastrophic to be unscrupulous in money matters. To keep this from happening, it is best to be extremely careful.

Therefore even this time – remember attentively and be aware of what and where and whom you owe for all this time. After all the obligation lies on the debtor, and not on the creditors. The latter are not obliged to remember and remind.

Like Polonius, I will recite to you instructions on how to live. This is because I would very much like you to accept freedom and independence not in the outer – stupid and selfish aspect (as often happens with young people), but from the other important, inner, altruistic aspect. To be free you have to look to the freedom of others. And so: travel as a gentleman, not only in the fashion of dressing in the Khokhlov style, but with your soul in the Anton Pavlovich Chekhov style. When and how will you travel? We (oh horrors!) thanks to Granny's blindness will remain in the Caucasus, that is Kislovodsk.

[...] The most dreadful thing of all is that we have no apartment, they've kicked us out of our old one, there's nowhere to store our belongings, and I am wracking my brains how to get out of this situation, sitting here, at a distance. Soon everyone will be gathering here, and not a hint of an apartment. So that is the dark side of life. Another cloud is Kira's romanticism. She has a child's understanding of independence and for its sake keeps travelling in tandem with some blackguard of a guide, wanders around the steppes all night on her own. Not only I, but all the locals wonder why you have to walk into a pack of wolves without a pistol. And so I am literally sitting on the edge of my seat... [...]

I got a letter from Volodya Sergeev.[37] First of all, they detained him in Moscow and wanted to try him in a court-martial for swearing at a district police superintendent. This frightened and upset him. He sent me a telegram, and I was supposed to write a letter to all the people in government that I know. They managed to hush up the affair.

Second disaster: precisely because he graduated from this new pedagogical institute, they won't hire him anywhere in Moscow and suggest he go to the provinces. He cannot refuse, because he is obliged to work in education for 3 years, wherever they order him.

I am much concerned about him and you. How will you get on without him these last years?! Again you have to write and think how you will deal with this. [...]

Your tenderly loving Papa. [...]

To **Olga Gzovskaya**. 22 July 1913, Essentuki.
Dear Olga Vladimirovna!

[...] How are you to approach the roles. Let's start with Toinette. The through action of the role is: 'to mock, to discredit medicine in the eyes of Argan,' of course, in order to rescue Angélique.

So make an effort not in principle, but *in fact* to verify this goal. What do I mean by in principle and *in fact*?

In principle is with the intelligence, coldly, unenthusiastically, so that you can say: yes, that's right, and reassure yourself.

In fact is to verify and feel yourself in this situation. To tell yourself: this has actually happened. Sidorov, Ivanov, your brother, your husband, no matter who, no matter what for, has become a fanatic about illness or erudition or religion – the kind of fanatic doesn't matter. What would I do right now, in the given situation, on Lago Maggiore or in Moscow, where doesn't matter. Here he is coming over and asking me to give him my seat. And if he needed this seat, as Argan might, for his mania, what would I do or what would be the best way to discredit the doctors and getting him, the fool, into a mess? So you are to seize on every event you meet with in your present real life and relate it to the through action with the aid of naïvety and imagination, which you possess, invisible to anyone, and so there's no reason to be embarrassed. Acting like this will get you used to believing in the through action. You will get used to facing an event and its whole context from that point of view.

In the first place, it will be easier for you to face the facts of the play itself with the same feeling of truth and belief, that is, for you to experience them emotionally, and, on the other hand, those practices will stimulate and quicken in your mind authentic true-to-life tasks, related to the given circumstances or adjustments.

When you verify the through action – you will attentively test whether or not it is forced, overemphatic, is your partner in real life being fooled, when you look one another in the eye closely. Then you will *constantly be verifying*, whether you can do all this not in that somewhat heightened situation of overheated excitement and energy which activity provides you in life, but in that calmness and simplicity when you are at home with your family, when no one is looking on or listening in; that is, do everything in the condition we call '*in robe and slippers*'. Do not take this term to mean indolence and indifference. *God forbid!!!* In such a case it is far better to carry out the task energetically, only without embellishment and retouching, without pressure, without underlining, but as evenly as needed to carry out the task (but not imagining you are doing it for yourself or others).

When you have inculcated this in yourself, then remember that the chief mental characteristic of Toinette is that she does everything through clowning and having fun. Everything makes her happy. Now tell yourself: I am indeed in such a state. And what if I were in this state and the same things are happening around me that are happening around me now at Lago Maggiore? What would I act? Try for practice to take on hundreds of such tasks, which are met with or can be met with in life and actual reality. When you are used to it, then you will practice to associate this state of clowning and merry-making in Toinette (which is the kernel of the role) with the through action, which is identical – to impede Argan's medical mania.

Completely independent of this. *Meanwhile by no means connected with the preceding, -- on the contrary, assiduously keep separate* the practices I just described from those I shall describe now.

Begin to look for the external image of Toinette, that is the Frenchwoman, cook, village girl. How does she walk, talk, run, laugh, sit? What kind of voice, costume does she have. How does she clean up a room, rinse out the chamberpots and so on.

Meanwhile separately from the through action and the core emotions, but only to accustom your muscles to the gait and movements, which you will come to fulfil mechanically in time.

How are you to connect the first part, the spiritual one, with the second, the physical one, -- we will discuss when we meet.

I forgot to add to the first part, the psychological one. Here's a good method of forcing you to verify the through action or, in particular, the tasks. Recall analogous situations in life, when, one way or another, you had to tend to a tiresome gentleman or gentlewoman, to be their companion.

Say to yourself: could it actually be that this person is here, in this room, in which you're reading this letter, that let's say, he is pestering me, -- what would I do then? And what if I had to have a slanging match with him to protect my husband, brother or sister?

Look for other analogous opportunities from life, that is analogous to the situations of the role in the play. Shift them to yourself and the through action and the kernel of the role.

That's all for now.

Lord! How simple this is in reality (without fail remember and keep in mind that it is awfully simple in fact – the things that you at different times and in different occasions have done a thousand times in life). And Lord – how complicated it is to put it down on paper and describe it. [...]

As to the Shaw [*Fanny's First Play* for the Studio] -- I am very interested and will help any way I can, but I cannot write now, because I have to discuss something else. Yes, as Mirandolina think of only one thing. How you, through your inherent femininity, might tame such a subject as the Cavaliere. Femininity and feminine strength in its broadest sense, but only genuine, sincere, and not artificial - strained.

Heartily and affectionately yours K. Alekseev

News that the MAT was to dramatize Dostoevsky's The Devils *and Nezlobin's Theatre* The Idiot *enraged Gorky in Capri. On 22 September his polemic 'On Karamazovitis' appeared in* Russian Word *and it was followed by a heated debate in the press and another angry letter-to-the-editor from Gorky. He deplored the sadomasochism and 'god-seeking' of that 'evil genius', especially on the eve of 'great events' in Russian public life. Benois was asked to respond on behalf of the MAT.*

To **his daughter Kira**. 23 September 1913, Moscow.
My dear and priceless Kiryulya!

I was worried, but when I learned about the jaundice, I confess, I began to get upset. Don't be cross, it's my being unaccustomed to living far away, and my awareness that I am chained to Moscow and the theatre, finally, perhaps, this old man's egoism. Another concern is the incipient strike. I'm thinking about how this might flare up and stop train travel. So we'll be cut off. But, God willing, this won't happen. Somehow this is not yet the time. These days remind me a bit of 1905. The trams aren't running, and the rumour spreads through Moscow that the electricity, waterworks, telephone will go on strike. This will not come to pass, but today the printing works went on strike. Again suspicious-looking individuals are walking the streets, and, of course, this proves nothing, but -- gatherings sometimes on Tver Boulevard, sometimes on Trubny Square dispersed by Cossacks, patrols prowling around. Workers tearing along in all directions on bicycles, Caucasian fur hats are turning up – it's reminiscent of 1905 in miniature. Add to all this a letter from Gorky denouncing the theatre. I append it in case you haven't read it. You remember dear charming Gorky on Capri? Compare him with this narrow-minded, obtuse and illiterate S.D. [Social Democrat]. What a difference! Of course, the letter did not achieve its goal. Almost everyone takes a very negative view of it and, while injuring Gorky, serves as a magnificent advertisement for *The Devils*. But it is painful that we, the whole theatre as a company, have to issue a rejoinder to him in a rather authoritative and sharp form. This is how we replied. Not saying that it's a pity that Gorky is attacking the theatre. Both the theatre's repertoire and its activities, which are apparent to all, are the answer to that. The pity is that Gorky has underestimated the genius of the God-seeker Dostoevsky and except for F. Karamazov, has found nothing but hysteria and morbidity. We, as the whole company of actors, consider it an obligation to explain that with our whole lives we have served and will serve the spiritual needs of a superior intelligence. To deprive us of this purpose is to deprive us of our soul and exterminate art.

And therefore we shall stage Dostoevsky. We shall love him and be inspired by him, we shall see in him one of the most precious treasures of Russian and world cultural achievements. Signed: the troupe, the directors, the administration, the board of the Art Theatre. [...]

Tenderly loving Papa

To **his daughter Kira.** 25 September 1912, Moscow.
Dear, sweet and precious Kiryulya!
[...] It's been a long time since there's been such a good atmosphere in the theatre. The studio has given everyone work and everything follows a common denominator. And it is fun to work. Now the theatre is giving the studio a good, even beautiful building (Governor General's square opposite the Skoblev monument). It isn't ready yet, but it will be finished very soon. The youngsters' work is going on in every corner. Boleslavsky is preparing Volkenshtein's play *Wandering Minstrels* (a wonderful thing). Sushkevich is preparing Dickens's *Cricket on the Hearth*. Leonidov is preparing and acting *Othello*.[38] Nikolay Andreevich Popov is preparing Wilde's *Florentine Tragedy*.[39] Then they are reviving Hauptmann's *Morbid People*[40] -- in short, work is bubbling away in every corner. [...] The competition – the Free Theatre – is in rehearsal... Tales and tattle about

it are going the rounds. It turns out that they are staging the operetta *La Belle Hélène* this way: the first act – the stage represents an enormous Greek vase. It is girdled by the gods in bas-relief. Lower down are the kings, at the base are the people. The second act depicts Kislovodsk (?), and the characters are in modern dress. But here I am tattling away to amuse you, my poor little thing. [...]

Papa

To **his daughter Kira**. 7 October 1913, Moscow.
My dear little girl Kiryulya,

Today at one o'clock the dress rehearsal of *The Fair at Sorochints* went on at the Free Theatre. I, Mama, Benois went there. The effect is magnificent. Sanin's a clever fellow. Musorgsky's opera and music are wonderful. The youngsters are very well trained. And despite the competition – my heart was merry and delighted. The theatre is excellent. Somov's[41] curtain made out of rags is beautiful. The success is great and encouraging. You believe in the theatre again and in its power. [...]

On 23 October the MAT season opened with a dramatization of Dostoevsky's The Devils under the title Nikolay Stavrogin, adapted and directed by ND and Luzhsky, with settings by Dobuzhinsky. The production was impressive, but strictly for connoisseurs. Lilina was outstanding as the Gimp.

To **his daughter Kira**. 24-26 October 1913, Moscow.
Dear and tenderly beloved little girl,

I've gone quite off the rails and God knows how long it's been since I've written to you. The reason is the beginning of the delayed season. We had to rehearse in every nook and cranny. The most dreadful work fell to my lot – rehearsing old plays, inserting alternative actors in place of the ones who've fallen ill and on the quiet assisting the Stavroginites, whom Nemirovich didn't have time to take in hand. During this time a lot took place. One can't even remember it all. Did I write to you that the Free Theatre opened with *The Fair at Sorochints*? Despite a great many defects, it wasn't half bad and quite enjoyable. Then there was *La Belle Hélène*, directed by Mardzhanov [on 16 October]. This was such a horror that it's ghastly even to remember it. It was a nightmare, a madhouse. Tasteless, garish, dazzlingly lavish scenery by Simov, a curtain by Somov, street-corner witticisms, of this kind: Yelena Swanovna (la belle Hélène was born of a swan). To top it all as the audience was leaving Mardzhanov's wife got jealous and slapped him, and they had a disgusting brawl. It left a dreadful impression. That poor fool Koonen!

Finally the time came for the dress rehearsals of *Stavrogin* and the excitement they entailed.

The production came out imposing, remarkable, not for a big audience, but rather for connoisseurs. It is performed well. Of the sets by Dobuzhinsky, many are good, but the word among clever people is that Dobuzhinsky is ponderous, and a novel is not a play etc. The production had no clamorous success, but people listen well, the reviews are good.

Today, that is just now, I held one more try-out. Gzovskaya played Toinette. Very good, merry, with brio, she was successful, and this pleased me very much. Yes, I forgot to say that in *Stavrogin* Mama took first place. Everyone likes her a great deal. [...]

With all his heart your Papa

Vakhtangov's staging of Hauptmann's The Peace Festival *opened at the Studio on 15 November. He and KS had a serious falling-out over this production, leading Vakhtangov to form a school which would become the MAT Third Studio, while continuing to work at the First Studio.*

KS began investigations into the subconscious and 'methods of stimulating the activity of those feelings beyond the reach of the conscious mind'.

The Mistress of the Inn,[42] *directed by KS and designed by Benois, opened on 3 February 1914, with Gzovskaya as Mirandolina and KS as the Cavaliere di Ripafratta. Only he seemed to have the buoyancy and pace needed and exuded a sense of improvisation. He enjoyed himself tremendously in the part, especially when Gzovskaya would provide home-cooked dishes for his eating scene. Her departure from the troupe in July caught him unawares and remains unexplained (she continued to take part in occasional performances in 1915). KS was even more stricken by this defection than by Alisa Koonen's.*

To **Lyubov Gurevich**. 24 February 1914, Moscow.
Dear Lyubov Yakovlevna!

[...] Last year, after three years of intense activity, Koonen left. Now, after four years of work, Gzovskaya is leaving. I do not understand why my female students run away from me. Are there some flaws in me or are we to suppose that everyone or most of them get as far as the gates of art and, having reached its very essence, betray it?

Work is becoming ever more difficult and impossible. Again two theatres have been born, break-aways from the Free Theatre[43], and both aided by pecuniary temptation are luring away that raw material which is beginning to show promise and after they leave do not live up to it. In a year's time, corrupted, they begin to knock on the doors of the theatre again. Just think, Koonen who was lured away for a salary of 6000 – now, after the theatre has failed, remains at a hundred rubles – a month. It's appalling what they're doing to the poor youngsters! [...]

from your cordially devoted K. Alekseev

On 12 March 1914 Norman Hapgood invited KS to stage a play at the New York Theatre Guild.

Three days later ND pursued his devotion to Andreev with the opening of Thought, *a play about a professor with a Jekyll-and-Hyde complex, again with Leonidov in the lead. It lasted for nineteen performances.*

On 28 June, Archduke Franz Ferdinand of Austro-Hungary and his wife were assassinated in the Bosnian capital Sarajevo by a Serb. Austria delivered an ultimatum

„ХОЗЯЙКА ГОСТИНИЦЫ". М. Х. Т. О. В. Гзовская.
Изд. А. А. Горожанкина, Фот. К. Фишеръ. Москва, 1914 г.

Figure 53 Gzovskaya as Mirandolina in *The Mistress of the Inn*. Photo: K. A. Fischer, Moscow

that Serbia give up its independence; Germany backed up Austria and forbade any outside interference. This led to a breakdown of peace efforts on part of other powers.

In late June KS and Lilina had gone to Marienbad for a cure and wound up being caught in the outbreak of hostilities.

To **Leopold Sulerzhitsky**. 15 July/28 July 1914, Marienbad.
Dear, good Lev Antonovich!

How I would like to be with you now, near the children and in Russia. It is disgusting here. The weather is 4-10 degrees. The seventh day of rain, so that the treatment has had to be ended. Marusya has been over-medicated, and she seems to have had temporary anæmia, terrible headaches and her stomach went on strike. I think we ought to run away as soon as possible, but if we run home to Russia, there are no tickets to foreign parts, because they are mobilizing troops here. On the other hand, they say that the strikers are stopping the trains and now you can't travel and have to stay put; that there will be no war; that Russia cannot fight. In any case, we have to get out of here –it's become so nasty here for Russians. For a long time there were no newspapers, so that we couldn't even get information as to what was happening at home. Our imaginations ran riot, and therefore our minds stagnate. […]

Yours in spirit K. Alekseev […]

To **Nemirovich-Danchenko.** 15/28 July 1914, Marienbad.
Dear Vladimir Ivanovich!

I am writing on behalf of everyone, and not telegraphing, because telegrams do not arrive and letters do. […]

We are waiting here in great anxiety in case there's war. We would have to return to Russia, but, except for Carriage Row, there is definitely nowhere to go, and we are afraid to be marooned.

My wife takes it all very lightly, but I, on the contrary, am gloomy and cannot control my over-active imagination and therefore I do not sleep at nights…

Our colony here is much reduced. V. I. Kachalov, Gurevich, my wife and I remain. We shall meet again somewhere! The children are with Suler on Knyasha Mountain near Kanev in Kiev gubernia, and grandmother is in the Caucasus. […]

K. Alekseev

Russia did not declare war on Germany and the Central Powers until 19 July (1 August n.s.), which led KS to fear there might be a revolution at home. He, Lilina and Kachalov left for Munich in hopes of getting to Switzerland and from there to Russia.

Diary. Marienbad, summer 1914

The first train to leave Marienbad; a fight for places and to get the luggage aboard. People behaving like animals. Total absence of porters and cabs. Carried my own luggage; changing trains all the time, inspections, dragging hand luggage hither and yon. Lost some of the hand luggage. Journey in third class amid hostile glances, and every other minute belligerently-inclined trains passing by. Arrived in Munich in the evening. Want of porters…

In Munich they were arrested along with other Russians as spies, becoming the first prisoners of war. They were transferred in the dead of night to Lindau. KS was sure the men would be shot. They were imprisoned in the fortress along with Dalcroze students from Hellerau and the painter Vasily Kandinsky and fed on bread and water. On 22 July they were allowed to travel by boat to Switzerland.

To **Nemirovich-Danchenko**. 26 July/8 August 1914, Berne.
Dear, good Vladimir Ivanovich!

We've only just arrived in Berne after captivity in Germany and all possible romantic and melodramatic adventures, which ought to be shown on a cinema screen.

L. Ya. Gurevich so yearns for her family that she decided to risk her life and speed through Italy and the sea to Russia. Her cousin – the philosopher Ilyin – promised to get her a ticket. But we cannot board the steamboat, first, because tickets had to be reserved well in advance, and the demand was enormous, and second, because there is *no money*, although the whole Russian colony assembled here has more than enough letters of credit. Nothing can be bought with letters of credit and, what's more, they won't change any kind of money, even French francs (they will change around 100 francs per person). So for you and for me a desperate situation has developed. The embassy at least sends off the poor Russians, but we are advised to wait, until dominion over the seas falls entirely into the hands of England and until it becomes clear how the enemy is now treating Italy, which didn't join the Triple Alliance. Who knows, they are starting to fire on Italian ships in the Adriatic. All other routes are, needless to say, cut off and for a long time.

What's going to happen to the theatre!!! The whole troupe is here. Kachalov, Massalitinov, Podgorny, Khalyutina, Lilina, myself are here. Raevskaya only just got to Italy. Leonidov seems to be in Italy as well. Perhaps, the moment has come when we need radically to change the whole structure of the theatre?! I mean, move to a studio-touring system? At a distance I can only sympathize with you and ache for your agitation. Here, after all the persecution, captivity and humiliation we've been through, it is impossible to think about anything but ways to tear ourselves away from this savage Europe.

To Moscow, to Moscow.

May God grant you strength and wisdom. I would be glad to help and be with you, but when and how will we meet again?! Thank you for the telegram from Sebastopol. We thought long and hard earlier about how to extricate ourselves, but the trains had stopped running, thanks to the secretly initiated mobilization. [...]

Meanwhile good-bye. I embrace you.

K. Alekseev

Address: Berne. Switzerland. Poste restante.

To **his brother Vladimir.** 27 July/Saturday, 9 August new style 1914, Berne.
Dear, good Volodya!

Whom should I write to if not to you. Although I know that your situation is even more dire than ours. Your children are at war,[44] and mine – alone, out in space. I don't know what's going on with them, and to be ignorant in our situation is ghastly. We have fallen into the kind of trap from which there is only one way out – to fling oneself into certain death, which we only just encountered. We were arrested in Germany and proclaimed prisoners of war in Lindau. Then we were pardoned, sent to Switzerland, which didn't want to take us, and for 3 days we lived in semi-captivity and thought they would send us back to the German fortress (Lindau). After strenuous efforts they let us in, and we got as far as Berne, where the embassy and other authorities are located. But... except for letters of credit, they won't give us money. I was provident and at the first rumours of war I put together 3000 francs by letters of credit. But they won't change them into Swiss money. Here we will make an effort to be sent back to Russia by steamer, or, if we get some money one way or another, we will try to get back to Russia via Italy. But – meanwhile there is no way to find things out. Today, let's assume, people say with assurance that there is a way through the Dardanelles, then tomorrow it will turn out that they are closed and mined. The same thing concerning roads through Rumania, which, it turns out, has now closed the frontier to Russia. It is also impossible to stay here, because Switzerland might be sealed, and await starvation.

Today Kachalov left here, because his family, the Sanins, the Efroses (who were convalescing in Italy) had long reserved him a ticket for the steamer. Whether they will arrive or not, whether they will get home or perish – who knows. We are distressed that we cannot go with our own group but have to go with strangers, but – what's to be done – right now it is impossible to get out. Besides, our tragic adventures of the last few days (the recipients of our letters will tell you about them) have so shattered our nerves that it is essential to catch our breath in order to figure out the situation and work out a new plan.

I understand what's going on with you. You are torn into 10 parts. Shamshin as well, especially if Tikhon Aleksandrovich has been drafted into the army.[45] Nikolai Vasilievich Yegorov[46] is also torn, but to whom am I to turn, except for him or Vasily Petrovich Telepnev, in order to set up some kind of financial and other support for the children. First of all, I think one would have to bring the children to somewhere safe. Up to now it seemed to me that Kiev gubernia was a safe place, but with Austria's declaration of war it will move in the direction of Kiev, and I am afraid *most of all* that the children, who don't follow politics, will wait until the *last* minute, which means flight and panic. And therefore my chief concern is to secrete them in *a safe place in good time*. Where? I suppose somewhere away from here, in Moscow. I do not think the foe will think to invade there and repeat Napoleon's mistake. I entreat Nikolay Vasilievich or Vasily Petrovich to send them money for the trip. How much? If the road is open, then less (but with something for emergencies), if the road is not open then more – 1000 or some such! If it is difficult to post it, then it will have to be sent by *special messenger*. I also beg Nikolay Vasilievich and Vasily Petrovich to ask my housekeeper Dunyasha to come to the office and arrange with her for the minimum for their maintenance and the upkeep of the apartment. Have her ask Markov (the landlord) to postpone the rent on the apartment until I return (if I ever find a way out of this critical situation and get out of here!). The main thing is that there be an apartment where the children, their granny and the Sulerzhitsky family can live. Well, even if the banks hand out money in rubles, how are we to get francs here? Then we will have to turn our minds to death by starvation and anticipate it... and in that case throw ourselves on the advice and practical experience of you, Nikolay Vasilievich and Vasily Petrovich.

If Igor is to be drafted into the army and they require of him a doctor's certificate of military exemption, -- copies are in my desk and in the chancellery of the university. The *exact address* of the childen: Kiev gubernia, Kanev city, Knyasha mountain, Belyashevsky farm. Care of Leopold Antonovich Sulerzhitsky (for Kira or Igor).

Granny (Olga Timofeevna) will have to be moved to our home, if they can manage to transport her from the Caucasus. [...]

Now what sort of plans do we have for returning to Russia. That's why we are sitting here, because in Germany nothing makes sense. Best of all would be to get information in Milan, but there is still a question of whether we can cross its border, which is now fortified, and, second, in travelling to Italy – could we return to Switzerland if we were kicked out of there. At the moment Kachalov is making an effort on both counts, that is the right to travel and return, but it is not known whether he will succeed in this and whether all these documents, visas and so on, the formalities of the local Russian, Swiss and other powers will be carried out and actualized. Meanwhile let us explain the way things stand here, because this is the administrative centre. The problem is that at the moment nothing is being explained and we know absolutely nothing of what is going on in Russia and other countries. It is the same here as in Germany and we are its enemies. Of course, they are not throwing us out now, like mangy, whipped, cringing curs, as they did in Munich, Lindau; but... they are not fond of us here, and that is very hard to take. But the plus here is that we understand each other, and in Italy we will not be able to speak, not knowing the language. In addition, there are two Saint Petersburg lawyers here – [Zakhar Lvovich] Rappoport and [V. V.] Isaichenko. They are sorting out the situation better than I can. The ships on which they are sending back Russians for free are very flimsy and dilapidated For a good, expensive one you need money. Whether they will stop payment on letters of credit and exchanging money is a question of pre-eminent importance for us. Have them telegraph here, whether one can transmit money (and whether there is money to be transmitted here). The best address for telegrams is: Suisse, Berne, pension 'Eden', pour m-r Z. Rappoport – for me. Meanwhile we are living in the tawdry pension 'Montano' (on the Zieglerstrasse) and pay 4½ francs per person (tout compris). But... the prices will rise soon... Right now they are saying that America is organizing transports of Russians under an international flag. If only this were definite, because now under other combinations there is a 90% chance of falling into enemy hands and being landed on a Turkish shore which has happened recently. The poor Kachalovs and other needy persons are deciding on that sort of dangerous venture, but my wife and I have to stay here a while, until new (perhaps even more dangerous) events transpire. I am sending this letter with Kachalov. I make haste to end it, because he is leaving soon. [...]

If you see the children, tell them that they, more than ever, are the be-all and end-all of our lives. We are straining to be with them, but for their peace of mind we will stave off both ecstasy and insanity, will not risk our lives deliberately, especially since we do not now control our own fate, it controls us. We send all our relations, theatre colleagues, friends and acquaintances the warmest, most affectionate feelings and with all our soul we love and pity them. We are suffering for everyone.

Warmly loving you Kostya.

[...] What are we to make of this? Yesterday the embassy assured us that the Italian ships sail with mathematical punctuality, and today the secretaries at the embassy warned us that the Adriatic is in danger, and [Duma deputy F. I.] Rodichev sent a desperate telegram that there are up to 4000 people in Italy waiting for steamers that do not depart. And there is no one to turn to. I am not eager to wind up in captivity again. After all, if Italy mobilizes and abnegates neutrality and, as they are saying, enters the Triple Alliance again, we will be its enemies. If, on the other hand, Italy remains an enemy of Austria – we cannot travel on an Italian steamer, because it will be shot at!! What next?

To **Leonid Leonidov.** End of August 1914, Beatenberg.
Dear Leonid Mironovich!

Thanks for your letter, report and advice to go to Rome. We will take it, that is we shall go to Rome, but in winter, if we do not manage to get back to Russia. I ask you once more to put in a word for us with the hotel manager and make an effort to get us unlimited credit. However, before going to Rome, we shall try to get straight to Odessa via Marseilles with the 'Messagerie Maritime'. Either we will make it or they will turn us back – in Marseilles or in Italy. There is no other way out. The northern route through Paris and Switzerland with a mass of changing trains I could not endure now. I do not have the energy, because I do not feel well. The other way, through Marseilles, we can sit still and travel in place without any changes. We will risk it, because my nerves will not stand any more fluctuations and lack of information.

There is a dreadful atmosphere here: although everyone is kind and affectionate, though clearly inclined towards Germany, all kinds of distortions of news not to our advantage are depressing. What cheers us up is that a great company of us has gathered (too many women): the Kachalovs (three), Massalitinov, Podgorny, my wife, myself, the Rappoport family and, perhaps, Khokhlov with his wife and Aleksandra Pavlovna Botkina (the mother). The latest news is of a northern route through Paris. Khokhlov is propagandizing for it. A week ago he went from Paris to Geneva, saw Argutinsky[47] in Paris, who claims that it is easy to get through. But I do not believe it. From Paris and beyond it may perhaps be possible, but on the way to Paris, based on information from those who have just been there – travelling is very bad and dangerous. [...]

Yours K. Alekseev

In 2-3 days we are going to Geneva. [...]

This plan worked out: KS sailed from Marseilles on 31 August on the ship Equator.

To **Nemirovich-Danchenko**. 12 September 1914, Odessa. *Telegram.*

Kachalovs, Podgorny, Massalitinov, my wife arrived Odessa. We travel when possible. In haste, love. Trains delayed. Stanislavsky.

To **Lyubov Gurevich.** Tuesday, 16 September 1914, Moscow.

Dear Lyubov Yakovlevna!

[…] After your departure came the most irritating and unbearable period. Walks to the bank, consultations, telegraphing. Scraping together bits of money, efforts to get tickets. Discussion and selection of the route. 'The Dardanelles are closed!' 'The Dardanelles are open!' Fog in the mountains, longing in one's heart. I got weak and fell ill, lay in bed for a week. We sprinkled arsenic around, pumped bromine. The German papers lied, scared us and drove us to distraction. When we arrived in Geneva things began to get easier. In Lyons it was terrible and the nearness of the war was palpable. In Marseilles – a carefree version of Paris, heat, sun. Heavy swells as far as Malta. Then things went well. It was most dreadful in Turkey. Especially the episode with meeting the *Geben*.[48] On the Black Sea we expected storms, because it was the equinox, but we sailed without any pitching. […]

Yours K. Alekseev

As a result of the war Russian theatres (the MAT among them) tried to introduce stirring patriotic themes. German plays were blacklisted. The morbid Andreev and Dostoevsky were not performed. KS thought that three of Pushkin's blank-verse 'little tragedies' would provide a poetic respite from the war.

To **Lyubov Gurevich.** 2 October 1914, Moscow.

Dear Lyubov Yakovlevna!

[…] Our repertoire has changed as much as possible.

We are opening with a revival of *Woe from Wit* (Dobuzhinsky is improving the earlier production).

Then the Shchedrin goes on.[49] It makes no sense not to put it on, because it is all ready, and to discard a finished production – there is no money and time. And, to tell the truth, there's nothing to be said against the Shchedrin. It is satire, but it expresses Russia .

The third production is Pushkin. *The Stone Guest, A Feast in Plaguetime* and *Mozart and Salieri.*

It is very possible that *Wandering Minstrels* will be transferred to the main stage of the Art Theatre.

Autumn Violins will probably remain in the studio.[50]

In the studio they will soon be putting on Dickens' *Cricket on the Hearth.*

I forgot to let you know. All our baggage has been found. It was inspected in Munich – at the Hotel 'Roter Hahn', and then sent on to an expeditor in Lindau, where it got stuck in the meantime. With some effort we can retrieve the baggage, but, possibly, we won't manage it until the war is over. My wife will write you in detail about this.

I had to leave all my notes, materials and all your extracts in Geneva with Ernestine (the children's governess). But I am so melancholy without these extracts. Could you have them recopied at my expense and send them to me? Write how much it will cost, and I will send the money at once. [...]

Yours K. Alekseev [...]

In September the shareholders' meeting resolved that the next year's repertoire should not be affected by the war and that the old repertoire should be overhauled. The season opened on 27 October with a renovated version of Woe from Wit *and KS in a new makeup for Famusov. The evening began with the orchestra playing the national anthem and the Marseillaise followed by English, Serbian, and Belgian anthems. The pacifist Sulerzhitsky was outraged.*

Figure 54 Stanislavsky as Famusov in *Woe from Wit*, 1914. Photo: Granzburg, Moscow

To **Leopold Sulerzhitsky**. 27 October 1914, Moscow.

Dear Suler!

God forbid I should force anyone. Today's pomp is not a glorification of war (can I be war-like?)

It is only natural that the Art Theatre wants to illustrate the might of Russia, for which we need unity, golden screens, a big crowd, a mighty sound and the genius of Griboedov. The Art Theatre is glorifying an ally, which, like Belgium, is howling on behalf of the idea of peace and international law, which alone can prevent future wars.

If this is glorifying war, then we shouldn't play the 'Marseillaise' and the Belgian anthem, but the Prussian 'Wacht am Rhein'.

Yours K. Stanislavsky

Work on the Pushkin evening officially began on 14 November. KS was to play Salieri in Mozart and Salieri. *It proved to be his most recalcitrant role since Brutus. None of his recourses – Chaliapin reading the part aloud, hypnosis, different makeups, contradictory characterizations – seemed to work.*

On 24 November Cricket on the Hearth *went on at the Studio, with Gorky in the audience. He wept.*

The premiere of Saltykov-Shchedrin's Pazukhin's Death *directed by ND took place on 3 December 1914. With various cast changes it lasted well into the Soviet era with 142 performances.*

To **his daughter Kira.** 11 December 1914, Moscow.

My dear, charming, tenderly beloved clever little Kiryulya!

I have worked out the Pushkin, acted it a lot; that's why I haven't written these last few days. What would you care to know? First, the war; second, how *Pazukhin* went; third, the doll exhibition. I think there's nothing more of interest in this brief interim. A great deal is talked about the war and much nonsense. They have decided to surrender Warsaw, and people are very upset about it. Then rumours ran that a militia has been formed. It turned out that a militia had already been decided on a long time ago, and not on account of the surrender of Warsaw, which they had not planned to surrender. Now it turns out that efforts have been made for a militia, but it doesn't exist yet. Today people at the theatre were saying that some important officer, who has just arrived from the war, said that this time no information will be given out (or, more accurately, tidbits will be given out), because he is afraid that secrets will be divulged, even among the general staff itself, but we should expect joyous tidings any time now and our tactics are apparently brilliant.

I can be brief about *Pazukhin*. The audience and the press have welcomed the play drily, are a bit bored. Of course, the usual banalities suitable for such occasions have been uttered.

-- Why portray scoundrels on stage? You should only depict beautiful people – etc.

The exhibition was big, and the vernissage well-attended.[51] I was only in the doll section, and didn't see the paintings. I hear that downstairs, where the paintings are, there was a scandal. Some futurist artist [V. E. Tatlin] was late with his picture of the following subject:

[*Diagram of a square with a yellow bucket glued to half of it, and yellow wallpaper on the other half.*]

I didn't see the picture, but understood from what people said that it was like this. [The painter Vasily] Perepletchikov didn't want the picture to be admitted and made a scene, however the public demanded that the picture be hung, which was done. I like the idea of a doll exhibit very much. This can have a wonderful influence on children. There is a good deal of rubbish, but a bit of it is not without talent. Best of all were the dolls made by the Art Theatre with [Nikolay] Andreev (the sculptor), that is, caricatures of me as Famusov, Vishnevsky in *Mistress of the Inn* (very good), Knipper in *Tsar Fyodor* (very like), Smirnova in *Macbeth* (very good).[52] All these dolls began at 125 r. and now people are offering up to 250 r. for them. The Fabergé dolls with porcelain heads, hands and feet are very charming (I have to finish, I'm called to the stage).

Tight and tender hugs.

Yours Papa [...]

To **Lyubov Gurevich**. 11 December 1914, Moscow.
Dear Lyubov Yakovlevna!

[...] It is very hard to do any work. First of all, my nerves are in an appalling state. I cannot sleep, it is hard to act, the whole time states of alarm and nightmares – I wake up. I have thoroughly wrecked my nervous system for this summer. But, of course, I do not dare complain and consider myself lucky when I think of what others, almost all of them, are going through.

The work is moving in art. We have worked out a lot of new stuff. Especially in the realm of the subconscious and superconscious and in the techniques for the nourishment and workings of these extra-conscious emotions. [...]

Cordially devotedly yours K. Alekseev [...]

To **his daughter Kira**. 17 December 1914, Moscow.
My dear and priceless clever-dick Kiryulya!

[...] It's the same old story with us. The war. Things seemed to have calmed down, if you believe the rumours that our forces are not pursuing the Germans on purpose. Here's the version: near Warsaw our rear is spread far out and it is hard to break through it. It can be provisioned thanks to the railway. To move the forces from the whole rear is difficult owing to ravaged Poland, with its half-destroyed railways. It makes more sense to concede this ravaged part of Poland (since it is ravaged) to the Germans for their manoeuvres. Here it makes sense to weaken the German army, especially in a season of impassable roads. If we move to the German frontier, -- all those unfavourable aspects will come over to our side, and in addition we will cede to Germany her whole advantage, that is her well-equipped and fortified rear, an enormous network of railways for the constant transport of troops etc. It is better at this time to put an end as soon as possible to

Austria and Peremyzsl… There seems to be some confusion about the goings-on at the Russian frontier of the Caucasus at Batum (Sarykamsha). Does it mean the Russians have retreated? True, the telegrams inform us of victories here. […]

Your tenderly loving Papa

The Pushkin triptych opened on 26 March to a very uneven press. KS was a Mozart, said some, not a Salieri. He felt himself incapable of being genuine when speaking blank verse naturally.

To **Mariya Savina**. *28 March 1915, Moscow.*
Deeply esteemed and dear Mariya Gavrilovna!
[…] The Pushkin production is very violently abused. The audience listens well and does not seem to be bored. Probably it is our fault, and our modest talents are not up to Pushkin, but we have worked as best we knew how, and consider that only now we are beginning real work on the audience. I think that it is impossible to have a profound emotional experience of Pushkin all at once and in this profound emotional experiencing achieve that buoyancy, which the airiness of the verse requires. Sometimes the verse gets heavy – from over-emphasis, sometimes, on the other hand, the verse begins to take on steam, but conversely the emotion only lightly glides over the crux of the matter. We take our time, Muscovite-style, and do not lose hope. We are going to Petrograd, where they will sling mud at us good and proper. This is quite a normal event, we might even start to miss the mud. Then we come back to Moscow and, God willing, we will learn a bit next year. […]
Your constant admirers and fans,

Mariya, Konstantin, Kira and Igor Alekseev

To **Aleksandr Benois**, 1 April 1915, Moscow.
Dear Aleksandr Nikolaevich!
Thank you very much for both the article you sent (I liked it a lot)[53] and the sketch of Salieri's costume, and for the letter on the back of it.
Thank you for sympathizing with the condition of an actor who has gone a bit loony.
What a surprise!
I swear to you.
The last few days I have felt so awful that I decided to go to Dahl[54] to be cured by hypnosis. When I woke up this morning and remembered last night's performance, I immediately blushed and succumbed to a kind of burning, piercing chagrin. I remained in that state until they came to waken me. I acted during the night, while I was tormented by insomnia, and the more I repeated the lines, the more I forgot them. During the day, on the street and in a cab, I caught myself repeating my lines at every moment in the same unrelenting obtuse way. During the day, jaded, I lay down and could not sleep, constantly running over the lines. I arrived at the theatre completely knackered. I had to correct something in the

makeup to convince myself and encourage myself that I had come up with something. I swallowed a double dose of drops and (oh horrors!) secretly drank some wine to buck myself up. But I had only to put on the white breeches to feel fat in them, and immediately the emaciation painted on my face became a caricature; my heart sank, and I fell into total despair and felt clumsy, superfluous, comical and, mainly *ridicule* [*French in the original*]. What I acted… God knows, I stumbled through the lines, almost dried up. The more I tried to overcome my apathy, the more the audience coughed. Yesterday I went to the dressing-room with hell in my soul and felt that I could not put on the white breeches or, more accurately, I decided not to go on stage wearing them. Profiting by your agreement in principle, I sent someone to fetch some black breeches and stockings. I put them on and felt liberated. Confidence put in an appearance, gestures. Having gone completely astray in my inner design, I desperately decided, in actor's slang, to *pull out all the stops*, unleashing both voice and gestures for good and all. And I let loose!!! It was very easy, but I felt that only desperation could have led to such a disgraceful state of affairs. They listened as they had never listened before. They even tried to applaud after the first act. In the intermission Moskvin rushed round, said that that was exactly the way to play it. I don't understand anything!..

I played the second act the same way. This time there was no hissing, but there was a kind of general rustling at the end and some attempts to applaud. One can act that way 10 times a day. Moskvin and others are encouraging. (Encouragement for encouragement's sake?!!!) There is only one thing left to me now: to justify this by genuine living emotion. […]

Yours K. Alekseev

On 14 April 1915 Autumn Violins *by Ilya Surguchev, staged by ND, opened. It ran to 109 performances, because it suited the somber mood of the times, and because there were fewer novelties in the theatre during the war.*

To **Yevgeny Vakhtangov**. 20 April 1915, Moscow. *Inscription on a photograph.*

You are the first fruit of *our* renewed art. I love you for your talent as an instructor, a director and an actor; for your striving for the *real* in art, for knowing how to discipline yourself and others, to fight and overcome shortcomings. I am grateful to you for your great and patient labour, conviction, modesty, persistence and purity in piloting our general principles in art. I believe and know that your chosen path will lead you to a great and deserved victory.

For the first time in twelve years, the MAT did not tour to St. Petersburg. The shareholders' meeting in August declared the need to expand the audience and take performances to people's and factory theatres in Moscow.

The back-and-forth victories and defeats of the Russian forces turned sour in May 1915, when the enemy opened a strong offensive with overwhelming artillery support. By the end of June the total Russian losses from ten months of war amounted to 3,800,000 men. The Russians were driven out of Poland and Galicia.

Figure 55 Yevgeny Vakhtangov as Tackleton in *The Cricket on the Hearth*

To **his daughter Kira**. *September-October 1915, Moscow.*
My dear, loving, precious Kiryulya!

I am writing you a business letter. Pay great attention to it. It would be a mistake to conceal from you the seriousness of the situation. So far, thank God, nothing is yet hopeless, but we can expect great events and the Germans showing up in Petrograd, and coming to Moscow, and this may happen now or in March, and a revolutionary movement will burst out; one might even expect general victory and peace. Of course, everyone's mood is alarmed, specifically now when it has become clear: some time, somewhere the Germans will come. How is one to behave at such a time? Sit and wait for something to turn up? Of course not. Now is precisely when one has to act. This is what we have come up with.

1) To stay in Moscow with the Germans is out of the question, it is dangerous for the women, for Igor, who will be recruited as a soldier, for me, if I am entered on the list of the proscribed.

2) In that case – flight is inevitable. But to run away at the last minute, when one will not be able to secure horses or people or trains and Granny will have to go on foot to the station while we carry her baggage is a risky business. For youngsters it's fun, for us old folks it's agony, and for Granny completely impossible. It is not for us to throw a dear old lady to the mercy of the Germans. However, it may happen that at the last minute she will be unable to leave and in her wake we will all have to stay. I do not think that Granny wants to risk her own or our lives. Therefore first of all, until the enemy's plan becomes clear, we have to keep Granny in the Caucasus. Where are we to transfer her, when the sanatorium closes? a) either to Mariya Al. Voinova,[55] b) or to Kislovodsk, to Ganeshin, c) or in the worst case to Maslyankina in Rostov-on-Don (of course, if she agrees to it). Mama will write about this, *but on receipt of Mama's letter to Granny, you must prepare to carry out this business by keeping Granny in the Caucasus*, until the general situation becomes clear. Along with this one must think about *the need to send warm underclothes and money*.

3) If it becomes clear that the foe is advancing on Petrograd or halting and waiting for spring, holding back from an expedition in winter, -- you and Granny will return to Moscow; for the time being, I repeat, to come here simply to end up in a panic-stricken evacuation and get stuck here is imprudent.

4) If it becomes clear that the foe is coming to Moscow, we will go to you. But to do this we have to have a place to live guaranteed. Therefore *discuss this with Cherchikov and ask him to keep two rooms constantly at our disposal*. You and Mama will be in one, and I and Igor in the other (what can you do – 'beggars can't be choosers'). If Granny is in Kislovodsk, she will need a third room. Your present room, although it is heated, will be cold for late autumn and, who knows, even winter. Keep this in mind. So there are no misunderstandings, I shall explain what I mean by 'keep a room at our disposal'. It means that we might arrive at any moment and settle into it, that is, clear it of residents. *Let Cherchikov explain what needs to be done for this and how much to pay.*

5) Also one cannot go on living without things, let alone take them with you at the last minute. Many Muscovites have already had dispatched to their estates and to the east what they consider their greatest valuables and necessities. And we ought to send off something as well. For instance, dresses, some of the linen, shoes, fur coats, my notes and valuable material for them. Fortunately, we have nothing valuable in the way of furniture and therefore you can't pack God knows how many of such packages, only the most necessary. Ask Cherchikov: *whether he will store five or ten such trunks, if not, then discuss it and take advice – where can they be stored*. Thus, you have to carry out those assignments which

are underlined, but do it quietly, if possible in secret, so as not to create a panic.[56]

Write me an answer as soon as possible. [...]

Your tenderly loving Papa.

Before undertaking anything, wait for my letter, which I will send today.[57]

On the home front disillusionment in the hopes of greater liberty, which had been the chief cause of enthusiasm for the war, produced a pessimistic mood during the winter of 1915. 1916 would prove to be a disastrous year for Russia. Four million men had been killed in the first twelve months of the hostilities. Ill-equipped and incompetently commanded, the regular army evaporated, and the Germans made inroads on Russian soil. The government was in disarray. Refugees were streaming into Moscow and St Petersburg: food queues lengthened, leading to bread riots. The suicide rate tripled.

The First Studio confined its public presentations to an evening of Chekhov sketches. A Second Studio was created by several MAT students with a rather vague profile.

KS proposed that The Seagull, which had received only sixty-three performances between its opening in 1898 and its removal from the repertoire in 1905, be revived, employing both members of the original cast and young actors. The idea was postponed so that ND could rehearse his own adaptation of Dostoevsky's novella The Village of Stepanchikovo, with KS in his former role as Rostanev, the saintly landowner victimized by a canting parasite.

To **Aleksandr Benois.** 5 January 1916, Moscow.

Dear Aleksandr Nikolaevich!

[...] We have had a fantastic year financially (contrary to all expectations), but a completely dead one artistically. The expectation of a call-up makes the actors completely incapable of hard work, so all plans and proposals are problematic. The Merezhkovsky[58] [*Let There Be Joy*] will soon go on. [Ostrovsky's] *Wolves and Sheep* is stymied and temporarily halted, because the casting clashed with those actors who are intensely involved in the repertoire

Now we're mad about Dostoevsky's *The Village of Stepanchikovo* which has been made into a beautiful play (not an adaptation) [by V. M. Volkenshtein and ND]. [Mikhail] Chekhov is playing Foma, I'm the uncle, Bersenev the nephew, [...] the General's lady is played by Birman, Perepelitsyna by Uspenskaya.[59]

The Deluge has gone on in the studio [14 December 1915]. The acting isn't bad, and Chekhov [as Frazer] is acting very well. The play is inconsequential. [...]

I am giving classes (in the so-called System) at the Bolshoy Theatre?!! It occurred completely unexpectedly. I needed singers to freshen up the concert programmes on which we are working. I suggested, with the permission of the administration, the youngsters of the Bolshoy Theatre. To my surprise, all the stars showed up at the first lesson and were so attracted that now they won't let me go. I don't think that the attraction will last very long. Most of them are falling away, and only 2-3 persons remain, with whom, perhaps I can manage to do something.

I am acting a cruelly great deal, I am very tired. My nerves are even more strained from the war and the expectation of Igor's call-up. [...]

Cordially devoted K. Alekseev

To **Lyubov Gurevich**. *5 January 1916, Moscow.*
Dear, good Lyubov Yakovlevna!
[...] It is hard to make one's living by art. The season is dead. We expect more call-ups. We do not know with whom and what to set up. From a financial standpoint it's a runaway season. Full houses, but it brings no joy [...]

Cordially devoted K. Alekseev

The premiere of the Let There Be Joy, *a depressing play of modern life by the mystical anarchist poet Dmitry Merezhkovsky and directed by ND, took place on 3 February 1916 and ran for a mere thirty-eight performances. Merezhkovsky was grateful, but mistakenly attributed the achievement to KS.*

KS was beginning to emphasize action over emotion as the driving force in an actor's creativity, and regarded these rehearsals as an opportunity to explore his new ideas about the creative technique. There was emphasis on finding the 'sense of self' and the 'desires'. Rehearsals for Village of Stepanchikovo *began with laying out the 'bits' of the first act scene 'Tea Time'.*

To **Mstislav Dobuzhinsky**. 8 March 1916, Moscow.
Dear Mstislav Valeriyanovich!
May the power of Christ be with you! Why was your number up? You are almost the same age as Kachalov, and he hasn't been called up yet. Write why they recruited you. Do you hold a white slip[60] or did you serve in the past? This news has us all very upset and distressed. We have been working very wholeheartedly on *The Village of Stepanchikovo*. Set up: a) the Bakhcheev scene; b) all of the second and c) third acts. What am I waiting for from you – for now? As many scraps of paper as possible with pencil sketches of everything that comes into your head. The sketches of the tea-party were sent – according to the same ground-plan... but the next dispatch was the tea-party again, and of quite a different character, entirely the reverse. The more of these little sketches the better, otherwise we shall freeze on one type of tea-party and petrify in that enchanted circle, and if the project doesn't answer the demands of the ground-plan and so forth, -- then the director will have to do violence to the designer, to bind him to what did not evolve in him organically. If a large amount is sent, the director can choose what is the most appropriate.

Therefore I expect not such big drawings from you, but simply little sketches of all the sets, in the most *varied and contrasting* ground plans and viewpoints and so on.

Furthermore I would like to have similar sketches of the costumes, makeups, hair-styles, etc., which you consider characteristic of the period, not earmarking them in advance for any particular character.

What shall I say about the drawings that have been sent?. . . There are good hints at the mood. They are complicated. Lots of lines. Not very useful for the landscape outside the windows. I would like more of a sense of crampedness and a familiar haunt. Don't we need more portraits on the walls or some special elephantine sofa, gigantic cupboard or pot-bellied chest of drawers with samovars, an organ... whereby to express narrowness and tedium.

I would like the ground-plan to be richer, in the sense of indicated locations (three acts in one set). We need places for all the moods: the full-cast scene, the love duet at sunset, and mysterious with Mizinchikov, and the cruel scene with Foma, and the heartfelt effusions of the uncle and Sergey – a great plethora of all sorts of moods. I am awaiting the dispatch of sketches as often as you can. When there are a lot of such drawings of the scenery, costumes and makeups to choose from, then I would like us to get together to make a final decision. Or, on the contrary, if your imagination still can't get into gear and you need jolts from rehearsals and fresh discussions – it would just as useful to get together and talk it over.

Do not be cross at my criticism of the drawings. You understand that my goal is to extract from you as much dreaming as possible on paper. […]

Your heartily devoted K. Alekseev

In 1913, Aleksandr Blok had offered his symbolic play of courtly love Rose and Cross *to KS in hopes that he would also play the role of Bertrand. After three years of planning, it was finally accepted for production.*

The premiere of An A. P. Chekhov Evening (The Proposal, The Anniversary, The Lecture on the Evils of Tobacco *and a dramatization of the story 'The Witch') took place on 22 March 1916.*

To **Lyubov Gurevich.** 12 April 1916, Moscow.
Dear Lyubov Yakovlevna!

[…] Igor has been called up, and I cannot get my brains around the combination of these two phenomena – a half-invalid child and the war's ruthlessness to our enemies. I live in the hope that the doctors will understand the imbecility of such a combination and release him, because he really is no good at all to them owing to his health. It has been shown he has a weak heart, and exhalations in his lungs, and his stomach is out of order, and he is prone to appendicitis. What kind of war is this? So far all we've done is live and wait.

We shall not be going to Petrograd. And this time we say: thank God! – although the financial loss from this is enormous. In Moscow the box-office is failing, and there's no point to going to the provinces either. Why not go? Because, first, touring is not artistic, but purely financial. It is commerce, and not art. This year we could do nothing what with the constant recruitments. All the plays are messed up, the ensemble is destroyed, nerves are frayed. Under such conditions there is no way to perform. We had better stay home and work on *The Village of Stepanchikovo, Rose and Cross* and so on. You ought to come here. (Only that way will we be able to renew the interrupted work in installments.) The second reason why we won't be going is that there will be talk: look, they'll say, the Art Theatre is travelling to make money, just like all merchants nowadays. It hires waggons that are needed to transport armaments. Of course, 20 waggons when there are 1500 dispatched every day comes to exactly nothing, and they give them to us willingly, without any provisos and bribes, but it's impossible to make the crowd listen to reason and so it would be better to bear the losses and not cast a shadow over the theatre. So we're waiting for you here. In fact, do come. Take a look at *The Deluge, Let There Be Joy* and we shall discuss the reviews. [...]

Devoted with all his soul yours K. Alekseev

To **Leopold Sulerzhitsky**. 21 April 1916, Moscow.

Dear Suler!

Christ has arisen!

Thanks for the letter, otherwise we were getting worried and planning to send you a telegram. I didn't write, because I am going through a serious time of anxiety. On Easter I even get a gift. They are recruiting university students, and Igor among them. I dropped everything, begin to make phone calls, make inquiries; I went to one, to another in the Crimea. To a department office – it's closed. Dealings with the organization had already been broken off, and so the only alternative I am faced with is an infantry school for ensigns and the trenches, because there is no other place to go. I write to Stakhovich – so that he will make an effort in Petrograd to place him in the Mikhailov Artillery Institute. He throws everything aside and on the first day of Easter goes to Tsarkoe Selo, there he makes a fuss, and some Grand Duke proclaims loudly in front of everyone that Igor's grades are not good enough to get him admitted, but because it's the Art Theatre that's asking– one must make a concession and admit him... They admitted him. Meanwhile I sent Igor to the doctors: I cannot believe that he could endure what I have heard of barracks life and have seen in the Krutitsky-like barracks. Three doctors say that he is not fit, he shouldn't be taken, but... they do take his sort. Only one thing is left: to make an effort to have him examined.

All this took place at Easter, with performances every day, moreover I was even acting in place of Stakhovich (in the Turgenev).[61] I am acting, and from the theatre I rush to make appeals, to pay calls. It's a horror, I don't sleep at night and I am once again falling into the same abnormal condition (neurasthenia) I was in abroad after my captivity.

Finally yesterday, 20 April, Igor was examined at the town hall and declared unfit and given an exemption for one year.

No sooner was that over, I had urgently to put *Lower Depths* to rights, because when I got to the rehearsal, I felt I was in the back of beyond.[62] (Such swine have our folks become!) I made a scene, refused to act in the performance and demonstratively went home. Chase after me, explanations, then compulsory rehearsals. Today, the day of the performance, I arrived, corrected things all day long and right now I am acting and writing to you in the intermission.

So far everything is going well in the studio. They still haven't given me my own production. Massalitinov's school has closed, and they want to form a second studio.[63]

It is warm outside, almost summer. I am sitting in my dressing-room, but it is impossible to open the window, because in front of the dressing-room toilet and all around there is litter, heaps of litter and bloody, abscess-covered bandages, which go on decomposing and rotting.[64] I made a fuss, a scandal, a protest. Aren't we swine! They said that there is nothing to be done, because the town council won't cart it away. After the putrescent blood reached two pounds, the question was resolved: they simply made a bonfire in the middle of the courtyard, and all day long they burned this demi-plague. [...]

Yours K. Alekseev

We are not going to Petrograd, thank God.

In spring 1916 KS tried to launch an 'Organization of Popularly-Priced Moscow Theatres', an itinerant company. It had barely got off the ground when the Revolution aborted it. He also sent Suler a grant of 500 rubles to set up 'an agricultural colony' outside Evpatoria.

A new partnership was formed because the terms of the original contract had expired. On 10 August 1916 the founders of the MAT proposed that from 16 June 1917 it would hand over the operation and its holdings to the actors not just as a temporary benefit, but in complete ownership. To accept this 'gift with conditions' a partnership without limit of time was developed on cooperative principles with twenty constituents – actors and workers in the theatre, including the co-founders themselves.

To **Nemirovich-Danchenko.** 11 August 1916, Essentuki.
Dear Vladimir Ivanovich!

[...] I am doing everything I can to get well: moreover, I will probably have to travel as an invalid, because it is impossible to change my ticket. If only my weakened constitution does not catch a cold or an infection. They are saying that only God knows what's going on in Moscow. [...]

Concerning the administration. [...]

My indifference, etc., has its reasons. I was not always this way. There was a time when I was on fire. But there is, first of all, a basic difference of opinion -- and many other reasons. The shareholders and I have different goals, different paths, and different (how shall I put it) ethics, upbringing, culture, views, habits, nature.

The question is a financial one. It must be discussed in financial terms. The best way to make money is by building a lasting, solid, sound concern, whose strength consists in the fact that the *only thing* it knows how to do is never to produce anything but good merchandise. What's more, it is always *pleasant, convenient, enjoyable* to do business with this concern. Its power is used to *implement, facilitate,* and not to *forbid, make difficulties.* Here everyone is imbued with a single thought to *consolidate* the concern, -- its source of nourishment. Therefore every novelty, every innovation is caught on the wing and put into operation quickly, rapidly. Things that in other concerns take decades to be accepted are adopted at once here. In a concern like that there are ideas, plans, aspirations, a guide-line leading upwards. It makes profits as well.

But there are other concerns. They are much less interested in the business itself and its continual improvement, they are afraid of wasting time in a period of transition, so that their focus goes no farther than the current year of operation. Is it worth writing any more, when everything has been understood and said a hundred times over? Our theatre possesses many assets in comparison with all other theatres not only in Russia but throughout the world, and what distinguishes it from other theatres is what sustains me in the theatre; but that is where our aims and paths part company, there is only one solution left to me, -- to close my eyes, to keep from seeing, and pass by as quickly as possible, deliberately develop that indifference which allows me to work in a concern whose aims differ from mine.

There is yet another reason that reinforces everything that has been said. I am well provided for, others are not. It is easy for me to take risks, others not. I, seemingly, take no financial risks in the business, and others, seemingly, do. In this case I bear the dangerous label of an impractical scatterbrained genius, etc. And it is true, I am impractical, as to the current season, but I am practical – as to future profits of the concern. Naturally, under those circumstances, I have no vote (and seek none, don't take this as a hint). Meanwhile I bear the greatest responsibility in the financial respect, because I am the most prosperous debtor and depend on banks and stock markets. For me the soundness and durability of a concern is more important than next year's profits. And there our interests and objectives radically part company from those of all the other shareholders. In addition, I, as a true-born Muscovite, surrounded by the traditional prejudices of a certain group of people on whom I and my family depend, financially and in other ways, -- must be scrupulous in another realm as well, known as *public opinion*: the '*que dira-t-on*'. And the ethical standing of the theatre is at present very low and I frequently have reason to be pained, embarrassed, and get into a ghastly state. Nowhere is there more drinking and drunkenness than among us, nowhere is there such self-importance and contempt for others and such insulting outbursts. In state theatres this is mitigated by the bureaucracy, which we, thank God, don't have, but we don't have the aristocratic traditions of an aristocratic house either. And in addition to that -- Moscow is proud of us, and so certain individuals have to maintain the prestige. So there is another set of compromises. Here and there our darker aspects pop up, and we have to stop up those holes. In Rostov, an impresario put up a poster that misled the public, and the local wool-merchants wrote to me: 'Tell Alekseev how he allows his actors to be such swindlers!' Another conflict. When all is said and done a stupid situation arises. 1) De facto I have no rights, -- no vote, no administrative and ethical authority, no power, I can make requests and act capriciously, but it is I -- I who has to answer for it, in the opinion of society and of Moscow. 2) Total lack of time, because I am playing and directing and when necessary experimenting and working for the future (so I am working on two, three fronts) and then whenever necessary I raise money. 3) I am also financially responsible, whatever a lawyer may tell you. 4) In the discretionary and objective sense of the agreement, I bear no responsibility, and so it is awkward for me to manage other people. 5) When I am needed -- I am put on display, my name is used; when I am not needed, -- I do not even know what is going on backstage contrary to my principles, habits, views. I often conceal what I have to put up with. 6) When a signature is needed at the bank – I have to provide it. In short, I must give my name for risks the concern takes and to conceal what I am out of sympathy with. 7) When we are dealing with things dear to me, for whose sake I would give my life, -- a thousand invisible threads hamper my movements at every step. That's how it was with the System, that's how it was with the two studios (not now, but before), that's how it will be with the new studio now,[65] that's how it will be with my new plans. And this is only natural. The things that are advantageous for the future, the things I care about, are in the most cases disadvantageous for the present.[66]

Can all this be reconciled? -- No! It cannot. I have either to convince everyone or give up and step aside. I don't know how to do the former, so I have to do the latter. The only possible way out (I repeat) is the following. I will stay at Carriage Row, and have my own studio (in general or with an independent troupe). People will come from the theatre and say: 'Stage this, perform that or help with the other.' -- 'Fine… Here are conditions' (not financial, of course). (You know all these conditions by heart.) A good play is put on in my studio --- excellent! I will bring it to the theatre with my troupe and perform it for 10 seasons. Actors in the Art Theatre are free and want to act with me – excellent! -- 'Such-and-such a play with the participation of so-and-so!' Everything is clear, everyone knows that I am responsible for the studio and *you* for the theatre and there is no false situation.[67] If there are financial losses -- please lean on me. If you need actors -- come to me.

To sum up. To my mind, you are making two mistakes which have brought about all the misunderstandings:

1) You want by force to unite things that cannot be united. -- Poland and the Baltic provinces cannot be united with Russia. They need autonomy if they are to come closer and befriend one another.

2) You are afraid to let power out of your own hands and want to keep a grip on the reins both great and small.

Time is passing. Convene the shareholders. They must sort out everything for themselves (apart from questions that regulate performances and artistic matters, of course) but you and I must stand to one side and *close ranks*. (Just you and I, without any third party.) They, that is, a whole group of people, want to put on a wretched play. Let them stage it and show it. If it's worthwhile -- we will put on the finishing touches and help them. If not -- they will learn from their mistakes. In everything and without fail -- we must once again revive a moribund initiative. And we must not be afraid of one thing, -- a season which creates great losses. Otherwise -- it's misery, bankruptcy, which I fear and which I will guard against in every way.

I gave fair warning of this a long time ago and, were it not for the war, I would have taken measures.

Rereading this letter I note the off-putting tone, which I do not tolerate in others or in myself. The tone is somewhat offensive, touchy. What am to I do? It came about involuntarily. I wanted to write in the most friendly, business-like tones and with an appealing attitude.

I am very fond of many people, but I don't agree with all of them all of the time.

Another problem – I don't know how to persuade people.

As far as the repertoire is concerned let's talk the next time we meet, and I'll finish this letter with a few remarks tomorrow. I'm very tired today.

Yours K. Alekseev [...]

[...] I love to discuss art, especially with you, but – time, time, damnable time. But we must, we very much must. But to do it, we have somehow to change something in our whole concern. [...]

After all, this is all I think about in my 'System': how to attain the most sublime feelings and beauties, only not through mere prettiness and sentimentality, violent emotional display and clichés. If I succeed in my lifetime to lay the first stone, solid and steady, I will consider myself happy and I will trust that our grandchildren will see the actor I dream about. But just as you can't make an elephant out of a fly, you can't make heroes out of us, eighty-year-old bourgeois. There is no technology for such a remodelling. Convinced that my path is a lonely one, but precisely because it is authentic, it is very long.

Rabindranath, Aeschylus – they are the genuine article. We cannot perform them, but should try.[68] Writers will help in this.

[...] *Suler.* I have information about him from the doctor. Suler can still be a worker, but in conditions of lengthy and systematic treatment, to the very end. If he shows up now – in the next week or month he will be of no use whatsoever. It will be a repetition of the old situation in a much worse form, and will result in a complete and irremediable invalid state. A question of life and death. Therefore I took it on myself, on my own responsibility, and wrote to him that he does not dare to return until he gets the appropriate permission. Meanwhile, before October, there is no way to count on Suler.

[...] *The Blue Bird. Either nothing is to be done, or a great deal.* We should convene the Council of Studio folk without delay and assign them to put on the play in the [Second] Studio as soon as possible. (In secret I will say that I would hire two midgets: the one who is performing at Solodovnikov's in *Madam Butterfly*, and the other to be sought.) If people learn that there are new performers at the centre of the play, and children at that, *The Blue Bird* will become the play of the season. Meanwhile let it be rehearsed. [...]

Owing to the breakdown in transport, some sectors of Russia were slipping out of control and food and fuel deliveries became sporadic. Serious signs of disaffection began to appear among workmen and army recruits. The Bolsheviks began to distribute defeatist literature among POW's in Germany.

To **S. A. Kharitonov.** 5 September 1916, Moscow.

Konstantin Sergeevich Alekseev (Stanislavsky) most humbly requests deeply esteemed Mr Kharitonov to allow him four and a half cubic metres of firewood every month, because my apartment is cold and spacious, because it contains rehearsal rooms for work with actors of the Art Theatre. The whole apartment is heated by firewood alone. Fulfilling my most humble request will greatly oblige your obedient servant

K. Stanislavsky

Kira had shown her paintings in the 'Knave of Diamonds' exhibition, the last of a series of decreasingly scandalous shows (begun 1910) featuring the works of such avant-garde designers as David Burlyuk, Aleksandr Ekster and Natan Altman.

To **his daughter Kira**. 21 September 1916, Moscow.

Dear, precious Kira,

[...] All we talk about is the mobilization. At the moment there is a vast recruitment. Besides the employees, skilled workers etc. they are taking from us Moskvin, Massalitinov, Gotovtsev, Trushnikov, Chekhov (another examination).[69]

In October they are taking the white-slip holders up to 1910, and in November the rest of the white-slip holders, that is the whole studio, which will probably have to close. In addition, Leonidov has again refused to act (but doesn't refuse to receive his salary). Stakhovich has also gone and is being obstinate, whereby he does not punish the theatre but me, because I have to act in the Turgenev in his place. Our season is in full swing. This year there is the impression that the last season hasn't ended but there was a Great Lenten break. It is hard to act one and the same thing, and there's no one to rehearse anything new. And *Stepanchikovo* has been taken off because of Moskvin. [...]

A minor little incident happened to me at the factory, and I refused both incredible profits and salaries. True, it hits the pocketbook, but does not tarnish the soul. (This is between you and me.) [...]

I hug you tenderly, love you, miss you, am worried about you.

Loving you with all my soul Papa

Olya and Misha Chekhov have a daughter. Misha hates her for having tormented Olya[70] during and after the birth. It ended with his handing over his daughter to his wife's mother.

To **Nemirovich-Danchenko.** End of September 1916, Moscow.

Dear Vladimir Ivanovich!

[...] *Vakhtangov.* Among my conditions for this year was a studio with its essential staff. Among the indispensable persons was Vakhtangov. At the start of the year he wanted 100 r. But I explained to him that first he had to prove himself in the studio. His salary remained 75 r.

This year he has worked wonderfully. He devoted himself to the studio, and to do this he had to turn down rather remarkable earnings on the side. He must get a raise. His labour is considerable, although inconspicuous. The benefit which he has inconspicuously brought to the theatre is also considerable, not only pedagogically but ethically. […]

K. Alekseev […]

The Second Studio officially opened on 24 November with Zinaida Gippius's drama of disaffected young people, The Green Ring.

To **Nemirovich-Danchenko**. 4 December 1916, Moscow.
Dear Vladimir Ivanovich!

It is depressing and difficult for me to declare once again *absolutely* and categorically that *under no circumstances* will I sign any paper, officially or legally binding me to a new partnership. I have already notified you of this more than once, and now, with the departure of Stakhovich (and after him all the investors and people who might share my financial responsibilities), – I do not have *any right at all* in regard to my family and my late father, for whom debts carried certain moral responsibilities, to risk my children's financial welfare.

In addition, for me to assume a responsibility which falls on me alone, I would need to have all rights and general support and love. I do not have any legal vote (and seek none), no right and no moral or any other authority. Under such conditions -- it is not only frivolous, but stupid to take on more responsibility than I can manage by myself.

It depresses me that in this case no one wants to help me and enter into my position and that they approach this problem only on behalf of the theatre's interests. Therefore my refusal is all the more energetic and categorical.

It is even more depressing if this refusal is seen as a desire to withdraw from something I have worked at all my life. That is not the case. I will do everything in my power, with even greater zeal, to safeguard our concern and the security of our colleagues in these dark days. Financially, without any legal document, I willingly assume my share of the risk and losses equally with the other shareholders, although I am not one of their number.

My decision is sufficiently categorical for me to ask you urgently not to return to this matter again. It is too difficult and oppressive.

Yours K. Alekseev

I make no secret of this letter, but I do think it would be better if it were not bruited about too much. I say this not for my sake but for the concern's.

In the minutes of the shareholders' meeting of 17 December 1916 KS and Stakhovich were still listed as constituents.

Notes

1 In an article in *Rech* (*Speech*) 6 April 1912.
2 Gribunin who played Dr Shpigelsky in *Month in the Country* and First Gravedigger in *Hamlet* had fallen seriously ill and could not go on stage till spring of the next season.

3 Mariya Aleksandrovna Zhdanova (1890-1944) played Anya in *Cherry Orchard*.

4 Kachalov would collect the comic accidents to which ND was prone.

5 Moskvin played Yepikhodov on stage; ND exemplified Yepikhodov's 'ton of troubles' in real life.

6 It was proposed for the first time that studio activities be connected with the preparation of the MAT repertoire, for which *Imaginary Invalid* and *Tartuffe* had been scheduled.

7 Aleksandr Aleksandrovich Vyrubov (1882-1962) later became a prominent actor in the Russian émigré colony in Paris.

8 Refers to improvisation from collectively created scenarios.

9 Vladimir Platonovich Bazilevsky (stage name Boltin, d.1932), acted at the MAT 1908-15.

10 Gzovskaya was replaced by Baranovskaya as Ophelia and by Lilina as Vera in *The Weakest Link*.

11 Koonen played Anitra in *Peer Gynt* and Liza in *Yekaterina Ivanovna*. In *Peer Gynt*, Bazilevsky played Mr Cotton, Baksheev the master of the Gstaad estate, Pavlov Ingrid's bridegroom; they had no part in *Yekaterina Ivanovna*. Pyotr Alekseevich Baksheev (Barinov, 1886-1929) was admired for his charm and 'stamp of Russianness'; KS saw him as a budding tragedian, ND did not. He acted with the Kachalov group and the MAT abroad, but ended his career at Korsh's Theatre. Polikarp Arsenievich Pavlov (1885-1974), acted at the MAT 1908-22, then became a leading figure in the Russian émigré theatre in Paris.

12 *Tartuffe* rehearsals were held from 5 November. Stakhovich was to play Cléante, Luzhsky Orgon (he was not in *Yekaterina Ivanovna*; in *Peer Gynt* he played the Button-moulder). Damis and Elmire were intended for Bersenev and Germanova, both were occupied in Andreev's play as Alyosha and Yekaterina Ivanovna.

13 In *Tartuffe*, Knipper was preparing Dorine, Koreneva Marianne; Vyrubov was assigned Valère.

14 Benois insisted that the music be that specially written for the 'Ceremony' in *Imaginary Invalid* by Molière's contemporary Marc-Antoine Charpentier: he remembered it from a performance at the Odéon.

15 KS planned to work on the interludes in *Imaginary Invalid* through improvisation in the spirit of folk comedy.

16 Ivan Nikolaevich Bersenev (Pavlishchev, 1889-1951) had classical good looks, height, a resonant voice and intense blue eyes; Mardzhanov, who had worked with him in Kiev and Odessa, recommended him to ND. He entered the MAT in 1911, and after Fortinbras in *Hamlet*, made his mark as Pyotr Verkhovensky in *Nikolay Stavrogin*.

17 The nightcap for Argan was in a sketch sent on 15 February 1913 and Benois suggested it be put on in place of the headscarf as a sign of respect when the doctors arrive.

18 The Antique Theatre (Starinny Teatr), St Petersburg, was founded in 1906 by Nikolay Yevreinov and Nikolay Drizen to reconstruct performance practices of the European past.

19 Benois: 'The cupids appear simultaneously with Aesculapius, who, in my concept, must enter with them from behind the backdrop and thus begin the apotheosis. They form a group, and then, after Aesculapius has embraced you and you ascend to the clouds, they accompany you and form a kind of tail for you and just so can bear your train. At the end you will kneel before Minerva, and the two beside you both kneel, while those behind you can play with the train.'

20 Benois considered the pre-apotheosis curtain 'trop compliqué' and offered another variant with a coat of arms. With that variant they would probably have to sacrifice the procession with chamber pots and clysters on poles or change the staging.

21 The dancer and choreographer of the Imperial Theatres Mikhail Mikhailovich Mordkin (1881-1944) staged the dances in *Imaginary Invalid* and the whole 'Ceremony' at the end of the show.

22 Viktor Dmitrievich Zamirailo (1868-1939), draughtsman, scene-painter and set-builder.

23 The blackamoor was to bear the train of a lady guest. Meyerhold had used blackamoors in Molière's *Dom Juan* at the Alexandra Theatre in 1910.

24 Aleksey Tolstoy's tragedy had long gone unplayed and was being revived for the second week in Lent.

25 Rehearsals, begun on 16 September 1912, were numbered in the tens (from 9 to 27 February there were only 19), but their sequence was interrupted.

26 Nadezhda Vsevolodovna Krestovozdvizhenskaya (Bazilevskaya) was an actress at the First Studio 1912-19.

27 Nikolay Osipovich Massalitinov (1880-1961) was an early adherent of the System, though it was thought his intellectualism lent a certain heaviness to his work. In 1913 he would open the acting school of 'the three Nikolays' with Aleksandrov and Podgorny. From 1925 he was a leading theatrical activist in Bulgaria, spreading the gospel of KS.

28 Nikolay Afanasievich Podgorny (1879-1947), joined the MAT in1903 and remained there until his death, becoming an influential assistant to KS.

29 Nikolay Fyodorovich Kolin (1878-1973), one of KS's first students, prominent in the First Studio; emigrated in 1920.

30 Boris Mikhailovich Sushkevich (1887-1946) had joined the MAT in 1908, playing small parts; he helped create the First Studio (MAT 2) and was a member of its administration to 1933.

31 The adolescent Kolya Larionov played Argan's little daughter Louison. At KS's suggestion he had been tutored by Gzovskaya.

32 That was possible, because in the fourth week of Lent public performances in theatres were not permitted.

33 In Petersburg the studio played only *The Wreck of the `Hope'*. *The Peace Festival* was shown during the next spring tour in 1914. No studio productions went to Odessa.

34 It did not happen.

35 An unsigned article 'In the Art Theatre Studio' in *Russian News*, 6 April 1913.

36 Benois believed that the modern actor would not improvise, but simulate it.

37 Vladimir Sergeevich Sergeev (1883-1941), historian; a ward of the Alekseev family.

38 Leonidov did not play the role until 1930.

39 It remained unfinished.

40 A reworked version of *The Peace Festival* was performed on 15 November 1913.

41 Konstantin Andreevich Somov (1869-1939), artist and designer associated with the World of Art.

42 The earlier production of 1898 had been entitled *Traktirshchitsa* (*The Landlady*); to make a distinction, this version was entitled *Khozyaika gostinitsy* (*The Mistress of the Inn*) in a new translation by Nelidov.

43 The Sukhodolskys opened a new theatre, the Moscow Dramatic Theatre, in the same building that had housed the now defunct Free Theatre. Another group of actors joined the troupe formed by Fyodor Komissarzhevsky. Shortly thereafter Aleksandr Tairov began to form the Kamerny Theatre with Koonen, now his wife, in leading roles.

44 All three of his sons were mobilized.

45 Tikhon Aleksandrovich Shamshin, senior engineer at the Alekseev factory and one of the company's partners, had been refitting the factory to deal with a deluge of military orders for coils of cable. KS refused any profits from the military orders.

46 Nikolay Vasilievich Yegorov (1873-1955), an employee at the Vladimir Alekseev firm, later became an administrator at the MAT.

47 Prince Vladimir Nikolaevich Argutinsky-Dolgorukov (1874-1941), art collector and member of the World of Art.

48 A warship under whose guns the *Equator* sailed. It almost ran them down in its course, panicking the passengers, passing within a hair's breadth of the other boat.

49 *Pazukhin's Death*, a sardonic comedy by the nineteenth-century satirist Mikhail Saltykov-Shchedrin.

50 *Minstrels* stayed in the studio, *Violins*, a sub-Chekhovian play by Ilya Surguchev, was transferred to the main stage.

51 KS attended the vernissage of the 'War Victims' exhibition set up by Moscow artists 'with military-charitable aims'.

52 Soft dolls in elaborately sewn costumes and plaster heads: KS as Famusov in a dressing-gown, Moskvin as Zagoretsky, Leonidov as Skalozub are in the MAT Museum.

53 Benois defended the principles of the MAT approach to Pushkin's 'little tragedies' in *Rech* (31 March and 7 April 1915). The dismal reception of the production led him to cool to the MAT.

54 The neuropathologist Nikolay Vladimirovich Dahl (1860-1939?) was a fashionable Moscow psychotherapist.

55 Mariya Alekseevna Voinova owned a boarding-house in Essentuki.

56 The passage in brackets was crossed out and there was added: 'N.B. It is premature to talk about this. Cherchikov might blab and start a panic.'

57 Written in Lilina's hand.

58 Dmitry Sergeevich Merezhkovsky (1866-1941), a symbolist who disdained Chekhov, was an unlikely author for the MAT and the choice shows how desperate it was for relevant contemporary plays.

59 The eventual casting had Moskvin as Foma, Massalitinov as the simple-minded uncle, Raevskaya as the General's Lady, Uspenskaya did not appear.

60 White slips were exemptions from military service given to the physically unfit, heads of families and other special categories; they were provisional and could be rescinded in times of need.

61 With Stakhovich away, KS had no alternate in *The Lady from the Provinces*.

62 The MAT was reviving the long-unperformed *Lower Depths* and KS considered that work on it was bringing the Studio's work to nothing. On 21 April KS played Satin for the first time after a three-year hiatus.

63 The School of Dramatic Art, where Massalitinov, Aleksandrov, and Podgorny ('the school of the three Nikolays') taught.

64 The Liazonov building next to the MAT housed a hospital in wartime.

65 The creation of the Second Studio in 1916. 'The two studios' are those on Povarsky and the First.

66 Line crossed out.

67 ND had claimed that no one was responsible for the Studio and that without Suler it ran itself autonomously.

68 Productions of Rabindranath Tagore's *The King of the Dark Chamber* and Aeschylus's *Prometheus* were planned but never completed.

69 Vladimir Vasilievich Gotovtsev (1885-1976) acted at the MAT 1908-24 and 1936-59; Georgy Aleksandrovich Trushnikov (1886-1945), a MAT employee. Most of those named either received a deferment or were found unfit for service.

70 Olga Konstantinovna Chekhova (Knipper, 1896-1980), niece of Olga Knipper-Chekhova and first wife of Mikhail Chekhov, later divorced him and became a superstar of German cinema, a favourite of Hitler.

him into a very morose state of mind. The confiscation of his factory and personal fortune, the threat of eviction from his home, and the growing awareness that he was out of step with a new way of life only exacerbated his depression.

Sulerzhitsky died of chronic nephritis on 18 December 1916 at the age of 44.

To **Aleksandr Benois**. 5 January 1917, Moscow.
Dear Aleksandr Nikolaevich!

[...] Again last season, during the dress rehearsals of *The Deluge*, Suler was taken ill. From that time on attacks of uræmia recurred periodically and there was no persuading him to leave Moscow. He was advised to go to Badmaev[1] in Petrograd, others told him to go somewhere warm. But Suler was stubborn and insisted that in a week after his arrival in Evpatoria he would be completely well and laughed at the doctors. However his expectations did not come true. In the summer he was very nervous and felt bad. The attacks kept recurring, as in the winter. And in August there was talk of moving to Kislovodsk, because the seaside was having a deleterious effect on the patient's health. In September Suler began to yearn for Moscow, for the theatre, and escaped Evpatoria on the pretext of being examined by doctors. He showed up at the theatre, then at the studio and in two days' time provoked an attack; finally he was persuaded to stay at home, but he invited various individuals from the studio to his house and dreamed of staging a particular play, although he could not even articulate his ideas: his tongue slurred the words. The doctors demanded a rigorous and systematic medical treatment. They moved poor Suler to the Military Hospital, and he was glad about it at first, because at home his temperamental children would give him no peace. But soon his patience gave out, and he demanded that he be moved back home, where the attacks recurred again. And again they moved him to the hospital. After that attack his strength failed him, and he could not get out of bed for a long time. We set up a duty roster, and the actors and studio folks kept him informed and entertained. Suler began to get better. He started to go out into the open air and left the house to call on his friends. This was his last farewell to his house. In a few days I went to the hospital to keep him informed, walked to his room, and then – total chaos, blood-letting, the whole bed and walls were covered with blood. It turned out that he had had the most violent of attacks. It was fatal and final. After that attack, strictly speaking, Suler was no more. He lay there, a wasted, spent semi-corpse, who could not speak a single sentence. Only his expressive eyes could speak. Day and night his wife (ever-present), studio folks, my wife, the wife of the late Sats, Moskvin and I were in attendance at his bedside. The whole time he tried to say something but could not. Various doctors were summoned (to ease our consciences), who sprinkled him with musk and other specifics (to diffuse the smell!). He passed away quietly. His heart stopped beating, but he kept on breathing for nearly two hours. At midnight, they brought him to the studio and laid him out in the foyer. The two days that he lay there were very moving. Everyone immediately understood exactly who Suler had been and what the studio (and the theatre) had lost. The studio folks carried him by hand

8

THE REVOLUTION
AND THE CIVIL WAR
1917–1921

In her memoirs, Sofiya Giatsintova, a young actress in the First Studio, remembers that she and her colleagues were so caught up in rehearsals for Twelfth Night that they paid little attention to the February Revolution. They did attend speeches by Kerensky the leader of the Provisional Government and saw KS in the audience. This artistic insouciance could not long withstand the pressure of events. The Bolshevik take-over in October, with its contingent bloodshed and civil conflict, turned a confused situation into a rout. Theatres dependent on government subsidy had no sense of how they were to exist; those dependent on the box-office saw empty houses due to unsafe streets and the devaluation of currency.

From the outset the Bolsheviks promulgated legislative measures to control the theatre. On 9 (22) November 1917, a fortnight after their power grab, a decree of the Soviet of the People's Commissars (Sovnarkom for short) placed the theatres under the authority of the arts division of the brand-new State Commission for Enlightenment, which was to become the People's Commissariat for Enlightenment (Narkompros). In January 1918, by order of Narkompros the theatres of Moscow were placed under the authority of the art and enlightenment division of the Moscow Soviet. At the same time, a theatre section (TEO) was tasked with running the performing arts as a branch of the government with uniform regulations.

Almost immediately, conflicts arose concerning the appropriate path for the Soviet arts to take. Left-wing radicals, working through an organization called Proletarian Culture (Proletkult), urged the new state to reject the historical legacy of world culture which, they declared, was elitist. The party leaders, however, were conservative in their tastes and held fast to the traditional touchstones of the pre-Revolutionary intelligentsia. Throughout this period, the central figure was the first Commissar for People's Enlightenment Anatoly Vasilievich Lunacharsky (1875-1933), an old-style intellectual and committed Bolshevik. Lunacharsky saw his task as reconciling the aims of the Revolution with the needs of the artistic community, and, ideally, merging the two. He proved to be the MAT's best friend in the first decade after the Revolution, protecting it from forces eager to liquidate it as an irrelevant vestige of a bourgeois ethos.

A tsarist under the tsars, the apolitical KS eagerly offered his artistic ideals to the service of the Revolution, misjudging its objectives. He posited a Pantheon of Russian Art. Its failure to come into being, along with the Studios striving for independence, put

Figure 56 Stanislavsky 1916–17

through all of Moscow to the Polish church.[2] There was a whole concert, because singers from the Bolshoy Theatre wanted to take part in the funeral and sang a whole series of concert liturgical pieces. They bore him back by hand the whole way through Moscow and buried him in the Russian cemetery, where Chekhov lies, next to Savitskaya, Sapunov and Artyom. On the fortieth day we organized a civil memorial at the studio. Many people wanted to read out remembrances of Suler and sing his favourite works of music. [...]

K. Alekseev (Stanislavsky)

A daily journal of MAT performances was kept, which recorded all the shortcomings due to the unsettled state of society and the ongoing war. KS was one of several directors who made plaintive entries over the course of the next few years.

Performance Diary, 27 January 1917. *Woe from Wit*, 139th performance.

During the first act, after we had begun, the Italian [delegates] arrived; in the flies, stage left – the firemen were making noise as if they were at home and stamping around as loudly as they could. [...]

In the last act only women came on stage with Famusov. Where did the men get to? Please let me know who was not there and for what reason.

And there were actually European guests in the theatre.

K. Stanislavsky

To **Nikolay Rumyantsev. Performance Diary**, *Blue Bird* Matinee. 12 February 1917.

Today I showed up unexpectedly to review *The Blue Bird*. After 'The Azure Kingdom' I crossed the courtyard to the stage. All the outer gates were open, and they were moving scenery, as if the show were over; they didn't even let those participating leave the stage. All this is being done so that they can run home all the faster after the show.

On stage and, finally, under the stage and everywhere backstage there are drafts, etc., blowing through. I ran on to the stage – in the centre stands Iv. Iv.[3] busy hanging a set, which, carelessly dragging on the ground, they threw out. When I walked over to them with a remark – they got embarrassed and immediately ordered the doors to be closed. I go to Uralsky[4] and protest. He tells me that he was on stage, then that he was in the corridor, then that he could not close the door (that's why he hadn't gone on stage – but into the vestibule). He is in charge of the show and does not know what is going on on stage. Then he says that there is an intermission now. But – he didn't say what matters – that he admits his mistake. I insist that this case be investigated in the most thorough manner and I request that I be told the results of the inquiry. I insist that the culprits be punished in due form. If this case goes by without consequence, then I will be compelled to take certain measures to safeguard, at the very least, my own productions from such assistant directors, who do not wish to follow the rules of the theatre and my requirements.

I called for someone from the administration – no one showed up. Can productions be going on and no one from the administration be on the spot?

S. A. Trushnikov was in the box-office, and his overcoat was not in its place, therefore everyone in the theatre had thought he had left. Obviously, they do not understand how important is the constant presence of an administrator on day duty. He ought to be, all of them ought to be somewhere where they can be contacted. If something happens – someone faints, an accident, the electricity goes out – he must reassure the spectators, re-establish order, call a doctor. If someone comes – he must greet him.

K. Stanislavsky

The actor who plays Time[5] is making no progress. It is not eternity, it is not abstract, it is not mysterious – alas, and it is a commonplace philistine. And what's more, you simply can't understand passages of what the performer is saying and trying to express, although the words are audible. Time should be impassive, but not indifferent. He has to rethink the kernel throughout, from the very root of the through action.

I watched all of the last scene. A pleasant, and in places a very pleasant impression.

For S. V. Khalyutina (I only saw that act) the through action – 'the pursuit of happiness' – is more apparent than it was before, and wherever she fully achieves it, the role goes clearly beautifully in its essence.

The awakening is very good technically, but there is still not enough through action in it. No desire to ply the mother as soon as possible with questions and stories, share the through action with her. The meeting with Berlengo is not *significant* enough. This is the upshot, the apotheosis of the whole play. The awareness of where the Blue Bird is has improved, but still not enough. But the role is getting smoother, straighter – and gimmicks for the sake of gimmicks no longer distract from the main thing. And I think... How talented [Khalyutina] is... ah, if only...!

I liked S. V. Giatsintova[6] very much. She avoided the mistake of the earlier performers – simpering, playing childishness, – and if it doesn't produce real childlikeness, which cannot be counterfeited, she understands it well and tastefully. The performance is alive, warm, in essence. And what I say relates in some degree to S. V. Khalyutina as well.

The finale, the play's denouement is a bit more imposing. There is a certain gimmickry for the sake of gimmickry.

I liked Miss Tokarskaya.[7] There is simplicity, and she plays the essence. Only, once she has taken the bird, she doesn't have to play excitement, but simply behave energetically, i.e., thank whoever needs to be thanked, take the bird nicely in hand and go as quickly as possible to care for the patient. That involves rapidity and restrained acting, but not direct action.

Morozov [as the father] is not progressing in the role. He is not a father, but a little boy, he is not a woodcutter. Everything he does is not artistic, but craftsmanship. And something has to be done about his long dangling arms. Give some thought to being a forester, what a hard-working, business-like man he is.

Present an image, and do not simply glue on a goatee – Berendey;[8] as if craftsmanship could contrive a living artistic life.

K. Stanislavsky

February saw two Revolutions: one took place in the streets and overturned the monarchy, installing a Provisional Government. The other occurred at the MAT when ND, after 150 rehearsals of Stepanchikovo, took over as director and immediately disagreed with KS about his interpretation of Rostanev. The much-needed production, cast with MAT veterans, had been delayed by KS's disquisitions on Good and Evil during the preparations.

Notebook, 13-20 March 1917.

I may not be able to beget Rostanev himself on Dostoevsky, but our son in common will be reminiscent in many ways of both mother and father. Nemirovich, like all literary men, demands that father and mother give birth to a second father or a second mother, point for point. But why give birth to them, when they already exist. All I can provide is Rostanev-Stanislavsky or, in the worst case, Stanislavsky-Rostanev. But let the literary critics come up with a Rostanev. He will be just as dead as their critical essays. It may not be right, but it will definitely be alive. That is better than the thing itself, dead.

To **his son Igor**. 15 March 1917, Moscow.
My dear, beloved Igorechek!

[…] I cannot provide much information on the political front. It looks as if everything is getting back to normal; it looks as if everyone is starting to get fed up with the Bolsheviks and the soldiers with the workers. It looks as if discipline in the Moscow troops is restored. There is no doubt that the soldiers salute with special smartness. One concern is whether the Germans will invade or not. These last few days there has been a lot of frantic talk about the discontents and even the quasi-revolutionary uprisings in Germany. […] I am rehearsing with might and main and hope to open the play the sixth week […]

Papa

After the dress rehearsal on 28 March 1917, KS broke down on stage and was unable to carry on. ND relieved him of the role of Rostanev, which was bestowed on Massalitinov. KS's relevant chapter in My Life in Art *calls this 'my tragedy'. It deeply shook his self-confidence as an actor, and he refrained from ever taking on new roles.*

Performance Diary, 8 April 1917. Matinee: *No Fool Like a Wise Fool.*

Serious attention has to be paid to the *walking and noise* offstage during the action. At some moments it becomes so dreadful that if the audience were to hear it, a panic might break out. It is hard for actors getting ready to make an entrance even to concentrate. The assistants and stage managers do what they can, but it is not enough, the backstage workers have got to understand the importance of quiet.

K. Stanislavsky

To **Vera Kotlyarevskaya.** 23 May 1917, Moscow

Dear Vera Vasilievna!

[…] I heartily sympathize with you. I feel that your nerves must be in tatters. Well, that's only natural. You were in the very thick of the Revolution [in Petrograd] and are sitting in it at the present time. Even now I have not forgotten what I went through in 1905. Without wishing to play down the significance and dreadfulness of the times, without wishing to belittle your concerns, I will say that personally I cherish high hopes. The rebirth of peoples cannot be consummated without upheavals. Of course, you are observing events close up, and we only at a distance, and therefore you have the better view. But… the atmosphere in which you live is making you morbidly sensitive. Things are calmer here with us. And so it is good that you are leaving Petrograd. Come here, catch your breath, and then you will have a better idea of how to figure out what is going on and appraise events.

There's nothing for it, financially speaking we shall have to tighten our belts for the time being. But that will not be for long. I too have been swept into the street and will be again before this is over. I am looking for new lodgings, and not just because they've evicted us from this one, but also because it is now beyond our means. I kiss your hand and shake your husband's. Hold tight. Everything will work out.

Devotedly yours K. Alekseev

Performance diary, 31 May 1917. *The Cherry Orchard.* [Last performance of the season.]

The lighting in Act I is beneath criticism. The backcloth remains almost entirely in the dark, when it is v. bright in the room. The splendour of early morning in the country and its poetry are not felt by the electrician. It was a crude, workmanlike, operatic play of light.

K. Stanislavsky

To **Vera Kotlyarevskaya**. 19 August 1917, Moscow.

Dear Vera Vasilievna!

I have only just returned to Moscow, after a difficult journey from Ufa with three invalids (Igor, my wife, who gashed her leg in a fall, and myself -- with my stomach and a temperature of 38.3). […]

I heartily sympathize with you, but I know that you are bold and steadfast and will endure the trials sent to all of us for our great sins. All this is dreadful and inevitable. Revolution is revolution. A mortal illness. It cannot flash by like an amazing dream. The horrors and beastliness are inevitable. Our time is coming. We must as quickly and energetically as possible cultivate an *aesthetic* feeling. That is my sole creed. That is the only thing that preserves the smallest particle of God. The war and the Revolution have got to be *aesthetic*. Then it will be possible to live. We must perform – to sow beauty and poetry hither and yon and have faith in their power. Even dissonance can be moderated by good music. […]

Yours K. Alekseev

In late August KS embarked on a restaging of The Seagull *with Olga Knipper recreating her original role as Arkadina and Mikhail Chekhov as her son. His belief was now that the play was about art, not love affairs, and his submergence in it was a kind of refuge from present hardships.*

To Nemirovich-Danchenko. 15 September 1917, Moscow.
Dear Vladimir Ivanovich!

I do not know what prompted your letter! I have initiated nothing and said nothing special to anyone, particularly since I see no one. I am going through a very difficult time; I feel depressed and am unendurably bored. But I am contending with what is going on inside me, silently.

As to vanity and, in particular, *The Village of Stepanchikovo*, the problem is that I am very glad not to be acting, and now all I dream of is: to forget everything connected with that ill-starred production.

Nor do I think about future roles, because I can do no more, at least, at the Art Theatre. In that regard, after the complete collapse of my plan, my energy has completely bottomed out. Maybe, in another sphere and in another place I might be reborn. I am talking, of course, not about other theatres, but -- about the Studios. *Othello –free!.. [In English in the original, KS's paraphrase of 'Othello's occupation's gone'.]*

Yours, K. Alekseev

The opening night of Stepanchikovo *on 26 September, which initiated the twelfth season, was the first time in the history of the MAT that KS was neither on stage nor in the audience, although he had come backstage before the performance to give the youngest performers gifts. Nor were the names of the directors KS and ND on the programme. It ran for sixty-five performances and would be the last premiere at the MAT for almost three years.*

KS played Famusov on 25 October (7 November n.s.) 1917, officially the first day of the October Revolution. Performances were called off the following day. The Cherry Orchard was performed at the Theatre of the Soviet of Workers Deputies, an audience KS praised as attentive. KS was elected to the team of delegates charged with dealing with the crisis in theatrical organization: should the theatres remain closed or not? He himself believed that the MAT should 'present performances for the broadest circles of the democratic public without regard to political coups'.

The Maly Theatre suffered not only from shots from street fighting but also vandalism and hooliganism by the Red Guards who occupied its building.

To Aleksandr Yuzhin.[9] 8 November 1917, Moscow.
Dear Aleksandr Ivanovich!

Just last night I learned from O. V. Gzovskaya the horrible details of the sacrilege committed on the Maly Theatre.

I feel grief and rage. It is as if they had raped my mother, as if they had insulted the memory of Mikhail Semyonovich [Shchepkin]. I would like to go to you and with my own hands cleanse the dear theatre of the foulness churned up by the unleashed insanity. I would like to say many warm words to you now. But, happily, unleashed insanity cannot insult art and its glorious representatives.

All civilized Russia is with you. In misfortune it loves and values you more than in good fortune.

May God grant that we shall soon forget this dreadful nightmare so that with redoubled energy we can carry on with distinction the work begun this season. [. . .]

I remain devoted and grateful to the Maly Theatre.

Alekseev-Stanislavsky

In solidarity with the Maly, the MAT did not resume performances until 21 November, during which period the state theatres were dark. Olga Gzovskaya requested the loan of Sofiya's costume for Woe from Wit, *because the Bolsheviks had stolen all the Maly's wardrobe.*

Performances were resumed, following KS's belief that art was the sine qua non *of culture. Bersenev and Podgorny, on ND's initiative, had taken on part of organizing the work and reconciling the internal conflicts of the day-to-day operations.*

To **Ivan Bersenev and Nikolay Podgorny**. After 10 November 1917, Moscow.
Dear Ivan Nikolaevich and Nikolay Afanasievich!

Just now Kachalov told me that today workers built the new stage for you, which probably insulted you and made you lose interest in the good, kind and laborious act of assistance, which you had taken on.

Knowing well this feeling of isolation and dissatisfaction in a great personal experiment, I consider it my duty to address you at precisely this moment, to assure you that you are not alone and your feeling of offence is painfully reflected in us. Indeed they are insulting and humiliating not you personally, but the whole profession.

But... we have to be prudent! We cannot let ourselves be insulted by the savagery of people who have not yet received the blessings of culture. If we serve enlightenment, we must be very wise at this precise moment, when the whole nation is becoming bestial and savage. Try to respond to insults which cannot sully you with sympathy and tolerance and do not turn them to scorn. Even try to keep from being upset, because your being upset only rejoices the savages.

Patience, restraint and calm reasonable words – those are the only weapons which we can use in the fight.

Courtesy in response to boorish bullying.

And no show of irritation. That is the best punishment for those who want to bully us and frighten us.

Accept from me and my family sentiments of sincere affection and gratitude for what you are doing, and believe that nothing will escape our attention and that we feel and understand all that you are going through: charitable impulses, and agitation, and fatigue, and effort, and responsibility, and risk, and bitter offence,

370

and isolation, and ingratitude, and disappointment, and the coldness of human souls... For all this you will be rewarded, but not because you expect it, but quite the contrary: not all at once, but gradually.

Only don't let your energy flag and your initiative expire.

Be courageous and patient and believe in your friends.

Affectionately and gratefully K. Stanislavsky

On 17 November the MAT company was convened to figure out how the theatre might serve the Moscow Soviet. KS was determined to welcome the Bolsheviks and bring 'the masses to art'.

Performance diary, 26 November [1917]. Evening. *Cherry Orchard*.

O. L. Knipper asks that a special person be assigned to the dog, to keep an eye on it, as was done with the hired dogs. At the moment the dog is making her life a misery and preventing her from acting. It is to be tied up and looked after all evening long. It is a nuisance. Today, just before the Act I entrance, the dog disappeared. There was a hue and cry, which spoiled the mood.

[...] The flute playing is dreadful. A symphony by some German composer on Russian life, the work of Mr Katzenellenbogen.

In Aleksandrov's room there is an insidious spring in the sofa. When you get up it plays a whole chord. All these little noises, squeaks, trampling create an atmosphere of backstage life that prevents one from acting and observing in peace.

K. Stanislavsky, A. Sanin

It is crucial to focus the attention of everyone taking part in *The Cherry Orchard* (and maybe other plays!?). Everyone has acted himself well into the play and the roles. It's all nice and cosy, and they're beginning to live for themselves, their personal lives. Much of this is valuable and good. But, living for themselves, they forget about the play, about Chekhov, his ideas and feelings, which they are to convey to others, they have forgotten about the through action and don't keep to the path set down. Here's the result: while one performer is carrying on an important scene, speaking an important thought, -- another overwrought performer very nicely and realistically overdoes the details, trivia, a newly interpolated *mise-en-scène* -- one kills the other. The result is a general vivacity, authentic, lifelike, but as in life a hodgepodge, and not the clearly and simply manifested life of the spirit, purified of the extraneous, as it ought to be in art. One must avoid overstatement, one must remember the chief landmarks in the play and the through action.

K. Stanislavsky

In December the Soviet of Workers' Deputies had arranged free performances for workers and the military. The MAT's shareholders protested.

The Alekseev cable factory was nationalized and renamed for Timofey Baskakov, a young cord-maker who had stormed the Kremlin in October.

Performance diary, 9 December 1917. *The Cherry Orchard.*

In the space under the stage there is red cloth all over the place. It is covered with dust, people walk on it. But nowadays four and a half yards of cloth cost 200,000 rub. Wasteful. [...]

The sound of chopping down the orchard is dreadful. It simply drives one to distraction that there is no real artistry in having to *repeat* something that has *already been devised* and put into operation. [...]

In the first act – the trees – the cherry branches were worn to shreds. They are dreadful, they have stopped being white and have turned grey. They have become shabby and devoid of all poetry. In general we always had a *Cherry Orchard* without a cherry orchard. The kind of cherry orchard we have now *ought to be* chopped down. Well, the hell with it. Fix the trees and add branches with fresh green leaves.

K. S.

Twelfth Night at the First Studio had got off to a rocky start by stressing the lyrical and elegiac moments, but KS turned it into a romp. Although he discounted it as a patchwork of old bits and pieces, it was well received.

The company meeting on 31 December discussed KS's proposal to divorce the studios from the theatre, to create a Third Studio, and to stage all the MAT's productions on a workshop basis in the studios, with only the best results presented on the main stage. ND protested against this and the practice of protracted experimentation; some of the old-timers referred to KS as a 'destructive and marauding Bolshevik'.

Performance Diary, 6 January 1918. *Three Sisters.*

Take note of the piano. Repair the legs. A white board has been put on it. It isn't painted. *I simply do not understand such negligence.* What does it cost to paint it; they make it and leave it unfinished . A grand piano with a pinewood insert looks like an old barrel or an old kitchen table. And this in the home of the three sisters, who personify culture.

Every beginning and end of an act at the Art Theatre is going for naught. Not one of the stagehands, dressers and maids and watchmen cares to pay any heed to what is going on on stage. They run around, stamp their feet, in defiance of the quiet demanded by the play. After Act 2 (not a bit of quiet) I myself had to stop a wardrobe mistress and some stagehand boys. And I have to admit that the actors themselves set the example, and they have no care for the stage.

K. Alekseev

Sergey Lvovich Bertonson (1885-1962), formerly on the staff of the Imperial theatres, in late 1917 had been running the procurement sector of the state theatres for the Provisional Government. On 27 December he wrote to KS about his desire to work at the MAT in any administrative position. He was accepted, and remained at the MAT from late 1918 as secretary to the administration and head of the troupe. He was to accompany the Kachalov group to southern Russia, then the parent company and the

Musical Theatre on the American tours. Efficient, studious and tactful, he was looked down by the actors as a bureaucrat, and from 1928 he lived in the US.

To **Sergey Bertonson**. 7 January 1918, Moscow.

Dear Sergey Lvovich!

[...] A certain happy coincidence has occurred, which promises success. The fact is that yesterday there was a meeting, which discussed the question of the reorganization of our concern in relation to the new oppressive and abnormal living conditions. At this meeting we talked about how we have no business-like, knowledgeable administrator, who understands both the concern itself and its artistic requirements. Today – your letter! I am superstitious and think God sent you to us. Really delighted that you had the bright idea of writing to me. Thank you for your frank and friendly appeal. [...]

Figure 57 Sergey Bertonson

The only problem is that Nemirovich is a dreadfully slow man. He drags out every piece of business. I will hustle him, but keep this in mind. [...]

K. Alekseev

To **Yelena Malinovskaya**.[10] 11/24 March 1918, Moscow.
Deeply esteemed Yelena Konstantinovna!

[...] The two spare rooms of my apartment which might be requisitioned as required for partitioning happen to be a department of the Art Theatre, in which rehearsals continually take place. These rooms are needed especially now during my ongoing illness. Therefore, if you are willing to believe that I have not sought personal protection, -- I once again thank you for your good relations to the theatre, and in particular to me, and I profit by the occasion to testify to my complete respect.

K. Stanislavsky

Meanwhile, KS was plunged into rehearsals of Blok's Rose and Cross. *ND had commenced staging this poetic drama of the Middle Ages with most of the older actors and Dobuzhinsky as the designer. KS, interested in simplifying the concept, brought in Ivan Gremislavsky to design a more emblematic production, and experimented extensively with younger actors on the System. The production never seemed to make progress.*

On 22 May KS proposed at a meeting of the MAT Fellowship that a Pantheon of Russian Art be created (in 1917 Podgorny had opened The Actor's Studio *which was to be part of the Pantheon). The founders of the MAT were to unite with the studios with a single creative method. Then its present productions of* Autumn Violins *and* In the Clutches of Life *would seem banal and obsolete. He was voted down, however. A later meeting requested him to take on the role of 'dictator' in reorganizing the MAT.*

To the **General Assembly of the MAT Fellowship.** Before 27 May 1918.

As I have already written, it is a question of saving Russian art – this is a civic duty, which no one has the right to refuse. Therefore if the assembly finds that only my appointment as dictator can lead the theatre out of a dead end, let it order me to be this dictator. I do not believe I have the right to refuse, but I alert you that although I will take on myself any administrative and economic matters, I will limit my role only to carrying out the general artistic plan, already familiar from my past report. I cannot carry out anything contrary to my views. [...]

In May 1918 Alla Tarasova, who had rehearsed Nina in the renovated Seagull, *took a leave of absence from famine-ridden Moscow to recover in the well-provisioned Ukraine. As a result, the following month the production was abandoned.*

Vsevolod Andreevich Chagovets (1887-1950), theatre critic and author of many works on the MAT, had invited the troupe to tour to war-torn Kiev. This never occurred, but KS's reply evidently refers to the proclamation in spring 1918 of a Ukrainian Region independent of the government.

374

To **Vsevolod Chagovets**. 25 June 1918, Moscow.
Dear, good Vsevolod Andreevich!

Forgive the bad writing, I am lying in bed. I have nephritis. That is one of the many reasons that prevent our coming to you. Other reasons – fatigue, the difficulty in travelling, the impossibility of transporting 50 carloads of baggage, the peril of losing all this theatrical property on the road, which, under present conditions, it would be impossible to replace. Finally –the total impossibility of covering expenses. What sort of profits would be required to pay for the trip? Sitting here in Moscow and bailing out the theatre, two studios and various incidental performances at 9-13 thousand rubles for 250 performances, we only cover the budget, which is reaching fantastic proportions. In any case, in a few days I will send a letter to the board, but I think nothing will come of this trip. How much we would like to see all of you, our friends in Kiev, and Kiev itself, ever since they took our dear blood brothers from us. We do not believe that they have turned their backs on us. God willing, this is only a temporary derangement, and the family will be reunited once more. It is difficult to suffer what is going on around us, although I must admit that the relationship to us actors is a good one and the new spectator loves us. But our nerves are in such a state that we can barely wait for the end of the season so we can take a breather. Fatigue is only one of the chief reasons that prevent us from moving from place. […]

Cordially devoted K. Alekseev-Stanislavsky

To **Vasily Luzhsky**. August 1918, Moscow.
Dear Vasily Vasilevich!

I think that after everything that's happened we cannot unilaterally settle the question of the performance [at the premises of the Theatre of the Soviet of Workers' Deputies]. What will the troupe say? What will Malinovskaya say? What will the Maly Theatre say? This evening the committee on artistic affairs will meet. Yuzhin should be there. Send a little note – if you don't forget (the meeting is in the Fellowship's room). On Sunday there will be a general assembly of actors. I don't think we can make a decision until after that. Or have a referendum.

For my part I would very much like to do a reading. But the first appearance has to be good. *The first impression* is very important. Somehow I wouldn't want to take part *off the cuff*. It is not suitable to recite individual scenes. Only a whole act is feasible and, to my mind, a *first act*, because something plucked from the middle will have no effect and will merely be boring. Nothing whatever should be recited from *Uncle Vanya* – an old man and an old woman, without makeup, reciting a declaration of love. What can a soldier make of that?

To my mind, the best of all would be to recite individual scenes from Chekhov and easy-to-understand, complete poems. But you have to show Chekhov whole. I repeat, a first *resounding* success is very important. We need to prepare a performance in all haste, but for a recital limit ourselves to individual excerpts.

Yours K. Alekseev

The TEO was created under Narkompros in September to run the theatrical activity in the country on a wide governmental scale. Mariya Andreeva, as a long-time Bolshevik sympathizer, was appointed Commissar for Theatres and Spectacles in Petrograd and co-founded the Bolshoy Dramatic Theatre where she acted 1919-21.

On 30 September KS saw an evening of studio work at the Hebrew-language company Habima, which he recommended to Vakhtangov.

The twentieth anniversary of the MAT was marked chiefly by the presentation of loaves of white bread to KS and ND.

The Bureau of Commissars of Safes had been created directly after the Revolution to help with the nationalization of banks. The Moscow Soviet of Workers' Deputies on 18 April 1918 allowed 'actresses and actors, actually in need, in accord with a certificate supplied by the artistic-educational section, to withdraw from safes and loan offices anniversary and nameday presents without the imposition of any sort of tax'.

To **Yelena Malinovskaya**. Tuesday, 15 October 1918, Moscow.
Deeply esteemed Yelena Konstantinovna!

I hasten to thank you for your new help and concern for us actors: for sending an affidavit to the Bureau of Safes. [...]

How is our complex and unwieldy art to react to the rapidly speeding great events? The greater they are, the greater the need for time to rework and reflect them in aesthetic works of stage art.

Meanwhile we have one thing left to do: give good performances of good plays. And the greater the events, the better must be the performance, the more time it demands for its preparation. [...]

With deep respect and gratitude
K. Stanislavsky (Alekseev)

To **Nemirovich-Danchenko**. *After 15 October 1918, Moscow.*
Dear Vladimir Ivanovich!

Forgive me for bothering you with family matters, but, I think it has some connection to the theatre.

And here is how. The fact is that my sister Anna Sergeevna and her family are starving. She is quite ill, almost bedridden. She has on her hands a son ill with tuberculosis, a daughter who is needed at home, and a little boy. Of the other children: one has been called up, the others are working for pennies. And as a result – starvation and cold. Nor is this all. My support so far can be expressed by very little help, because I will not stoop to hackwork except in the greatest extremity.

My sister can be saved by her safety deposit box, which they want to confiscate. There has to be testimony that she is now working for the theatre.

My request is that she be listed as an actress of the MAT. Of course, this is pro forma, and she will receive no salary, nor even appear in the theatre. Now the question is: why, one might wonder should the theatre do me and her such a favour?

1) In my time, when the theatre was financially in need, she showed it her own kind of favour, playing a few roles free of charge [under the name Aleeva 1899-1903]. Now the theatre can pay her back favour for favour.

2) If the theatre does not come to her aid, then the whole family will land on my shoulders, because my elder brother is unemployed, and my sisters similarly eke out a miserable existence.

Compelled to save my nearest and dearest, I will have even more strongly to devote myself to hackwork, that is, withdraw even farther from art and the theatre, just at the time when I am becoming essential to it.

It would be good to settle this question at the emergency meeting, because time won't stand still. Once the safety deposit box is confiscated, there will be no way to recover it for her. [... *Rest of letter torn off.*]

The affidavit was provided.

Performance diary, 29 October 1918. *Woe from Wit.*

In Sushkevich's place Svarozhich[11] played without a rehearsal. Last or next to last time Pavlov played without a rehearsal. . .

I understand the need for understudies, but. . . *Woe from Wit*!!! Without a rehearsal!! In what backwater is the theatre located! After this how can one ask respect and genuine creativity of others? Why shouldn't the performers be given advance notice? We should find one little minute, amid our affairs. After all, I have a scene with him and an important one.

The basin in our washhand-stand looked unscrubbed since the last performance of *Fyodor*, the faucet is clogged, rusty -- and dirty water stands in the basin!! Quite the picture of gradual ruin and decay.

K. Stanislavsky

On 4 December Uncle Vanya, was shown on that stage of the Polytechnical Museum as a public dress rehearsal, so that the actors could be paid. KS noted 'First paid hackwork (!!!?) 300 rubles'. He claimed he had to support thirty unemployed starving persons and hence had to go on acting. Tokarskaya and Muratova were playing Marina and Voynitskaya. Lilina was supposed to play Sonya. For mobile performances of Vanya, KS devised a special light-weight 'soft set', with draperies made of cloth saved from the tenth-anniversary celebration.

KS categorically opposed naming the group of MAT studios the People's Art Theatre. On 15 December Lenin saw KS as Krutitsky and roared with laughter, calling him a real artist. The following March he spoke his appreciation of him as Astrov

To **Vasily Luzhsky**. Before 18 December 1918, Moscow.
Dear Vasily Vasilevich!

You know that I *will under no circumstances* take part in a performance of a hackwork nature. Now more than ever, because hackwork is becoming our chief activity.

Therefore I consider that the performance on 21 December is risky and in this regard I have to talk things over with [the organizer R. A.] Gurvich. The fact is that inserting Tokarskaya without a rehearsal is *completely impossible*. She requires much work in order to achieve merely a decent interpretation. I thought of going through the Tokarskaya and Muratova scene on 18 December at 2 o'clock (theatre) after the meeting about the repertoire. It cannot take long, since there is nothing for us to perform.

If necessary, I am ready to go over *Fyodor* in the evenings or rehearse after *Fyodor* in the evening. On 20 December we have to schedule a rehearsal, but what sort of rehearsal it will be I don't know.

The fact is that Marusya from morning on has to stay with the safety deposit boxes. Otherwise: everything locked up in them will be lost and confiscated. She will probably stay there until 3 o'clock.

But at 3 you can't be there.

I'm ready as a last resort to rehearse even on Thursday, after *Ivanov* or on the morning of 19 December on an *Ivanov* day. However I'm afraid that I won't be up to it, because an enormous amount of work has been piled up on me for the performance of *Uncle Vanya*.

It is for all our sakes that the performance on the 24th be not only good, but stupendous. Among other things, everyone is talking against it.

Therefore, I plead with you to reserve the following days (we need two of them).
18 Wednesday, 2 o'clock (theatre) *Uncle Vanya*.
In the evening *Tsar Fyodor*.
19 Thursday – 1 o'clock (at my house).
Evening after *Ivanov*.
20 Friday, 1 o'clock p.m. – theatre.
Evening -- during *Clutches*.
21 Saturday, 1 o'clock –my house.
We need two of them:
1 – only scenes.
1 – talk through the whole play.

Yours K. Alekseev

Performance diary, 16 January 1919. Matinee: *No Fool Like a Wise Fool*.

[...] I have read the preceding report about how things had got so bad that no one was there at the start of a scene. In earlier times, when Baranov once failed to show up, he was dismissed from the troupe in no time, although he was a v. important figure in the troupe. Now people are not only not dismissed, but they even earn a reputation for it.

I shout for help.

I insist, demand, request an immediate investigation of what happened – exemplary punishment of those who are *criminally* guilty in regard to the theatre and art. Otherwise I will consider the theatre quite impotent, over and done with.

On 11 January the *assistant director* Pons[12] *himself* did not show up. And he is a beginning young director just entering the concern. What is this? Where are we heading? And this sort of thing goes on with just a single formal notification – he cannot be dismissed without the strictest punishment. Pons himself should *plead* that he be chastised as an example to others. Or…he will lose any right in future to mark latecomers in this book and call others to account for this.

In his place and in the theatre's place I would punish Pons in the harshest way, to teach others not to do it.

K. Stanislavsky […]

In February 1919 the question arose of touring through Russia and to Petrograd. KS felt that a new reformed frame of mind was needed first. He wanted to resuscitate the spirit of Pushkino with a second generation of youngsters. By March worsening conditions led the troupe to discuss touring to the Ukraine, along the Volga, the Caucasus, even Siberia. KS was against it, some of the leading actors for it; ND temporized.

To **Lyubov Gurevich**. Before 3 May 1919, Moscow.
Dear, sincerely beloved Lyubov Yakovlevna!

What a very, very long time since I last wrote to you! I couldn't, I wasn't in the writing mood. Too much has happened in last few years!.. My life has changed completely. I have become a proletarian and still want for nothing since I'm moonlighting (that means acting on the side) -- almost every day when I'm free from the theatre.

Meanwhile I have not fallen so low as to give up making art. Therefore I am acting only in whatever can be well staged outside the theatre. I'm ashamed to talk about it. Our old friend *Uncle Vanya* lends a hand. We are playing him in the Polytechnic Museum in a new style, without a curtain, but with sets and costumes. The resulting performance is highly original. Incomparably more intimate than in the theatre. Of course, it is no longer appropriate for us to play young people. We know, recognize and are tormented by this compromise. But still this is better than vulgar recitals and platform readings, for which they are paying insane money. Sometimes we play *Uncle Vanya* at the First Studio too. That's very pleasant as well… Any day now I'll be acting *The Mistress of the Inn* in what used to be the former Great Hall of the Assembly of the Nobility.[13]

In addition, to increase my income I'm having to set up an opera studio for the Bolshoy State Theatre.[14] The fact is that the Bolshevik gentlemen are forcing us to take on the whole Bolshoy Theatre and they say this about it: the Bolshoy Theatre is a corpse and the Art Theatre is half-dead as well, so let's join them together. Our corpse is breathing great life into the corpse of the Bolshoy Theatre. Everyone has revived to a great extent. Luzhsky and Nemirovich are staging [Rimsky-Korsakov's] *The Snow Maiden* there, I have refused point-blank to work right away on a production and have only agreed to the studio. The Bolsheviks were forced to give in and offered millions to the studio. It's the same way that people ensnare naive girls, once they have been lured and confined in brothels. The first concern is to get them even more into debt. But I didn't take this bait, because I was afraid that this studio would instantly get overrun with swindlers, so many of whom have attached themselves to theatres nowadays. One fails to

379

notice how a good half of these allocated millions seeps away. Therefore I proposed the following conditions. The studio will pay for itself — by the performers themselves. And now on 4 April at the former Assembly of Nobility we shall be giving a concert. All the singers of the Bolshoy Theatre are singing, and we (that is, Gzovskaya and I – teachers at the studio) will play a scene from *Mistress of the Inn*, which hasn't been performed for several years.

My wife is also in a tight spot. First of all, the whole problem of provisioning is up to her. Thanks to her we eat reasonably well. This is enormously important for the children, since Igor has tuberculosis and Kira is predisposed to it. Everything we earn we spend on food. We refuse ourselves everything else. We've been ground down. Our clothes are worn out. Our living quarters have been reduced. The result was a successful arrangement whereby all our property (the library above all) has so far remained intact. The vestibule, dining-room and sitting-room are assigned to the Studio (the First Studio, and the Opera Studio of the Bolshoy State Theatre); one room is rented out and we huddle together in the rest...

I've lingered over this letter for a few weeks, finding no time (even in the intermissions of the performances) to finish it... Of course, one can find half an hour, but you don't find yourself in a mood suitable for a letter.

Since I began the letter, a lot has changed. We travel nowhere, because it is impossible to travel anywhere now. Who can guarantee that all the sets and costumes won't be taken from us on the road. In what form [*unfinished*]

And we ourselves, what if we returned during raging typhus? Especially along the railway lines.

Our artistic life is bubbling over, though we are not actually opening anything new. The fault lies not with the performers but with the stagehands. There is nothing to be done with them. The boorishness and thievery has been such that our descendants will not believe it if I were to write it down. We stand firm on [*unfinished*]

Today the last convoy of studio folks is being dispatched [on tour to Petrograd] and I decided to send off what I have already written and left unfinished. I hope that I will find a chance to write because I would like to.

I know that my silence will not disturb you – and you know that I love you whatever the circumstances and am constantly devoted to you. I embrace you.

Yours K. Alekseev [...]

The armistice with Germany had humiliating results: without an army, the Bolsheviks could not prevent the Central Powers from penetrating Russia. The Ukraine and the Baltic nations sought independence from the former Empire. Resistance against the Bolsheviks increased from the East and the South. 1919 was decisive, as the Whites launched a concerted attack. The White advance led the Reds to tighten controls, institute ruthless terrorism and look for enemies within. Many of the intelligentsia hastened to leave the country. Those who remained were not fully trusted, and mass arrests were made of intellectuals and cultural figures. The hard-line of the Cheka, the security arm, often prevailed over Lunacharsky's more tolerant policies.

On 1 June a group of actors, Kachalov and Knipper among them, went on a three-week tour to the cities of the Ukraine. When they were caught in Kharkov by General Denikin's White Army and cut off from Moscow, the actor Ivan Bersenev led them through southern Russia and the Caucasus and eventually abroad.

On 6 August ND informed the theatre that the Kachalov group could not return to the theatre any time soon. The council resolved that the theatre would have to reorganize its work and repertoire to open the season without the absent portion of the troupe. Despite the militant atheism of Marxism, the Revolution spawned numerous theatrical projects of millennial and apocalyptic character. KS was ordered to resume work on Cain, which he conceived as a mystery play performed in a Gothic cathedral (an idea Reinhardt would later develop in The Miracle). The actors were to be true believers who behaved like human beings even when playing supernatural figures. KS saw Byron's poem as a contribution to the cause with Lucifer 'a terrifying anarchist', God 'an awful conservative' and Cain 'a Bolshevik'.

He also worked on Tchaikovsky's Yevgeny Onegin at the Opera Studio. Rose and Cross was finally eliminated because of the reduction of the troupe and Kachalov's absence.

On 7 August Lunacharsky named the MAT an autonomous theatre with a subsidy. On 26 August 1919, Lenin signed the decree 'On the unification of theatrical activity' which nationalized 'all theatrical property (buildings, properties), in view of their cultural value' and centralized the whole economy of the theatre under a Central Theatrical Committee ('Tsentroteatr') answering to the Narkompros. It also instituted a censoring function by calling for an inspection of the repertoire by the authorities to make sure it was serving the socialist ideal. To protect the cultural legacy, Lunacharsky named six pre-Revolutionary theatres – the MAT, the Maly, the Bolshoy, the Alexandra, the Mikhailovsky, and the Mariinsky -- 'Academic Theatres'. They were to serve both as museums and as conveyors of the best traditions of the past. Henceforth the acronym of the Art Theatre would be MAAT (MKhAT).

Owing to the breakthrough of the White Army, on 30 August KS and Moskvin were arrested on the direct order of Feliks Dzerzhinsky, head of the Cheka or Secret Police. The only card-carrying Bolshevik in the MAT was Valentin Sergeevich Smyshlaev (1891-1936) who had joined in 1913 and began to act at the First Studio in 1915. He organized brigades at the front in 1919 and taught at the central studio of Proletkult. Smyshlaev agitated for his elders' release, but because Lunacharsky was out of town, that did not take place until 6 p.m. the same day.

Igor, exempted from military service because of his health, began working for the theatre and continued to draw a salary until 1927.

To **his son Igor**. Before 26 September 1919. Moscow.
Dear Igorek!

Congratulations on your birthday. It's a great pity that we aren't together, although even we couldn't talk for long. At the moment I am terribly busy, for I am in over my head with business: a) the theatre – I am acting and directing Cain, b) at the 2nd Studio I give lessons twice a week and direct current plays, for which I get a salary (7000), c) the same at the 1st Studio, where activities have not yet begun, d) I act as consultant to the Comic Opera[15] (that is I indirectly take part in the production of *Mme Angot*), e) the Opera Studio, f) [*illeg.*] (I still haven't begun).

And all the same this is better than moonlighting in hackwork in all sorts of theatres.

We are all very excited by *Cain*. The theatre is buying a big church organ for 20,000 r. There will be a whole oratorio with religious processions below, above [?]

I think a great deal about you, your future, as you asked me to do. It is most difficult of all to decide what to consider as a foundation – your spiritual condition or your health, that is your physical one. They are tightly bound to one another. We will have to decide once and for all what you need: south or north -- and act and prepare the future along those lines, meanwhile nothing serious can be begun during the current debacle.

Well, let's talk it over. Hugs and love to you and Kiryalya. I'm hurrying to rehearse *Cain*. Chesnokov will play the music and arrange it to be performed with the text.[16]

Your Papa

I am somewhat concerned that I cannot send you your new exemption from military service. The fact is that if it gets lost, it will be impossible to obtain a second one and you will become a deserter. I have it here, but I am afraid to send it with Mikhail.[17] The way we live now – here, in town, in wartime conditions, this document is extremely critical, to lose it would be a disaster. [...]

To **Vasily Luzhsky. Performance diary**, 15 October 1919, Moscow.
Help.

I entreat, insist, demand, shout help – to impose automatic fines *immediately*.

If the people who consider themselves actors do not understand everything that I have been ramming into them at lessons for a whole month, we have to stop any sort of lessons and replace them not with artistic but with the simplest penalties... Before, when the actors loved and protected their theatre, such fines would have been an insult, but now with this sickening hackwork attitude – a fine is unavoidable. And I *insist* on it. Unless the employees and students sort themselves out and stop this outrage.

Please give me now and every time a list of those who are late. If even now they do not heed the call, I will lose any faith.

On 30 November Twelfth Night *opened in the First Studio. KS was shocked by the impoverishment of the physical production. For similar material scarcities, he had to abandon the original concept for* Cain *of turning the whole theatre into a cathedral and look for something else. A vision of phantoms and shadows came to mind.*

In December 1919 all Russian theatres were nationalized, which meant that the MAT could not remain out of step with government policy and survive. In a letter to a meeting of theatre workers presided over by Lunacharsky, KS insisted on his belief in politics in art, so long as it is not compulsory.

Diary, February 15, 1920. [During *Uncle Vanya*, KS as Astrov had to] step before the curtain and explain to the audience the meaning of quiet for the progress of the production and the acting. The announcement met with approval. The whole show proceeded in total silence. They didn't even venture to laugh. If they did the same at every performance, within a month, I wager, you wouldn't recognize the audience. They would spruce themselves up and would not dare come into the theatre in overcoats and hats. After the second act I demanded that they expel a drunk from the auditorium. He was expelled.

On 16 February Lunacharsky named the MAT one of the special theatres to be protected by the government. This was necessary because many of the officials of the TEO, Meyerhold and Andreeva among them, regarded it as obsolete and irrelevant, if not counter-revolutionary.

To **Yelena Malinovskaya**. 31 March 1920, Moscow.
Deeply esteemed Yelena Konstantinovna!
    Tomorrow, Friday, at 12 o'clock and Sunday evening at 7 o'clock are the dress rehearsals of *Cain*. Tomorrow it is semi-rough, because many of the production elements have not been made and are unfinished. On Sunday, I hope, the rehearsals will be cleaner. I will be glad to see you at either of the rehearsals. Do not judge them harshly, because we have worked under conditions under which no one else would have agreed to work.
    See you soon.

K. Stanislavsky

Cain, opened on 4 April, on a stage draped with black velvet (for financial as well as artistic reasons); it was too static and seemed unfinished. Met with the public's apathetic and bored response, it ran only eight performances.
    On 2 June Lunacharsky had written to Lenin about KS's difficult living conditions and asked that he not be evicted from his apartment. He gave him an academic bursary because KS had had to buy his last pair of trousers at a flea market. The following month he asked Lenin to procure KS an academician's ration. Lenin found the Alekseev family a detached house with spacious rooms and a garden, appropriate for rehearsals, at 6 Leontiev Lane, although it was in no state to be moved into. A tenant on the ground floor protested in a flurry of letters that so much space was being assigned to a lot of 'has-beens'.
    Meyerhold had been the first prominent man of the theatre to leap on the Bolshevik bandwagon and was appointed head of the TEO first in Petrograd, then in Moscow. He launched the movement 'Theatrical October' to create a new proletarian theatre and founded a studio to teach 'Communist acting'.

To **Vsevolod Meyerhold**. 11 November 1920, Moscow.
    In accord with your promise and intention, I ask that the representative of the Third Studio of the MAT be given a document stating that you have no objection to the Third Studio being under the M. Art Theatre and thereby affiliated with the State Academic Theatres.

K. Stanislavsky

ND directed the nineteenth-century comic opera The Daughter of Mme Angot, *while KS worked on Cervantes interludes at the First Studio,* The Government Inspector *with Mikhail Chekhov on the main stage, and Rimsky-Korsakov's* Vera Sheloga *at the Opera Studio. He also lectured to the Hebrew troupe Habima, the Armenian Studio and other amateur groups. He often missed rehearsals or was late because he was trying to avoid eviction.*

To the **Sovnarkom RSFSR**. 14 January 1921, Moscow.

I have lived for 20 years in this building, where two and a half years ago a motor-vehicle garage was installed.

Now the Opera Studio of the State Bolshoy Theatre is located in my apartment. From the moment the motor-vehicle garage moved in, my family and I have lived in terror and under constant threats of eviction in three days' time. Most recently the threats were of such a character that they gave us no possibility of working or resting after work, or making plans for the future, or laying in the necessary stock of fuel etc.

It began a year ago when our living space was reduced in accommodation per person. After this, regular talk of my eviction began. Strangers without a by-your-leave began to come in and walk around; they trespass on the studio's rehearsal room during the work of the artists of the Bolshoy Theatre, about which in my time there was a report drawn up, they even break into my room while I am sleeping or dressing.

In spring of this year an order was received for the eviction of all the residents of the building. Efforts were undertaken through A. V. Lunacharsky, Ye. K. Malinovskaya and V. P. Menzhinskaya,[18] which were not crowned with success.

A person unknown to me spoke about my eviction with V. I. Lenin, who on his own authority changed the order.

After an explosion on Khodinka Field and a fire in the storehouse of the motor-vehicle garage again there was talk of eviction. I went to V. D. Bonch-Burevich.[19] He told me that all the residents in the building had to be evicted, so that I and my family, to use his own expression, 'could sleep in peace'.

In a week they started talking again about my eviction on the grounds of some resolution of the Supreme Agency of the Administration. Once again strangers began to intrude into my apartment and behave provocatively. Especially zealous in this regard is an ex-manager of the motor-vehicle garage. Twice people from the Cheka showed up, allegedly to effect my speedy eviction.

After one of these visits the back door was locked and entrance to the yard forbidden to anyone residing in my apartment. Thanks to the fire in June provisions and slops have been decaying over the past eight days and the stench pervades the entire apartment.

Despite illness, I was ordered to remain in Moscow, in order to inspect all the apartments to be shown to me by the motor-vehicle garage. Not one of them met the minimal requirements of the Opera Studio of the Bolshoy Theatre.

Thanks to the obligatory inspection of apartments I was detained in Moscow while on leave until 15 June. After this time thanks to the efforts of the office of the State Bolshoy Theatre – my leave was extended to the end of August. In this way, though a leave of two and a half months is due all performers, my leave was abbreviated to one month. I was deprived of the possibility of treating my chronic illness.

From August the threats, terror and demands to inspect apartments were renewed, because all the locations offered seemed unsuitable. The Bolshoy Theatre studio itself was made to inspect apartments and within a few days found a new one that met only the most minimal requirements.

The manager of the motor-vehicle garage suggested moving me in within three days. I failed to make him understand that I cannot turn over the theatre museum, which was put in my care, nor my personal papers and writings concerning art, accumulated over the course of my forty-years of activity and of value only when they are arranged in systematic order, nor, finally, my director's library, which I have cause to use hourly, especially at the beginning of the season, when the stagings of new plays for the season are developed. All these valuables require my unfailing personal involvement in their packing and removal, for which I must have time and corresponding leave from those five establishments in which I work and which were put under my authority (the MAT, Studios 1 and 2, the Dmitrovsky Theatre and the Opera Studio of the Bolshoy Theatre).

For the sake of my most speedy eviction the manager of the motor-vehicle garage took upon himself the preparation of my future apartment for me. He ordered the parquet floor of the two big rooms to be scrubbed; unfortunately, I failed to convince him that this is not enough for the move, because the apartment is filthy to the nth degree and requires not only complete redecoration, but a disinfecting, because the residents had included sick people, and the apartment is full of bedbugs and parasites. I failed to make him understand that I can live in impoverished surroundings, but I have a right to those minimal demands of cleanliness for a cultured human being. Besides, the new apartment requires lots of alterations, which have still not been carried out.

Until very recently some rooms in the new apartment were occupied by telegraphers from field headquarters. In addition, other establishments are making claims on this apartment, among them the Arts and Crafts Museum.

The orders for my eviction were not presented to me.

In the last few days with the onset of cold weather 40 square metres of firewood from the TEO were delivered to the Opera Studio. The wood was brought to the yard, but the man in charge of the motor-vehicle garage Mr Medevedev via the manager Mr Abramov ordered the wood put in the street, despite the fact that before the load of wood had been delivered we had informed them that wood was to be delivered, and no one at the time had protested this until the wood was loaded and delivered. The draymen who brought the wood insisted on unloading it immediately, threatening to leave the wood in the street. My situation as the party responsible for government property was inescapable. The situation was complicated by the fact that, as an actor, I had to hurry to the theatre for a performance just as the wood was being delivered. Luck enabled me to find a way out of the predicament. The wood was deposited in the apartment of an acquaintance.

Despite the fact that the residents who work in the motor-vehicle garage have a standard wood supply in the yard of the garage, and despite the fact that my shed lies at a great distance from the petrol storage and other inflammable matter, I am forbidden to haul even a minimal amount of wood into the yard. The Studio of the Bolshoy State Theatre and I are obliged to live in an unheated apartment. This inevitably produces a difficult situation: I cannot remain in an unheated apartment, because with the nephritis and ague from which I suffer, I am risking my life. On the other hand, I cannot move to the other apartment, because people are still living there and the apartment is not ready to be moved in and heated, and after a two-year heating shortage the apartment and its walls are damp through, and the stoves are useless and in need of repair.

In view of the fact that my forced eviction from the apartment can not only hinder but completely halt work of five organizations, I petition for the following:

1) protection from coercion and the same opportunity as other citizens to take advantage of the decree forbidding eviction after 1 November, at a time of cold and frost,

2) postponement of my removal to early spring, at which time my possessions will be fully prepared,

3) permission to keep deliveries of up to 30-40 square metres of wood in the shed of my apartment and studio in cold weather,

4) protection from constant terrorization and threats of eviction, which prevent my working in peace and making plans for the coming months.

K. Stanislavsky

Lunacharsky and Malinovskaya have made efforts in the Sovnarkom — Lunacharsky himself supported it, but to no avail. After this I was repeatedly brought every possible order for my eviction. The terror was renewed with redoubled strength. Finally I was forbidden to bring in wood, even from the street into the apartment (not just into the yard). The wood was hauled on the sly – by hand. The back door was conclusively boarded up. The servant girl had to get a written order to go to the cellar.

Every day, they have poisoned my life with comings and goings, threats, demands from the motor-vehicle garage and the Cheka. They have hounded me from this apartment, but residents have gone on living in Leontiev Lane. Finally between New Year and Christmas, when it was 18 degrees of frost, on returning home late after the show one of the men from the garage was waiting for me to hand me notice of my eviction in 5 days' time. I did not accept the notice, because I had received an order from the State Theatre Office not to accept any demands, but to send them all to Malinovskaya.

The next day men arrived from the Cheka with an order for eviction – I received them in bed before witnesses, and on my refusal to accept the mandate a man from the motor-vehicle garage provocatively declared: this means you don't recognize the Soviet government. Luckily, I had witnesses to this conversation on my side. Despite the declaration of the Office of State Theatres that it was impossible to live in the new apartment, despite the official act of the Sanitary Commission that the apartment appears to be in an unhygienic condition – on 14 January 1921 the MChK has demanded my eviction in a single day's time.

On 29 January 1921 KS got a letter from the head of the motor-vehicle garage that the building in Leontiev Lane was definitely under renovation and put in suitable shape and 'at the present time nothing can prevent your removal there'.

By 1921 military operations had ended, and with the pressure lightened, the centralized government was reinforced. It was ruling over a destroyed country, racked economically by inflation and deficits. Five-sixths of industry was gone, transport for anything but military purposes had broken down, the suppression of private trade initiatives led to an active black market. Farmers produced only enough for their own needs, and a devastating famine emptied the cities, partly by flight, partly by starvation.

To the **All-Russian Central Executive Committee**. 22 February 1921, Moscow.

From the actor of the Moscow State Art Academic Theatre Konstantin Sergeevich Stanislavsky (Alekseev).

Figure 58 Georgy Alekseev

Statement

My brother, Georgy Sergeevich Alekseev, was arrested in the Crimea, his wife, Aleksandra Gustavovna Alekseeva, is seriously ill, and their daughter Valentina Georgievna Konyukhova is in a difficult financial situation.

To save my brother and his family, I turn to the All-Russian Central Executive Committee with the following requests:

1) To give the order to provide an affidavit of the reason for Alekseev's arrest.

2) If possible, to free him from arrest or mitigate his grievous plight. This should be done as soon as possible, because Alekseev is a sick man.

3) In case of the prisoner's release, to allow him and his family to move to Moscow and to provide the proper authorization for that.

My brother's address, at our last meeting, is Crimea, Yalta, New Miskhor, former estate of the former Princes Dolgoruky. [...]

Inquiries were made, but the case was not altered. KS's brother had already died in 1920, unbeknownst to him, and the fate of his sister-in-law remains unknown.

To **Fyodor Mikhalsky**.[20] End of February 1921, Moscow.

Dear Fyodor Nikolaevich!

Again the situation is becoming desperate. The case has not moved. Everything has stopped short. Technicians have removed the electric wiring and plugs from the theatre and nothing works. Mukhin was supposed to break open a doorway

Figure 59 The house in Leontiev Lane in which Stanislavsky lived and worked for nearly twenty years

and hasn't come. In my apartment on Carriage Row there is frost in the rooms, and on Leontiev Lane they cannot stoke the stoves, because there is no firewood. If matters go on in this way – we will catch our death of cold, and *The Government Inspector*, Cervantes and so forth will not go on this year.

K. Stanislavsky

The Alekseev family was installed in 6 Leontiev Lane by March, but the move was not without discomfort.

To **Fyodor Mikhalsky**. 11 March 1921, Moscow.
Dear Fyodor Nikolaevich!

You should know what's going on. I am in bed. So is Igor. They are pestering everyone for residence permits. The chairman of the housing committee requires us to get a warrant for the apartment from the housing department so that everyone has a residence permit – at once. The only way to get it is with the help of theatre tickets. Don't you have any acquaintances and protectors in the housing department? You will greatly oblige me.

Cordially devoted K. Stanislavsky

Once residence at Leontiev Lane was officially confirmed, the Opera Studio commenced its activities there.

To the **Electoral Commission of the Mossoviet**. After 25 April 1921, Moscow.

At the pre-election meeting of actors, convened [25] April at the Bolshoy Theatre for electing deputies to the M. Soviet, I was inserted in the list of candidates, despite my refusal on three separate occasions.

I wish by the present letter once more to state categorically my request that my candidacy be removed from the ballot. The reasons which impel me to this are the following:

1) I am swamped with work at the following establishments: M. Art Theatre, MAT 1st Studio, MAT 2nd Studio, Opera Studio, Bolshoy Theatre, Chekhov Studio, Griboedov Studio, 'Habima', Armenian and Latvian Studios. In all these studios I carry on a series of experiments – to work out the question of how to train the actor's creative process, which is to be the chief aim of the last years of my life.

2) In connection with this I am occupied with arranging and analysing an enormous amount of material in my special field, collected by me for my almost forty years of work in the theatre. I invest great significance in this work and consider it remarkably urgent in view of the fact that little time is left me for an active life.

3) My tasks as an actor, my domestic and financial conditions allow me no possibility of refusing all my tasks and work. On the other hand, my health and ever worsening chronic illness, age and time deprive me of any possibility of taking on new obligations.

4) If I were to be awarded the honour of election to the number of deputies of the Mosc. Soviet of Peop. Com. – I could not involve myself with my new obligations

except wholly conscientiously. I would consider it my obligation as representative of an actors' company to respond to the innumerable solicitations which may be directed at me. Therefore I know for certain that a new obligation would strip me of all my time and all my strength – and would deprive me of the possibility of devoting myself to my special field and carrying out the basic tasks of my life. In other words, I would have to betray my art for the sake of public service, for which I have never felt a calling. My call is to serve society in the theatre and I must remain in the realm of art.

In view of all the aforesaid I am compelled categorically to refuse the supreme honour which they wish to bestow on me by election to the deputies of Mosc. Soviet.

On 1 May 1921 Meyerhold and Bebutov published 'Stanislavsky's Isolation' in Vestnik Teatra (Theatrical Herald); *it praised KS's special genius and urged him to abandon the moribund MAT and link arms with the ongoing Theatrical October.*

At this time KS was in fact rehearsing a high-spirited and cartoonish Tale of Ivan the Fool and His Brothers *adapted by Mikhail Chekhov at the Second Studio.*

In the 1920/21 season at the Bolshoy Theatre Studio he prepared a Rimsky-Korsakov programme (prologue to Maid of Pskov *and* Tale of Tsar Saltan, *scenes from* Night before Christmas *and* Sadko, *and some staged ballads),* Tchaikovsky *(first three scenes from* Yevgeny Onegin *and staged ballads) and Massenet's opera* Werther.

To **Yevgeny Vakhtangov**.[21] From a convalescent home in Pokrovskoe-Streshnevo, summer 1921.

My dear, good, beloved Yevgeny Bagrationovich!

I learned of your illness just before I left Moscow.

Every day I have thought of phoning you from the clinic here, but the telephone is out of order and there is no contact with Moscow. So we sit here and fret. Today a nurse from the All Saints' sanatorium came by and said that you are getting better. God grant that it's true. Until they repair the phone I will look out for any news of you I can.

Please believe that we care for you very much, treasure you very much and await your return to health.

With heartfelt regards, K. Stanislavsky

This is only my third day off, since my season this year has only just finished and will start again on 15 August, I hear. In that time I have staged three operas, and if you add to that *The Government Inspector* and *The Tale*, plus three revivals, it turns out that I am not eating Soviet bread for free and am entitled to a vacation.

The Lord keep you.

KS had set up his sister Zinaida Sokolova as a leader in the Opera Studio and she tended to get on the nerves of her colleagues. Her counterpart Viktor Ivanovich Sadovnikov (1886-1964), a singer and conductor who worked at the Bolshoy Theatre and Opera Studio from 1919, had offered to leave the Studio, because 'others', i.e., Zina, were distorting KS's ideas.

To **Viktor Sadovnikov**. After 19 August 1921.

Dear Viktor Ivanovich!

Excuse me for writing with a pencil. I have neither paper nor ink.

I already told you when I saw you that I will not take part in any way in all the squabbles of the studios. My rule: go around quagmires, don't wallow in them. If a studio is necessary and viable, you know how to reconcile yourself to the shortcomings of others and emend your own, if they are dearer to you than the studio – close it down and – serve it right! This means it was a miscarriage, a stillborn infant.

If you would care to be ruled by my opinion, here it is. My wisdom is not complicated. It consists in the fact that I stand on the plane not of personal interests but of business, and I reason practically.

A studio cannot exist (under the ever more complicated conditions, when I myself am torn to pieces) – with a person, who would give his all to the business, that is work 36 hours, almost for nothing, run to the telephone, open the front door, do the dusting, pack the costumes, set up the scenery… etc., etc., without receiving a simple thank-you for courtesy's sake. This needs to be appreciated most of all. The shortcomings of such a person are secondary. I have seen three such persons in my lifetime: Sulerzhitsky, myself and Sokolova. You are a lord! You need things ready-made and therefore you do not understand the way that I, an unskilled labourer, appreciate such people. It is a pity, in this case, that Sokolova is my sister (I am especially strict with her), because it is harder for me to say that she is just such a person. Simply because in my whole lifetime I have found only three of them, it is stupid to hope that a new one will show up in a week. There are none. There is only Sokolova. If she leaves, I shall have to take on her work. I cannot refuse beforehand.

Ergo: Sokolova seems to me indispensable not because she is my sister, but because without her I have no one to lean on.

Sadovnikov is a disciple of the studio, a trained studio actor. A tenor. The only other tenor we have is [Vladimir Nikolaevich] Verbitsky.[22] It is impossible to build a repertoire on him. If Sadovnikov leaves, we will have to end the performances for the year, until we find and grow a new tenor. The studio folk cannot work anymore without wages. The studio will disperse and close temporarily or forever.

Ergo: if the studio is to exist, Sadovnikov will have to come to terms with Sokolova's shortcomings and check his own, while Sokolova will have to come to terms with Sadovnikov's shortcomings and keep an eye on her own.

They can do this work themselves. I cannot help them in any way.

If Sadovnikov and Sokolova love the studio, they will do it very quickly. And they will find a 'modus vivendi', because they are not savages but people of culture; if they love themselves in the studio, then they will both have to remain – alone without a studio, while I, regretting the past, will be cleverer in future and will seek a better application of my strength. That is what the most primitive, realistic, practical life and its demands tell us. […]

Yours K. Stanislavsky

Kira was expecting a baby; her daughter Kirilla Romanovna Falk was born on 4 September 1921 in a clinic in Trubnikov Lane.

To **his daughter Kira.** August 1921, Pokrovskoe-Streshnevo.
My dear Kiryulya!

The telephone is out of order, the phone-poles were downed by the storm, and therefore I am profiting by the occasion to write. Whatever has happened to us that is too uninteresting to relate in a letter you can learn from the bearer. I do want to profit by the occasion to talk about what disturbed me not long ago in a discussion with Mama. She thinks that you do not want to go to the clinic, while I, what with my imagination, had assumed that you have a secret intention of giving birth at home.

I understand you very well, I don't care for clinics myself, but, God knows, for all my hatred of them, I insist in case of an illness that demands attentive care that I be brought specifically to a clinic. *All* the multifarious dire conditions of our debacle have made this an urgent requirement. In cases of childbirth attentive care is everything; it is essential *to the nth degree*. On it, in the majority of cases, both the health of mother and the fate of the child depend. Believe me, what I find most distressing is that I cannot surround you at the moment of your first birthing with all the comfort that surrounded women lying in in our time. But this is not our fault. Right now my obligation is to do everything I can to provide you all the amenities in a clinic and to persuade you to refuse childbirth at home. Just recently, before the debacle, such births were already being considered unhygienic and were rarely practiced. Need I remind you that now under modern conditions one cannot achieve that ideal cleanliness that was available in the past. In the past the whole room and its ceiling were scrubbed down and hung with fresh sheets. But let's assume that, with effort, this much can be done. There are other untoward obstacles. Medications. For all my efforts, I procured a few little vials of carbolic, but what's needed is a bucketful. There are none of the essential utensils. A clinic will not let a private family have them. There's not enough linen. In the clinic there may not be ideal cleanliness or pharmaceutical supplies, but all the same there will be a sufficient quantity there. Moreover, there is medical help. How important it is at the proper time during childbirth. How many accidents happen from incompetence and ignorance. It is a simple matter to tie the umbilicus, but if it is done ineptly, it can almost create a rupture in the baby etc., etc. Of course it is possible, under present conditions, to count on the doctor arriving in time and, if need be, staying the night and even living in the house. The same thing might be achieved with a midwife. But at night, will they really come? There are no cabs, and don't count on Anton – he will let you down. But the main thing is no doctor will come. In the past they were starving and would come running at the first call, but now they swim in banknotes and don't need the patient. In a clinic they are more answerable than in the past for every blunder, and therefore they pay attention. But my chief worries are the disorganization at home and our advanced age. After all there is no one to send. Mikhail?! Not the

Dunyashas. Ivan?! And he won't go, but only pretend to. Nataliya Gavrilovna[23] is needed at home. That leaves Mama (needed at home) and myself. All right, if I have to make a run during the day: I will hire a horse-cab, but what can I do at night; how much time will I take getting to the doctor; do I have enough effrontery and resourcefulness to wake up a whole house; otherwise can one knock loudly enough to be heard at night. So when I think about all of my responsibility and measure it against my strengths, I start to get scared and no joke, and I would like you to be aware of my apprehensions and take them into consideration. Since I do understand your feelings – to leave home at such a moment! – I sympathize with you with all my heart and will do all I can to make sure you will not be far from home or on your own. Only, for heaven's sake – do not take the risk. This letter requires no answer. You don't have to sit down, bent over a piece of paper; explain everything to whoever is bearing this letter or have him note down the gist. If Zina is at home, have her say what's going on with her as well, and the state of Vakhtangov's health, if she knows.

The weather here is diabolical. We sit within four walls. Luckily, I have a private room of my own in the dacha [*illeg.*], on the 2nd floor with a balcony, on which, true, one cannot stand without risk of falling through.

> Hugs, love, thoughts.
> Your Papa

The premiere of KS's brainchild The Government Inspector *took place at the MAT on 8 October 1921. It was a huge success because of Mikhail Chekhov's eccentric interpretation of Khlestakov. It ran for 52 performances, ending only because Chekhov left the MAT to run the First Studio as the MAT 2.*

From this point on, all new productions were staged by the studios, and the main stage of the parent company saw only revivals. The evening of Turgenev one-acts, The Blue Bird *and* Tsar Fyodor *were all revived during the 1920/21 season.*

KS started to rehearse The Fruits of Enlightenment, *although it would ultimately be banned.*

Smyshlaev, who had agitated for the release of KS from prison in 1919 (something of which KS may have been unaware), published a Theory of Processing the Theatrical Spectator *with the Proletkult of Izhevsk. KS was upset by the superficiality and eclecticism of the process put forward for the actor's work on a role and Smyshlaev's unrestrained use and perversion of the idea and premise of a 'system'.*

Diary, 1921. What keeps me from promulgating my work has proved no obstacle to Smyshlaev. Having failed to understand the primary, basic essence of my quarter-century of work, having mixed up all the basic premises, with a levity and arrogance that defies description, he has published a so-called Stanislavsky system, sheltering behind the now fashionable screens of collective creativity.

[...] Smyshlaev does not have the courage to admit that he has borrowed everything from me, he does not think it necessary to refer to this in the book. This is a matter for his conscience. But this is what is important for me. He has

Заслуженный Артист М. А. Чехов
« Ревизор »

M. X. A. T. 2.

Figure 60 Mikhail Chekhov as Khlestakov in *The Government Inspector*. Photo: Tea-Kino-
Pechat, Moscow

shown himself to be a bad and backward disciple. He reports old news and reports
it inaccurately. He has misrepresented my ideas. My practice at the MAT has
gone far beyond his at this point.

*In November 1921 the Third Studio opened on the Arbat. At a meeting of the Board of
the First Studio, Vakhtangov urged Stanislavsky to abandon the MAT and build a new
collective based on the First Studio. No decision was taken, but when he was informed
of this proposal the next day 'K.S. wept'.*

Vakhtangov had two major successes: under his direction, the Hebrew troupe Habima had staged an expressionistic version of An-Ski's mystical play The Dybbuk; *and the Third Studio had had a phenomenal public (though not critical) success with Gozzi's* Princess Turandot, *with commedia dell'arte techniques adapted to modern tastes. When the preview of* Princess Turandot *took place on 27 February 1922, Vakhtangov was too ill was attend, so KS stood in for him and phoned him during the intermissions. Vakhtangov died a few days later at the age of thirty-nine. KS wrote, 'My God. My hopes have died... my best student...'*

Notes

1 Dr P. A. Balmaev practiced Tibetan medicine.
2 Sulerzhitsky had been christened in the Roman Catholic faith.
3 Ivan Ivanovich Titov (Stepanov, 1876-1941), head of the scenery division, a founding member of the MAT.
4 Aleksandr Nikolaevich Uralsky (Bagaritsky), assistant director, at the MAT 1908-18.
5 Aleksandr Nikolaevich Morozov acted at the MAT 1914-19.
6 Sofiya Vladimirovna Giatsintova (1891-1982) entered the MAT in 1910, when five were chosen from a hundred applicants; her first substantial role was the shameless Pelageya in *Let There Be Joy!* (1916). She became a stalwart of the First Studio.
7 Mariya Alekseevna Tokarskaya (Tokarevich), student at the MAT school 1901-05; at MAT 1913-21.
8 The long-bearded king in *The Snow Maiden.*
9 The letter is addressed to him in his function as Chief Director and Administrator of the Maly Theatre and was published in *Russkoe Slovo (Russian Word)* on 23 October.
10 Yelena Konstantinovna Malinovskaya (1875-1942), active in the party hierarchy, was at this time head of Akttheaters.
11 Konstantin Georgievich Svarozhich (Turusov) acted at the MAT 1913-19.
12 Yury Yegenievich Pons, assistant director at the Second Studio and the MAT 1917-22. As Georges Pons, he later became a manager of the Chauve-Souris cabaret abroad.
13 It opened in the Columned Hall of House of Unions on 11 April.
14 The Opera Studio of the Bolshoy Theatre was created in December 1918.
15 This was KS's derogatory term for ND's Musical Studio.
16 Pavel Grigorievich Chesnokov (1877-1944) wrote the music and trained the chorus.
17 Mikhail, a former Polish soldier, wounded at the front and on leave from the hospital, was living with KS's family, doing various chores around the house.
18 Vera Rudolfovna Menzhinskaya (1872-1944), government and party worker; in 1920 chief of the TEO of Narkompros.
19 Vladimir Dmitrievich Bonch-Burevich (1873-1955), government and party worker; historian and ethnographer.
20 Fyodor Nikolaevich Mikhalsky (1896-1968), from 1918 in administrative work at the MAT.
21 Vakhtangov was now at the All Saint's clinic-sanatorium after two serious operations.
22 Vladimir Nikolaevich Verbitsky, singer; at the Opera Studio 1921-24.
23 Nataliya Gavrilovna Timasheva, maid in KS's home.

Figure 61 New York 1923: A publicity shot for the MAT tour. Front row, left–right: Morris Gest, Vishnevsky, Moskvin, John Barrymore as Hamlet, Kachalov, Stanislavsky, Ethel Barrymore, Arthur Hopkins (Barrymore's director), Robert Edmond Jones (Barrymore's designer). Back row, left–right: Nikita Baliev and Olga Knipper-Chekhova

9

INNOCENTS ABROAD
1922–1924

Faced with the critical situation prevailing throughout Russia, in early 1921 Lenin had put in force 'a tactical retreat', the New Economic Policy (NEP). Private enterprise was once again permitted, although on a reduced scale; centralized food allotment was replaced by a limited market economy. This brought about a revival of urban life and an improved standard of living, with an accompanying rise in prices. At the same time, subsidies to the theatres were severely reduced; companies were expected to survive on the basis of their box-office receipts.

In January 1922 the Communist Party began interfering ever more actively in the business of the academic theatres, bypassing Lunacharsky. By November the Mariinsky and the Bolshoy were in danger of being liquidated as remnants of a tsarist past; theatrical budgets were about to be transferred to public schools. The danger was averted by drastic cuts and staff reductions. Between this moment and March 1924, the administration of the state academic theatres was in a constant state of crisis.

KS published an article that the starving theatre should be relieved, for it was not a luxury but an essential for society. American aid agencies had sent packages to needy actors, funded by concerts organized by Russians abroad and sponsored by a US government agency headed by Herbert Hoover.

To **The American Famine Aid Administration**. 9 March 1922, Moscow.

We have had news that in the name of culture America is ready to come to the aid of the Russian theatre in every way.

Sincerely moved by such an attitude, with profound gratitude we would be willing to receive support from the American people during the material need which our art is suffering at the present time.

I refer to the technical supplies for the stage of canvas, paints, electric light-bulbs, fittings and accessories, fabric for costumes etc.

Supplying this need of our theatre would be an unforgettable service for Russian art.

We hope that we Russian actors in our turn will manage to do comradely service to our American colleagues in art and in the name of general human culture.

The Chairmen of the Moscow Art Theatre:
Vl. I. Nemirovich-Danchenko
K. Stanislavsky

When Isadora Duncan came to Moscow in April with her students, KS did not seek to attend her recitals or see her privately.

On 1 May, the Opera Studio rehearsal hall in Leontiev Lane offered its first public performance of Yevgeny Onegin, *with KS working the curtains.*

To **Sergey Rachmaninov.**[1] 26 May 1922. Moscow.

Dear Sergey Vasilievich!

I have occasion, once more, to thank you, but this time not for myself personally but in the name of the Art Theatre for the five parcels of rations you sent me. You do not know how you touch and melt my heart – by your attention and remembrance of us. At the same time the theatre will give you an accounting of how the rations were distributed. You are doing a very good deed, because the actors are actually starving, but nevertheless do not stop working and supporting the theatre. [...]

Perhaps you will be interested in the result of the public show and concert, whose preparation I wrote about before. We did not succeed in getting a real theatre. The Bolshoy Theatre offered us Beethoven Hall (the former foyer of the imperial box). I turned it down, because it is in the very thick of the Bolshoy Theatre's operatic atmosphere. I am afraid to let my green youngsters into it; they will immediately be poisoned by operatic histrionics. I managed to stage a whole opera (*Onegin*) without cuts, with choruses and both balls – at home in the studio which is almost located in my apartment. It is hard to let strange people off the street into one's own home, but I managed to do it because without performances there is no way to keep the apartment. In this way, my apartment has been turned into an opera theatre, where two or three times a week fifty or sixty members of the public show up (at 3,000,000 rubles a ticket). The hall, where the performances go on, is divided by a small archway with four columns. The house is old-fashioned, dating from the beginning of the last century. We managed to use all the peculiarities of the period for *Onegin*. At times we made the columns into the first-scene balcony, at other times we put Tatyana's bed between the columns (scene 2), at still other times we clad the columns in covers of tree-bark with painted snow (duel, forest). Then we fashioned the columns into the governor's box at Gremin's ball and so on. The performance was done, of course, to piano accompaniment, because it is impossible to fit our orchestra into the hall.

Onegin is having an enormous success. The audience weeps, and our young Tatyana (Gorshunova[2]) has already become a minor celebrity, so she has to be protected from admirers and being spoiled by precocious success. You have to give the youngsters credit – they created the success and sometimes even make a great impression on me. Silly operatic cliché is totally expelled, and I have even convinced case-hardened artists of the Bolshoy Theatre that even in opera one can live by the authentic creative feeling of the actor. Meanwhile I have succeeded in making sure that every word of the text is understood, and even in the crowd scenes (the choruses), in quartets and ensembles – and there the most important words for thought and action reach the audience. To do this some of the singers intentionally pronounce the text less distinctly, and pronounce the emphasized

Figure 62 The ball at the Larins' in Tchaikovsky's opera *Yevgeny Onegin*, staged by the Opera Studio in Stanislavsky's salon

words more distinctly; this way, of course, the musical aspect (led by Golovanov[3]) is not slighted. Another minor achievement is that I have succeeded in making all the movements and actions of the performers, chorus, lighting effects (this aspect is arranged rather well in the hall) rhythmically correspond to the music. In this way I do not permit a martial rhythm, that is staccato in tempo, but manage to make the rhythm palpable, but not conspicuous. This provides precision and finish to the performance. The audience senses something unusual in this regard, but cannot account for how it is achieved.

Besides this, I have succeeded in getting all the soloist actors, not playing leading parts, to take part in the chorus and themselves fill all the functions of props men, scene dressers, makeup men and so on. Our financial conditions require this. Constant participation of the performers in small roles and the chorus forces them to get used to the stage quickly and spread their wings. Besides, all together it creates a good artistic atmosphere – backstage. To give you an understanding of the miniature quality of our theatrical space, I will describe what happens in the adjoining (and only) room by the stage, in which my sister [Zinaida] lives, who helps me run the Opera Studio of the Bolshoy Theatre. In this room, serving as her bedroom, dining-room, study and drawing-room, all the performers make up, men and women change clothes (screens are set up for this), prepare furniture and props for the performance. There the peasant chorus (Act I), the maidens' chorus (the party) sing. In the same room scenery is stored, platforms are carried through. In short, it's sheer bedlam. At the end of the performance all the students in a general effort straighten up and sweep out the room, freshen it, so that my long-suffering sister can go to bed, take tea, etc. This example will show that many of the students work in a self-sacrificing way, receiving nothing for their labours. This is genuinely moving given the oppressive conditions in which they live. Our orchestra makes even more sacrifices. [...]

K. Alekseev (Stanislavsky)

In June the Kachalov group returned from abroad and was treated coolly by KS. With a fully constituted acting company, ND worked out a plan with Tsentroteatr to tour components of the MAAT at regular intervals under the guidance of European and North American impresarios. The purpose would be not only to spread the renown of 'Soviet' art, but also to make much-needed foreign currency (valyuta). The tours, enthusiastically supported by Lunacharsky, were opposed by Feliks Dzerzhinsky, head of the Cheka, on the grounds of 'brain drain'. Other artists permitted to go abroad had not returned.

Just as KS finished the protracted rehearsals for Fruits of Enlightenment *on 17 May Baliev, whose cabaret* The Bat *(now known as* Le Chauve-Souris*) had been the toast of Paris, London and New York, wrote that the MAT should tour America under the management of his own agent, Russian-born Morris Gest. KS's presence and name on the poster would be indispensable.*

After an initial veto and a flurry of memoranda, the First Studio was given permission to play in Europe as a test. When it came home after a successful tour, the parent company was then granted support to visit Germany, France and the U.S. Before then, ND's Musical Studio opened La Périchole *and KS held rehearsals of* Tsar Fyodor Ioannovich *for its revival with Kachalov as the alternative lead. He was now taking his summer rest cure at an elite government-operated sanatorium outside Moscow.*

To **his son Igor**. 22 August 1922, Moscow.
Dear Igorek!

[...] I got a telegram from Nemirovich and Leonidov[4] (the impresario) from Berlin that we will go to Berlin in October, Paris in November, London in December and America in January. On the phone Vishnevsky said that Rumyantsev had come in person, and said that the tour will begin on 24 September – in Berlin.[5] There was a fuss, because neither the scenery nor the actors have been assembled. Then came a telegram that we will be informed of the day the tour is to begin. Since that time there has been nothing, and we are waiting for news. Meanwhile Rumyantsev explained that the Lessing Theatre in Berlin would be rented and the manager Barnowsky[6] is wiring to tell me that as soon as I visit his theatre, he will consider himself at my service. Then we are supposed to go to Dresden and Prague. In Paris we will perform at the Champs Élysées Theatre – for 25,000 francs the engagement. The same French impresario[7] will take us to London.

As soon as we turned down Gest's American terms, he immediately agreed to all our conditions, that is 8,000 dollars (16,000 rubles) a week (8 performances) and another 50% of the profits. Rumyantsev told us about America: how much an apartment or a pound of meat costs, how each apartment shares the kitchen in which meals are prepared, they write a little note how they want their food cooked or prepared, they phone; they let down baskets of crockery and bowls of provisions; and downstairs the food is cooked and returned.[8] We could not learn any further details about everyday details from him... [...]

I tenderly love and hug you.
Papa

To **Nemirovich-Danchenko**. 12 September 1922, Moscow.
Dear Vladimir Ivanovich!

I am leaving with the firm intention of returning to Moscow 'either with my shield or on my shield'.[9]

Either I will succeed in rallying the first group, and then it will be possible to try and carry on the concern; or this will not succeed, and then we will have to end it. At least I am unlikely to remain on the stage.

If the group falls I do not envisage any further horizons.

I look forward to the forthcoming jubilee[10] as onerous, unnecessary, boring, compulsory, and I would very much advise you to think about cancelling it. How? Quite simply – by postponing our arrival and returning to Moscow 17 October, using the time before then for a more elaborate preparation abroad of *Fruits of Enlightenment* and *Cain* with Kachalov in a new staging.[11] [...]

K. Stanislavsky

Diary, 13 September 1922.

The eve of departure. Heavy luggage dispatched by sea, small stuff left. A bit of packing. Was at the theatre, spoke with the students newly enrolled in the recently-formed school of the first MAT group. Handed them over to Demidov and the 2nd Studio.

Farewell visit to Fedotova. Unrecognizable, in pain. As before treats guests to her favourite coffee, but no nuts now. Beyond her means. Made sign of cross over one another. She wept a lot.

Came home. Opera Studio there in full. Group photo taken... But spirits not very high. A long admonitory speech to the studio folks. Main precepts: 1. *Before saying or doing anything, think if it will be good for the Studio*; 2. *Wipe feet outside the Studio door. [Leave] the bad outside, take the good inside...*

KS left for Berlin on 14 September 1922, travelling through Riga; that same day the company headed for Petersburg to sail thence to Germany.

To **Nemirovich-Danchenko**. Between 10 and 17 October 1922. Berlin.
Dear Vladimir Ivanovich,

I really don't know what to write! Shall I describe the successes, ovations, flowers, speeches?!... If they had been prompted by new breakthroughs and discoveries in our work, I would not spare the colours and every rose handed us in the street by some American or German woman and every kind word would be

Figure 63 Stanislavsky as Vershinin, 1922. Photo: A. Pybchev, Moscow

endowed with great significance, whereas now... It's ridiculous to be delighted and gratified by the success of *Fyodor* or Chekhov. When Masha and I do the farewell scene in *Three Sisters*, I start to feel embarrassed. After all we've lived through, it's impossible to weep because an officer is going away and his sweetheart is staying behind. Chekhov delights me not. On the contrary. I don't feel like playing him... To go on in the old way is impossible, but we lack the people to embark on a new way. The old-timers who could cope do not want to relearn, and the youngsters cannot, and besides are too frivolous. At times like this one wants to throw over the drama, which seems to be in such a hopeless state, and take up either opera or literature or ply some craft. That's the kind of mood our triumphs evoke in me.

[...] There has proven to be a tendency at present to introduce us as a Soviet theatre. For love of intrigue they do not want to admit that we are apolitical. We have got to be very careful. One interviewer wrote that I find that the Soviet government treats us well, warmed to us, and gave us a subsidy... All this is culled from different parts of the conversation. So, for instance, the interviewer asks me: 'Is it as cold with you as it is in the Berlin theatres?' 'No,' I reply. 'Our theatres are warm'. And that's all. In another part of the conversation the question is asked: 'How do you manage during this inflation?' I reply: 'The theatre plays to full houses. Beyond that there is a subsidy.' Out of all these answers a phrase is cobbled together, beyond what was said. They write brazenly whatever they want and not what you say to them.

The actors are behaving decently. If you ignore the chatter and racket in the dressing-rooms, which are so close to the stage that everything can be heard. Some of the actors have the half-formed intention of peeling away. Despite the fact that they were warned that their wives would cost them dear – they claim that no one cares that they are not on their own, but are themselves plus someone else.

Meanwhile there are good relations all round. [...]

God keep you. I understand how hard it must be for you, and constantly think about you over in Moscow.

To **Nemirovich-Danchenko**. 5 December 1922. Paris. *Telegram.*
Colossal success, general acclaim, fantastic press.

To **his wife Mariya Lilina**. After 10 January 1923, New York.
I am writing this letter on the boat. It's pitching. I am writing badly. [...] From Paris to Cherbourg we travelled without incident: the train runs right to the landing-stage. All sorts of formalities on the spot: customs, medical examination, passport. They put you on a decent steamboat with cabins and a big common room, and not just one...

We waited a long time, because the *Majestic* was late. It was already dark. The landing-stage was lit up with lamps. Rain came down, then hail. When they found out that we hadn't been examined by the doctor, they rousted us and the children out on deck. That's probably where our children (the Bulgakovs' and Tarasova's little boys) caught cold and are now ill (38°). Finally we slipped in the darkness into water as black as ink. We travelled calmly stopping and starting for nearly an hour, but still no *Majestic*. All of a sudden there loomed up a huge hulk lit by a thousand lights. It is as long as all of Kammerherr Lane from the Obukhov building to Tver Boulevard. In front of us – on the side protected from the wind, a few steamboats were moored, moving ahead of us. Our boat, stupidly, insisted

Figure 64 Staterooms on the *Majestic*

on mooring, no matter what, on the windward side. It knocked and banged around the hulk, listed from the waves and wind, oops – it turned over. Finally, to our general joy, it went and moored where it should have done. This episode was unpleasant. So now we were moored, but they didn't let us on board. It turns out there has be -- a medical examination. They're mostly afraid of an eye disease. Gryzunov and Uspenskaya[12] for some reason seemed under suspicion. They were held back. Uproar, protests. They let them go. We boarded the steamship, which, despite the waves and a slight choppiness, stood as if rooted to the spot. We boarded. The lavishness is tasteless, but grandiose. The people in first class stare at us. We don't look like Europeans! I'm in galoshes, Vishnevsky in a fur hat, and all the Europeans are in summer clothing, and at the moment we came on board they were in tuxedos after dinner. They took us to meet the manager of the steamship company – in an office, on the boat. He said something to me in English, and I bowed and replied in French. Stupid! In second class it's more comfortable – simpler. Nothing special, but cosy. The cabin is small, with a double bunk-bed (upper and lower, on the upper lies my hand baggage, on the lower I sleep), a bookcase, a washhand-stand, hangers, hot-water heating. A basket of flowers from the steamship company, with greetings to me. I washed. I went to the dining-room. An enormous room with columns. A grey public – immigrants of all nationalities, mostly, of course, Jews. We can order nothing ourselves. People had been assigned to help Knipper and other 'English people'. [Simeon] Gest [Morris Gest's brother] who travels with us helps and Sholom Asch (playwright, author, Jew) comes over to us. After dinner in the big common room an orchestra plays Negro-style, with whistles, rattles, noise-makers and everyone hideously dances new-fangled dances. People stare dully all around. Next door is a big room. There men are playing cards. Of course, our actors wasted no time in setting up 'chemin de fer' (the shameless lot). The foreigners were amazed!! On the other side of the common room are two parlours with desks and an upright piano. Around all the cabins and rooms in second class is a wide, enclosed deck, that is a promenade with a view of the sea. On the windward side they let down tarpaulin awnings, and during the day you lie there on long deckchairs. The ship is always in motion. It rocks. Just a bit, but all the same it was an unpleasant surprise for us, because this is a very large ship, and you would think it would be impossible to rock it. The air is so warm that one can lie in bed with an open window, because, evidently, the heating is not regulated individually in each cabin (it turns out that I was getting heat for no reason, because the steward and I could not communicate. The heating in the cabin was regulated splendidly, which I took advantage of later on.)

At 7 in the morning – 'tom-tom'. Half an hour later – a second 'tom-tom.' They bring cups of coffee with milk and buttered toast into the cabin. At 11 they pass bouillon round the decks and cabins (I don't take it). At 12:30, lunch (at first they brought it to my cabin, but then I went to the dining-room). Before lunch an orchestra in the common room plays high-brow music (so-called, like the overture to 'Dichter und Bauer'). After lunch everyone lies in armchairs on the enclosed deck and sleeps, at 4 they bring coffee and toast. At 7 dinner or, more accurately, supper, at 10:30 you go to sleep. I might take a bath – of sea water. There is a Zander-style gymnasium with machines for riding, camel riding, rowing, a bicycle, chest expanders, etc.

I must admit that the crossing was difficult. We were two days late on account of storms. [...]

There's been pitching and rolling the whole time, except for two days and two nights. During that time we were in heaven. It's warm, because of a southerly wind or breezes from the Gulf Stream. Moonlit nights. During the day (and ill-disposed nights) we wear jackets. We lie in the armchairs, they bring us bouillon, tea, coffee. The children make mischief on deck. Most of all – little Fanna [daughter of Faina Vasilievna Shevchenko]. A general favourite. Moskvin served her as a kind of nursemaid – didn't leave her side. Even I was surprised. Which means he has stopped drinking. Some are even more sensitive to the rolling of the sea, and suffered intensely the whole time, among them: Pashennaya,[13] Yershov, Gudkov[14], Podgorny, Ripsimé[15], Bokshanskaya – and they were on deck. But... suddenly a squall blew up, and, wonderful to tell – for a quarter of an hour this vast hulk rolled... [...]

The outstanding event of this time was a concert on board. The custom is that travelling performers should play or sing for the benefit of the sailors. And they forced us to do so. The concert was held in the enormous 2nd class dining-room, where we would go. This was the night of 1 January. The program was: 1) Pushkin's *Godunov* (Vishnevsky and Burdzhalov). No one heard a single word because the boat's screws were making so much noise. 2) Brutus and Antony – me and Kachalov. We declaimed and so were heard. 3) Moskvin and Gribunin – 'The Surgery'. This was understood by all, especially when one punches up the comic bits. The second part was improvised. Knipper sang her little ditties to Yakobson's[16] accompaniment. I am not an admirer of her as a singer, but this time it was all right. [...] The audience are immigrants of all countries and for the most part Jews who understand nothing.

On the eve of the concert we very modestly saw in the New Year. We went to the dining-room and drank a bottle of champagne in a small company of old-timers (it was impossible to do more – for want of money, we had reached the end of it.)

Another event in our life was a visit from the famous psychologist from Nancy Coué.[17] He is a great celebrity. He paid me a visit, because he is interested in my theory. But as a matter of fact he did the talking and I listened. What is important for me is that he supports my method, -- that is, that it is impossible to manipulate and fortify the will, but one must act on the imagination. This is the basis of his method of treatment, and mine of an actor's creativity. All my visits to him took place in 1st class. This is the way it's done – 2nd cl. goes to 1st. The Americans and English are very punctilious. Thank Sholom Asch, who helped me find my way. Thank a particular American actress.[18] Incidentally, this actress is an interesting phenomenon. She is a bit like Gzovskaya. She can perform whole scenes, a whole show by herself. For instance, a Rumanian and a Chinese converse on shipboard, praising their nations. She speaks neither Rumanian nor Chinese, but splendidly imitates both accents. Or another scene. A girl has married an Irishman, and someone is criticizing her for this (who? – I didn't understand). At first an old woman talks. The actress puts a kerchief over her head and mimics old age. Then the mother talks. The kerchief drops to her shoulders. Then the girl herself talks. The kerchief is tossed aside. She does seem talented! [...]

Finally we got good weather, as I have already written, it was balmy when, reaching America, we rode the Gulf Stream. But in a quarter of an hour, early in the morning, on the eve of arrival, everything changed. Snow fell. It was cold, snow on deck. We reached the shores of America on the evening of Wednesday, 2 January. The boat travelled at its calmest speed. That night all the major baggage was to be distributed. The next day, early in the morning – we were to expect the doctor, different officials for the inspection, visas, etc. Everyone went to bed early. I dropped off and was awakened by a shout. I am ashamed to write about this for general consumption, and therefore I write it separately, in the notes – for Vl. Ivan. *See note I.*

The next day, that is Thursday, 4 January, they awoke us around 8 o'clock. We were all herded into one room. The interviewers arrived. Like birds of prey. They started photographing us one by one, in pairs, etc. (I enclose snapshots.)

I forgot to say that back in Paris there had been an uproar. The American papers printed a letter from the American National League, in which the public was warned that we were coming to propagandize and half our profits would be sent on a secret mission to Russia. Back in Paris we had been interviewed about this, and now, naturally, everyone swooped down on us and interrogated us, just as if we were under investigation.

The formal medical examination (a Punch-and-Judy show). Cross-examination by the officials: why have you come here? Passport and visa inspection etc. are dreadfully stupid formalities (Americans are the greatest sticklers for formality). During the cross-examination it turned out that Mar. P. Grigorieva's[19] ward cannot be allowed into America, because first, she has no parents. And second, she works in the theatre, though she is only 16. This too is a crime. They have to put her on some island for an inquiry. A tragedy. The girl is crying and so on.

The steamship was moored. On account of the interviewers I missed the Statue of Liberty and the arrival. I only saw the shoreline, buildings covered with snow, landscape reminiscent of the Volga and its peaceful shores. Our enormous boat had already entered the river, and lots of little steamboats had encircled it. In the distance whole factories of some sort or, more accurately, a row of railway stations – covered. This is the landing dock. At the end stands a crowd waving handkerchieves. You can recognize Baliev, Boleslavsky, Kairansky,[20] Ziloti (husband and wife[21]), Rachmaninova and her daughter (he himself, unfortunately, had left for a 3-month train trip). Gest himself with his whole suite (I forgot to mention that his youngest son had come on the boat with us from Europe and acted the whole time as translator). From that moment the farce began. Gest arrives on the boat. Things were arranged so that they had already taken our picture together –film and still photographs. In such a way that I wasn't aware of it. Then they snap me alone, as if greeting an enormous crowd (which didn't exist). An awesome reception had been arranged. Gest wanted without fail that we be met by the local Russian archbishop (or some ecclesiastical dignitary) *in full regalia*. The archbishop himself refused, and, fortunately, Bertenson (who came over with Luzhsky and Gremislavsky earlier) talked Gest out of it, saying that it might offend religious feeling. What's more – the mayor of the city was supposed to hand us *the keys to the city*. And this had been set for the 3rd, when we were expected, but there was an important meeting on the 4th, and no one could come. Local societies were to meet us with bread and salt. But they didn't meet us, because the boat took so long pulling into the pier, and they were all busy people. Therefore all these tributes were put into an automobile, which was waiting for me. Then these gifts were taken out so that I could be photographed with them. Where they are now – I don't know. Maybe they had all been rented!!! The chief of police sent a magnificent policeman to accompany me from the boat. And so, as if arrested, I alighted with the policeman. He stood on the running board of the automobile and travelled upright, blowing his whistle to let all the policemen know that they should stop all the carriages, trolleys, buses, motor-cars, pedestrians. In short, everything stopped dead, and we sped down all the streets of New York (probably, a dozen cameramen were filming us). Gest, of course, sat with me. Had he arranged this cheap effect for 10 dollars? Having settled me in at the hotel, Gest went off to rescue Nyusha – M. P. Grigorieva's ward. Here he showed his good side. He went to the island, took charge of her, escorted her off it, settled her in an apartment, calmed her down and only then went home. Then there began the most dreadful fuss and formalities about costumes and scenery. Each item had to be described, measured, weighed…

I am not living in a hotel, but in furnished rooms at 208 Fifty-Sixth Street, the Thorndyke Hotel.

The theatre in which we are performing is Al Jolson's Theatre on 59th Street, New York, U.S.A.

I arrived, took a nap, took a bath, had a meal (mediocre). At 8 o'clock I went to a party at Baliev's. A cost-free evening, with famous millionaires invited. I had to arrive by 8:15 to meet the millionaire Kahn[22] (I think that's right). Evidently, he is the one paying, in case of losses. On entering the theatre of course, ovations, flowers. After the welcome I had to speak – in Russian, but Gest translated it into English. I thanked them for the reception and for the past years' deliveries to Russian actors. […]

The theatre is decent. Everything meant for the audience is even very good. It is enormous but at first sight looks quite small. It is so cleverly contrived. If you stand in the very last row in the orchestra, the impression is as if you were standing in the gallery – of the Bolshoy Theatre. People look like pygmies. But if you sit in the stalls, the impression is similar to the dimensions of the MAT. The acoustics are, I suppose, all right. The stage is small, but there is room to store scenery. The stagehands and lighting men are quite remarkable. On Saturday 6 January at 12 o'clock the show of the company that preceded us ended. Before 4 o'clock p.m. their scenery had been removed. After 4 they began to haul in and hang our sets. Work all night long. Yesterday, the 7th, Sunday (the first day of our Christmas), at 1 o'clock there was already a technical rehearsal – with all the actors. At 8 o'clock an inspection of makeup and costumes and a dress rehearsal for the supernumeraries – the 2nd and last scenes. We ended at 2 o'clock. The stagehands did not leave the whole time. They only asked – before the dress – to be let go at 1 o'clock. They were told that one was too early, maybe half past, and they agreed uncomplainingly and with good will. What's more, the work goes on cheerily, amicably; and several times our Russians were told to smile and not have gloomy faces. The electrician here is a true artist. We have already given him an ovation. Perhaps, all this is going so smoothly because it's early days! I fear the evil eye. But meanwhile the atmosphere in the theatre and all around is benign, which helps us a good deal. The same atmosphere we had in Zagreb.

And I like the city itself and its inhabitants. It is tasteless, but cosy. It is not true that there are nothing but skyscrapers here (they are in fact rare). There are big buildings and small ones. Nor is there such movement as people said. I don't see any great difference from Paris. I have not yet seen a single suspension railway. True, on one of the avenues there is a train on pillars, but vehicles travel underneath the pillars. But this is 1st Street, which people try not to travel on. However it is difficult without the language. Thanks to Yekat. Vl. (Gzovskaya's sister). She comes every morning to extricate me from difficulties.

Do I need to describe the rehearsals of our colleagues, which, as in other cities, go on in some garret somewhere, where they paint the sets, or in specialized big rooms, dedicated to this. Down below, under our rehearsal room there is a dance hall for ordinary workers, where for a certain price dance partners and their ladies stamp non-stop, attracted by the horrible modern dances. This working-class hall is remarkably clean, decent and boring. There is nothing to let you know that the dancers are ordinary working-men and -women. The lessee of the dance hall is, of course, a Russian Jew, who dreams about Russia, but never made a bit of money there. I even skip over the technical rehearsals. Let me say once again that such stagehands and stage discipline are unknown to us in Russia and undreamt-of. This is where we should send our workers to learn how they work in a free country with equal citizens, under the supervision of a union. The stagehands have told us: at rehearsals you talk and we'll make notes of whatever you need. Likewise leave to us the responsibility for whatever you need for the performance. After that not one of your people has to touch or move a single set or prop, and if they do, we will stop working and leave. And actually: they did take notes of everything, then each of the stagehands was tested on it, explaining to us: this prop goes over there, then is moved over here and so on. Their diligence, patience and endurance are totally astonishing. I have already written about it.

[…] We have never had such a success before, either in Moscow or in any other city. Around here they say this is not a success, but a revelation. No one knew what a theatre and actors were capable of. I am not writing this out of personal vainglory, because we are showing them nothing new, but the oldest stuff we've got. I tell you so as to show what a rudimentary state art is in here, and with what avidity and curiosity they clutch at everything good that's brought to America. Actor, entrepreneur, celebrity – they all merge in a general chorus of enthusiasm. Some famous actors and actresses grab your hand and kiss it in ecstasy. Such a treatment, which, perhaps, we do not deserve, is remarkably moving.

This is how the day is played out. At 10 o'clock Gzovskaya wakes me with a phone call. I tell her what I want served, she phones the hotel desk, a kind and stupid Negro arrives, carrying an enormous cut orange with sugar (I don't know what to call it). It is an exotic fruit. For it alone it is worth living in America. It pays to eat it on an empty stomach, and then your digestion becomes a chronometer.

Then I am served coffee and ham. At 12 or 1 rehearsal. Before that some interview, a meeting. At 5 dinner at the hotel or in some restaurant, where everything is cooked on a skewer before our eyes. Then a nap – and to the theatre, to act or check the set-up. Again guests, interviews and so on. After the show tea at the hotel or restaurant. […]

Yes, it is not easy to be a spokesman, a director, a manager, an actor simultaneously, in a company of 60 people, with wives, husbands and children. Nevertheless I do not complain. Our journey is interesting. Whereas it is a hard way of life for you poor things, we are told. As soon as we have sorted out our finances, we will organize some superhuman means to send dividends to the Moscow shareholders. But maybe it's not dividends that are needed but something else?! Write.

I hug you, remember you, love you.

K. Stanislavsky

Note 1. So, I was awakened by a shout. Our crowd is already making a scene! I open my door. I hear Russian words. I get dressed, go out. On the stairs are a few stewards, who have also been awakened. Below is the steward on duty, who calms me down. The shouting has already abated. In the little common room, in half-darkness, sit Leonidov, Bulgakov,[23] very dishevelled, and Gryzunov.[24] It seems that Baksheev (we had just seen him before – and he was not drunk) had played his favourite role --- the *genius*, à la Chaliapin. He was shouting that he was a genius, that no one appreciated him. He walked up to Bulgakov and out of the blue started to insult him in foul language, working himself up into the drunken ecstasy of a genius. Finally he began to make indecent remarks about Bulgakov's wife. Then the husband really got outraged. Thanks to Leonidov (the actor) we managed to avoid a major scandal. But some people saw it. And the steward on duty came up to Baksheev and shouted at him in a threatening manner. […]

On arriving in New York all the shareholders assembled and summoned Baksheev, because my reprimands had already lost their edge. All the colleagues spoke their minds. They chewed him out good and plenty. It seems to have made an impression. But for how long!?

To **his wife Mariya Lilina.** 14 January 1923, New York.

[…] I don't need to describe the premiere and its auditorium (maybe I already told you about it). Every distinguished individual, such as only exists in New York, in the sense of the intelligentsia was there in person. The second performance was sold to millionaires and like the first brought Gest about 8000 dollars (and we got the same amount for the whole week).

The toilettes, the diamonds were dazzling – the stones knock your eye out. (In view of the fact that it is dangerous here to wear real diamonds they leave them at home, but at the theatre wear copies of the real ones, that is, paste.)

I remember that I told you about the ovations which were even more clamourous than in Paris; I also told about how the local god is the director Belasco[25], who never goes to opening nights, came to ours twice (the second was the next premiere, when Kachalov and Pashennaya and I acted). Belasco is the father of Gest's wife, she kissed our hands (!!!). I suppose it's a local custom. Belasco overdid the modesty and said that he, nothing, not a thing, could compare with us. All the others arrived, various people and said everything that one says in these circumstances. There were many Americans – actors, writers, professors. After this they took us to a (Russian) restaurant, whereas in all the other cities the waiters were former princesses and princes, the doorman happens to be a former commander of at least a squadron, generals and others. This restaurant is Gest's favourite, because, evidently, he sincerely loves everything Russian and dines and sups there – every day. At the banquet they let in only performers of the MAT and the 'Chauve-Souris'. An exception was made for Sudbinin (the sculptor) as an old performer at the MAT. A quartet from the Mariinsky Theatre played.

This is the same restaurant from which, a few days before, Gest had wanted to extricate me, saying that I must not show myself before the first stage appearance. The furnishings are in semi-darkness, red candles, painted sleeping-shelves, as in *Fyodor*, benches. The doorman is costumed like a guardsman in *Fyodor*, with the double eagle on his back and chest. [...] I sat with Rachmaninov's wife and left early, because I was tired.

Only I found it unpleasant that, by general demand, we had to put on a scene from *Orchard* and *Boris*. This managed to undercut *Fyodor*. But... they say that, thanks to the fact that the performance began at 8 and ended at 10:40 – the success was greater than expected.

A week has gone by, in which we played *Fyodor* eight times. [...] On Friday matinee there was a performance for actors (a full house, no comps, but paid tickets. A box-office of 5400 dollars.) Reception, ovation at the finish. After the performance fraternizing with actors.

Gest lavishes gifts, flowers, enormous baskets, even a metal chest full of American candy and sweets on us. It's so nasty with mint that no one can eat it, and I don't know where to put it. I asked him to send it to Moscow along with the parcels of rations.

The first pay packet of dollars will come soon, and I will send shipments to Moscow. Some of them are at Zina's disposal. [...]

They have snapped us in photographs and films. All the local celebrities have come to us, against the *Fyodor* backdrop, shook our hands, brought flowers etc., as is the custom. Probably the picture will be screened in all the cinemas of Europe in a Pathé newsreel. Here in all the cinemas they show pictures of our arrival, and all the pictures are met with applause, and they have started to recognize us on the streets and in restaurants.

I did not act in that performance because it was Luzhsky's turn. I acted on Friday evening (at the Jewish performance – Sabbath eve). On Saturday there is both a matinee and an evening performance. Meanwhile constantly packed houses. Gest and his company are dumbfounded by the unexpectedness and the success. He, along with us, has become the hero of the day. True, he has done a great deal. He so conditioned and aroused the city of multimillions that they knew of the theatre's existence in advance. In Paris without sufficient *publicité* and advertising, we had to blaze the trail ourselves. And that is why it fell out that by the end of the tour when the last 5-6 performances were sold out, the public bestirred itself and moved, and we were about to make money – we had to leave. I am afraid that the same thing will happen even here. Everybody is making money except us, and we arrived as we shall leave – as beggars. Gest has the right to extend the tour – up to 6 months. This right is so much in force according to local law that we do not have even the right to refuse and leave here before 6 months are up. We cannot even change the financial arrangements. An extension has to be on the same terms as the first 3 months. Of course, Gest will take advantage of all his rights and detain us for not six, but five months, that is till mid-June. This way we lose very profitable London, and in June there is no way for us to join you. At the very moment when we conquer America and free ourselves from Gest's eagle-eye – we have to leave. With the 8000 dollars that Gest pays us, besides the 1200 a week that has to be paid to the supers and the chorus, we earn nothing, the more so since the scenery, which was trotted around Europe for weeks, will be left in America.[26]

Barnowsky, Hébertot, Gest make money and we only wind up with new jackets. Meanwhile just sitting here, in America, seeing these endless queues at the box-office, aware of this crowd of 7,000,000 in New York, we understand how easy it would be for a success to make us millionaires. Of *Fyodor* one may say with complete assurance that it could now be played for years – to sold-out houses. With horror you think how people can do this. But worse than that, in my old age, to return to Moscow to die, and, lest I croak from starvation, to start moonlighting in hackwork again. Here they make me offers to write articles for the papers and for this pleasure, that is for every article – they will pay something like 3000 dollars, that is three times what Gest pays for a whole week. My only weapon against Gest is that by contract the repertoire is in our hands. We can perform what we like, and here it is very important not only what we perform, but who performs, because the public is used to going to see the actor. Everything I said relates to *Fyodor*, but how things will be with the rest of the plays and especially the Chekhovs?! – who knows. I don't think that the rest of the repertoire will go like *Fyodor*. The reviews, which, as they say, are unprecedented here will be sent to Moscow. I made a selection and enclose them – what I could get my hands on. Now it's Sunday, and there's nowhere to go. I went to the movies where there is room for 6000 people. A good orchestra, violinists, a female singer sings bass, and a very boring picture, during which I fell asleep. I dined in a special kind of restaurant without waiters. You take what you want by yourself, pick up forks, knife by yourself. Cheap, but uncomfortable.

I hug you all.

K. Stanislavsky

412

To **his family**. 19 January 1923, New York.

Dear Marusya, Kira, Igorechek, Kirilka!

[…] The day is immediately broken down not only into hours, but into minutes. And if half an hour is left over, you rush to lock the door and lie down. I cannot say I don't get tired, but all the same I manage to get a lot of work done. And it's not so much the business itself and the acting that wear me out, but chiefly the actors. Worst of all, most of all is the cost to the nerves, the unpleasantnesses and constant pestering of that dreadful Koreneva. She and her emoting have become utterly insufferable. Once she refused to play Mstislavskaya because the Garden scene in *Fyodor* isn't being performed and it is beneath her dignity to come on only in the last act. I took no end of trouble with this role in Berlin and now for some reason I have to take trouble with another [actress]. […] Now a new nastiness is beginning – with *Cherry Orchard*. Who will be the first to play Anya – she or Tarasova. If it's Tarasova, then she will destroy her life and career, will cross the sea on foot, but will not tolerate such a disgrace. She rants and raves till you want to throw up. I am rehearsing Irina with her in *Fyodor* for her sake, because we already have 2 tsarinas. At the rehearsal she makes mischief, puts on airs, shows off, aims rude remarks at Bulgakov. We all put up with it. I make a remark to her that she takes the wrong way. Suddenly she's offended – she stops talking, she acts out a tragedy. She stops to sob and overacts tears very badly. Bulgakov calms her, she rounds on him and calls him filthy names. I was patient, patient – for a long time. Finally I started to yell at the top of my lungs and threw her out and took the part away from her. She is three rabid devils and not a human being, when she thought that we needed her. All these incidents with her and other actors make me desperately tired. […] Knipper is the best of the lot.

[…] Every day mobs of people line up at the box-office. They are selling tickets 2, 3 weeks ahead. We have already played a week of *Fyodor* and will play a week of *Depths*. Today is Friday, there was a matinee for actors. After it more fraternization. Now it's evening. I am sitting at home and writing. I go nowhere. The theatre and my room. Attempts are being made now to change the terms with Gest. The millionaire Kahn who took on himself the risk of our tour wanted to speak with me personally. Some people visit me. Some ask me to write articles. They still have not specified the price of an article, but Sholom Asch is sure that they will pay from 2-3000 dollars an article. I am already writing for tips, in any case. Others inquire about publishing a book. Meanwhile they still don't explain what this might pay. I am living like the Miserly Knight. I have decided to make money in order to provide for you. If we are clever, it can – and only here can it – be done. Anyone else in our place, with such an unprecedented success, would leave here a millionaire. I feel that this is like Paris, just at the moment when we were starting to make real money, -- we had to leave. It has become clear that we have enslaved ourselves to Gest for the whole 6 months, that is until June. If he wants to extend it, we cannot prevent him, and moreover at the same financial terms as before. We have only one ace up our sleeve. The repertoire. We can play what *we* want and *with whom* we want. We cannot play *Fyodor* with Moskvin. Would anyone prefer Bulgakov -- !!²⁷

413

L. M. Koreneva

Théâtre Artistique de Moscou.

Figure 65 Lidiya Koreneva. Photo: A. Gubtschewsky, Berlin

But that way is awfully repugnant and unacceptable. Leonidov (Davydovich), it seems, has already tried to play on that string. Gest immediately stopped him and said that he is an honourable man and that if there is a success, he will offend no one and knows what he has to do. Only he has to do the right thing. We shall see!

So far I have felt no homesickness. But when I learned that you are not easy in your mind in Europe – I began to feel homesick and wanted to see you again as soon as possible.

[…] Yesterday was my birthday – aged 60. […] God, how fed up I am with going on in old plays!!! Last night I had a rest (my first this week) before today's matinee for actors. Yesterday only Podgorny, Ripsi and Bokshanskaya stopped by. They brought gifts.[28] Podgorny 3 pair of socks (what a shame. He hasn't got any money himself). Bokshanskaya and Ripsimé half a dozen handkerchieves (!!). Then Richard Boleslavsky came by and brought a wonderful leather document-case. It is interleaved like a notebook. Then there was Leonid Davydovich and his wife Yuliya Karlovna and he brought 4 neckties (!?!). All night long I lay in bed and slept. Then I took a bath and again turned in. Tonight after the show I am sitting at home as well, having excused myself on grounds of all sorts of business. I am writing to you. It is late now, I have to finish.

We have a frost – snow. Sometimes wind, and sometimes, like today, suddenly a sunny, wonderful day – Indian summer. Our idiots – the young people – immediately put on summer blouses, then catch colds, and I'm stuck with having to bring in new people in their place. […]

I embrace you all tenderly. I love you. I miss you, I'm worried. How is Kirilka? How I'd love to lay eyes on her. She's walking! She's talking!! Has she forgotten me? I want to send her toys. But, they say, it'll cost you an enormous customs fee. In general it's hard to send parcels here. I would send you sugar and other things but – there's no way. How is Igorek? That's the main question that is tormenting me. […]

I embrace you all tenderly and tightly.

Yours K. Alekseev

To **Nemirovich-Danchenko**. After 14 February 1923, New York.
Dear Vladimir Ivanovich!

I am writing you the most confidential letter, which only two persons should know about – you and I. Once you and I sat in the Slavonic Bazaar for whole days on end, talking about the future. Now I have occasion to write you about the future from afar.

One must get accustomed to the idea that the Art Theatre is no more. You appear to have understood this before I did, for all these years I flattered myself with hope and salvaged the mouldering remains. During this trip everyone and everything has come into quite sharp and well-defined focus. No one and nothing has a single *thought*, *idea*, outstanding *goal*. And without such things a concern based on ideas cannot exist. There was a time when we were at an impasse, in the sense of artistic questing. This is now no longer the case. We and we alone can learn to perform the great, so-called romantic plays. All the other theatres that endeavour to do this inevitably have to travel the road that we have paved. Otherwise they will not achieve what newly-fledged innovators are seeking so hastily and superficially. Our crowd understands this. When I tell them and demonstrate what rhythm, phonetics, musicality, graphic delineation of speech and movement mean, -- they understand, get excited, aspire. But when it becomes clear to them that this cannot be achieved without great preliminary work, the only ones who respond to it are those who ought not even to think about romanticism, while those who were made for it think to themselves: we'll manage with the old methods.

Do you want to serve Russian art? Do you want the MAT to exist? They all answer coldly: 'No – it's over and done with!' And this coldness is more eloquent than words, it bespeaks the ruin of the MAT.

415

I have no energy to begin new work on the same old foundations.

'Why,' they cry. 'Give us new foundations to produce new work.' But it is impossible to teach them to speak literately, move rhythmically and so on – while working on a role. That way they only jerry-build a role and patch it together. A rehearsal cannot be transformed into a lesson. There is no way to explicate one and the same thing to each one of them – individually. A stage director has no time or patience. But the actors don't take this into consideration. What they call work is rehearsing new plays and learning their lines, but not art itself. It is impossible to overcome this prejudice. I give it up. But work by the previous method appalls me. And I no longer have the strength for it.

So: they don't want to do it a new way, and the old way is impossible.

Where am I to direct my energies? To whom am I to give what, to my mind, is the most important thing that I have learned during this time and that life and practice continue to reveal to me now. 60 has struck. Is there any way to dream sensibly about breeding a new young generation to whom to transmit what I know? I won't live that long. One can talk about rhythm, phonetics, graphics with a great, consummate, experienced actor. It's premature to hammer this into the head of youngsters.

What's the good of you or I staging another 5 plays, which will have an enormous success; for when we are not around us our students will not even know how to revive the productions as they could not do with either *Depths* or *Ch. Orchard* or *3 Sisters* during the time of the Kachalov tours.

Now that we have followed in their tracks, we have been convinced of this by those who had seen them and then compared them with us.

'Don't let them out by themselves!'

That's the refrain uttered by the witnesses of the political, not artistic, successes of the Kachalov group...

I have no one to whom to give what I would like to give! (Nor do you.) Nothing more remains for us but to write and perhaps illustrate in films what cannot be represented by the pen. With this work we can conclude our artistic life.

But how can we discard and disperse the basic MAT group?

After all, for all its drawbacks it is *unique* (in the whole world). Now, having travelled this world, we can state conclusively that these are not mere words. Of course, it is the best theatre in the world, the best, rarest group of artistic personalities.

Without presenting anything new, it can and must be shown. Nor is that all. Only it alone can be shown abroad.

The total, wretched collapse of the 1st Studio (not of [Mikhail] Chekhov) confirms this idea. Those tours left a bad impression everywhere, and I'm thinking, won't it be dangerous if they go back to touring? Such is the opinion of those who have seen the tours.[29]

But – Europe! – one has to forget about it. There is nothing to be gained there but losses. To act for a month (that is the maximum) and then travel for 10-15 days to a new spot and spend everything you've earned – that is not business!

Anyone who has been to America and experienced this vast expanse, anyone who has seen the endless queues of people all day long – at the box-office. And there is no end to this queue... Anyone who has heard the voice and call from the provinces, from hundreds of towns with millions of inhabitants, a majority of whom are Russians, will understand that one can do business only in America.

'Stop writing about the MAT or let it come at once!' exclaim the papers in Chicago. What a great financial boon it is to have a success in America.

Financially this is expressed by 5700 dollars (that is, 11,400 gold rubles) a night. Non-stop, over the course of a year.

What kind of Europe can vie with America in this respect! But...!!

Anyone who has seen the America of managers, theatrical trusts, courts which are all disposed to favour the theatre owners and impresarios will understand what a horror, what a catastrophe it is to fail to be a success here.

Now that I am here, I understand and tremble at the thought of what Gest, Shubert, Joseph [sic] Kahn could do to us, if we were not a success and were to incur losses.

Since I understand this not only intellectually but viscerally, the same conviction with which I praise America when one is a success leads me to warn everyone against failure.

I would let Chekhov tour here. I haven't seen the performances of the 1st Studio. There's no point in talking about the 2nd Studio, the 3rd Studio would do for a month or two with *Turandot*.[30] Possibly! But not one impresario will take a troupe with a repertoire of fewer than 4-5 plays! Futurism is not in fashion here.

It is a great mistake to think that America is not acquainted with good actors. They have seen all the best there is in Europe. Perhaps that's the very reason that America so values individuality. The whole theatrical business of America is built on artistic personality. A certain actor is a genius, and the rest are mediocrities. Plus the most magnificent staging, which *we know not*. Plus *wonderful* lighting, of which we have no conception. Plus a technical stage which we haven't dreamed of, plus a staff of stage hands and their foremen of which we have never dreamed and would not dare to dream. (We begin *Three Sisters, Cherry Orchard* at 8:05 and end at 11:10. We begin *Fyodor* at 8:05 and end at 10:25. The interval before Act II of *Ch. Orchard* lasts 8 min., before Act IV of *Three Sisters* 10 min. And this on a stage 28 yards deep!!!)

So, we are far from being able to amaze America in every respect. An actor such as Warfield[31] who plays Shylock we do not have. And Belasco's production of *Merchant of Venice* exceeds in magnificence and lavishness anything I've ever seen, but as to the director's contribution – the Maly Theatre could give him grounds for envy.

Barrymore[32] as Hamlet is far from ideal, but very charming.

Such a Peer Gynt as young Schildkraut[33] we do not have in Russia. There are many famous-name actors whom we have not yet seen. The opera, when it comes to voices, can withstand comparison with any theatre in Europe

The symphony orchestra, conductors here are like nowhere else in the world.

To tell the truth, I frequently fail to understand why the Americans so extol us. The ensemble!

417

Yes, that is impressive.

But they are incomparably more impressed by the fact that in a single troupe there are 3, 4 artistic personalities, whom they immediately identified.

The rest, they say, is the work of the directors. This they can do even with our American rank-and-file actors. But three, four talents in a single play – that stuns them. True, there are some in our troupe they have not examined closely, have overlooked! But those who are on show and who have the right to first place, they immediately identified and appreciated more than Europe did.

Without America you can't live in Moscow, but the only machine for extracting dollars can be *the first group alone*. It would be crazy on our part if we don't try to stay here to feed the Moscow theatre, the studios. Let those who are incapable of greatness stick to that profitable, but far from interesting role. But there are a few who still want to work in art. To them I would add a few more – you, myself. What's to become of them? In all fairness, we have to establish a pecking order.

Sitting in Moscow, it may seem that the enviable role is to travel around with the troupe and enjoy success. But it is far from sweet and for the most part annoying and exhausting. You wouldn't put up with it for long. Moscow may have seemed onerous, but now I am convinced of the opposite. The heavy onus is not in Moscow but over here. It would be fair to give me a vacation and recall me to Moscow, and have you come here. As you have carefully preserved the studios, so I, I give you my word, will carefully preserve K.O.[34] at your bidding.

To leave the group here alone is impossible. They absolutely need a guardian.

You would be refreshed here, perhaps you will stage *Anathema, Karamazovs* for them, and I will be refreshed in Moscow, I will observe what is happening with the Opera Studio.

This is the only place where I can work in the meantime, for lack of anywhere else. In my free time I do some writing, so as to publish a book in America in time, for the whole world.

I am firmly convinced that you and [your wife] would not only be refreshed, but would earn enormous sums for the rainy day of old age – and not only profits from the theatre, which under a new contract might be huge and support the Moscow theatre and the studios, which are awaiting assistance from the government to no avail. Besides the theatre, you could give lectures, write articles, teach lessons at 50 dollars for half an hour and so on.

Then, when it becomes as unbearable for you as it is for me now, I will replace you.

If we do not do this, then the prospect that lies before me is tragic. Dragging my weary lot along with the 1st group to the sneers and insults of the Soviet newspapers. Beggary. Old age. Death in a refuge for superannuated actors and the complete impoverishment of my extended family and [your wife].

All this can be improved and provided for forever in some 4-7 months of an extended American tour.

Once our actors are financially provided for, then, who knows, maybe they will be able to become artists once again and work for art.

Under such conditions I see many of our old-timers involved in their leisure hours with phonetics and intonation and graphics and rhythm.

I am ready to believe that, provided for, they could give good performances with new tasks 3 times a week – and then manage to speak a new word in art.

Resumé:

1) As promised, we shall return in autumn – to Moscow (but this will be a fatal mistake).

2) We need to figure out whether the troupe is to remain, -- as a dollar pump – in America.

3) I shall return to Moscow, and you will travel to America. It would be good for us to move here and transfer by hand everything that is left here.

4) The first time it becomes necessary, after I bring the family to Russia, I shall set up Igor in Switzerland, over the course of the season I shall preserve whatever is left in Moscow, I shall supervise and encourage the Opera Studio – I shall return to America and replace you, if that is required.

5) Having provided financially for the troupe and studios with American dollars, everyone will return home, while preserving a close bond with America. (O. Kahn is building a theatre for touring foreign troupes, read in parenthesis – for the MAT.)

There is still one stumbling-block. It seems you are prejudiced against America and, besides, you won't enjoy the preliminary sea voyage.

Don't believe it, America is not at all what you think it is. Enormous buildings, streets like corridors, a piercing wind, darkness, soot, head-spinning movement. All that, probably, is there, to some degree, in various parts of the city. Certain places, 1st and 2nd streets are in constant movement. (You don't have to go there.) Certain places, in the business districts of the city, probably have big buildings, the famous American rhythm of life is oppressive. But all this is somewhere else.

What we see in the centre of the city mostly reminds me of a bigger Moscow.

The people are fascinating, affectionate, good-natured, naïve, athirst for knowledge, utterly spontaneous, without European snobbery, looking you in the eye and ready to accept whatever is new and genuine. It is not true that the American will only go to a musical revue. He is as alert as a German, tries to understand Chekhov, and the women shed tears when they see *Three Sisters*. It is not true that at 11 o'clock everyone gets up and leaves. Komissarzhevsky[35] ended his public dress rehearsal of *Peer Gynt* at 1:30 in the morning and everyone stayed in his seat and said: for the sake of a revue we wouldn't lose sleep, but for a real play – *yes*. And not only the middle classes but even the aristocrats are unusually kind. [...]

There is no doubt that Americans sincerely love Russia.

Not long ago I read a letter from O. Kahn, written after a certain report on Russia. In it he acknowledges the completely exceptional bond of America to Russia, a unity or kinship of spirit and concludes that the MAT has played an historic, political and national role. We are the first and most eloquent and persuasive envoys from Russia, who have brought America not the cut-and-dried clauses of a commercial treaty, but the living Russian soul, for which America has felt a bond.

In some other gathering it was said that the political role of the MAT is enormous. It returned to Russia many Russians who had remained in America. Once they experienced the Russian soul, these Americanized Russians again burned with a desire to return to their homeland. This is the cultural element that will play a very important part in the life of Russia's future industrialization.

Have Yelena Konst. [Malinovskaya] explain this to the Communists. It is worth their knowing. Instead of thanks, we read quite often in *Izvestia* and other papers caustic and insulting remarks and threats directed at us: 'what are you going to show us now that you've been abroad?'

Meanwhile, if you provide no new instructions, we shall arrange to return in the fall.[36]

We shall return as beggars, much as we left, in order to die in an actor's asylum. Indeed at the present moment we are covering the losses incurred in Europe. Then, before summer, we shall earn something. We shall lose the summer, because there is no sense in going to England (where business is very bad) for 3 weeks. According to Gest's contract we belong to Gest until June.

We will live on the little bit of money we earn till summer. In fall we will earn a tiny bit more. It will be enough for me to afford Igor a year's stay in Switzerland. But to cure him 3-5 years are absolutely necessary. Therefore I will again at the earliest opportunity, for the sake of my son's life, have to go to America alone.

In short, I can't keep all this bottled up. Some kind of foolishness will result.

Bear in mind that during the tour the work is so heavy, with all sorts of extraneous incursions, what with illnesses, capriciousness and other reasons, so many that there is no way to think about new plays. Once I have earned extra money, I have to go to a country with a cheap currency (even if it's Russia) and there prepare a new repertoire. To begin in Moscow with the old one is tantamount to closing the theatre.

Now that the troupe has sniffed dollars, everyone has started saving. Drunkenness has decreased, things have become quieter and easier, and only Koreneva rants and raves, out of her overweening vanity and envy. Yes! It is difficult to glorify Russia with a troupe of male and female hysterics. You know how to deal with them – it will be easier for you, but they are afraid of me when they needn't be and aren't afraid of me when they should be.

Just now I've been told that O. Kahn gave a speech somewhere. 'Russia owes us so many millions, but she has sent us Rachmaninov, Chaliapin, Diaghilev, a whole series of artists and, finally, the MAT. – She has paid all her debts. We are quits.' Tell that to the Komfin. [...]

To the whole theatre, all the studios friendly greetings.

Yours K. Stanislavsky

N.B. We have begun the 6th week (*Cherry Orchard*). So far full houses.

On 9 February 1923, a decree of the Sovnarkom created the Chief Committee for the Control of the Repertoire (Glavny Komitet po kontrolyu za repertuarom, known familiarly as GRK or Glavrepertkom). Not subject to Lunacharsky's control, it demonstrated the weakening of his influence and began increasingly to interfere in theatrical matters.

Before the MAT left on tour it was obliged by the Special Committee for the Organization of Foreign Artistic Trips to give a charity performance in the US every month on behalf of the Commission to Fight the Effects of the Famine (Pomgol). Since the contract with Gest made no provision for such a contingency, the theatre contracted with the Russian representatives of the Red Cross in America; it implemented the Pomgol obligation, enabling the MAT to pay out the mid-month profit from one performance (in 1923 it consisted of 1175 dollars.) On 30 March Olga Bokshanskaya handed Pomgol a check for three months for $3525. Later on, when the troupe's receipts lessened considerably, the problem of paying the Commission greatly complicated its life.

To his brother Vladimir and his sister Zinaida. End of March 1923, New York.

Read this letter after the Chicago one.

Dear Volodya and Zina!

[...] Everyone everywhere is interested in the [opera] studio. Especially in Zagreb and New York. Tours can be arranged. In Europe with losses, in America with a little profit. It can't be done without an orchestra. An orchestra costs crazy money. Everyone has caught fire at the studio: Rachmaninov and Ziloti and chiefly Coates[37] (from the Mariinsky Theatre). Coates is looking for a millionaire. Gest has taken an interest. He wants to talk with me, but... I suddenly learn from the Moscow letters, various sources (some of them from Malinovskaya's crowd) that all is well – they are performing and successfully and there's progress in the singing, and full houses three times a week, but the discipline of the studio folks is becoming the talk of the town.

All at once my shoulders drooped, my heart sank into my boots and a dreadful idea pierced my brain. The concern is defunct! Without discipline a theatre actor has no art! Art is discipline! For such a crowd of loose-living singers to appear in America!! To fall into the clutches of Gest!!! And be the only one to answer for all those who are unwilling to take orders. After all, the slightest misstep – and the contract is broken. Go home overseas on foot. And here everything is done to the profit of the entrepreneur, not us, the actors. The lawyers themselves say: it is not worth going to court in America. Their own crowd always wins, they know them and regard them as close relations.

So I lose heart and put off the appointed day for discussions with Gest. Now I keep thinking: what's going to happen to me? Will I have to take on all the responsibility on my own? What for? That's crazy! Only with utter, blind faith in one's forces can one undertake a new grand tour. Our troupe is made up of old-timers, with whom the studio folks cannot even compare in discipline, and they are far from disciplined enough for this trip. And meanwhile here's what they are capable of. The Cherry Orchard is scheduled – 8 performances in a row per week, and next week 8 performances of Three Sisters. On the day of the first performance of Cherry Orchard Knipper fell ill – 38.5°C in the morning (at night they were afraid to take her temperature). There's no one to replace her. I fly to Gest. 'The show must go on. I will not allow you to change the play. Let anyone who likes go on. What do I care if you haven't brought a sufficient number of actors. You will pay for all the losses.' Knipper, sick, with a fever of 38-39.5°C , played all 16 performances and saved us. 'You modern-day lot! How about that!'

[...] Of course they have swindled us to the top of their bent. Everything possible has been sucked up in a few months. They had good reason for renting one of the biggest theatres (over 2000 spectators). Things are managed in the most profligate way, because all the plays open with sold-out box-offices for 2 months, the expenses have been repaid and now they will pay us in the provinces. The press has rattled away after every opening like machine guns. They have written about nothing but us, on the first page, non-stop, every day, because premiere after premiere has been opening. When everything had opened, the press had to fall silent, but Gest was able to come up with topics for interviews etc. This, naturally, had its effect on the box-office. Receipts got worse. From 5700 every night (in tsarist money = 11,400 r. per night) they dropped to 3000 dollars (in tsarist money = 6000). This is an awful lot, but nevertheless it gives Gest the right to comment on and point out the drop in receipts in order to put pressure on us in discussions about the tour and future terms. All this is performed as if to music. As a result – there is nothing to be earned per performance here.

It is possible to make money by other means. For instance, the cinema, lessons, setting up a studio, articles. They pay a lot of money for this, but you have to stay in one place, and that is impossible with a troupe, because there are too few plays in the repertoire. […]

The cinema. I have come up with quite a unique scenario (which we will perform in Moscow). A grandiose one, which might be entitled *The Tragedy of the Peoples*. It has Ivan the Terrible and Fyodor and Dmitry and the Russian people, excellently characterized. For America, I am told, all this can serve as background. Centre stage you need a romance of two young people, with impediments to their love. We curse, wrangle. I am afraid that nothing will come of it. If the cinema doesn't work out, there is no way to stay here, because there is no way to perform in the summer, and the 50 members of the troupe have to be fed. We will probably go to London (summer), Paris, Scandinavia (autumn). Then we will meet again in November. If things work out with the cinema, we shall stay in America and return in February, but… whether we return with money!? – That is the question. And for Igor it is the fatal question of his life, because you cannot live abroad on Soviet money, and it will take 5 years to cure him. Meanwhile I'm fed up with the wandering life, and being alone, without my family, in America, at my age! I am completely alone, I live alone in a hotel, where they don't speak any language but English. The hotel is shabby, the servants Negroes. When I need something, I phone either Engel (ran a hair clinic in Moscow) or Yek. Vl. Gzovskaya. These two ladies comprise my companions, they are involved with publishing the book, the studios, the articles. I doubt that anything will come of it. […]

….What should I tell you about America! Well, for instance. You travel by underground railway. In the car there is a recorded voice. They say: 'Such-and-such a station', 'do not get out until the doors open' and all sorts of other instructions. There is no conductor. It's all automatic. The same with the trolley. The doors open by themselves, you put in 5 cents by yourself. Here's another picture of life here. A child lies down to sleep. The mother hurries to the theatre. She puts a radio (a special machine in each home) in front of him, and it tells a story, which one man at the station tells to all of New York at night. Such machines are also in the villages, in the deepest backwoods. They also catch radio waves in it and connect them to the opera, our theatre, a lecture, etc. [...]

To **his wife Mariya Lilina**. First half of April, 1923, Chicago.
Dear, priceless Marusya, Kira, Igor, Kirilka!
[...] The fact that we spent 3 months in New York and had an enormous success means nothing in Chicago. Here no one even knows about us. We start at the beginning. The press is fantastic, 10 to 14 curtain calls, but the box-office is not sold out and in proportion the extent of the tours keeps getting longer. The last week there will be full houses. There are supposed to be – that's how America works. You have to prove yourself first, and at the very last the public actually forks out its dollars. So, the financial aspect is not the most brilliant. In New York the movie deal fell through. This means a loss of about 20,000 for me. But there was nothing to be done. We composed a brilliant scenario, which, sooner or later, will be filmed somewhere. A serious, intellectual one. So action-packed that it doesn't require a single intertitle. They tell us: it's fine, but not for America. Let it stay in the background, for front and centre we need the romance of Natasha Mstislavskaya and Shakhovskoy. She should be a peasant girl, in love with Fyodor, and Fyodor with her. Irina must be jealous of her. And to get rid of her rival, she tries to marry her off to Shakhovskoy. They put him in prison, and Natasha in the costume of a Strelitz goes to the prison, rescues him and they reach the Kremlin by crawling along the housetops. They climb the wall up to the dome of the church, everything ends in a marriage. With a picture like that we would be unable to show our faces in Moscow.

Gest [...] doesn't swindle, everything is above board, according to the contract, but is so devised that all the assets go to him and all the liabilities to us. Despite the splendid box-office (especially in comparison with other theatres). For instance, at the moment we are making around 3500 dollars a performance (with 10 performances a week), while the most popular theatre with a new play makes 1500 dollars. Everyone is astonished that a foreign-language theatre can take in such receipts. What's more: 3500 = an even 7,000 rub. We never made this anywhere in the old days – neither in Moscow nor in Petersburg, where the maximum was 5000 rubles. And, despite the receipts, God willing, we have left 250-300 a share, including yours, which comes to 5 to 6,000 dollars. In the best case and in the current tour of the provinces we are earning that much. 10,000 altogether. The articles I will write -- ? The book... exists and the publisher, but the contract is not yet drawn up. The studio and lessons will evaporate, if we do not come back here next year. And it likely that we shall not indeed return. We need a new repertoire: *Uncle Vanya*, *Karamazovs* (all of it), *The Government Inspector*,[38] *In the Clutches of Life* (Kachalov's request). Consider what the scenery, transport of costumes will cost, we shall have to support the troupe all summer long, because there is no way to go to England, they won't let Russian actors in (unemployment and poor theatrical business). Either we return to Moscow or, living out the summer in communal conditions, we go to Paris (with the addition of 1-2 plays). Belgium, perhaps, Sweden, Denmark, Holland, Scandinavia. So far all these plans are fermenting. But no doubt by the end of the present provincial tour (end of May), we shall go to Europe and see one another soon.

Love, hugs, miss you. Very lonely. Love.

Yours Kostya [...]

To his daughter Kira and grand-daughter Kirilla. 24 April 1923, Philadelphia.
Dear, good Kiryula, Kirilka!

[...] Philadelphia is a very cold city in terms of the public. The local residents were surprised that we have received up to 10 curtain calls, and it struck us that our reception was worse than we expected. And here, despite the fact that Philadelphia is 2 hours' journey from New York, most of them know nothing about us. [...]

Papa [...]

To his wife Mariya Lilina. 25 April 1923, Philadelphia.
Dear good Marusya!

I am informing you under the most solemn seal of secrecy (otherwise some great unpleasantness might result) that the preliminary contract for America is signed and sealed. I have had to turn down Gest and move to Hurok.[39] First, because Gest insisted on a contract that went no longer than May (and our leave to February), and second, he is giving himself airs, is under the bad influence of Baliev, who has turned out to be a downright boor. Hurok offered a brilliant contract, twice as profitable as Gest's. He has secured the money and offers an advance of 25,000 dollars. We need a new repertoire (he demands: *Government Inspector*, *Karamazovs* (1 evening), *Uncle Vanya*, *Wise Fool*, *Clutches* (?!!)). I am afraid that in 3 months (November to February) one will not earn much, because one has to pay for the scenery, which has to be made anew, and the travel there and back. On 7 June we go to Europe. Perhaps we will be able to get to Paris for discussions about October. From Paris to you is a long journey, because there is no way to go the usual route through the Ruhr (they blow up a train every day) and we have to go roundabout somehow. [...]

To his family. 13 May 1923, Boston.
Dear, kind, beloved Marusya, Kira, Igorechek and Kirillochka!

I am writing from Boston. The city is good, quiet, a success, same as everywhere. The first night the audience, as in the other cities, responded in a wishy-washy way, and the second, probably, will come in droves, because in the provinces they don't believe the press. We got here on a Sunday, nearly 5 o'clock (having left Philadelphia at 9:30 a.m. the same day). We were met by a rather large crowd with two loaves and salt. One from the Russian colony – a superb gilt platter with a salt-cellar and a delicious kulich, and the other from the city, carried by the mayor – on a silver platter – with black (almost) bread and a wooden salt-cellar. A priest (a refined gent in a fancy jacket and buttoned waistcoat, on which he hangs a cross, tucked into a side pocket. That's how the priests dress around here) spoke at length – in Russian. The mayor spoke at length – in English, I briefly in Russian. No one understands anyone else and so we bowed and spoke our thanks all the more cordially, each in his own language. Meanwhile a committee of a few men and ladies were present, chosen to escort us to our meetings in Boston. That very evening there was a rehearsal of *Fyodor* (?!!!) with supernumeraries and actors and the next day we performed. The reception was great. Now the routine days flow by again: matinees three times a week etc., etc. It's boring to write about it…

Some of what I wrote in my unfinished letter (appended) has changed. For instance, the repertoire. Since I wrote [Americans] rushed to put on *The Government Inspector* and it cruelly flopped on the American stage.[40] The play was abused by the press, and Hurok (or more correctly Yurok) swore off it. We conferred at length. We need a Russian play – *Woe from Wit*. Big, expensive cast -- in the loss column. *Pazukhin's Death* they won't understand. *The Village of Stepanchikovo*. Who will play the darling uncle? There are three possibilities: myself, Leonidov and Kachalov. I do not have the strength, and after all that has happened, I cannot! Leonidov is empty words. Kachalov – one could not come up with anyone better. Whereupon a whole tragedy erupted (only, for heaven's sake, do not write and tell him about this. Otherwise there will be a whole to-do.) Its cause, of course, is clear to all. There are two real roles in it, Moskvin's and his competition. And the role of Foma wins. This led to an (epistolary) explanation, with which I, of course, sympathize. How Kachalov is hurt and insulted, how he *was not shown* to America, how he is losing his reputation. He is an alternate to myself and Moskvin. All this is, of course, Ninka's[41] doing. He doesn't need the tour, it isn't worth the sacrifice. It's a disgrace to travel for dollars (while he himself acquired a fistful of pounds sterling from this tour). He is refusing to do anything, but would like to be released. All this, of course, in the most delicate style without a hint of blackmail (just like Koreneva!).

When we were agonizing ingloriously in Moscow for 3 years and starved, while Kachalov was going around Europe picking clean our fame and money, that was all right. But when he has to help us for one little year, it's a disgrace to chase after dollars etc. The new contract has caused turmoil in the troupe. Some are to be sent back, others, perhaps, dismissed (for instance, Germanova).[42] Again Koreneva behaved like a housemaid, and asserted that she had saved the theatre (in some past era she once stood in for an indisposed Bulgakova[43]). Bulgakov, who happened to have played Fyodor twice, is at a loss as to why he is not given more to play. […]

In short, the swamp begins to stir again and again it become abundantly clear that there is no theatre, that the souls of our actors are stinking muck and that one must run away from this cesspit. One has to protect one's family from this, and therefore one has to be patient. Let Vas. Iv. [Kachalov] be a noble idealist, while I am a dollar-hound.

After long discussions and deliberations it was decided that of the plays proposed the easiest, fastest and most profitable of all to stage is *Fruits of Enlightenment*. [...]

Uncle Vanya will remain. *Clutches* ditto. *Karamazov* ditto. *Wise Fool* ditto. The costumes for *Mistress of the Inn* will be brought over again for a few charity performances on behalf of Moscow actors. Mirandolina will be played, in English, by the charming Laurette Taylor,[44] who dreams about this. This is a secret too. This medley of languages will be reproved, but, first, it is not a scheduled performance of the MAT, but an incidental one, like all charity performances, -- a gimmick. Otherwise you wouldn't collect lots of money to feed the Moscow actors. The end justifies the means. And second, she will be such an ideal Mirandolina that they will forgive the medley of languages. Which is better: a vile Mirandolina in Russian or a brilliant one in English. To my mind, for art's sake the latter, foreign Mirandolina. [45] So, on 7 June we go to Hamburg (for about 10-12 days). Another change: I will not be going to Paris. From Hamburg straight to you, with Vishnevsky. I will not plan to go to a spa, but if you do, I am ready to be with you, if only to meet with Igor and Kiryulya. Experience has convinced me that spas are dreadfully wearying and any effect is very short-lived. You feel much better if you constantly take salts for gout over the course of a whole year, with the help of diuretics and similar 'Vichy' waters. [...]

The best thing in America is travelling in a Pullman car. The fact is that they are giving us a whole train with a restaurant. Wonderful cars, with warm water, separate smoking-cars. I have a great drawing-room compartment. The stagehands are travelling with us. We have got used to one another. For the first time I am living quite alone. So, for instance, today I did not act. I sit at home – I wrote, and lolled about half the night in bed and sang under my breath (I have transposed my voice). Well, good-bye, dear ones. Now, God willing, it won't be long. We'll still have to be parted next year, but not for long. And then to Moscow, to Moscow, to Moscow. Tender hugs, love.

Yours Kostya

To **his family**. 21 May 1923, New York.
Dear, good Marusya, Kira, Igor, Kirilka!

The journey is over – and yesterday we returned on Sunday, 20 May to New York. I am sitting again in the same room at the Thorndyke and today we begin with *Fyodor* – at the same Al Jolson theatre. (By the way: in Boston we saw the famous Al Jolson, in whose honour the theatre is named. He is something like a clown or, more accurately, a chatterbox à la Baliev, only refined, in evening dress. He spouts all sorts of piffle on topical themes. Talented.) In Boston I came down with a cold. [...]

Under the most solemn seal of secrecy (although our blabbermouths have had time to trumpet it everywhere. Nevertheless we are keeping it a secret, and if anyone asks us, we deny it as a rumour). Yesterday I met with Hurok (Chaliapin's new manager). [...] I suppose Gest sniffed danger. Yesterday he came to meet us, was very affectionate, spoke a lot of flattering compliments. Tonight he made an appointment with Leonidov (Davydovich) to discuss the future. I don't know the results. In the past he behaved like a boor, and in every way gave us to understand (obviously, he had prepared a more advantageous contract) that we were already finished in America, squeezed dry, we are of no interest, and offered an even half of the previous terms. But then, I don't remember if I wrote you this, on our arrival in Philadelphia I had to do the following in one day: at 12 o'clock take the train to New York – to make a public appearance in a stage-box with Belasco, Reinhardt (and I). Then have my picture taken with them. Rush back to Philadelphia (2 hours' travel). From the station to a women's club, where local millionaires (around here they count as aristocracy) gave us a reception. I was late because that day, the same as in Soviet Russia, the clocks were set back an hour (that's where all our news comes from). In the evening the Russian colony organized a banquet, and I made toasts. A few days later Reinhardt paid us a visit and came to Philadelphia for the 1st performance of *Cherry Orchard*. A packed house, full to the rafters, extra seats, and lots of the public turned away without tickets (*Cherry Orchard* has the greatest success in the American provinces). Fortunately, in terms of acting it was an extremely successful performance, and the Philadelphia audience, famous for its restraint and coldness, went wild to the surprise of everyone present. Reinhardt and a beauty – a Rumanian actress sitting with him in a box -- burst into tears. Reinhardt said that the play is remarkable and the interpretation unprecedented. After this he gave an interview to various papers. (I enclose it to be preserved in the MAT Museum.) This was the performance that, to all appearances, caused perturbation in Gest, which led to some sort of disagreement with Reinhardt, who was his chosen one. For *The Miracle*, a pantomime, he needs a beauty and, of course, an actress to play the Holy Mother of God. But Gest sent him all his mistresses – little short of street-walkers. Evidently, there are now three entrepreneurs chasing after us (I forgot the name of the third!). But, so far as I'm concerned, the deal is concluded with Hurok. On 7 June we board the boat (a big German one), sailing straight for Hamburg. [...]

On 23/4 May the director of the American Defense Society R. M. Whitney published in the Boston Evening Transcript *a report that the theatre was sending 25% to 33% of its receipts to the Third International. Two days later, in a letter no longer extant, KS wrote to Morris Gest, asking the impresario to take all possible measures to 'refute the mendacious report which has a tendency to present our mission to the American public in a false light'. The theatre's only propaganda is propaganda for art, he insisted, and has no financial obligations to the Soviet government. Gest quoted this letter in print to contradict the newspaper account.*

To his brother Vladimir and his sister Zinaida. After 7 June 1923.
Dear, beloved Volodya and Zina!

[...] I know and grieve that you are distressed by the news that we signed (so far it's a secret) a contract with Gest for next season. What was I to do? If I were to refuse, -- everyone would be deprived of the possibility of going to America, besides we had only prepared the ground, opened up the American public, especially the provinces. [...]

I have completely changed my opinion about the Americans. I do not know what these people are like in regard to dollars, that is in the commercial sense. Probably, they are very unpleasant, but in everything else they are remarkably compatible with Russians. They sincerely love us Russians. In America even without the language you feel completely at home. You can talk and shout in Russian. They all like it, whereas in Germany, for instance, you have to hunch over and speak in a still, small voice. The local so-called aristocracy is a typically bourgeois family, reminiscent of the best Russian merchants' homes. Big rooms, lots of everything, lots of servants, lots of entertaining. The difference is that the audience is very naïve and tolerant. We sing Russian songs everywhere – 'The sun comes up' (I wrote you that even Marcella Sembrich[46] sang in our choir), and everyone goes crazy. Well, good-bye for now. [...]

KS began to write My Life in Art *on the boat in June. He also sent suggestions for renovating the scenery for* In the Clutches of Life, Mistress of the Inn *and* Ivanov *in Europe. For reasons of economy, the designs were often simplified for touring purposes, with sections of scenery from other plays pieced together. Gremislavsky had written of the difficulty of adjusting Benois' dimensions to the specifications of the American stage and quick-changes, and reported that he would not get the scenery from Moscow before August.*

To his brother Vladimir and his sister Zinaida. 15 September 1923, Berlin.
Dear, good Volodya and Zina!

[...] The fact is, my eyes do not allow me to work (that is, write) for more than three hours, and I have to finish the book – my autobiography (which I have turned into a history of the MAT) – by the deadline. They've ordered 60,000 words. And I have written them, but out of inexperience I did not reckon on the amount of material and have only reached the founding of the MAT. I sent the hastily written material to the publisher and he liked it very much. I am asking him to do it as 2 volumes, because I do not know how to abridge my through action into 1 volume. And the history of the MAT itself, God willing, will fill up a whole volume. The publisher sent to say that it is impossible. America absolutely requires a single volume, and even Shakespeare himself is published in one volume. So now I'm in a fix. It is crucial to publish the book, because now it is crystal clear that in America you can't make money from the theatre, despite the colossal box-office. Indeed at this time we are travelling with no more, no fewer than 8 American railway cars of scenery (which is equal to 16 Russian cars). A whole goods train, which is to travel across all America. On the other hand now, with success in the making and the publicity, there is a dreadful demand for the book, pictures of the theatre etc. But it has to come out while we are of interest to America. Once we leave – then it's a different story. The book, issued in time, will have a minimal press-run of 30,000 copies. That is the set number because all the libraries will buy a book that's in the public eye. That is why it is crucial to publish it now without fail, while we are acting in America, that is, interesting society with our personalities. Afterwards – things will be quite different. The press-run might reach only 5000 copies. And it is crucial for me to provide for Igor's stay in Switzerland (a secret, because Switzerland is hostile to Soviet Russia) for 4 or 5 years. And this costs a dreadful amount of money. So I'm writing, but now rehearsals have begun morning and evening, because we have to set up the new repertoire, with new performers, of 6 plays (*Enemy of the People, The Mistress of the Inn, Karamazov, Wise Fool, Clutches of Life* and *Ivanov*). I write at night. Once the performances begin, there will not be enough time or strength to study difficult roles twice a day and then write a book. So I am in a tearing hurry. There is no time for letters. [...]

I do not have time to write to Aleks. Vlad.[47] that I am *horrified* that the Bolshoy Theatre wants *to appropriate our costumes* [for *Yevgeny Onegin* and *Werther*]. If this is so, we have to assume that we are pounding water through a sieve. We are working to create our own repertoire, while the costumiers are dismantling the main thing necessary for an independent life – the actors' costumes. I know what it means to hand over even one single costume to somebody else. It means saying good-bye to the whole production. For instance. We gave 2 costumes to the 2nd Studio for a Molière production. Now the costumiers declare that we have given away almost all the costumes to somebody, and only half from the Benois production are left. Moreover, when I say that the costumes are not in order and soiled (all of them) – they reply that it's the fault of the 2nd Studio (which borrowed 2 costumes, not all of them). The same thing will happen with the Bolshoy Theatre. Our costumes will be devoted to hackwork, and they will assert that we were the ones who soiled and wore them out. When we come to stage something at the Opera Studio the first and essential condition is the following. A costume, in which I have invested part of my soul, cannot be at the disposal of anyone other than the studio for which it was created. Otherwise they will lose heart and their imaginations will go numb. Cannot someone plead with El. Konst. [Malinovskaya] not to let them confiscate our costumes. [...]

Kostya

To **Aleksandr Bogdanovich**. Atlantic Ocean, The *Olympic*, 2 November 1923. Dear, good Aleksandr Vladimirovich!

[...] When I am in Europe – decaying, worn out Europe – the wailing about Russia becomes too much. In America it's somewhat easier. But even so no promise of dollars, no prosperity will make me trade Russia the tormentor for darling America. If I do not go home this year, it is only because of ailing Igor. I am afraid that this season will not bring us many dollars. We hope we will be successful, because the Americans have sincerely fallen in love with us and in the Parisian American newspapers they call us *their* theatre. But... All our plans and budgets are wrecked thanks to the German revolution, which we had to escape, because we were afraid of losing our property, costumes, scenery.[48] We had to live in an expensive country (France), where we lost dollars and the cost of living was rising, -- for more than a month and a half, instead of a week. The new scenery for the foreign repertoire is also being made at steep prices in Germany or at expensive Paris prices. And keeping 60 people in expensive Paris instead of in inexpensive Germany!!! And the tours cancelled in Berlin, which were supposed to serve as dress rehearsals!! And the rail travel with prices raised a thousand times!! And the delay of the scenery and the cancellation of performances with full houses in Paris!! And 4 months of living without performing in the off-season (10 June to 8 October)!! All this forced us to begin the season with big debts, which had to be covered before aught else. True, in America we will have enormous receipts. For instance, in June at the daily performances of which there were 3 a week at a temperature of 50° (the asphalt melted), -- the theatre took in 5,000 dollars. But all this goes to the impresario, his pocket, his company, and Otto Kahn (a percentage of the advance [for travel]. In comparison we get small change. [...]

K. Stanislavsky

To his daughter Kira and grand-daughter Kirilla. 11 November 1923, New York. Dear, good, beloved Kiryulya and Kilyalya!

[...] In Cherbourg we expected a horrendous inspection, because valuable Gobelins had been stolen from Versailles, and now they're looking for them everywhere. But everything turned out all right. They didn't inspect us [...]

The crossing [on the *Olympic*] was excellent the whole time, but it was freezing and there was nowhere to sit on deck, because all the best places had been snatched by yids. The upper deck is enormous, spacious, but open, and it was wonderful there on sunny days. They were very hot, but few. On the first crossing thanks to a tidy deck we could all sit together, but this time we're all separated. I've been writing almost all the time.

[...] Gest arrived on the boat with his whole staff. He began his policy, that is to praise Duse, who is doing, according to him, terrific business, 'like nobody ever'. That's a stone meant for our yard.

'How many times a week did she perform?' Moskvin asks.

'Twice,' replies Gest.

'And do you think that if we performed twice, the box-office would be any good?' Moskvin explained.

We came on shore the next morning. Everyone disembarked at a different time. I went to the Thorndyke. At first they put me on the top floor (the upper ones are more expensive). Then I moved to my previous room. Everything there is familiar and 'all things here bring to mind the past'.[49] There's the broken chair I broke last year, and there's the torn curtain. You know where you can hang things, where you can put things. I'm at home. And actually, in all the world, the Thorndyke is most my home, because here I am my own master. Not in Moscow where I do not have my own room, where everyone breaks in on everyone else. Not to mention other cities where you live in barracks. As a result everyone moved to the Thorndyke (it turned out to be the cheapest): Knipper, Moskvin, Raevskaya, Bertenson, Leonidov, Gremislavsky. Then the surprises began. The theatre, which should have been turned over to us for a week, was turned over only on the day of the performance. Gest blustered and impudently exclaimed, 'I'm supposed to provide a theatre. Any one. Forget about the Jolson Theatre. Here's the Princess Theatre for you' (and the stage is three times smaller there). How we are to get out of this mess I don't know. Meanwhile we rehearse in rooms at the hotel. What's more, Gest scheduled us for the 31, but the performance is 19 November. No theatre, no rehearsals, and we have to have dollars to pay the troupe. In this way, we are starting with a debt of some 30,000 dollars (60,000 [gold rubles]). There is no way to expect profits from the percentages. Thank God, the salaries are guaranteed. My only hope is the book. Here the editor and the translator praise it a good deal. They assert that it will be eternal, meaning edition after edition, because it is full of pedagogical and directorial and actorial advice. God grant it be so. But first it has to be written, and has to be a success. The profit, if it is to make one, will come no sooner than autumn of next year. That is why you must not be angry if I write infrequently. I don't have eyes enough. All my free time has to be given to the book, especially now that I am in New York. I have to finish the main thing, otherwise disaster. When I am travelling, there is no time to do anything.

From here we go to Montreal and some other city in Canada.[50] (We were dreaming about the sun, and we get snow.) Canada is the same latitude as Moscow (we most humbly thank you). And I have no fur coat (it was stolen). I'll have to have one made. Disaster! It may go down to 25 degrees of frost there. We'll be there 2-3 weeks, and from there to Boston, Philadelphia, Chicago, Washington. I don't know where beyond that. There is a lot of talk about setting up a permanent studio here under the general leadership of the MAT. That will constitute a subsidy for the theatre. Yesterday there was a celebration – for Duse's performance. At 2 o'clock the whole troupe went to the theatre for the matinee. An old woman – the ancient of days… with dreadful asthma. She can hardly walk. It is painful to see. She can no longer act, but there is a certain music in her. After the performance Knipper and I went on stage, brought her a basket of flowers. I made a very long speech in French. Now and then it was interrupted by applause. Duse was very moved and grateful. I feel sorry for her. […]

Your Papa. […]

On 10 September 1923 the Moscow Evening News *reprinted a squib from other papers under the headline 'Lord Stanislavsky Waxes Wroth'. It stated that in American interviews KS praised the reception by the American spectators and disdained the Soviet spectator. On 28 October the Soviet comic journal* Krokodil *printed a caricature*

*showing him bowing to American bankers saying, 'Ladies and gentlemen! How glad I
am not to see before me that Soviet scum.'*

To **Nemirovich-Danchenko**. 20 November 1923. *Telegram*.
Report of my American interview lies from start to finish. Repeatedly, before
hundreds of witnesses, I said direct opposite about new spectator, -- boasted, took
pride in his instincts, offered as example philosophical tragedy *Cain*, splendidly
welcomed by new spectator. I thought my forty years' activity and long-standing
dream of people's theatre would protect me against insulting suspicions. Deeply
offended, wounded to the heart.

*The same day he had been named an honorary member of the Maly Theatre and a People's
Artist. Narkompros accepted his letter exculpating himself from newspaper accusations.*

To **his wife Mariya Lilina**. 27 November 1923, New York.
Dear, darling Marusya!
 […] 2 premieres have gone by.[51] The success is enormous, perhaps bigger than
last year's. Especially *Mistress of the Inn*, which went unprecedentedly well.
Kairansky had a look and says that it can't be compared with Moscow, that
Pyzhova is incomparably better than Gzovskaya. Even Gzovskaya's sister
Yekaterina admitted that. But… the box-office is paltry. Perhaps it will improve,
although it's doubtful, because Gest is not making any efforts and advance
publicity. We cannot understand his behaviour. The newspapers do not print long
articles, saying that Gest gives them few advertisements. In all likelihood, Gest is
very anxious about the expenses for the production of Reinhardt's *Miracle*.[52] He is
here and extraordinarily charming. He is a rabid enthusiast for the MAT and in
particular for me as an actor. He approves of no one but me and Duse.
 Duse was at the opening, because the performance was in her honour. But after
Act 1 she left (because she was acting at a matinee the next day), having left me
a note with all possible praise for *Karamazov*. I figured that her words were the
standard compliments. The next day, that is 20 November in the afternoon, she
acted, and in the evening they phoned me that she had arrived and was sitting in
the back rows, to finish watching the performance of *Karamazov* (this is after her
matinee performance). I went to the theatre, sat with her. She said that she knows
nothing superior, that this is not a theatre but a church, that we are the only
troupe in the world. Who could play that scene ('The Nightmare') but Kachalov
[as Ivan Karamazov]. She praised Tarasova [as Grushenka]. Then Knipper joined
her, she expatiated on the same idea and said that she had learned a lot from the
last performance. If she is feeling well, she will not miss a single one of our
performances, etc. But the box-office is poor. The opening night made 3000 dollars
(at the higher prices). The second performance 1800 dollars. The opening of
Mistress of the Inn – 1500 (regular prices) etc. This week already we are not being
paid our full salaries, because deductions have to be made for the debt. Therefore
our financial affairs are in this sort of situation. Out of the 9000 deposited here in

the current account I have to hand over 1500 dollars to the theatre. I have 7500 left. I have figured on half-salaries, that is 700-800 dollars a week. We will receive this for no more than 4 months, because I doubt that Gest will extend the contract. It is very likely that in March we will have returned to Europe. *I write all this as a great secret, because if we let this be known, people will say that we have flopped, and that is not the case.* We are having a great success, but the man in the street has not yet come, because there is no publicity *at all*. Gest's hocus-pocus may be a way of ridding himself of our concern and turning us away after 4 months. After all, he has on his hands, simultaneously, 1) Duse, 2) Reinhardt, 3) us, 4) Baliev. Now the fashion is for Duse – and everyone wends his way there. But after all she acts only twice a week. No wonder she makes money. [...]

Karamazov has gone on. The theatre and the actors have had a greater success than last year, but they panned the play and especially the narrator [played by Sergey Bertenson]. *Mistress of the Inn* has gone on 4 times. The success and the critics are unprecedentedly enthusiastic. We played improbably better. We found a completely Italian tempo. The roars of laughter are huge. Pyzhova is good and successful. They praise me more than in all my previous roles. But... Gest provides no publicity of any kind. The press is angry with him and if it writes about us, and doesn't keep silent, it's only out of respect for the MAT (an editor told me). Gest is fixated on Reinhardt. All the hoopla is saved up for him (as it was for us last year). We are stepchildren. That's why nobody knew when we opened our shows. We play at reduced prices and do quite bad box-office. [...]

Hugs. Kostya
27 November 1923

[...] I am grateful most of all that you have thought things over and have understood my mental condition and isolation. Now there is no doubt that the MAT can exist as no more than an object of pity. Yesterday, for instance, we opened *Ivanov*. It was like Easter. According to the public, everyone wanted to exchange kisses. Everyone ran up to us on stage. The curtain calls were endless. Gest thanked us and declared that if we had begun with this play, everything would have been fine and this mistake had cost us 100,000. Just try and make sense of that. We were afraid to put on *Ivanov*, and it turned out to be just to the taste of America. And the receipts for the opening night were 1400 dollars. With us it's the same old story. [...] Leonidov has become intolerable again. Even Vishnevsky has gone rotten. To Moscow, to Moscow. [...]

ND had written that it was hard for Lunacharsky and Malinovskaya to defend them if they seemed to be fence-sitting politically. The two commissars were themselves on the defensive, and Malinovskaya was soon to be replaced.

To **Nemirovich-Danchenko**. 28 December 1923, Philadelphia.
Dear Vladimir Ivanovich!
[...] You are absolutely right that Moscow may get the idea that we are sitting on the fence! Yes, we actually are sitting there, but it cannot be otherwise, since

we find ourselves not in Soviet Russia, but in a state openly hostile to it and dogging each of our steps in the so-called political sphere. I willingly grant that Moscow's attitude towards us is malevolent and suspicious in regard to our 'loyalty'. But that is nothing to the conditions that surround us abroad, we are involuntarily compelled to take devious action. For our part we do all we can to put off not only celebratory, grandiose ceremonies for the jubilee [for the MAT's 25th anniversary], which are being organized on every side, but even the least slight on the government. As soon as we arrived in Paris, the Russian colony, which now includes nearly half a million people, sent a whole deputation to organize a celebration. I and all of us, at the risk of offending the organizers, refused point-blank. Suddenly, without asking our management, Hébertot posted an announcement at the box-office that on 27 October, on the occasion of the jubilee, there would be a gala performance. I quickly made a scene and ordered him to pull down the sign, but even so the rumour got into the papers. On the day of the jubilee all our old-timers wanted to forgather in a close circle of companions, but I forbade even this, because I knew that even the most private gathering would be blown up into a jubilee celebration. In order to give a routine appearance to the scheduled performance of *Three Sisters*, which played on the jubilee day, I scheduled the alternate performers, did not come to the theatre myself, because I had heard that a presentation was in the offing, that the audience was gathering in evening dress. They sent for me at home three times to come to the theatre, because the assembled audience was waiting for me and would call for me. Even so I did not come to the theatre. There is nothing more I could do and was glad that the danger of the jubilee passed.

A long time before the jubilee the Union of Russian Writers had sent us a request to perform *Wise Fool* on a free day before the trip to America on behalf of literary men who were literally starving to death and going barefoot. For a long time we tried to find a way to put on some evening on behalf of our Moscow comrades. In America it is impossible to arrange such an evening, because Gest, referring to the contract, will not allow a charity performance under any pretext. We decided to take advantage of a suitable moment to put together an evening's performance on behalf of our comrades and Russian men of letters, and complied with the Union's proposal, agreeing to split the profits fifty-fifty. We will send you the financial account of this evening when we get it from Paris. We performed this show in dreadful agony, after a heavy Paris season, in feverish haste on the eve of the voyage, we played modestly, without publicity, without selling tickets at the box-office, and only distributing them by hand, we didn't even play in a theatre, but in a hall in the Hotel 'Lutèce', on a little platform without scenery. After the performance the organizers urgently invited us to join them for supper. We tried to refuse, but it turned out to be impossible, because among the guests were many French literary men, scholars, socialites, well disposed to us. [...] And my wife and I didn't even have evening dress; we had to send home for clothes. An immense supper, about fifty people. Milyukov[53] turned out to be the master of ceremonies. But you will agree that, after we learned this, there was no way to leave, especially since Milyukov is the editor of the only Parisian Russian newspaper, which it is impossible to ignore, since we were appearing in Paris and principally for a Russian audience besides. After all, you know perfectly well that outside of Russia almost the entire Russian press, the smallest rag included, is of an anti-Soviet tendency. And it was impossible to ignore it either, for if it comes to that, abroad it is most necessary to close off any access to oneself that might impart to one any kind of definite political colouration. And abroad more than anywhere else we have to insist on our thorough apoliticism. [...]

You will say that, all the same, it counts as a celebration. Yes, but who could prevent it? You will say, but why did we have to give a performance on behalf of men of letters? Well, simply because it is unthinkable to refuse Russian writers dying of starvation, because this performance is the only possible way to collect some money for our Moscow comrades. Why did we have to accept a banquet? Because to turn it down would have been tantamount to organizing a political demonstration, whereby every door in America would have been slammed in our faces (just a year ago a *Times* correspondent came to me in Paris and warned that we had better not go to America, because the local papers had published telegrams from Paris, saying that we were Bolsheviks and that we should be boycotted); because abroad we are OBLIGED to remain strictly neutral, so as not to compromise ourselves in a definite direction in the eyes of the governments of those countries where we have to live and work. And finally simply because it is HORRIBLY, HORRIBLY DIFFICULT for us. Moscow accuses us of disloyalty. But people regard us even more askance abroad. They barely let us into France. We managed to achieve favourable results only by circumventing French laws. In Paris a considerable portion of the public, both French and Russian, boycotted us simply because we are from Soviet Russia and, consequently, Communists. Now they won't let us into Canada, with the official explanation that we are Bolsheviks – and all our plans for a tour collapse. Who knows how many more hardships lie ahead of us?! You only have to remember last year's press persecution, stirred up against us in the Boston newspapers. As a matter of fact a definite conviction has taken hold there that we pay the Russian government nearly half of our profits, which provokes great displeasure in certain circles here, and to alter public opinion in this regard is very hard to do. If in future we maintain some clearly expressed Moscow political views, there might arise new, ever newer major complications, and Gest will be obliged to impose *force majeure* on us and break the contract. What will become of the 40 persons taking part in the tour and the 8 carloads of stage machinery? To decline a banquet of the sort that took place in Paris, only because some active members of the Russian emigration are present, would be equivalent to a political demonstration. [Not] To go to it would be impossible, or else we would have had to leave quickly, which was also unthinkable. I remind you that last summer and early autumn all our plans and projects connected with Berlin got so embroiled that we ended up in a financial impasse. We managed to incur debts on the prospective American receipts, and if we wanted to leave now, it would be impossible until we pay off what we owe.

435

Here both Russians and Americans frequently castigate us for using our theatre to glorify present-day Russia. In Moscow they sling mud at us for preserving the tradition of bourgeois theatre and because old plays by Chekhov and other authors of the 'intelligentsia' are popular with Russian émigrés and American capitalists; they assume that we are rolling in dollars, and in fact we are up to our eyes in debt. After all, it's not for my own pleasure that I've been travelling from place to place, from town to town, for nearly two years, I take on tasks beyond my powers of endurance, spend my time on things I'm not used to, not the things I love and dream about, and every day I risk losing what's left of my health. My morale is low, I've simply lost heart, and at times I've even thought of giving it all up. Meanwhile Gest will not put up with losses, but does nothing special. And we get no percentages and still have to pay off the old debts. If this keeps on, then, starting from week 11, they will stop paying a salary to us shareholders. Live as best you can! It is especially hard for me, because the very idea of bringing Igor back to Moscow is tantamount to condemning him to certain death. Is it such a crime on my part to try with hellish labour to save from death my son, who fell ill from our being evicted from our permanent apartment, from living in unheated lodgings. Despite all the abuse heaped on me in Moscow, I am refusing every conceivable kind of profitable proposition made me in Europe and America, and am yearning with all my soul for Russia, the very Russia which has now spat upon my soul. I do not know what to do. I do not have the strength to stay here, but I do not see that I have the strength to go on working in Russia under the conditions that are developing.

Yours K. Alekseev

To **Aleksandr Bogdanovich**. End of December 1923.

Dear, good, beloved Aleksandr Bogdanovich!

[…] They are interested in the Opera Studio here (bear in mind that they track the life of the Russian theatres very closely and know them all). It is easy to draw up a contract with Gest and Hurok and especially Rabinoff.[54] But… given the shape our studio is in now, it is not worth the transport. Therefore all talk of a speedy arrival (and there is a great deal) – I decline, of course, on various plausible pretexts. Honestly, there are actually no more malicious enemies of the studio than the studio folks themselves!!! To tell the truth, America is very spoiled for choice when it comes to music and singers. All the best in the world are here. All the best German, Italian, French singers, Chaliapin, etc. are at the Metropolitan. All the best pianists – Auer, Rachmaninov, Ziloti, Paderewski, etc., violinists – Hoffman, Heifetz, etc., – are all here. Only the greatest vocal celebrity can come here. Smirnov has no success.[55] I don't think our stars will have any, taken individually. But if we were to bring an ensemble – that might have an enormous success. Americans have no concept of this. Of course, the musical aspect as well as the dramatic must be at its peak. When I tell them about what is going on in the Moscow studio, their eyes light up. I can write no more. I am off to act… […]

Yours K. Stanislavsky

The Soviet papers published a photo on 20 January 1924 captioned 'What the White Emigration Is Up To' and claimed that a charity bazaar visited by MAT actors was selling treasures filched from Russia. Knipper and, KS were photographed standing next to Prince Feliks Yusupov, the assassin of Rasputin and a leader in White Russian society.

To **Nemirovich-Danchenko**. 22 January 1924, New York. *Telegram.*

Bazaar opened by American ladies on behalf of poor Russian actors. We turn down all invitations, but must attend this as representatives of Russian actors in America. Only things sold portraits of actors, silly birthday gifts of American make, unrelated to Yusupov's valuables. Thousands of people at bazaar, many snapshots taken. When we learned of photos, categorically insisted on their destruction. Stanislavsky.

To **Nemirovich-Danchenko**. 12 February 1924, New York.
Dear Vladimir Ivanovich!

[…] There can be absolutely no talk about earning dollars. Our sole concern is to manage to get out of here free of the debts incurred in revolutionary Germany and expensive Paris last summer, which increased our budget almost five-fold. I also want to pay off Gest and get him out of the red and so keep him on our side for the future. We also have to consider, once we have paid our debts, how and with what money we are to get from London to Moscow and safely transport 60 people and eight waggon-loads of property. Where are we to put this property? Where do we get the money to prepare a new repertoire as none of our folks agrees to appear in Moscow except in a new play. If that is not possible then personally I propose a temporary or permanent closure of the MAT groups. Our concerns about dollars and their expenditure are bound up with my whole future and perhaps the very life of ailing Igor. Here is where I must provide for his life, perhaps for many years to come, because he is seriously ill, and to bring him back to Moscow now is tantamount to a death sentence. One can hardly blame me for this chasing after dollars. I personally will return home like a beggar as I left it, and I pray God only that I earn the damned dollars to provide for the life of my children. But one will earn nothing by means of the theatre, one must forget about that now and forever. We will have to figure out another way, that is by writing a book. You can hardly suspect me of doing this for pleasure. You know my attitude to pen and paper. I am doing this out of the most extreme necessity. Whether the book will bring in anything and whether it will bring in what it was written to bring in – the future will show, moreover, unfortunately, not the near but the more distant future, because there is no way to expect that the book's success, if it is fated to have one, will be decided any time soon. Likewise this upsets my most immanent financial planning and budget. It has to be based on proposals and conjectures. To avoid losses, I have to make utterly incredible efforts which you in Moscow cannot imagine. This does not mean, of course, that we suppose your life there to be blissful. We know what it costs you to run the theatre, when the whole thing is splitting at the seams and there is no help from any quarter except the K.O. group which is dear to you.

Our work is different. The fight against compromise, the superhuman efforts to avoid it or, when it becomes impossible, to mitigate it. Do we succeed in this? Of course, not always. Those performances in which I personally take part come off all right. But I cannot vouch for those that take place in my absence, and to be at the theatre every day is beyond my strength. With hand on heart, I say I do more than I can and should in this respect.

Except for a few painful exceptions on the artistic score, I cannot complain about our old-timers. Artistically they behave well. I will tell you about the rest when we get together. The young people labour in a workmanlike way, enthusiastically, as walk-ons, sound effects, they play footmen, carry trunks in *Cherry Orchard*, chop wood in the last act and are daily occupied with some tiresome chore in the theatre. In respect of art, except for a few individual youngsters such as Tarasova, Pyzhova – there's no one to get especially enthused over. They may be willing, but few are able. As to ethics and the rest, I can speak only in relation to a few: we shall have to take a good broom, vigorously sweep out and find new ones. Then, perhaps, we can talk about a group, a troupe. There isn't one now. The old one is aging, and the young one is hardly maturing. Travelling, of course, has demoralized everyone, except for a few individuals, such as Luzhsky, whose conduct and work I respect, Knipper, most financially strapped of anyone, least complaining of anyone, who always agrees to everything, and a few others.

The demoralization has increased remarkably at this moment, when everyone has learned that it impossible to expect profits. You should know that a weary, broken and disorganized army is returning to you in Moscow, one which can no longer shoulder heavy packs and great loads. Four days a week, a matinee on Sundays by the young people with minimal participation of the elite actors and talents, that is the absolute maximum that can be counted on. Moreover, budgets must be reduced to the point that we may have to play all new productions against drapes, in old costumes ·· and all our calculations for success must be based exclusively on superb acting. In America only that, and nothing else, is successful. Therefore it was worth it to have the last performances and revivals of *Uncle Vanya* and *Pazukhin* in particular staged against drapes (true, they were neatly and snugly adapted), thanks to which the critics and the audience were able to concentrate on the actors. Yes, a company like that, with such personalities, does not exist in Russia or anywhere abroad at the present time. Only they might be able to discover those things in the new art of the future which we are all so avidly seeking. But whether they will seek it or rest on their laurels is a question I find worrying.

Everyone will return, at least the ones we need. Rumours circulate about the young people, but these are only rumours, because Lazarev and Boleslavsky have shown that it is not so simple, without the MAT trademark, to extricate oneself from American sensationalism, bluster and 'business'.[56]

It would be frivolous to count on our company to cover the theatre's incredible expenses. It occurs to me that everybody recognizes this and would even agree, albeit with great reluctance, to a significant reduction in former lavishness of productions and in other things rather than work beyond their strength, because half the company is really ill and half of that group are cripples. One, two, three, four, five, six, seven – of the people we need, the most talented ones, are genuinely ill and some of them fatally. I am writing you all this to whittle down any hopes you may have of the help which, I know, you need badly. We must make reductions, be more modest, base ourselves on pure art, technical experience and talented people – that is the future motto for this group

There is one individual who makes me rejoice – healthy, strong, intelligent, passionate, ready to observe the essence of art, she who in many plays is a remarkable replacement for Knipper and Germanova, someone we need to the nth degree. This is Tarasova. She is coming to Moscow, she became attached to the group, became a general favourite, knows how to get on even with Leonidov and Koreneva, but all this, of course, for the time being. We have to see to it that she doesn't get spoiled or corrupted. But she is having the greatest of successes here. After Reinhardt saw her (this is a secret), he badgered me to let him have her for *The Miracle*, at least for the first eight performances. I am steadfast when it comes to art and, since this was not difficult, I, of course, refused .[57] We have to do everything possible to make life easy for her and her family, and chiefly her husband, when they return to Moscow, at least by looking for temporary lodgings.[58] Another secret is that without her we cannot stage a single play, and it would be idiotic to rely on the studios, because for two years we have scattered in all directions and can hardly understand one another at any time and merge.

Don't think I have been inactive. I have been working indefatigably, working on the things I consider to be most important, which in this age of charlatanism have been forgotten by everyone, except you. And that gives me strength. We are strong in other things as well. We are accepted in America. (I'm not counting Europe as we can expect nothing there except success and good reviews.) America is the only audience and the only source of money for funding on which we can count. I consider that we cannot do without America and am almost convinced that now America can't do without us. This indispensability was created not so much last year, when we had a strident, clamorous, so to speak, general, public success. It was created during the second visit, this year, among the real intelligentsia and the few Americans of exceptional culture and a thirst for real art. In essence, they possess the nerve that might be the evolution of progressive art in America. The American people are capable of theatre. They understand, feel and appreciate individuality like no one else. In this respect it is easy to do without the German and Frenchman, but not the American. He has so anatomized bone by bone the individuals of our troupe, was so able to distinguish those who are crucial in the first rank from those who are crucial in the ranks of utility, that I was often quite surprised. But it stands to reason! Almost in every American theatre and American production there is one leading and very good actor. Some of them with a beautiful actor's personality. When they go to the theatre, they are used to watching him in particular, and this habit has become ingrown in the public. They so value personality in an artist and actor that they wind up completely perplexed and excited by our prodigality. Six excellent actors in a single production. From the 'business' standpoint this strikes them as incredible, because each of them could keep a theatre going, and with all the best actors in the troupe, perhaps, even a dozen 'commercial' theatres.

The success of the present year is not public, it's more exclusive. Last year they made our acquaintance, now they know us and love us. I can't fight off all the offers – to write a book, start a class and a studio. Some individual actors are accepted in local society and benefit not only from respect but genuine affection.

Our art has so deeply entered all the pores of the local theatre that they cannot do without us, especially if I manage to write the book so that it piques their interest but doesn't tell all. Both Gest and Rabinoff would forge some connection with us, I don't mean they themselves, but those who back them. Without coming to a decision, I will keep my eyes and ears open and try before our departure to sow as many seeds as I can. Even now I could sign many contracts, but given the barbaric attitude to us prevalent in Russia as a reward for 25 years of truly honourable service, I will agree not to do so, not even to write about it, not even to enter into serious negotiations.

Your remarks that there is art over and above the dollar, that we have to think about new paths, work, experiment, provide for Moscow – here, in the conditions of our life, raise only a kindly and indulgent smile. Do you know where we rehearse to put new players into old plays? In the shabby rooms of the seedy hotels where we are lodged. Are you aware that if they lend us the nastiest so-called foyer, or more accurately, the lobby of some theatre, then within five minutes Comrade Cleaning-woman shows up and brazenly starts yelling, shouting and making a racket to show that our cultured actor's labour means nothing, whereas theirs, unskilled, is what America's all about. Soviet Russia is the America of the future in this sense of the worker's power over the actor. When the chief stagehand, truly, a wonderful, splendid fellow, comes to put up the scenery – the actor steps aside, clears the stage, on the double, American-style! But when the actor comes to play a delicate, tender Chekhovian duet or a pause, the workers backstage walk around, stomp, play cards, and if you speak to one of them sternly, all of them, to a man, put on their overcoats and drive home in their motor-cars, and we have to swim back to Europe without our trousers.

To think about creating something new when you play ten shows a week would be crazy. Save your strength for what they suck out of you and don't think about the big picture, because you will overexert yourself and everything will grind to a halt. Believe me, when I have brought back our whole crowd and their belongings, dumped them at the Art Theatre and handed them over, I will be the happiest man on earth. And I will not sign on for that voyage a second time, at least not on the same terms under which we are working now. […]

I confess to you that I have been thinking frequently about a total renunciation of the stage and art. I shall probably do it if I feel that I am too old for it and if the young people have outgrown me. I cannot be a parasite in art. For forty years I have worked, acquired a certain inertia which keeps me moving forward, I cannot stop at that. I will study, teach, write, if I don't get my way, because I know for certain that it is needed, people are waiting for it, that without me they will not recognize it, just as without you they will not recognize what you can do – something essential for the art of the future.

I embrace you, I constantly think of, love and admire your energy.

Warm greetings and tight hugs to all who remember me and do not nurse a grudge

K. Alekseev

Postscript

I forgot the main thing – to straighten out the involuntary messes which our spies here have caused you. Thank heaven that I am the spokesman of the troupe. You know how I hate any politics and how afraid I am of getting involved in it. In this realm my caution and punctilio reach comic proportions. I am weak enough, thanks to cowardice, to turn down all invitations. Put yourself in my place. You would be resolute enough to accept a good half of them, and things would get even worse. We appear only where it is impossible not to be absolutely, positively, without any ifs, ands or buts. And in that case a great deal of effort has to be expended to convince me to go, before I agree. Don't forget that we are hedged round on all sides by obstacles. On one side, the whites, who do not accept refusals so simply and docilely, but imbue them with their sympathies, which are dangerous for those who are involuntarily living among the whites; the red obstacles, as you see, are also fraught with consequences. And then there's Gest, who insists on lots of public appearances; then there are simply close acquaintances, friends, whom you do not throw out of your flat when they come with greetings; then there's the press, whom the theatre cannot do without; then there are the intelligentsia of every possible political party, who also contribute to success. Upset this or that obstacle, and you'll have to swim back to Europe without your trousers. When there are sixty of us, and all without trousers, -- you can imagine. In Moscow they want us, when we get to Germany, to meet only with Frenchmen, and in France deal only with Germans; in the land of the whites, spend time with the reds, whom you can't find here with torches, because they are in hiding. All this is as impossible as, coming to you, in the land of the reds, fraternizing with whites. Here's an example for you.

A few days ago a few strangers come up to me on Broadway and offer the usual greetings actors get. Who they are I don't know. Lo and behold, from a big shop window a camera is aimed at us. I turn my back on it. Lo and behold, from around the corner someone is snapping us with a hand-held 'Kodak'. Maybe the people who were talking to me are foes of Soviet Russia – how do I know? Maybe tomorrow another article will be published with a vile illustration – what can I do? All that is left is to yield to fate, reconcile yourself and remember that in Russia a whole blameless life, utterly pure in certain spheres of public life, cannot be safeguarded against the gossip of some scoundrel or notorious swindler. He only needs to say one word to the press, and people believe him and not the man who for sixty years has proven his rectitude by deeds. Of course, I will not get over this bitter insult to the end of my brief life. God be with them! [...]

Yours K. Alekseev

To **Nemirovich-Danchenko**. 12 March 1924, New York.

[…] All the Meyerholdian, Tairovian and other achievements are wholly borrowed from the krauts, where they have already bored everyone stiff. In America, all the vaudevilles and revues, they so knock your eye out that the Americans are unable to listen, which explains the failure of Komissarzhevsky's *Peer Gynt*, which, really and truly, if you leave out the design aspect, is staged pretty well. This is far from meaning that I am bewailing Chekhovitis and all our earlier acting techniques, which have turned into the bad cliché of the Art Theatre. It means that I bewail my personal future, that I will never more stage Shakespeare the way he appears to me in dreams, as I see him in my mind's eye and hear him with my mind's ear. Shakespeare on the basis of harmonics, phonetics, rhythm, feeling for words and action, on the basis of a simple, noble, gradual, consistently logical development of feeling and course of action. The old-timers, who alone could do this, don't want to relearn, while the youngsters and the studios, who, evidently, do want this and are experimenting with work in this direction, are too untalented for such a great task. I am trying to take an interest in productions of a contemporary and spectacular nature, there are many amusing plans, gimmicks, out of which Meyerhold might construct principles for some kind of new art, but all this hocus-pocus excites me for no more than a few hours, and afterward I get fed up and cool off. […]

At a shareholders' meeting in Cleveland on 28 March it was proposed, in view of losses, to stop paying shareholder's dividends. Gribunin categorically refused and threatened to drop out of the troupe if his money was stopped. When at the 31 March meeting KS asked for caution and restraint, Gribunin insulted him and said he had no money because he had bought a new apartment in Moscow. Knipper rose and described his behaviour as offensive to the MAT.

To **his family**. 6 April 1924, Chicago.
My dears – Marusya, Kira, Igorek, Kirillochka!

[…] And so: in Cleveland things were not bad, in the terms of reception, artistic success and reviews more than brilliant, but financially – Gest had neither losses nor gains. Here it was explained to us with perfect clarity that however fine our business had been over the last 5 weeks, we, actors of the MAT, could no longer receive a dollar of our pay, because everything we earned was not enough to cover Gest's debts, for scenery, for the return trip, as far as London (by contract with him). Similarly, the debts incurred in the summer, the whole weight of which is still incumbent on, have to be paid out of the personal salaries of the shareholders themselves. Besides that, the return trip of both the whole troupe and the scenery etc. from London to Moscow must be deducted from their salaries.[59] The outcome was that until the contract runs out we, the shareholders, can be paid only a minimum of living expenses, while all the rest will be applied to the indicated ends. In other words: total collapse. In the very best case I can bring back only around 4000 dollars. This is to cover everything. To provide for

Figure 66 Stanislavsky as Prince Ivan Shuisky and Vasily Kachalov as the Tsar in *Tsar Fyodor* backstage during the tour, 1922–23

Igor and for us to get back and return to Moscow and live there. The result is a dismal one. The only thing left is the book… To tell the truth, reading it – for the first time – from beginning to end, I don't expect a great success. It might, God willing, make a trifle, 3-5 thousand. Dreadful news arrives from Moscow and Nemirovich. A telegram was sent, notification of receipt requested, announcing to the troupe that they are all obliged to show up by a certain date. Certificates of illness will not be accepted. Those who do not show up will be considered political fugitives and not allowed back into the country. In order to remain here, one has to get permission from Nemirovich-Danchenko. Of course, one can receive it,

443

and therefore decide whether to go or stay. Igor is outside the discussion. He, of course, will remain abroad. Maybe you can live on what I bring you (4000 dollars) – plus 3-4-5000 from the book (questionable). Should we return together or separately? Despite our importunate pestering, N.-D. has not wired us the date of return. There is no point in closing our eyes: the latest is 15 August. Even if a later arrival date were possible – one would have to return by that time. While there is still no frost, not all the apartments distributed – we would have to settle down in Moscow before the frost. Who knows, maybe, what lies ahead is the renovation of the apartment, stoves, cleaning, and finally a move to the new apartment (on what money, they write that now you need 10,000 dollars to get a permit for an apartment). From Moscow N.-D. writes that he sits all day long with the authorities and representatives of Narkompros, Glavnauka and some other agency. They are deciding the fate of the MAT. It appears there will only be the MAT and the 1st Studio. The 2nd will be abolished and stuffed into the other, the 3rd will remain as it is, so will the 4th. The 1st Studio is getting Shelaputin's theatre (New Theatre). Their building 'The Alcazar' is going to Habima. Where K.O. will be put no one knows yet. We, that is, the MAT needs to stage 5 shows a week. We couldn't handle any more. I suppose they will move us to K.O. for a few days. Well… of course, there N.-D. himself won't forget and on the pretext of a synthetic theatre or other impressive phrase will hang the lion's share of general expenses round our neck. The troupe is waiting in trepidation to learn who will stay and who will be chucked out. They have become extremely tractable. […]

There is still some doubt about Moscow. It is the apartment. I don't understand what will happen with it. They closed the studio.[60] They said that it is temporary, that is, until I get back. But Malinovskaya is gone – entirely – both from the Administration of the Academic Theatres and the Bolshoy Theatre. In her place they have appointed Ekskuzovich[61] from Petrograd (a boor). He will be our official in charge of the MAT. For the Bolshoy Theatre they appointed Lapitsky.[62] He is my personal enemy, who will take revenge on me for in my time having served on a committee that arranged to take his first theatre, Zimin's, away from him and give it back to Zimin. There is no reason to suppose that he will stand up for the continuation of the studio. But the building belongs to the Bolshoy Theatre. What will be done with it. Chase us out or settle someone else in it?.. Or will the Bolshoy Theatre simply be stripped of it… and then the whole building will become my headache.[63] I cannot support it and will have to leave it quickly. Where to?... All these questions have to be considered. Perhaps it would be better for us to stay abroad, until everything becomes normal. Or could Kira and Kilyalya move temporarily into somebody's apartment? Whose? This has to be settled by letter in good time. I cannot personally think about all this in the meantime. Now, at a time when the financial picture is shaky, we have to be on our guard, because the putrid, decomposing rot is everywhere poisoning the troupe. So, for instance, Gribunin declared that he was unwilling to pay the debt, let those pay it who have money in the bank (an allusion to me). But he himself bought land outside Moscow and an apartment in Moscow. 'I have no money,' he insists. When I began to appeal to his conscience at the meeting, he answered so rudely that Knipper got upset and expressed a protest (true, by herself. The others kept silent.) Gribunin demonstratively left the meeting, but, when he got home, he agonized for two days and finally sent me a gracious letter with an apology. Now we have good relations again, and he is subdued. Every minute one can expect not dangerous but unpleasant excesses from various quarters.

I embrace, bless, tenderly love, miss, burst with impatience at the waiting.

Your Kostya and Papa and Granddad

Christ has arisen.

Buy a toy for Kirlyalya on my behalf. But don't spoil her for no good reason. The life that awaits her will be hard, but interesting.

I embrace her, miss her.

Granddad

To his **sister Zinaida** and his **brother Vladimir Alekseev**. April 1924, New York.

[ ] I am writing my autobiography, starting with Adam, as do all beginners and inexperienced quasi-littérateurs. Diabolical! I cannot write down things that have already been described 20 times in all the books about the MAT. So I made a shift. I began to describe the evolution of the art I have witnessed. Now it's going with more of a swing. I scribbled away, with no let-up, all summer. I wrote 60,000 words without even getting to the main theme that had been ordered, i.e., the founding of the MAT. I telegraph from Germany, I send what I've written, after every ordeal you can imagine over copying it on a Russian-alphabet Remington. They send permission for another 60,000. I write, but there's the deadline staring me in the face – 1 September, and I've begun three rehearsals a day in Waren, near Berlin.

[…] I get to America – the publisher immediately puts pressure on me. He still isn't threatening, but insists that he will suffer great losses. I summon up what's left of my strength. I barely sleep and write whole nights on end. As soon as a play opens, there are free nights and hours of the day. But all sorts of interviews, deputations and a horde of acquaintances who invite me to a lunch or a dance or a concert etc. etc. prevent me from working. I have to find refuge somewhere. I tried outside the city. Too inconvenient. Besides, I'm alone, not knowing the language, I waste time on all sorts of household necessities and chores, and even the trip to town takes lots of time. They assign me a separate room at the splendid New York Public Library.

[…] In the new room, the work began to hum. I wrote like a convict with only a few days left to live. I wrote another 60,000 words. And still the theme is not exhausted. They give me 30,000 more, to a total of 150,000. But not one line over that limit, or else the book would be too thick to bind. I write and write and write. Already there are advertisements everywhere, already individual chapters are appearing in all sorts of periodicals. Already you see announcements all over the place that on 26 April the book will be on sale at the price of 6 dollars a copy (instead of the original 2 dollars). I write during intermissions, and on the trolley, and in restaurants, and on the avenue.

[…] The absolute deadline for turning in the book is the end of February. But March has come, then mid-March, then March ends and still the book is not ready. It all has to be crammed in hugger-mugger, any which way, just to get it finished. I just finished it, at long last. I have simply ruined my eyes. Now I await 26 April in fear and trembling. What will come of the book, I don't know. Will it go over well? What it's like I have no idea and never will, because they've abridged some things and eliminated things without my knowledge, and I could not even look the whole book through from beginning to end. […]

To the **American People**. Before 17 May 1924, New York.

On leaving this country, I wish in the name of the Moscow Art Theatre to state my gratitude to the American people for the hospitality which it has shown to us over the course of these two seasons.

I am quite unaccustomed to the means of expression I have chosen. Trained in the life of the Russian stage, so very remote from you, I am not used to addressing the public through the press, but then everything in this country is strange for us. In America the newspapers address the whole country. They are the ears, eyes and mouth of the New World.

So, no matter how unusual and intense are my feelings at this leave-taking, this strange, unwonted means of expression strikes me as appropriate for the valedictory words to a nation that has treated our fifty-three-week tours in a foreign language with so much attention and respect.

I would like, in accord with your standard custom, to tell your readers that the whole troupe of the Moscow Art Theatre will never forget the heartfelt and sincere hospitality that America showed to us.

We bid you farewell with regret. During these two seasons spent in your country, many of our erroneous opinions about it were dispelled. Now we understand and appreciate the American attitude towards art. No other nation feels it so deeply as the American, and in this regard American and Russian souls are close.

We will never forget how the American actors attended our performances time and again. We shall bear away with us a special memory of our meetings with David Belasco, that distinguished actor of the American theatre, and the satisfaction we felt when we found in his theatre the same atmosphere and efforts, the same devotion to the field of theatre, that constitutes the soul of our own native business.

All the events of these two years, that have come to pass thanks only to the daring and perspicacity of Morris Gest, seem to us a dream. We will not cease to wonder at the co-ordinated work of your railways, theatres and stagehands and will always owe an unpayable debt to your press, which followed us with such intelligence and understanding, despite the difficulties of a foreign language.

If we have possibly succeeded in revealing to you the previously unknown mysteries of Russian thought and the Russian soul, then we can boldly say that we take back to Russia with us both a desire to unite our two nations and a profound respect for you, our generous hosts.

We firmly hope that if some time in the future American actors come to Russia, they will feel as cosily 'at home' as we did among you.

Konstantin Stanislavsky on behalf of the MAT

To **his brother Vladimir**. Late May 1924, Paris.

Dear, darling, beloved Volodya!

[…] The book has come out now, in a magnificent, sumptuous, wonderful format, much better than the contents themselves. I am bringing a copy with me to send you. You won't be able to read the text, but can simply look at the illustrations. But an accident happened. Boarding the steamer, the packet with the books, like all inanimate objects, was dropped into the automatic baggage hoist. I suppose I didn't fasten an official label on it. All our things were sent to our cabin, but not the packet. They looked for it for three days. I don't think it can be lost, but because I sent it with those who are going straight to Moscow (Luzhsky, Moskvin, Gribunin, Burdzhalov, the dressers etc.) and I can get my baggage when I leave the boat at Cherbourg, when they disembark our group, I will then be at loss how to convey my book to you and Nemirovich. I'm afraid of it going by post, because they will start to flip through it and they will publish it without my permission. […]

The second reason I didn't write is that there was a lot of trouble and worry with the troupe. An actor is a person who is good and obedient so long as he is being paid. Stop paying him and he turns into someone else. So it is with us. From the moment they stopped paying salaries in order to clear off debts, everyone at least did his duty but the putrid poison of depravity set in. The actors stopped obeying and fear only me. There was trial and tribulation, and I could not wait till the moment when I could slough off my responsibility for them. It was depressing, difficult and revolting, but… thank God, it ended, and ended with honour. The last few months were again a thoroughgoing triumph. In Cleveland, Detroit, Chicago and the last weeks in New York business was magnificent (too late, because none of it devolves on us, and everything has gone to clear off debts to Gest). More flowers, receptions, speeches and street demonstrations. In Chicago, for instance, we ended on Easter night. Morning and evening of Good Friday and Holy Saturday there were two shows a day, after which we entrained for Canada and Detroit. The whole street was blocked with people. The crowd burst into the hotel (which is located in the same building as the theatre). A rain of flowers on stage and the street, ovations and so on. They came to the station, there was a crowd there too, they burst into the carriage and so on. The same thing recurred in the other cities. In New York the farewells were very moving. We gave a concert on our own behalf. The house was sold out and some 300 people were without tickets. Flowers, ovations, etc. And the next day a moving farewell, reviews and treatment – as if we were their own. Now America considers the MAT is an American theatre. […]

Hugs, love.

Kostya

Notes

1 Sergey Vasilievich Rachmaninov (1873-1943), composer, pianist, conductor; lived abroad from 1917.

2 Galina Nikolaevna Gorshunova (1900-73), soprano at the Opera Studio 1919-33.

3 Nikolay Semyonovich Golovanov (1892-1953), conductor, pianist, composer; musical head of the Opera Studio (1919-22) and the Opera-Dramatic Studio (1935-38).

4 Leonid Davydovich Leonidov (Berman, 1885-1983), impresario, who before 1917 had tried to get the MAT to tour outside Russia; one of the organizers of the Kachalov Group, the MAAT and the Musical Studio tours abroad; in 1925 KS asked him to organize personal 'director's guest appearances' in Berlin and Vienna. In 1934 he launched a proposal to bring Reinhardt to Moscow.

5 It started on 26 September.

6 KS knew Barnowsky from the first tour abroad in 1906.

7 Jacques Hébertot (1886-1970), innovative French impresario; promoted the MAT's tours to Paris in 1922 and 1923. The tour to London did not take place.

8 This seems to be a garbled account of the working of a dumb waiter.

9 According to Plutarch, 'Come back with your shield – or on it' was what Spartan mothers told their sons when they went off to war.

10 The 25th anniversary celebration of the MAAT scheduled for 14 October 1923.

11 The government had originally forbidden a tour during the season, but this plan did not work out.

12 Mariya Alekseevna Uspenskaya (1887-1949) acted at the MAT 1911-24; from 1924 lived in the USA. As Maria Ouspenskaya taught at the American Laboratory School and then in Hollywood, where she was a frequent character actress in movies.

13 Vera Nikolaevna Pashennaya (1887-1962), a leading actress at the Maly Theatre and wife of Gribunin, was brought into the company purely for the US tour.

14 Vladimir Lvovich Yershov (1896-1964) acted at the MAT 1916 until his death. Ivan Ivanovich Gudkov (1887-1962), a charter member of the MAT, from 1923 in charge of the technical production department; 1931-55 chief electrician; occasionally went on as an actor.

15 Ripsimé Karpovna Tamantsova (1889-1958), secretary to the MAAT administration and private secretary to KS from 1924. She had joined the MAT in 1919 as an assistant director and ran the repertory office 1919-24 (she and Bokshanskaya were known as 'the office wenches'). In 1927 KS sent her to France to edit the French translation of My Life in Art. When he was in France and Germany 1930-32, she kept him apprised of events in Moscow.

16 Miron Isidorovich Yakobson, pianist and composer.

17 Émile Coué (1857-1926), French psychotherapist, famous for his slogan 'Every day in every way I am getting better and better.'

18 Ruth Draper (1884-1956), American actress and diseuse, famous for her one-woman shows. Her diary reads 'Marvellous ship, very rough crossing. Recite for Coué and at the Concert. Nice talk with Stanislavsky – wonderful man.'

19 Mariya Petrovna Grigorieva (stage name Nikolaeva, 1869-1941), actors and wardrobe mistress.

20 Aleksander Arnoldovich Kairansky (Koiransky, 1884-1968), man of letters, critic, designer, friend of Kachalov; emigrated first to Turkey, then the US, where he assisted KS in writing My Life in Art. Later he taught at the American Laboratory Theatre School.

21 Aleksandr Ilyich Ziloti (1863-1945), pianist and conductor; living abroad from 1919; and his wife Vera Pavlovna Tretyakova (1866-1940), daughter of the founder of the Moscow art gallery.

22 Otto Herman Kahn (1867-1934), American banker, art collector and patron; he had underwritten the MAT tour.

23 Lev Nikolaevich Bulgakov (1888-1948), actor; at the MAT 1911-24; stayed in the US, acting and directing, with his wife Varvara, often with the Yiddish theatre.

24 Aleksandr Ivanovich Gryzunov (1894-?), acted at the MAT 1919-31.

25 David Belasco (1853-1931), American playwright, director, actor, known as 'the Bishop of Broadway'.

26 There had been no time in Europe to finish painting the scenery for *In the Clutches of Life* and *No Fool Like a Wise Fool* and it had to be repaired in America; this cost the theatre a lot of money.

27 Lev Bulgakov prepared the role of Tsar Fyodor and played it a few times in America.

28 KS's birthday fell on 5/17 January.

29 The First Studio toured in the summer of 1922 to Riga, Tallinn, Berlin, Wiesbaden and Prague.

30 Vakhtangov's *PrincessTurandot* was still playing in Moscow.

31 David Warfield (1866-1951) was one of Belasco's star players in such tear-jerking melodramas as *The Music Master* and *The Return of Peter Grimm*.

32 John Barrymore (1882-1942), scion of a well-established American theatrical dynasty and a popular matinee idol, was considered the Hamlet of his generation.

33 Joseph Schildkraut (1895-1964), Austrian-born actor, son of Rudolph Schildkraut, made most of his career in the US.

34 Kamernaya Opera, the Chamber Opera, the official name of the Musical Studio.

35 Fyodor Fyodorovich Komissarzhevsky (1882-1954) directed at the theatre of his sister Vera Komissarzhevskaya in St Petersburg, before opening his own theatre in Moscow in 1914; he worked in London, Paris, Riga, Turin and New York, before becoming a British subject. In England, as Theodore Komisarjevsky, he popularized Chekhov. On the outbreak of war in 1939, he settled in the US.

36 On April 1923 ND wired him that the authorities had allowed the tour to be prolonged to 1 February 1924.

37 Albert Coates (1882-1953), English conductor; at the Mariinsky Theatre 1911-19.

38 It was not brought to America, and *The Brothers Karamazov* was condensed to one night.

39 Sol Hurok (Solomon Izrailovich Yurok, 1888-1974), Russian-born theatrical entrepreneur who expedited a number of Soviet-American cultural exchanges.

40 The Classic Theatre Company production of *The Inspector General*, directed by the Yiddish actor Maurice Schwartz, opened on Broadway on 30 April and closed almost immediately.

41 KS's slighting nickname for Kachalov's wife, Nina Litovtseva.

42 Germanova took part in neither tour but remained in Europe, first as a member of the Prague group, then as a free-lance in Paris.

43 Varvara Petrovna Bulgakova acted at the MAT from 1916; with her husband she stayed in the US and taught acting for many years.

44 Laurette Taylor (Loretta Helen Cooney, 1884-1946) was married to the British playwright J. Hartley Manners, who provided most of her vehicles, including the long-running *Peg o' My Heart*.

45 Neither the Tolstoy play nor the Laurette Taylor *Mistress* was produced.

46 Marcella Sembrich (Prakseda Marcelina Kochánska, 1858-1935), Galician soprano, had sung at the Metropolitan Opera in New York from 1883; at this time she was retired as a singer and taught vocal classes.

47 Aleksandr Vladimirovich Bogdanovich (1874-1950), singer, teacher.

48 It was proposed to open a second tour in Berlin on 26 September, but given the political situation in Germany it was put forward to 18 September in Paris.

49 The start of the Prince's aria in Dargomyzhsky's *Rusalka*.

50 It did not happen.

51 The New York tour opened on 19 November with a one-night *Brothers Karamazov*; the second premiere was *Mistress of the Inn* on 22 November.

52 *The Miracle* employed a cast of 700, besides the orchestra and chorus.

53 Former minister of the Provisional Government Pavel Nikolaevich Milyukov (1859-1943) published the Parisian Russian-language paper *Rech* (*Speech*).

54 Max A. Rabinoff (1877-1961), a Russian-born impresario who had managed tours of the ballerina Anna Pavlova and the Imperial Balalaika Orchestra.

55 Dmitry Alekseevich Smirnov (1882-1944), tenor; lived abroad from 1920.

56 Dmitry Alekseevich Smirnov (1882-1929) acted at the MAT 1902-03, 1909-20. Richard Boleslavsky (Boleslaw Ryszard Srzednicki, 1889-1937), Polish-born actor in the First Studio and cavalry officer in the world war. They both came to the US in advance of the MAT and were living in poverty. They discovered that by exploiting the MAT trademark they could create a more or less flourishing studio which became the American Laboratory Theatre.

57 When the tour ended, KS gave her permission to appear in nearly 30 performances of *The Miracle*.

58 Aleksandr Petrovich Kuzmin (1891-1974), Tsarist naval officer and marine midshipman; in 1915 as guardsman had been transferred from Odessa to Tsarskoe Selo to protect the imperial family. In April 1917 he married Tarasova and they travelled a trail of tears during the Civil War. They joined first the Kachalov group and then the MAAT during its tours abroad (in 1918 he worked for a short time in the Second Studio as foreman of the workers taken on for crowd scenes); at the MAAT recording rehearsals and appearing in crowd scenes until 1930. He later organized art exhibits.

59 The trip to London, organized by Hurok, was thwarted by Gest who refused to pay the return trip from there to Moscow, although he promised to organize a tour for the next season.

60 The Studio was not closed, but no longer subsidized by the Bolshoy Theatre from February 1924; it was moved in the fall to the Glavnauka Narkompros (Chief Scientific People's Commissariat of Enlightenment).

61 Ivan Vasilievich Ekskuzovich (1883-1942), theatrical official.

62 KS had known Iosif Mikhailovich Lapitsky (1876-1944) from 1903 when he had a private debut at the MAT but was not accepted into the troupe. In 1920 Lapitsky headed the Maly State Opera, heir to Zimin's Opera, and, favoured by the Union of Theatre Workers, was appointed to head the Bolshoy.

63 After long bureaucratic convolutions, the apartment in Leontiev Lane was allotted to KS for life.

Figure 67 Stanislavsky and Nemirovich in 1928

10

ADJUSTING
TO A SOVIET WORLD
1924–1928

In the two years that KS and his companions had been abroad, radical changes had taken place in the Soviet Union. After Lenin's death in 1924, the nation was run by a triumvirate: the Party Secretary Iosif Stalin, Trotsky's brother-in-law Kamenev, and Zinoviev, president of the Third International. The New Economic Policy was increasingly reduced and eventually cancelled. Foreign travel was still allowed, with special permission, until the borders were closed in 1926.

Meyerhold had become the pre-eminent figure in the theatre, his constructivist stagings and theory of biomechanical acting gone viral throughout the republics. In the arts in general, widespread experimentation was the rule, often on the premiss of finding new proletarian forms. Lunacharsky, ever more sidelined, attempted to maintain a balance between the exuberant experiments of the far left and the more conservative tastes of party officialdom.

In spring 1924 ND wrote to the State Academic Council laying out plans for the following season: 'Of the old repertoire of the Moscow Art Theatre one must exclude a) the works of literature unacceptable for our modern times (example: the whole Chekhov repertoire, -- at least in the interpretation in which these plays have been produced at the Art Theatre up to now); b) productions, fully acceptable as works of literature but lacking interest on account of their obsolete stage format (example: No Fool Like a Wise Fool)'. He proposed to revive The Drama of Life *and* The Brothers Karamazov *and stage the plays of Jules Romains. These schemes remained unrealized.*

With much of the company abroad, the vacuum at the MAAT had been filled by the studios. ND devoted most of his time, attention and energy to his Musical Studio, whose goal was to apply Art Theatre principles to opéra-comique and other musical dramatic forms. When KS returned, ND was officially the administrator of the MAAT, its dramatic theatre and school, artistic director of the Musical Studio, and the Second MAAT, created out of the First Studio. He was also chairman of the Art Theatre's board of directors. KS's titles were Adviser to the Dramatic Studio and School and one of ten stage directors of the MAAT and its studios. In 1924 ND had appointed as his assistant, Ilya Yakovlevich Sudakov (1890-1969), who would eventually become one of the leaders of the theatre. Sudakov had drawn up a report on the new relationship between the MAAT and the studios.

To **Nemirovich-Danchenko**. 10 July 1924, Chamounix.

Dear Vladimir Ivanovich! […]

I read Sudakov's letter and accept and approve all the measures you have taken. The First Studio – to be a separate entity. This long-standing disease in my soul calls for a drastic operation. (A pity that it will be called the 2nd MAT. It has betrayed it -- in every respect.) Privately I call the studio Goneril's Studio.

To cut the 3rd Studio adrift – I approve. That one is Regan's Studio. To absorb the Second Studio -- Cordelia. They are dear and there is something decent about them, but, but and but again … Will they mate – the fiery steed and the trembling doe… It is a difficult task, but you know them better at the moment, I, at a distance, cannot imagine what they will do with themselves after their Futuristic romps.[1]

Baksheev (and Tamirov[2] too???) have left – one pigsty the less. As actor he is useful, but not as much as he fancies. His Mitya Karamazov is gobsmackingly disgusting. His Lopakhin is disgusting without being gobsmacking. It will be difficult without him, but I'm not sorry, indeed I rejoice. I should have chucked out lots of them!! Who is playing Baev – Yershov?! (he is eager for character roles).[3] Podgorny, Batalov.[4] I don't see anyone else.

To open with *Government Inspector* – I agree, more readily than you. I am no great fan of having it performed. Except for [Mikhail] Chekhov [as Khlestakov] (in some performances), no one stands out.[5] Some things need to be corrected in *Inspector* – I agree to everything, because, as I already wrote to you, having been abroad for 2 years, I understand nothing of what Moscow needs. Obviously, not what I need. I fully comply and for the year I will completely set aside my own initiatives and dreams. Believe me, I am doing it without the least ill feeling. On the contrary. With the full realization that this is necessary to the nth degree. If it is still possible to save the MAAT, then only one man can do it -- you. I am powerless. I have lost my edge completely. For two years I've had to shout so much abuse that now I have no authority of any kind while you, on the other hand, have acquired an enormous amount. Therefore I personally stand for granting you total dictatorship. I will try to keep myself in hand as far as I can and always give you my vote. But the most important thing is not to hold any meetings. Not a single one. If you need advice, you will call me into your office or simply call a *consultative meeting*. You will learn what everyone thinks and you will decide by yourself – alone. The actors – and especially our unruly and narcissistic ones – cannot run things.

I don't want to refuse anything whatsoever for a year, but if it is possible – please remove me from the administrative post. And again – with no bad feelings, only with an awareness of my own unsuitability.

I also agree to play in *Fyodor*, but don't be fooled -- Kachalov and I are playing badly.[6] Or more accurately, no way at all. At least Kachalov's makeup and figure aren't bad --- icon-like, while mine are like a painting by Nevrev.[7] Whether I have the time to come up with another makeup and costume I don't know, and is it worth it?

But, I repeat, I will play, since the theatre must be saved. And I will go at it with a good will. To the best of my knowledge. But do not count on the effect.

The productions must be beautiful – I agree with all my heart, but how is this to be done? How do we bring together superb, very experienced actors with beautiful personalities (at the moment we no longer have creative players, but mere actors) – with the dear spoiled puppies of the 2nd and 3rd studios. And nevertheless – it is a good idea. Let people insult us, let us flop. So long as there is a group of people who *love the theatre*, who are wishing for *something*, who work hard for *something*.

Yershov as Godunov. [8] Well, you've seen him a hundred times. He is still the same. Very handsome in the makeup, very upright, with rigid arms and legs. Big and very imposing, plus after Vishnevsky the fact is he speaks well, intelligently, grammatically and distinctly. Vishnevsky at least had the temperament of a beast, but Yershov is cold. When he tries to be impulsive, he gets a bit ridiculous, like a good-natured little boy who is trying to come across as an imposing and substantial grown-up. The audience may like that.

Woe from Wit is, of course, difficult. But there I cannot judge even approximately, because I saw Yelanskaya only in 1 recital performance – except for the laryngeal-nasal voice, everything was good. I barely know Prudkin and have never seen Livanov,[9] only know that some people consider him a genius (especially as a director). That is bad. We have to make a sharp differentiation between Chatsky and the rest. Of course. That is what I wanted for the first production. How and with what techniques we are to achieve this now, I don't know. My techniques, based on emotion and distinct enunciation, gesture, phonetics, the rhythm of graphics etc. – will not work, because they require preliminary training. It's up to you with the books [from the 1906 production] in hand. I will heartily do whatever I can, and will learn with the greatest, most sincere interest.

But the problem is that I am dull at what does not organically flow from me, and when I begin to copy, then something bad happens to me, which makes me even forget my lines – something happens to my memory. In general this faculty of mine is very badly out of order. My memory and vision have failed greatly. These are the awesome harbingers of approaching old age. There were nightmarish performances, when I completely dried up in a well-known monologue that had been wedged in my mind for years. Tarasova had to prompt me.[10] Rumyantsev shouted from the wings, and I understood nothing.

Tarasova. [11] Will she actually show up? I doubt it. It's a question of husband and money. Who will guarantee that her husband isn't molested under the present circumstances. Without such a guarantee she will not agree to it. All the money she earned – Syupik (her husband) lost in some chocolate deal. She acted this summer to earn dollars for Moscow. I don't know whether she succeeded in this, but she had a great success, along with some tempting offers. Add to this the allurements of our marauders under the leadership of Sharov.[12] I'm almost convinced that they will make off with her, especially since she has changed greatly of late. Success has turned her head, and she has become unrecognizable.

Become the supreme lord and master over the Studios? Fine, I agree and will try to do what I can. But this time you must sustain me in my faith or at least offer some sort of ray of hope for the Studios. They have disappointed me so much that I have no more faith in them or good feelings. All the studio folk are petit bourgeoisie with tiny, practical, utilitarian spiritual needs. A smidgeon of art and lots of compromises. And all this is diluted by boorishness, faulty education, laziness, vulgarity, narcissism and satisfaction with the cheapest success. These darling little minor theatres, into which the studios have metamorphosed, are odious to me. And I can do nothing to set them an example, because even our theatre, the old-timers' theatre, has metamorphosed from a theatre into a big, mediocre show business with an enormous tap-room 'for the consumption of alcohol on the premises and to take away'. A business where talented people turn into drunks. But in life the demands on art have become harsher than ever. These demands and harshness weigh heavily on me personally, on my bad character. I am almost incapable of compromising, and when I do – they credit it to my account, take advantage of my weakness and abuse it. And when I stand firm – they say I have an insufferable character and run away. What I can give nobody needs. The little they already possess is enough for them. As a result – I am all on my own and am becoming even more anti-social. Indeed, for two seasons, I sat all by myself in my room at the Thorndyke Hotel in New York. When it comes to harshness and demands I need to hold back. I am not very fond of actors. And I am ready to throw them out. That is the only possible way to purify the atmosphere. If I were to let myself go and talk about actors the way I think about them, after what I have seen: when a certain Russian performer, when he isn't being paid… You wouldn't recognize me. But I control myself, because, obviously, in such an unstable situation I am not the judge. But, now that I am back, I will build a wall – and submit to your wisdom. The actor stays in the theatre, but when I'm at home he won't cross the threshold.

Yes, it's a great tragedy about Kachalov, and not in the way you think. The problem is not that he has no roles. He would not be very cheered up even by Stockmann, which he wanted to play, because it's the best role on tour – you can't imagine. He will do whatever you want, if he is promised annually to be allowed to tour for part of the season– abroad. He cannot do without these cheap and lucrative laurels any more. The problem is something else, something more important. He is ill, seriously so. He is an authentic, incurable alcoholic. All the changes in him that were so striking – in his appearance and his face and his acting – are the result of the disease. […] I am afraid that the way things are going with [his wife] Litovtseva, matters will not be put right. Neither she nor Kachalov love the theatre (but then, what is there to love about it as it is?). Most recently Kachalov has become remarkably more affectionate than after we returned to Moscow the first time, before the trip to America.

Fruits of Enlightenment. A play created for contemporary fashionable sensibilities. Why don't they like it? Because nowadays they are all touring, and it has no touring roles. We don't want to act as we did in the old days, but when they experimented with the avant-garde, futurism scared them. They didn't acknowledge the studio folks of the different studios as they were, but when they started to teach them, Leonidov jumped for joy.

Yes, a great deal of business lies before you, and I am ready to help you with all my heart, in the role of an assistant.

Now, having had a look at America, it is crystal clear that our administration does not know how to work. In America, during our nomadic life, a single manager did everything that a whole bunch of administrators does over here. They will say... Yes! That's America, but here in Russia, with Stanislavsky and Nemirovich-Danchenko!! Reply to them that even in America Stanislavsky was there as well as the actors who were even more spoiled than before, but had nothing to complain about Gest's management, but, on the contrary, praised it. And I was no less demanding than in Moscow. [...]

I am afraid that Chekhov is overacting the Government Inspector.

Podgorny. He is the most devoted fellow: to you, to me, to the administration, to the work – and the greatest hater of actors, who have put him through the mill. You would have to be an angel to do business with Ninka, Shevchenko, Bulgakov, Leonidov, Bondyryov[13], Baksheev and the rest of those gentlefolk. Whose fault it is I do not know, but the fact is that Podgorny 's relationship with the troupe was impossible. He has a sort of quirk, which, for all his good will towards the work exasperates everyone who deals with him. It was tactless (but understandable given the psychology of the persecuted) of their triumvirate: Ripsi [Tamantsova], Ol. Serg. [Bokshanskaya] and Podgorny. They were together everywhere – separate from everyone, their own kind of 'ménage à trois'... Neither Sudakov nor Podobed[14] nor Bertonson takes an interest in the old-timers. The only one who might is Sushkevich, but he is in the 1st Studio and wants to be an actor. Bertonson is very irritating with his Petersburg [i.e., bureaucratic] tone , which he cannot discard.

Mariya Petrovna [Lilina]– there is nothing to say for the nonce. Everything depends on Igor's health. God sent Doctor Manukhin to us here completely by chance.[15] We will have to decide: whether to have Igor treated by him or continue the slow method. A lot depends on money. [...]

We are opening with *Government Inspector*. People are expecting the old-timers. The acting of all the old-timers in *Government Inspector* is so-so.

People are expecting an ensemble, but with the newly introduced youngsters you won't achieve one.

As a result only Chekhov is a success, and the public says: he's one of our own, he's beaten the 'American bunch'; they have lost touch, they've changed and so on. Shall we give a smart riposte to our enemies?

What to begin with? Maybe *Pazukhin*?! I know it's not very effective... But on the other hand the old-timers can show off in it – juicily, in the spotlight (just the opposite of *Inspector*). After that alternate *Tsar Fyodor* and then *Inspector*, and have the old-timers prepare *Woe from Wit* as soon as possible.

Please understand, I am not criticizing, but only tossing out an idea. Think about it, don't say anything, and the question will be taken up when the time comes.

Also by way of a personal opinion. I continue more than ever to doubt that we alone – the dramatic troupe – can perform all 7 shows a week. The old-timers cannot do it, and the youngsters of the 2nd Studio are not mature enough for the MAAT. In our building meanwhile a few cannot sustain interest without us. I believe that we need help. Now that the 1st Studio has broken away, and there are no other studios – who will be with us, if not K. O.

If in terms of budget the dram. troupe cannot pay its own way (which is indubitable for such a numerous troupe), there is nothing left but to skim the cream and discard anything superfluous, leaving 4-5 shows a week. Don't forget that the old-timers are all ill: Moskvin – heart (he's had serious attacks), Gribunin – I am afraid even to mention him. Between you and me, he is, to my mind, seriously ill. Luzhsky – heart, Aleksandrov – his days are numbered, Kachalov – ill, Leonidov – utterly unfit for work, to my mind, but not through illness but through dissipation.

I have heard nothing about Meyerhold and the Third Studio and cannot imagine how this could happen.[16] I will either work in a new, renovated MAAT and its studios, or give up the stage entirely --- for the sake of some other work, which it would be premature to speak of for now. [...]

Yours K. Alekseev

[...] there is no doubt that the [Prague] group's effrontery is going beyond all bounds. Even their well-wishers waxed indignant at the behaviour of Sharov, who in Paris publicly proclaimed that Stanislavsky doesn't have the right to prevent them from using the MAAT's name, because they are the original MAAT (this is Sharov, who never was an actor with us). And they will show us... All this, of course, is empty threats, but there is no doubt that they are vulgarizing and tarnishing our name (with the connoisseurs). S. Makovsky[17] personally told me that we shouldn't let our children out on their own. This is dreadful. Russia must not be embarrassed at such a moment. And this was said back when Kachalov was still with them. You can imagine what's going on now. There's no doubt that, by exhibiting our plays and our style of playing them ahead of us, they have skimmed the cream, and in their wake, with skimmed milk, it will be hard to attain the success that the theatre might have if it were the only one abroad and could make an appearance after a long hiatus. The constant flaunting of the MAAT name on posters cheapens us. Now, if they go to Paris and London and flop there, -- you will never convince America that we weren't the ones who flopped. They're slow-witted over there, and cannot understand these combinations of multiple MAAT troupes. Gest is planning to take the theatre to London, and in time to America. But, of course, he will refuse if the MAAT trademark flops in London before we get there. There is an even greater problem – if it succeeds. But in Paris, they might go down in flames. Paris is not Czechoslovakia. This is how I would proceed. In the sternest formal terms I would warn them that we will no longer tolerate the exploitation of the MAAT trademark without our express permission. If this does not work, instruct Gest to safeguard America, and [the manager] Leonidov to ask that we be informed about Europe. And in case our proscription fails – send telegrams not to them, but to those theatres and cities where they are performing. In the telegram make a protest and explain that they are using the trademark illegally. If even this does not work, then we will have to go to law. It is impossible to remain indifferent to this phenomenon, because they are luring all our best actors away from the MAAT and ruining our tours abroad so much that we will have to give them up forever. I personally will not weep, because, of course, a second time, without you, I will not go for no matter how many dollars. [...]

Your sincerely devoted and affectionate

K. Alekseev

On 8 August KS returned to Moscow from Saint-Gervais near Chamounix; and on 24 August ND returned from abroad as well. They discovered that the MAAT administrator Mikhalsky had been exiled.

To **Fyodor Mikhalsky**. 29 August 1924, Moscow.
Dear, dear, Fyodor Nikolaevich, heartily beloved by all of us!

If you could peer into our hearts and understand what is going on there, you would be surprised and proud. You are one of the few who knew how to deserve the general, unanimous love and gratitude of all, starting with the actors and ending with the stagehands.

When news of your misfortune reached me – abroad, we could not get over it nor think about anything other than the fatal mishap you have suffered. But God willing, everything will work out, and you will be with us again. When overseas amid difficult conditions of work I thought about our return to Moscow and mentally painted a picture of our arrival – I saw your beaming face, felt how you and I would exchange kisses and share a tight hug. I know that you were waiting for the old-timers more than anyone and yearned for us. Vl. Iv. cannot think of you without tears, and he is far from sentimental. [...]

We will try before your return to sort out the unravelling theatre...The First Studio has turned us down. Good luck to it. Half the Third too. The Second and part of the Third have remained faithful and with them we shall now put together a troupe and a school. There are plenty of them, and hence there is some choice. The youngsters, to all appearances, are not bad and want to work. But they have all been brought together from various quarters, with the most diverse and variegated approaches to art. Some from cabaret sketches, Futurism, some from hack mannerisms, some from craftsmanship, some from genuine art. How can they all be integrated into one common denominator? This is especially difficult in the school, where there are some interesting talents. Our school, prepared by Demidov,[18] evidently, stinks of – God. The Third Studio school as well. But the folks in the Second are not bad, but they have already partaken of the stage and professional ways of doing things. It's good that we will, apparently, have youngsters, that is, a good actress for young, powerfully dramatic roles – Tarasova (who will arrange an apartment for her – if you are away?). In addition there are also Molchanova,[19] Yelanskaya and a few from the 3rd Studio. Of the men,

459

Zavadsky,[20] Prudkin, Livanov. We always had a lacuna in this line of business, which, evidently, will now be filled. We will immediately rehearse *Pazukhin*, *Government Inspector*, *Woe from Wit* and *Fyodor* with a new team [...]

I am having trouble with the Opera Studio. The Bolshoy Theatre has no money, the subsidy has been reduced, my whole private household depends on me. If I withdraw from the Studio (a pity, because it might be made into something good), other people will be moved in, and it will be impossible to live, because the apartment is set up so that it cannot be divided into 2 parts. In order to live, I have to support the STUDIO. And how am I to do that without money? [...]

On 11 September a revival of Pazukhin's Death *opened. The party-line critics found it irrelevant and even Lunacharsky, in defending it, felt it needed more bite to suit the times. In the meantime KS was rejecting the work of the studios and insisting on harder work.*

To **Natalya Degen-Volkhonskaya**.[21] 12 October 1924, Moscow.
Dear Natalya Viktorovna!

[...] In art there are the eternal and the fashionable. The eternal never dies -- the fashionable passes by, leaving but little trace. What we see around us is ephemeral, fashionable. It is not without its use because a little crystal is formed from it, probably a very small one, which will fuse its minor accomplishments with the eternal in art and give it a stimulus. All the rest will perish irretrievably.

All that we have been living through will undoubtedly create a new literature that will represent the new life of the human soul. New actors will reproduce this new life in terms of the eternal, immutable laws of creativity, common to all humanity. From ancient times they have been studied with relation to acting technique and this is being enriched to a remarkable degree by whatever is contributed by art, all the latest researches of serious innovators in our profession.

Do not show this letter to anyone, because my opinion is extremely superficial and unfounded and might confuse people who love to be clever about art, but have no feeling for it. [...]

To **Vasily Luzhsky**. Before 19 October 1924.
I cannot yet very clearly figure out the full scope of my work in the aggregate:

1) As *actor* I am to play – a) Shuisky, b) Famusov, c) the Cavaliere, d) Satin (?), e) Krutitsky, f) Count Lyubin...

A new complication has arisen, thanks to my age; on the days when I have a performance I cannot conduct rehearsals. (Old age is evidently to blame; I come down with something like asthma.)

2) Revivals as *director* – a) *The Blue Bird*, b) *The Landlady* (*The Mistress of the Inn*), c) *Woe from Wit* (in part), d) *The Lady from the Provinces*.

Simultaneously, rehearsals of Famusov, the Cavaliere, Satin, Krutitsky, Lyubin.

3) To reorganize the entire *school*... To give my own lessons in delivery, rhythm, exercises and self-awareness with music, phonetics, graphics.

To organize and direct excerpts and student performances; to organize a crowd-scene class and turn crowd-scene productions into a class.

4) To organize the *Studio*…

5) To organize the Opera Studio…

6) My own personal undertaking, to earn dollars for Igor – to write two books for America; one on my travels and the other, a didactic novel.

I am still rather at sea in this plethora of things to do… I say again, I will refuse nothing that is not done in name only. That would spoil the general atmosphere, which appears to be settling down just now.

Mikhail Chekhov opened in Hamlet *at the MAT 2 on 12 November. His former colleagues in the original company attended on 17 November. KS refused to rise from his seat or meet with Chekhov afterwards. He noted, 'A real tragic actor is a great rarity, not everyone possesses the necessary qualities. Not even Misha possesses them. Khlestakov is his sort of thing, in this role he is really helpless… instead of authentic tragedy he has hysterics. And then, that flirting with modernity, that leather jacket. In short, I left right after the performance nursing my chagrin.'*

During this time ND began work on a deliberately 'revolutionary' play, Pugachyov Times *by Konstantin Trenyov, an historical chronicle about a peasant uprising under Catherine the Great. It was the first melding of youngsters from the Second Studio with the old-timers. Meanwhile, KS got into serious difficulties with the new censorship board the Repertkom, which demanded major changes and abridgements to* Blue Bird *that called its continued survival into question.*

To **Georgy Burdzhalov**. 4 December 1924, Moscow.

Dear, kind, beloved Georgy Sergeevich!

We are all most sincerely aggrieved by your poor health and regret that *Depths* has to be played for the first time without you [as the landlord Kostylyov]. I would like you to learn not to take too much to heart all the various kinds of annoyances that beset us. Honestly, everything has become so demented and petty in this world that it is not worth paying it much mind. Whatever happens to us, somehow, all the same, life will turn around and bad as things are, things will work out, until the next set of annoyances. Just as if we were in Luna Park strolling past every kind of ballyhoo. They are silly, just as they are there, and not worth paying the least attention. At the moment, like you, I am under fire from Vserabis;[22] it is the third month now that a certain bastard is poisoning my life and wants to shut down the studio and take possession of my house. From the moment I said, 'Shut it down. Things can't be any the worse,' I began to live more easily. They want to haul me into court, but who at the present time isn't taken to court!! Well! They will sentence me to a reprimand. Well! Let them sentence me. All this is scare tactics, because we have committed no crime at all. We are so pure in our art that they are embarrassed and afraid of us – the other. Let us rejoice and be cheerful again, as ever, and healthy. May God keep you. I embrace you tenderly and lovingly and kiss your wife's hand.

With cordial affection yours K. Alekseev

Burdzhalov died a few days later on 10 December.

In 1925 a Repertory Board for the MAAT was established, packed with young Communists, which, in the words of Aleksandr Popov, quickly 'degenerated into a controlling and infiltrating ideological force, pretending to be a 'democratic institution representing the majority'.' Next came an Artistic Council and then a mestkom or trade union committee, its leaders appointed by the party, which could call meetings of the collective on political matters. Its chairman was a stagehand. ND tried to avoid attending these meetings whenever possible.

Meanwhile, KS was working with Lyubov Gurevich on the revision of My Life in Art for the Soviet reader. It involved shuffling of passages and whole chapters, cuts and additions. Many revisions had to be made to the socialist and atheistic temper of the times. She tried to talk him out of a chapter purporting to be a letter from 'one of your Petersburg friends' to remind the reader of what importance the tours there had for its intelligentsia, but he included it anyway.

To **Lyubov Gurevich.** Before 10 February 1925, Moscow.
Dear Lyubov Yakovlevna,

I am overwhelmed, disconcerted, touched and grateful for all your efforts. You should not stand on ceremony: cut out all superfluities; I am neither attached to nor enamoured of my literary 'creations' in any way and my self-esteem as an author has not yet had time to develop. I worry when something needs to be recast. For example, what should be done about the tours to St Petersburg and the provinces? They could be eliminated, since, as you so rightly observe, they are abominably, badly described.

In the strain I am under at present, I am physically incapable of concentrating enough to give heart and soul, as I should, to our St Petersburg friends.

As for the good times and hard work in the actor's life, I felt that all the trials and tribulations I describe give an idea of the work involved. I shall have to insert somewhere something that will convince the working class.

I have no life at present, thanks to this book. The publishers are exigent. They are insisting that I stick to the deadline and bear all the expenses and losses myself. They are swamping me with questions and galley-proofs. I don't understand the marks they use... And we end up with a skit entitled *The Cobbler Should Stick to His Last.*

When I have handed in the last page of manuscript and the last proof-sheet I shall be the happiest man alive, but when the book comes out, I daresay I shall start looking for a suitable hook to hang myself from. Yes indeed!.. It's ghastly enough to be an actor, but to be a writer!

I kiss your hands and send my best to your daughter.

I enclose with apologies a manuscript on Chekhov. I beg pardon and I thank you. The more you trim and cross out the better.

With warmest love,
K. Alekseev

The manuscript was submitted to the publisher on 16 April 1925. The article on Chekhov was published separately.

Sergey Dmitrievich Balukhaty (1893-1946), a literary scholar, had asked KS to let him use the score of The Seagull *for a comparative analysis of the productions at the Alexandra and Art Theatres. Eventually Balukhaty published the director's score for* The Seagull *and in his lengthy introduction reproduced KS's letter.*

To **Sergey Balukhaty**. Moscow, 14 February 1925.

I am very grateful to you for your interest and request, and should sincerely like to help you in your interesting work. Bear in mind that the mises-en-scène of *The Seagull* were made according to old, now utterly discarded methods of the enforced imposition of one's own personal feelings on to the actor, and not according to the new method of a preliminary study of the actor, his attributes, the material for his role, in order to create a mise-en-scène that will suit him and be useful to him. In other words, the method of the old mises-en-scène belongs to the despotic director, against whom I now lead the fight, while the new mises-en-scène are made by directors who submit to the actor.

With this in mind, I would appreciate it greatly if, before you discuss my *mise-en-scène* in the book, you would provide a foreword clarifying all that I have just stated.

With sincere wishes for your success,
K. Stanislavsky

KS and the MAT troupe left for a tour of Tiflis, Baku, Rostov-on-Don, Odessa, Kharkov, Yekaterinoslav and Kiev which lasted from 2 May to 20 June 1925.

To **Aleksandr Bogdanovich**.[23] 10 May 1925, Tiflis.

Dear Aleksandr Vladimirovich!

[...] I read [Puccini's] *The Girl of the Golden West* and liked the libretto a lot. It might be a good thing to stage. And if I then learn Italian, it could play even in America, i.e., they know the opera well there. Caruso sang it, and the libretto was composed by New York's darling David Belasco. [...] It might be very interesting for me to stage it. I have asked around and will continue to ask around in all the cities where there might be singers, and especially tenors. It would be good to find a tenor with a youthful passionate sound and a temperament. [...]

Cordially devoted K. Stanislavsky

To **his son Igor**. After 3 June 1925.

Dear, beloved Igorechek!

[...] When I got back, I found enormous changes. First of all – in the makeup of our spectators themselves. Where had they come from? Many are from the provinces. At first they thought us strange. (I'm not talking about our former spectators. There are few of them left and they don't go to the theatre.) One would think that the theatre, on its return, should have had full houses, but it was quite the opposite. At first the box-office was worse than later on, when the new spectator became acquainted with us. In the past, when we, the actors, would walk down the street – the passers-by recognized us. Even in New York towards the last now and again people would give us a glance, a nod or say a few kind words. But on our return to Moscow we felt completely alien, and nobody knew us. Now, gradually, we are becoming more popular. There's no point in bringing up the way the newspapers and our other enemies treated us before and do the same now. 'Their actors are good, but nobody needs their theatre' – that's the gist of all the obituary notices for us. In the higher circles the attitude is quite different. They understand perfectly well that the traditions, kernels of Russian art, knowledge, experience, talent, actor's individuality exist only in our theatre. And therefore they do all that is incumbent on them to ease the difficult situation of our theatre. A new institution, the Repertkom (repertory committee), has banned our entire repertoire. What's more, we have to lodge two bears in one den, that is we (the elders and the affiliated youngsters from the Studio) and Nemirovich's K.O. We are left with 3 days and 1 matinee. What's more, during our absence Nemirovich incurred a debt of more than a hundred thousand rubles for his inept operetta company. Of course, this is listed on the books as a temporary loan, but everyone understands perfectly that this is only nominal, and there will be no talk of repayment whatsoever.

Now that I have started talking about art, I shall go on about the theatre. First of all – I'll say 'in general' what's going on in that world. The situation is a difficult one. The most insulting term is 'academic theatre'. Even more abusive is this MAAT (of course, the first like the second is quite the – specific -- doing of Bersenev). Some of the academic theatres do good box-office, of course, first of all ours (with a purely artistic repertoire, without compromising with my conscience). The Maly (with compromises) and the Bolshoy Theatre (although on the whole it incurs great losses). The rest of the theatres are empty and hungry, if they do not perform topical vulgarities (such as *The Empress's Conspiracy*, that is the story of Rasputin on stage.[24] This vileness was composed by Aleksey Tolstoy[25] who is debased and defiled by it. The plot is a good one, but how trivially, how sensationally he treated it. Now, after a spectacular success and packed houses for this vulgarity, he is writing a new history of Azef and wants to call it *Son of a Bitch?!*).[26] Many theatres have been burned down. Not a single theatre pays salaries in the summer, because there is no money. We are in this situation thanks to that bastard the K.O. musical studio. It is the most ignoble of institutions – untalented, hopelessly stuck to us like herpes or a carbuncle. On various pure or impure pretexts and hearsay [?], Nemirovich has arranged things so that we are nondetachable, our bookkeeping is intertwined. That's why in our old age we have now to wander around the provinces to earn money to get 1½, 2 months of rest. The season, as I have already written, was more difficult because we had to assemble the whole troupe again this year out of old-timers and youngsters (devils bound to babies). All the youngsters are corrupted in the worst sense. Some start to Turandotize themselves, others, like the Second Studio, have been warped by all sorts of new warping methods.

We had to be joined together in *Woe from Wit* (no joke) and *Inspector* (?!). This was difficult. Just like a troupe put together from different, very diverse theatres. It was the same with *Fyodor, Blue Bird, Depths. Pazukhin's Death* particularly paid a price for this, because almost everyone in it plays old folks... [...] For the end of the season we prepared and [on 25 August] played *Pugachyov Times* by Trenyov (an old author). Moskvin is Pugachyov. The leading female role is played by Tarasova. The rest of the numerous roles are divided among all the performers, almost the whole troupe. Lots of scenes (7 or 8). And the staging and the scenery and the directorial work and the performance turned out to be a failure. I do not expect success (the play will go on next year).[27] Nemirovich, who is staging the play, is not downhearted, but during our absence he has contracted a certain kind of self-assurance which is not always justified by the work. He has a very bad and unfair attitude towards the old-timers, who feed him and his good-for-nothing studio. For this reason and, of course, because he and Luzhsky now come off as dictators, they curse him and Vas. Vas. – and do not love them. That is not always justified either. Now the turn to me is complete (just as in America – they stuck like glue). I have become very popular, and no later than 21 May (3 June) on my nameday they organized a celebratory tea (of comic character) in Odessa. [...]

To **Lyubov Gurevich.** 14 June 1925, Kharkov.
Dear, good and sincerely beloved Lyubov Yakovlevna!
[...] My brain can still not cope with the idea that editing a book can produce such joy. I picture this labour to be hellish, and would not be capable of doing it with care. Therefore my thanks are enormous, unlimited. What should I do for you?! Thinking about the future book, naturally – my ideas fly to you. Without you I cannot write what I need to and what I know. Help me. But this help can be realized only on the condition that you and I find some 'modus vivendi' acceptable to both of us. Let's plan it out and start the great work – I have devised a clear scheme for the next two books on the theatre.
First – a student's notes.
Second – the history of a production.
First – work on oneself.
Second – on the role.
These three books will offer a rather large part of my experience and material. Art has need of it.
I have already written about 50 (printed) pages – of the diary of a student.[28] This too will turn out to be a rather large book. As to the American notes, there's been a hitch. I cannot screw myself to this work. I suppose my mind is so used to moving in the direction of the first book, which is an introduction to the system, that now, out of inertia, the just completed book lingers on. To make a long story short, it is easy for me to write the system and the diary, but the American notes are not getting written. [...]

Yours K. Alekseev

To **his son Igor**. 26 June 1925, Kiev.

My dear and beloved friend Igorek!

I am in Kiev after successful tours to 6 cities (Tiflis, Baku, Rostov-on-Don, Odessa, Kharkov, Yekaterinoslav). Yesterday we arrived and at night I performed *Depths*. I don't like to act on the day I arrive, but yesterday was especially unlucky for me. On the train, at night – my lumbago acted up and I could not sleep, because the jolting of the carriage and the movements of my body produced twinges in the sore spot. We got to the 'Continental' Hotel (I think you've been there. You remember, there was a little garden with a restaurant in it, where the music made a din all day long and there were little balconies all around, where the actors lived and we talked back and forth. The little garden is still there, but there's no restaurant.) They allotted me a room with a bath, and soon I was dreaming of taking a hot bath, but it turned out to have neither warm nor cold water. While I was trying it out, the door slammed shut and there was no way to open it from inside. The way to the bathroom is through the bedroom, and on the other side of the bedroom is the living-room, which is locked from inside. What was I to do? I was trapped, in solitary confinement, in only my shirt, with lumbago, in a damp room. To add insult to injury – the lights went out. I was in the dark. Can't lie down, can't sit down, it's cold, no window, just a door with a broken lock. But I have to get to the rehearsal and perform in the evening. There was nothing left to do but bang and holler. But how were they to get to me even if they heard me. How could I explain what had happened. I could hear nothing from my prison. I banged and hollered so much that I was surprised I still had hands and a voice. Luckily for me, one of the windows in my room opened on to the roof and one could go along the roof to one of the adjacent rooms, and a window to the roof turned out not to be locked, but only tightly shut. A chambermaid shoved the frame, it opened. I was saved.

The performance began. We performed the first act, without an intermission, we had to start the second. The lights were already dimming out in the audience. We were running around for the actor playing Zob. It turns out that he had not even arrived at the theatre. How this had happened, that nobody had mentioned it, I can't understand. The actor who played Zob – Maloletkov[29] – is one of the most punctual and diligent. It turns out he had fallen asleep, no one had woken him. We had to start without Zob, because the audience was already plunged in darkness. We didn't know what we would say or how we would say it, and, chiefly, how we would end the act (after all, it's Zob who ends it). We had barely come offstage, I sent couriers to find him and told them to make up Gudkov as Zob. Maloletkov soon showed up and had time to get on at the end of the play. No one noticed. Not even Al. Iv. Adashev (a former actor of ours, who had acted in the play at the time when it was first staged.)[30]

I learned that Kilyalya is ill. She has chicken-pox. If only it were limited to that, it wouldn't matter. Yustinov came from Moscow and said that Mama had trouble obtaining papers for abroad. Whom is she travelling with is the question. At the moment Kachalov is playing *In the Clutches of Life* for the last time and tomorrow he will leave with those who are going farther abroad. But Mama doesn't have time to go with him. Margulis[31] is letting her go, but she wants to meet with me and make arrangements for the future. I will transfer the money in the American bank to you in installments. [...] We are making more on this tour than we expected, and this will help us through the summer – to the start of next season (they don't pay us a salary from 1 May). When I get to Moscow I will have to put the finishing touches on staging the play *Jacob's Dream* for Habima (scenery by Falk.[32] The 1st set is enchanting, the second not so good, and the third is quite bad). I know that you will bawl me out, but there's nothing to be done, I got embroiled in this affair, left before I finished the job, and they signed a contract for a trip to Europe and America and they will have to pay a forfeit if I don't stage the play. I curse myself... but I deserve leniency.[33] Until I can provide you the amount that will allow you to be cured completely, I cannot live at peace in this world.

[...] The acting profession in Russia is on its last legs. Soon no one will be left who might preserve past achievements, and this has to be done, because you cannot imagine how absurd this business of theatre has become. For instance. Did you know what the new theatre is like? They hang up nets, as in the circus, trapezes, trampolines. The actors -- employees in the circus uniform of a ringmaster -- help other actors clamber up on to trapezes, turn somersaults, declaim. They stand on their hands, feet in the air while speaking their lines and playing their roles. Here on the Ukrainian stage the new art is expressed by the women wearing Little Russian embroidered sleeves on their legs and standing on their hands and performing scenes with one another (head first). This is how they *renovate* the oldest of plays (*Natalka-Poltavka* or *Coursing Two Hares at Once*, etc.) for want of new ones. This is called renovating a play. Meyerhold, being a clever man, has turned back to realism. He was just in Kiev (in our very theatre). Some say it was a terrific success. Others say no. Some assert that they made money, others deny it. His prices run from 10 k. to 1 r. 50. Ours are 5 r. Today *In the Clutches of Life* has a full house. Yesterday *Depths* (for the first time in Kiev) didn't make it, about 500 rubles. The movies are to blame. They deprave the public dreadfully, corrupt its taste.

The tour ended with KS inscribing a group photograph 'Actors of all MAAT Theatres and Studios – unite!' He returned to Moscow on 30 July.

To **Anatoly Lunacharsky**. 31 July 1925, Moscow.
Deeply respected Anatoly Vasilievich! [...]
This is what happened in Baku. As in all the cities, there too we offered the profsoyuz [Professional Trades Union] one performance at prices reduced by 60%. After discussions the profsoyuz proposed that instead of one performance we should hand out 300 tickets at the 60%-reduced price for each of the six performances advertised in Baku. In all we were supposed to hand out 1800 tickets, and this number corresponded to the number of seats for each individual complete performance. Three days later the profsoyuz demanded of us another

special performance, because not all the workers who wanted to attend our performances had been accommodated. It was simply technically impossible to put on a double performance, along with the plays advertised here, and it was also impossible to be detained in Baku an extra day, because that would have broken up our itinerary and the order of the performances advertised for Rostov and other cities. Our advance man on the tour V. V. Luzhsky telegraphed all this to Moscow so that the theatre turned to you with a request to help us by sending a telegram to the Baku profsoyuz saying that the MAAT, having fulfilled its appointed mission, cannot remain beyond the advertised performances. On 20 May the telegram from you in V. V. Luzhsky's name was received, and, it goes without saying, helped us a great deal. I append a copy of the telegram.

As for the notices in the newspaper *Labour* let me fill you in: we sent it an exhaustive explanation with the request that it be printed in the next issue. The editors of *Labour* replied to us on 8 July that the letter we sent will be inserted in *Labour* only after they have received an explanation from their Baku correspondent, who had sent the report on the MAAT tour to Baku. (I append our exchange with the newspaper's editorial staff.) Unfortunately, I have found no refutation anywhere.

In other cities, if memory serves, performances were offered to the profsoyuzs. As to the inaccuracy of opinions and witticisms concerning 'Our MAAT in the Sticks', I can only say that in Tiflis the workers presented us an address during the performance, and the All-Ukrainian Profsoyuz of Railway Workers a testimonial, a copy of which I append. [...]

Once again I think you for your good relations towards me and the theatre.

On 15 August, the Ukrainian author Mikhail Afanasievich Bulgakov (1891-1940) presented a sixteen-scene dramatization of his novel The White Guard to the MAAT troupe. It had been solicited for use by the younger actors. When KS became acquainted with it, he was reluctant and thought it 'Soviet agitprop'.

Pugachyov Times, directed by ND, Luzhsky and Leonidov, opened on the main stage on 19 September 1925. This chronicle of a peasant revolt in the reign of Catherine the Great was not well received by the leftist critics and ran for only forty-one performances. KS was shocked to see advertisements in the programme for his forthcoming book; the commercialism next to the beloved Seagull insignia scandalized him.

Rehearsals began for two classic comedies, Beaumarchais's The Marriage of Figaro and Ostrovsky's The Ardent Heart. Lunacharsky's call for a return to Ostrovsky had resulted in Meyerhold's deconstructed and constructivist Forest, which ND loathed. KS inspired his actors to all manner of monkey-shines to the point of caricature.

In October 1925 ND left for New York with the Musical Studio. He would remain abroad until January 1928, partly because of the old-timers' supercilious attitude to the Studio's American success (which was, in fact, decidedly mixed).

Nicholas I and the Decembrists, adapted by Aleksandr Kugel from a novel by Dmitry Merezhkovsky, began to rehearse on 14 December, with Kachalov in the role of the martinet tsar. For permission to organize a special matinee in honour of the centenary *of the Decembrist uprising, KS turned to the Commissar for Defence, Lev Davydovich Trotsky (Bronshtein, 1879-1940), who was no fan of the MAT. He referred to them as insulars, no better than the poet Anna Akhmatova.*

To **Lev Trotsky**. 1 January 1926, Moscow.
Much esteemed Lev Davydovich!

First of all thank you sincerely for your good letter. I learn from it that even you, in your first collision with the theatre, are disturbed and beginning to be bedevilled by the same malady of modern theatre from which we suffer. No plays and no playwrights. Everyone chides the theatre for the staleness of its repertoire, but after all it is not the theatre that writes plays, but men of letters, and therefore, one would think, before chiding us, one ought to address them. Here is a specific case: there is a good actor V. I. Kachalov, he has created an interesting profile, which one can use to express much of what the modern spectator needs. But there are neither plays nor playwrights who could perfect what is being shown from the stage, and therefore the actor's creativity has to remain under a bushel. If we had to employ a writer of mediocre talent, the result would be one of those plays on an ostensibly political theme, which are now cramming the theatres.

We are wracking our brains to show off Kachalov in a successful role. We are being urged to revive the *Matinee* in the form in which it has already been presented. But we do not find it possible to make gifts paid for by others, and so the fate of Kachalov as Nicholas I remains for now undecided.

Thank you for the ideas you have suggested. I am in full agreement with them and will continue to seek a talented man who could perfect what has been begun in an artistic manner.

The Ardent Heart opened on 23 January, with KS listed as 'In Charge of the Production'. He himself was ill and could not attend what turned out to be a mirthful success. Olga Knipper's brother Vladimir wrote, 'Everything exhales the charm of your talent and throughout it all one can feel the enormous culture and power of the school of Russian acting and directing that you created.' Hard-line Bolshevik critics were outraged, but Meyerhold had nothing but praise for this exercise in the grotesque. It turned out to be the MAAT's biggest hit in years and chalked up 607 performances.

The Hebrew-language troupe Habima which had been guided by KS and Vakhtangov was leaving Russia for an American tour. This letter was intended to herald their appearances abroad.

To **Habima**. Before 26 January 1926, Moscow.

[...] We happened to play a small part in the history of the Jewish theatre. And I am very glad, because I fulfilled thereby one of the important missions of an actor. Art is the realm of the spirit, in which people come together with the purest and most sublime concepts, beyond politics, beyond petty personal aims, but for the sake of beauty and aesthetic delight. In art there are no differences of rank, religion, nationality. Art is the realm in which the brotherhood of peoples might exist. In this sublime and pure sphere of art I met the members of Habima Theatre and its talented leader – my friend – N. L. Tsemakh.[34] Now, during this temporary parting I send them a heartfelt and friendly desire to continue to propagate beyond the borders of our homeland that which we and they and my student Ye. B. Vakhtangov (chief director of *The Dybbuk* from its inception) loved, valued and created.

On 25 January 1926 Bulgakov read a revised, twelve-scene version of The White Guard *to the actors who were enormously interested. Both generations wanted to act in it and rehearsals began at once.*

In late 1925 KS initiated the creation of an artistic laboratory, where not only new styles of scene design but new material for building scenery were researched. In an attempt to interest Igor in such matters, he advised his son on a puppet theatre he was building.

To **his son Igor**. Before 14 February 1926, Moscow.
Dear, beloved, good Igorek!

You write that the theatre is done for, but your imagination is dozing. I want to waken it and give you a plan for working and even, perhaps, a command. At the moment we are busy with working out new plans, contexts and possibilities for the stage and the theatre. The question is dealt with in general, and not specifically for any given play or production. All sorts of colours and lines and forms of the scene-painting designer are over-familiar and obsolete. We have grown disillusioned with them. The most correct path of all is Meyerhold's. He is proceeding from general scenic and directorial possibilities and principles. And he determines them boldly and simply (it is impossible to say the same thing regarding the acting aspect, which is weak in him.) So, as an example. Most of all we need to contend with the stage and proscenium. Its enormous dimensions crush the little space taken up by the scenery and the very personality of the actor. How are we to do away with this enormous and oppressive space of the proscenium. Curtains, draperies, borders and so on. Meyerhold has abolished even them. With him the whole behind-the-scenes area of the stage is shown. It is whitewashed and clean. This is the building itself, a continuation of the auditorium. He does not hide this and in this great hall (as if united with the spectator) displays small screens, whatever furniture is needed, etc. Along with this he comes up with all sorts of gimmicks. Sometimes the furniture rolls on, sometimes it appears as part of the wall (the furniture is fastened to the wall), sometimes it rises from beneath the floor and so on.

I do not exclude the kind of possibility shown by Meyerhold; I should think that it is necessary only to turn the wings of the theatre into an architectural construct – as a continuation of the auditorium. I mean, to reduce them to a common denominator. [...]

To **Mariya Margulis**.[35] 16 March 1926, Moscow.
Dear, good Mariya Vladimirovna!

Instead of the usual letter of thanks for your new over-indulgence (fruit, caviare), -- let me tell you a fairy tale.

Once upon a time there were two friends. Both were rich and lived well. One was a factory-owner and a merchant, the other a scholar. They constantly called on one another, talked about business and science, took an interest in art.

But then... they both became poor. All each had left was a little cottage, which it was hard for them to maintain. Each one, as best he could, helped his friend. If the hen laid an extra egg – he would take it to his friend. If the cow gave more milk, they would churn extra butter and share it with the friend.

'It is awkward,' the scholar once said, 'to accept gifts. One must make a present in return.'

So on Easter he sent flowers to his friend.

In reply the friend sent him an enormous box of chocolates. The next time they sent one another an enormous vase of flowers and a big basket of grapes. Then came champagne, wine, pictures, furniture, carriages, a cow, a horse. In order to cover the expenses, they had at first to mortgage and then sell their houses and move into hovels.

There came a time when there was nothing left to give and nothing left to sell.

But their friendship remained unaltered. Again, as before, they shared the necessities: a stale crust of bread or a potato. With it they would say tearfully and lovingly: 'The gift does not matter to me – what matters is the love.' That's the reason we are ruined, and the gifts had nothing to do with it! [...]

Soulfully devoted and loving
K. Alekseev

ND's letters from the U.S. raised a question about the further fate of his Musical Studio and the colleagues at the MAAT, who had taken part in his tour abroad. From the time of its creation the Musical Studio had been on the budget of the MAAT, occupying a spacious rehearsal space (the so-called K.O. Hall). The reorganization of the theatre (the merger with the Second Studio and the divorce from the other studios), the complicated financial situation, and the refusal of an independent government subsidy deprived the Musical Studio of the possibility of further funding, especially since the theatre had incurred enormous debts while the MAAT had toured abroad in 1922-23. All this plus the aesthetic differences roused the 'old-timers,' headed by KS, to demand a territorial and administrative separation of the Musical Studio from the parent company. This deeply stung ND. It persuaded him to stay abroad for another two years, particularly when he was offered a contract as an idea man by MGM Studios in Hollywood.

To **Nemirovich-Danchenko.** After 31 March 1926, Moscow.

I got your letter and hasten to answer it. [...]

It is distressing for me to speak of the feeling of revenge, which you suspect in us. This is a matter for your conscience.

I will not speak about what you do not see and do not feel at a distance. This will be cleared up on its own when you return.

Finding myself in the very thick of the fermenting life of the theatre and all the other conditions of our life, I feel like an undivorced spouse, [36] I venture to offer you some advice.

Do not repeat the old mistake, do not return the Musical Studio to the building of the MAAT. It is impossible to imbed a lover in a family. Do not load new burdens and taxes on the shoulders of the old-timers and the starving youngsters. The glass is filled full to the very top, one more drop and catastrophe will be inevitable. Do not force onto people others in whom trust is undermined. Mariya Petrovna [Grigorieva][37] as a costumier and Sergey Lvovich [Bertonson] are not popular. [...]

You often talk about the old-timers' unfairness to the K. O. But try for a moment to put yourself in our shoes and think whether there is even greater unfairness on your part to us. I ask you. What more can the K. O. demand of us. We did not create it, it was created against our will. We know now what our docility cost us.

1) The K. O. *took you away*, and, you needn't hide your eyes, -- irrevocably. Your heart is no longer with the MAAT nor will it be, even if you worked in it, and we know what work without a heart leads to.

2) The K. O. completely *betrayed the character* of the MAAT profile and me and the general taste – betrayed it not for the best. The semi-musical K. O. is of no interest to me or any of us. We and the public itself became convinced of it this season, when the MAAT became a dramatic theatre again.

3) The *idea* of a synthetic theatre is not only completely *alien* to us and me in particular, but even antipathetic. I consider such a theatre amateurish. A pianist or a violinist cannot be great in his own art and at the same time be as good at painting pictures as someone with a genuine vocation, at building a house as a genuine architect and at inventing choreography as a genuine dancer. If he dissipates his energies, he will get no farther than charming, talented amateurishness. And it's the same in our concern. The most a synthetic actor can achieve consists in dancing charmingly, but as an amateur. Singing charmingly, but as an amateur, acting charmingly on stage, but... as an amateur. This *but* will always pursue him and turn him into a dilettante. No. The synthetic theatre cannot be high art, and therefore this concept, to my mind, is deleterious. Let a singer dance, fence, practice acrobatics. All this is useful, but first of all, let him sing beautifully, and for this he has to spend the greater part of his life.

4) I myself have been involved in opera for over seven years now and I know for sure that the singer's psychology will never and cannot be understood and accepted by a dramatic actor. These are two types of performer – *they will never be compatible*, like water and oil. The MAAT in its person stood for just such a combination of oil and water at the time when it cohabited with singers. We recall in horror our spiritual condition during those years and at no price can we think of returning to what for us is completely unacceptable.

5) I don't wish to speak about *financial sacrifices, squabbles over money*, etc. However when I think what starving Raevskaya, Vishnevsky's children, my children and most of the families paid and are paying now for this, and that you and I receive a salary of 600 r., -- I do not find justification for such sacrifices and do not consider it right for us to continue to make them.

6) Over the course of 7 years the whole big collective, with people attached to it like L[eonidov]., who have constantly compromised you, has erected a thick wall between us, the old-timers, and you. We have received many humiliations, unjust harsh insults from them and from you, because during this time the old-timers of the MAAT became a term of abuse. But we, withdrawing upstage and observing the hullabaloo taking place within the walls of the theatre, saw clearly – who your real friends are. Whether those who constantly flattered you and abused you behind your back, or those who silently put up with the constant insults, which went so far as suspicions in a secret correspondence with Leonidov or suspicions of cruelty and injustice to old comrades and servants.

To **Firmin Gémier**.[38] After 8 April 1926, Moscow.

The idea of uniting the actors of all nations struck me too during my two-year travels with the Art Theatre to all the lands of Europe and America. I saw with my own eyes that the theatre is suffering a dangerous crisis everywhere.

Weakened at first by the cinema, and subsequently dealt the final blow by the war, the theatre is compelled to cater to the sharply lowered standards of taste of a new element that arose at that time, a special class of profiteers who possess capital and abound in the capitals of all countries and set the tone in them. The modern repertoire of the theatres and productions adapt themselves to their taste first of all. They are the intended audience for the display of unheard-of luxury and the tawdry wealth of spectacular hokum with nude women and sordid plots, much like the cinema's.

I am struck by the fact that the people who govern these countries, in charge of the ethical, moral and aesthetic development of the peoples subject to them, have, with the others, forgotten the lofty purpose of the theatre and, as it were, stricken it off the list of educational and improving media of mass influence, leaving it only the role of entertainment and amusement to distract people from politics. In conversation with a highly-placed person of the ruling class, whose name I am not at liberty to reveal because our talk was private, he said to me candidly: 'I warn you, I hate the theatre.' 'Which one?' I asked. 'The depraved and debased theatre that I hate more than you do, or the high-minded and noble theatre that should serve in the hands of every government as one of the best and principal means for the reconciliation and mutual understanding of peoples?' After that a long-drawn-out debate raged between us about the theatre as one of the weapons for achieving world peace, of which so much is spoken in all corners of the globe now that the war is over.

In nearly all the countries where I had to act in a language unknown to a foreign public, who were totally unknown to us, watching a foreign repertoire of a far-away eastern country entirely unknown to them, we heard such remarks as: 'One such performance tells us much more than all the conferences, expeditions, congresses, lectures and scientific treatises that strive to define the soul of a nation in order to understand it better.'

This capacity of the theatre is quite understandable. If a national genius in his comprehensive work of art describes the most typical and profound features of his people's soul, and if the most gifted actors of a country, in collaboration with the best directors, designers and other experts of our collective theatrical art, who convey by common effort the work of this genius, the soul of the people and the details of its life that influence its psychology, if these living interpreters appear in person in foreign countries and speak heart to heart about the things that make up their spiritual nature, it is not at all surprising that such art and such a performance will transmit more of the unseen and intangible, supra-conscious human emotions that are more essential than anything else for the knowledge and understanding of a foreign people and its country. Neither a scientific report, nor a lecture, a treatise, a conference, nor an inert book or newspaper can do this.

They have their own field of operation, which is transmitted by word of mouth and print. The field accessible to the actor radiates invisibly from soul to soul.

I told this anonymous person, whom I mentioned, that it is their obligation to encourage that sort of theatre, a theatre of humanity, a theatre of mutual understanding of the world

On 9 February VOKS (the All-Union Society for Cultural Relations with Foreign Countries) had forwarded KS a letter from the Norwegian theatre critic Olof Ljusell, asking for precise information about the organizational structure of the MAAT and its relations to its studios.

To the **All-Union Society for Cultural Relations with Foreign Countries**. 25 April 1926, Moscow

In reply to your inquiry I respond that the question of the relations between the Moscow Art Academic Theatre and its (now former) studios has the following history.

The studios were my brainchild, while their foundation was laid as early as 1904.

At that time it was explained that performing the current repertoire and the staging of new plays, always very few at the MAAT, since their artistic preparation requires a great deal of time, do not provide, on the one hand, for complete freedom for directorial research, and on the other, the possibility for young, beginning actors to perform leading roles, because they were cast in such roles only as great exceptions, and, as a rule, the leads were always bestowed on experienced actors.

In this way, the Studio, as I conceived it, was supposed to be a place of directorial research both in regard to the actor's performance and the outward shaping of plays, and at the same time to be a nursery of young actors, who were supposed to be perfected on the studio stage so as later to perform leading roles at the MAAT itself.

Originally it was proposed, and at the start it was so, that the studios were supposed to be mere branches of the MAAT, subject to its artistic and administrative-financial leadership, and the actors of the studios were supposed to come on in crowd scenes and in less responsible roles on the stage of the MAAT.

Those hopes, which guided me in establishing the studios, were realized only in part, while the notion that the studios were to be nurseries, from which the troupe of the MAAT was to be replenished, went completely unrealized.

The studios almost from the very moment of their existence began to strive for independence from their own mother country, first in the administrative-financial sphere, and then even in the artistic one; at the same time the actors of the studios began to appear in MAAT performances with diminished enthusiasm, because these appearances distracted them from work in the studio, and that work had become nearer and dearer to them than participation in the concern of which they themselves were the creators.

In this way, the studios gradually became, on the one hand, completely independent from the MAAT, and, on the other, turned into ordinary theatrical enterprises, having lost the 'studio' quality.

At the end of the day this de facto situation was even affirmed legally.

Before 1924 under the MAAT there existed four dramatic studios and one musical studio founded by one of the administrators of the theatre, Vl. I. Nemirovich-Danchenko.

In 1924 a reorganization of the MAAT took place, as a result of which the MAAT took on the following structure:

1. The MAAT (basic troupe) merged with the former Second Studio, thereby ending its own independent existence. The MAAT performs on two stages: the main and the small. The main is given over to plays of the classical repertoire and especially significant productions. The small is for the directorial and acting experiments of the youngsters.

2. The Second MAAT, created out of the First Studio of the MAAT, completely independent of the MAAT.

The former Third and Fourth Studios lost any association with the MAAT, do not bear its trademark, act as independent theatrical enterprises and are called: the Vakhtangov Studio and the State Fourth Studio.

The musical studio of the MAAT is detached as an independent theatre. In this way, the MAAT is responsible for neither the artistic nor the ideological activity of its former studios.

There are no rules for the MAAT and its former studios, because the rules for state academic theatres are only now being worked out in a legitimate fashion.

As to your third inquiry my reply is that, owing to the aforesaid independence of the former studios no rules regarding the transfer of actors from the studios to the MAAT exist, besides general cases of admission into the MAAT of actors from other theatres are extremely rare, and the troupe of the MAAT is filled preferentially by students from the school which it established. At the present time such a necessity is not felt in the school, because in 1924 young actors from the former Second Studio and students of the school entered the ensemble of the MAAT troupe.

People's Actor of the Republic K. Stanislavsky

On 26 March KS was shown two acts of The White Guard; *he approved and refrained from making any alterations.*

Nicholas I and the Decembrists *opened on 18 May, and Kachalov was praised for his interpretation of the reactionary tsar. KS, however, was now focused on scenery for* The Marriage of Figaro.

To **Aleksandr Golovin**.[39] 28 May 1926, Moscow.
Dear, beloved and highly esteemed Aleksandr Yakovlevich!

You yourself, your talent, your designs are enchanting and entrancing, as always. Specifically so and necessary, not a Carmen Spain but a Frenchified one. Otherwise it wouldn't suit Beaumarchais. I feel that it will be your most enchanting work. God grant you strength and energy to carry it out, and I will answer for its enormous success. [...]

Heartfelt devotion K. Stanislavsky

On 15 June Merchants of Glory *opened with KS 'in charge of the production'. It was another foray into the grotesque, caricaturing bourgeois profiteers. It achieved 103 performances (it should be borne in mind that at this point the government was subsidizing theatre parties from factories and military services).*

KS took a hand in rehearsing Bulgakov's play during the early summer. A closed dress rehearsal of The White Guard, *now renamed* Days of the Turbins, *was held on 24 June. KS feared the government might close the theatre on account of this play. However, the Repertkom allowed it to open, pending certain drastic revisions.*

To the **MAAT Collective.** 26 June 1926, Moscow.
My dear, good friends!

This year we have been through a very difficult, but heartening season, which I would call in the life of our theatre a second 'Pushkino'.[40]

In the last few years people have tried to bury the MAAT and its founders, calling them obsolete and backward. They tried to segregate the parents from the children, that is, the basic Art Theatre, -- the 'old-timers' -- from the youngsters. But this season, thanks to a great common effort, the parents have become more closely acquainted with the children, and the children with the parents, and we again have created the harmonious Art Theatre family. The youngsters have realized that intuition and inner emotion are not enough for a real actor, and that there is no art without virtuosic technique, without traditions built up over the centuries, and that this was something they could get from none but the 'old-timers'. As for us 'old-timers', we understood the enthusiasm of the youngsters, appreciated their talent and diligence, and this has aroused in us the desire to share what we know with them.

The harmonious work of actors, directors, the musical and vocal division, all the technical and working staff, the administrative, bureaucratic and service divisions, have yielded rich results: *six* completed productions and *two* with the actors' performances fully prepared.

476

Figure 68 Act 2, scene 1, "The High School," in *The Days of the Turbins*, 1926

All of us have worked not out of fear, but conscientiously, unstinting of our strengths.

We have earned attention, from the government down to the new spectator, who is getting to know us. Now people look at us with different eyes.

In bidding you farewell until autumn, I should like to embrace every one of you and to congratulate you on a brilliantly consummated season, and to express the hope that our future work will be still more harmonious and joyful.

Cordially and affectionately yours K. Stanislavsky

To **Viktor Simov**. First half of 1926, Moscow.
Dear Viktor Andreevich!

[...] As to the fact that people have become trash. There's nothing new about that. The same thing is happening throughout all Russia. But even so one can do something with these people, because in a certain respect the foregoing tragedy has given them backbone. In other places there's none of that. The fact that they are no-talents. So what is to be done? You can't add talent to them, but God is not sending other, more talented ones. [...]

To **his wife Mariya Lilina and his son Igor**. 7 July 1926, Darino.
My dear, beloved Marusya and Igorek!

Today, Wednesday, 7 July, I am sitting with Kira at the tea-table, in Darino, 9:30 p.m. – a dismal sunset behind a cloud, promising rainy weather for tomorrow. It is cold outside. 10 degrees, so the windows are shut. Kilyalya is napping in her

Figure 69 Stanislavsky and his granddaughter Kirlyalya, 1922

nursery, but cannot fall asleep (she has begun to nap badly). Her new governess Nina Petrovna, a modest, skinny, charming woman, is in her room. Out of the kitchen sound the voices of Fyoklusha – the fat, far from old, glorious (for the moment) cook – and ever so young Anyuta, also from Vologda gubernia, a friend of our previous Vologdan housemaids. Quiet, boredom, but it's soothing after the urban hustle and bustle. And now you are by the sea, under a hot sun. I can envy you that. I can now write to you more often than in winter, but there are few occasions on which to send you the letters. Meanwhile I myself do not know how frequent they will be and how to make use of them. Meanwhile we all feel well, if you don't consider Kira's slightly upset stomach and a certain tragic-comic event with me. The very day of my arrival I headed for the outhouse, unbuttoned my trousers… I hear bees buzzing, I look, there are two enormous wasps in flight, a third lying in the little window. I swat at it with a piece of paper. Suddenly, like an aeroplane, it darted headlong at me in a bee-line, stung me very painfully on the chin and flew like a dart out the window. I ran out almost without my trousers, because a whole uprising broke out in the place. It turns out that the wasps had built their nest there and ten of them had settled in. My wound stung rather painfully, and I expected my whole kisser to swell up, but it turned out that the devil is not as black as he is painted: there is barely a swelling. They gave me some ammoniac chloride. I dabbed my whole chin with it. Then, on advice from Fromgold, who happened to show up at the dacha,[41] Kira made me a hot compress, and I went around, 'à la malade imaginaire', all muffled up. Soon it all went away, except for a burned part of my chin, which prevents me from shaving. Against my will, I have to let a goatee sprout from the injured spot. Everything else is fine. [...]

I am very concerned that Kilyalya is growing up without fresh air. I am ready to do anything. I wonder whether I should send them and you to Kislovodsk in the Crimea? Or to the MAAT estate, rented specifically (?) for the actors' vacations. It's 2-3 hours from Moscow by r.r. and 12 versts (along a surfaced road) by horse-drawn car. [...]

I understand and admit that I have to meet with Igorechka and talk about his future. Meanwhile I will write to him on this subject, but again what is to be done with Kira and where. I am afraid to leave her alone. Right now I could not, to speak frankly, leave. And I am tired and my heart is dilated. What will happen next? We shall see. On 1 September I have to be in Moscow, because on 4 September the season has to start. Otherwise we will all starve to death. [...]

Kostya. Papa.

Despite its artistic success with most, though not all, the critics, the Musical Studio had incurred debts abroad that had to be repaid to a Berlin bank. The MAAT Collective was very much against paying off the debts out of its own budget. Stanislavsky agreed to guarantee the sum from his own salary as a 'point of honour'.

To his wife Mariya Lilina and his son Igor. *23 July 1926, Moscow.*
Dear, beloved Marusya, Igorechek!

[...] In the theatre it's all pecuniary questions. Again there is no money, but our playboy Nemirovich keeps sending desperate telegrams to send him money for payment to the bank. Sometimes he is under arrest. In addition, this incident occurred. One of the nitwits and scoundrels of the K.O. Studio sewed into the linings of their personal baggage bolts of cloth, stockings etc. When the baggage was inspected, which was carried out with remarkable care, the hidden items were uncovered. Just imagine what a disgrace and embarrassment for the poor old M. Art Theatre. Nobody has a good word to say for it and nobody understands that every personal low act by some blackguard will put a blot on our good name. An actor of our theatre cannot allow himself such disgraceful behaviour just to snatch an extra ten rubles from compulsory customs duty. It resulted in such disgrace and shame – I cannot even describe it... They drew up a report. Poor Podgorny had to risk getting involved again, because naturally all the baggage of all the studio folks was in danger of confiscation. [...]

Now Podgorny has left for the MAAT collective farm. This is an estate we have rented for 60 years (from the late Doctor Yakovlev, a tuberculosis specialist, who treated Igor). They made repairs and built a rest home --- for about 40 persons. In time it will be an almshouse for the MAAT's old-timers. Everyone who has come back from it is in seventh heaven. They fatten people up (our Aleks. Aleks.?)[Prokofiev, head of the MAAT catering division]. The place, people say, is wonderful. At the moment Leonidov, Aleksandrov and various youngsters are resting there. The Kachalovs are in Gurzuf, at Ol. Leon. Knipper's place. Vishnevsky is in Kislovodsk (his heart is being treated). Luzhsky at the seaside in Riga is caring for the ailing Peretta Aleks. [his wife]. Baklanova[42] is living there too. She has hooked up with some unprepossessing chorister from the K. O. For this reason or some other Nemirovich is angry with her. They are exchanging insults and are at daggers drawn. Baklanova is taking an engagement and won't come back to Moscow. Nobody knows what is to be done. She sent for her son to come to Riga. Moskvin, as always, is fishing on the Oka. Aleksandrov is taking the cure for alcoholism. A dreadful accident happened to him. The fact is that he was splendid in the role of the newspaper editor [Richepin] in the play *Merchants of Glory*. Just before the very start of the premiere, which was organized in short order, they had to rehearse the music. The fact is that the play begins with a symphony – by a full orchestra. Aleksandrov pestered me that it had to end, because soon it would be 7 o'clock and the audience would already be assembled (but no one had yet gathered). Suddenly for no good reason he felt offended (an alcoholic) and hid. At the start of the performance, when all the powers-that-be had assembled – Rykov, Yenukidze, Lunacharsky, Semashko[43] and the rest of the Narkoms, who have attended our theatre very zealously this year, -- Aleksandrov was already drunk. You can imagine my feelings, when I sat in my seat and heard our friend's slurred speech. The performance went on. I made up my mind to prepare a replacement. Aleksandrov's comrades talked to him. I pretended to know nothing, because the next day there was another performance, and after it an interim. Just let him play the second performance, and then we'll take steps. He will not be drunk at the second performance!

But he was drunk, and even drunker. He had to be sent home – Gorchakov[44] came on in his place, for he and I had staged the play and he knew all the roles by heart. The audience never noticed. After this, by the decision of the Supreme Soviet, Aleksandrov was stripped of all his roles and all his duties. He is temporarily expelled – and is under examination and taking a cure. If he gets better – he will come back, if not things will be bad. Let's hope that the incident will do him good and he will get better. At the moment he is undergoing intensive treatment. [...]

Kostya [...]

Before the new season began, KS met in August with Pavel Aleksandrovich Markov (1897-1980) of the literary department, Sudakov, and Bulgakov to revise the text of Turbins, *which he worked on a good deal the following month.*

When ND went abroad, Luzhsky had become an administrator of the MAAT.

To **Vasily Luzhsky**. 18 August 1926, Darino.

Dear Vas. Vas.!

[...] Don't be angry, but I do not agree to make any replacements in *Woe from Wit*. The old repertoire makes sense to me only in its most brilliant ensemble. I will say frankly that in the last few years of my life I can act only under such conditions. In the contrary case I will definitively leave the stage as an actor. This decision of mine is so definitively immutable that I would not like to argue and quarrel any more in its regard. [...]

Cordially affectionately yours K. Alekseev

Yours K. Stanislavsky

To **Aleksandr Golovin**. 29 August 1926, Moscow.

Dear Aleksandr Yakovlevich!

[...] Despite being in a tearing hurry, I cannot refrain, in my intense delight, from giving vent to my growing excitement at this time over the wonderful designs you sent me. Among the prosaic modern horrors, my scrutiny of them was a true delight, for which I sincerely thank you.

Now let me pass to the main current issues.

[...] 5. I will try to relate how I envisage the whole act, of course in its most general features, without the logical sequence of scenes.

Fanchette is looking for Cherubino. She slinks along alleys, thickets. The audience sees her move along the forestage on the turn-table. She passes one piece of scenery and comes up against a side of the box-set, let's say the left side. She sees Figaro and hides in a gazebo. Figaro runs after her. Again the audience sees him running, but he does not exit offstage, because the revolve turns in synch with him. He runs along the balustrades of some circular gazebos and the half-revolving scenery of the turn-table, arriving at the gazebo at right, sees a group in front of him: Basilio, Bartholo, and plays a scene with them. Soon the Countess and Susanna steal out of the gazebo, along the forestage. And behind them Cherubino. Figaro hides and then runs after them. Two female pranksters steal past that part of the scenery, whence Bartholo and company have just emerged. The revolve turns again. They pass some staircase of a second gazebo and find themselves in a kind of bosky thicket, the appointed spot for the rendezvous. This thicket is built so that the trees have apertures on all sides, and perhaps even high up so that all the jealous characters can observe the unexpected meeting with Cherubino that goes on within it. The Count has not held back, he has run after Cherubino. There is a race through all the nooks and crannies of the complicated set. The turn-table revolves and again winds up at the first gazebo. All the rest of the scenes down to the ending take place there, that is until the vaudeville.

At the moment of the vaudeville music and song gradually arise from every corner of the complicated set, somehow illuminations are lit. At the start of the vaudeville music and song sound in every corner of the garden and the court. It will be composed of old-fashioned tunes, and the blending of sounds from the

Figure 70 The garden scene in Beaumarchais' *One Mad Day, or The Marriage of Figaro*, designed by Aleksandr Golovin, 1927

various parts of the garden will blend into a musical harmony.[45] The wedding procession with the common folk bearing torches will start out and ultimately fill up the entire garden by itself, crowding out the nobility. As it processes, this torch-light parade will pass all the earlier nooks and crannies of the set. In each of these nooks of the set they will meet the individual characters: Basilio, the Count and Countess, Cherubino etc. On meeting them they will sing the verses and couplets that make up the vaudeville. At the very end the procession and all the characters will come to the main space, where all the dancing is concentrated, where the globes are illuminated, where the fountain is playing. The songs and dances of the finale will take place there and the vaudeville and play will come to an end. [...]

6. Knowing that they are staging this play (as if for spite) in Leningrad, I would ask you to keep as a very great secret the scenes as I have described them to you just now, as well as the concept of the production itself, based on the common people, the marriage of the chamber-maid in the kitchen, and not, as usual, in ceremonial rooms. [...]

K. Stanislavsky

In the projected production of Prometheus, *Koreneva was to play Io, but, because she kept begging off on account of illness, Tarasova was put in the role. Koreneva suddenly recovered and demanded that Tarasova return to being her alternate. The Supreme Soviet got involved and declared that whichever was better in rehearsal should act at the opening.*

To **Ripsimé Tamantsova**. 10 September 1926, Darino.

In this given case, I am trying to avoid specific personalities, I mean I am trying not to think about Koreneva or Tarasova. Let them be simply X and Y. The principle is important, it is important not to destroy the tradition. As soon as that happens, then one precedent will lead to another, a third, and everything will get mixed up.

This is the theatre's tradition: there is a primary performer and his alternates. The basic performer rehearses and plays at the first three consecutive performances. The work of the alternate (*who must get an adequate number of ordinary and dress rehearsals*) goes on simultaneously. To be secure in the role, he has the right to two performances in a row. If the alternate is perceptibly better than the primary performer – then in a special staging by the director in chief and other directors he can be moved to the first rota, that is he can become the primary performer.

This is, I believe, a long-standing tradition of alternation. *I would enter it into the minutes of the Supreme Soviet* and work for its acceptance. Tarasova performs incomparably better than Koreneva – let a special discussion be held on this topic. Meanwhile Koreneva is the chief performer. Tarasova must *without fail* get the necessary number of rehearsals and dress [rehearsals]. When she is to act is a matter for the director and the head of the repertoire to set up.

It would be good if this issue were discussed in the Sup. Soviet not as a specific, but as a general case, relating not only to Koreneva and Tarasova, but to all the rest, the whole theatre.

K. Stanislavsky

To **Vasily Luzhsky**. Before 11 September 1926, Darino.
Dear Vas. Vas.!

[...] I will act *Uncle Vanya*[46] wherever necessary. I am afraid of one thing – the proximity of the audience, what with my old age and gait, being close up. [...]

The loafer K. Stanislavsky

The Russian edition of My Life in Art *was published in September in 6000 copies, a very large number for the period.*

On 26 September, KS attended Meyerhold's Magnanimous Cuckold *at the State Theatre No. 1. He was extremely displeased, seeing nothing new in it, and was disappointed. When asked to put a remark in the distinguished visitor's book, he wrote: 'Vsevolod Emilievich my old friend. At every moment I saw searching, casting about, mistakes and achievements. What I love about him is that at all these moments he was enthusiastic about what he had done and sincerely believed in what he was striving for.'*

Fearing the reaction from the critical establishment and the government, KS had forbidden any one not connected with the production of Bulgakov's play to stay away from the theatre. The public preview on 23 September had gone brilliantly. On 5 October, Days of the Turbins *opened to a more restrained response but it was a success, not least because of the 'Chekhovian' flavour of the domestic scenes. The official directors were Luzhsky and Gorchakov, under KS's supervision, although Sudakov and*

Bulgakov himself had been important contributors to the staging. The play was immediately attacked by the far-left critics for its sympathetic portrayal of the Whites and public meetings were called to denounce it. Eventually the play was banned in March 1929, but three years later Stalin requested a revival and ultimately it enjoyed 987 performances, becoming one of the signature productions of the Soviet MAAT.

On 12 October, the old-timers, Moskvin, Leonidov, Kachalov, Luzhsky and others wrote to KS pleading with him not to take on administration of the Opera Studio for fear he would not have the time and strength to carry out his duties at the MAAT.

KS saw an inspection of Prometheus by the MAAT Council and the Repertory-Artistic Collegium on 4 November. He condemned it as 'ballet music plus Kachalov'; it needed 'action' not kitschy loveliness, stern religious ecstasy and not 'Duncanism'. The whole was 'vulgarity, treacle, vileness'. He drew up a new plan but the production was put off sine die.

A week later he enthusiastically accepted Leonov's Untilovsk for production as a real Soviet play. It would ultimately be banned by Glavrepertkom.

To **Maiya Meltser**.[47] December 1926, Moscow.
Dear Maiya Leopoldovna!

[…] Here are a few ideas concerning act 2 [of the opera *Zazà* by Leoncavallo]. I would put it in a hotel room. That is more evocative of an actor's bohemia. Actor-style chaos in the room. Zaza, à la Duncan, loves bearskins too. She rolls around the floor, goes home in some ordinary outfit. The love scene with her tenor can take place in the most unusual mises-en-scène. For instance, on the floor, on the bearskin rug with cushions. Her dressing is a whole scene in itself. She flings away the dressing-gown – it flies in one direction, the slippers in another. The maid, same as the actress, is a sloven, -- kicks a slipper off her foot so it won't encumber her. Zaza, theatrical-style, dresses awfully quickly. All these trivial details, irrelevant to the main theme, can be indulged, because the subject of the opera is banal and insipid. Everyday details, superfluous in a work of profound subject, are necessary whenever the subject is shallow and colourless. Everything that lends the role a tinge of music-hall extravagance will, I think, enliven the uninspired, amorously moaning puppet Leoncavallo wrote. A certain specific colouration can turn the role into an interesting characterization. And one can animate the play by a sharp comparison of music-hall bohemia with boring, God-fearing middle-class felicity.

I kiss your hand, regards to your husband.
K. Stanislavsky

To **Fyodor Ostrogradsky**. 22 December 1926, Moscow.

Today, 22 December, at the [dress] rehearsal of *Onegin* there was an unusual cold and draught. All the actresses and actors without exception caught colds. Some say that a window is broken (?). Some say that the iron door wasn't closed (?). I cannot sort it out at a distance. If the door is responsible – assign a watchman to keep it shut (whatever the cost).

All the performances and the theatre are in danger. The time is coming when they will start to come down with colds, one and all, and the performances will have to be changed. I warn you there will not be time to alternate new performers for those who have come down with colds.

Before it is too late, save the day. I warn you that everyone in *Onegin* is wearing low-cut dresses! There will be far more catching cold than in *The Tsar's Bride*. *Onegin* is the most dangerous play in terms of catching cold.

Be careful and take preventive measures.

K. Stanislavsky

Yevgeny Onegin opened at the Dmitrov Theatre on 24 December. The move from the little ballroom in Leontiev Lane to a big stage did it no favours. KS found that the faulty lighting spoiled many scenes.

To **Aleksandra Mitropolskaya**.[48] 10 January 1927, Moscow.
Dear and heartfully beloved Aleksandra Vasilievna!

What does it mean to serve in the theatre for twenty years? It means: over the course of almost a quarter of a century on a daily basis making uninterrupted sacrifices great and small for the sake of art: it means: not knowing the cost of the work and the reckoning of the time devoted to it, uncomplainingly to endure cold, heat, stuffiness and draughts; to know how, when necessary, to wear out your pants sitting for a full evening in a hole under the stage, on stage, in the dark wings, on the boards or in the flies; patiently waiting for hours at rehearsals for your turn to work and, without getting to the end, going home without malice and grumbling.

To serve the theatre means voluntarily turning oneself into a victim, standing back, doing the impossible, taking monastic vows, subjecting oneself to military discipline, handing over all one's talent and knowledge. Actors are lucky, they receive laurels and fame for their sacrifices. But the backstage workers, on whom not infrequently depend the progress and success of the performance, remain in the shadows. The spectators do not know them. They (some of the creators of the performance) peep from behind the wings and rejoice at the success of others; people often forget even to thank or congratulate them for the success of the common labour; not infrequently they are exploited in the theatre.

Among such important agents in the theatre one of its most remarkable, exemplary, modest, self-sacrificing, invisible collaborators is You, dear Aleksandra Vasilievna! I must take advantage of your jubilee day today, when the heart is open and the tongue has come unstuck from the larynx, in order to express to you the feelings of love, respect and gratitude to you stored up over ten years. May you long be for all of us a paragon of the ideal relation to a concern bordering on a religion. May you remain an essential, useful and talented participant in our dear old and young MAAT.

Affectionate and grateful K. Stanislavsky

To **Aleksandr Golovin**. 4 February 1927, Moscow.

Dear Aleksandr Yakovlevich!

At the start of the letter I cannot refrain from excitement at everything: your intuition, which catches the director's concept in mid-flight, and your wonderful knowledge of the stage. (I confess that the striped Harlequins, which seemed to me unstageworthy in the sketch, turned out to be wonderful lit by the footlights.) You saw what my director's eye did not. The mises-en-scène, which you are remarkably adept at arranging, and the dazzling colours which are placed wherever necessary, not the contrary, are in aid of the basic action and the prime essence of the play. Your colours do not leap to the eyes, despite their brightness, and serve as a background for the costumes. You have a remarkable feel for the body of the actors by knowing the fall of the fabrics and their cuts. In short, if I was once your enthusiastic admirer, now I have become psychopathic. Let us call you to mind every day and be concerned that we, actors, cannot attain your heights.

Now, when the production has opened, it would be useful to acquaint you with the general tableau produced on stage.

We were assigned the play with a particular ideology. Whatever else it was it had to be revolutionary. You understand how dangerous that word is and how it borders on a mere vulgar agitational skit.

But, fortunately, the work itself is in its essence liberal, and therefore we could meet this requirement without compromise. We needed only boldly and lucidly to lay bare the basic artery of the play.

Here are the concepts that motivated us in this. In the play the border between upper and lower classes is clearly marked, and given the contemporary requirement one does not have to gloss over this border, but, on the contrary, trace it clearly. The magnificent Count and Countess (the costumes have turned out remarkable in magnificence and colours), showing up in a poorly furnished cellar in a tower, delineates with unusual intensity, the basic difference the play needs. And at the same time the poverty of Susanna and Figaro, harmoniously and lovingly trying to turn some former storeroom into a cosy chamber for their first night, -- becomes unusually moving and charming. How moving are the common people coming to the newlyweds with peasant ornaments against the background of those grey wet cellar walls. What a splendid contrast is the magnificence of the gallery, how preciously dazzling, astonishing the rooms of the countess and the balcony with its staircase, baked by the southern sun. Probably, such preciosity and magnificence underline the era of luxury even more in the last act with its manicured trees, fountains and ponds. How good the people's court, coming in contrast to all this magnificence, and how essential it becomes to this commentary that the marriage take place not in the sumptuous palace of courtly façades, but in the secluded corners of the palace, where the servants huddle. Against this poor background, lit by the hot setting sun, naively, with heartfelt simplicity, the common people have set up a throne and seats of honour at the wedding table. The naïve luxury of groom's men and bride's maids, the shrill flute and bagpipes of the village musicians. The naïve village dances in the presence of the brilliantly dressed Count and Countess, the stupidly dolled-up Marcellina. All this, put in sharp relief, rounds out the planned and executed trajectory of the play and its construction. [...]

With warm affection K. Stanislavsky

Stalin came to power in January 1927 and encouraged the rejection of classical Russian art along with modern Western culture. All cultural organizations were re-engineered to create a new type of personality wholly devoted to communism. For the first time, a real attempt was made to bring the theatre wholly under party control by appointing Communists as producers and administrators, establishing 'artistic councils' within the theatre and emphasizing the role of 'activist' groups such as the Komsomol (Young Communist League) and trade unions to wage 'civil war in the arts'. Party officials and proletarian representatives from factories and unions served on the councils to prevent deviation from the party line.

KS still assumed, naïvely, that one could offer alternatives or modifications to government policy. On 21 February 1927 he made a speech at a Narkompros meeting about the development of Soviet theatre; this is his outline.

That we are gathered here proves that theatre is necessary. We are lucky. We must make better use of the theatre. Our business as actors is to explain the nature of art.

1) To extract the soul, to insert new demands is tendentious.

2) To take bare-bones tendentiousness and transpose it to the stage results in an agitational skit.

3) To ban old plays that do not coincide with new demands (*Othello, May Night, The Blue Bird*, Chekhov) results in anecdotes; there is nothing to perform.

4) New plays that are in no way revolutionary, although talented, do not answer the demands. The contemporary subject matter is too great.

5) Left-wing art. Revolutionary forms, not subject matter, outward shows of portentous events... result in boredom.

To sum up: art has its own nature, which you cannot go against... One must be patient, not rush things, help the poet to take shape. Let him learn from his mistakes.

Get rid of tendentiousness, but strive to reveal the essence.

Do not be afraid to criticize what is contemporary.

Get rid of isms.

All forms and means are good so long as they are artistic.

Othello was in fact under way at the MAAT with Leonidov in the leading role.

To **Boris Ivanov**.[49] *10 April 1927, Moscow.*

To be an actor first of all you have to have talent.

What is talent?

It is a combination of many human abilities. This complex includes physical gifts and human qualities and memory and imagination and excitability and sensitivity and attentiveness. All these gifts, taken separately or together, must have charisma on stage and be harmoniously blended. It is possible to be homely in life, as was Roshchin-Insarov[50], but this homeliness became charisma on stage, and then it was better than good looks. It is possible to have a little bit of everything and become a powerful actor thanks to one's charisma on stage. Next to this one can have plenty of everything, but, if this plenty is devoid of an attractive presence and stage charisma, it has no value on stage.

As you see, to define talent is not an easy thing and it cannot be unpacked all that quickly.

K. Stanislavsky

Beaumarchais's comedy One Mad Day, or The Marriage of Figaro, *solely directed by KS with Golovin's designs, opened on 28 April 1927 and made a big hit. It stacked up 430 performances.*

To the **Administration of the State Academic Theatres**. 14 June 1927, Leningrad.

Representatives of our theatre, present at the session in UGAT [an organization for state academic theatres] on 6 June, have informed me that the colleagues of the Narkompros for all academic theatres have passed a resolution which proposes the establishment of artistic-political soviets as consultative organs, with the adhesion of social and party organizations.

I consider it my duty to express the following observations on this matter.

The idea of the Narkompros on establishing artistic-political soviets is nothing new for our theatre, because the theatre on its own initiative has already from the start of the current season invited prominent party deputies of the Soviet community in the persons of Messrs. A. K. Voronsky, V. P. Polonsky and D. G. Ryazanov,[51] to participate in the work of its artistic organs, and in individual cases (in discussion of some modern, socially responsible plays, such as Untilovsk)[52] has set up extensive conferences with the participation of a series of other representatives of the community, art and literature. Along with this one needs to bear in mind that if involvement in the work of the theatre of the aforesaid representatives of the community has taken place, that is only because they understood the nature of the theatre in general and the subtle and complicated organization of the Art Theatre in particular; if someone ends up in our theatre who does not understand its nature, he will be a great obstacle to artistic work, needlessly hindering the business and offering no advantages.

Therefore I consider that all the practical measures that can be taken in this matter should occur in advance and strictly in co-operation with me and the responsible leaders and spokesmen of the artistic will of the theatre.

At the present time, being on tour in Leningrad and considering our first post-revolutionary appearance before the Leningrad spectators of remarkable significance, I, thoroughly overburdened with work both in opening a new play and inspecting the old ones, devoid of any possibility whatever to give sufficient attention to the questions you raise both about the artistic and artistic-political soviets in the theatre, and about the administration, I therefore ask that any resolution about them applicable to the Art Theatre be put off until I return from leave, which, by doctor's orders, I must use for timely treatment when the tour is over.

Administrator of the MAAT people's artist of the Republic K. Stanislavsky

To his daughter Kira. 17 July 1927, Kislovodsk. The TsEKUBU[53] rest home.
My dear Kira and Kilyalya!

[...] I am not living in the main house, where it is very noisy, but in its out-building not far away. Thoroughly well-equipped. A completely separate room, in a separate wing. Next to me are the serving-maids – two enchanting women, elderly, of the good old sort. They call me professor and vie with one another to care for me. One of them, Tatyana Ivanovna, has her own little cottage in Kislovodsk. She sent for two pots of geraniums from there and decorated my room with them. The sanatorium also constantly changes its vases of flowers. The ladies of the sanatorium, my new literary admirers, sent me flowers.

My room is small, but comfortable. By it is an enchanting little covered terrace with a good view. In the room itself is a washhand-stand with running water. It drips, and this is unpleasant at times, but my earlier lodging taught me to turn on the thinnest-thinnest trickle, and then you get an uninterrupted sound which isn't annoying and is easy to get used to. The quiet is the most complete, only the music from the kursaal can be faintly heard. Where is our rest home located? At the very end of the Rebrova gully. On the mountain itself. This is no longer a street, but little cottages along a country road. If you go out of the lattice-gate of the big house, you come upon the cross-road to the Mountain of the Cross in the Red Stones. If you go down the path along the field, then in ten minutes you come upon the Red Stones. If you go out of the lattice-gate more to the left, then you wind up in a wonderful spot – the promontory of the Mountain of the Cross, where a cross was erected at one time. Now it has been cast down and sprawls on the ground. Hence the remarkable view, which can be compared only with the view on the Tiflis with Griboedov's tomb. At night in the moonlight, which is shining now, you get a fairy-like picture. You seem to be standing on the prow of an enormous ship, and beneath you, far below, extends an enormous city, like New York. [...]

Tender hugs, love and constant thoughts to all. I bless you.

Kostya

To his wife Mariya Lilina, daughter Kira and grand-daughter. 19 August 1927, Kislovodsk.
My dear Marusya, Kira, Kilyalyogie-froggie!

[...] Half of *Armoured Train* has been banned. It's a pity the whole thing wasn't. *Turbins* and *Uncle Vanya* are also banned. They suggest instead of *Uncle Vanya* staging *Cherry Orchard* (Ugh!!!). Raevskaya came upstairs on foot to see me. She's skinny, but seems to be getting better. Kachalov had got better, started to look like his old self, got younger, the tumour is gone. Evidently, he isn't drinking. [...] They don't allow anyone to annoy me, thanks to my benefactress El. Bor. Bronner.[54] The public here are thoroughgoing boors and daughters of bitches. There's no other way to put it. They go around in their drawers, with bare, nasty, hairy bellies and chests. You walk through the park and spit in disgust. You think you've wound up in the hospital or the bathhouse. The dreadful thing is that this wonderful fashion is followed even by the intelligentsia, even our own folks: Izralevsky,[55] Kachalov. [...]

I love you and miss you.

Kostya

Originally the designer of Armoured Train *was to be Leonid Terentievich Chupyatov (1890-1942), whose sketches attracted KS by their foreshortening, when he saw them at an exhibition in Leningrad. The MAAT veterans preferred those of Viktor Simov.*

The Days of the Turbins *was prohibited, to Lunacharsky's exasperation.*

To **Fyodor Mikhalsky**. After 23 August 1927, Kislovodsk.

Dear Fyodor Nikolaevich!

[...] I fear that there will be a new failure of communication with the sets for *Armoured Train*. Everything makes it obvious that Simov is back. Everyone is on his side. Let him do it. I am happy for him. As for waiting for me to arrive before the matter is decided for such rushed productions, that will evoke a great postponement. The decision is that Simov should do it.

Wait with *The Turbins*. Have Nik. Af. [Podgorny] and the others circulate a rumour about the ban (it's fresh publicity) and among other things tell Markov that Meyerhold via Fevralsky[56] recommends a debate on it with...[57] (perhaps not now, but later, when the general efforts begin).

Have the book-keeper draw up a list of losses from the prohibition of *Turbins*. Make sure he does not forget to put in those losses that will result from the general situation for all the other plays. We have to get the organizations together and make half-promises. But have them start making an effort when the general call is given out. The more of them the better. [...]

Yours K. Stanislavsky (Alekseev)

To the **Collegium of Narkompros**. 5 September 1927, Moscow.

The Moscow Art Academic Theatre included in the production plan for the coming season presented to Glavrepertkom the play *Days of the Turbins* among others. In private conversations (the administration of the MAAT received no written communications) it was explained that Glavrepertkom does not find it possible to permit the production of this play in view of the devolving resolution of the Collegium of Narkompros to allow its production only a year from now.

In view of considerations of a financial nature, which are extremely important, as well as in view of the admitted success of the actors' performance of the play *Days of the Turbins* – the Moscow Art Academic Theatre requests that the

Collegium of Narkompros permit the production of the aforesaid play in the current season.

Administrator of the MAAT people's artist of the Republic K. Stanislavsky

To **Anatoly Lunacharsky**. 13 September 1927, Moscow.

Deeply respected Anatoly Vasilievich!

Illness prevents me from requesting a personal meeting with you to make a report on the state of affairs of the MAAT. But there are matters which have to be brought to your attention at once:

1. The banning of *The Turbins* and *Uncle Vanya* has wrecked our entire schedule for the whole current season.

The attached report will acquaint you with the sums our losses would amount to if the ban were to go into effect. These losses cover not only the daily drop in the box-office for performances of *The Turbins*. We will incur losses on other days thanks to the fact that our repertoire will be much sparser. We shall have to stage old plays several times a week.

2. With the replacement of this play, the work load represented by performances of the youngsters in *Days of the Turbins* will actually be transferred from the shoulders of the youngsters to the shoulders of the 'old-timers', occupied in those plays which will have to be substituted for the 70 performances of *Turbins* excluded from the repertoire, which, for a number of reasons, appear to be undesirable.

3. To increase box-office receipts we would have to take swift measures to revive old plays that are not in the repertoire at the moment. That would take a very great deal of time, when every working hour is extremely precious to us as we have urgently to mount *The Armoured Train* for the 10th anniversary of the October Revolution. The work is colossal and demands the undivided effort of the whole theatre. It contains a great many crowd scenes, in which the whole troupe is involved almost without exception. There is a very great deal of work involving acting, design and staging.

The presence of *The Turbins* in our current repertoire would act as a guarantee of the emergence of other new plays. Now we must either risk not being able to stage a show for the anniversary of the October Revolution, or deliberately go on suffering financial losses.

I would also like to inform you that *Armoured Train* has still not been finally approved by the censor. We require extensive and complicated changes from the author who has gone abroad for a vacation. We have sent him a telegram, but meanwhile we can only await his arrival.

To rehearse an urgent production, when the text itself has not been set, is almost impossible. Uncertainty is the worst enemy of theatrical work, sapping the actors' energy and creating difficulties and delays by the minute.

In the light of all I have said I make the following request:

1. that you take a hand in the decision about *Turbins* and
2. ask the Repertkom to reconsider its decision concerning *Armoured Train*.

Given the fact that I know that the question of the repertoire, to wit *Turbins* and *Armoured Train*, will shortly come under scrutiny, I heartily beg you to intercede so that the theatre will receive a favourable decision, because in the contrary case, we will incur unavoidable losses which, at year's end, may be expressed in a big number.

ND's time in Hollywood had been frustrating: all the scenarios he submitted were either rejected as too pessimistic for American audiences or subjected to drastic adaptation. He became eager to return to Moscow and so mended fences with KS by letter.

To **Nemirovich-Danchenko**. 21 September 1927, Moscow. *Telegram.*
Infinitely happy. Shake firmly hand long extended for complete reconciliation, complete oblivion of all mutual offences, complete merger as of old. Live together, die together. Await you with great impatience. Stanislavsky.

To **his daughter Kira and his grand-daughter**. Before 1 October 1927, Moscow.
My dear Kira and Kilyalya!
[...] I will not write about all the theatrical vileness. On Sunday the Opera Studio opens. Suk[58] will be conducting for the first time. Everyone is wildly excited about it. People say the orchestra and singers are unrecognizable. I haven't heard it myself, because I don't go out these days.

Turbins is still not licensed. Nemirovich sent a telegram of reconciliation. Before the open grave of a friend (Yuzhin) – he makes peace and asks that bygones be bygones. Perhaps he is not lying this time. [...]

Your Papa

In October Days of the Turbins *and* Armoured Train *were both passed. In addition, KS had been directing the nineteenth-century melodrama* The Sisters Gerard (The Two Orphans), *its setting on the eve of the French Revolution the justification for reviving this old chestnut. At the Opera Studio, it was Rimsky-Korsakov's* May Night *with its supernatural* rusalki *or water-nymphs that had caused concern.*

To the **Board of the State Academic Theatres**. 3 October 1927, Moscow.
For the present I inform you that the work assigned for the October celebratory play by Vs. Ivanov, *Armoured Train*, will go full speed ahead, despite my illness, under the direction of I. Ya. Sudakov and N. N. Litovtseva. At the present time 7 scenes (there are 9 scenes in all in the play presented by the author) are being worked on. The remaining 2 scenes are subject to approval by the Glavrepertkom.[59]

The same increased tempo will be observed in the work on the production part of this play under the leadership of this show's designer V. A. Simov.

I propose to show a rehearsal to the Glavrepertkom at the end of October. I cannot inform you of the day and hour, because that depends on the author and the Glavrepertkom. In any case, UGAT and the Glavrepertkom will be informed of this showing at the same time.[60]

492

As to A. V. Lunacharsky's orders and the devolution on me of personal responsibility, I consider that I am responsible only for the production meeting its deadline, but as for its artistic execution,[61] that is prevented by: 1) the holding-up of the text of *Armoured Train* by the author and the Glavrepertkom. 2) the overwork of the 'old-timers' at rehearsals of *Armoured Train* and consequences of individual appearances in the plays that have gone on instead of *Turbins*.

Administrator
People's Artist of the Republic K. Stanislavsky

To **Herbert Graf**.[62] 11 October 1927, Moscow,

I hasten to apologize for my delay in replying to your letter. It was waiting for my return to Moscow, after my summer treatment. Due to my illness my arrival was delayed. I thank you very much for your confidence in our Art Theatre. But before we get down to the business that interests you, I have to explain that the Art Theatre is a purely dramatic theatre. Its artistic principles are based entirely and chiefly not on the stage director of the Meyerhold and Tairov[63] type, but on the stage director as the actor's teacher. Our theatre develops chiefly the intrinsic technique of creativity, and after lengthy work it has achieved remarkable results in this realm, on which basis the theatre operates, making progress in the directions indicated. The external production concerns us only inasmuch as it is required for the actor's intrinsic creation.

Meyerhold and Tairov have different principles. While the stage director with us is the actor's midwife, who delivers the actor's new-born creation, my comrades in art, Meyerhold and Tairov, consider the director to be at the head of everything, he must create single-handedly, while the actor is no more than putty in the hands of the prime mover. We consider the external approach to art, prominent in our country in the last few years, to be obsolete.

The essential difference between the two tendencies compels a newcomer to our theatre to study all the principles of the intrinsic creative laws we have developed. We consider them the only medium of future art, its development and progress.

The two opera studios, one bearing my name, and the other bearing the name of Nemirovich-Danchenko (the latter has been touring Europe and America) are also based on the Art Theatre principles of intrinsic creation. There is also a slight difference between my studio and Nemirovich-Danchenko's. Mine trends towards almost entirely intrinsic work with the singer. In N.-D.'s studio this trend merges with the newest external forms of production.[64] Both studios are passing through a formative phase. Their financial resources are extremely slender. They are not able, therefore, to pay the workers in this concern as much as they deserve. Unfortunately, this deprives us of the opportunity to approach persons active in Russian and foreign art who have attained a prominent status in art.

I have written everything that might be expressed in a letter on the matter that interests you. It grieves me that our terms are not likely to be acceptable for you. But if I were to be wrong and you would wish to work with us under the circumstances set forth, -- I shall be only too pleased.

Thank you again for your consideration.

Best wishes, and I ask you to convey them to all the actors of the German stage who still remember us.

To **Susanna Yegorova**.[65] 12 October 1927, Moscow.

Respected Susanna Vladimirovna!

Creativity is what creates the life of a human soul. Is it possible to imitate another's soul? No. One can imitate only the externals. It is possible to imitate the manner, the behaviour, the outer appearance of a character.

However outward imitation cannot provide feeling itself. Gogol said: 'Anyone can *ape* a character, only a genuine talent can *become* the character. He who does not know how to become a character has nothing left to do except to ape him.'[66]

One of the contemporary innovators has heard that there is an art of representation. It is a very complex and difficult art of the French and German schools. I was trained in it, was at the Paris Conservatoire and therefore I have the right to speak. This art is based first of all on the emotional experiencing of the role. Once or a few times the actor experiences the role at home and at rehearsals. But having experienced it and explored how it appears to him, he studies to transmit the results of his original emotional experiencings with the help of technique, brought to perfection. Such actors as Sarah Bernhardt know how to work in a way not one Russian actor can, except, perhaps, the late Karatygin and Samoilov.[67] The Russian actor is completely incapable of this art. Instead he simply practices craftsmanship. Russian craftsmanship reminds me of a toy from Troitsa.[68] The French is a sophisticated statuette of ivory. The Russian technique of imitation is an axe. Can you fashion the most refined ivory carving with an axe? In much the same way coarse acting methods will not convey the incredibly complicated life of a human soul.

I profess the art of emotional experiencing.

At the rehearsal of 27 October of Armoured Train *KS gave Batalov, whose character was extolling Lenin to a North American soldier, an influential line-reading: the name must be whispered 'as the most treasured most precious, most important thing in life… for you must put into speaking the word Lenin your soul, your love for humanity and your country.'*

Two days later, The Sisters Gerard, *Vladimir Mass's adaptation of the creaky melodrama* Les Deux Orphelines *by Dennery and Cormon (which D. W. Griffith had made into the epic silent film* Orphans of the Storm*) opened, with KS named as the supervisor of Gorchakov's and Telesheva's staging. Meyerhold held it in contempt, but its popular appeal led to 171 performances.*

To **Nemirovich-Danchenko**. 6 November 1927, Moscow. *Telegram.*

Much obliged deposit Guaranty Trust Company of New York Fifth Avenue Office one thousand dollars to account Alekseev (Stanislavsky). Today public dress *Armoured Train* immense success, applause throughout act after each scene

Figure 71 The scene of the partisans on the church roof in *Armoured Train 14-69*, designed by Viktor Simov, 1927

and enthusiastic ovations at end. 14 November aktheatres honour ten year activity of Narkom Lunacharsky and Narkompros. Cordial regards, hugs. Stanislavsky.

The eighth of November saw a celebratory performance devoted to the tenth anniversary of the October Revolution of Armoured Train 14-69 *by Vsevolod Ivanov. KS was listed as 'in charge of the production' by Litovtseva and Sudakov. It was the first revolutionary, party-approved Communist play to be a success at the MAAT and ran for 327 performances, becoming a showpiece of the troupe.*

To **Vasily Kachalov**. 9 November 1927, Moscow.

Yesterday at the premiere, in the presence of Rykov, the government, the critics and other theatres, at the moment of the first showing of our eight-months' work, at a time when the theatre is trying with its remaining strength to win back its former position and right to exist in a new Russia, in front of the new severe audience – *you were drunk.*

A greater insult, offence and pain I have never experienced in all my life.

With KS billed as 'responsible director', Untilovsk opened on 17 February 1928 and was taken off after twenty performances. Lunacharsky considered it a step backwards for the Art Theatre. Bulgakov's Flight *was then turned to for a modern play, while adaptations of Dostoevsky's* Uncle's Dream *and Kataev's* Embezzlers *were in rehearsal, with* Boris Godunov *at the Opera Studio.*

To **Yekaterina Vavulina**.[69] 25 February 1928, Moscow.
Respected Cit. Vavulina!

[...] We will not stage *Hamlet* because they are performing it at the MAAT 2, just next door. And the state academic theatres do not allow the same play to be in the repertoire of two separate theatres. The MAAT 2 with Chekhov as Hamlet will come to Leningrad.

As for my book, it exists precisely so that grown-up actors might become children on stage. Without a system and a technique, there is no way to do this, and because I admit only such acting, practice has led me to a system. I have happened to know many actors, who in their time have thrilled audiences, such as Duse, Salvini, Yermolova. They were all hard on themselves, entertained great self-doubt and worked a very great deal. Legends about the easy inspiration of an actor's creativity are depicted in melodramas like *Kean*, but it does not exist in a serious actor's life. [. . .]

UGAT had requested information as to how the MAAT planned to celebrate the 100th jubilee of Ibsen in Oslo in March, and KS replied to Aleksandr Ivanovich Galin, deputy director of state academic theatres.

To **Aleksandr Galin**. 27 February 1928, Moscow.
Much esteemed Aleksandr Ivanovich!

We ourselves wanted to commemorate a great writer, whose plays we performed a great deal in his time. But this has turned out to be impossible, because the sets and costumes of the earlier productions of the plays no longer exist and since the works of Ibsen have been acknowledged to be unsuitable for modern demands. There is not a single one of his plays in our repertoire at the present time. Nor are there many of the former performers of those plays. To produce a performance would demand many months of work.

Instead one can only suggest a recital. But even a reading requires great preparation. One of us chief directors is necessary for this work, Vl. I. Nemirovich-Danchenko or myself. Vl. I. Nemirovich-Danchenko has so far not received clearance from Narkompros and therefore cannot even consider work as a director. As for me, I am simultaneously running rehearsals for *Embezzlers*, *Cherry Orchard*, *Mistress of the Inn*, *Othello* and *Uncle's Dream*. Moreover, three of these plays will be staged in very rapid succession to satisfy the subscribers in good time. The rest must be ready for inspection by the end of the season. I do not have the strength to take on new work. Besides, the actors capable of performing a recital in memory of Ibsen are taking part in this hurried work. [. . .]

Administrator of the MAT, people's artist of the Republic K. Stanislavsky

KS had first come in contact with Elizabeth Reynolds Hapgood (1894-1974) and her husband, the influential journalist and reformer Norman Hapgood (1868-1937) in

1924 during the MAAT tour to the US. She had served as interpreter when he met Calvin Coolidge at the White House. She later claimed that, at that time, she had urged KS to publish his experiments in acting and actor training. Her effort to renew the acquaintance would have significant effect, for good and ill, both in terms of improving his material circumstances and in the legacy of his writings on acting.

To **Elizabeth Reynolds Hapgood**. 22 March 1928, Moscow.

I was delighted to get your kind letter. It exuded the warmth and charm with which nature has so generously endowed you. I clearly recalled the unforgettable days spent in America – your wonderful husband, your extremely hospitable Mama and dear children. I remembered the tea parties I attended, our meeting at receptions, opening nights at other theatres and backstage at the Jolson. Again I was surprised by your unusual linguistic abilities, the beautiful Russian which you not only read and write, but which you know how to feel. I envy your ability, when I recall your proficiency in English. The little that I learned at the time, I have now forgotten.

We have a proposal to go to America next year and would very much like to take advantage of it, to see our dear American friends again. Since we returned from America, instead of one theatre under my leadership and direction there are three in all: the Art Theatre with two stages (our old-timers and the Art Theatre 2nd Studio, which have merged and been made into a renovated theatre troupe with a large number of splendid young people, very capable and talented, who aid us old-timers) and, in addition, my Opera Studio, which I founded in order to teach phonetics, drawing, verbal rhythm in drama and which has expanded to the dimensions of a great theatre. I have managed to stage many operas during this time: Rimsky-Korsakov, Musorgsky, Tchaikovsky, which I hope in my time to show to New York. Right now I am busy with very interesting work at the Opera Studio. I am staging *Boris Godunov*, but not in the Rimsky-Korsakov version which F. N. Chaliapin sings, but in another, much better one, that was written by Musorgsky himself and from which Rimsky-Korsakov adapted the current *Boris Godunov*. If F. I. Chaliapin were to learn about these discoveries that were made in the score, he would be in seventh heaven.

As to the Art Theatre, the problem is that all of our new productions that might succeed in America, are, according to the testimony of M. Gest (who was with us in Moscow twice), either remarkably awkward and difficult to translate or else unsuitable for American life for censorship reasons.

Another problem is that when we leave to tour Europe and America all three theatres in Moscow must definitely function equally well. We have to prepare and rehearse a repertoire so that two theatres are working simultaneously in Moscow and one abroad. Likewise the opera theatre named after me has to work as well. This is a difficult task. If we manage to achieve it, we shall have the great pleasure of meeting you again and your whole dear family.

At this time we have had occasion to work a great deal and stage a whole series of new plays. Photographs of these productions were inserted in the American papers. We staged *The Ardent Heart* by Ostrovsky, which, according to M. Gest, might interest America. Then we staged *The Decembrists*. Although this is a revolutionary play, M. Gest thought that it might be brought to you. In addition we staged *Merchants of Glory* by Nivoix and Pagnol. This play was banned by the censor abroad and probably won't make it to you. A great fuss was made over the play *Days of the Turbins*, which is on in theatres abroad right now, and perhaps will come to you. This is a rather cumbersome production, which is difficult to transport in the form in which we perform it. Its staging requires a revolving stage. A very good production was done of *The Marriage of Figaro* which was executed by our very best Russian designer A. Ya. Golovin. This production greatly attracted M. Gest, but there can be no talk of bringing it over, it is too cumbersome and difficult. This season we staged two plays by modern authors: *Armoured Train* by Vs. Ivanov, clear-cut and revolutionary but hardly suitable, and the other is *Untilovsk* by Leonid Leonov, very profound and dark, which requires a good knowledge of Russia.

As you can see, there are no plays for America among the new productions. So we shall have turn to our earlier productions, the ones that have not yet been shown in America. They are very difficult to translate. So now we are busy picking out a repertoire suitable for America.

What is there to say about our life? From 10 in the morning to 12:30 I am busy at my Opera Studio. From 1 to 5 p.m. I work at rehearsals at the Art Theatre, from 5 to 7 I am occupied with routine business. As you can see, it is a hard life. So it goes from day to day, with a few months for rest and convalescence, and all this with a failing heart and vision. My son is still ill as ever and lives in Davos which greatly depresses me. My wife acts in many of the theatre's productions, and my daughter and grand-daughter stay at home and keep busy with housework, games and mischief. [...]

At a rehearsal of Embezzlers *on 22 March, Lilina offended the assistant director Batalov in some way. KS chided her for this 'unethical behaviour'. Lilina apologized to Batalov and the incident seemed to be over. However, Batalov began to complain of her 'high-falutin ways' and roused the leading actors and workers to have her behaviour judged at a meeting of the Mestkom.*

To **Nemirovich-Danchenko**. 6 April 1928, Moscow.
Dear Vladimir Ivanovich,

In recent times such an atmosphere of mockery and derision has been created in the theatre that it is impossible to work in it.

I am forced to terminate my attendance at rehearsals until a more propitious time, when I shall be given the possibility to resume them.

My wife is also deprived of the possibility of being at rehearsals. If you find it essential to replace me as director of *Embezzlers* and my wife as one of the performers, I cannot, of course, protest.

After this letter, the matter was formally regulated, the initiators apologized to KS and on 12 April he resumed rehearsing.

After 100 rehearsals emphasizing the System, Embezzlers *opened on 20 May, with KS billed as 'artistic leader', Sudakov as director and the constructivist Isaak Rabinovich as designer. It was taken off after eighteen performances.*

On 10 May 1928 The Workers' Gazette *published a crudely tendentious article claiming that the MAAT 'had no connection to the community of workers,' that it did not appreciate young actors and over ten years had not attracted a single Soviet dramatist. It also cast doubt on the personal honesty of Yegorov and Podgorny (without mentioning their names).*

To the **Editors of** *Izvestia,* **Pravda** **and** **Contemporary Theatre**. 15-22 May 1928.
Respected Comrade Editor. [...]

The evolution of our theatre along the paths of contemporary socialization is taking place with great difficulty, but I think that each of our contemporary plays staged by the theatre, not to mention *Armoured Train*, has explained much and given much to the theatre.

At the moment we have ordered a series of plays by contemporary authors and next season we shall stage two contemporary plays and two classics, because we consider it our duty to present a classic repertoire as well.[70] [...]

A few newspapers and magazines published remarks with personal attacks on individual workers of the theatre. I consider it my bounden duty to say that the persons wounded by such remarks, who occupy responsible positions as members of the administration and my closest assistants, have worked and are working with me in full contact and at my direction. I frankly and passionately stand up for my wonderful assistants and co-workers. They have been well known to me over a long period of time as talented, highly respectable and honourable people, seasoned in the business over the course of many years, infinitely devoted to the concept of the MAAT, with an outstanding track-record – each in his own speciality. I categorically protest against the entirely unfounded attacks and accusations, deeply wounding the most honest and most devoted to the theatre of my assistants. [...]

People's Actor of the Republic
K. Stanislavsky

On May 15 the revival of Cherry Orchard, *co-directed by KS and ND, opened; the directors received twenty-six curtain calls.*

To **Boris Syromyatnikov**.[71] 23 May 1928, Moscow.
Dear Boris Ivanovich!

Your letter sincerely moved me. At the present time, what with the current crude manners, people seldom treat one another with warm human feelings. Therefore one values them ten times more, especially at the difficult moments of life.

The Art Theatre at the moment is experiencing an epidemic, which is running through the whole theatre. It is quite painful, but not fatal. The problem is that it deflects us from our real concern – art, and when a bit of life is left over, one becomes very parsimonious of one's time and work to be done.

We will not be protected from the attack of the contemporary gutter press in the future, until we are working for real art. Those who are unfamiliar with the real thing would, naturally, rather it not exist and would prefer insolent craftsmanship to prevail on stage. It is this contest of craftsmanship and histrionics with authentic art and those who serve it that provokes and will go on provoking the endless attacks on the theatre. One has to reconcile oneself to it. [...]

To **Viktor Belyaev**.[72] 27 May 1928, Moscow.
Deeply esteemed Viktor Mikhailovich!

I am very interested in [Kurt Weill's] opera *Der Tzar lässt sich photographieren*, the same as those new operas, especially the Russian ones, which you have kindly found for our studio.

I would very much like to meet with you and look over all your finds, to which end I am on the lookout for our concert masters, who are presently on leave. As soon as I find some of them, let me send them to you for appropriate instructions, and after that we will discuss the day for the review.

I am sure that I will be able to figure out the musical subtleties, and I judge an opera by its instructional value, in which you, I hope, will not refuse to be my general guide. [...]

Performance diary, 28 June 1928.
Chekhov's plays exist in the pauses, as do almost all our plays. They demand total quiet. Half the energy has to be provided by the establishment of indispensable order backstage. Neither requests nor persuasion have any effect. Today after everyone departed in the last act of *Uncle Vanya*, while I was on stage, there was a dreadful noise, footsteps, conversations. The scene, which required the utmost quiet, was spoiled. When I came to the end of my role and went offstage, i.e., during the most important final monologue, there were a *very* loud slam of an iron door (this on Uncle Vanya's estate) and loud conversation. [...]

I ask that the most definite measures to be taken to establish order on stage during the act and suggest to the firemen that they have to *behave themselves*.

On 12 August 1928 the Opera Studio-Theatre was granted the status of a theatre (as was the Musical Studio).

The first production that ND was allowed to supervise on his return to Russia was a small-cast Soviet comedy Squaring the Circle *by Valentin Kataev. It opened on 12 September and proved to be so popular that it had a run of 646 performances. From this point on, the bulk of MAAT productions would be staged by ND, with the occasional contribution by Sudakov and others. KS would devise, supervise or touch up a particular work, but almost never ran rehearsals in the theatre.*

In mid-September KS travelled to Berlin on his way to meet his family in Badenweiler.

To **Nikolay Podgorny**. 20 September 1928, Berlin.

Dear Nikolay Afanasievich!

I am writing to you about the following subject. The fact is that here in Berlin, long before my arrival it was given out that I was coming to Germany. Some said that this trip was connected with the tours of the MAAT, others claimed that Reinhardt had signed me to work with him, still others asserted that, like [Mikhail] Chekhov,[73] I was moving here to work, and so on. That is why I am presently besieged by interviewers and I have to hide from them any way I can. But now my only defence can be Mariya Petrovna, and she has plenty of things to do without me. Despite all our precautions, yesterday I was trapped – and chatted with some charming gentleman in a café. He purported to be an admirer of mine, addressed a very short speech to those sitting in the café and asked to pay me a call. All this gave me no chance to find out if he was a journalist and not a fan. What he is writing now I have no idea. Of course, I said nothing in particular to him, but you don't have to say anything for all sorts of nonsense to be written in an interview. The writer, as you know, dreams up whatever excites and interests him. In addition, yesterday I was at the Deutsches Theater and saw *Die Artisten*.[74] In the intermission some people followed me around and sketched me from various angles. Obviously, my portrait is to appear, and they will write whatever caption they please.

Nor is that all. I am being made every possible kind of offer… to act, to direct, to teach, to make movies and act in them. Every Russian who is working here without exception purports to be one of my students and thereby astonished the Berliners who imagine that there is no one in Russia except Stanislavskians. This has popularized my name a good deal. Just now a photographer showed up – and I will evidently have to go and have my picture taken, because he arrives at my home just when (dinner-time) you can't dodge him. What will happen next – I don't know. I hear that they are preparing more bizarre offers. The only recourse is to leave here as soon as I can, before some gossip or vileness takes place. But the problem is that Igor can be in Badenweiler only on Sunday, while all kinds of business is keeping my wife and family and the doctor, who has to examine my grand-daughter here.

So I decided for caution's sake to write to you about this and ask you to see Al. Iv. Svidersky[75] to tell him how matters stand. There can be no doubt that everything that goes on here will be echoed in Moscow and stir up rumours that I have fled Russia etc. Let Al. Iv. know and at the critical moment tell me his considered answer. […]

I should also like to know: if the Russian actors here ask me whether it is possible to return to Moscow and how they will be treated – what am I to say to them? There may be talk (meanwhile, I want to make it clear that I have had no specific questions from anyone. I only know that some of them find themselves in conditions of hardship) of the members of the Prague troupe: Kryzhanovskaya or Bondyryov or Serov.[76] I repeat, I have seen none of them, but if they read it in the papers, they might turn to me. […]

The Russians here are having an insane success. The cinema (ours) is considered the best – better than the American one. […]

Yours K. Alekseev

KS returned to Moscow on 15 October.

To **Max Reinhardt**. 25 October 1928, Moscow.

I am in Moscow and, casting a mental glance over what took place in Berlin, I relive everything that happened to me there, and my heart glows with warmth and joy. I feel connected with your distant and beautiful city not only outwardly, formally, that is with my new title of honorary member of all your theatres, which I very much treasure and take pride in, but by other, more intimate, inner chords, which now unite me to you and the members of your numerous theatrical family.

Figure 72 A caricature by Kukryniksy of Stanislavsky on the 30th anniversary of the MAT. *Krasny proletariyat*

This new feeling warms me and brings me great joy

The life of an actor does not proceed on the plane of everyday life, but in beautiful memories of the past and dreams of the future.

Everything I experienced thanks to your special relationship to me provides great nourishment for such memories and dreams.

The visit of your representative, a very charming and courteous man, the simple, cordial and intimate meeting which you arranged for me at your Deutsches Theater, the many undeserved honours, kind words, addresses and the rank of honorary member, the gift of a beautiful motor-car,[77] the refined manner in which this was done, the splendid supper in hospitable company. All these memories are dear to me.

I remember another evening, even more intimate, at your apartment. This was an evening of dreams about the future.

All these memories of what I have just experienced cheer me, but the dreams of the future rejuvenate me. […]

The previous day the production of Flight, *which had been under attack as counter-revolutionary from the Union of Proletarian Writers (RAPP), Pravda and other official organs, was cancelled. (Stalin himself described it as 'anti-Soviet'.) The MAAT's co-founders were in a perturbed state as they approached the celebrations for its thirtieth anniversary.*

On 27 October 1928, during the evening ceremony, the Communist Party Leader Mikhail Kalinin proclaimed that the theatre should 'march hand in hand with the working class'. In his response, KS abandoned his scripted remarks and spoke from the heart. He congratulated the government for letting the old-timers come to terms with the revolution in their own, gradual way, and described ND and himself as 'the modest wife and the philandering husband'. (Some in the crowd shouted 'Kiss the bride'.) Fuddled after a sleepless night, he praised the deceased supporters of the MAAT, mentioning the pre-revolutionary millionaire Morozov, 'beloved by all'. 'I bow to them all and cherish my memories of them.' Everyone stood at these words, including Stalin and the other party officials. Still, awareness of his gaffe weakened his resistance.

Two days later, while playing Vershinin in the first act of the jubilee performance of Three Sisters, *KS experienced acute heart pangs, but finished the role to the end. Only then did he collapse with a serious heart attack, later diagnosed as angina pectoris and myocardial infarction. It was to be his last stage appearance. He later explained why to an interviewer.*[78]

First Berlin, where the stay lasted ten days. Every day I had to go to bed at three in the morning. Every day a bottle – a different wine, you can't refuse when they drink to your health, and wine is the most harmful thing of all for me... Then Moscow, preparing for the jubilee, banquets without end and, finally, a speech which I had to give. In general public speaking is a torment for me, but in this case things had to be arranged so that nobody was forgotten and nobody was offended. The next day, excerpts from an old production: *Three Sisters*. I play

Vershinin. I made my entrance – an ovation. Of course, we knew that it would be that way, so I was completely unmoved. The only thing that bothered me was the uniform, it had become tight, and out of coquetry I didn't want to have it let out. But never mind... So, in other words, I make an entrance, there's an ovation, I speak the words and suddenly – I feel ill! I almost fall, but I got a hold of myself, fought it down, and ended the act. However, when I withdrew upstage (as the blocking required), I sent for my doctors: they were both in the theatre. Finally, the act ended, I twice came out to take a bow and... collapsed, people were already carrying me in their arms. The audience noticed none of it, only wondered why I didn't come out for more bows.

The government granted KS an extended sick leave on full salary and $3,000 in foreign currency.
On 5 December the Council decided that, in view of the worsening financial situation, The Cherry Orchard should be made a regular item in the repertory, with Yershov in the role of Gaev, previously played only by KS and Kachalov. ND reassured him that neither his family nor the theatre would suffer financially or artistically.

Diary, after 5 December 1928.

Force majeure circumstances prevent me from working. The question remains – how to save the theatre. This is how I figure it. All other questions fall away, because if we have to stage *The Cherry Orchard*, we have to stage it, there's nothing to discuss.

But here's my opinion as to why we have staged old plays – *Uncle Vanya, Cherry Orchard*. I invest *enormous* significance in this, and it's been proven: whenever we insert revivals of old plays into the season, that's the moment the theatre comes to life. But there is no one able to do it. It's been forgotten. And the only ones who can offer such an ensemble are the old-timers. Our youngsters need it, our new audience, which has never seen such an ensemble, needs it... As to *Othello* it has also entered the programme to show what a tragic actor is and what a tragedy is. This is a luxury, which brings in no money, but cinches the brand-name. And that's the only attitude I take to that production. Therefore I have nothing against rehearsals beginning under the aegis of Leonidov, because that way nothing can go to waste. And if Leonidov runs the rehearsals, he will carry out the work until I have a look at it. It has to be taken into consideration that this play cannot be put on twice a week, but only once a fortnight.

My opinion is to rehearse not *Flight* but *Three Fat Men*[79] with a lively tempo.

Notes

1 This seems to be a reference to Boris Vershilov's stylized productions of *The Robbers* and *Thunderstorm* in the style of Meyerhold.
2 Akim Mikhailovich Tamirov (Tamiroff, 1899-1972), actor; at the MAAT 1920-1922. Stayed in the US as a much-used character actor in Hollywood.
3 The ancient 'serf uncle' Finagey Baev in *Pazukhin's Death*.

4 From a peasant background, Nikolay Petrovich Batalov (1899-1937) appeared in *The Green Ring* at the Second Studio in 1916; at the MAAT to 1937, he was a prime factor in 'Sovietizing' the company, bullying it into submission and trying to reconcile it with RAPP (the Proletarian Writers' group). KS cast him as Figaro and Vaska Okorok in *Armoured Train*.

5 The season actually opened on 11 September with *Pazukhin's Death*.

6 KS's performance as Ivan Petrovich Shuisky was almost unanimously admired by the public and colleagues and critics.

7 Nikolai Vasilievich Nevrev (1830-1904), painter of historical genre scenes.

8 Yershov had first played Godunov abroad during the tours.

9 Mark Isaakovich Prudkin (1898-1994) was at the Second Studio from 1918, the MAAT from 1924; he played Chatsky in most of the second-generation performances. Boris Nikolaevich Livanov (1904-72) had been invited by ND from the Fourth Studio in spring 1924 and began to rehearse the role of Chatsky.

10 Tarasova partnered KS in *Uncle Vanya*, playing Sonya.

11 Podgorny had written to KS that he had a letter from Tarasova inquiring whether it was safe to return with her husband, and he was loath to reassure her, because the official Mikhalsky had been exiled 'despite all his acquaintances and all his influence'.

12 Pyotr Fyodorovich Sharov (Peter Scharoff, 1886-1969), a former assistant director, had been a member of the Kachalov troupe, and was now a director with the so-called Prague Troupe of the MAT, subsidized by the Czech government. KS feared he might offer a contract to Tarasova, as he had to other young actors.

13 Faina Vasilievna Shevchenko (1893-1971), buxom character actress at the MAT from 1914. Aleksey Pavlovich Bondyryov (1882-?) left the MAAT in 1922.

14 Porfiry Artemievich Podobed (1886-1965), business manager of the MAAT 1921-26.

15 Ivan Ivanovich Manukhin (1882-1958), physician and social worker.

16 ND intended to merge the Vakhtangov (Third) Studio into the MAAT. Meyerhold, who was against this, asked KS to help him in finding the studios 'some place where they will aspire'.

17 Sergey Konstantinovich Makovsky (1877-1962), art critic.

18 Nikolay Vasilievich Demidov (1884-1953), actor and teacher.

19 Raisa Nikolaevna Molchanova (1897-1980) acted at the Second Studio and the MAAT 1916-33 and 1936-55.

20 Yury Aleksandrovich Zavadsky (1894-1977), a student of Vakhtangov, who played Prince Calaf in *Turandot*; he left the First Studio when it proposed to 'go Soviet' and joined the MAAT, where he became a favourite of KS, who cast him as Chatsky and Count Almaviva, and defended him when he was arrested.

21 Natalya Viktorovna Degen-Volkonskaya, writer, translator; close friend of Lyubov Gurevich and fan of the MAAT, was writing from abroad.

22 Short for Vserossiysky professionalny soyuz rabotnikov iskusstv (All-Russian Professional Union of Art Workers).

23 Aleksandr Vladmirovich Bogdanovich (1874-1950), singer and teacher.

24 Staged at the ex-Korsh Theatre in spring 1925.

25 Aleksey Nikolaevich Tolstoy (1882-1945), writer, former anti-Bolshevist, known as the 'Red Count'; pillaged Russian history to find counterparts to contemporary events.

26 Staged as *Azef* at the ex-Korsh Theatre in January 1926.

27 It opened the season on 19 September and was in sixteen scenes; it ran for 41 performances.

28 KS picked this form for *The Actor Works on Himself*.

29 Boris Sergeevich Maloletkov (1900-41) acted at the MAAT 1922-41.

30 He played the shoemaker Alyoshka.

31 Mikhail Semyonovich Margulis (1879-1951), neurologist and psychiatrist.

32 Roman Rafailovich Falk (1886-1958), artist and designer, KS's son-in-law.

33 Sushkevich completed the production.

34 Nahum Lazarevich Tsemakh (1887-1939), founder of Habima, would stay in the US with some of the actors, while the rest went to Palestine, eventually to become the national theatre of Israel.

35 Mariya Vladimirovna Margulis, a sister of Olga Gzovskaya.

36 ND had used that expression.

37 Mariya Petrovna Grigorieva (stage name Nikolaeva, 1869-1941) ran the costume shop at the MAAT from 1898 until her death.

38 Firmin Gémier (Tonner, 1869-1933), French actor and director; founder and leader of the Théâtre National Populaire in Paris. He had sent KS the first issue of *Cahiers du Théâtre*, an organ of the Worldwide Theatrical Society, which proposed an international union of theatrical arts and crafts.

39 Aleksandr Yakovlevich Golovin (1863-1930), designer, a member of the World of Art; 1908-18 designed sixteen productions for Meyerhold at the Imperial theatres. Basically a painter, his scenery had flat perspective, but he created every article in the production. During the work on *Figaro*, he fell ill and never left his home, with only one meeting with KS. During *Othello* his health worsened and Gremislavsky employed a good deal of diplomacy in taking over the scenic work.

40 In Pushkino outside Moscow 14 June 1898 where the work on the MAT began.

41 Yegor Yegorovich Fromgold, KS's regular doctor, a student of the endochrinologist Vasily Shervinsky.

42 Olga Vladimirovna Baklanova (1893-1974), leading actress of the Musical Studio, playing Mlle Lange, La Périchole, and Carmencita, remained in the US where she appeared on stage and in film (most memorably in *The Man Who Laughs* and *Freaks*).

43 Party officials: Aleksey Ivanovich Rykov (1881-1938), People's Commissar of Communications 1931-36; Avel Sofronovich Yenukidze (1877-1937), a friend of Stalin, headed the TsIK Committee to Manage the MAAT till 1935; Nikolay Aleksandrovich Semashko (1874-1949), People's Commissar for Public Health of the RSFSR.

44 Nikolay Mikhailovich Gorchakov (1898-1958); his version of Dickens's *The Battle of Life* was admitted into the MAAT repertoire and he was allowed to direct the younger actors in *Woe from Wit*. His big hit was the Soviet farce *Squaring the Circle*, for he had a gift for comedy. His first independent work was Bulgakov's *Molière*; official displeasure with it compelled him to prove his political reliability.

45 The original concept was to make a selection of antique tunes; eventually the task of selection and composition was assigned to Reinhold Glière.

46 Luzhsky had suggested that, with all the activity at the MAAT, *Uncle Vanya* be put on on the Small stage.

47 Maia (Mariya) Leopoldovna Meltser (1899-1984), singer, director; at the Opera Studio 1923-50.

48 Aleksandra Vasilievna Mitropolskaya (1882-1942), pianist; from 1906 concert mistress of the MAAT.

49 Boris Grigorievich Ivanov (1908-64), film director. He had asked KS which external and internal qualities an actor should possess.

50 Nikolay Petrovich Roshchin-Insarov (Pashenny, 1861-99), actor, father of Vera Pashennaya.

51 Aleksandr Konstantinovich Voronsky (1884-1937), literary critic; Vyacheslav Pavlovich Polonsky (Gusin, 1889-1965), literary critic and publisher; David Borisovich Ryazanov (Goldendakh, 1870-1938), director of the Marx-Engels Institute.

52 Leonid Leonov's talky play had to undergo five drafts before it was accepted for production. *Untilovsk* (from the English 'until') is a hamlet in the far north inhabited by political exiles from all regimes; the debating dissidents agree only in falling in love with Raisa, a Soviet exile.

53 The Central Committee for the Improvement of Scholars' Daily Lives, founded in 1921 by the Sovnarkom, was an elite organization that provided rations, clothing, travel expenses, medical care, and the like for 8000 intellectuals and their families.

54 Yelena Borisovna Bronner (1881-1937), director of the TsEKUBU sanatorium in Kislovodsk.

55 Boris Lvovich Izralevsky (1886-1969), instrumentalist and conductor; at the MAT 1903-53.

56 Meyerhold was resting in Kislovodsk along with KS and told him to act through the academic secretary of his theatre. Aleksandr Vilyamovich Fevralsky (1901-84), theatre scholar; academic secretary of GOSTIM.

57 Ellipsis in the original.

58 Vyacheslav Ivanovich Suk (1861-1933), violinist, composer, conductor; at the Opera Studio 1924-53.

59 The final version had eight scenes.

60 The Repertkom was shown *Armoured Train* on 31 October in the rehearsal hall without sets, costumes and makeup.

61 Lunacharsky's orders had made KS personally responsible for the timely preparation and production, but had said nothing about quality.

62 Herbert Graf (1904-73), Austrian director, head of the Breslau Opera Theatre; as a child he was featured as 'Little Hans' in one of Freud's studies of juvenile sexuality. Inspired by the tours of Tairov and Meyerhold, he staged a series of operas in a new style and wanted to work with the MAAT.

63 Aleksandr Yakovlevich Tairov (Kornblit, 1885-1950), former lawyer turned actor and director, worked at the Free Theatre, before founding, in 1914, the Kamerny (Chamber Theatre) devoted to the 'synthetic actor'. Married to Alisa Koonen, his leading lady, he was often under fire for his 'formalist' productions.

64 In a letter to Ostrogradsky of 9 July 1927 he said: 'We have completely contrary objectives. Nemirovich goes from drama to music. And we go from music to drama.'

65 Susanna Vladimirovna Yegorova, actress; 1925-27 pupil at a school organized by the MAAT actress T. V. Krasovskaya; later entered the MAAT Second Studio.

66 Free quotation of Gogol in a letter to the actor Ivan Sostnisky, 2 November 1846.

67 Vasily Andreevich Karatygin (1802-53); Vasily Vasilievich Samoilov (1813-87), actors at the Alexandra Theatre.

68 Wooden toys in the style of twopence-coloured broadsides, made by inhabitants of the Troitsa-Sergiev suburb.

69 Yekaterina Nikolaevna Vavulina, artist; taught drawing and painting. In earlier letters she had persuaded KS of the necessity of staging *Hamlet* with Kachalov in the lead and imparted her impressions of *My Life in Art*.

70 The 1928/29 season opened with the comedy *Squaring the Circle* by Valentin Kataev and *Blockade* by Vsevolod Ivanov, and discussions were held about works by Trenyov, Leonov, Bulgakov, Olesha and others.

71 Boris Mikhailovich Syromyatnikov (1874-1947), legal historian; KS had known him for years, having met him on vacation in Kislovodsk.

72 Viktor Mikhailovich Belyaev (1888-1968), music scholar, folklorist, pedagogue, member of the Association of Contemporary Music, one of the founders of the Society of Friends of the Opera Studio, author of the pamphlet *K. S. Stanislavsky's Opera-Studio* (1928).

73 Mikhail Chekhov, who had arrived in Germany in early July, signed a contract with Reinhardt to appear in his theatres.

74 *Die Artisten*, an adaptation of the American play *Burlesque* by Arthur Hopkins and George Watters, was directed by Reinhardt with Mikhail Chekhov as the clown Skid. The impresario Leonidov had written to KS that it was 'just such rubbish as *Dreigroschen*

Oper, which you and I could not watch to the end and escaped to a café', but daily played to full houses.

75 Aleksey Ivanovich Svidersky (1878-1933), official of the Glaviskusstvo of Narkompros 1928-29.

76 Mariya Alekseevna Kryzhanovskaya (1891-1979) acted at the MAT 1915-19. Georgy Valentinovich Serov (1894-1929), actor. None of them returned from emigration.

77 Owing to financial and organizational problems, the car was not brought to Moscow until June 1930.

78 B. Zon interviewed KS on 11 August 1934; the unpublished interview is in the Stanislavsky archive.

79 *Three Fat Men* by Yury Olesha (performed 1930) is a childish allegory of capitalism, militarism and clericalism.

Figure 73 Stanislavsky's expressions watching a rehearsal at his home

11

AN INTERNAL ÉMIGRÉ
1929–1932

Now General Secretary of the Communist Party, Iosif Vissarionovich Stalin (1879-1953) launched the first Five-Year-Plan to turn the USSR into an industrial nation, enlisting the full participation of the arts in its unrealistic goals. Two important policy changes effected in 1928 had a considerable impact on the theatre. Sovnarkom created an Arts Sector of the Commissariat of Enlightenment known for short as Glaviskusstvo. Glavrepertkom was incorporated as an inflexible censorship office within it, charged with monitoring and approving all plays prior to production. The emollient Lunacharsky was removed from office.

The 'Bolshevization of literature' was consolidated by the creation of RAPP (Russian Association of Proletarian Writers). Militant to the point of fanaticism, its members asserted the 'hegemony of the proletariat' in literature, with a mission to create a genuinely revolutionary culture. Backed by the Party, in 1929 RAPP embarked on a campaign of terror aimed at breaking the will of fellow-travellers in their rival institution, the All-Russian Union of Writers. The theme of the realization of the Five-Year-Plan was declared to be the only one worthy of a Soviet writer's attention. When RAPP's periodical At the Literary Post *lauded* My Life in Art *and showed an interest in the Stanislavsky system, the journal* Modern Theatre *rebuked this 'uncritical' view and regarded this interest to be counter to 'the social demands on the theatrical front'.*

From the time of his heart attack through the near decade before his death, KS became a shut-in. He rarely left his lodgings except to go to sanatoria either abroad or, as the European political situation worsened, at home. He continued to draw up staging-plans, chiefly for operas. Rehearsals were held in his ballroom, reports were made to him by toadies, and he was kept coddled and away from day-to-day Soviet reality. He devoted much of his time to preparing the written version of his system with the aid of Lyubov Gurevich and Elizabeth Reynolds Hapgood. He also provided an article on 'Directing and Acting' to the Encyclopædia Britannica, *which included sections on scoring a role and breaking it down into component parts, as well as building the character along an unbroken through-line.*

Unfortunately, in his relations with the MAT, he was dependent on a trio of trouble-makers and sycophants: the actor-administrator Podgorny, his private secretary Tamantsova and. Nikolay Vasilievich Yegorov (1873-1955). Yegorov had been a book-keeper at the Alekseev factory from 1891 until its confiscation; then a member of the board of the Moscow Association of Cable Factories. In 1926, at KS's initiative, he was invited to the MAAT to run the financial-administrative division as comptroller and consultant, along with Podgorny. KS trusted him implicitly, but he came in conflict with part of the troupe and had to leave in 1929. The burden of the operation of the MAAT fell entirely on ND's shoulders, supported by the more competent team of Bokshanskaya and Sudakov; it is to his credit that it did not mummify over the next decade. The lion's share of KS's attention was directed to the Opera Studio rather than to the MAAT, in part because his siblings Zina and Volodya were in charge there. He sent a warm note to the company before the dress rehearsal for Boris Godunov.

To the **Opera Theatre**. 1 March 1929, Moscow.
My dear Studio folk! Every last one of you!!

I am writing you this note on the sly from the doctors.

Do not give me away.

Please know: you only think I'm not with you, but I'm there invisibly, in spirit, and in my thoughts I am feeling and imagining everything that is going on with you.

You have approached this matter honestly and conscientiously; you have worked unstintingly and emerged from the difficult situation in which my illness put you.

This is a very great deal. It proves that a studio is viable, that you all have energy, persistence and self-sufficiency.

Well done! This is a great joy for us all and for me, in particular.

What happens next depends not on us, but on chance. But I am sure that work performed from the heart, lovingly, will never fail. Go boldly on stage and remember that the success of a performance is not created by opening nights, but by a series of repetitions and the passage of time. Today is only a public dress rehearsal. And another ten, fifteen such lie ahead. Only after that will the production be steady on its feet and create a consensus of opinion about it over the course of long years.

When the curtain goes up or the time comes for each of you to go on stage – remember that this is not the decisive moment, but only the first appearance before an audience, which is already disposed to admire you. [...]

My greetings to each of you individually and a big hug to anyone who cares.

K. Stanislavsky

To **Lyubov Gurevich**. 16 March 1929, Moscow.
My dear and dearly beloved Lyubov Yakovlevna!

To tell the honest truth, this is the first letter I am writing, on the sly from the doctors, since I fell ill (not counting the notes I sent the Studio folks the day *Boris Godunov* opened).

I am writing flat on my back and therefore illegibly – forgive me.

I have missed you so much. I do not know when we shall meet. You are terribly busy and under the weather, and I am still not strong enough to be able to discuss the worrisome matters and issues we will not be able to avoid when we do meet.

That is why I am writing.

The need to speak with you has been fermenting within me for a long time. Ever since I was first shown the new edition of my book.[1] I take no credit for that edition. It is entirely the work of your hands. All the greater, then, is my need to thank you for ever and ever. I do not know how to repay you for all that you have done for me. Of course, owing to your direct supervision the book came out wonderfully. Everyone likes it, even more than the first edition, which also won a meed of fame.

I had Ripsi order a specially bound copy for you and will send it as soon as it is ready. Vast, sincere, friendly thanks for your great help. If it were not for you and your continual support and encouragement, I would not have written the book. You are my literary godmother.

And so now, with the second book [*The Actor's Work on Himself*], I cannot do without you, without your criticism. [...] I soon will be going abroad and that's where I shall work. During this time, despite the most exceptional conditions that were created for writing in my present complete isolation – it is hard to work, at least to write anything new. I can only sort out and systematize what I have already written. I just managed more or less decently to patch together two chapters, the most difficult for me: affect, memory and contact. They need reworking, major revisions, additions. Nevertheless the approximate character of what is to come can be gauged from this rough draft.

If you have the time, look it over and *when we meet* (and not in writing; I beseech you not to burden yourself with this work) tell me your candid, severe, ruthless opinion.

What most troubles me is that I do not know for whom I am writing? The experts or the general public?

Of course, I want to be understood by the latter, that is the general public. For that I am trying to be accessible. But I cannot figure out whether I am succeeding or not.

Another problem is that I feel the book will be boring compared to my first book. The reason is obvious. Those were reminiscences, this is a grammar. But could this actually interest a reader? He wants even a grammar to be amusing, or else he won't read it. Maybe the diary format is boring in itself. The fact is that I have only to start rereading what I've written -- and I nod off and rage at myself. [...]

Yours K. Alekseev (Stanislavsky)

Meanwhile I don't feel very cheerful. Arrhythmia has started to plague me. I just can't manage to get well enough to go off somewhere warm.

To **Mikhail Margulis**. March-April 1929, Moscow.

Dear and heartily beloved Mikhail Semyonovich!

I have not written to you because I wanted to write the first letter well, in some special way.

I don't know whether I have managed to do it in this.

How I should like to be Tolstoy or Chekhov in order to put down on paper the feelings about you that have long dwelt in my soul in regard to you, and now, after winter and all that you have done for me are in the past, I am filled with quite a remarkable affection for you, about which it is hard to write. It can be transmitted between the lines and words the way great writers know how to do it so well.

The supreme thing left to me in this world among all the awful and depressing things humanity is suffering at the moment is altruism. It alone will save people from that horror that life has prepared for us ever since the last war.

This year I was surrounded by the kind of loving care that falls to the lot of the happy few. There is no way to give thanks for this love. It is superior to all the hackneyed and vulgar phrases customarily used to express a sense of gratitude.

I cannot find new expressions that would not echo the banality of the jubilee celebration.

All I can do in the meantime is to try and make you understand that I am not unmindful of a single moment or a single tremendous service, sacrifice, that you have made for me over the course of our long friendship and, especially, this year.

I even remember that evening of the jubilee performance, fatal for me, when you drove me home in the car. I remember how you, in your tuxedo, cared for me, inquiringly and lovingly gazed into my eyes to figure out whether I was ill or already dying. I will not forget the second night of anxiety, with even greater worries and inquietude.

I will never forget your innumerable, almost daily visits at the very commencement of my illness and afterwards – during the unprecedented cruellest of frosts. I understand how difficult it must have been for you to reschedule your manifold activities to show up on time for private consultations at the same time as the other doctors. And the telephone calls, the inquiries, advice and care of those around me! How can I make you feel that all these tremendous sacrifices were not made in vain, but are clearly and forever engraved, as if on tablets, on my heart, mind and memory.

I need these memories not only to recall the past but to give me the strength to live in the future and create, to know that the earth still holds people, friends, brothers, love and everything that gives a man a reason not to die.

You see how I lack the talent of Tolstoy, Chekhov and Dostoevsky to convey the great thing I carry in my heart. I have not spoken even a hundredth part of what I feel and would like to convey to you, although I am already covering a fourth page with my writing.

Believe me, dear Mikhail Semyonovich, I love you sincerely and I tenderly embrace you and will preserve forever in my soul an utterly extraordinary feeling of affection, which I have for very few in this world. Meanwhile, in this letter, I do not want to write about anything else. Soon I'll write in detail about my health. You know the general features from Yur. Nik.[2]

I kiss you tenderly.
K. Alekseev (Stanislavsky) [...]

In May KS was well enough to travel with Lilina to Badenweiler, and from there he closely followed the progress of the Opera Studio and its production of The Queen of Spades.

To **his brother Vladimir.** 26 August 1929, Badenweiler.

Dear Volodya!

[...] First of all I shall state the most fundamental of my conditions and demands; if they are not met, then the whole meaning of the Studio's existence disappears. They are to be read by everyone taking part in the production. This, my most pressing demand, relates to the director, conductor, chorus master, all the performers down to the lowliest props man: *everything that has heretofore been achieved by the Studio must be not only preserved, but brought forward. I refer to: a) perfect diction, b) perfect rhythm, c) the theatrical reflection of every moment in the musical score, moving along the through action, d) the whole chorus must be trained so that they may be placed not by voices, but by the inner meaning of what is going on on stage, e) and the soloists will accept the mise-en-scène not because of the conductor or individuals standing around backstage, but by the fact that the through action requires it, f) the question of the laws of speech cannot be disputed; this is the law for every literate participant in art, g) all this must be carried out, but never to the detriment of the musical aspect. One must do everything so that it be exemplary.* As seven years of practice have shown us, this is to be done with the help of proper training and rehearsals. These rehearsals must be held at all costs. [...]

K. Stanislavsky

To **Ripsimé Tamantsova.** 7 September 1929, Badenweiler.

Dear Ripsi!

[...] The book will turn out big and solid, and [Norman Hapgood] [3] the American who invited me to the Laboratory, when he learned that I cannot go there, offers me the sum of 5000 dollars, out of his pocket, so that I can live quietly and finish the book, which ostensibly the theatrical world is awaiting in America.

[...] I am awfully happy that Leonidov is better. If only he knew how much I want to work with him! Don't let him be angry with me for not answering him, and have him write two words: how is Golovin, are the costumes, designs finished and what is being done on *Othello* in general? I have tried to write the staging-plan, but am still agitated, and my imagination is morbid. What's more, I've lost the knack of writing staging-plans. [...]

Yours K. Stanislavsky

For half a year the MAAT had been run by the so-called 'quintet' (Batalov, Markov, Prudkin, Sudakov and Khmelyov). On 5 September 1929 thirty-four-year old Mikhail Sergeevich Geitts (Heitz,1893-1937) was appointed 'Red' administrator, to deal with organizational and administrative questions. He posted a banner, 'We shall transform the entire Komsomol into shock brigades in order to fulfil the Five-Year-Plan.' Every collective had to sponsor some industrial organization, so the illustrious Art Theatre wound up as big brother to the Moscow Ball Bearing Factory.

To **Leonid Leonidov**. 15 September 1929, Badenweiler.

Dear Leonid Mironovich!

Ripsi has informed me that a Red administrator has been appointed. I had discussions on this subject with Svidersky several times, and not long ago we exchanged telegrams, whose subject I will explicate below. Now I have to account for my actions to the old-timers – the ones who founded this concern.[4] Whom shall I send this letter to? Moskvin, Kachalov, Luzhsky (he's ill), Podgorny (they say that he's the favourite)... You know our old-timers – they will read it, talk it over and put it aside. Therefore I address myself to all the old-timers and the youngsters, but through your kind mediation. In the first place, you are energetic, bold, you know how to state your opinion straight out, tactfully, and best of all you know my opinion on the present state of the theatre. You better than anyone, you understand what can and cannot be said – therefore permit me to reveal all my thoughts and feelings to you as they came to me in fact.

You know better than anyone the atmosphere in the theatre, its mood and you will keep silent about what ought not to be said at the moment. Do not be surprised that I am not writing myself but dictating – this is not because I am too weak and cannot write, but because letters of this kind upset me a great deal, and combined with my own handwriting it will quickly wear you out, I am having to delay the process of writing over the whole week, as happened with this letter, but if I had tried to write it myself, the delay would have been much longer. I am dictating the letter to my son, whose probity and silence I can guarantee. Besides, he knows all my business anyway, because I also consult him for advice on the subject.

Do not be cross that I have not answered your letter before now, but this whole time I have been either immersed in letters or felt poorly and could not engage in any correspondence.

I append my confession regarding the Red administrator.

I embrace you tenderly and lovingly.

K. Alekseev (Stanislavsky)

The question of a Red administrator, as is well known, has been dragging on for a long time. It began before Svidersky's time, but at that time I was fit and the administration was in the hands of people whom I consider business-like. After this, as you know, I fell ill. Vladimir Ivanovich was left on his own, the business administration was swept under the rug, Vladimir Ivanovich could not deal with the administrative-financial aspect, and the financial-administrative aspect fell into the hands of the present administration. I like them very much, they are good actors, but where is their business sense? Why do they deserve our trust in this sphere? How could they take on handling such complicated matters? Their inexperience and ignorance of this business became all too clear when, as a first step, they got rid of the two experienced and business-like people, whom they should have held on to, in the face of their own inexperience [Yegorov and Podgorny]. [...]

You understand that at my time of life I cannot undertake administrative responsibilities and in my old age be hauled into court on account of the inexperience of a green administration. I myself, who has founded three factories in my lifetime and dealt with businessmen over the course of 30 years, candidly confess that without an efficient administration, in other words, Nikolay Vasilievich [Yegorov] and Nikolay Afanasevich [Podgorny], I am afraid to remain an administrator. I have made this last remark before, I am making it now and will continue to make it. I spoke of this with Svidersky, when he visited my home during my illness before I left.

The question naturally arises: what is the next thing to be done? I am ill and cannot work as I used to. Vladimir Ivanovich is overburdened and also cannot work as he did of old, he can hardly keep his hold on the literary-artistic and directorial department. But I told Svidersky that the only way out I could see was to appoint a Red administrator and even then I hastened to present him with a huge 'but'. No two administrators are alike; one administrator can bring great benefit, another can wreck the whole business. To destroy the finely-tuned organization of the Art Theatre forever, irrevocably, takes only a moment, one stroke of the pen, to create it is an event of the rarest chance which occurs once in a hundred years. That is why for us the selection of a Red administrator is a question of the continuing existence of the theatre, its life or death. A good administrator can be an enormous aid to the theatre in its present circumstances. I say that from my own personal experience of the Opera Theatre. When questions of a political character arise, we, the non-Communists, cannot speak to that with authority, we are barely heeded, but the picture immediately changes when a Red administrator, a Communist, addresses the question, because he is heeded, matters are discussed with him in a different way than with us, and he speaks with others in quite a different way than we can. We knew the importance in the theatre of Communists who understood its nature and carefully fought for whatever needed to be lovingly saved and preserved. That kind of Red administrator, even if he does not understand the nature of the theatre but wishes to understand, is, I am profoundly convinced, indispensable. [...]

I reported my conversation with Svidersky to Vladimir Ivanovich by phone as much as a telephone call and the medical monitoring of my pulse allowed. If I am not mistaken Vladimir Ivanovich agreed not to a Red administrator but to a Red board member, but, after all, that's just a play on words, what is important is not what he is called but that he is a Communist officially briefed to supervise the running of the business. I believe that a Red administrator who has unmediated contact with us, the other administrators, is much better, more useful or, in the case of a bad appointment, less dangerous, if only because he is constantly associating with us, not estranged from us, and because officially he has one vote while we have two if we manage to come to terms. It is not difficult to come to terms with a business-like, cultured person of Communist discipline who loves our theatre and art, and I know this from many, many instances in my personal experience during recent years. But the most important thing is that they appoint to the function of administrator some prominent Communist, who has agreed to accept the function not simply as one of the members of the board. What if he's a minor Communist, with no authority, who will take not an artistic-social line, but a personal, bureaucratic one? With that sort of politician, invested with power, it will be more difficult to come to terms than with a cultured, intellectual individual who understands and loves the theatre.

On parting from Svidersky, I formulated my view in this way: there should be a business-like group of people (I don't know their names); a Red administrator, Yegorov and Podgorny (people may say they are hard to get on with, but the Communist will deal with them). This troika will run the administrative-financial department. Vladimir Ivanovich and I will not meddle in it except when the business touches on the artistic, performance, staging side of things, and the present administration will have no access to this department. This is to be done for the salvation of those actors who ought to study, study, study, and who, instead of that, are involved in matters alien to them, of which they understand absolutely nothing, and by which they are diverted and corrupted in exercising a power beyond their abilities. They cannot be representatives of the Art Theatre in capital letters. They could not even be administrators of the Second Studio of the First Great Art Theatre. As actors they are rapidly moving backwards, and as managers they are reducing the theatre to the MAT in lower-case letters. Besides, I am afraid that under their administration we shall soon return to a time when the theatre again stops paying salaries punctually, as was the case under Dmitry Ivanovich [Yustinov]. [...]

I embrace you and all the old-timers.

K. Stanislavsky

On the appointment of Geitts as administrator, a collegium was instituted to serve as a consultative organ which, besides the troika (Geitts, KS, ND), included the previous quintet, but without Zavadsky who was politically suspect.

To **his sister Zinaida.** 15 September 1929, Badenweiler.
Dear Zina!

No model for the first act [of *The Barber of Seville*] was made. In the drawing the mise-en-scène seemed to be interesting, but when we assembled the model that was sent, it came out pure Bolshoy Theatre. In order not to redo everything from scratch, I would have to modify in some degree the general details of what has been arranged

The portable model sent will show those small changes which will ostensibly (though far from ideally) get us away from stereotypes. The result will be a good or bad, I do not know which, realistic set. But after all the following act is stylized. The result will be sort of two principles: first – the standard theatrical one, the second stylized. I am trying to reconcile them. Igor had put stylized draperies on the enclosed collapsible model. Here's what they mean: they belong to the decorative part of the staging, that is to the 18th century, to that hall in which presumably the performance takes place and which serves as a basic background for a realistic tableau. The meaning of this stylization is that we will show only those parts of the realistic setting necessary for the action: 1. two windows,

Rosina's and Bartolo's, beneath them two pillars, a grille. 2. portions of a café with jalousies and 3. a portion of a house with a window and Figaro's sign. [...]

To write a detailed mise-en-scène without a keyboard and hearing the singing is impossible. Wouldn't it better to sketch out, describe the trajectory of the day in a general, undetailed mise-en-scène. Beginning: night; somewhere a distant lantern is gleaming, just before dawn. The musicians are hidden behind the pillars; Fiorello can barely keep them in the background; they are undisciplined and now and then crawl out with questions for him, half emerging from the colonnade or coming out on the background of the grille, to stare at Rosina's window. Meanwhile tardy musicians (3-4 or 5 individuals) have wandered in and look for where they are to forgather. One of them comes down the stairs, another goes up to meet him; a third has entered from the staircase stage right and moved along the wall to the café. Meanwhile a fourth has entered stage left from behind the corner of the café and headed right to the nook between Bartolo's house and the stairs. Amid all this we lose sight of the people wandering about and trying to find their way. Probably the best thing would be pick them out in the dark, give them lanterns. Fiorello has an incredibly hard time keeping them all in line, showing them where to go and keeping them there. Finally at the top of the stairs at the corner of Figaro's house the Count appears. Fiorello runs over to him. Meanwhile there is excitement among the musicians, each one wants to bow and slavishly kiss the hem of the cloak of the man who will be paying them. A new uproar, new efforts on Fiorello's part to impose order. The Count has entered, stolen over to the window, the grille, taken a look to see if Rosina is there, and has taken a stand where he cannot be seen from the window, but he can see the window. In other words, he has stood on the well. [...]

The musicians play underneath the arches, only their faces and the tips of their instruments are visible (it would be good if real musicians were playing and not supernumeraries). Fiorello backed against the grille watches to see if the window opens.

Sequel.

Cavatina. At the end of the cavatina a dramatic pause. Fiorello and all the musicians look around to see if Rosina is there. After the pause the Count's line to Fiorello continues. After the words 'No, signor', another dramatic pause, during which the Count slowly crosses to the fountain and sits downcast. Fiorello cautiously comes over to him, says that [it is getting light?]. The Count is rapt in thought. (N.B. It is not necessary that the Count slump, so that he can chase off the musicians energetically, obviously, a new idea has occurred to him.) The Count begins to pay out money, -- chatter, inconsequential noise. Fiorello is afraid of a scandal, chases them off, imposes order. He chases them off stage right, some return to the Count from the left. The musicians, impudent and obsequious, kiss the hem of his cloak.

Fiorello: God grant that the noise did not awake the neighbours, looks into the café nook to see if they woke anyone up. Meanwhile the Count has gone over to the grille, looks in the window, back to the audience again.

I suggest that the line 'I want to talk with her' and the rest up to Figaro's entrance, -- I suggest that this musical aside be turned into dialogue with Fiorello.

At Figaro's first sounds Fiorello runs away, while the Count goes behind the columns.

The four lines and more, as many as the conductor demands, Figaro appears in the window. Working clothes, apron. He is holding two wigs to wash them in the well.

At Figaro's first sounds the landlord of the café wakes up, looks around. (N.B. The tables have been out there all through the night. The landlord merely puts down a stool and a bottle of Chianti, wherever the musical aria permits it.) N.B. There is no way to indicate the place where this is to be done without the score; it will depend on the rhythm. I can only indicate the action: 1) at some point Figaro wets his wigs at the fountain, 2) pours something into a bottle and shakes it up or stirs it around with a little brush (evidently dye for wigs), 3) somewhere at some point he knocks at the café. The landlord's head pops out, he gives him a bottle and a glass, a stool (?). 4) Figaro drinks wine and sings, while the landlord listens. Figaro does a little dance.

Figaro illustrates what he sings. (N.B. Try to make these illustrations clear, as the Italians do, if the actor can only achieve a simple waving of hands.) Perhaps the landlord comes out and sits beside him at the table.

Another variant of the entrance. Perhaps people will miss the traditional barber wandering down the street. This will be difficult to make new with inexperienced actors. They will easily fall into a stereotype. Try the following entrance. Figaro comes in (in this case the shop does not have to be seen). A guitar on his back and some sort of little box with various utensils. Hung all over with all sorts of razors, basins, tongs, brushes, combs etc. He also sells cosmetics, and he can set it up for shaving.* In short, he works both in the shop and on the street, wholesale and retail. I remember that in Rome I was awakened by a boy who was shouting in the shrillest voice. He was selling all kinds of wine, stopped his cart, put out his wares and walked around the square, shouting and showing his wares in windows. The same thing should be shown here as well. An itinerant barber, who like my alarm clock will wake up everyone on time, offer his services and wares.

At some point in his glee he can take the guitar and play it a bit, if there are enough opportunities for it in the music. Perhaps he can even do some dancing, displaying his wares in a window. The important thing is that these dances arise from the sincere merriment of the performer, and not from the desperation of a singer who is singing a difficult aria, as always happens. And this variant can be supplemented, if necessary, with wetting the wigs, and pouring water in a phial of bleach, and knocking at the café, and drinking wine with the landlord.

The scene of the Count and Figaro. The Count has been watching closely. He comes out from behind the columns. The landlord of the café has sat at the table with Figaro, sees the Count, nudges Figaro. Figaro, seated, take a good look at him (he had been sitting with his back to the Count).

They recognize one another. On the words: 'Quiet, not a word of this' – the Count goes back under the colonnade and with a sign beckons Figaro. All the rest of the scene will be conveyed by the diction. They both stand under the colonnade, separated by the columns.

Change the words 'Someone is coming on to the balcony' to something else, because there is no balcony, and the awning let down (it doesn't matter that it was let down at night – they might have forgotten to roll it up) has long ago been cleverly raised on the sly (the awning is raised from inside the room). Rosina emerges. The Count steps out a bit from the colonnade. Rosina steps back a bit, preventing the Count from seeing her, and says: 'Although I am ashamed, I will throw him the letter.'

Meanwhile, as this scene takes place, a similar awning on the corner window is covertly raised. Bartolo's phiz appears. Dialogue from the window. Bartolo stretches mightily to see Rosina and whether there's anyone in the street. The Count and Figaro beneath the colonnade roar with laughter as the 'futile precaution' and all the deft subterfuges that Rosina makes with great calm.

Rosina: 'Ah, what a nuisance, I dropped my page.' Deftly played. Chuckles from underneath the colonnade. Bartolo has lowered the awning and disappeared.

Rosina very hurriedly gives a warning. With great haste the Count leaps over the grille, and Figaro pulls out of his pockets some scraps of paper and scatters them along the street,** but almost gets caught – Bartolo has come out. Figaro has not lost his head, quickly dons a wig which lay on the café table, pulled off the table cloth, put it on and has sat with his back to Bartholo as an habitué of the café. Rosina in the window, the Count staring from behind the grille, the landlord of the café – they all die laughing. Bartolo walks along the street and picks up all the soiled handbills tossed around by Figaro. Bartolo has realized his mistake, gets frightfully angry, throws the papers he's picked up in Rosina's direction so that she retreats inside at once. He waits until she disappears. Bartolo exits. A pause of loud laughter.

Rosina appears in the window again in a minute. The Count, having climbed over the grille, has run under the colonnade, also roaring with laughter. Figaro, having cast off the wig, runs to the Count as does the landlord of the café.

The laughter is a cappella. Find some chord or tonality, because, so far as I recall, this scene has no recitative.

Reading the letter under the colonnade. The line 'I explode, I explode.' The Count leaps up in rapture, almost dances in front of Rosina's window. Figaro dances too, plays the fool. Both quickly return to the colonnade. Figaro eggs him on. Under the colonnade the Count gets carried away in his malice at Bartolo, looking forward to his battle with him, but Figaro, standing by a column, pops out on one side, then the other, speaking his line afterwards.

The door opens. They run out from underneath the columns, they don't know where to hide, and exit into the cloth draperies that conceal the end of Bartolo's house. Bartolo enters followed by Ambrosio.

While Bartolo crosses, only the heads of the Count and Figaro pop out of the folds of cloth.

Ambrosio crosses, yawning, to the grille to get a breath of fresh air and sits on a stone of some kind.

All the rest of the dialogue, now that Ambrosio is on stage, takes place in the folds of the draperies. Ambrosio has fallen asleep.

The awning is quietly raised. The Count and Figaro leap out from behind the folds of drapery. Figaro eggs on the Count. Ambrosio sleeps on. The Count puts one foot on Ambrosio's knee, the other on his shoulder, and, just as if on a stepladder, climbs up and sits on the grille. Figaro gives him his guitar. The Count sings, and Figaro sits on the lap of the sleeping Ambrosio.

*Perhaps he can shave the landlord of the café.

** He scatters most of them away from the house, so as to lead Bartolo farther away aside.

To **Leonid Leonidov**. 17-22 September 1929, Badenweiler.
Dear Leonid Mironovich!

[...] Now all my hopes are directed at 1 November. God willing, I will be better and then I can hug you in Moscow, at the *Othello* rehearsals. If only it remains at least relatively warm here! This delay is not too harmful, because, God willing, it will give Kachalov time to be free of *Resurrection*.

Yes, I just remembered something else! Some experiments have to be made with the moving gondola: either move it by means of an electric motor, or by means of two levers, like children's bikes or a railway handcar.[5]

Preparations will have to be made for the thunderstorm and whirlwind during the 'Senate' and the arrival in Cyprus. You will have to think about the music: 1) to greet Othello and some signals from the sea and the shore. In addition, some sort of gathering with Oriental music, local, Cypriote, accompanied by Turkish instruments. That march goes on offstage, and they will process along the fortress wall, whereas the procession of the local citizens takes place on Othello's arrival in Cyprus. 2) Some sort of signals in the corps de garde, stirring, summoning the corps de garde to arms. 3) Iago's song. 4) Give some thought to the noises of the popular uprising and the hammering on the fortress gates behind the fortress. I'm told that Volodya Popov[6] has invented something with a radio for sound effects, -- can this be used here? I am wracking my brains how and where to show off the wonderful costumes of the natives provided by Golovin? They will pass by in the scene of the gathering in Cyprus, but how can they be seen in the dark? In the reception of Ludovico, on that staircase, they might be shown off, and they would be appropriate to the through action, because this would fortify the whole line of Othello's growing state of mind. In fact, after this Othello becomes contorted with anguish down in the cellarage, makes a vow beneath a star-lit heaven in his grief, goes so far that during an official ceremonial reception of an ambassador he strikes his wife in the face in public. 6) Desdemona's song. Who is the composer? Vasilenko, Glière, Zueva's husband (I've forgot his name).[7]

However, how are we to keep an intimate production from going off the rails into something overly pretentious. A certain balance has to be found. The arrival of the victor in a subjugated town or the official reception of an ambassador even in an intimate production must not be skimpy. As far as Cyprus goes, everything has been provided for there, so that it does not divagate too far in the staging sense. All there is for passage is a single little path on top of the walls, and down by the door and on the stones one can show the indignant natives, sticking to the

Figure 74 Design by Aleksandr Golovin for the opening Venetian scene in *Othello*

walls and staring out in the distance at the advance of Othello's ships (once again in order to show off Golovin's costumes).

As for Ludovico's reception, it has turned out more theatrically than I had expected, but Golovin very much wanted a staircase, and I could not refuse him. And once there is a staircase, you cannot create real intimacy on it. The set itself demands a certain spaciousness. [...]

I embrace you tightly.

K. Stanislavsky (Alekseev)

The government dismissed Nikolay Yegorov on 1 November 1929.

To **Mikhail Geitts**. 2 November 1929, Badenweiler.
Dear Mikhail Sergeevich!

I accidentally learned that in Moscow, in our theatre, a purge has begun. I am thinking about those who are critical to the concern and are exposed to danger.

N. V. Yegorov. To some he is a pain in the neck. I take the liberty of writing to you about him.

Why do I defend him in every conflict that has broken out in the theatre. Out of partiality? No. Because I am most sincerely pained by the matter.

523

For the same reason I now address myself – to you personally, with the first and great request, on behalf of the concern. Promise me that before you make any definite decision about Yegorov's fate, you will attentively take a closer look at him, call him in and have him describe in detail everything that he and I and N. A. Podgorny achieved together despite hardships during the three years of my personal administration of the MAT.

You should inquire into all the torments, nocturnal meetings after a working day, sleepless nights, webs of intrigue woven around us, the organized campaign against Yegorov and Podgorny, on account of me and the measures I had to take for the sake of saving the concern. How could I be removed in this matter from my assistants at the time. If Yegorov is at fault, then so I am, first and foremost. I am not asking you to do this retrospective in order to air old linen, but to establish fairness.

You cannot punish a man for selfless work, for overstrained nerves and heart, for irreproachable honesty. He should be cherished and used, because he showed his mettle not in words but in deeds. By chasing away such persons, one may undermine trust in and love for the concern in those devoted to it.

I am far from the idea of accusing anyone in this letter.

Every theatre and especially ours is a very complicated machine. There will always be intrigues and abuses of confidence. This makes it all the more essential to have a man like Yegorov, who stands, like Cerberus, for safeguarding the concern's interests. Having lived all my life in the theatre, I have dreamed all my life about such a man. Now, in my declining years, when I have found him – shall I have to part with him. I know full well that no one else like him can be found. Does one have to speak of his experience and knowledge of his business? Let me offer only one example. There was a time when the former heads of the finance division stopped wages on a monthly basis; they paid out advances by the quarter to stop the mouths of protestors any way they could. I declare that I entrusted Yegorov with the financial responsibility – at a critical moment for the pecuniary side of the theatre.

From that time on I do not recall a single delay in paying wages.

Forgive me, dear Mikhail Sergeevich, for pestering you with my requests, but I make so bold as to believe that in short space you will thank me for helping to preserve a necessary, loyal, knowledgeable and incorruptible man, devoted in every fibre of his being to the basic concept of the Art Theatre, which fostered him and made him famous. For this one can forgive him a few of his shortcomings, which lurk in every man.

I shake your hand and send heartfelt greetings and wishes for successful work.

Sincerely devoted K. Stanislavsky

Geitts could do nothing.

To the **Art Theatre Collective**. 31 December 1929, Nice.

[...] The time will come, and very soon, when a great play, a work of genius, will be written. It will, of course, be revolutionary. No great work can be anything else. But this will not be a revolutionary play in the red banner sense. The revolution will proceed from within. We shall see on the stage the regeneration of the soul of the world, the inner struggle with an obsolete past, with a new, not yet understood, unrealized present. This will be a struggle for equality, freedom, a new life, and a spiritual culture, the extirpation of war... This is the time when we will require authentic actors who know how to speak, not just in words and voices, but also with their eyes, soulful outbursts, radiant emotions, commands of the will. The new play will require entirely new scenery, stage dressing. Not, of course, the kind I have cultivated for so long and which have come to be the cliché known as Stanislavskian naturalism. Nor the kind that is now considered new and fashionable, but quite a different kind, that will help and not hinder the Actor (with a capital A). But where is one to find this *Actor*?

I assert that his place of origin is here, and only here, in our theatrical family. In so saying, I am not limiting this family merely to our homeland, but the whole world.

For the time is coming soon, when *only first-rate* theatres will exist. All the rest, the mediocre ones, will be recast as talking pictures. This will be only natural. With great pleasure I will pay 20 kopeks to hear Chaliapin, Caruso (reborn), Toscanini, [*indeciph.*], etc., etc., rather than a mediocre live troupe, passably performing a passable play. Theatres will have to pull themselves together or they will be jettisoned.

A struggle with the cinema of the future is pointless when it comes to production values. I am told that here, in Europe, they are devising instruments for projecting operas in the open air, loud-speakers that can help amplify sound to the limits fixed by the power of an orchestra to some thousand people. A certain great connoisseur of operatic matters told me that recently in Rome he heard a diminutive soprano with such an impressive voice that its sound flew throughout an enormous theatre and seemed to pierce the ear. To the man who told me this it seemed as if she were standing right beside him. When he went backstage to express his excitement, it was explained to him that the soprano herself was good enough when it came to singing ability, but her voice was so small that it could hardly be heard in a room. The new loud-speaker lent it strength. So it will be in our dramatic art. The competition with the cinema will be arduous.

Nevertheless the cinema will never be able to vie with a living, creating human being who not only knows how to speak but also to *radiate*. Film can never possess this capability.

Our theatre alone is capable of this and knows how to do it technically.

The traditions of this art still linger within the walls of our theatre. They are deeply implanted in the souls of our old-timers, some of whom acquired our art unconsciously. They know no other. But... we are getting old. Therefore... I should wish to see all of our youngsters, all our replacements, make use of us before it is too late, while we can still tell them a great deal and teach them a great deal.

Probe more deeply what the old-timers say!

Ask us more questions and try to piece together what you learn from us.

Take your places beside us before the footlights more prominently and more often. The things I am talking about are learned not only in the theatre, not only in the classroom, not only in rehearsals or working at home, but mainly before the footlights, before a full auditorium, soul to soul, at the very moment of creativity. […]

In a letter of January 1930 Geitts had praised Olga Knipper as the social climber Moskaleva in ND's adaptation of Dostoevsky's Uncle's Dream *(one of her first new roles in a long time and a comic gem. On the other hand, he was extremely dissatisfied with the direction of Kseniya Ivanovna Kotlubay(1890-1931), which he found 'unimaginative, somewhat narrowly pedantic'. As for Gorchakov's staging of* Three Fat Men, *he opined that it was hopeless, devoid of creative afflatus.*

To **Mikhail Geitts**. 9 January 1930, Nice.
Esteemed and dear Mikhail Sergeevich!
[…] Who, where is there a director among the present ones who could replace Nemir.-Dan. However dismaying it may be, in all my life there were among all my numerous students only two such directors: 1) Sulerzhitsky, whom I consider to have been a man of genius, and 2) Vakhtangov – not so good, but also capable of becoming an artistic leader. They are both dead! Meanwhile no one new has appeared, nothing is left but to pair off directors. The trouble is that there are directors of all sorts of abilities and functions: a) the administrative stage director, who can implement a performance and support systematic work and organization. This is very difficult, and not everyone is capable of the little note that gets people to obey. b) the producing stage director. He is the one who knows how to talk to designers, stagehands, who can bring to life his own or someone else's physical production. c) the literary stage director, who can turn a play into a performance along a faithful literary line. d) the artistic stage director, who by himself can create (without copying) the artistic aspect of the performance. e) the psychological stage director, who can accurately proceed along the inner trajectory. f) the pedagogic director, who can correct and educate the actors. These functions are rarely combined in one person. They are met with separately. So one has to combine the psychological director with the producing director and give them a general directive. […]
I am very worried about Leonidov. He is a special kind of actor. He constantly needs to be supported, encouraged and not too badly fatigued (he is ill).

To the **Opera Theatre team**. 14 January 1930, Nice,
My dear friends and studio members,
[…] Answer me: do you believe that the fundamentals and principles of our theatre are the right ones? Do you want to work according to different fundamentals? If so, our ways must part, for nothing will ever come of our work together. Do you believe that it is not the stage production, not the director's contrivances, not the adoption of ephemeral and quickly passing fashions in our art, but the creation of the singer and actor, based upon the organic laws of nature, truth and artistic beauty that constitute the theatre needed by the people and Russian art? If you believe this, then cherish, strengthen, love, and protect the fundamentals of our art.

Does our theatre have any meaning, any necessity without them? If not, then you will realize yourselves that its salvation lies in the principles upon which it is based.

Once you believe in the fundamentals of our art, once you take them to be correct and are not willing to work in any other way; if you have learned the methods for achieving your goal and carrying on your work so as to be able to say to yourself: I have done everything I am capable of, the rest is beyond my powers – if all this is so, then what has cast some of you into despair? Worry about whether you'll be a success or a failure? You know in advance -- if you have put a great deal of love, integrity, knowledge and nature-given ability into the new productions, success is bound to come sooner or later. Therefore, cast away all doubts and advance directly towards your goal without any hesitation or road-blocks.

Let me ask you one more question: are you sure that good fortune has not spoiled you? You cannot complain about us. Your theatre is in its fourth year, and you have already been noticed in Moscow and abroad. Many of you are already famous actors; the theatre enjoys a good box-office; not a single concert goes by without someone from our company taking part -- is that not enough for you? Do not frighten fortune away, and be satisfied with the big things that it is giving you in these hard times for all mankind. You are lucky, you were born fortune's favourites, compared to others. It is wrong of you to lose heart and get depressed.

Might you be troubled by the future of our theatre? Then let me tell you: anyone who wishes to live in our day and age must to some extent be a hero. If you are stalwart and doughty heroes, welded into your collective, -- rest assured that you are flourishing and will overcome all obstacles and survive. If a little craft is dashed by the first wave, cannot breast it and forge ahead, it is not seaworthy. You should understand that if your collective is unstable enough to be dashed by the first wave that washes over it, then your cause is predestined to a sorry fate.

Therefore let your mutual artistic and comradely ties grow strong and forged together. This is of such importance that, for its sake, you must sacrifice vanity and caprice and bad character traits and favouritism and everything else that drives a wedge into the collective intelligence, will and feelings of people, and disintegrates, demoralizes and destroys the whole. The point is that you should be well organized, and on that I will be able to advise you.

I am tired now, and can dictate no more, but day by day I will note down how I might be useful to you from afar to firm up your collective and develop in it an intrinsically conscious and heartfelt discipline.

I embrace you, affectionately,

K. Stanislavsky

While in Nice, KS renewed his acquaintance with Elizabeth Hapgood. She later claimed that he had come to Nice specifically to meet her and her husband, who urged him to combine the two sections of the proposed book – the actor's inner preparations and the external technique for creating a character -- into a single volume.

To **Ripsimé Tamantsova**, 22 January 1930, Nice.
Dear Ripsi!

[...] A long time ago I sent you a list of those newspapers in which extracts from my forthcoming book might be published in America. There will have to be a lengthy correspondence with them. Yelizaveta Lvovna [Hapgood] is waiting very impatiently for an answer as to which of these papers we can treat with. I think you are holding back on this for fear that I will publish something that has not been vetted by Lyubov Yakovlevna [Gurevich] or that I will sell it too cheaply. Don't worry, nothing will be done without Lyubov Yakovlevna; the book has been sold for a fixed sum, so that I'm not dependent on publication – that's a matter for the book sales. My concern is that nothing should be printed in such publications as might seem improper to the authorities. If a reply is delayed too long, then misunderstandings may arise, so please hurry.

But the most important thing I need to know is: does the [Yale] University of New Haven want to publish my second book and any subsequent ones (not printing them in newspapers, but publishing them). Find out as soon as you can

Figure 75 Stanislavsky and Elizabeth Reynolds Hapgood in Vichy, with Yu. N. Chistyakov and Leonid Leonidov, 1930

and write whether Yelizaveta Lvovna can start negotiating with them. There's a Theatre Faculty at the university there and they need my book. I should think they would be the most receptive one. In any case here's the address: *Professor George P. Baker, Yale University Press, New Haven.*[8]

As to my book *My Life in Art*: what has been decided about the Polish publication, as well as the German and French?

Another request: the museum has a photo of our group – the whole troupe – in America, taken with Yelizaveta Lvovna and her husband in Washington. Have it copied as soon as possible and send the copy to me.[9] [...]

What lies ahead is writing the staging-plan for *Othello* – the Desdemona/Cassio scene, the scene with the fountain. I haven't seen the design – how am I to conceive the staging? Is it possible to send me a photo? Ditto for the set for 'The Staircase' (the reception of Ludovico).

Tell Leonid Mironovich that in the set with the fountain, whose ground-plan I have, something is unclear: there is no door on one side, and Othello and Cassio definitely have to make separate exits.

A set for Emilia's room was also ordered from Golovin but I don't have the ground-plan for that set.

I have a great request for Nikolay Vasilievich [Yegorov] that he repair the flaws in my apartment and Kira's. For instance, in my room and Igor's during a cold spell in winter there is a draught from underneath the balcony doors. Ask him to see to it that there is no draught coming from them or the windows, especially in a cold spell.

In our apartment here there is an apparatus for heating water by gas, which has been laid on. There have been two explosions here. This has worried me quite a bit. The apparatus was cleaned and for a few days there was no gas. The same thing might happen in our apartment – what would happen to the kitchen then, what would we cook on?

They say Leonidov has a Russian stove or cooker – ask how much does it cost?

Is there heating in the bathroom? It is impossible to take a bath here, because the room is cold.

I very much fear that a smell will emanate from the toilet throughout the whole apartment. Shouldn't we install an electric fan. What does Nikolay Vasilievich say about the apartment in general? [...]

ND had another major hit with his adaptation of Tolstoy's Resurrection, *using a narrator played by Kachalov to recite passages from the novel and serve as the voice of the author. (He had not employed this in any of his Dostoevsky adaptations. The device had first been used at the First Studio in* The Cricket on the Hearth.*) It would run 726 performances. He followed this up with another success, the American sensation drama* Chicago *by Maurine Watkins under the title* Publicity. *It achieved 245 performances. Under these circumstances KS felt impelled to urge on Othello. Leonidov, rehearsing the title role, had complained that in the soliloquy 'Forgive, peace' there was 'too much declamation, pseudo-emotion' and he found the 'soliloquy in the bed chamber difficult'.*

To **Leonid Leonidov**. 10 February 1930, Nice.

Dear, kind Leonid Mironovich!

Forgive me for not writing myself, but dictating. This comes about because I have to write a lot these days – on one hand, the staging-plan for *Othello*, and on the other, the book which I must complete at all costs before I leave. Furthermore, I have a sizeable correspondence. All in all, I would never be up to it, if I were to write it myself, bent over my desk; that is why I dictate lying down. That is quite an achievement, because in the past I could not even so much as think about the theatre or the productions, or to carry on a correspondence without getting overwrought. That sort of work quickly came to an end in heart palpitations and spasmodic chest convulsions. [...]

I want to come as quickly as possible to the scene which you feel isn't working for you, but which, as I recall, I liked at the trial run of *Othello*. There was no declamation in it then. In any case I will try and help you with a few pieces of advice.

Let us analyse the nature of Othello's state of mind. He has been incredibly happy with Desdemona. His honeymoon is a dream, the climax of amorous passion. This climax is for some reason rarely acted in interpretations of Othello, the author himself has paid scant attention and space to it, but nevertheless it is important to show what Othello is losing, what he is bidding farewell to in the scene which you feel isn't working for you. By its very nature this scene is transitional. Starting at this point, Othello hurtles downward. How can he suddenly bid farewell to the bliss he has tasted and to which he has grown accustomed? How easy can it be to realize his loss? Whenever a man is deprived of what he has lived for, he at first loses his voice, his equilibrium, and then begins a harrowing search for it. Once he had his bliss, but how is he to go on living without it. A man undergoing a crisis reviews his whole life in torments, in sleepless nights. He mourns for what he has lost, he values it more highly still when he compares it with the future that lies in store for him and which he conjures up in his imagination.

What does a man need to carry out this immense inner work? He needs to withdraw into himself to examine the past and see his future life. That is a moment of tremendous self-fathoming; so that it is no surprise that a man in such a state does not notice what is going on around him, becomes distracted, strange, and when he returns again from dreams to reality, he becomes even more terrified, perturbed and seeks a pretext to vent the grief and pain stored up during his self-fathoming.

That, I think, is roughly the nature of Othello's state of mind in that scene. That is even the source of the scene design. That is why Othello at one point runs to the top of the tower, as he does in that scene, at another dashes down to a kind of cellarage where they store weapons and all sorts of broken household goods and there he hides from people so that they won't see what a state he's in.

That is why the trajectory of this scene, as I conceive it, should go as follows. He climbs the tower to experience [*perezhit*] the words, 'Ha! Ha! False to me?' I utterly reject the words 'Ha! Ha!' because there is a threatening undertone to them, while there is no threat in Othello's condition. That is why when I played

Figure 76 Leonid Leonidov as Othello and Alla Tarasova as Desdemona, 1930

this scene, if I recall correctly, I replaced 'Ha! Ha!' with 'What! What!! False to me, to me!!' What does this mean, the emphatic repetition of 'me'? It means: in the face of our love that once was, in the face of my total devotion to her, ready to make any sacrifice, she could have spoken those three words to me: 'I love Cassio', and I would have done everything in my power to carry out her wishes, I either would have gone away or I would have stayed beside her to protect her; but how could she repay this devotion, this complete self-abnegation by betraying me underhandedly, deceiving me, and doing it with such diabolical deftness and cunning?! She is indeed the devil disguised as an angel. I insist that Othello is far

531

from being a jealous man. The petty jealous man, as Othello is usually portrayed, is Iago. It turns out – I see it clearly now – that it is Iago who is jealous of Emelia in a petty, sordid way. Othello is an exceptionally noble soul. He cannot live in this world with an awareness that people are unjust to one another, that they can with impunity sneer at and spit on the sublime love that dwells within him! And this in the guise of ideal beauty, akin to a goddess, of divine purity and chastity, of unearthly kindness and tenderness! All these qualities are so artfully imitated that they cannot be distinguished from the real thing!

To come back to the scene, I insist that it is not jealousy, but a morbid disillusionment in an ideal woman and human being never before seen on earth. It is an exquisite pain, an insufferable torture. Othello sits for hours in the same position with his eyes fixed at a point in space, his whole being turned inward in order to understand and believe in the possibility of such a Satanic lie. This is why, when Iago cautiously creeps out from below, like a snake, unnoticed, and says, as a doctor would to a patient, with unwonted tenderness: 'Why, how now, General? No more of that,' Othello trembles with a premonition of the pain this torturer can cause him. When the doctor approaches with a huge probe to poke it into the aching wound, the patient groans at the realization of the torture to come. Usually, performers of Othello fly into a rage at this point. In reality this is still a harrowing pain. It is so painful that the earlier cheats and illusions of happiness seem to him at this pre-operational moment to have been happiness. He contrasts this illusion of happiness with what has now happened, and begins to take leave of life. In all the world he has only two passions – Desdemona and the warrior's occupation, like a great actor whose life is split between the woman he loves and his art.

Hence, 'O, now for ever, farewell the tranquil mind! Farewell, content!' etc. is a valediction, a lament, a lament for his second favourite passion and not at all a scene of emotional rapture over the soldier's life, as it is usually played. I shall applaud you most enthusiastically when you freeze into a given pose, motionless, oblivious of everything around you, and envisage in your mind's eye the whole picture that is so infinitely dear to a true master of the art of war. Stop, wipe away the tears that course in great drops down your cheeks, stifle your sobs, and speak in a barely audible whisper, as people speak about what matters most to them, the things they treasure.

This soliloquy may be broken up by long pauses, during which he stands rapt and silent, contemplating to the bitter end what he is losing. During other pauses he might lean over the stone and sob soundlessly and at length, trembling and shaking his head, as though bidding farewell. That is not the emotion of war-like exultation, but a mournful leave-taking on the edge of the grave. After he has bloodied his soul with this farewell, he feels he must vent his torment on someone else. That is where the venting of his pain on Iago begins. And when he has seized him and almost thrown him off the tower, he is appalled by what he is capable of doing and runs to the open space of the flat stone, and drops upon it, racked by unvoiced sobs. Then he sits up straight, like a child, in a child-like pose, on this

532

crag, and asks forgiveness, and pours out his pain to Iago, who stands below him, and at the end of the scene, when it is almost dark, the moon rises and the stars begin to twinkle. Othello, standing on the eminence of the rock, summons Iago, and there, on a promontory between sky and sea, outraged in his finest human feelings, calling upon the moon and stars as they rise above the horizon to be his witnesses, he performs an awesome sacrament, *that is his oath* of vengeance.

Bulgakov's play is very interesting.[10] Will he give it to somebody else? That would be a pity.

Keep the following in mind: if it is set in Molière's period, there is *absolutely* no one in Russia at the present time who could have a feeling for the XVIII century [sic] with the exclusive exception of Golovin. He is ill and works slowly. Once it is settled that the play will be produced next year, the idea should be immediately to order the scenery from him well in advance, all the more because he is unemployed right now and in need. [...]

In reply to your argument that you are an uneven actor, I will answer once again in the mise-en-scène for the next scene. [...]

Yours K. Stanislavsky

Keep an eye on Sudakov. He can so improve the mise-en-scène that it will make you blush.

K. Stanislavsky

To **Leonid Leonidov**. 24 February 1930, Nice.
Dear Leonid Mironovich!

[...] Here is my reply to your two objections:

On Cyprus you want to enter and rush at once to Desdemona. I advised you to receive the deputation first, and then let them go and play your meeting with Desdemona.

You and I want the same thing, that is to push your scene with Desdemona out into the foreground. It was to achieve it that I reasoned in this way: you dash in and embrace her and play a passionate scene. That is what everyone does. That is exactly what everyone in the audience is waiting for. Therefore there is nothing surprising in such an entrance, and without that, you have no edge.

Another sticking-point: how can you play the scene of receiving the deputation after the tender meeting with Desdemona? That meeting requires great intimacy; afterwards you must go home and to bed. But if I see the actor cool down after this and take up his duties as governor general, it would reflect badly on the love interest. As a spectator, I would stop fantasizing about what might go on after the scene ends, in the intermission, when the love will take fire.

It occurred to me, when I wrote out this scene, that it would be more vivid, powerful and advantageous for the love interest in this scene, if Othello first discharged his gubernatorial obligations, during which he would be excited, looking around as unobtrusively as possible, seeking a glimpse of Desdemona. The formalities over and done with, there would be a very intimate scene and exit.

I think that would better achieve what both of us want. It is impossible to tell without trying it out.

As to your next objection: You are against the uprising on the island and explain your reasons. Your reasoning may be correct. Now let us ask Shakespeare: what do he and Iago want? Look at line 46, Iago's words: '...am I to put our Cassio in *some action* that *may offend the isle...*'

This is so clearly expressed and so supports my comments that no further explanations are needed.

Of course, the director can carry out Iago's plan to its conclusion or cut it off at an earlier point. In other words: he can show the uprising (this is a good illustration of Iago's plot) or he can conceal the uprising from the audience, that is to say not let the spectator in on the plot Shakespeare devised for Iago. In the first instance, the whole figure of Iago, Cassio's terrible transgression, Othello's unreasoning love for Desdemona, for the sake of which he flouts military discipline, increase in scale.

In the second instance the whole shrinks to the dimensions of a minor street brawl among drunks, instigated by a wily little blackguard of an intriguer, Iago – and Desdemona would scarcely display any influence over Othello. It is this reduction in scale that I have always found unbearable in all productions of *Othello* without exception.

Only once, at the Hunt Club, I managed to stage it in the way I dreamed of. This was one of the most powerful moments in the production (winning the approval of Rossi[11]). You cannot conceive of how this minor matter magnifies the scale of everything that ensues. If I were there with you, nothing could be easier than to prove the truth of my words, so strongly do I feel this and know it to be true. But at this remove all I can do is keep silent, and leave you to do what you can and feel like, but I warn you that this is very deleterious to the play. It will be on an entirely different scale.

It is awkward in one respect – one has to include a crowd scene in a play that one would like to keep intimate. This is a great liability, I agree. For my part I should do everything to minimize it. I should cut the crowd scene down to the size of the width of the gates, with the rest of it moved to the forestage and entrusted to about ten participants.

I believe that one should never reduce Shakespeare and always try to expand him.

[...] Of course, the deadline that has been set is for a Punch-and-Judy show, if not simply a conspiracy. Do not give in and ruin the performance. Here is a better way to go about it: mount *Othello* as quickly as possible, sort out the mise-en-scène and give the stage to *Fat Men*, but be sure to finish up whatever is still unripe. In the worst case let *Fat Men* go first. Does the kingdom of hackwork have to reign in our theatre? [...]

Yours Stanislavsky

To **Fyodor Ostrogradsky.** 2 March 1930, Nice.

Dear Fyodor Dmitrievich!

[...] 1) After long consideration and inner struggle I have decided to withdraw from participation in the production of [*The Golden*] *Cockerel*. It is impossible to direct from a thousand versts away. Such work will end in misunderstandings and delays. […]

2) […] Now that several years have gone by, they are urging me that a modern opera is needed. Once it exists the theatre can take a risk. What could be better. One need only rejoice. To stage a new opera is not that much easier than renovating an old one. If the opera is a success, it will be a great trump card for the theatre. The whole question lies in its artistic value. I am not speaking about the political aspect, because once the Soviet has passed it, that means that requirement is met.[12]

3) They ask me about the issue of the constitution of the troupe and chorus. In the ten years of the theatre's existence I have insisted on one and the same thing. The ideal is that everyone be a singer who can meet the high demands of the theatre, a good actor – and can sing both solo and in the chorus. Every year we are drifting farther and farther away from this. Quite recently a chorus was engaged. Let them answer on their conscience – can all the singers and choristers sing solo parts and meet the ever greater increasing artistic demands made on our theatre by critics, audiences and the authorities? […]

To be a good operatic actor, you need, of course, not only a voice, but intelligence, culture. Those who have small voices must rely on technique and art. Such a singer will be heard and of use everywhere, in both great and small buildings. Perhaps we have already developed actors of this kind, but because we have not sufficiently tracked their development, must they vegetate in the chorus?! That is, of course, unacceptable. Testing must be more individual and fundamental. I do not recant any of these, my earlier stipulations, stifled and muffled under drop-cloths.

4) […] To have a classical repertoire you have to be in constant rehearsal. When a good modern opera turns up – stop all preparation of classical stuff and switch over to the modern. But until this modern opera appears, --- what is the sense of sitting by the seashore waiting for the weather to change, while the whole troupe is bored and grumbles without new work? Carrying on things this way, of course, we are frittering away all the singers with good voices. […]

Yours K. Stanislavsky

Othello opened on 14 March, but it was weeks before KS had any news of it.

To **Fyodor Ostrogradsky**. After 15 March 1930, Nice.
Dear Fyodor Dmitrievich!

[…] Let me repeat and insist on the *simultaneous preparation of several operas*. Example – the Art Theatre. There for nearly 20 years they didn't listen to me and staged 1 play a year, and now?.. How many have they staged this year? And only because they rehearse up to 7 productions at the same time and work on them for a long time – years.[13]

'Giving birth to a baby takes 9 months, but giving birth to an opera not under a year.' Everything that is done in haste produces nothing but miscarriages and still-births. […]

535

I will not do hackwork, any old way, to a deadline, nor, in view of my health, can I do more. If I am going to be rushed, I will have to refuse such work. This does not mean, of course, that I will deliberately waste time. You know that I do not like to spin my wheels in place during the work process. But I will not open an unfinished piece. I have deserved this right by my long work in the theatre. I will open it only when the production is ripe. I am obliged to say this, and here is why. Nothing spoils young actors and demoralizes the profession so much as roles and plays that have not been placed on straight rails. When this is done well, the actor will grow by himself. Otherwise, he will fall back on his own devices and move in reverse. [...]

To **Leonid Leonidov**. Before 18 March 1930, Nice.
Dear Leonid Mironovich!

Below I list the letters you've sent me. Thank you very, very much for them. You are the only man in Moscow who hasn't forgotten me recently and, despite being mired in work, keeps me up-to-date with what's going on. Ripsi has fallen silent again and sends nothing – neither the reviews of *Chicago* nor any tidings of *Queen of Spades* nor their reviews. The Opera Theatre also keeps mum.[14] This is very depressing for a man like me with a vivid imagination. So thank you all the more. Do not be angry with me for not answering every one of your letters. I do this not because I do not want to, but because I *do not have the strength*. I have put off the book, everything, and am occupied only with *Othello* – so far as I have the strength to do so. Igor is also working as much as he can, because he too is ill, and he has his own regimen, yet he has to write out two copies of my staging-plan. One is for Moscow, the other stays here, in case of loss. Today I sent you 'Desdemona's room' ('The Handkerchief'). (Earlier, a few days ago, I sent 'The Study' and 'The Tower'.)

Today, from your letter, I learn to my dismay, that 'The Handkerchief' will take place in the study. Doing so will destroy the whole *trajectory of the day*, which is so necessary to the play.

Yes! This is a great comedown for the theatre! Once it allows itself to stage *Othello* under such conditions! Classical plays are relevant nowadays only in an *exemplary production*. One must not forget that we are staging it not for Moscow, but for *the whole world*! Here [in Europe] they know everything, they keep track of everything. A foreigner who comes to Moscow is going to see not a contemporary play, but *Othello*. He will use it to evaluate the successes and errors of the theatre. The classical repertoire, especially someone like Shakespeare, is a demonstration of the theatre's reputation for foreigners. This is very important of us at the moment. To achieve fame is very difficult; to lose it takes a minute. 2, 3 serious flops, in the eyes of the whole world, and they will start talking in quite a different key than they do now. Stuck in Moscow, we cannot conceive the significance our theatre has abroad. A unique oasis of art, that's how they refer to our theatre. Gémier dropped in on me (he's here too – ill) and I learned a good deal from him concerning our theatre and its influence. Even the French know all about it. We have not sufficiently appreciated the fact that with the decline of our theatre the tradition of artistic acting will come to an end. This is absolutely the case! Strange as it seems! Yes indeed! Not only the Art Theatre. But you should hear what they are saying about my opera! You wouldn't believe your ears. Suddenly, after all this – *hackwork*.

I swear to you that, with such a production and the administration's treatment of the performance, I would be delighted to remove my name from the poster. I do not do this only for the sake of you, Moskvin and Kachalov. Once you convince me, it means it can be staged, but if I have to make those changes you write about, -- that means that it is no longer my production plan. A consistent *trajectory of the day* has paramount meaning to it. By destroying it (if only by moving the scene 'The Handkerchief' into the study, on the next day, after 'The Tower'), you lose the whole sense of 'The Cellarage'. This last is needed only if Othello, under the impression that the handkerchief is lost and Desdemona is guilty, -- in his despair goes he knows not whither. He went down, down, down and ended up in the *cellarage* – he sat down on a step, stayed there all night long, not even noticing the rats running around him. It is in such a mood that he learns or, rather, sees that Cassio has wound up with the handkerchief – that is why, under this fresh impression, he shouts 'I would have him nine years a-killing!'

If all this takes place the next day, after a pleasant night, in the surroundings of a study – the whole thing changes. Now it turns into *premeditated* murder *aforethought*, and the setting of the *cellarage* has no point. What's worse, it looks like a *director's conceit* to seem *original*. Meanwhile I will go on writing the staging-plan. But I do believe I am wasting my time now. After all you cannot perform what I am writing, what with the existing *hackwork*. To tell the truth, this work costs me a good deal and is difficult to achieve. Write to me candidly. If it is too late and the matter is irreparable, let it come into being as best it can. I know that you are suffering more than I, and sympathize heartily with you and understand your dreadful situation! That is why I want to act so that matters improve for you. But... It may very well be that my demand to take me off the poster will cause a reaction. In short, I leave it all to your discretion. As you see fit. I embrace Moskvin. Thank him, he is lending a hand a second time. He should be put on the poster. And Kachalov too, perhaps. Thank him. [...]

There may be another way. If my name remains on the poster – there is nothing to be done. Maybe, later, when the production is running and they are tearing me to pieces for *eccentricity* and *trying to be original* in the settings, it might then be possible, unobtrusively, to take my name off the poster. [...]

Tamantsova wrote that there was a great distance between Golovin's designs and the finished sets.

To **Ripsimé Tamantsova**. 9 April 1930, Nice.

[...] I am appalled! Why in the world stage *Othello* in that manner?! What have I and my staging-plans to do with it? It's pure illiteracy. I took on *Othello* precisely to try and correct such illiteracy and now it has burst out worse than ever. What's new about it? Where is there any trace of Stanislavsky's staging-plan? I blush for myself whenever I think about it. Could I not somehow have my name unobtrusively removed from the posters? Send me a poster and the reviews (*Othello* and *Queen of Spades*). The French and (I'm told) German newspapers are reporting that *Queen of Spades* was a flop. I know nothing, I'm being hoodwinked. I'm playing the part of the fool, because I don't know what's going on in my own theatre, others do but I, the administrator, don't. I'm not terribly fond of fool roles. Send me the reviews, postcards. Consult Nik. Af. [Podgorny] as to how my name can be taken off the posters but without offending either Leonidov (I understand what he's going through) or Moskvin (who worked on it). On the other hand, why should my name be linked with hackwork? [...]

Don't tell Leonidov that I am upset. Get him to write to me. But do let me know how his health is. Bloody flux is no good. Especially for a diabetic. [...]

Othello enjoyed success with audiences and did great business, but left the stage for reasons unconnected with art. After the ninth performance, 25 May 1930, Livanov got drunk, injured his leg and was bedridden for three weeks. Boris Maloletkov was supposed to step in as Cassio but on the night of 29 May Sinitsyn, the only player of Iago, fell from a fourth floor and was killed. There was talk of Kachalov taking over, but it didn't happen, and the play that promised so much for KS, Leonidov and Shakespeare dropped out of the rep.

Over the next seasons, more Soviet plays were frequently performed. KS, however, rarely saw or commented on them, and only occasionally would take a hand in working with an actor on them. He did not even concern himself with a restaging of Mistress of the Inn *in 1933.*

On 22 April 1930 KS granted Mrs Hapgood power of attorney to negotiate contracts for his writings. Ultimately, she would hold the rights to all of Stanislavsky's writings outside the USSR and its sphere of influence until they were bought by Theatre Arts Books.

To **Ripsimé Tamantsova**. 23 April 1930, Nice.
Dear Ripsi!

[...] Today I sent you the first registered parcel (the same as the staging-plan for *Othello*) of my book, 50 pages from different chapters. On receiving the following packets you will have to sort out these pages, they are numbered. As soon as you get them, immediately with no loss of time, *wire* me: reçu. And nothing more, no extra words. Economize, for heaven's sake, money for telegrams. I have spent all my money here and will return up to my eyes in debt. [...]

One must keep in the mind that the book begins with a plan of the whole scheme, that is all three volumes. Otherwise, I believe it will be impossible to publish the book in parts. In fact: if the first book is issued (Diary of a Pupil. Work on Oneself. Emotional Experiencing.) it might seem that emotional experiencing is of an ultra-naturalistic character, and the book will be violently abused. If at the start of the first book there is a general plan and an explanation that the whole system leads to superconscious creativity, the naturalism of the early phases will be justified.

Of course, they will say that the whole book ought to be published at one time. But if so, it wouldn't see the light for five years, and in the meantime someone else will grab hold of the system and publish it.

But there is another reason why it is inconvenient to issue all three books at once. It consists in the fact that no one will buy three books at once. No one abroad or in Russia has any money. Issuing it in parts, in instalments, so to speak, the edition will be bought up all the sooner.

So, the first book is to be called 'Diary of a Pupil. Work on Oneself. Emotional Experiencing.'

By my calculations it will be nearly 700 pages as published by 'Academia'.

The second book: 'Diary of a Pupil. Work on Oneself. Embodiment.'

Third book: 'Work on the Role, Creative Sense of Self and the Unconscious.'

I don't remember the other books at the moment, where I will speak of the three tendencies in art. [...]

K. Stanislavsky

To Ripsimé Tamantsova. 11 May 1930, Nice.

Dear Ripsi!

I am not writing to Leonid Mironovich because I feel bad. I cannot calm down after the news about Nik. Vas. [Yegorov's dismissal]. L. M. has nothing to do with my silence. All I've heard about him is good things, but about the production, for the most part, they write bad things in the foreign, that is the local papers.

Of course, I'm sorry that I wasted such labour in vain and that my dreams took on a Sudakovian form. But L. M. is not responsible for Sudakov's lack of talent and that the Art Theatre has turned into the Hack Theatre. When I get a hold of myself, I shall write.

What upsets me even more is there is talk again of my not returning.

Can there be no faith in human decency! How cordially and responsively have I been dealt with, how can I not come back after this! The theatre is heading downhill. So is the opera. How can I not return. After all I have devoted my entire life to this business. I have written a book and can now speak about *the fundamentals of dramatic and actor's art*. How can I not return.

Please try to dispel these rumours. [...]

What I am to do with the motor-car? Before I can bring it, I need to know: where are we to put it? It can't be transported and parked in the middle of the yard. Figure out some way of arranging things so that it will cost nothing and everyone – me and my closest relations – can ride in it. Where am I personally to go with it; from home to the theatre and back? It's cheaper to take a taxi. I don't foresee any other excursions. What sort of a passenger am I? Wherever we want to arrange it, I can travel alone. In other words, the motor-car will not move. Best of all would be to sell it when it arrives. But... Do I have the right and who could buy it? With the current miserable financial conditions who would need it! [...]

Yours K. Stanislavsky

In June in Badenweiler KS met often with Elizabeth Hapgood's family and worked with her on translating 'An Actor Works on Himself' into English.

Spring 1930 had been a fraught period for Russian drama. Vladimir Mayakovsky had committed suicide, following the attacks on his comedy The Bathhouse. *Mikhail Bulgakov had spent two years as a literary outcast, his writing forbidden publication and his plays banned from the stage. In despair he wrote to the supreme authority, Stalin. Bulgakov asked to be allowed either to emigrate or be granted a position at the MAAT. On 18 April there came a phone call from the GenSec, allowing him to join the theatre. He was taken on as an assistant director and dramaturg, his first assignment the dramatization of Gogol's epic comic novel* Dead Souls *('I'll be asked to adapt the* Brockhaus-Ephron Encyclopedia *next,' he complained.) He eventually was also named an actor and played the Judge in* The Pickwick Club, *to KS's delight.*

To **Mikhail Bulgakov**. 4 September 1930, Badenweiler.
Dear, kind Mikhail Afanasievich,

You cannot imagine how glad I am that you are joining our theatre!

I had the opportunity of working with you only during a few rehearsals for *The Turbins* and then I sensed the director in you (and perhaps the actor?!).

Molière and many others combined this profession with that of literature!

I welcome you with all my heart and sincerely believe in your success and look forward to working with you as soon as possible. […]

Sincerely and fondly yours K. Stanislavsky

KS was back in Moscow no earlier than 3 November. As she edited the book, Gurevich had scolded KS for immersing himself in his idealistic world and shunning reality, as if aloof from the life of the Soviet Union for the past decade. In a draft reply he explained that he was writing on commission from New Haven University, i.e., Yale University Press, with a deadline of New Year's Day, 1931. He was concerned to provide examples that would suit a capitalist country.

To **Lyubov Gurevich**. 23/24 December 1930, Moscow.
Dear, good and beloved Lyubov Yakovlevna!

[…] Something that I have feared most of all has come to pass. Not the fact that I've lost touch with modern life. It could not be otherwise, I have never left rehearsals or my bed over the course of 5 years. Add to that two years in America – that makes 7 years. But life goes forward at a gallop! All the pages, like 212 'd' and 'e' I showed you, have to be cut and changed. But… *I do not know how to sort out my enormous amount of material and I am drowning in it.* Even more important is that I cannot get going all at once and let the reader in on what comes next.

Every man takes his nourishment by a certain method obligatory to all, chewing, swallowing, digesting etc. This was obligatory for people who lived B.C., and will be those who will live for a few hundred years. It is a physiological matter.

It's the same in our concern; every man takes a play, in a certain way analyses it, swallows it, emotionally experiences it and so on. This is also a psychophysiological matter, obligatory for past and future generations.

In my book I would like to speak *only about this*, not entering into the *who* and *what* and *when* is to be performed or created by the actor. This is a *psychophysiological, psycho- and physico-technique of creativity, and that's all.*

Obviously, I do not know how to organize this in a substantial way. My material will not fit into one or even two books. I consider that it will take no fewer than 5 volumes – 8 volumes. Perhaps these dimensions conceal my inexperience.

My plan for the whole great work is this:

1) *1 volume.* The published book My *Life in Art.* Preface, introduction, the same amateurism, leading to the system.

2) *Work on oneself.* It is broken into *Emotional Experiencing* and *Embodiment.* At first I thought of combining them into 1 volume. Then, abroad, I counted up the pages, I figured out that the text would come to 1200 printed pages. I took fright and decided to make two books (Emotional Experiencing and Embodiment). Now after huge abridgements it seems to become possible again to make the second volume 'Work on Oneself' out of Emotional Experiencing and Embodiment together.[15]

3) *Third book,* or volume, *Work on the Role.* Some of this material you know (it has to be reworked), because Yelena Nikolaevna [Ostrogradsky's wife] copied it out in her time and she still has a copy. In this book in the most detailed form there will be talk of both the *bits* and the *task* and the *through action.* This can only be discussed in regard to a whole play. It cannot be discussed in regard to a little étude. How I tormented myself over this question! How much paper I scribbled over and tore up! Not to speak of the *task* as one of *the elements of the sense of self* is impossible. You barely begin to say one word – all the rest, that is the whole system of the *scoring* and the *through action of the role,* is dragged in, and there is no chance of stopping. If you start to talk about this in detail, it demands no fewer than 30-50 printed pages. This completely digresses from the theme of the second book, devoted to *sense of self on stage* and its elements, and only that ('Work on Oneself').

4) The *fourth book* (and perhaps, this will also fit into the third, that is 'Work on the Role') will speak of the *very creation of the finished role,* leading to the *creative sense of self* (the sense of self on stage, as it moves through the play, develops into the creative one) in capital letters, beyond the bounds of which are found the *creative subconscious.* Only here will the last anonymous banner be unfurled, on which (3rd of the whales)[16] will be inscribed: *The subconscious by means of the conscious.* (This is clearer in the rough draft.)

5) *Fifth book. 'Three Tendencies in Art.' About the art of emotional experiencing* everything is already said. Therefore the book is dedicated to the *art of performance* and *craftsmanship* (in a remarkably expanded sense). Emotional experience will be set forth in the form of a grammar. The problem is it is impossible to begin to talk that about the art of performance until everything about emotional experiencing has been said. In the fifth book I will begin from this: everything that is said about the *art of emotional experiencing* relates for the most part to the *art of performance* +

more – what is experienced has to be amended in its own style and learned to be produced mechanically. If what is performed is still not experienced, -- that means, it's craftsmanship. One can speak about this last point only after they know about the first 2 tendencies.

6) The *sixth volume* is devoted to the *art of the director*, and one can begin to talk about this only after the discussion of the *three tendencies*, with which the director constantly deals and which he is called on to guide and unite into one general *ensemble*.

7) The *seventh volume* will be devoted to *opera*.

Such are my plans, which obviously reveal all my inexperience and impracticality in the realm of literature. Now that I have explained to you my general plan, it will be easier for me to answer specific points.

I have to say as well in guise of preface that I have read much of what I have written (in its unabridged form) to some actors. To Leonidov (who complimented me, but with the aside that the book is so overloaded that it becomes ponderous). I also read it to Marusya. She cannot stand any kind of theory, but in this book she made a grasp at every line, assuring me that it is very useful for the actor and has a remarkably great deal to say.

In addition, an American actress[17] came to me in Badenweiler to take lessons. She also criticized the prolixity of the book, but now writes enthusiastic letters about the successes she has had when she worked there according to the 'system' (I imagine that she skimmed 10-15 lessons?!).

I say all this not to put up defences or boast, but so that you will understand my helpless and confused condition. Hapgood (the husband) offered me first aid with his red pencil. Following his example I too began to cross out more and the book took on the form it has now.

As to your first paragraph I seem to have answered everything. Now the two parts of 'Work on Oneself' – *emotional experiencing* and *embodiment* – are combined. Today I'm sending Ripsi 'Contact', soon I'll send 'Adjustment' as well as 'Sense of Self on Stage', in which I talk about how all the elements combine together and how *the sense of self on stage* is formed from them.

As to your second point, it seems to me I have also answered a good deal. Yes!... I forgot to say something very important. There is an *eighth book*, in which I want to speak about revolutionary art. Don't be surprised by my audacity. But I, ensconced in my own conclusion, know a good deal about the new actor (about their technique, of course). They all come to me in their despair and ask for my advice as to what to do and where to find the truth. When I speak to a Meyerhold or a Tairov actor about the most general features of the principles of the system, they grab on to it. I say the same about the youngsters whom I now observe through my sister at the Opera Studio. As never before – the system is having a success. I am certainly not saying all this to convince you that I am right and not lagging behind the times. Yes, of course, you're right, I am horribly obsolete and admit it. I say it to show only that the question does not exist on the plane of new or old art and its tasks, but on the plane of *psychotechnique* – we understood one other perfectly. [...]

Change, point out, cross out whatever I have written. I give you *carte blanche*. I believe fully in your knowledge. So, for instance, page 212 'd' and 'e.' Here is it's story. (Don't forget that I intend to write about revolutionary art). In the book we're talking about there are discussions of old art that was not created under the Bolsheviks. That is why the examples are bourgeois.[18] If that's a mistake, it has to be corrected. After all many chapters were written 20 years ago (psychotechnique knows no era). Teach me: should they be translated into modern examples? Which ones? (This is what scares me. The book *My Life in Art*, so far as I know, enjoys success with the youngsters even now. They understand it perfectly. I get letters from them that say as much.) [...]

You are afraid of changing my personality. But the problem is that I myself don't know my own personality. [...]

Yours K. Stanislavsky [...]

From 1931 a nurse, Lyubov Dmitrievna Dukhovskaya (1871-1947), was in constant attendance on KS until his death.

To **Mikhail Geitts**. After 12 January 1931, Moscow.
Dear and much esteemed Mikhail Sergeevich!

[...] 1) The troupe is completely exhausted. The old-timers are all ill, and, if the concern needs them, they need to be taken care of.[19] One has to be an actor oneself to understand how difficult it is to act tragedy four days in a row.* I know that the leading roles are alternated. Nevertheless such a stint is difficult. In addition, it is very expensive. The costumes for *Fyodor* are worn out, are barely holding together, and it is no longer possible to repair them. There is no such fabric for costumes. And it is impossible to obtain museum pieces (which are taken from my personal items).[20]

Before a big tour it is best that the public forget about us for a while. This will increase our success many times over. This year our actors have made far too many appearances in Leningrad. People have got used to them, and this diminishes the success of a big tour.

2) It is impossible to move [*Marriage of*] *Figaro* from place. If it were otherwise, I would long ago have taken it to show in Leningrad. But I did not allow this, to spare the material. In addition, without a real revolving stage – precisely to the dimensions of our theatre – there is no way to do the production decently. It is dangerous to stage the production on revolving *platforms*. We risk the stage not turning at the right moment, and will have to let down a curtain between scenes. Meanwhile the production and its rhythm are calculated on a rapid change of scenes before the eyes of the spectator. Without this – the play will become unrecognizable.

The scenery in Golovin's tones will not endure the jolting of railway cars. They are painted and will lose their chief splendour – the colour. They will have to be freshly repainted. It is impossible to demand that this work be done with all the care as it was originally. It will cost too much. The repair will be done as hackwork, and we will have one good, fresh production the less. Requests were made to take this production to Berlin and Paris. I refused for the same reasons I am stating now.

Need I mention the costumes. What will be left of the panniers, laces and white silk netting of the XVIII century! And the cut-out scenery! These are reasons which force me to protest against including the play in the Leningrad tour.[21]

3) It should be remembered that there was also talk about next year's repertoire, which has been remarkably delayed. The fact is that I myself staged five plays in the course of one season [1925/26]: 1) *Pugachyov Times* (Nemir-Dan.), 2) *The Ardent Heart*, 3) *The Decembrists* (2 versions), 4) *Merchants of Glory*, 5) the public dress rehearsal of *Turbins*. All the plays were carefully worked out, and were not hackwork, because this repertoire was prepared a year before it was produced (except for *Decembrists*). In our theatre it is extremely important that a play be installed in the mind of the actor a certain number of times. Only under such conditions do our actors know how to perform well. They are bad at hackwork.

At other theatres it is the opposite. There they are good at hackwork, but do not know how to prepare and think about a play for a long time. After10, 20 rehearsals they no longer know what to do with it, and they feel that it's high time for them to perform the production. [...]

Respectfully K. Stanislavsky

To my mind, one has to make an effort to shorten the travels, excursions and tours.

* Moskvin didn't mention this, I did. He is not complaining and has given no thought to this.

To **Genrikh Yagoda**.[22] Moscow, 26 January 1931.

Deeply respected Genrikh Grigorevich!

Forgive me for disturbing you with a personal request, but the matter on which I am writing gives me, an invalid, no peace.

My nephew, Mikhail Vladimirovich Alekseev, his wife Aleksandra Pavlovna Alekseeva (née Ryabushinskaya) and her sister Nadezhda Pavlovna Ryabushinskaya[23] were arrested in June of last year and so far have been kept in confinement in Butyr prison.

A few days ago in the apartment where the prisoners' children live, by order of MOUNI (Disposition of Real Estate of 28 December 1930 no. 1021/8 on the occupation of rooms of those officially exiled) residents were settled into 2 rooms.

This circumstance leads me to think that OGPU has come to some decision regarding the Alekseevs and Ryabushinskaya and, obviously, they will be exiled.

I do not know what they were arrested for, how great is their guilt and whether there is any possibility of their remaining in Moscow.

If there is absolutely no way of doing this, then I beg you, deeply respected Genrikh Grigorevich – to alleviate their lot as much as possible and not to separate husband and wife. And if they are indeed exiled, then allow them to travel at my expense to the place assigned them.

In addition, I beg you to allow their children to be given the property under seals and grant them the right to occupy the sealed room, especially since at the moment they are living in a single room 134 square feet in size – four of them together: two very elderly women, my nephew's daughter Tatyana Alekseeva, aged 18, and her brother, Sergey, a youth of 15.

I know no peace thinking about them, especially my nephew who suffers from angina pectoris.

Knowing your kind relations with me, I am deeply certain that you will do everything you can, and I beg you very, very much to help in this matter. Believe me, by this help alone you will alleviate my torment over persons near and dear to me.

Once again I beg you to forgive me for troubling you, and allow me to hope that you will not dismiss my request without some follow-up.

The phrase: 'Accept my sincere respect and devotion' was blue-pencilled in the manuscript by Podgorny.

Geitts was meeting with non-cooperation from the younger members of the troupe which led to inactivity. The crisis of discontent came to a head: Sudakov and Batalov, supported by RAPP, were ready to move with their supporters to TRAM, the proletarian theatre movement.

To **Mikhail Geitts.** 1 March 1931, Moscow.

Deeply esteemed Mikhail Sergeevich!

Forgive me for writing on such a scrap of paper but my writing implements are in disarray owing to illness.

If everyone is against the strenuous work that has to be done to improve the neglected artistic aspect of the concern, one has only to note with sorrow a new token of the downfall of our art.

I cannot force them to do it, it is impossible to bring them together for discussions and attempts to persuade them either.

All I can do is warn of the serious danger threatening our concern.

The oncoming season cannot be artistic, but must perforce be hackwork, without any preparation.

When I am free I will devote 1½ months to the opera business and try to show through it the results of the work which the MAAT has repudiated.

At the earliest opportunity, as soon as the doctor permits me, I shall phone you and be glad to talk about the matter.

With sincere respect K. Stanislavsky

To **Lyubov Gurevich.** 9 April 1931, Moscow.

Dear, kind Lyubov Yakovlevna!

Forgive me for writing on paper with little holes in it. I have no other at hand. Thank you for your letter, in answer to which I repeat once again: do whatever you find necessary.

Inner human life. Leave it as is.[24]

As to *organic authentic feelings*. You don't write what to call them. I agree to your name for them.

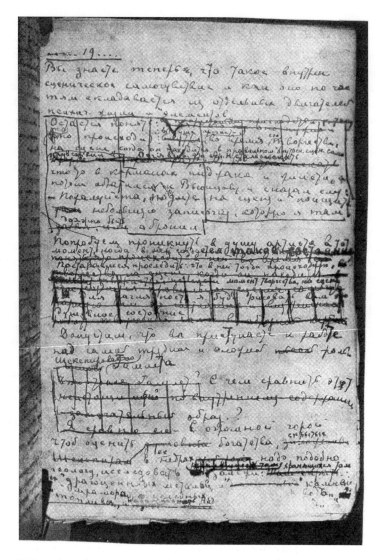

Figure 77 Page from the manuscript of *The Actor Works on Himself*

I also make a distinction between theatrical and authentic emotional experiencing. Obviously, this distinction is not clear enough the way I put it. I say that on stage the performer lives by a feeling that is authentic but of affective origin, that is, prompted by affective memory, whereby the feeling is purified of everything extraneous.* This feeling is the quintessence of all the feelings that resemble it. Thanks to this purification and condensation it is sometimes more intense than the authentic real-life feeling.

546

Not long ago I was told that a certain female patient, convalescing after an operation, all but went out of her mind, and suffered the most violent nervous derangement not during the operation and not directly after it, but when she had returned home, to her own room, and remembered how the illness had begun and all its consequent events. And there are plenty of such examples. When I was in the sanatorium in Streshnev, there were many such people who had gone crazy from memories of tortures and punishments inflicted on them many years before.

The actor lives on stage precisely by such memories of the past, and I call them the authentic ones.

When we stimulate these affective memories on stage, they and their ilk are instantly animated. What animates them is the quintessence – the synthesis. To my mind, this is stronger than the authentic feeling of a single private instance. There is another minor nuance: why actors love the word 'magical'. It says: *if* the case had been thus and such, what would you have done? To speak in all candour, however I may have behaved this very day, it is essential to perform exactly the same thing that goes on in life; to rack one's brains the same way, to put out the antennae of intuition in the same way. At those moments or instants the performer completely forgets the stage and lives the most authentic human life. The only difference is that at those instants he sometimes feels the authenticity of his experiencing more deeply than in real life. Do these moments lead to madness? Fortunately, no. But they do lead to unconsciousness, as well as to a kind of exalted feeling. (At a public dress rehearsal of *Tatyana Repina* Mariya Nikolaevna [Yermolova] fell under such a peculiar spell that it alarmed the audience. The spectators thought that she had actually poisoned herself. Yermolova herself could not give a lucid account of what had happened. This is not madness, of course, but moments or instants of a kind of strange abnormality.)

I am telling you things that you know better than I do. But this is not the point. The point is an imbecilic, untamed and untalented audience that has no understanding of or feeling for art. Moreover, -- an ignoble audience that gets caught up in nit-picking words, like Afinogenov,[25] when not long ago a certain gentleman asked him: can you understand what Stanislavsky means when he says 'when you play a villain, find the good in him'. To which Afinogenov replied, 'It does me more good to understand the things I say.'

You go on to say that they arise at the desire of the actor himself, through the magic *if*. Therein lies the magic quality of the *if*, that they arise not at the actor's desire, but by the actual necessity of life.

The secret is that the actor neither desires nor does not desire. He answers the question he sets himself: what would I have done, if ... and so on. He would do absolutely the same thing as in life, and if he would want to behave differently, then he would be falsifying, underacting, would not be experiencing in the right way, and would not believe what he is doing on stage.

But, now I repeat, this is not the point, the point is the idiotically clever audience. One has to adjust oneself to it which I do not know how to do and in this I trust you completely.

You go on to write that they (that is, behaviour and emotional experiencing on stage) take place impersonally, by means of the magic *if*, removed from *personal* interests. To my way of thinking, this is not quite right. Creative moments on stage are *the only ones* evoked by the magic *if*. Therefore I will discuss them now. If I sincerely answer the *if* question when it is posed, at that moment I am living my own personal life.

At those moments there are no *roles*. There is myself. All that remains of roles and the play are the conditions, the *circumstances* of its life, the very same vestige of my personality that relates to me personally, because the whole role in every one of its *creative* moments belongs to the living individual, that is to the performer himself, and not to the dead schematic individual who is the role.

All the particulars and details of life left out by the poet are restored in the actor's playing of the role. This occurs invisibly, in pauses, in the subtext, it is contained in the feeling itself, which is transmitted by the actor, who has become the synthesis of all the analogous experiencing with all its accompanying details and proposed circumstances included by the poet. These last, I repeat, are restored by the actor to the life of the role with the help of his fancy, imagination, which enshroud them at all times as clouds do a mountain.

You go on to write: 'They result in consolidation, compression in scoring the role by means of the creative consciousness.' Yes. First of all they result in consolidation – the imaginative concept. Which I just spoke of. What is compressed is only what is irrelevant to the actor in real life, what goes unnoticed there and only distracts him from the essentials that do matter. To my way of thinking, this fortifies and does not vitiate the organic quality of the emotional experiencing.

You go on to say that in real-life events unfold not through the creative consciousness but involuntarily.

But actually is there not the greatest lack of volition and complete unconsciousness in creative intuition, imagination, which conceives its fancies or, more accurately, divines authentic life and prompts its feelings. Authentic life will never prompt us on its own to what goes in the life of our imagination. That realm makes possible things that are undreamed of in real life.

But once again I repeat that all this matters to me and you, and not to that idiotic audience, which will nitpick the terminology to show off its dull wits.

The *magic if* replaces the *creative if*. If necessary, make the replacement. It will be necessary to add a footnote or put (magical) in parentheses, because it has gained immense popularity among actors here and abroad. Not long ago I read an article by Charlie Chaplin who bases all his creativity on the magic *if* (presenting it as his own invention).

I completely agree with you that this requires a specialist. What is curious is that I am writing about the most difficult psychological moment – the creativity of the mind, but I myself have never read a straightforward account or even a couple of books on psychology. This amuses me and surprises me at the same time. I am totally ignorant, and therefore your help and the help of a specialist are indispensable to me. I have already asked Podgorny to talk over this matter with

548

Shpet.[26] He did, apparently, but I don't know the result. Today Podgorny returns from Leningrad, and I will ask him.

What do you think, what financial inducement should I offer him? This question is beyond my abilities to decide, so removed am I from all kinds of scholarly and literary matters. [...]

I embrace you. Christ has arisen. I kiss you thrice.

Yours K. Stanislavsky

* I agree that it is not the affective memory itself that has performed this purification, but by whom, what and how it is done – I don't know.

To the **Supreme Prosecutor of the USSR**. Petition. Between 26 April and 11 May 1931, Moscow.

My nephew german Alekseev Mikhail Vladimirovich and his wife Alekseeva Aleksandra Pavlovna were sentenced by the Collegium of OGPU to 10 years in a concentration camp. At the time of their exile from Moscow two children were left behind – a daughter Tatyana Mikhailovna Alekseeva, aged 19, working at the present time in Moscow, at the Lenin Library, and a son Sergey Mikhailovich Alekseev, age 15, studying at School No. 42 of the Baumann Department of People's Education in Moscow. They both reside at no. 12 Little Kharitoniev Lane, apt 22.

In view of their desperate financial condition, as well as the lack of any close relations outside of Moscow, I request permission to provide them with a residence in Moscow and take their maintenance on myself.

I request that my petition be granted.

People's artist of the Republic [K. Stanislavsky]

The petition was granted. However, Mikhail Alekseev had died in the prison hospital and on 27 May KS had to write to Yagoda to be appointed guardian of 'his orphaned children'. Tatyana Mikhailovna Alekseeva (Chetveryakova, 1912-40) became a physician, but died of tuberculosis in 1940. Sergey Mikhailovich Alekseev (1916-?), became a construction engineer, was exiled after Stanislavsky's death, and died in an old-age home in Syktyvkar in the remote Komi Republic.

To the **Art Sector of Narkompros**. 20 September 1931, Moscow.

In reply to your memorandum of 10 Sept. 1931 addressed to all the state theatres of Moscow and Leningrad and in particular to our theatre, I consider it necessary to inform you that as a result of discussions with Com. M. S. Epshtein[27] concerning the artistic-productive work of this season Com. Epshtein found it necessary to give our theatre special treatment, exempting it from excessive obligations to conduct specific political campaigns and charging the MAAT in given cases to carry out such requirements only with the official stamp of the Narkom for Enlightenment or his representative.

Administrator of the MAT
People's Artist of the Republic K. Stanislavsky

On 11 October KS inspected the work that Telesheva, Sakhnovsky[28] and Bulgakov had done on Dead Souls. *He told them they had gone up a* cul de sac, *and the work had either to be restarted from scratch or discarded totally. He objected to the lack of reality, the hyperbole, and particularly the use of a narrator. The production had to be a showcase for the actors, not the directors.*

Although KS's letter and Gorky's intervention in the struggle with RAPP had prevented the MAAT on coming fully under government control, its Committee for Political and Artistic Affairs was liquidated and on 20 October the Red administrator Geitts was relieved of his post. KS invited Nikolai Yegorov to return and fill the gap. In hopes of refreshing the repertoire with plays by Bulgakov and Erdman, KS chose to go directly to the top and addressed the GenSec.

To **Iosif Stalin**. 29 October 1931, Moscow.
Deeply esteemed Iosif Vissarionovich!

Knowing your abiding interest in the Art Theatre, I turn to you with the following request.

You already know from Aleksey Maksimovich Gorky that the Art Theatre is deeply interested in Erdman's play *The Suicide*, which the theatre regards as one of the most remarkable works of our era. In our view, Nikolay Erdman[29] has managed to expose the various manifestations and ingrown roots of the philistinism that puts up opposition to the construction of the nation. The technique, with which the author has revealed the philistinism of real people and their hideousness, constitutes an original innovation which is, however, wholly in keeping with Russian realism in all its best representatives, such as Gogol and Shchedrin, and is close to the traditions of our theatre.

Therefore, after the author completed the play, the Art Theatre thought it important to apply its expertise to demonstrate the comedy's social significance and artistic authenticity. However, at the present time this play is banned by the censor. So we would like to request your permission to set to work on the comedy *The Suicide* in the hope that you will not refuse to inspect it prior to its opening as performed by our actors. The fate of this comedy could be decided after such a showing. Of course, the Art Theatre will not involve you in any expense for the production prior to its showing.

Stalin's reply which came ten days later offered a low opinion of the play and referred KS to the Repertkom report, but allowed the theatre to 'experiment' with the assistance of an official from the Department of Culture and Propaganda. At the same time he recommended to the Politburo that the Art Theatre be turned over to the TsIK.

To **Lyubov Gurevich**. 9 November 1931, Moscow.
Dear Lyubov Yakolevna!

My delay in fulfilling your request, that is, sending the unfinished chapter about speech, is not my fault, but due to Rips. Karp.'s ill health. I am sending the only manuscript, which is left from my book. There is nothing more. I don't understand what 'Gymnastics' chapter you are talking about. Besides what has been written I have nothing to say. My goal is to lead the student up to that lesson, but I do not intend to teach the subject. My goal is to say: a) gymnastics prepares the basic, raw muscular centres; b) dance goes much deeper and selects subtler centres. But neither gymnastics nor dance can provide plastiques, but only prepare the student for a new subject; c) plastique.

All I wanted to say about ethics *somewhere* (?) in this book is that it is one among several general conditions. But I did not want to discuss ethics in detail until the students wind up on stage, and that will occur only in book 2. Before I write that chapter, I have to read and research material and various definitions of 'ethics'.

'General sense of self.' There will not be a separate chapter, because one needs only to say two words about it, that is 'unite inner and outer senses of self, and you will achieve a general sense of self'. I said so in the chapter about *external senses of self*.

On training I thought I would stick to what is said (if I'm not mistaken) in the very last and final words of the whole book.

On gesture I said (I don't remember where) that I allow on stage no gestures, but only *action*, movement. In relation to movement plastique everything is said in the corresponding chapter.

On mimicry I said (I don't remember where either) that one need only develop and exercise all the facial muscles. Then they themselves will do whatever is necessary and naturally reflect emotional experiencing. I cannot say any more about mimicry, except that from now on it is wrong to study it out of existing books which teach actors to make grimaces imitating fear, joy, sorrow, etc.

Nor can I say anything about the mimicry of the eyes, because it is impossible to make the eyes glisten. That happens instinctively.

If I knew the latest researches, perhaps, they would prompt me to something. […]

Yours K. Stanislavsky

To **Lyubov Gurevich**. Autumn 1931, Moscow.

I do not understand how to convince you that I agree in advance to everything you will delete, insert, rewrite, change, rephrase in different words. I assure you that I have absolutely no ambitions or vanity. I am not a writer and do not wish to be one. I need only to present what I have learned during a lifetime in art. Once more I give you complete *carte blanche* and thank you in advance for every excision. I myself would excise half the book, but I have stopped understanding it. I understand those concerns you are feeling. I would like to relieve you of them by assurances that I believe in you alone –unconditionally.

What third person should I appoint? I have no one who would really have a feeling for the system. My wife?.. But she doesn't understand contemporary life at all. Leonidov? He is not very contemporary either and… lazy. Truly, I have no one. You alone, and so I have all the more faith in you and once more I ask you to do with the book whatever you please. My trust is total. […]

Yours with all my heart K. Stanislavsky […]

In early December 1931 at a plenary meeting of RAAP the MAAT was accused of 'idealistic and metaphysical roots' counter to socialist experience. The 'system' was condemned as ahistorical and abstract. (Meyerhold was also attacked for his biomechanics.) On 16 December the MAAT was subjected to the authority of the TsIK and was officially renamed the Moscow Art Academic Theatre of the USSR. The high status this conferred made it a 'court theatre' with the attendant benefits and restrictions. A government committee headed by A. S. Yenukidze decided not to appoint another Red administrator or deputy administrator, because Yenukidze realized that the appointment of someone unfamiliar with the theatre's work would create undesirable results. And there was no one appropriate at the moment.

The opening of Fear, *a very apposite play about the reluctance of elderly intellectuals to accept the Soviets, took place on 24 December, directed by Sudakov. It was regarded as a powerful and politically acceptable move to a Soviet point of view. At the eighteenth curtain call KS bowed from his box.*

To **Delegates to the VIII All-Union Congress of Art Workers**. 8 January 1932, Moscow.

I am writing this letter because I cannot greet in person the delegates to the congress whom we have the honour of welcoming today within the walls of the MAAT.

The questions which we are gathered here to resolve strike me as important precisely now that theatres have the possibility of proceeding directly on the path of renovation and rebirth of their art.

The foundation of our future work must be based on the beautiful and salvational principle of the high *quality* of the productions created, and not simply their numerical *quantity*.

We are to set ourselves to the difficult and engrossing task: we must help each other, especially the beginning actors and those who have erroneously been led astray from authentic art.

Where are its fundamentals and what do they consist of? *In the natural organic laws of the creative nature of the actor.*

Unfortunately, we devote little study to these laws.

We do not know much about the physical nature of the human being, starting with the food he consumes. But how many of us have studied the ways we consume the artistic impressions which serve us as material for creativity. How many of us know how they are converted internally and externally? For after all the consumption is carried out by the laws of organic nature, and one cannot deviate from them with impunity. That would entail an inevitable displacement in the direction of crude craftmanship, which causes the destruction of art itself.

The crucial thing is to make haste and study not 'fashionable', but authentic, natural, organic laws of our creative nature and the fundamentals of art. Such a decision forces us to pay great attention to the age-old traditions of past art and study them more thoughtfully and perceptively. We must make haste as well, because there remain few representatives among us who preserve the original tradition of a departing art of the past. They may quickly and forever disappear from the earth, as happened with ancient art, *bel canto* singing and so on. Indeed the creativity and technique of an actor disappear with his death.

We must make haste, because the final period is upon us.

Theatrical art, which has deviated from the true path, has been carried away by external form, having forgotten the most important thing – the inner essence. This common mistake has led us astray, seeking easy paths to the line of least resistance. Therefore it behooves us to begin with the serious study of organic laws of creative nature for their practical application to our art.

This will be the first measure in work that improves the *qualification* of actors and stage workers.

Such an improvement is particularly important now when the outlines of the theatre of the future are beginning, if only very faintly, to be drawn.

Young drama has achieved a few successes in the technique of writing, but a revolutionary theme will be deepened within the psychology of modern human beings. Russian literature, which up to now in the vast majority of its works is grounded in negative types, seeks positive images of heroes.

Their personification on stage requires of us and in no short order new methods of creativity and complicated artistic techniques. Are we prepared for this? If not, it may happen that the beautiful plays we are waiting for will not be suitably performed. An inaccurate overestimate of our assets has been mistakenly created by valuing what is easier and more accessible.

Hence *formalism* and *the lack of personal responsibility*, so dangerous to our art.

Each theatre requires its own approach. What is useful for one is harmful for others. The proof of this is the rapid deterioration of the powers of the best actors, heart dilation, nervous and other ailments and the general overstraining in not only old, but even in the youngest actors. A more careful treatment of them is essential, especially for those of us who work on stage not with the external means of hands, feet and bodies, but the most hidden parts of our innermost creative organism.

Nowhere is 'egalitarianism' more dangerous than in our creative activity. In this question we come close to resembling our dangerous competitor, that is the cinema, as well as our chief enemy – *hackwork* – in all its various manifestations and noble camouflages. It is essential to establish a correct reciprocity with our competitors and regulate, plan, organize the work of actors on the side. Under contemporary conditions it seems to be inevitable for financial considerations, and this leads us to the question of the everyday conditions of those who labour in our art.

They are dreadful and demand improvement for many as quickly as possible. A pay scale for most stage workers is needed. Living expenses, queuing, workloads beyond one's strength, inadequate rest, sanitary conditions, cold and, chiefly, residential conditions, that bring on a special species of psychic ailment. If these everyday living conditions are not regulated first of all, then all the rest of the objectives we aim for will be impossible to achieve. The housing question affects even the fact that many actors perish in the backwoods, where they can neither perfect and develop their talent nor employ it in proper measure and form. There are more than a few cases when capable actors, unable to find a niche in the capital, leave for the provinces where there is no possibility for the further development of their talent. We must tackle this question and get down to the building of homes.

In conclusion I consider it my duty to direct your attention to the new explorations and requirements, which offer the theatre and its art a new life.

In various places of our boundless country they are building gigantic theatres, counting on almost fifty thousand spectators. It is proper to resolve the question – is it within an actor's human powers to fill these gigantic buildings? Will these new conditions not lead to a mighty abasement of art? And is it not proper for specialists and this assembly to address this question and define the maximal dimensions of buildings, appropriate, on one hand, for dramatic, and, on the other, for operatic and ballet performances.

On 18 January 1932, before his departure abroad, KS's seventieth birthday was celebrated and he was decorated by Kalinin at the Kremlin with the Order of the Red Banner. From Nice, he strove to procure a new studio which was granted him. His return to Moscow was greeted with great pomp.

To **Elizabeth Hapgood**. 7 April 1932, Moscow.
Dear, good Yelizaveta Lvovna,

I am not writing you but dictating, not because I don't have the strength to hold a pen in my hand, but because I am most strictly forbidden to do so by the doctors. The fact is, after influenza in January and February, during which I was bedridden for six weeks, I am back in bed, lying here for the fourth week. Now the illness is passing, but it was serious: influenzal collapse of both lungs; over the course of two weeks my temperature soared very high, up to 39½ (our top number is 40½). Now my temperature is nearly normal, but I am as weak as after a very serious illness, and I am still in bed, probably for the next two weeks if not more.

I write you all this to explain my protracted silence, during which I had time to receive two or three of your wonderful letters. The last one upset all of us very much, because you write me about a certain unusual post-war disease of the mouth, associated with the teeth (and everything connected with them horrifies me) and the tongue, part of which, as you write, had to be cut out. What does this mean? Did they cut out the small uvula at the back, in the throat, or are you talking about the tongue proper? The latter is incomprehensible and terrifying. Write when you get the chance. To finish with illnesses, I will say that my kidneys and heart function splendidly and those are my most vulnerable spots. This last year influenza was especially virulent among us; everyone fell ill, Gurevich too. We, two moribund old folks, she an editor, I a writer, have completely exhausted you, a young translator, with our seventy-year-old pace: here it is April already, and not a single chapter has gone to be copied, and meanwhile there's nothing to send you. Not for a single second do I attribute this to any malicious intent of Gurevich herself, because she is an utterly exceptional person in terms of conscientiousness, honesty and nobility. I cannot rush her, because she herself is madly embarrassed and upset by the delays that have occurred. You won't understand this, but when you consider that all our work has, by the laws of our country, to be checked against dialectical materialism, obligatory for everyone, then you will grasp how this affects an enormous work all the more since it must not violate the very fundamentals of my system, to be presented in a form clear and comprehensible for the West. In the last analysis, it all has to do with terms and words, that won't alter the essence, but finding and selecting these words is difficult and painstaking and requires great tact. So don't hold it against Gurevich. Now she has to have a meeting with me, but meanwhile no one is allowed to see me and that means a new delay.

What is one to conclude from this? I think that she will not succeed in finishing the book soon; I think that chapters will begin to be sent for copying comparatively quickly, and then we will start to send them to you for translation. When will you get the whole book? In the very best and happiest case – before summer, maybe, and during the course of it. I have to think that when it starts to get warm, which is not the case here yet, Gurevich and I will be able to meet more frequently. If you only knew how difficult it is, how ashamed I am to write all these words, how guilty I feel towards you and the publisher – but what is to be done? 'The cobbler should stick to his last.' I've taken on a task beyond my strength. Forgive me, do not get angry and apologize to the publisher. I have to close – I am tired.

I kiss your hands and send heartfelt regards to all your family.

Affectionately K. Stanislavsky [...]

In April 1932 the Central Committee's resolution 'On restructuring literary and artistic organizations' marked the official end to radical experimentation in the arts. The Politburo resolved to liquidate independent organizations of writers and replace them by the monolithic Union of Writers. Ten days later, RAPP was suddenly disbanded without any warning, removing one of the MAAT's inveterate enemies from the cultural landscape. Meanwhile, yielding to Stalin's solicitations and promises that he might reorganize the supervision of writers, Maksim Gorky returned to Russia from Sorrento. Socialist Realism was now the approved method for every branch of culture.

To **Maksim Gorky**. 28 April 1932, Moscow.
Welcome back, dear Aleksey Maksimovich!

I send you greetings both on my behalf and that of all the comrades in our theatre. First of all we want to thank you for what you have done for the MAAT.

We have received what we have long dreamed of, heaved a sigh of relief and can gradually readjust our affairs, which were in the process of complete disintegration.

Thank you for your help and the trouble you have taken.

I have had a very bad winter. At various times I have been bedridden for some four months in a row, and am still not on my feet. But I hope to be so soon and then -- I shall shake your hand in person and sincerely thank you once again.

Sincerely devoted K. Stanislavsky

To **Mikhail Arkadiev.**[30] Before 17 May 1932, Moscow.
Deeply esteemed Mikhail Pavlovich!

Our theatre has received strict instructions in writing and by telephone from the Sector on arts to put on suburban performances in the KOR theatre in mid-May (17 and 19).

Of course, if you find it necessary to insist on it, your command will be carried out.

But allow me in this present letter to abnegate the responsibility for much that this demand can entail, in connection with other conditions probably unknown to you. This is what they consist of:

1) After an enormous delay, which came about because of the collision of two productions, ours and the N-D Mus. Theatre,[31] we had to take on massive staging work on *Gold. Cockerel* in a hurry – under dreadful conditions: in the dark, without scenery workshops, with the general decline in energy thanks to all the adversities which fell to the lot of the theatre this season. The work went cumbersomely, and the troupe, like the whole collective, is tired to death. This is especially dangerous in operatic matters, where we are dealing with singer's voices.

2) In view of the Mus. Theatre's departure and our daily performances with a great number of matinees, the troupe has enormous work in prospect, which will exhaust it even more, especially since our team of choristers and prepared soloists did not count on daily performances.

3) Before the theatre goes on tour it is absolutely indispensable to inspect and improve all the scenery and costumes for all the plays that are being sent to Leningrad.[32] Even the actors' performances require such review, for during the season in many ways they deviate from the true line. This also demands enormous work, which will wear out the actors of the theatre even more.

4) The away performances for the suburbs, which you require of us, coincide with the time for repairing and sending the scenery to Leningrad.

5) The newly improved scenery will be spoiled and broken in a strange suburban theatre unfamiliar to us and will require fresh repairs. You know, of course, that travel ruins scenery, which is frequently torn and spoiled to make it fit a strange stage.

6) Besides rehearsals with the actors, arduous rehearsals with the orchestra are required. There are few days for them, thanks to the matinees and other work. The 17 and 19 are very necessary to us at once for these rehearsals.

7) In agreement with A. Serg. Bubnov and Moisey Solom. Epshtein[33] and you, it was settled that each theatre will perform public service. At other theatres, which know how to and can moonlight in hackwork -- -- this work can be carried out in tours to suburbs and collective farms. But we, and in particular I, do not know how to and cannot moonlight in hackwork. Therefore a different public service was laid on us: the formation of cadres. We have begun preparations for

that work, although we have not been issued the means for this. We are working with young people and are preparing for broader activity. To do two jobs, that is, moonlighting and school, is impossible. One cancels out the other. Therefore, as was decided – assign us to forming cadres.

Nevertheless I have agreed to the arrangement of *well-organized systematic* performances at KOR. For this I mustered my strength to prepare youngsters and perhaps a whole troupe and have not repudiated this intention for the moment. However I agreed to do this under the single condition that the performances would be *organized*, the suburban theatre prepared for this kind of established troupe.

What they are demanding of us now appears to be *pure hackwork*. Under the existing conditions away performances cannot be anything else.

Judge for yourself: in the morning they transport the scenery. During the day somebody, free from the ongoing work of the theatre, goes to arrange the lighting and scenery. There is no order in the theatre. Often they have not called on and waited for an answer from the necessary people and secured the necessary assistance of the local officials and workers. The dressing-rooms and the lighting in them are in disarray and there is no way to make up. Dirt, darkness, costumes lie around on chairs, tables and often on the floor, because often there are no hangers. The actors, worn out by the disorder and disorganization, cannot act decently in the slightest degree. This is especially felt by us, with our creative method. Add to this a paltry orchestra of 20, playing an opera with complicated orchestration. A large number of musicians cannot be seated in the narrow space for the orchestra.

How can such a performance be called anything other but hackwork?

My half-century of service to the theatre gives me the right to expect that in the last years of my life I will be exempt from what I have been fighting against all my life.

But if I am needed for hackwork and there is no way to exempt me from it, if it is impossible to settle and confirm once and for all what has been already been contracted with you and my other superiors, if the constant meddling and changes of mind by new individuals who have joined the Arts Sector team, is unavoidable, then I most respectfully beg you to tell me so straight out, so that I know what is required of me and how am I to conduct myself and how I am to be freed from this work which I find to be intolerable.

With utter respect [K. Stanislavsky]

In 1932 under TsIK, the MAAT was renamed for Gorky. An extensive plan of building, expansion and improvement of its theatre buildings, as well as of solving the problem of housing staff, was put in motion. The major repairs began in the summer of 1932. KS was afraid that the renovations just begun at the MAAT would drag on and force the theatre to tour to Leningrad, but that did not come to pass. An architects' competition for constructing a new building for the Opera Theatre was also held. In 1934 building began on Glinishchev Lane of a house for the theatre workers and the construction of apartments for actors and sitting tenants at 22 Kirov St.

In May Nikolay Yegorov had been appointed deputy administrator, though he was on bad terms with Sakhnovsky. Although his bailiwick was supposed to be the financial department, he often interfered in artistic affairs and behaved like a surrogate KS.

To **Nikolay Yegorov**. 15 August 1932. Pension Klein. Badenweiler in Baden.
Dear, good Nikolay Vasilievich!

Just a few days ago when we had hellish autumn weather, I envied anyone who was broiling in Moscow. But today, after our weather turned heavenly, I think a great deal about you, whose fate it is to be boiled in a cauldron and breathe the dust of construction sites. I very much fear for you! You have to think about your vacation. I know little of what's happening with you. Someone wrote here that the construction is proceeding with great difficulty. I decoded this phrase: withholding of materials. That is worst of all – agonizing and helpless. Obviously, I conclude, the season will begin after a great delay.[34] If that is the case, what is to be done? Touring? Or rent one of the theatres that happens to be vacant? The latter is probably better for productivity, but the tours are more pleasant for the actors. But here's what's bad about touring: scenery which has only just been repaired gets tattered on the road and on its return there is no time to fix it. Besides, while on tour, you have to forget completely about the production plan. That is very bad. This year we were to present on the main stage *Dead Souls*, *The Suicide* and *Molière*.[35] I think that *Talents and Admirers* is finished. Let me say in secret that I have hopes that the play will go well, if two or three roles are replaced, and that the production might be presented on the main stage. Besides that, Gorky on the Small stage.[36] Yes! All this on condition that Nemr.-Dan. will return and *be able to work*. I am not up to it by myself, because once again I stayed home all winter long and sank into bed the same as last year – nearly five months. What's bad is that travelling, if it becomes necessary, will offer nothing new (except for performing *Fear* in Leningrad). A repetition of old news. That is bad. Every one of our tours should be a new revelation. [...]

Dear Nik. Vas! I don't want to burden you with a new chore and ask you to write to me. But if you could have someone else answer me, even if in the most cut-and-dried manner, the following questions:

1) How is the turn-table being repaired? Are there delays?

2) What is the new electrical wiring like? Does it work well? Is there a shortage of material?

3) Is a building being constructed in place of the annex with the collapsing walls?

4) How is one of the most important and troublesome questions being decided, building housing for homeless actors, such as Stepanova, Livanov etc.?

5) Did we get the adjacent Rabfak building and is it being adapted? If so, then how. Whom are they going to accommodate there and how?

6) How is the renovation of the Small stage going? Will it be heated?

7) How about the question of fuel supplies for the winter for both theatres?

8) Are there any changes: instructions, individuals in the administration?

Figure 78 The façade of the Moscow Art Theatre on Kammerherr Lane in 1930

9) What about the question of advertising the competition for the new theatre and what have you heard about this work? […]

1) My lifelong goal: to consolidate the existence of the theatre and the position of the old-timers in it after my death. If they are to be placed on the proper level of respect, then their positions will be fortified. And not only the three of the troika, but through them the other old-timers. This is to be done not for the sake of protection, but because, when Nemirovich and myself are gone, only they can maintain the true traditions of the MAT. If this does not happen, then the government will install the Sudakovs, and, as practice has shown, in a few months it will be turned from the MAT into the former Second Studio, with all its bad habits of acting. Then – woe to the old-timers! They will put an end to them! We are led by these speculations to appoint a *troika*. To which Leonidov remarked: 'But what will happen if we fail?' This danger impels him to be especially cautious.[…]

Now a few words about myself and the family. We are living with the family (the one pleasant thing and the sole justification for this trip). Igor's wife is very sweet and fits in with the household.[37] It's as though we had lived with her for ages. She is not good-looking, but her figure is all right. Igor is more or less well, but horribly thin and, far from putting on weight, is actually losing it, which is very bad for him. Kira has lost weight and looks charming. My grand-daughter Kilyalya has shot up frightfully. She speaks French like a Parisienne and I worry that she's too Frenchified. But she's very slim and svelte, and with our family history (tuberculosis) that is very alarming. She's funny, talented, highly strung and temperamental – to the nth degree. In addition, poor little thing, she's about to undergo an unpleasant operation – removal of her tonsils. This absolutely has to be done here, abroad, before they return to Moscow. In addition, she now requires a frightfully nutritious – and, moreover, specially doctor-prescribed – diet. She is ordered to be wary of colds and 'flu. All these reasons and conditions would make one think twice before taking her to Moscow, and the same for Igor. We'll have to spend yet another year alone! But on the other hand you can leave Bryusovskaya in the apartment for another year. [...]

To **Nikolay Yegorov**. Before 24 August 1932, Badenweiler.
Dear good Nikolay Vasilievich!
    I am writing to you about Vl. Iv.[Nemirovich-Danchenko].
    Evidently his is a difficult situation: penniless, in debt, in Berlin the mood is dreadful on account of the political events. His condition is very depressed and extremely debilitated. There is no doubt that he is seriously ill. Something has to be done for him. I asked Leonidov and Kachalov to visit Nem.-Dan. in Berlin and figure out in some detail what might be done for him. Just now I received the information that he has been sent money for living expenses from Moscow, but quite an insignificant sum. If efforts could be made to supplement his money, perhaps even my opinion will be required. In that case I asked Vl. Iv. to write to me a letter in reply to my advice as what to do to be able to return to Moscow eligible to work. In this letter I am writing my opinion and I sent the letter to you. Perhaps, it will be necessary.
    It is beyond doubt that Vl. Iv. is seriously ill and his condition is a difficult one. We have to help him. There is not much he can do in Moscow, but all the same he is able to shape up a couple of plays as desk work. And this is a great help to me, because I am alarmed by the enormous amount of work ahead of me, which has to be carried out. Otherwise the troupe will start to get bored and will boil over again.
    What is happening with you I do not know.
    Now people are saying that the reconstruction is going successfully and that it will all be ready on time. Most of all I fear your overexertion! Give this some thought. [...]
    The most urgent necessity for the coming season is not to overtire the troupe with a large number of performances, to provide more time for the work in rehearsals and organizing groups of ten and their re-education. [...]

                                                                    K. Stanislavsky

Yegorov replied on 30 August that in June Yenukidze had sent 500 dollars to ND in Berlin; in addition he had been given 2000 marks in Spring. The Sovnarkom decided to allow ND another 1000 dollars, and, this, in Yenukidze's opinion, exceeded the amount originally requested for the trip.
    At the beginning of the season the Committee of the TsIK instituted a reorganization of the administration of the MAAT; Sudakov, on its recommendation, was appointed chief

of the planning-industrial portion in lieu of the stage director Boris Arkadievich Mordvinov (1899-1953), who had worked at the Second Studio and MAAT from 1921.

To **Vasily Sakhnovsky**. 2 September 1932, Badenweiler.
Dear Vasily Grigorievich!

[...] Once the committee promotes Sudakov, I cannot fail to take their wishes into consideration and agree to put him in the position granted to Mordvinov. Please try to see that this does not make a bad impression on the latter and undermine his energy. However with this agreement I would like Av. Sofr. [Yenukidze] to know my following views of Sudakov.

1) I do not consider him especially malicious, but he has a bad penchant for theatrical intrigue. He cannot be considered a student of the MAAT when it comes to ethics and traditions. Moreover, he is a typical representative of the old 2nd Studio, which had good artistic strengths, but very, very bad traditions, which were created, along with others, by Sudakov. That is why I always maintained that after our death the chief danger for the MAT was to be expected from Sudakov's part. He will quickly turn the theatre from the MAAT into the 2nd Studio, in which the chief task will be the family protection of the ringleaders.

2) I consider Sudakov an exceptionally energetic, industrious individual. Such an activist (minus his shortcomings, which cancel out his qualities) is extremely necessary to us, and if he might be turned into a sincere follower of the traditions of the MAT, it would be very fortunate for the concern. But for this Sudakov would have to be completely reborn and re-educated, reformed, instructed. He is unintelligent, ignorant, conceited through and through, smug and self-satisfied. Many of these gifts are necessary, but in proportion. His are out of proportion.

3) As a go-getter and producer (administrator, but not an artist), I consider Sudakov very powerful and valuable. But as an artistic stage director and adherent of the MAT – as weak as can be. His fame as a director is much exaggerated. He has not staged a single play on his own, and when he has had to do so, it was bad (*Othello*, the first version of *Ardent Heart*). Bulgakov's *Turbins* – the inner line. *Armoured Train*: the scenery, I and Simov (in that performance more powerfully and better than in the others where I appeared myself). *Grain* – Moskvin, *Fear* – Leonidov. When Sudakov has good advisers (he knows how to listen to them), then he can prepare a play well. But he cannot finish it according to our demands. This is no surprise. But the strange thing is that he does not want to learn from this.

Sudakov is the ideal director for hackwork, when one can skim along the surface of plays. He knows how to cast actors, rehearse quickly with them and skillfully put on a performance which (considering the speed of the production) is successful. But if you took him off a rushed production and provided the time for a good artistic performance, -- he would be in a tough situation. And look more closely at such performances – how many of the merits in them are superficial.

4) I write all this to put you on guard against one particular danger. As a go-getter – Sudakov will hurry a production along. This is good. But in so doing will

he remember what is most valuable for all of us and, as it now appears (to the great fortune of the MAT) for the Committee of the TsIK and the Party. Will the productions Sudakov drives to open on time be truly artistic, worthy of an Academy, and can he understand how to achieve that artistic quality, does he know that if you start talking about opening a production ahead of time, too early in a period dangerous for its formation, it can dislocate the artistic process. How many such dislocations Sudakov would have had, had I not held him back and delayed the opening of unprepared productions.

So one must always reckon with this shortcoming or Sudakov's actor's nature in future. Sudakov in the role of a go-getter can be uniquely useful and – dangerous.

5) One must convince Sudakov and demand of him that he begin to study everything from the beginning. If we move to his work with actors, it seems that he works with actors entirely the way he performs himself. He does not know the elementary things essential for an actor, but what he does know, he understands superficially. Most typical of his lack of understanding is his audacious proposal for *Mary Stuart*.[38] It bespoke the naïvety of his lack of understanding. He flits through art and the repertoire, which he wants to create completely the same as fluttering through all of Europe in a few weeks of a schoolboy's summer vacation.

In his career he has always done everything: staged a series of new plays, put on the classics – Shakespeare, Schiller; he staged operas, he taught, set up as a professor, became an authority... all this is no more substantial than his travels through Europe in 20 days.

He plumes himself on these achievements of his, but in my eyes, on the contrary, he depreciates himself precisely by this prematurely extensive but shallow surface activity. Can he study everything from the beginning again now? If yes – he is saved. Nothing more will ever come of him, but he can easily become a 'worldwide celebrity' à la Sanin. But if he begins to set down to business seriously, and in all earnestness (and not in frivolous hackwork) tries to understand what the MAT is, he can become in future a great man and a necessary one – badly needed – for the future MAT, in which so much hope has been invested.

6) I consider Sudakov unbusinesslike, in the purely administrative sense of business. He has shown this in all the duties he undertook in the theatre (management, troupe, a member of the group of five, promoter in the production side). He has to learn from the very beginning, it's a good thing we've got such an expert in business affairs as N. V. Yegorov. And in this realm there are laws, traditions, techniques, knowledge of how to get on with people or retain them. This has to be known.

[...] A few words about *The Suicide*. Ask Av. Sofr. straight out: are we to stage the play or turn it down? I stood up for it for the sake of saving a brilliant work, for the sake of supporting a writer's great talent. If the authorities cannot view the play with our eyes, only trifling and delays will come of it. What's more, if I am not mistaken, we accepted the play before our admittance to the TsIK. Perhaps the TsIK is against the play.[39]

At this time there was talk of creating an Academy of Theatrical Technique under the MAAT. This idea originated with Gorky when he met with the MAAT's 'old-timers' at KS's lodgings in September 1931. Almost a year later Yenukidze 'was speaking in clear-cut terms about an Academy' that gave a push to starting organizational measures.

To **Leonid Leonidov.** 26 September 1932, Badenweiler.
Dear Leonid Mironovich!

[...] Can it be that [Aleksey] Tolstoy has written a good play, suitable for our theatre?![40] I am afraid for *The Suicide* in the sense that the actors do not believe in the possibility of its being realized, and therefore the work will proceed without energy, and meanwhile it is most important from the artistic aspect... and difficult!![41] [...]

It seems to me that the old-timers have earned the right to act only on the main stage. Merely walking up the staircase deserves that. Even the youngsters complain. What a pity that the Small stage can't be replaced by another, more suitable one. Meanwhile this will not be done – the financial crisis and niggardly wages will not be eliminated.

Pillars of Society! Good Lord, what a crashing bore. I cannot forget that dreadful production and my ten fits of sweating while I played Bernick [in 1903]. Can Khmelyov really be enthused about it!?[42]

Here's where the doubt comes in. Can all 15 plays be put together so that they can be rehearsed so that none will overlap and the work be delayed, as was the case with *The Suicide* and *Dead Souls*? In secret I tell you I can appreciate Sudakov. Yes, he is capable and has the energy to drive the directors with two whips and torment the actors in order to distinguish himself and fulfil the plan. But this is the most dreadful thing about Sudakov that you will have to endure. Sudakov's tempo is mechanical, he cannot produce artistic results. When it comes down to this energy of Sudakov's, -- remember his excursion abroad: 'around the world in 80 days'. He travelled but saw nothing. Just like now, he has staged everything one can in a long career as a stage director, but, in fact – he has not one single production that can be called an original artistic work. Under such hurried conditions it is impossible to speak of an Academy and exemplary performances. I repeat, now even I most fear after my death 'Sudakovitis', meaning his activity, which destroys an *artistic* theatre. [...]

Affectionately yours K. Stanislavsky [...]

To **Nikolay Yegorov.** 19 October 1932, Badenweiler.
Dear, good Nikolay Vasilievich!

[...] I am so depressed by all the blows which fall upon me that my nerves are completely shattered. That's why, perhaps, everything appears to me in an extraordinarily gloomy guise. I have long felt, and now I know, that things are not going well with you. Between you and me, I did not like Leonidov, when I spoke with him here. I was very moved by the attention and confidence of the powers-that-be, but a few lines after the advertisement of the course on the 'system', on classic drama --- I then read a declaration of Ilya's trust... Sudakov's Academy!!

[…] All this paints a chaotic picture of the work awaiting me in Moscow. Add to this the sharp rejection of Lyub. Yakovl.'s book which I did not expect. And my completely altered financial situation here, that is the impossibility of a big advance for the book which my children need; finally – the meeting and quick parting from my family, with the thought, natural for a 70-year-old, that encounters and contacts may be the last ones. All these conditions, along with the jittery mood of the West, have completely broken me, and I am more tired than I have ever been, and cannot wait until I get out of here. If it weren't for the children's poor health and my wife's overstrained state, I would have escaped from here long ago. With every moment things seem to be getting worse and worse in Europe. We may have it hard, but at home there is something to live for, whereas here is a void, a grave, dying and appalling boredom. […]

K. Alekseev […]

On 28 November 1932 Dead Souls *opened, but the critical reaction was hostile. The Communist press condemned it as unconcerned with social and class questions; belletrists such as Bely thought it missed the whole grotesque facet of Gogol. Nevertheless, as a showcase for veteran actors, it remained in the repertoire into the 1960s, playing 1,039 performances.*

Goldoni's commedia play The Servant of Two Masters *was prepared by group of MAAT youngsters to be performed on club stages. Sudakov decided to move it to the Small stage. KS saw it on 4 December 1932 and categorically rejected it; Sudakov reworked it a bit but Yenukidze upheld KS's veto. The MAAT mimeographed bulletin then printed an openly hostile note against KS, which created a great stir in theatrical circles (almost all the Vakhtangovians were on KS's side). This publication turned even Sudakov's adherents against him. Others complained to the TsIK and Yenukidze, who, after seeing the play on 26 December, decided it could be performed. The next day KS convened the troika which resulted in an address to the Committee.*

To **Avel Yenukidze**. 27 December 1932, Moscow.
Deeply esteemed Avel Sofronovich!

After inspecting *Servant of Two Masters* on 26 December 1932 V. G. Sakhnovsky informed me of your decision to open the production as a public performance, as well as of the request of I. Ya. Sudakov – in accord with his agreement with you – that I give him a visa for the public performance of this play after my second review. Nevertheless I consider it my obligation in all candour to inform you once again of my personal opinion of the production, which has taken firm hold in me. I consider that this production is dangerous for the art of the MAAT, because the actors of the theatre contract professional clichés in it, with which they then, inevitably, will infect other plays. I consider that this production is superficial, devoid of 'through action' and therefore internally meaningless. These fundamental flaws can be avoided only by way of deepened work, having attentively and profoundly opened up the play and having worked out both it and every role along the lines of the through action. For this the few rehearsals held by I. Ya. Sudakov and the collective of actors are insufficient. On 5 December of this year, after my inspection of this play, I informed I. Ya. Sudakov and the actors of my opinion of the necessity of prolonged and profound work on the production, because to perform it in the presentational manner in which *Servant* had been performed, means contradicting the very system of the theatre; indeed this very 'presentational manner' demands great technique in the mastery of speech, voice, movement, knowing how to wear costumes, which the performers of *Servant* by no means possess.

Therefore I consider that from the artistic standpoint the production of *Servant* in the guise in which it was shown me cannot have a place in the MAAT USSR named for M. Gorky.

I am steadfast in this stand, especially given those directives I received from you, which I accept in full and which define the line I take in the theatre. I have instructions from you about the need to educate a Theatre-Academy, the unimportance of haste in opening plays with regard to their quality, deepening the content of the production, the training of great, internally rich expert actors. I agree with you that only by this path can the theatre our country needs be created in our time.[43] The production of *Servant* contradicts all these principles utterly, and, in opposing it, I am only upholding the line of the theatre you have set down.

I cannot regard the production of *Servant* outside the general question of the theatre. It is merely a sample of that abnormal condition, which is destroying the line of the theatre and which will develop into a deviation from the proper actor training, called for by the government.

The industrial plan accepted in my absence is, in essence, infeasible. It promotes a phony trend for mounting productions rather than promoting the actual artistic growth of the theatre. Plays created over the course of 2-4 months cannot live as works of art, because they skim along the surface and do the actor irremediable harm, cultivating in him a light-minded relation to creativity and foisting on him a workmanlike, stereotypical approach to a role. The actor, working simultaneously on 2-3 roles, dissipates his energies and, without creative concentration, offers an assortment of stereotypical devices, leading him from life to the worst shams, and the longer it goes on, the more incapable the actor becomes in conveying great themes. Therefore the proposed plan will inevitably eliminate the actor's art and is alien to the ideas of the Art Theatre.

Servant seems to be only an example and consequence of this plan. It is supported and led by a specific faction within the theatre. Since there have arisen between me and the adherents of this plan very great differences in principle, which concern the very essence of the art of the MAAT, I propose as the only way out the following measures, set forth in the attached address to the Committee to this letter from the Board of GABT and the MAAT USSR named for M. Gorky.

If, despite my explanation (which I have been obliged to lay out), you are pleased to have the production of *Servant* go on on the stage of the MAAT USSR Gorky Theatre, I submit to your command, but allow me to abnegate responsibility for this failing work of the theatre.

K. Stanislavsky

The attached address suggested that Sudakov and his group form an independent collective in the former Korsh's Theatre. The Committee acted on the proposal, making it an affiliate of the MAAT, with both theatres under KS's general leadership. KS insisted on Sudakov's departure from the main stage of the MAAT so that the leadership was in the hands of the troika. Servant did not open on the MAAT stage; after reworking it played in suburban clubs. This victory indicated that KS was now assuming a more authoritative role in the government's eye: that of an exemplar and monitor of the excellence of Soviet art.

Notes

1 The second Russian edition of *My Life in Art*, published in December 1928 by Academia.
2 Yury Nikolaevich Chistyakov, physician, who accompanied KS on his trip abroad 1929-30.
3 In 1924 Hapgood had published KS's memories of Anton Rubinstein and Tolstoy in *The Forum*. As far back as 1914, he had proposed that KS stage a play at the Stage Society in London.
4 The familiar faces on the Board in 1928-29 were Batalov, Zavadsky, Markov, Prudkin, Sudakov and Khmelyov.
5 The moving gondola was an obsession: he had first proposed it for the *Othello* of the Society of Art and Literature in 1896; then in *Merchant of Venice*; he reworked the staging plan for the first two scenes of *Othello* in 1929 to have the gondola move in front of Brabantio's house.
6 Vladimir Aleksandrovich Popov (1889-1968), actor at the MAAT 1908-15 and 1936-68; he was the sound technician for the production.
7 The music was written by R. M. Glière. Sergey Nikiforovich Vasilenko (1872-1956), composer and conductor. Zueva's husband was Viktor Aleksandrovich Oransky (Gershov, 1899-1953).
8 George Pierce Baker (1866-1935), American professor, who founded the 47 Workshop in playwriting at Harvard (1905) and the Yale School of Drama (1925).
9 A group photo of the MAAT actors in front of the White House. Hapgood is next to Vishnevsky, Mrs Hapgood next to KS. Hapgood had visited Moscow and the theatre in 1923.
10 An early reference to Mikhail Bulgakov's play about Molière, sometimes known as *The Conspiracy of Bigots*.
11 Ernesto Rossi saw *Othello* on 22 January 1896.
12 V. M. Leshevov's four-act opera *Ice and Steel* had been accepted and KS had roughed out the first act, mailed 9 March 1930. One act takes place in a factory, another in a windstorm.
13 In the 1929/30 season the MAAT put on six productions: *Uncle's Dream, Resurrection, Chicago, Othello, Our Youth, Three Fat Men.*
14 The doctors had insisted that KS be kept from any excitement.
15 Later he divided it into two parts again.
16 A reference to the medieval Russian notion that the world was supported by whales.
17 Eunice Stoddard, an actress with the Group Theatre, had studied in the 1920s at Richard Boleslavsky's American Laboratory Theatre.
18 Gurevich had told him, in view of the frightfully impoverished condition of the intelligentsia, not to refer to jewels and fortunes, because they would embitter and depress some readers, offend others. In an early draft of the letter, KS explained that he is unsure the book will be published in the USSR, but that 'the most bourgeois country there is' will accept it, unless he includes Gurevich's examples, which will guarantee it will be banned there.

19 Geitts replied that the old-timers were not overworked at the theatre, but 'wildly, under nightmarish conditions, disgracefully and freakishly moonlighting' all over the place. 'Moskvin is beating all records in this respect (and he is far from having to.)'

20 The theatre was taking *Tsar Fyodor* to Leningrad 3-6 February, hence KS's concern.

21 Geitts had not allowed *Figaro* to go to Leningrad and was surprised KS did not know about it.

22 Genrikh Grigorievich Yagoda (1891-1938), dreaded head of the secret police; from 1924 deputy chairman of OGPU, from 1934 Narkom of the NKVD.

23 Mikhail Vladimirovich Alekseev (1886-1931), KS's nephew, a physician. Aleksandra Pavlovna Alekseeva (Ryabushinskaya, 1888-?), his wife, also a physician. Nadezhda Pavlovna Ryabushinskaya (1887-?), her sister, also a physician.

24 In line with dialectical materialism, Gurevich had proposed to change 'life of the human spirit' to 'inner human life'.

25 Aleksandr Nikolaevich Afinogenov (1904-41) headed the theatrical sector of RAPP and was a Marxist dialectical-materialist who opposed the MAAT. At a RAPP conference in Moscow (25 January-6 February 1931) he had criticized the MAAT and the Stanislavsky system as hostile to proletarian theatre.

26 On 24 May Gurevich wrote to KS that Gustav Gustavovich Shpet (1879-1937), philosopher and vice-president of GAKhN, 'has already pored over' half the book in order to 'bring it in line with modern European science'.

27 Moisey Solomonovich Epshtein (1890-1937), Deputy Narkom of Enlightenment.

28 Vasily Grigorievich Sakhnovsky (1886-1943), historian and critic, began as a director under Komissarzhevsky; anti-realistic, he sought romanticism in his productions. In 1932, he became deputy administrator for the artistic division of the MAAT. Cold and sarcastic, he loathed his opposite number Yegorov and his stagings rarely met with KS's approval.

29 Nikolay Robertovich Erdman (1900-70), playwright and cabarettist, whose satirical comedy of hasbeens and parvenus *The Party Card* (*Mandat*, 1925) had been a great success for Meyerhold.

30 Mikhail Pavlovich Arkadiev (1896-1937), an official at Narkompros.

31 The Musical Theatre was putting on *The Fair at Sorochints* on 12 January 1932 which delayed the opening of *Golden Cockerel*.

32 The tours to Leningrad opened on 6 June with *The Clandestine Marriage*.

33 Andrey Sergeevich Bubnov (1883-1940), Narkom of Enlightenment 1929-37.

34 The 1932/33 season opened on 1 September with *Fear*.

35 In 1932 only *Dead Souls* was produced.

36 *Out in the World*, a dramatization of the third volume of Gorky's autobiography, which opened on 25 September 1933.

37 Igor Alekseev married Lev Tolstoy's grand-daughter Aleksandra Mikhailovna Tolstaya (1905-85?).

38 *Mary Stuart* was included in the repertoire schedule as an experimental work for the 1932/33 season with Yelanskaya in the leading role.

39 Rehearsals had begun 16 December 1931 and went on till 2 May 1932.

40 The literary department was working on Aleksey Tolstoy's *Patent No. 19* but it was not produced.

41 Leonidov replied that work on *Suicide* could continue for the exhibition performance.

42 The play was not revived.

43 Yenukidze believed that only one person should have authority in the theatre recognized by all. Anyone who did not obey should leave. The MAAT should not be producing hackwork.

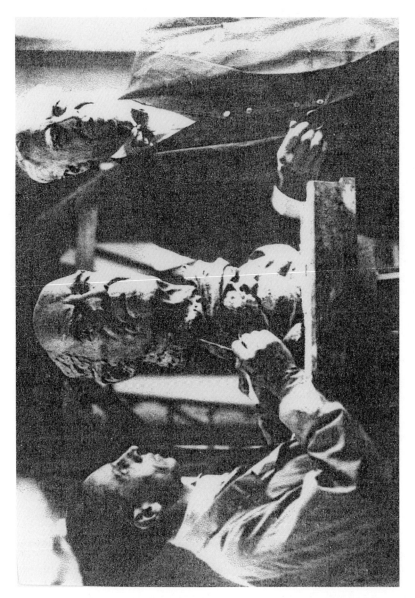

Figure 79 Stanislavsky sculpted by N. P. Gavrilov in his studio 1935–36

12

BECOMING A MONUMENT
1933–1938

As the second Five-Year-Plan was put into gear, there was a return to traditional family values among a new middle-class. The assignment of housing and communal apartments allowed for greater scrutiny of family life and the repression of individuality. The population became more passive in its obedience to dictates from above. A cult of Stalin began to take shape.

The diminution of individuality in private life was replicated in the arts. 'Levelling' and 'standardization' were the bywords. In August 1934 at the First Congress of the Writer's Union Gorky and Andrey Zhdanov pronounced Socialist Realism to be the style for Soviet art. Plays, films, ballets and other performances were to be reviewed by the censors at least ten days before their official opening. On 16 December 1935 the All-Union Committee for Artistic Affairs was established to bring every aspect of cultural life together under one roof. This latest phase of centralization turned the spotlight more directly on the performing arts, as all the theatres were put under the Committee's supervision in December 1936. More than half the new plays and productions produced by the leading theatres of the Soviet Union in the 1936/37 season were forbidden by Glavrepertkom as insufficiently socialist-realistic or too formalist.

Individuals and institutions branded with formalism or 'Meyerholdism' were severely reprimanded, transferred, stripped of authority, arrested, exiled or, in the most extreme cases, executed. Denunciations, the gloating of the favoured and the demoralization of the rest, were the order of the day. Quarrelling among intellectuals served as a prologue to the Great Purge which began with the murder of Sergey Kirov in 1934 and ground on for another five years. An estimated ten million citizens were arrested, interrogated and banished to labour camps. In February 1936 the Second Moscow Art Theatre was closed.

Now classified as a cultural treasure, KS found himself insulated from much of this turmoil. He was in an ambivalent position: constantly honoured with lip-service to his achievements, he was distrusted by old-timers and youngsters alike. They feared his unending rehearsals and reiterations. He would happily have given up staging plays in favour of research on acting, but worried that if he were merely a teacher, no one would come to his classes. His system of acting was converted by the educational bureaucracy from a living, evolving art form into a dogma. The rapidly rigidifying principles of the MAAT were reconfirmed as the correct aesthetic system for the development of Soviet theatre: the directive to actors and directors was 'study at the MAAT', a tenet of conformity that severely stunted the stage's artistic development.

Gorky's new play Yegor Bulychyov and Others, *a character-study of a dying merchant beset by charlatans and faith healers on the eve of revolution, had been produced in 1932 by the Vakhtangov Theatre in Moscow and the Bolshoy Dramatic Theatre in Leningrad with considerable acclaim. The MAAT was slow to take on the play.*

To **Maksim Gorky**. 6 January 1933, Moscow.
Dear Aleksey Maksimovich!

I am getting to work on *Bulychov* [*sic*] [. . .] In this play I see the best pretext for laying bare my relationship to theatre and the modern world. I would like to work on the play seriously, within the schema of our art, without haste, because its meaning lies in the depth of ongoing problems, and not in a chronicled depiction of actions. On your arrival I hope to have material for discussion with you of our approach to the play, because by that time several scenes in *Bulychov* will have been worked out with the actors.[1]

I am very sorry that I didn't manage to meet with you during your last stay in Moscow, because I came back from abroad after you had departed. At that time I would have liked to discuss a range of problems with you, which have the highest degree of significance for the principles of the theatre. At the present moment they have become so exacerbated that they demand a very clear, unequivocal and categorical resolution. At their base lies a single quintessential problem of how to understand the role of the MAAT at the present time, the understanding of its special and particular art, unlike the art of other theatres. Within the theatre we formulate it as a question of 'breadth' or 'depth'. That is: should we devote all our strength to understanding, deepening, and developing our art, without pursuing a number of performances, or should we – following the example of other theatres – attempt to give a swift and therefore transient response to topical matters, without thought of deepening our art?

It would be naïve to think that, confronted with such a question, I would cut myself off from the demands of contemporaneity; on the contrary, I believe that the MAAT is obliged profoundly and not superficially to respond to current events; to look into the heart of a matter, and not its outer surface. I want a theatre of *ideas*, not a theatre of recorded fact. In all sincerity I want to say that I do not see a different role for myself in our time – I want to devote the remainder of my days to the education of actors and the enrichment of the actor's mastery, so that it is capable of conveying the deepest and strongest feelings and thoughts of humanity in our time.

I had the impression that your position in regard to the MAAT coincided with my views. You were not far off the mark when you defined the position of the MAAT as a theatrical Academy.

There are, however, many obstacles to this growth in 'depth'. In the last few years the theatre has greatly increased in 'breadth' – it has a team of more than 120 actors of whom many demand work which we cannot give them and which they cannot sustain in the MAAT; there have been productions in which the art of the MAAT has not achieved the requisite standard, -- that caused dissatisfaction and depression. As a result a group has formed, which to our watchword 'depth' has opposed a striving for 'breadth' – the rapid-fire and prolific output of plays and a new conception of the actor. I see no way out except to partition the theatre, so that the basic MAAT can pursue its chosen line with consistency. I consider it essential to concentrate all our forces within a *single* theatre without any affiliated stages – and with that single troupe, with a shared understanding of art, I hope to achieve the necessary results. It seems to me that outside the theatre the entire seriousness and acuteness of the situation that threatens the ruin of the MAAT will not be properly appreciated if the measures I have proposed are not adopted quickly. I have sent A. S. Yenukidze two papers (I will send you copies) with a request for a decision. I hope that you will help us in this critical moment in the theatre's life.

I firmly shake your hand and send regards to your whole family.

Sincerely devoted K. Stanislavsky

To the **Participants at the Birthday Soiree**. Mid-January 1933, Moscow,

[…] One of the reasons why I declined an official celebration was that I did not want to tire out actors, already much harassed by new public appearances. If, despite it all, you wished to gather today, today's festive occasion touches me even more and intensifies my feeling of gratitude to all the organizers and performers in the celebration, to every one of its participants and to all the guests without exception. [. . .]

At the time we are living through, when the human heart and mind are unsettled by historical events, it is difficult to unite a large group of people with one common idea that will bind them together. We artists are lucky that way, because we are united by our art, which at every historical moment grows ever more necessary for people's inner life. However, nowhere more than in art are there so many different opinions, viewpoints, ways, 'systems', discoveries, differences, enmities and quarrels. They all divide people. Yet, in spite of this, we are bound to each other. It may be said that at today's gathering my friends and comrades in art, my students and people of like mind – we are united by *Stanislavsky's 'system'*. What is that?

At the present time this system in each of the theatres that has grown out of the Art Theatre has developed into quite a different, new, often contradictory one, and, in spite of this, we are not strangers and are bound by a common element that unites and guides everybody along the path of art.

What sort of bond is it? It is a bond to a system, but not only Stanislavsky's system, but to a system of the greatest of artists, the 'creative nature of man'.

This nature and its creative laws are the same for all people, all trends, all persuasions of genuine art. In regard to these creative laws, we are all kith and kin. Whenever the matter involves a deviation from nature into the domain of countless stylizations, we become strangers and stop understanding each other.

I write all this to make our bond clearer, more lucid and well-defined. I devoted my whole career as a performer not to creating a new art of my own invention, but purely to a most thorough and painstaking investigation of the creative nature of the performing human being in myself and in other performers, in my pupils, in amateurs, musicians and singers. My labours were not those of an inventor, but of an investigator. They have not been in vain. This gathering of my friends, comrades in art, collaborators and pupils, united by a common faith in the 'system' of the greatest of artists, human creative nature, proves it. It alone is eternal, understood by all and essential to everyone who approaches art.

My second bow is for my friends and to people of like mind as a mark of recognition for the idea in art common to all, and that unites us.

The theatre is in the throes of a worldwide crisis, and in our country too all is not well with art, but nevertheless, thanks to the concern shown by our government, art is advancing and not dying. When we think of the future and of our dangerous rival the cinema, we already foresee the gloomy future for all the bad theatres in the whole world. They will have to make way for the Great Silent One, which has begun to speak so loudly.

But, despite all this, I predict a rosy future for the theatre. There will be fewer theatres, but, on the other hand, those that survive will be splendid, imbued with genuine art, and genuine art springs from the laws of creative nature. Those who study them and follow these laws may rest assured that no danger threatens them, and the flower of renewal awaits them. But those who have departed from nature should return to it as quickly as possible.

Human nature is infinite in its diversity, and therefore an endless number of attitudes and trends in art will be created from its laws. So much the better. It is something we should welcome, because if all types of art resemble each other like two drops of water, they would be boring, and there is nothing worse in the world than boring art.

Therefore let everyone create as he wishes, as best he can, let him do what he wants, let him draw a few eyebrows and circles on his face, provided everything he does is inwardly justified by the eternal and compulsory laws of creative nature.

My third bow goes to the like-minded, who are destined to perform the immense role of rescuing the dying art of the actor through a return to the eternally young and unfading art of that greatest of artists – nature.

To **Nina Tikhomirova**.[2] 20 January 1933, my 70th year, Moscow.

I have lived long. I have seen much. I was rich. Then I became poor. I have seen the world. I have had a good family, children. Life has scattered them throughout the world. I have sought fame. I found it. I have been honoured, been young. I have grown old. Soon I must die.

Now ask me: what does happiness on this earth consist of?

Gaining knowledge. Of art and of work, in the attainment of it.

By gaining knowledge of art in oneself, one will gain knowledge of nature, the life of this world, the meaning of life, you would gain knowledge of the soul -- talent!

There is no happiness greater than this.

What about success?

Passing fancies.

How tedious it is to accept congratulations, answer greetings, write thank-you letters, give interviews.

No, it is better to sit at home and watch as a new artistic image is created within.

K. Stanislavsky

To the **Art Theatre Cloak Room Attendants**. 23 January 1933, Moscow.

Dear friends!

You remembered me on the day of my seventieth birthday and sent me greetings that are so very dear to me. I was sincerely moved by them. You are our colleagues in creating productions. Our Art Theatre differs from many other theatres in that its performance begins the moment people enter the theatre building. You are the first to meet the entering spectators; you can prepare them to accept favourably or unfavourably the impressions coming from the stage. If the spectator is angry, he is unable to abandon himself to the impressions and becomes distracted and unreceptive; if, on the other hand, he feels at once that he is respected as soon as he enters the theatre, he regards the performance quite differently.

That is why I consider your work extremely important, and I greet and thank you for your congratulations as my collaborators in creating the performance.

Please accept my sincere and heartfelt gratitude.

K. Stanislavsky

To **Maksim Gorky** [in Sorrento]. 10 February 1933, Moscow.

Dear Aleksey Maksimovich,

I am bedridden as I write to you. After my jubilee (its celebration came as a surprise to me) I fell ill and could not reply to your splendid and wonderful letter until now. […]

I have been lucky in my life. It shaped itself entirely on its own. I was a tool in its hands. But this luck obliges me to hand on to others before I die what life has bestowed on me. Yet how difficult it is to impart to others one's experience in something as complex as an actor's creative process. In one's personal contact with a pupil one can demonstrate, illustrate, portray things that are difficult to put into a verbal formula. Portraying is our sphere as actors. But when you take up the pen, the words needed to define sensations run away and hide. Since our last meeting in Capri, where you did not hesitate to con my initial lines and attempts of the pen to create something like a 'grammar of dramatic art', I have racked my brains to convey to paper concisely and clearly what a novice actor should know. A book like that is needed, if only to put an end to all the false rumours concerning the so-called 'system', which, as it is now being taught everywhere, only wrongfoots young actors. The matter has to be put in order.

But apart from that, theatrical art, or, more accurately, the art of acting is perishing. One by one the great talents and technicians are departing the stage, leaving behind nothing but the recollections of their contemporaries and a few wretched photographs in Bakhrushin's Museum. That is why I decided and am afraid to write down my experience. It is a job for a real writer. Yet writing about art 'scientifically', as attorneys once used to do in the Literature and Art Circle, is boring and pointless.

Help me in this work (which has been redone three times) with your sage advice and experience. What with the demands for 'dialectical materialism', finishing what I have started is getting to be beyond my strength. [...]

Your heartily devoted and loving

K. Stanislavsky

To **Avel Yenukidze**. 15 April 1933, Moscow.

Dear Avel Sofronovich!

[...] Here is what's going on with us.

The former Korsh Theatre had its own contingent of spectators, schooled to the theatre over decades.[3] The first order of business is one has to win over this spectator. Therefore special attention is now directed to the productions at the affiliate. A few productions from the main stage have had to be transferred to the affiliate (a few performances of *The Lower Depths*, *At the Gates of the Kingdom*, *The Days of the Turbins*), because we did not have at present the repertoire for a big new (ex-Korsh) stage ready; it is only now being created (*The Mistress of the Inn*, *Out in the World*, a dramatization of Gorky, *The Pickwick Club* by Dickens, Bulgakov's *Flight*, perhaps Ostrovsky's *The Ward*).[4] Some productions, which were successful on the Small stage, had to be removed from the repertoire, because they made no effect on a big stage. When at least part of the newly prepared productions see the footlights, then we might not have to worry about the fate of the affiliate.

Between 20 and 30 April we hope to open a production of *The Mistress of the Inn* at the affiliate. This is the independent work of the youngsters and the first directorial work in our theatre of Mordvinov and Yanshin.[5] I haven't seen a rehearsal myself, but am acquainted with the concept of the production. It has been done with imagination.

In three or four weeks after *Mistress of the Inn* we will open the play *Out in the World*. And in this independent work of the youngsters under the direction of Kedrov there is much that is interesting, if one may judge by the concept, which the director related to me.

The remaining two productions for the affiliate: *The Pickwick Club* by Dickens and *The Ward* by Ostrovsky will go on next season. *The Ward* was shown to Sakhnovsky a few days ago, and he was very enthused by Telesheva's independent work. The greenest youngsters take part in it exclusively.

Despite the present impoverishment of the affiliate's repertoire, the financial aspect of the new theatre is going well. As soon as tickets went on sale they were entirely snapped up, but, on the other hand, what with the change of performance due to the actors' illness (unfortunately, very frequent most recently) a large number of tickets were returned.

[…] The production of *Molière* has had almost no rehearsals, because a few of the actors are busy in the basic stagings of the affiliate. As to the design aspect of this production, it is gradually being carried out. Beautiful sketches of the sets and costumes by the designer Ulyanov are ready, most of them I find persuasive and are partially being executed.[6]

The second production of next season, *Yegor Bulychov* [sic], is also being enthusiastically worked on, and, it is hoped, the play will be roughly completed by the end of this season.

The next scheduled production is Afinogenov's *The Lie*. The play is written. A few days ago the author wanted to read it aloud, but now, for some reason unknown to us, the reading has been cancelled.[7]

Trenyov will shortly be bringing us a play. But, evidently, it is more suitable for the affiliate than for the main stage.[8]

[…] Right now it is the turn of the revival of Hamsun's play *In the Clutches of Life*. New performers will be introduced in it, among whom our new member of the troupe Ktorov[9] has had to be introduced sooner than the proper time and sooner that we should like; he has been very well accepted by the theatre, as have his comrades at the ex-Korsh theatre. They are working vigorously with him in order to bring him up to our techniques of acting. It is just a pity that time will not allow us to carry on work with him that would be appropriate. We have to introduce him urgently, and not another performer. The play has to go on on 10-15 May.

After *In the Clutches of Life*, [Ostrovsky's] *Talents and Admirers* will also be opened this season.

As cause for the delay of the production of this play, through the illness of Yershov and Kachalov, I played a major part. Constrained by doctor's orders not to leave the house in the wintertime, I still cannot adapt to the new conditions of my present work 'at home', in absentia, not seeing actors and productions on the stage itself. A play and the acting of its performers sound quite different in a room than on a big stage, and it is not easy to judge this difference. The same with the production itself, and the sets, and the mise-en-scène. On the model they produce a different impression than on stage, and you cannot always judge this in absentia. That is why it is essential for me to see rehearsals in the theatre itself. But now, when they will soon let me go out, as if on purpose the main stage cannot be used for *Talents and Admirers*, because it is occupied without interruption by the revival of *Clutches of Life*. Therefore work on *Talents and Admirers* continues to go on at my place on Leontiev Lane.

What we are doing with this play cannot be called mere rehearsing. It is rather a lesson, a school, a testing and improvement of the technique and creative lines of the actors. As the result of daily acting and various difficult conditions of theatrical life and nerve-wracking work our technique has begun to show signs of serious illness. And if at the proper time the actors are not to be led to the proper path and are left uncorrected for a long time, are not shown their mistakes and the means to correct them, then the art of every member of the troupe will imperceptibly move backwards and will acquire such habits which it will not be easy to uproot later on. Thanks to such a general testing the actor's technique will be reformed in short space – up to the next drill – and go forward.

Most recently one can perceive a great striving among the actors to improve their capabilities. They have become interested in a better understanding of the meaning of technique and expertise in our concern. Those who wish to work in this direction are quite numerous. I do not have the ability and strength to comply with the very large number of requests of this kind, despite my great wish to do so. Therefore a delay is occurring in this sphere, and the involuntary culprit for this again appears to be me. This is all the more vexatious since this work on the improved capabilities of our actors I consider one of my most important tasks.

But the bad thing is that such rehearsals, transformed into lessons, take a great deal of strength and time, that in respect to productivity it is inconvenient, because it delays the opening of *Talents and Admirers*.

Another reason for the delay in opening this play is that at the moment I am swamped with work. A whole series of new productions has devolved upon me, which I must plot out or let slip through my fingers: *Talents and Admirers*, *Molière*, *Yegor Bulychov* [sic], *The Barber of Seville*, *Carmen*, *The Maid of Pskov* and a new opera by Polovinkin, *The Playboy of the Western World*.[10]

Furthermore, major work is going on for the organization of the Academy.

I am forbidden to overtax my powers, and so I have to take care to husband my strength. I can support only one major rehearsal a day, leaving the evening for all likely meetings. This also creates delay.

A new reason for delaying the opening of *Talents and Admirers* is that we have too small a troupe for two big theatres. Instead of double, we have wound up with one outfit and a half. Now the result of our mistake comes abundantly clear, in that for a long time the theatre has been left without the school that earlier augmented our cadre. At the present time nothing remains but to accept actors from outside. But it is harder to re-educate an already formed specialist than to develop a young, beginning and, in our sense, unspoilt student. An incomplete troupe leads to the clash of some actors in various plays, which also delays the progress of the work and allows no possibility of casting roles as one would like. Hence a whole series of compromises, that similarly not only affects the directorial side, but complicates and delays the work.

Talents and Admirers will be opened after *In the Clutches of Life* this season.[11]

Finally, a new delay – from the dreadful overexhaustion of the actors' organisms. All of them are somewhat ill. Illness, changes of performance, rehearsals are now the usual result, very forcefully postponing the work and damaging the performances, and therefore, so as not to harm the coming season, a good summer vacation for the actors has got to be provided.

As to the financial side of the main stage of the MAAT, the box-office receipts leave nothing to be desired.

In conclusion let me say a few words about our work on the Academy. A few committees have been formed, which are working enthusiastically, boldly, with great inspiration and faith in the proposed interesting work.

We are working hard, we are presenting a maximal programme and will try to include in it everything that our theatrical practice and culture have led to – at the present moment. If this plan cannot be realized right now, let the programme sit in the museum or be executed in part. Such a programme is to be a demonstration of the practical execution of the so-called 'system'.

The chief principles we laid down in this programme are that the school graduate not individual students but whole troupes, with their own producers, directors, designers, administrators, makeup artists and even chief stagehands; with their own repertoire of a few plays.

All the learning takes place not in class, not at lectures, but in the production-line of the school itself. So, while they are studying literature – history of costume, historical period, everyday life, -- the students recite roles and perform excerpts from plays chosen for this. But before they are unleashed on the public, they have to know a great deal of literary, historical, artistic, social and other information. So that they benefit from this, a series of specialists will relate the information that an actor has to know. As they receive and implement it in practice, the students will regard such 'elucidation' not as they do boring lessons which have to be learned by heart and then forgotten, but as they do creative material which will become essential for them in their immanent work and the school's recitals for the public. All sorts of knowledge acquired, as well as applied to practical matters, will be firmly fixed in the memory. The new methods demand careful inspection of the preliminary programmes and training of the new teachers. And this work and preparation will be carried out by the committees. [...]

To **Iosif Stalin**. May 1933, Moscow.
Deeply esteemed Iosif Vissarionovich!

Knowing your exceptionally responsive and attentive relations with the Art Theatre, I have made bold to trouble you with a request that has a very important significance for the theatre and that moves us all. It concerns my closest comrade in work, co-administrator and co-founder of the theatre – Vladimir Ivanovich Nemirovich-Danchenko, who is presently abroad and has no funds for travelling to the USSR. So far as I know, Aleksey Maksimovich [Gorky] has written to you about this. I have only to add that this request is addressed to you by the whole collective of the theatre, which at the present time is greatly in need of the presence and work of Vladimir Ivanovich.

The circumstances under which Vladimir Ivanovich remained abroad for such a long period are these: in winter and spring 1931 he suffered a serious heart attack. Then, in summer 1931 he went abroad for treatment, while he received for the treatment a paltry sum which he had worked out in his agreement with the Narkompros. In autumn 1931 he could not return to work, because the state of his health continued to prove perilous. In winter 1931-32 he subsisted on the money he got abroad as an advance on finishing his book, and got no money from the USSR. With the coming of summer he addressed a request for financial aid from the USSR for treatment and return, which was promised him in the amount requested, but was sent gradually and with great delays. The fear of remaining abroad without funds to live on has compelled him to take on a series of directorial jobs in the Italian theatre. Answering urgent requests of the MAAT to return quickly to work in the theatre, Vladimir Ivanovich broke off his foreign obligations, but at this time the sums he has received from Moscow are insufficient to clear his debts and make it possible to return to Moscow. At the moment he needs 1,500 dollars to cover all these expenses.

However one may judge the reasons for Vladimir Ivanovich finding himself abroad at the present time, in so difficult – even threatening -- a position, I cannot forget, even for a minute, his colossal role in the history of Russian theatre, nor his energetic, talented, self-sacrificing work in the revolutionary years, when he gave all his strength to support the MAAT and the development and creation of art in the great new epoch. The theatre is in dire need of his work now – it is difficult for me to carry out alone the fulfilment of all those remarkable and necessary tasks which the Government and the Party have set for the theatre: both the creation of the Academy (since Vladimir Ivanovich is a remarkable pedagogue) and the running of two theatres – the parent and the affiliate, and further work with playwrights, and hands-on directing of productions.

I am deeply convinced that, once he has received the financial possibility of returning, Vladimir Ivanovich will devote all his strength to the nation, as he has done throughout his years of work, and will justify the trust of the Government and the Party.

On 5 July ND returned from abroad, but at the end of the month KS and Lilina went to Berlin and then to a rest home in Nice.

To **Ripsimé Tamantsova**. After 5 September 1933, Rouen.
Dear Ripsi!
[...] I remind the actors [of *Talents and Admirers*] that they are not to go on stage without preliminary exercises for entering into the creative sense of self, without verifications and exercises of the scheme of the lines of *the life of the human body of the role.*

In every act – eliminate 95% of the effort.

Don't let them forget the little truths and little beliefs in every physical movement.

Let them test and perform the role or its scheme without any gestures, sitting on their hands.

Don't let Tarasova harp on one note and every day have her practice the whole range of her voice, to amplify it, to justify not only the high notes, but the *low* ones in the register while speaking. [...]

Yours K. Stanislavsky [...]

The fourth edition of My Life in Art *was issued in January 1934 and sold out in three days, making KS the third Soviet best-seller after Pushkin.*

Talents and Admirers, directed by Litovtseva under KS's supervision, opened at the MAAT on 23 September. The Barber of Seville, with the staging attributed to KS but carried out by three directors including his brother Vladimir, opened at the Stanislavsky Opera Theatre on 26 October.

To **his sister Zinaida and his brother Vladimir**. 8 December 1933, Nice.
Dear and beloved Zina and Volodya!

[…] I now have the impression that *Talents* has flopped, but *Seville* was a success. I am sorry about my work on *Talents*. Very important advances resulted from of it. Judging by the rehearsals at my home, I was made to transfer a play with mediocre qualities to the main stage. Was something lost along the way or was I mistaken in something? How depressing to begin laboratory experiments, not to bring them to a conclusion nor even see on stage the result of all the work.

To **Aleksandr Bogdanovich**.[12] 4 January 1934, Nice.
Dear, good Aleksandr Bogdanovich!

[…] I have written to no one (I don't count my brother and sister), because I constantly feel bad, full of apathetic, gloomy thoughts. All this can lead to tedium, and not provide good cheer, which you now need for work. Therefore I write nothing to you about my gloomy thoughts and ideas about our theatre, which I do not see flourishing and renewed. […]

Whatever I say is to explain the reasons for my silence and indolent work or, rather, its absence in new productions. There is another reason as well. It is, for instance, *Carmen*. I have the text of the libretto for the third act (the vaguest), made by [its director] P. I. Rumyantsev. How easily I could set to rights a text like this – in drama. But in opera, without music, without the playing of the piano – I am completely inert, and everything in me keeps silent. To arrange such piano-playing here entails thoroughgoing and very costly work. Not to mention that the instrument has to be in one's home, in one's room, because I do not go out and will not go out. Secondly, even if one had the instrument, could it be used quietly enough, otherwise in an hour the tenants on the floor below will be coming to protest that the music is disturbing the residents.

It is not worth borrowing anything from the French. They understand absolutely nothing about our business and are so far from what we are seeking in art that it is impossible to discuss it with them. There are Russian performers who would work with great pleasure for very little money (the French are insanely expensive), but all these Russians are émigrés, and therefore I cannot associate with them. What's more, my finances are in such a state that I must save every franc. So every day I open up Rumyantsev's notebook, I read, I cannot concentrate, I squeeze inspiration out of myself, but nothing emerges and nothing will, so long as I do not hear the music. As soon as this happens, I shall immediately understand which direction to take. Meanwhile I can share with you and through you with Rumyantsev a few sensations, premonitions, which, I think, are on the right track.

The main thing is to find a new approach to the opera, which would lead straight to the supertask of the work of Bizet (not Mérimée) and along with that you should keep away from that banal, vulgarized road that always leads to *Carmen*. First of all – that folk, factory-rural-highway robber milieu, and not darling Carmen and not her pretty boy Escamillo. In the first, second and fourth acts it is a bit marked, lots of places in the mise-en-scène and in the treatment are prepared for that. Of course, if all this is too saccharine, then we've overshot the mark in the direction of the earlier *Carmen* of the Bolshoy and all the other theatres. But it can also be intensified in the direction of folk drama, wherein Escamillo is an episodic hero, flashing brightly and then disappearing. Note that in the second and fourth acts Escamillo is far from the man he is in the third act. In the early acts he is brilliant, but no one stands up to him, but here no one, except Carmen, swoons over him. He is among bandits, smugglers, in a very dangerous milieu, and he has to be defended with firearms.

This and many other moments, some scraps of remembered music jolt me to imagine that the third act is different from how it is usually presented, distinct from what we suggested in our conference. We have to get away from candy-box smugglers. They have to be made authentic, amid great dangers, hiding, stealing, and not marching with packs on their backs. And in the music I can feel precisely that mood. Based on this I envisage a setting – something like the Crimean Chufut-kale.[13] Some ancient town on the top of a high mountain, half in ruins, with caves and grottos and corridors, carved into the rock face, with windows, carved out of the rock face. I don't yet see whether the action takes place inside or, on the contrary, in a narrow crevice between the crags, which are carved out with paths and bypaths, in which it is easy for smugglers to hide. Snow, because this is the very top of the mountain. Everyone muffled up, a snowstorm, there is fur too. The smugglers approach, along the corridors, hiding their booty in the grotto. Down below, beneath the stage (a single head is visible, lit from below by a camp-fire), in one of the carved-out windows, salvaged from the old town in the rock-faces, Carmen is visible telling fortunes. And at the same time on the second level gay Spanish women are also telling fortunes, but young, carefree ones. I see José and Escamillo, duelling along the lengthy corridors. They flash first in one window, then in another. And the darling simpleton Michaëla drops right into this set-up. Let us feel the self-centred devil Carmen in this staging. In this set-up her break-up with José will be more powerful, more profound, more fatal.

All these fancies float around in me and fail to find a well-defined form, because they are not guided by music. This is agonizing, and I cannot urge myself on in any way and I fear that I will not be able to do so. [...]

Yours K. Stanislavsky [...]

After assisting KS as director on Marriage of Figaro *and* Dead Souls, *Yelizaveta Telesheva worked with the youngsters of the theatre for a year on Ostrovsky's* The Ward, *with more than a hundred rehearsals, but after the dress rehearsal it was decided not to include the production in the regular repertoire of the theatre.*

To **Ripsimé Tamantsova**. 18 January 1934, Nice.

Dear, good Ripsi!

[…] Nice is wonderful, and you can't find such another place without winter, but it is not for working. I have no energy. It takes all my forces to write a letter. It takes many days to write one. And I have more letters to answer than ever. No wonder. Before I always had Igor with me in the role of secretary, but he's not here now, and now and again I have to write to him. […]

Marusya is also starting to turn into a human being. She has become more cheerful, begun to laugh. But she cannot walk by herself and can go out only when she's with a companion. In short, we are two typical ruins. I hope all the same that we will be better by summer.

Kira is worn out with looking after us. She is cook and maid and housekeeper and errand-boy for the shopping and chief furnace-tender who has to get up at night and stoke the stove. She is tired, but does not complain, because when we're away she is so lonely and keeps worrying about her own heart, which is not all it should be. At first Kirlyalya was fine. Big, massive legs, arms, flanks, a feminine torso and even a stout one. Kira toughened her up, and she went around barefoot all the time and in a light overcoat. But she caught the 'flu and, just like me, it will soon be a month and she still can't get over it. That means, a weak constitution. Constant bronchitis, laryngitis, sore throat, coughing. When you think about our heredity – I become concerned about her and my dreams about resettling them in Moscow begin to fade. No, she will not endure our conditions! It is obvious that we, the old folks, will have to die – solo. […]

The day goes by without your noticing. You've done a bit of writing in the morning, done some more during the day, had lunch, and now it's cold, the sun's gone down. So the day is over, because the evenings here are boring, especially now when we have been so long apart from Kirlyalya, who very much beautifies my life. She has become very clever. […]

Our spirits are low, because the actors are going without work.

It seems to be a simple truth: give someone work – and everyone will be cheerful and there will be lots of productions. No sooner do I schedule the kind of year with big preparations which will be spoken of throughout the season, -- when Sudakov comes along and smashes it all. Everything has been smashed up this year again. I cannot pursue my method in the concern. Only after America, for one or two years I managed to get things right and there were 5 productions and a cheerful mood.

Vl. Iv. was worn out all summer. I am very much afraid that this will happen with me. Therefore (now that I've started to talk about this) think about the following.

Where am I and my wife to live – in the summer? Evidently, on Leontiev Lane they will be tearing down the shed in the yard and building a house. It will be impossible to live there. It is impossible to acquire a dacha for 2 months. TsEKUBU is good, but the water there is awful. I cannot imagine where we are to go. […]

Lyub. Yak. took the manuscript. I am very glad and am afraid that nothing will come of it again. A great deal will depend on you. Don't hand over everything to her, but only what will not confuse her. So, for instance, what we are to do now.

It is extremely difficult to figure this out. The fact is that she was horrified by the chapter 'Speech', judging it by the raw material for the chapter that was sent to her and which she took to be the chapter itself. Now this chapter is written. I think that it is acceptable, does not slip into science, does not teach, but only guides the student to the subject, as do all the other chapters (gymnastics, dance, singing etc.) about physical culture.

How can I tell her now that this chapter exists, that she does not have to work on it to no purpose?

If I tell her, she will be horrified again and cry: give me everything. I will give her everything, on my arrival.

Now let her finish the first half – *emotional experiencing*, and let her start *embodiment* on my return. They don't have much to do with one another.

She regards me as a man of letters. But I don't think I am one. I am an unhappy martyr, who knows a lot and feels obliged to transmit to others what I accidentally managed to learn. No one in future will be as lucky as I was to lead such a life, and no one will learn what I have learned only by chance. I have to write down what I can, what I am able to write. I have to. So I ask for help. Not for myself, for the theatre of the future. If people want to subscribe to me – let them sign on. Fame is not important to me. What is important to me are the secrets which no one is willing to disclose. Famous actors usually keep them to themselves. That is why our art is marking time. I want to turn over everything. But I need help. Imagine that at all costs you have to eat a piece of meat with the whole house. Indeed it can be done following a plan drawn up in advance, especially if your stomach is so weak and incapable for such work, like my own head and brains. I bite off a piece. I have to reheat it, time goes by – I bite off another bit. And so over the course of thirty years I keep biting and biting, and only after I write down something, I reheat, I meditate, I rewrite, I forget, I reread, -- I start to understand how I have to write. I cross everything out and start all over again. Only now have I arrived at being able to read and recognize in what is written what I wanted to express. This is appalling work. My brains are not up to it, nor is my knowledge and now my strength is beginning to be not up to it. I feel sometimes that my head has stopped working, so hard is it to make sense of the vast material, when I'm not used to this sort of thing. Of course, I have done it badly, but what I do is important, and I need help, because the work I am carrying out is Sisyphian. […]

Yours K. Stanislavsky

Issues no. 8 (1933) and no. 4 (1934) of the magazine Theatre and Drama *printed 'Talks about the Initial Elements of Actor's Mastery' in which Sudakov commented on the system. Sakhnovsky contributed articles which presented problems from his planned book on directing.*

To **Ripsimé Tamantsova**. 1 February 1934, Nice.
Dear, good Ripsi!

I got the five issues of *Theatre and Drama* you sent and to my great sorrow and spiritual humiliation I have learned that my system has already been printed by

Sudakov and is being prepared for the press by Sakhnovsky. I've been walking around all day as if I'd been hit hard by a stick — on the head.

The point is not an author's vanity, but that the beloved essence to which I gave given my whole life is cynically violated and turned over in a distorted shape to the judgment of the crowd.

What is so dear to me will now be drenched in slops, because in that shape it is presented, my distorted creation will deserve no better treatment.

Sudakov has an exceptional ability for simplifying to the level of 'simple-minded' everything that he comes in contact with. The first impression of the reading public will immediately be – in such a shape – of a petty-bourgeois simplification, and I shall suffer from it, the way a father suffers by a raped and defamed daughter.

Well… good luck to him! What is done cannot be undone. But why does he write me a letter afterwards with protestations of love and loyalty. What is this – contempt, mockery?

But I am not writing this letter on account of my spiritual torments, this is what it's about.

They write me from America that my publisher is beginning to lose patience, especially since my system has already been put forth in Russian books?!. . . What this means I do not understand myself. The supposition arises in me that these books you sent me are perhaps already famous in America? Perhaps, individuals who attended the Moscow excursion last spring[14] subscribed to the Russian magazines and follow everything that goes on with us? This is very possible and probable.

Compare that with my obligation to my American publisher.

I do not remember whether it is stipulated in the contract or not that I am obliged to make sure and prevent it from being printed anywhere before my system appears in America. I know that I wrote about this more than once, in a letter, which can also appear as a document against me. I remember that I wrote in a letter either that it be stipulated in the contract that I must take measures and not allow and prevent the appearance of my system in print.

I don't have the contract at hand, and I do not remember and cannot judge where and in what form I subscribed to that obligation.

What Sudakov did and what Sakhnovsky plans to do undermine me both morally and financially. I do not know what laws about this exist in America, but I'm told that the laws regarding printed matter are strict there, and I risk either breaking my contract or some fine, which the publisher can deduct from my profits on the next book.

Is there no way to discuss with a lawyer or a notary whether I should write a letter now to somebody, perhaps to the publisher, perhaps to Sudakov, to confirm my loyalty, and perhaps protect myself from financial losses. I believe you have a copy of the contract.

This dropped on me just at the moment when I had undertaken a correspondence with America relating to an advance for the second book (Work on the Role) to cover the debts incurred here and get back to Moscow and pay for the trip and the doctor's fee. [...]

Yours K. Stanislavsky

P.S. Yel. Serg. [Telesheva] wrote me about a proposal to put on *Marriage of Figaro* in Leningrad. Although it pains me, I cannot agree to this, given my life. There are productions, artists, that cannot be moved from place, and if you move them, you spoil them forever. Golovin cannot be trotted through the [workers'] clubs.

Yegor Bulychyov and the Others opened on 6 February 1934. It had already had a wildly successful production at the Vakhtangov Theatre in 1932 which stood as a challenging standard of comparison. The Vakhtangov production stayed around for years; the MAAT production closed after twenty-eight performances because the critics considered that Leonidov in the lead had simply played himself.

To **Nemirovich-Danchenko**. March 1934, Nice.
Dear Vladimir Ivanovich!

[...] Cordially and joyously I congratulate you on the great success of *Bulychyov*. It is most important that this production should go so well, first, because it is a play by Gorky, and, second, because the production is performed in Moscow. It is hard to compete with first impressions. All the more honour to you and the performers. Yes! We have lived to the point that we are lagging behind the 3rd Studio and other theatres! This is not a task and matter for a theatre such as ours. For this I very much blame Markov, who let all the men of letters slip out of his hands and does not pursue an international repertoire.

We have got to correct this shortcoming of ours, and approach some of the more talented ones, and egg them on to write and help them more. About *The Lie* and Afinogenov I can say nothing. The play got past me owing to Sudakov, and I didn't read it. I agree with you that they will not allow us to do *Flight*, just as we didn't succeed in putting on the magnificent play *The Suicide* by Erdman.[15] To tell the truth, ask him to read this play to you some time. His reading is quite exceptionally good and very instructive for a director. His way of speaking conceals a new principle, which I cannot figure out. I roared with laughter so that I had to request a long interval, because my heart couldn't take it. [...]

I have done nothing in particular on *Molière*. I looked it over and spoke my opinion (with an appropriate knowledge of the play), or, more accurately, my impressions of the designs. And that's all. If necessary, I will not turn down any sort of work. But people should consider: is it possible to produce such a theatrical play in one's home. Won't that create new delays? Now, in view of my illness, I cannot work – quickly. How I will endure rehearsals after my heart failure this autumn I do not yet know, but only hope. I'm glad of any kind of work, because I'm bored without it. A strange fate for the role of Molière. Two come to mind at once: Moskvin and Tarkhanov. Now both have fallen ill. What's going on? I like Stanitsyn[16] very much as an actor. He needs a very responsible role. But what Moskvin would make of it! Won't they jostle one another. This has to be well sorted out. I'm ready to work with either one.[17] [...]

It seemed to me that we cannot create a second MAAT and run it on a par with the old MAAT. You and I are not up to it, and the old MAAT is suffering from such competition. But nevertheless we need the affiliate very much. What for? To create the theatre that will exist after our death – the old MAAT. Let the Sudakovs and others show us their talents for management during our time. Or, more accurately, let the whole group of actors, running the theatre like Vakhtangovians, show us what they can do. Let them study to run not only the artistic sector, but even run the whole theatre during our lifetime. When they have learned, then let them cross over to the old Art Theatre – to replace us, and let a new group be created for the affiliate. It does seem that at the base of all the discussions about new cadres and changes which we have had with our officials, -- the path I propose will solve their problem best of all. But my project was not accepted. They arranged for the affiliate to be run by three old men, and I will (for appearance's sake) head it. Sitting at home and not having been in the theatre building even once after it was made over to us, -- I cannot create it.

Were I in the place of Sudakov and his friends, I would think I could expect nothing better. What an absurdity – to be handed a theatre, and such a long-familiar one. But Sudakov is used to licking other people's plates, signing his name to other people's work and speculating and earning money for it. Evidently, my misgivings were correct: Sudakov can satisfy club demands, but not the demands of the MAAT 1, nor even his affiliate's. That's why he stubbornly begs off the responsibility of running an independent theatre. He was almost never at Korsh's Theatre and didn't follow its performances. I verified this personally and more than once phoned there. Not once was he there. If Sudakov begs off his assigned business, one has to find a group who will. [...]

I still have to give you an answer about one very important and very painful question – the purge [of superfluous actors].

Yes. Most unfortunately – it is essential. [...]

Yours K. Stanislavsky [...]

Congratulations on the enormous success of Shostakovich's opera.[18] If he is a genius, it's a comfort!

To **his brother Vladimir**. 3 April 1934, Nice.
Dear, good Volodya!

[...] You have succeeded through long patience, obstinacy, honesty, talent. Unfortunately, you don't always know how to demonstrate things effectively to the idiotic actor. Most often he has to be 'shocked'. The actor is an idiot, and this stupidity is more charming than his intelligence. Intelligence in an actor is vulgar and repulsive. [...]

[Rigoletto] is the kind of opera that can be staged by anybody. It's an easy opera in its cast: 2-3 choruses, which can be done after the soloists are ready. The small parts are easy to prepare – spaced out, and almost all of acts 2, 3, and 4 can be rehearsed neatly with 5 persons. I have often been told: why don't you give an order for it? Give an order – and everything will be done. I gave the order for

Rigoletto 5 years ago, and no one paid any heed, but said 'Very good, sir!,' 'Aye, aye.' Is it the fault of my frailty and administrative incompetence? I agree. This is where my tragedy lies. All my life I have had to be something I am not. All my life I've played the role of 'administrator', 'chief', 'hard-nose', 'tough guy'. In my old age this role is getting beyond my strength, and more and more frequently I miss the mark and give it up. It is hard for me to play this role, and there's no one I can hand it over to! You haven't worked this year partly because of my fault, and partly through the obtuseness and lack of talent of our whole staff. Their obtuseness and lack of talent is driving me to despair! I am writing so frankly because I am in Nice. When I get back to Moscow, I will have to be the 'boss' again and I am starting to forget how to play that role.

[...] As to the through action and supertask of *Rigoletto* I cannot speak at the moment. As to Monterone, you may, perhaps, be right.[19] But, possibly, approaching it from that side is dangerous. If you highlight an aspect which has not been highlighted by the author, a non-contemporary approach may result. There is a contradiction in the opera: a depraved society and oppressed slaves, who when all is said and done rise up in rebellion. A modern spectator will expect this aspect. I would highlight it. Is it necessary, when one puts on an opera by *a composer*, to pay overmuch attention to his source (V. Hugo)? I think there is very little Hugo in Verdi. Something of Verdi's own emerged, and, to my mind, rather better than Hugo himself, whom, to tell the truth, I am not overfond of. Given our tenor – who is short and quite unlike the audacious duke (Francis I), -- we have to make the role a nasty, spoiled, mischievous infante – a little boy, who has violated a 14-year-old girl. None of our folks can play a king à la Hugo.[20] [...]

Of course, best of all would be to reconcile everyone and preserve the staff in its entirety. I don't believe that this is possible. In the life of a theatre (as at the MAAT – with its 4 studios) there comes a moment when one has to release from the depths of the theatre a whole group of people who had been admitted for a great many reasons – a wrong-headed approach. So it was with the 1st, 3rd and 4th of our studios. If this divorce, very important for the work of the group, had not been allowed, -- it would have destroyed the whole theatre. Now the same story is recurring with us at the Art. It would be a bad thing if these disaffected people were not released. They have either to be reformed or united into an independent group. I think that such a moment has come to a head with us. People want freedom, independence. They should have it. Another question: will they be able to handle it. At the First Studio, the Vakhtangovians have personal initiative, administrative types. Is there any of this among our leading actors? I don't know and I doubt it. But they are not petty. Of course, this should not be done all at once. We have to have discussions and gradually help them form groups and either leave or submit to our demands. One thing is impossible: to keep up our present relations with the government – in the government. That is my opinion. [...]

Evidently, Shostakovich is talented, and we are letting him slip through our fingers. [...]

Yours Kostya [...]

To **Ripsimé Tamantsova**. 18 April 1934, Nice.

Dear, good Ripsi!

[...] I find very interesting what you write about Meyerhold.[21] He always was a naturalist, but without actors who could perform simply and well. He cannot teach them and therefore they need to be camouflaged by all sorts of trickery. Is it true that they have celebrated his 60th birthday [on 10 February]? If so, you made a great mistake by not writing to me about it [...]

I don't remember this Balukhaty or when I promised him the mise-en-scène of *The Seagull*. Until I have looked over a copy – I can say nothing. I think that all my notes are antiquated. Besides, it is inconvenient to lend my mise-en-scène just now when the theatre is reviving the play – in a new way: a tone of protest and challenge will result for my part. Until I finish my first two books on the system, I cannot take on any work. Afterwards I am thinking of making mises-en-scène for a few classic plays of Shakespeare. The ones I never managed to perform in my lifetime.

That's correct, copies of *The Seagull* and others cannot be let out of the museum. [...]

K. Stanislavsky

To **his sister Zinaida**. 19 April 1934, Nice.

Dear, good, beloved Zina!

It's not my fault that I was so late in writing to you. Before I leave I have to copy out everything I wrote down here (two chapters anew: 'Speech' and 'Tempo-rhythm').[22] These are awfully difficult chapters, which have held up the book. I don't know how it came out, but I cannot do it any better, because the chapters are excruciatingly difficult. To say what I need to, without slipping into the swamp of science, so that things are always interesting and conversational, vivid. The question of copying here is complicated. Starting from the fact there you can't get a typewriter here. I have to write by hand, and with my awful handwriting on top of that, which I can barely make out myself. I have to correct the manuscript itself from scratch, dictate much of it to myself, and after copying it out again correct a mass of errors. And the chapters are enormous. 100 pages each. You can't carry on such convict labour a second time, because in Moscow you won't manage it what with all the business. What's essential is a long period of complete, isolated serenity, which can only be found here, far from Moscow. Correspondence is rushed, because it is dreadful for me to go back with only a rough copy. What if it gets lost with the baggage or confiscated at the German border? [...]

The theatre is a special realm, the most difficult of all existing arts. Collective work and creativity demand enormous tact and sensitivity to the general condition and atmosphere of all the work of the theatre. For the general mood you constantly have to watch keenly, constantly have to heat things up or cool things down to the proper degree. There are occasions when with pain in your soul you have to sacrifice artistic quality, to some degree. The stage director must know how to create a suitable atmosphere for work.

Not infrequently a thoroughgoing rectitude and inflexibility are harmful to the theatre's general concerns. True, there are occasions when you cannot allow any deviation from the strict artistic or administrative line. At a time like this I don't think you'll manage to get 500 performances of a play.[23] You have to refresh an opera once it has opened, you have to provide some sort of satisfaction even to someone who has performed the drudgery of a run of 500 performances. To perform such a number of performances more or less conscientiously is no easy task. It is important to refresh the through action so that the opera comes to life again over a bit of time. An anniversary performance is of no great significance in itself. On one occasion they will perform well, and afterward again everything will go as it did of old. But if the through action and supertask are revitalized, then the renovation will be in evidence for a long time. This is a difficult and important directorial task. For such occasions in the theatre museum there must be a director's instructions, reminding one of the whole line of the production of the play. Reading such instructions, the actors should remember and feel everything that once excited them. To your lot has fallen this difficult and burdensome but important work. It will have to be done with the whole operatic repertoire to keep the actors from falling into cliché. It worries me that this work has come and been laid on wearied nerves. At your age you should husband your strength thriftily. I am learning this art, but you still have not recognized the necessity at a certain age of studying to make others work and giving instructions yourself. […]

Yours Kostya […]

To **Ivan Moskvin.** 22 April 1934, Nice.
Dear, good, beloved Ivan Mikhailovich!
   […] The other day I happened to see Chaliapin's film *Don Quixote*. A wonderful figure and makeup. Untalented director,[24] Fyodor Ivanovich's voice is unrecognizable in the talking pictures. It has taken on quite a different timbre. He speaks French – very badly. He tries to imitate French declamation, instead of teaching them how to act. In short, the film is not a success. […]

Yours K. Stanislavsky

The Bolshoy tenor Leonid Vitalievich Sobinov (1871-1934), who joined the Opera Studio in 1934, had referred to the upheaval caused by the demand that the Opera Theatre tour to Kharkov and Voronezh and 'the catastrophic state in preparing a new repertoire, about which Narkompros harps at us unambiguously'.

To **Leonid Sobinov.** 4 May 1934, Nice.
Dear, good Leonid Vitalievich!
   […] Touring is our bane, and especially for me. Spring and autumn are exactly those months in which I could go to the theatre and work actively, because all winter I'm kept locked up, as if under house arrest. The second bane is this bureaucratic chivvying of productions by the industrial-financial plan. But there

one has to do business with people who have absolutely no understanding at all of our field and specific conditions of work. Normally the Art Theatre in the best case stages two productions a year, which remain in the repertoire for some ten years. Other theatres stage many plays in a season or two, with some specific exceptions. The difference: staging for ten years, for an eternally sold-out box-office, or for two seasons with an unsold box-office. Entirely two different methods. One relies on staging techniques and directorial gimmicks, the other is pedagogical, for the actor's development. To mix craftsmanship with art 'is for the host of hunters, I'm not of their number.'[25] They demand of us both the creation of cadres and 'productivity' (in quotation marks). We cannot meet these demands; I personally cannot meet it, because, first, I am ill, and second, I have fought against hackwork all my life. This is a bureaucratic demand, and I have to make a formal reply against my will, because these people do not understand the subtlety of art.

In addition: there are two troupes in our theatre, but after all the theatre – stage, workshops, rehearsal space etc. – is one. They want there to be twice the number of productions in one theatre. No, in our theatre under our conditions (be it one, or two, or ten troupes) one can stage at most three operas (I – one, Nemirovich – two). Or two – we + one – Nemirovich). Nemirovich is more on form and therefore stages more quickly. We go deeper, and this takes incomparably longer and is more difficult.

And this simple thing the bureaucracy does not understand.

All that is left to do is the maximum that can be done. And much can be done. For instance: the Art Theatre in some years put on five productions a season: *The Ardent Heart, The Decembrists, Merchants of Glory, The Sisters Gérard* and a public dress rehearsal of *Turbins.*

Those plays were cast so that an actor played no more than a single role. Rehearsals went on simultaneously. And I opened all those plays by myself, because Nemirovich and his troupe were in America. Such timely preparation allowed us to excel now and then in quantity. [...]

At my age I cannot countenance the star system which has been spreading. I demand first of all that kind of conscientious relationship to the matter from the conductors and chorus masters. They, more than anyone, have to understand the needs of the whole enterprise. [...]

Yes, I agree with you: my brother and sister are devoted to the business and good workers. As their brother, I have to mistreat them. If you sometimes find it necessary to stand up for them, I will be glad. [...]

To **Nikolay Yegorov**. 17 May 1934, Nice.
Dear, good Nikolay Vasilievich!

[...] I have only one refrain here: 'To Moscow! To Moscow!' How sad it is to be parted from my dear ones, but to be stuck here by illness torments me (just like all the debts dribbling in drop by drop). Meanwhile I imagine that people are telling you: he won't show up, he's a defector, and similar nonsense!

All these worries and disturbances ruin my life. [...]

A few days ago Moissi drove to me here in a motor-car. He had returned to Italy (his homeland), became an Italian actor, is an enormous success.[26] He's touring through all the cities. He was next door in San Remo, learned that I am here, and got here in 2 hours. The night before, he acted *The Living Corpse*. The next day he flew in the morning to me. At 2 o'clock he left for somewhere near Genoa; that same day, at night, he played Hamlet there. And so it is every day. But nevertheless he's cheerful, young as always, -- charming. In Italy they are most occupied with renewing the theatrical business *according to the principles of Russian art*. So the Art Theatre plays an enormous role there. Not long ago a staggering success was had by the Jewish troupe 'Ohel', which was created by a student of Stanislavsky – Halevy (it's the first time I've heard of him).[27] This troupe is going to Paris. They are waiting for it with bated breath. Even the Prague troupe is starting to perform in Paris (*Krechinsky's Wedding* with Khmara as Krechinsky (oy!) and Pavlov as Rasplyuev). Those are two more opportunities for people to write about the MAT. [...]

Yours affectionately K. Stanislavsky [...]

To **Nemirovich-Danchenko**. 30 May 1934, Nice.
Dear Vladimir Ivanovich!

[...] This is what I think:

1) The two of us have barely enough spare strength left to set the MAAT to rights. If we are to sort out other theatres, then we had better consider that the MAAT is finished, and the affiliate has to be closed.

2) My health does not allow me to take on any work *with a deadline*. It is beyond a doubt that on my return to Moscow I will catch 'flu more than once, which will make me bedridden for no less than a month.

3) I cannot stage *The Seagull* – in a new way – I do not see any performers for staging it in the old way. To stage it with the existing ones, one would have to carry out enormous work or, more accurately, a complete course of study. And even so the results, it strikes me, would be mediocre. [28]

4) The prospect of repeating myself in old work does not appeal to me. I have little time left for work and for life. When you come down to it I would like something new, and not a repeat of bygones.

5) What kind of work I can do after my recurrent autumn seizures is a question. Therefore, to be firmly reliant on me, you would have to try me out in advance.

6) I will do everything I can to assist in the coming anniversary. I fear that I cannot offer much strength.

7) Everything that relates to my work obtains only on condition that the question about the Academy be liquidated. If there is to be an Academy, then we have to scrutinize our whole plan very closely and have to gauge our strength. Tomorrow I go to Paris, *at risk*. What will be shall be. There is no way to stay here any longer.

My wife feels a bit better than the last time, but she still cannot go to Moscow. I am going alone – with a doctor.

Yours K. Stanislavsky [...]

In mid-July 1934 KS met Harold Clurman and Stella Adler in Paris. They were prominent members of the New York Group Theatre, its founding inspired by the MAT's 1922-23 tours. According to them, KS worked with Adler for five weeks from four to five hours a day on a scene from John Howard Lawson's Gentlewoman, *in which he emphasized action and supertask. KS is also purported to have diagrammed the system on a blackboard, emphasizing 'given circumstances' and the 'magic if' in preference to emotional memory.*

KS returned to Moscow on 4 August 1934, nauseated with the Fascism and anti-Semitism he had observed in Europe. He was eager to plunge into work, especially 'to restructure everything' with invigorated allegiance to Soviet audiences.

To **Leonid Sobinov**. 1 September 1934, Moscow.

[...] Now the big news. Suddenly P. I. Novitsky[29] comes to me. He was always my most hard-bitten enemy, a desperate opponent of the so-called system. It turns out that in the past he had approached it 'a bit superficially'. But recently 'he delved into' the question and found in the system... Here beginneth an expression of ecstasy. The upshot is he asks me on behalf of the Narkompros to set up a school to create cadres. This school has to be a model for the whole Union. Which means, someone gave an order for something! Right now the question has been raised about granting us 150 thousand for the first year to create the concern. A question about instructors and pupils. These latter have to be sought not only in Moscow, but throughout the whole USSR... I am also busy with this matter and have taken an interest.[30] [...]

KS began to rehearse Carmen. *On 31 October he previewed the work that Gorchakov and Bulgakov had been doing on* Molière *and tried to apply some of the System's techniques.*

To **his wife Mariya Lilina**. 19 November 1934, Moscow.

[...] Moscow is being beautified not by the day, but by the hour. You can find everything in the shops. On Tver Street an enormous Filippov shop has opened. Whatever you can think of is there, including live sturgeons. It's expensive, but good quality. No one needs to complain about food.

Craig is to stage *A Midsummer Night's Dream* at the Maly Theatre[31] (who will suffer from his drubbing there?). They say he has aged terribly!

The Pickwick Club is on at our place. I was at a performance.[32] A very interesting production (Stanitsyn). Wonderful sets (Vilyams)[33]. Everything in the best of taste. The youngsters are acting, many of them not badly, for instance, Gribkov (Pickwick), Massalsky in a character role,[34] but many of them are mediocre in an acting sense, some are even wretched. Over all, a good, upbeat performance. It is having a great success with the Repertkom and the audiences.

People are beginning to praise *Thunderstorm*. [35] Nemirovich is working well. He wants awfully to show me up in Ostrovsky. After the ill-fated *Talents*.

I don't recall whether I wrote about *Talents*, that I'd seen it. A dreadful performance. My heart bled. I couldn't watch the last act.[36] [...]

Figure 80 A socialist-realist painting by V. P. Yefanov of an idealized Stanislavsky addressing
students of the Military Aviators Academy at a banquet in his salon

To **Mariya Chekhova**.[37] 3 January 1935, Moscow.
Dear and ardently beloved Mariya Pavlovna!

You ask me to recall and write to you when and under what circumstances I
presented photographs of myself to Anton Pavlovich.

I cannot remember. I shall try to provide you with a few memories.

I blushed when I read over the inscriptions I had written on the photographs
listed in your note. Dry, formal phrases.

Now that the memory of dear Anton Pavlovich has become a cult for all of us,
the cold tone of my dedications seems inexcusable to me.

How is this to be explained?

One of the photographs is dated 17 January 1904, which was his birthday and
also the date of the opening of *The Cherry Orchard*.

That was an unforgettable and awesome day; an opening, a wonderful new
play, a new role, a new production of the theatre, a birthday and finally –Anton
Pavlovich's health! Everything frightened us.

But besides all our worries I was also concerned about a birthday present. What
might please Anton Pavlovich? A silver pen, for a writer, or an antique inkwell?
What would he do to me if I offered him such gifts? A piece of antique, gold-
embroidered fabric? What would that matter to him. But I could find nothing
better and presented it to him with a wreath.

'I haven't a study anymore! It's a museum now, don't you know!' complained
Anton Pavlovich.

'Well, what should I have given you?' I enquired.

'A mousetrap! We do have mice! Now Korovin sent me a fishhook. Listen, that's a marvellous present!'

Those are the circumstances under which I signed my photographs. Perhaps this will serve as my excuse. [...]

Your loving and always soulfully devoted
K. Stanislavsky

Throughout March, KS was conducting rehearsals of Molière *at his home. Bulgakov was appalled by the 'naïve' nature of the director's analysis and his attempt to rewrite the play as a romantic biography. Some rehearsals devolved into pedagogic exercises or protracted arguments between the author and the director. They dragged on through April and May in an atmosphere of exasperation, hysteria and KS's efforts to introduce actual scenes from Molière's plays. On 28 May, the play was taken away from KS and returned to Gorchakov. KS resolved to concentrate more intently on 'the truth of art'.*

On 2 June, a general meeting of the MAAT ordered the troupe to study the speech that Stalin had given at the Military Academy graduation ceremonies; this occasioned a discussion among the actors of the MAAT that raised complaints about the current depressed state of things. The delays in producing Molière, *formalities and red tape, the theatre's remoteness from real life, and the lack of a congenial atmosphere were among the complaints addressed to Stalin. Sakhnovsky pointed out the lack of unified leadership meant a lack of clarity. The authorities believed that KS and ND 'take no interest in the theatre whatsoever' but engage in 'mutual squabbling'. The Stanislavsky faction was accused of counter-revolutionary behaviour. The upshot was a resolution that KS and ND be relieved of the administrative-organizational work and a new director put at the helm of the theatre. It was proposed that KS and ND be retained as artistic directors and honorary administrators, but that a member of the Central Committee of the Communist Party supersede them as actual administrator.*

29 September saw a soirée devoted to the beginning of the school year at the Opera-Dramatic Studio. These sentiments KS conveyed to his sister were to be conveyed to the students. They are clearly meant to appease the authorities. He himself hoped it would be a stepping-stone to the longed-for Academy.

To **his sister Zinaida**. Before 29 September 1935, Streshnevo.
Dear Zina!

[...] I would like to express personally how much we appreciate the efforts of the government and the Narkompros, [which] are touchingly concerned about our theatres, our art, the cadres old and young. All this is very important and moving, especially when you look over at the West, where up to now they make demands of the theatres beyond their strength.

[...] What do I wish [for the students]?

First and foremost – that they understand (and this means, feel intimately) what our government summons them to and expects of them at this historic moment, when only heroes have the right to life. They must serve in every *way*, in every

Figure 81 A publicity still of Stanislavsky with the American contralto Marian Anderson, 1935. Photo: Konsertbolaget. He offered to work with her on Carmen, but she preferred not to perform opera

relationship. They must work to become the actors the country needs: Soviet actors, in the highest and noblest sense. They must not only understand the present and the future, but they must also absorb all of the past, because this is the last opportunity for this: the old-timers who can speak of the past are leaving us one by one. The youngsters must understand what collective creativity is, what such comrades are – in fact, when everyone is linked by the same overall great social and artistic concept. Discipline, cohesion, understanding each other for the sake of the basic idea. [...]

I embrace and congratulate you.

Kostya. [...]

Craig, who had not commented on the chapter 'Duncan and Craig' in My Life in Art *when the book was first published, took offence when the book was reprinted by Little, Brown. He believed that the story of the falling screens diminished his prestige and prevented producers from commissioning his scenic designs.*

To **Gordon Craig**. October 1935
Dear friend and colleague!

When I wrote the chapter about you, I was genuinely moved by fond memories of our work together.

I wanted to depict you as your image is preserved in my memories.

You did not strike me as a standoffish Englishman, but as a passionate Irishman. Hence the mistake that got into my book about your origin.

It seemed to me that you resembled us – Russian actors – in your stormy temperament, audacity, freedom.

You are preserved in my thoughts and imagination – next to Sulerzhitsky, whom I honour highly and love to this very day. Your two figures: the tall, powerful artist Craig and the short, talented Suler – is what I wanted to describe in that chapter.

That is why I did not leave out details about how I became acquainted with you in your bathing costume, how you stood out from everyone in the street with your eccentric appearance, in a fur coat from Griboedov's *Woe from Wit*. And I put down other details of the same sort because in my memories I sincerely admired your original and beautiful personality.

I do not think that you would like me to look upon you with a different gaze.

Thinking of you as a brilliant artist, I lacked the glowing colours to describe your creation *Hamlet* on our stage and your wonderful concept, which I did not succeed in displaying in full measure.

I described in the book my efforts, the tests we carried out, my inability to bring to fruition what the screens had to give us.

I was very dissatisfied with myself and my work as your assistant on *Hamlet*, and exposed myself, and mocked myself and my unsuccessful trials. I wanted in this way to extol you all the more.

The catastrophe with the screens obliged me to mock myself but not the idea of the screens.

And I was right in my self-criticism, because to this very day I grieve for my failure as your assistant in that remarkable staging of *Hamlet*.

But, obviously, I am a poor writer and did not succeed in conveying what I felt.

My fellow-countrymen, it seems to me, understood me correctly and view you with my eyes. But abroad your ill-wishers read my words differently.

I believe that this is the case, and I am aggrieved with all my heart that I did you harm and not good, as I had wished.

I should not have written about the ill-fated fall of the screens. You are right that I should not have provided fodder for malicious tongues.

I thank you also for not taking me to court. That would have been a dreadful finale to our beautiful acquaintance.

Before turning to the question of how to correct my blunder in the next editions (if there are any), let me correct a mistake of yours.

You accuse me of lying and declare that the fall of the screens and the various tests (cork, wooden, etc. screens) didn't happen.

I append a testimonial affidavit by the chief stagehand and the stagehands who are still alive and are still working for us. They affirm that the catastrophe with the screens and the various tests of materials for them did occur in reality and that you are mistaken in denying it.

I send this document in order to convince you that I am not a liar and not even a fantasist.

I pass to ways of correcting my blunder.

I will write to my publisher in America about your wish. He owns the rights to reprint the book in England and all English-speaking countries.

If the book is reissued in a separate edition, it will be easy to grant your wish. But it may very well happen that the book's letterpress is affixed once and for all to big pieces of pasteboard with printed letters (I don't know what this kind of printing method is called in your language).

If that is the case, then there is no way to expunge or even change what has been printed.

In that case there is one thing left: to insert in the publication a kind of explanation, at the end of the book, the sort of thing that is in your book on Ellen Terry; or a foreword, in which I explain what I am writing to you now.

To avoid fresh misunderstandings I would very much like you to provide me with a rough text of what you would like to see in my letter to the reader. Do not refuse to send it, while I, for my part, will write to the publisher.

Once again I express my sorrow and commiseration for what has happened. I hope that my blunder will not alter our good relations and fond memories of our encounter and work. In one's declining years, before bidding farewell to life and you, I hold dear the re-establishment of our good relations and the knowledge that you do not harbour in your heart an unkind feeling towards me.

The story of the screens was removed from the Russian version of My Life in Art *in 1936, but has always remained in the English-language editions.*

Molière *rehearsals resumed in December under ND's control. Then KS was confined to bed with a recurrence of 'flu-like symptoms, loss of weight and what his doctors thought might be a tumour.*

To **Iosif Stalin**. 1 January 1936, Moscow.
Dear, deeply esteemed Iosif Vissarionovich!

I received your greetings, conveyed to me by Com. Zhivotova[38] (asst administrator of the MAAT), and am deeply moved by your attention and your concern. I learned from her that you are interested in the situation of the Art Theatre, and this obliges me to express to you the whole truth about it. I understand that I must do this very briefly, bearing in mind that you are overburdened with matters of worldwide significance.

The immense upheavals that have taken place in every sphere of construction in our nation, a new people, a new everyday life, a new human civilization a-borning compel me, one of the oldest representatives of the theatre, sincerely dedicated to art, to be alarmed for its fate. Our Theatre can and must become the most advanced theatre in our country in its stage reflections of the entire fullness of the inner spiritual life of the working man, who has become master of the land.

Theatrical matters throughout the whole world are in a state of stagnation. Age-old traditions are vanishing.

But, happily, the USSR at the present time is proving to be the true heir to the best traditions of both European theatre and all that was good in the old traditions of Russian theatre. We must succeed in passing on what is most valuable to the rising younger generation and, together with them, not merely hold on to it, but also consolidate it for further development. The preservation of these seeds of age-old theatrical achievements and their development into a new beautiful art form must be above all the concern of us, the representatives of contemporary theatre. They can be preserved only by a theatre of the most supreme culture and the most supreme technique. This theatre must become the beacon to which all other theatres must aspire. In its time the Maly Theatre was such a beacon, and after it the Art Theatre. Now there are no such true beacons. The Art Theatre is slipping from its heights and is becoming at best a decently productive theatre. But the spiritual needs of the spectator are growing and may outstrip it.

I would like to devote all my experience, all my knowledge, all my time and health, all my remaining years, to the creation of a genuinely creative theatre. In my search for paths to creating such a theatre I have turned to youngsters, having organized a few months ago the Opera-Dramatic Studio, and to this end I am working on my second book, in which I want to pass on all my experience and all my knowledge. But one of the most important paths seems to be the preservation and development of the creative riches accumulated by the Art Theatre. These riches are treated carelessly by a certain sector of the troupe, which finds the great creativity that places great demands on them as human beings and artists to be unnecessary and inconvenient.

It is this whole struggle between high aspirations and petty, ephemeral interests that is going on at the present time within the Moscow Art Theatre and is tearing it to pieces. Creative experience and the aspiration to great art are on the side of the few surviving old-timers and some of the up-and-coming youngsters. On the other side considerable energy is being applied to minor facile tasks.

The struggle is hard, and timely help is needed by us two leaders, in our declining years, given the difference in our creative principles and the tangled state of our 40-year-old relationship, to lead the theatre out of the situation in which it finds itself. An experienced, cultured Communist administrator is essential, who could help V. I. Nemirovich-Danchenko and me to repair our mutual relationship for the creative leadership of the theatre. It occurs to me that the most suitable candidate for this complex, difficult work is Com. M. P. Arkadiev, official of the Administration of Theatre of RSFSR NKP [State People's Commissariat of Enlightenment], as a man with theatrical experience, tact and great energy.

Along with this it is essential to fortify the party organization of the theatre by a cultured and qualified leader.

A thorough and rigorous review and reassessment of the whole creative collective of the theatre are also essential to identify the people who are suited for the great creative experimental work, which can create genuine theatre.

It is necessary to require the theatre's workers with all speed to improve their qualifications to the level of genuine expertise in art, and to that end to institute shock-worker merit bonuses.

Our theatre must discard the slogan 'tempos to accelerate the actor's expertise', since the tempo of theatrical productivity accelerates naturally and on its own.

Those individuals incapable of joining a collective of qualified experts should continue to work under the former conditions in the affiliate under the leadership of the MAT, filling out its ranks with new actors to create a productive theatre.

The MAAT must be transformed into a beacon of theatrical art.

Knowing your love for the theatre, I hope for your assistance.

Your devoted K. Stanislavsky

This about-face on KS's part eased the appointment of Mikhail Pavlovich Arkadiev (1896-1937), official of the Art Sector of Narkompros, as administrator of the MAAT. ND's knee-jerk reaction was to oppose it. Arkadiev diagnosed the theatre's malaise as 'creative inertia' and prescribed more productions of Soviet plays. He also recommended salary rises and the bestowal of the Order of Lenin on the theatre; both measures were approved and executed. Pravda trumpeted his advent as a red-letter day in the history of the Art Theatre and he became greatly loved by the troupe.

In January 1936 the campaign against so-called 'formalism' was launched, and the Committee for Artistic Affairs, newly founded to make sure all theatrical offerings toed the Party line, saw value in retaining KS and ND.

To **his wife Mariya Lilina**. 6 February 1936, Moscow.
My dear, kind Marusya!

[...] Well, what else can I tell you about my boring life? Arkadiev has entered upon his duties during this time, inspected the whole theatre, found that it's dirty, is going to all the performances. There was a dress rehearsal of *Molière* [5 February], for papas and mamas, after Vl. Iv's tinkering with the play. Surprisingly, the rehearsal had a success. It is a new kind of production: the success is enormous for the designer (Vilyams), they praise all the stereotypist-actors (Stanitsyn?! Yanshin). They even praise Koreneva and Podgorny. They even praise Bolduman and, a bit, Sosnin.[39]

People chide Livanov a bit (*jeune premier*, a darling, he's showing off his good looks). Everyone abuses Bulgakov and the play. It cost me so much worry on account of the 'pure art' in this rubbish. Still, it's a good thing that the rehearsal had a success. We need it now, at this moment of transition. [...]

Kostya

Molière opened at the MAAT affiliate on 15 February, officially advertised as directed by Nikolay Gorchakov. KS's name was nowhere to be seen. The production was luxurious but failed to create enthusiasm; the powers-that-be found it subversive and it was removed after seven performances.

To the **Department of Private Amnesties of the TsIK of the USSR** from People's Artist of the Republic Stanislavsky Konstantin Sergeevich. February 1936, Moscow.

Statement

On the night of 17 to 18 June 1930 by order of the OGPU my nephew Alekseev Mikhail Vladimirovich, his wife Alekseeva Aleksandra Pavlovna and my relation by marriage Ryabushinskaya Nadezhda Pavlovna, Alekseeva's sister, were arrested – in their communal apartment in Moscow, on Kharitonev Lane, no.12, apt 22.

From the words of Alekseeva and Ryabushinskaya I know that their indictment was brought against them according to the 58-6 article of the UK [*Ugolovny kodeks* or Criminal Code].

What charge was made against M.V. Alekseev I do not know. 11 months after his arrest, 11 May 1931, he died in confinement.

They were each sentenced to internment in a concentration camp for a term of 10 years with confiscation of all property. The confiscation was carried out at Ryabushinskaya's. In Alekseeva's case the confiscation was countermanded.

On 18 May 1931 both Alekseeva and Ryabushinskaya were sent to Solovki. Now they are both in Lovents. In exile they are both working as specialists, Alekseeva as a bacteriologist, Ryabushinskaya as a physician. They are working irreproachably. I do not doubt that both can be attested to be irreproachable workers.

They both, Alekseeva and Ryabushinskaya, have been involved all their lives with socially useful labour.

In 1912 Alekseeva graduated from the faculty of natural sciences, in the war served as a nurse, and then served the Soviets in her speciality. From 1926 to the day of her arrest she served in this way at the Botkin Hospital.

Ryabushinskaya is a physician, she graduated in 1917 from two faculties – natural sciences and medicine. Until her arrest she also served in the Institute for the Defense of Labour and the Institute for Nutritional Physiology.

She was in conflict with relations who were abroad because of family matters (a will) and has no contact with them.

I know both of them very well, am very close to them. I know, I am sure that they cannot be guilty of such heinous crimes. For me there is no doubt that they are more slandered than guilty.

Now, five years after the arrest, it would not be expedient to pose the question of reopening their case, therefore I do not consider it essential to go into the circumstances of their case.

I only ask that there be taken in consideration that until their arrest and afterwards they have worked honourably and are working, that they are no longer young: Alekseeva is 48 and Ryabushinskya is 49. In terms of health they are both listed in the 3rd category. They are both in bad health, both suffer from myocarditis. The work in their place of internment is beyond their strength. They quickly get exhausted. They have a hard time enduring the climate.

Alekseeva's children, from whom she was torn, live in Moscow.

All the aforesaid prompts me to request an order to return them to Moscow and their family.

KS's request was not granted.

The Studio opened its doors in March 1936. In April KS addressed leading actors and directors of the MAAT about the method of physical action. 'It is clear to me that there is a director of the result and a director of the root.' When a director goes straight to the result, he forces the actor to play the result. KS preferred to stress the supertask and the through action.

Over the next few years ND and Leonidov were active at the MAAT, personally directing such ambitious and successful works as a spectacular dramatization of Anna Karenina *and a revival of* Woe from Wit. *In the face of this, KS decided to return to* Molière, *the original, not a recreation, and in May began to cast* Tartuffe *with young actors, in hopes of transmitting to them via this production everything he had learned about acting. Ironically, when the MAT had been founded, he had professed to hate* Tartuffe.

To **Elizabeth Hapgood**. 7 June 1936, Moscow.

Dear friend!

I am dictating, not writing, because I still cannot get well. This year was dreadful – the sixth month I am bedridden, have suffered every possible pain, illness and insomnia, and now my heart is very weak. Don't not be cross that I have written nothing and have delayed the last chapter. It was written with my remaining strength, a temperature, I mean with a fever. But now I can say that the book is finished – the delay is only with the censorship and the sending.

I could not receive Norris Houghton,[40] because I really was ill. Forgive all the unpleasantness and embarrassment that I caused you. This is my punishment for taking on something that is not my business. The publisher refused to publish it – he is right.[41] You are so dear and kind to have found a new publisher. I can only thank you and wonder at your patience. Now I can boldly say that you will have the entire book within a few weeks.

I shall answer your questions. For efficiency I sent a telegram with the following contents:

'Sending last, sixteenth chapter. Consists of six lessons. My book treats only process of emotional experiencing, physical embodiment constitutes separate big book. I trust your tact, taste, caution, correct, cross out wisely what's hard to understand. Do whatever necessary in your discretion for copyright. Names of students bear no relationship to their personalities, change names.'

Now I will answer you point for point.

1) How many chapters will there still be (I have 15). Answer – I am attaching a list of all the chapters.[42]

2) It is impossible to put the theory of emotional experiencing and the theory of embodiment into a single book. First, because it would create too large a book, second, I could not finish it next year. You say that there is no way to sell the 'system' in parts. But after all the 'system' is included in my following books: 1) 'Work on Oneself' (emotional experiencing), -- this is the first book, which is now being sent. 2) 'Work on Oneself' (embodiment) – that speaks of physical training of the body, voice, movement, rhythm, external characteristics and

inner (there is no way to distinguish them from tempo-rhythm). 3) 'Work on the Role'. Without this the first two books do not make much sense, because the sense of self on stage and creative real condition of the actor cannot be created without work on the role. 4) The last book is creativity itself: the realm of the subconscious and so on.

All this together constitutes the 'system'.

At age 73 can I guarantee that I shall write all these books and can I on that basis sign a contract, especially since in the process of the work itself the general plan of the whole labour will involuntarily change.

3) The copies sent to you have not been corrected in terms of style, therefore there are plenty of mistakes, but this is irrelevant to the translation. If we had to await a well-edited and well-revised text, I would be delaying you even more. When it comes to style, do whatever you want.

4) You speak of Russian expressions, not understood by English-speakers. I trust your tact and taste and leave it to you to cross out or modify whatever you find necessary. Sometimes there are images that are too Russian, -- I leave it to your tact and intuition to rework them for your nation or leave them out entirely, if it does not harm the subject and chief goal of the book.

As to the copyright – I trust you completely: act as you know best. If you find it necessary to show your translation to a specialist in copyright, then, of course, show it using your own discretion.

5) The names are all arbitrary, they bear no relation to the inner characteristics or characters of the people in the book.[43] I discarded that intention – it is too tendentious. Therefore in principle I have nothing against changing the names: let Umnovykh be called Umnov, but Maletkova instead of Maloletkova – no Russian will accept such a name. Therefore it would be better if when you change a name you talk it over with Uspenskaya or Deikarkhanova or one of the Muscovites. In short, do with the names whatever you like. But just one remark. A local lawyer says that it is essential that the names in the Russian and American editions be identical. If this is not the case, then the text will not be accepted as identical and the rights to the Russian edition will have to be assigned separately. [...]

I am now rereading the whole book.

The chapters in order.

1. Introduction. Amateurism.
2. Stage art and stage craftsmanship.
3. The magic 'if', given circumstances, action.
4. Stage imagination.
5. Stage attention.
6. Freeing the muscles.
7. Bits and tasks.
8. The feeling of truth and faith.
9. Emotional memory.
10. Interrelationships.
11. Adjustment and other elements, the actor's characteristics, abilities and talents.

12. Agents of psychic life. The mind, the will and the feelings.
13. Lines of tension of agents of the psychic life.
14. The internal sense of self on stage.
15. The supertask, the through action.
16. The realm of the subconscious in the actor's sense of self on stage.

On 8 June Gorky died, possibly poisoned at Stalin's behest. The newspapers were kept away from KS, but that very fact informed him of the death.

To **Boris Livanov**. 8 July 1936, Moscow.
To a dear and beloved actor, a good man.

Of him who has been given much, much will be asked. Answer me: what have you done with your beautiful talent? Have you understood the chief fundamentals of art? Have you studied them? Do you know that the one and only joy in life in our business is knowing the creative secrets of organic nature? Has talent suggested to you that theatre is ending forever throughout the whole world; that the only ones that will remain standing are those who still know what art is. There are more of such unique individuals, who know a bit about art, in our theatre than anywhere else. This is a great responsibility. But even those individuals are getting old and leaving us, and with them the Russian art of the actor is departing. Do not let them go, so that the secrets of our concern be not forever buried. The MAAT has the mission to save world art. You will answer for the non-fulfilment of this command of fate, since you are one of the living young successors. If you manage it, fame awaits you. If not, disgrace will dog your steps.

Lose no time! Cast everything aside, study anew, everything is very badly retarded! Art will discover brand-new laws!

The time has come.

You are one of those I have in mind, when the fate of theatre flashes before my eyes in the unprecedently beautiful conditions for its flourishing – in our country.

Affectionately and hoping in you
K. Stanislavsky

To **Lyubov Gurevich**. 2 September 1936, Barvikh.
Dear, good, ardently beloved Lyubov Yakovlevna!

[…] For me you have always been the authoritative spectator, the competent critic and the wise counsellor.

You know what such a connoisseur means to an actor among the ill-assorted crowd.

One needs to keep in mind that our life in art was passed in that time when the revolutionary struggle flared up in the theatres, when the old, obsolescent actor's craft was fighting with its last strength and trampling down the shoots of the sprouting new, delicate Chekhovian art. Among the attacks and encouragements, among the misunderstandings and overstated demands, among the disagreements and revolutionary chaos – a wise, understanding, impassive voice of a talented

602

critic, which you always were, had for us, the leaders and actors of a theatre of the new tendency, an utterly exceptional significance. [...]

When I was ready to tear up my prospectus for the 'system', you supported my wavering faith in myself. Thanks to your enthusiasm and great assistance I could bring my first book to light. And now, with the issuance of a remarkably more complex labour, you are continuing to cheer me on. [...]

Loving and grateful with all my heart
K. Stanislavsky

On 6 September 1936 KS, ND and Kachalov were named the first People's Artists of the USSR. A draft of his letter thanking Stalin survives, but it is unlikely to have been sent.

To **Iosif Stalin**, late 1936.

Accept from me, deeply respected and beloved friend of culture, the arts and of artists, Iosif Vissarionovich, my great, heartfelt gratitude for your paternal concern for me, my comrades-in-arms and the art which we serve and which is perishing in all the countries of the world, except the Soviet Union. [...]

The beautiful, well-merited words and epithets with which hundreds of thousands of citizens of our and other lands lovingly dignify you, have become too familiar, too habitual. People have grown accustomed to their sound, they do not convey the meaning concealed within them. I seek another way to express my feelings to you. [...]

That way is the candour of a confession. When the construction of socialist life began in our country, we did not understand and could not imagine the grandiose plans of the Party – those of V. I. Lenin and your own. Much seemed utopian, stirred up doubt, mistrust. This prevented us from boldly walking hand in hand with our leaders.

[Thanks to the government for demonstrating] a love and attention [...] to the theatre and the workers that is exceptional and unparalleled in any state, at any time.

Elizabeth Hapgood's drastic recension of Stanislavsky's acting text appeared in English as An Actor Prepares, *published by Theatre Arts Books, two years before it would appear in Russian. It created an immediate stir in the US, but its partial form and uncritical vocabulary led to the image of KS as devoted only to the actor's inner state.*

To **Elizabeth Hapgood**. After 6 November 1936, Barvikh.

If it weren't for you, I wouldn't have written this book. You encouraged me and were my inspiration. Thank you for this, as well as for the wonderful translation and your maternal effort to bring out the book. You are its godmother.

To **Elizabeth Hapgood**. Before 20 December 1936, Barvikh.

Dear, very best of friends!

I have to write a business letter, but I don't feel like it. It's been so long since I've written to you that you have stopped understanding our life here. In short, I want to tell you about what's happening with us, and at the end we'll talk business.

I have spent a dreadful year of illness. Last year, after a very unsuccessful summer vacation, I did not feel very hale and hearty. But the work was interesting and that kept me going. A year ago I opened my new opera-dramatic studio-school. Here is its origin: my sister Zinaida Sergeevna, whom I think you know, had for a long time a group of private students, whom she drilled so much that, despite their youth, they could be entrusted with pedagogical work in a new studio. They were formed into cadres run by my sister. All summer long, in the hot spell, they auditioned the young people who had come to them. They auditioned up to three and a half thousand people. This is how an audition usually goes: they set up an audition table, the instructors and chairmen take seats around it, a line of all sorts of people pass by, they recite and sing till you're blue in the face, but the wise auditioners intuit at once: this one has talent and should be admitted, and not that one. My sister acted differently, more cleverly. First of all she rejected all those who have no talent for the stage, and nominated for audition those who have some ability. Another selection is made. Around a thousand candidates are left, with whom the whole staff of instructors will be involved over the course of three months. They are not only auditioned, but instructed, and twenty people are chosen for the dramatic course and about twenty for the operatic. The entrance audition is held periodically and at set times. What we are creating is not simply a school where you come, study and – go to any theatre in the country. Our school does not graduate individuals, but a whole troupe (operatic and dramatic). Our studio creates *theatres* and graduates ready-to-work troupes with a small repertoire, its own directors, costumiers, makeup men, a manager and his staff. These troupes work together. The opera singers can perform drama, and the dramatic actors can perform in the chorus, as mimes in opera ballets. The performances will alternate: one day dramatic, another day operatic. Even more interesting is what ensues. Up to now we were dealing with young people who had grown up in the difficult conditions of world war with its famine, privations, blood and atrocities; in the tempestuous times of the revolution. These young people had not managed to receive a proper education. Now a new generation has grown up who have lived under the best conditions and received training. They really are new people. This younger generation is beautiful, eager and able to work. It is a pleasure to do business with them. Wonderful young people. In our crew there are many simple workers, peasants (from collective farms), Red Army men, there are the homeless, the students include Leonidov's son and daughter, Vishnevsky's daughter, there are engineers and intellectuals. Whenever they merge together, I cannot distinguish the collective farmers and artisans from the intellectuals. You would be surprised at how quickly people can be transformed and learn an alien culture. In short, a wonderful group of young people has been assembled, athirst for work and enlightenment. The method of education is also unusual. Here's an example. One of the students, a handsome boy, who is successful with the ladies, an intellectual – gave himself airs and sulked amid his comrades, saying that there was no one here he could talk to or befriend. His remarks were printed in the next issue of the bulletin-board newspaper. There was a storm of indignation: 'Denunciations! Someone's been eavesdropping!!' The students were outraged. The principal summoned all of them to a debate and explained that if such vague dissatisfaction were to be hidden in all the corners of the school, it would upset all our work. Therefore the diseased places had to be brought to light as soon as possible and the reasons for the dissatisfaction eradicated. The debate that followed was stormy at first, and then peaceable, and finally the students themselves explained to their conceited comrade the error of his ways and assigned him to put out the next issue of the newspaper under his editorship. That issue included not one, but three whole 'denunciations' or, as they now call them, three topics for discussion. This incident very much aided the cohesion of the young people and the eradication of the causes of dissatisfaction. [...] The so-called Stanislavsky system is now accepted– as essential and obligatory for all schools and theatres. Therefore our school has achieved special significance and attracts special attention.

To **Elizabeth Hapgood**. 20 December 1936, Barvikh.
My dear, best of friends, whom I thank infinitely, my favourite of favourites, to the business at hand!

Your attitude, care, excitement, concern over the publication of my book moves me to tears. I remember the whole epic of its origin: from signing the contract in Badenweiler, the absurd manuscript I handed to you for translation, all the copying, corrections, changes and other mistakes of an amateur, undertaking a task that was beyond his scope; all my delays, awkwardnesses with the first publisher, my despair on realizing my incompetence, your encouragement and faith in the necessity of the book, finally the break with the first publisher and the search for a new one etc., etc. I blush for the troubles and disagreements I caused you, and now I clearly acknowledge that if it weren't for you, I would not have finished this book. Now I confess that during that period I gave up the work time and time again, having come to the conclusion that it was beyond my abilities. And actually my head ached when I had to sort out the details of the creative process. At those moments, on one hand, your encouraging letters, and on the other the awareness of my obligation to you forced me to take up the pen once more. In truth you are the godmother of this book, and therefore the first order of business is to congratulate not myself but you for its publication. Congratulations for, obviously, succeeding in mastering the difficult task of translation (which it seems is brilliant) of a book that treats a very specialized subject and the life of a foreign people and nation, its local colour and daily life (which you also successfully assimilated to American customs). I believe that I understand how difficult your task was and I applaud you from the bottom of my heart. You deserved those ovations and flowers that were sent not to me but in truth to you. [...] In my mind, as a knight, I get down on one knee, bow to the ground and kiss your slipper, and then hug you tightly as a friend.

I welcomed the joyous news in bed after my collapsed lungs had just relapsed. I was very dangerously ill this year not once but many times. If you don't count short interruptions, I lay in bed and sat in a room --- at home and in a sanatorium – for exactly a year (that is, from December 1935). The last chapters of my book were written with a temperature of 37.5-38 degrees, with an aching head. Owing to various theatrical conditions I now have to correct the Russian edition. But here is my problem, let me explain it to you. What does it mean to write a book about the system? It does not mean to copy out something over and done with and ready-made. The system lives inside me, but in an inchoate state. Only when you start to search for a form for it is the system itself created and defined. In other words, the system is created in the process of writing it down. That is why so often even now I have to change things and write some more. Here's an example. Now, completely by chance, I came across a new means of approaching a role, which immediately became awfully popular, at first in my new studio-school, and then at the Art Theatre itself. You ought to be in on these events. So I will give you a short explanation.

This is how we do it now: today I read a new play, and tomorrow we are to act it. What can be acted? The play says that Mr X enters to Mr Y. Do you know how to enter a room? Then make an entrance. The play says, let's assume that it is a meeting of old acquaintances. Do you know how old acquaintances meet? Then go and meet one another. They speak their minds a lot to one another. Do you remember the gist? Then speak the gist. What? You don't know the words? Never mind, speak your own words. You don't remember the sequence of their conversation? Never mind, I will prompt you as to how the thoughts follow one other. So the whole play proceeds by physical actions. It is easier to gain an understanding and control of them with the body than with the fickle mind. That's why this physical line of a role is easier to create than a psychological one. But can the physical line of a role exist without a psychological one, when the mind is not inseparable from the body. Of course not. That is why simultaneously with the physical line of the body the internal line of the role develops on its own. This practice distracts the attention of the person doing the creating away from feeling and conveys it to the subconscious, which alone can correctly control and direct it. Thanks to such a procedure you avoid forcing the emotions and draw nature itself into the work.

When the actor, having created the physical line, suddenly and unexpectedly begins to feel the inner, spiritual line of the role, his joy and wonderment know no end. It seems to him that a miracle has taken place in him. This practice, of course, requires a technique all its own. I am busy now working it out. I impart to you the secret of my laboratory, because one way or another it will reach you. Meanwhile don't talk about it, so that it doesn't get bruited about and distorted in reception. It may mislead a great many people.

Meanwhile I am still in the sanatorium. Not long ago Leonidov and another of our actors, Khmelyov, were here. Now Kachalov is coming here. He is much, much better. He already goes out and walks in the fresh air, while this is the third month I have been sitting inside. The first two months my wife lived with me. She was also mighty ill. This happened just at the time when Kira and Kilyalya came to Moscow. We couldn't meet them or live with them. Now my wife has gone to the city, and I live here on my own. They come and visit me twice every six days. But visiting hours are so short (from 2 to 5), and the people I have to talk with so many, and my strength is so scanty that I can say that up to now I still haven't seen as much of my own family as I should. They arrived almost unexpectedly and settled into our little apartment, because their good apartment is occupied by other people during their absence and one can't toss them into the street. That is why they live in our rooms like sardines in a tin. [...]

Affectionate and grateful K. Stanislavsky

[...] One quick remark. I entrust to you the fate of my book. Do with it what you will, translate it into any language whatsoever, let it be printed in any country. However as to country and publisher work things out with our Soviet government. It is not proper for me to have dealings with just any country and, most important, just any publisher. If the publishing house is hostile to our country, it would be improper for me to do business with them.

To **Elizabeth Hapgood**. 11 January 1937, Barvikh.
My dear, best of friends!

[...] Today's letter will probably turn out to be a business letter. I planned to write to you long ago, but had the time to get sick again. Nothing serious, but the local medical men put me in bed and forbade any sort of activity. My sole consolation was Kachalov, who came to gossip and read to me. He is getting better and will soon go back to work. But, they say, Knipper-Chekhova will be coming here soon. Our old-timers are giving out, growing old.

[...] You ask: how many books should you send? 2 for me. 1 for the museum. 1 for Mei Lanfang (the famous Chinese actor).[44] A copy for you. I will sign it and send it back – 1 for Reinhardt. 6 copies for others. I thank you in advance and kiss your hand. I am only afraid that there are not enough blank pages to express my friendly feelings, gratitude and all my guilt towards you: all the trouble you overcame, the awkwardness for my periods of delay with the promised copies, the unpleasantness with the first publisher, the trouble in finding a new publisher etc. [...]

As to affective memory. This term derives from Ribot.[45] He was widely criticized for such terminology, because affect gave rise to confusion. Ribot's term was discarded and not replaced by a new, more sharply defined one. But I had to give a name to the most important memory on which almost all of our art is founded. So I called it emotional memory (that is, the memory of emotions).

It is a falsehood and completely idiotic that I have repudiated memory based on sensation. I repeat: it is an important element in our creativity. All I had to repudiate was the term (affective), and more than once to acknowledge the significance of memory, which prompts our emotions, that is the thing on which our art is built.

The rumour that I left the Art Theatre three years ago is also a lie. That rumour arose because, from the time I fell ill, I didn't go to the theatre, and here's why. In winter, at a time of frost, I could not leave my house. I had heart spasms (angina pectoris). In spring, when I might go to the theatre and see my own and other people's productions, the theatres, both the MAT and the Opera, are going on tour. In the fall, when the theatres begin to perform, I had a relapse. My work (for all the theatres and studios) goes on only in Leontiev Lane where I live. So I work with actors from all our theatres. There I present a preview without sets, costumes and makeup to a small, select audience. During the rehearsals designs and models of scenery and costumes are shown. There too, on specific rehearsal days, I examine makeups and costumes on the actors themselves, who come to my house and put on their makeup and costumes at my house. But the production itself, as a totality, I do not see. I did not see on stage *Dead Souls*, *Talents and Admirers* (Ostrovsky), *Carmen*, *The Barber of Seville*, *Don Pasquale*, *The Queen of Spades*, *Boris Godunov*.

To tell the truth this is a halfway departure from the theatre. The last brushstroke a painter puts to a picture — that's all. Now I fail to make that brushstroke, and therefore I am somehow losing the desire to put anything on stage. Only Nemirovich really does any work. He has gone wholly over to the artistic sector, and won't have anything to do with the managerial and administrative side. In great part it has been imposed on me. But it is impossible to run things at a distance, by telephone. Therefore I have had to request that they provide someone, a government official, to deal with the managerial and administrative side of the theatre. They have assigned us such a person [Arkadiev], and this has happened just in time because at this time I fell ill and now I've been ill a whole year and have dealt with almost no business, I had great difficulty in finishing writing the book. As you see, I never thought of leaving the Art Theatre and do not think of it now, but illness prevents me from working as I should. That's probably why the rumours started about my [leaving]. I trust my health will improve and I can get to work again.

[...] If you want to take my book under your protection for its translation and placement in different countries, I can only be infinitely happy that the book has been so lucky and that it wound up with you, in loyal and beautiful hands. I myself could only dream of this in secret, but wouldn't have dared to suggest it to you, because, even without that, I have worn you out with this book and made a lot of trouble.

If you find this interesting or amusing, then, I repeat, I can only envy the book and rejoice at its fate. Do with it what you will, translate it into whatever language you please, make deals for it in other countries. Of course, you will do this better than I or any agent and 'specialist' in these matters.

There is, however, one matter which absolutely must be observed. My book cannot be published in those periodicals, publications, publishing houses which *are hostile* to the USSR. In that case, if this condition is breached, my situation will be very uncomfortable, and it might cause a scandal. Which publishers are hostile to us – I don't know. This question can be resolved only by the legation in each particular country. Before dealing with any company in another country, I will write to the legation of that country and ask for information: whether it is proper to be published by such-and-such a publisher – I will name the company. To avoid misunderstanding one needs to have a document from the legation.

Therefore: the right of translation (by whom, which country and company) will depend on you (with the approval of the legation), when questions about publishing the book in other countries are addressed to me, I will forward the foreign publishers to you. Exceptions only for Germany, Italy and Portugal. I will have to sort them out from here. Until I know whether I can let them have my book and whether you have any sanction from Moscow or the legation – it's not worth drawing up a contract.

While I am writing all this, the idea is whirling around in my head: all this trouble – and it is, I do think, enormous – you are taking on yourself! I am afraid that, when all is said and done, you will curse my book. Besides that, there is the ticklish question; I will have to send you rewrites, corrections, make inquiries. All this is, I do think, a good deal of work. You cannot cope with it alone. You have to have an assistant. I do not think that my work will receive wide distribution. I will be satisfied if it helps me pay off my debts. But even if there isn't much demand for the book, there will be a lot of work in advertising it in other countries and increasing the interest in the book. In sort, all these observations come down to the fact that you cannot and should not do this out of friendship --- without payment, but should put it on a business-like footing. This way you give me the possibility of putting the book in your care and you will bring me great joy.

You write nothing about the contract. Where is it in force: Canada or London. As to Prague I think I can answer you as I did before: 1) You will have to sort things out about the publisher with the legation; 2) the book will be printed only in Moscow, I am sending the printed pages for 100 copies. They will be bound at a publisher's in Prague, and the bound book will be delivered to corresponding institutions, so that no one has the right to translate it from Russian into foreign languages, because conventions with countries abroad do not exist in the USSR.

If, let's say, some publisher would like to publish the book abroad in Russian independently (highly unlikely), I have nothing against it. I wanted to pass to the question of your trip to Moscow, a question which greatly excited and rejoiced me. But Kira has arrived, therefore I will have to cut this letter short, otherwise it will be a long time before I send it. Do not reread it. Forgive me for writing badly. I am lying or half-lying in uncomfortable positions.

[…] To all, all of you my heartfelt greetings. I embrace you, thank you and love you.

K. Stanislavsky

To **Elizabeth Hapgood**. 2 February 1937, Barvikh
My dearest friend!

I am still in the sanatorium and I still feel weak. […]

You signed a preliminary contract in your country, America, for the book-to-be and ask when it will be written.

What does the woman mean! Earlier instances haven't taught her, and you have already forgotten what it means to do business with a writer of my sort. There will be more delays: again you will have to be embarrassed on my account;

again the publisher will turn it down and you will have to take the trouble to find a new one.

Now I am afraid of specific deadlines! Therefore I can say nothing of when the book will be ready. I have to rest a bit from the previous work, and then we shall see how the business gets along.

Thank you for this new contract, I kiss your hands, but let it be without a deadline. That's the only way I will quickly write the second book: *embodiment*. As soon as I begin it, I shall inform you and keep you informed of my work.

Yes, there had to be a lot of rewriting for Moscow. I think it is to the benefit of the book. Right now I've only just finished the foreword to the book (Russian version). Therefore the work for the local edition is finished. [...]

Eva Le Gallienne is a familiar name, but I do not remember where we met.[46] Write what she will say. I don't need this out of curiosity, but for two reasons. First, to know what and how it affects the reader so I can take this into consideration in the next books, and second, in order to make corrections in the first book. Besides, everything that testifies to the necessity, the usefulness of the book, will spur me into beginning the new work.

[...] These are good times for me now: my wife is living here and so is Kachalov. In the evenings we meet and read chapters from my book and argue over it, make corrections. I can work a bit. So can Kachalov. But in five days' time both of them will be leaving, and I will remain quite alone. That will be bad. Before their arrival there was another lonely stint. It was dreadful. Before this lonely stint Leonidov was here and another young actor – Khmelyov. With them I managed to talk about the book and new techniques.

[...] I got the review from the *Times*, a copy of the letter from Chaplin and the letter from Taines (?). Thank you, what they write about me is very interesting and flattering.

I am impatiently waiting Gielgud's[47] article from some magazine. I'm also waiting for the article from one of the producers of the 'Guild'.

You write about the enthusiastic opinions of '*business people*'. This is completely unexpected. What can they find of use in my book?

I am very, very sorry that I cannot hear the opinions about the book, that I am not with you. [...]

Yesterday the letter of 15 January 1937 arrived and, oh joy, -- along with the books! Thank you, thank you! I like the format very much. It's simple, elegant. Because I wrote it so long ago, I thought it might be enormous, but it is totally normal. Although I don't understand a word, although I cannot read it and appreciate your work, nevertheless I simply enjoy looking at it and realizing that I am obliged for its appearance in print to my dear, wonderful friend – Liza. Thank you, thank you, thank you!

This means you have received my long letter.

I very much understand the professor of Russian about whom you write. Letters and words are so definite, concrete, that they do not convey the nuanced sensations of feelings. The greater and subtler this feeling, the harder it is to write it down. He wants to translate the nuances of a language and cannot. I want to translate the nuances of creativity – and cannot, I am dissatisfied and keep seeking and cannot be done with corrections. This was not how it was with me when I wrote my first book *My Life in Art*. To write about the facts and events of one's life, our language and our letters, words are sufficient, but for art and psychology one needs to think up a great many new words. Without them one has to tie oneself into knots and originate forms, moods, similes, metaphors, examples, whole scenes, and it's hard to do and takes time.

[...] There, all the letters are answered, with all the business questions, and I can turn to the most important, interesting matter, that is the question of your trip to Moscow.

The toughest thing is to pick a time when we can meet and visit, so that you can also see the theatres. This has to be weighed carefully. Usually our festivals for foreigners take place 1-10 September. The weather at that time is not too bad and not very cold. But at that time I usually linger outside the city, that is in a sanatorium or somewhere else outside Moscow, to breathe fresh air, because in October I have already shut myself up between four walls. If we were to meet, you would have to leave Moscow, subject to the visiting hours of the sanatoria. Their hours are strict: from 2 to 5. If you take into consideration that during that time I cannot protect myself from other visitors and visiting days and hours are not allowed every day, but approximately twice a week, then you will understand that during visiting hours we won't have time to talk as we ought.

As to the theatres, the beginning of September is a bad time for them. The actors begin the season lazily, the actors can't get into the swing of things, because of the heavy workload, double rehearsals every day – they get tired. All the productions have to be rerehearsed, after all, often to insert new performers to replace those who are delayed on leave or fallen ill etc. After October I shut myself in all winter at home in Leontiev Lane. This is the most suitable time. Even if I am busy, you can attend rehearsals. It might be interesting to you, because now you are a specialist in the system. For all the theatres, that's the height of the season. Perhaps at that time there will come to Moscow some of the national theatres of the Caucasus, the Ukraine, Kazakhstan, Uzbekistan etc. These are interesting performances, which you will see nowhere else. But during the wintertime there is a powerful cold spell. True, these last few years our climate has changed mightily and, as in this year, we do not know great cold. But days do occur, like today for instance, with a temperature of 30 degrees of frost.

Spring is good, and if I am not ill, in the month of May I begin to go out and move around, but cautiously. Sometimes in this time I am sent to the sanatorium, they may send me anywhere – to Kislovodsk. But that is the exception that proves the rule. As for the theatres, usually all my theatres are travelling on tour. Many of the other theatres are also on the move, and in their place there arrive troupes from the provinces, to show off and repeat their successes. I believe I have sketched the whole year for you. Decide for yourself, when and how our meeting can take place.

I'm told that this year they are sending the MAAT to Paris, to an exhibition, for one month.[48] From Paris everyone will return to the outskirts of Moscow, to the rest home for our theatre, and work will proceed there all summer long – preparations for the jubilee performance, on the occasion of the twentieth anniversary of Soviet power. I will probably have to go there and work, because I have done nothing with the theatre all winter long.

Meanwhile I will dream about my meeting with you and Norman Carlovich. How good it will be if we were to meet! In conclusion I shall tell you about myself. It's been a whole year now that I've been ailing on account of a bad bout of influenza. It wearied my heart and caused an illness in my right foot, which up to now is still limping (nervous inflammation). They conveyed me barely alive here, to Barvikh. Here I recovered and in gratitude organized a concert for the patients with my own young students. The concert had a great success, but I could not go to it, because just on that day my lungs began to collapse. Now I am recovered, but still weak. Those are the conditions in which I had to finish writing the book. My wife came here with me and here she underwent a sort of attack of high blood pressure. She was ill for a long time, and I had to look after her. Now she is in health, has gone to Moscow and is busy teaching in the studios with great success. There was a catastrophe there as well: both my sister Zinaida Sergeevna and I were out of commission (she had a heart attack similar to mine). The studio looked to be in a critical situation, and Mariya Petrovna came to our aid, with great success. During this time the MAAT had a new administrator. Vl. Iv. works with might and main, but even he, not long ago, had a rush of blood to the head. Now he has recovered. At the moment the theatre is rehearsing *Anna Karenina* (a dramatization) and *Boris Godunov* (by Pushkin).

Kira and Kilyalya came here to see me on the way back to Paris, so Kilyalya can finish school.[49] They meet with me very seldom, only on visiting days. They are returning to Paris now, when any day now war might break out, -- It's alarming. Meanwhile Kilyalya is studying here, in the French program, and is working on Russian, in case she has to transfer to a Russian school. My concern is Igor. His doctors sent him to Casablanca (Morocco), next to Spanish Morocco, and I am upset on their account. Such is our life.

I kiss your hands, embrace you, once more heartily thank you for the book. […]

Your grateful and loving friend K. Stanislavsky

Back at Leontiev Lane, KS rehearsed Tartuffe, Madame Butterfly *and* Rigoletto. *For* Butterfly, *he drew on his past experience with* The Mikado, *insisting on ethnologically accurate behaviour.* Rigoletto *was reinterpreted as a paean to the underdogs, surrounding the wronged jester with a crowd of professional fools who share his pain.*

ND's Anna Karenina *proved to be a huge success, in part because audiences flocked to view the props and set pieces, costumes and uniforms, crowd scenes and special effects, vestiges of a bygone Tsarist era.*

On 4 May KS was awarded a Lenin prize, along with ND, Kachalov, Moskvin, and Leonidov. Later that month Elizabeth Hapgood came to Moscow and spent ten days with KS from two to seven p.m.

In June 1937 Arkadiev was removed as administrator of the MAAT: the official reason was that he had given unauthorized interviews to French journalists about future plans for the Paris repertoire which had not been approved by Stalin. He was convicted of spying for Polish intelligence and shot. He was replaced by Yakov Osipovich Boyarsky (1890-1940?), a Party leader and chairman of RABIS, first deputy Chairman of the Committee for Artistic Affairs. He was removed in turn in 1939, liquidated and later rehabilitated.

Back in Moscow on 12 December 1937 KS insisted on leaving his room to vote in the Soviet Supreme elections. He caught cold and had to go back to bed, but the ballot box was brought to him there.

Over the previous years, attacks on Meyerhold had increased from critiques of his productions to ad hominem defamation of his personality and talents. They culminated in the closure of his Theatre, after which he was treated as a pariah by the theatre community. Despite past differences, KS phoned Meyerhold in late January 1938 and invited him to join the Opera Theatre. When his seventy-fifth birthday was celebrated, Meyerhold wrote to him: 'How can I tell you how much I love you?'

'How can I tell you the magnitude of my gratitude to you for what you taught me about such a difficult business as the art of directing turns out to be?!'

'If I have the strength to overcome all the difficulties set before me by the events of the last few months, I shall come to you, and you shall read in my eyes my joy over you, that you have already recovered from your illness, that you are hearty and merry once more, that you have gone to work once more for the good of our great motherland.'

That same birthday was marked by a number of measures passed by the Politburo: KS was awarded the Order of Lenin; Leontiev Lane was renamed Stanislavsky Street; a new building was devoted to the Stanislavsky Studio under the MAAT; five fellowships were funded in his name at the State Theatrical Institute. His complete works were to be published under the editorship of Lyubov Gurevich.

To **Iosif Stalin.**[50] 8 February 1938, Moscow.

Dear Iosif Vissarionovich!

I am deeply touched and moved by the special solicitude shown me by the Party and the government, which has commended my public activities so highly in connection with my 75th birthday.

I have now received a huge number of congratulations, letters and telegrams from all parts of our boundless socialist homeland, from the far-away austere North to the wonderful sunny South.

I can attribute the large number of letters I have received to just one thing: our people's great love for art, which never attracts so much attention as it does here with us. Where else will you find this thirst for knowledge, for the acceptance of real culture? Only in our country.

That is why I love my homeland. That is why I am proud of my homeland, the country where genuine theatrical art is studied not only by major stage directors and actors, but also by workers, collective farmers and school children who ask my advice.

Only our enemies or blind men could fail to see and appreciate what has been done in our country over the last 20 years. Under a government such as ours, a government elected by all the people, composed of those most gifted and most dedicated to the interests of the workers, led by the great Communist Party and you, dear Iosif Vissarionovich, working people, one may be confident about our homeland.

Your solicitude for humanity will always stir a feeling of admiration in me. That is why my thoughts are so often with you. And now, after the high valuation of my social activity in connection with my 75th year of life, I thank you for the special attention shown me.

Accept my humble appreciation and great thanks for everything you have done for our art, for the theatres and, in particular, for me personally.

People's actor of the Union of the SSR, medal recipient
[K. Stanislavsky]

To **Iosif Stalin**, 1938, draft.
There, where once in tsarist Russia lay barren fields, impassable tundra, and thickets, the spring of life now pulses, everywhere art blossoms forth into luxuriant flower, there too they are studying my system.

ND's wife, the former Baroness Yekaterina Nikolaevna Korff, died on 25 February.

To **Nemirovich-Danchenko**. 27 February 1938, Moscow.
My dear, good Vladimir Ivanovich!
There have been many misunderstandings between us in recent years that have troubled our good relations.

The grievous ordeal that has befallen you brings my thoughts back to a past that is so closely linked with the dear departed. As I think of her, I think of our earlier, good relations. Under the impression of these memories, I wanted to write to you. What about?..

I cannot pretend to console you in an inconsolable grief; there is nothing special I want to write about...

At this grievous moment I want to and need to say to you a few sincere and simple words, -- as I used to in times gone by. I feel that dear Yekaterina Nikolaevna would have liked that.

I would like, in a friendly way, to say that I sincerely and deeply feel for you and am looking for ways to help you.

It may be that this friendly, heartfelt impulse of mine will give you the strength, even in the slightest degree, to make it through this grievous ordeal visited upon you.

Sincerely devoted and affectionately yours,
K. Stanislavsky

Sometime in April-May Meyerhold joined the Opera Theatre and prepared its summer tour to Sochi and Kislovodsk.

To **his wife Mariya Lilina**. 5 June 1938, Moscow.

[…] I am well, Kira and Kilyalya are too. Kilyalya is taking exams, doesn't know her grades yet, is cramming. Kira and Zina bring me the news every day. My arm aches a bit, but that is due to my having my 15th massage session, which requires extension. I did diathermy in Barvikh for a few months, with absolutely no result.

I watched *Butterfly* twice [in the salon], a very pleasant impression, the production is almost ready, all the Japanese women are in costume, a very charming stage-set for the room is installed. There was another showing of *Vanyushin's Children* and *Three Sisters* for GITIS [the State Theatre School]. Great success. The headmaster said that he understands the difference between our approach and the approaches of the so-called experts. *The Cherry Orchard* was not shown in accord with your statement. I myself did not get to work again with the participants in *Cherry Orchard*, but managed to show Novitskaya a bit of how to strengthen the line of the concept. Every other day I sit a while on the balcony. When the sun goes down it gets cold, so I have to go in. […]

Life goes on monotonously and tediously, only my work in the studio cheers me up and stimulates me. It is impossible to write, I'm constantly being bothered. […]

To **his wife Mariya Lilina**. 7 June 1938, Moscow.

Dear Marusya!

Thanks for the letter, I'm glad you got our letters, that you're cheerful and not bored. Compliments and regards to Zarudny;[51] thank Nina Nikolaevna, Vasily Ivanovich and Dima [Kachalov] for the wonderful lemons and oranges;[52] tell them I feel like the Mayor [in *The Government Inspector*] who gets gifts 'on his saint's day, St Anthony's day, and on Saint Humphrey's too'. I feel the same as ever. Yesterday was a free day, I sat on the balcony and wrote, while the artist Ulyanov painted my portrait, then Kilyalya and Galya[53] came by, and Kilyalya told me that the previous evening she was at the Cultural Park with Roman Rafailovich. A picture had been commissioned from him – a group of some national minorities. He had gone there to select them; there was a kind of theatre on an island, evidently like the one in Leningrad. The audience sits on the shore, and the show is performed on the island. This time amateur actors of all nationalities went on. Kilyalya liked it a lot. At 7:30 I got in bed, in the evening I wrote an article for the komsomol, Zina came by, Kira was there and, as always, at one I went to sleep. The day before yesterday an interesting meeting was called of teachers of singing, public speaking and diction. They were supposed to speak on how to correct enunciation in singing, but Gukova fell ill, Nezhdanova fell ill and Shor-Plotnikova has been ill.[54] They had to postpone the meeting. Then I quickly gathered Novitskaya, Orlova,[55] Karp, Kruglyaka on the balcony and tried out a verbal exercise with them, I mean they were supposed to carry out all the set tasks with the aid of nothing but words and gestures.

They declared that they understood and will work with Novitskaya, and later on they will show me, but, of course, they understood very little. With this sort of thing you really have to get involved. […]

615

Today the Studio is going to show me two acts of *The Merry Wives of Windsor*. The weather is rather hot during the day, but turns cold at night. The days resemble one another like two peas in a pod, so that you simply don't know what to write about to keep from being monotonous. So, till next time, and meantime I embrace you tightly, love and miss you.

Yours Kostya

After 17 June KS's health worsened, with severe cardiac arrhythmia.

To **his wife Lilina**. 19 June 1938, Moscow.
Dear, sweet Marusya, I embrace you, I miss you, but I rejoice heartily that you are feeling well, and, as everyone testifies, cheerful and lively.

My problem is the recurrence of intermittent heartbeats, the doctors don't like it, they aren't accompanied by any great discomfort to me personally. My arm and my haemorrhoids are a much worse matter, they make me uncomfortable all the time. Today they decided to apply the smallest dose of mercuzal (a diuretic). The last time it immediately got me better, I don't know how it will go today. My temperature is 36.1. I have cut short all kinds of activities, and I probably won't have a chance to meet with the Studio any more. [...]

But my most grievous affliction is the articles on the occasion of the 40th anniversary for the Moscow anthology (two) and an article [about] the 20th year of the komsomol, which I rewrote twice, but not at all successfully. Worst of all is that for this kind of affliction there is no mercuzal that might promote the flow of ideas.

Kira conscientiously keeps me informed, as does Zina.

I do not breathe fresh air, because I am either bedridden (on warm days with an open window, but there are no warm days). Or else, when it's cold, I sit at home.

The artist Ulyanov drops by whenever possible to paint my portrait. Poor fellow! It can't be easy to deal with such a 'still life' as I am.

Kilyalya has gone to Fromgold [a rest home] with my heartfelt exhortations to be careful.

I have read over the reviews [of the Leningrad tour] you sent me. In the most brilliant period of the theatre they never praised us as highly as they do now. Doesn't this strike you as a sign of the degeneration of our art?

[...] I draw to a close. I embrace you tenderly. I miss you, look forward joyfully to our seeing one another again, but then too, am glad that you are resting away from Moscow. Don't worry about me, there's nothing special wrong with me, just the chronic indisposition.

Much love, Kostya

Ulyanov, who had designed The Drama of Life *and* Days of the Turbins, *remembered that he had to stimulate KS out of his torpor by mentioning Duncan ('Eye to the main chance' he commented) and Suler ('That's who I need now').*

On 13 June KS worked on scenes from Hamlet *with students of the dramatic division of the Studio. The last showing of* Madame Butterfly *in KS's presence took place three days later.*

To **his wife Mariya Lilina**. 21 June 1938, Moscow. *Telegram*.

Health good. Refused to attend recitals, don't worry, don't rush to return, rest. Hugs. Kostya.

To **his wife Mariya Lilina**. 24 June 1938, Moscow. *Telegram*.

Health good. We wait impatiently. Hugs. Kostya.

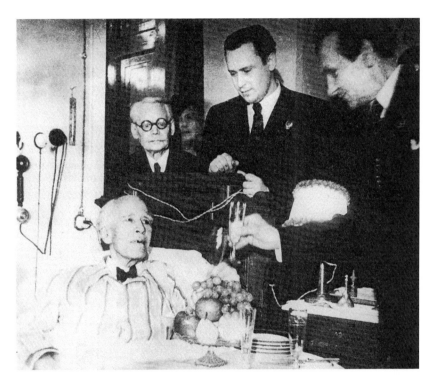

Figure 82 Stanislavsky on his sickbed on his 75th birthday, greeted by Yakov Gremislavsky, the MAT's first makeup artist, the actor Boris Livanov and the journalist Sergey Mozalevsky

Lilina returned to Moscow on 27 June. Because the summer was oppressively hot, she prepared to move KS to the rest home in Barvikh on 2 August. Before leaving, KS penned a few instructions for his disciples:

Do not go into a theatre with dirty shoes. Scrape off the mud and dust at the entrance and leave your galoshes in the vestibule, along with your trivial concerns... Too often actors carry with them everyday muck, gossip, intrigues, slander, envy, an etricated vanity. The theatre stops being a temple and becomes a garbage can. Think more of others and less of yourself. Take care of the common work and common state of mind, and you will be suffused with well-being... Let everyone care about everyone else.... and an atmosphere will condense which will be able to overcome the mediocrity of the every day. It will be easy to work. This joyful sense of expectation, this receptive mood I call in my language: the 'pre-work state'. This is the state that you must bring to the theatre... The first and indispensable condition for achieving the pre-work state is summed up in the motto: 'Love art in yourself and not yourself in art.' In consequence, above all, make sure that art is well felt in the theatre.

After he dressed with difficulty, KS suddenly collapsed on to his bed. He would not leave his room again. On 7 August he suddenly, half-consciously asked, quoting Lermontov, 'Who's looking after Nemirovich-Danchenko? He is now like a "solitary white sail". ... Is he ill? Does he need money?'

Mariya Lilina to her son Igor. 9 August 1938.

Your poor, poor Papa died on 7 August at 3:45 p.m. and was buried without cremation at 5 p.m. on 9 August in the Novodevichy cemetery, beside Simov and Chekhov. That trio began the theatre and now all three have ended their service to art. It is pleasing and comforting to me that they are together. Even now the grave is piled high with wreaths, real and artificial; but the real wreaths have dried up and the artificial ones have scorched in the sun; we shall have to plant some flowers and make a turf mound.

The autopsy revealed that for the past ten years KS had carried on despite an enlarged heart, emphysema and aneurisms. The report read: 'Acute arteriosclerotic dysfunction in all arteries, excluding the cerebral arteries which had not succumbed to the degenerative process.'

Three weeks after his death the Russian edition of An Actor Works on Himself *appeared, seen through the press by Grigory Kristi, but in a drastically abridged form. The author's preface announced that successive volumes would discuss the creation of a role, characterization and exercises. The war would interrupt attempts to marshal KS's notes into a coherent text.*

On 29 August, for the first time an Art Theatre season opened without his participation

Notes

1 KS did not work on *Bulychyov*, but only discussed the leading role with Leonidov and the sets with Konstantin Fyodorovich Yuon.
2 Nina Vasilievna Tikhomirova (1898-1976) acted at the MAAT 1924-64. She had played Olga with KS in *Three Sisters* on the 30th anniversary of MAAT, when he had had his heart attack.
3 The former Korsh Theatre, opened in 1882, was closed in 1932.
4 *Flight* never opened, and *The Ward* was prepared for club stages.
5 Mikhail Mikhailovich Yanshin (1902-76), acted at the Second Studio and the MAAT from 1922 until his death. He first made his name as Lariosik in *The Days of the Turbins*.
6 Nikolay Pavlovich Ulyanov (1875-1949) had worked as a designer with the Studio on Povarsky, where his immense wigs and wide panniers from *Schluck and Jau* had been much admired; he was brought back for *Yevgeny Onegin, Days of the Turbins*,

Molière and *Carmen*. Rehearsals for *Molière* were regularly put off, the first dress took place on 5 February 1936, Ulyanov was forbidden to work on the show so it was designed by Vilyams.

7 The theatre was forbidden to work on the play without reasons being explained. Stalin did not like either the first or second version.

8 Trenyov never wrote the play.

9 Anatoly Petrovich Ktorov (1898-1980) was at the MAAT 1933-80; in Hamsun's play he was cast as Blumenschön, a role created by Leonidov.

10 Leonid Alekseevich Polovinkin (1894-1949), modernist composer; his opera, based on John Millington Synge's play, and known in Russian as *An Irish Hero*, had won a competition held by the Bolshoy Theatre.

11 *Talents and Admirers* was shown at a closed dress rehearsal on 14 June, the official premiere was held over to the next season. It ultimately played 413 performances, despite the negative notices.

12 Aleksandr Vladimirovich Bogdanovich (1874-1950), singer and teacher.

13 A Tatar fortress in the Crimea, a remnant of Karaite culture.

14 The First International Theatre Festival for foreign art workers 1-10 June 1933.

15 ND blamed the ban on Afinogenov himself for staging the play in Kharkov too quickly where it made a negative political impression. It led to his voluntarily stopping rehearsals on Bulgakov's *Flight*.

16 The character actor Mikhail Mikhailovich Tarkhanov (1877-1948), brother of Ivan Moskin, joined the MAT in 1922 and later ran its Fourth Studio. Viktor Yakovlevich Stanitsyn (Geze, 1897-1976), who began in the Second Studio, acted at the MAAT from 1924; he was one of the directors of *The Pickwick Club*.

17 Cast as Molière, Stanitsyn told Bulgakov it was hard to speak many of his lines and wondered if the play was about him personally. Stanitsyn was getting a divorce while having an affair with Tarasova and Molière's situation reminded him of his own.

18 *Katerina Izmailova* (*Lady Macbeth of Mtsensk District*), staged at the Musical Theatre on 24 January 1934. Acclaimed at first, it was later attacked by an anonymous editorial in *Pravda* as symptomatic of formalist art and proscribed.

19 Vladimir Alekseev believed that *Le Roi s'amuse* by Victor Hugo should be retitled *Monterone's Curse*.

20 The Duke was eventually played by Anatoly Ivanovich Orfenov (1908-87).

21 Tamantsova had reported that Meyerhold's *Lady of the Camellias* was to be ultra-realistic.

22 Those chapters in the second part of *An Actor Works on Himself*.

23 The 500th performance of *Yevgeny Onegin*.

24 Georg Wilhelm Pabst (1883-1967), Austrian film director, one of the major figures of the German expressionist cinema; his best work includes *The Threepenny Opera*, *Pandora's Box* and *Kamaradschaft*.

25 A line of Chatsky's in Griboedov's verse comedy *Woe from Wit* (Act 3, sc. 3).

26 Moissi, an Albanian citizen, had been born in Trieste when it was an Austrian protectorate; after World War I it was annexed to Italy; on the ascent of the Fascists to power he lived in Germany.

27 Moisey Vulfovich Halevy (1895-1974) worked at the Tel Aviv studio Ohel (The Tent) on principles he had imbibed from Habima (which he had left seven years before because of artistic differences) first from Vakhtangov, then from KS's lectures.

28 ND replied that the whole theatre had come to life at the mention of *The Seagull*, and that KS's reaction had thrown cold water on their enthusiasm.

29 Pavel Ivanovich Novitsky (1888-1971), theatre critic.

30 This referred to the creation of an Opera-Drama Studio, one of whose instructors was Novitsky's daughter and later Novitsky himself.

31 Craig spent some time in Moscow in 1935, but staged nothing. He met with ND, but KS kept out of his way.

32 KS saw a dress rehearsal on 14 November. It opened on 1 December and proved so popular that it ran for 643 performances.

33 Pavel Vladimirovich Vilyams (1902-47), a graduate of VKhUTEMAS in 1923, student of Kandinsky. Began active work in theatre in 1930 and designed seven productions for the MAAT, including the caricatural backdrops for *Chicago* and *Pickwick* before being assigned to *Molière*.

34 Vladimir Vasilievich Gribkov (1902-60) joined the MAT in 1926. Pavel Vladimirovich Massalsky (1904-79), at the MAAT from 1924, his first assignment the sound of a nightingale in *Tsar Fyodor*; he played Mr Jingle.

35 ND's production of *Thunderstorm* opened on 2 December 1934.

36 KS saw *Talents* on 20 October 1934.

37 After her brother's death, she was made curator of the Chekhov Home-Museum in Yalta.

38 Yelena Sergeevna Zhivotova (1892-1972), assistant to the administrator of the MAAT 1935-36.

39 Mikhail Panteleimonovich Bolduman (1898-1983) and Nikolay Nikolaevich Sosnin (Soloviev, 1894-1962) both joined the MAAT in 1933. Bolduman usually played Soviet heroes, Sosnin was outstanding in Chekhov plays.

40 Norris Houghton (1909-2001), American scene-designer, had visited Moscow 1934-35 on a Guggenheim Fellowship to study directing; the result was his book *Moscow Rehearsals*.

41 Yale University Press turned it down because they believed it was too long and of limited interest. Theatre Arts Books agreed to take it, if it were thoroughly re-edited and abridged. Its editor Edith Isaacs took a hand in that process.

42 The second part of *The Actor Works on Himself*.

43 Originally KS had given the figures 'speaking' names, e.g., the teacher Tvortsov (Creativeson), the student Chuvtsov (Feelingson).

44 Mei Lanfang (1894-1961), Chinese star of Beijing Opera, expert in *tan* or female roles, had visited Moscow in 1932.

45 Théodule Ribot (1839-1916), French psychologist. His *Psychologie des sentiments* (1896) was translated into Russian by F. Pavlenko in 1898.

46 Eva Le Gallienne (1899-1991), American actress-manager, founder of the Civic Repertory Theatre. She and KS met on 4 January 1933.

47 John Gielgud (1904-2000), foremost English actor, especially in Shakespearean roles. His comments appeared in the July 1937 issue of *Theatre Arts Monthly*.

48 The MAAT went to Paris for the Universal Exposition in August 1937 with three productions, all directed by ND, Gorky's *Enemies*, *Lyubov Yarovaya* and *Anna Karenina*.

49 KS's daughter and grand-daughter had remained in Paris, where Roman Falk practiced as a painter. The worsening political situation in Europe brought them back to Moscow in 1936. After the war, they returned to Paris to live out the rest of their lives.

50 In the first collected edition of KS's work, at a time when Stalin's reputation was under a cloud, this letter was published as addressed to Mikhail Ivanovich Kalinin (1875-1946), the venerable Party figure-head.

51 Sergey Mitrofanovich Zarudny (1865-1940), lawyer; family friend.

52 The Kachalov family was congratulating him on his nameday (3 June).

53 Galina Leonardovna Bunotyan (Besyadovskaya), a school friend of Kira's.

54 Antonina Vasilievna Nezhdanova (1873-1950), soprano at the Bolshoy Theatre and teacher. Lyubov Yakovlevna Shor-Plotnikova (1873-1960), singer.

55 Lidiya Pavlovna Novitskaya, drama teacher. Varvara Pavlovna Orlova, singing teacher at the Opera-Dramatic Studio.

BIBLIOGRAPHY

A listing of the literature on Stanislavsky could fill several fat volumes. I have listed here only some of the works, chiefly books, I believe to be the most useful, particularly from the biographical and historical angle. I have also deliberately omitted handbooks and manuals about acting according to the Stanislavsky system.

Stanislavsky's Works

Stanislavsky, K. S. *Sobranie sochineny v devyati tomakh,* ed. O. N. Efremov, V. Ya. Vilenkin and A. M. Smeliansky. 9 vols. in 10. Moscow: Iskusstvo, 1988-99.

Vilenkin, V. Ya. and I. N. Solovyova, eds. *Rezhissyorskie eksemplyary K. S. Stanislavskogo.* 6 vols. Moscow: Iskusstvo, 1980-94. [*Hors-série: 'Dyadya Vanya',* ed. I. N. Solovyova (Moscow: Atheneum-Feniks, 1994).]

English Translations and Adaptations of Stanislavsky's Works

An Actor Prepares. Adapted by Elizabeth Reynolds Hapgood. New York: Theatre Arts Books, 1936.

An Actor's Work. A Student's Diary, trans. Jean Benedetti. London: Routledge, 2008.

An Actor's Work on a Role, trans. and ed. Jean Benedetti. London: Routledge, 2010.

Building a Character. Adapted by Elizabeth Reynolds Hapgood. New York: Theatre Arts Books, 1949.

Creating a Role. Adapted by Elizabeth Reynolds Hapgood. New York: Theatre Arts Books, 1961.

My Life in Art, trans. J. J. Robbins. Boston, US: Little, Brown, 1924.

My Life in Art, trans. [from the Russian version] by G. G. Ivanov-Mumjiev. Moscow: Foreign Languages Publishing House, n.d.

My Life in Art, trans. [from the Russian version] by Jean Benedetti. London: Routledge, 2008.

Selected Works, ed. Oksana Korneva. Moscow: Raduga Press, 1984.

Stanislavsky on the Art of the Stage, trans. and ed. David Magarshack. London: Faber, 1950.

Stanislavsky Produces Othello, trans. Helen Nowak. London: Geoffrey Bles, 1948.

Stanislavsky's Legacy: A Collection of Comments on a Variety of Aspects of an Actor's Art and Life. Rev. ed., ed. and trans. Elizabeth Reynolds Hapgood. New York: Theatre Arts Books, 1968.

Russian works on Stanislavsky

Balashev, S. S. *Alekseevy.* Moscow: Oktopus, 2008.

Efros, N. *K. S. Stanislavsky (opyt kharakteristiki).* Petersburg: Soltnse Rossii, 1918.

Gorchakov, N. *Rezhissyorskie uroki K. S. Stanislavskogo. Besedy I zapisi repetitsii*. 2nd ed., rev. and enlarged. Moscow: Iskusstvo, 1951. [English trans. Miriam Goldina *Stanislavski Directs* (New York: Grosset & Dunlap, 1962).]

Gurevich, L. Ya., ed. *O Stanislavskom. Sbornik vospominaniya*. Moscow: Vserossiiskoe Teatralnoe Obshchestvo, 1948.

Kalashnikov, Yu. S. *Estetichesky ideal K. S. Stanislavskogo*. Moscow: Nauka, 1965.

Kommissarzhevsky, F. *Tvorchestvo aktyora i teoriya Stanislavskogo*. Petrograd: Svobodnoe Iskusstvo, 1916.

Polyakova, Ye. *Stanislavsky*. Moscow: Iskusstvo, 1977. [Eng. trans. Liv Tudge (Moscow: Progress Publishers, 1983).]

Polyakova, Ye. *Stanislavsky – aktyor*. Moscow: Iskusstvo, 1972.

Radishcheva, O. A. *Stanislavsky i Nemirovich-Danchenko. Teatralnykh otnosheny 1897-1938*. 3 vols. Moscow: Artist. Rezhissyor. Teatr, 1997-99.

Shestakova, N. *Pervy teatr Stanislavskogo*. Moscow: Iskusstvo, 1998.

Sobolevskaya, O. S. *K. S. Stanislavsky rabotaet, beseduet, otdykhaet*. Moscow: Soyuz teatralnykh deyateley RSFSR, 1988.

Solovyova, I. N. and V. V. Shitova. *K. S. Stanislavsky*. Moscow: Iskusstvo, 1985.

Stroeva, M. N. *Rezhissyorskaya iskaniya Stanislavskogo 1898-1917*. Moscow: Nauka, 1973.

Stroeva, M. N. *Rezhissyorskaya iskaniya Stanislavskogo 1917-1938*. Moscow: Nauka, 1977.

Toporkov, V. *K. S. Stanislavsky na repetitsii. Vospominaniya*. Moscow-Leningrad: Iskusstvo, 1949. [English trans. Christine Edwards, *Stanislavsky in Rehearsal: The Final Years* (Theatre Arts Books, 1979); trans. Jean Benedetti, *Stanislavski in Rehearsal* (Methuen, 2001).]

Vinogradskaya, I. *Zhizn i tvorchestvo K. S. Stanislavskogo. Letopis'*. 2nd ed., enlarged and revised. 4 vols. Moscow: Moskovsky Khudozhestvenny Teatr, 2003.

Vinogradskaya, I., ed. *Stanislavsky repetiruet. Zapisi i stenogrammy repetitsiy*. 2nd ed. Moscow: Moskovsky Khudozhestvenny Teatr, 2000.

Individual Productions

Balukhaty, S. D., ed. *Chaika v postanovke Moskovskogo Khudozhestvennogo Teatra*. Leningrad: Iskusstvo, 1938. [English trans. as '*The Seagull*' *Produced by Stanislavsky*, ed. David Magarshack. London: Dobson, 1952.]

Chushkin, N. N. *Gamlet-Kachalov. Na stsenicheskoy istorii* Gamleta Shekspira. Moscow: Iskusstvo, 1986.

Efros, N. '*Na dne*', *piesa Maksima Gorkogo v postanovke Moskovskogo Khudozhestvennogo Teatra*. Moscow: Gos. Izd., 1923.

Efros, N. Vishnyovy sad, *piesa A. P. Chekhova v postanovke Moskovskogo Khudozhestvennogo Teatra*. Petersburg: Soltntse Rossii, 1918.

Nekrasov, V. M. '*Bezumny den ili Zhenitba Figaro*' *na stsene MKhAT*. Moscow: VTO, 1984.

Nemirovich-Danchenko, V. I. Gore ot uma *v postanovke Moskovskogo Khudozhestvennogo Teatra*. Moscow: Gos. Izd., 1923.

Roshin, A. Tri sestry *na stsene MKhAT*. Leningrad: VTO, 1946.

Rostotsky, V. and N. Chushkin. Tsar Fyodor Ioannovich *na stsene MKhAT*. Moscow-Leningrad: VTO, 1940.

Rumyantsev, P. *Rabota Stanislavskogo nad opery 'Rigoletto'*. Moscow: Iskusstvo, 1955. [Eng. trans. E. R. Hapgood, *Stanislavsky on Opera* (New York: Theatre Arts Books, 1975).]

Senelick, Laurence. *Gordon Craig's Moscow* Hamlet. *A Reconstruction*. Westport, Conn., US: Greenwood, 1982.

Works on Stanislavsky in Other Languages.

Amiard-Chevrel, Claudine. 'Stanislavski et l'occident. En marge de "L'Oiseau bleu" et de "Hamlet". La correspondence de Stanislavski- Suleržitski,' *Revue de l'histoire du théâtre* (jan.-mars 1978).

Benedetti, Jean Norman. *Stanislavski. A Biography*. London: Methuen, 1988.

Boleslavski, Richard. 'Stanislavsky: The Man and his Methods', *Theatre Magazine* 34 (Apr. 1923).

Carnicke, Sharon M. *Stanislavsky in Focus*. 2nd ed. London: Routledge, 2009.

Gourfinkel, Nina. *Constantine Stanislavski*. Paris: L'Arche, 1955.

Gourfinkel, Nina. 'Repenser Stanislavski', *Revue d'histoire du theatre* (avr.-juin 1971/72).

Magarshack, David. *Stanislavski. A Life*. New York: Chanticleer, 1950.

Merlin, Bella. *Konstantin Stanislavsky*. London: Routledge, 2003.

Mollico, Fabio, ed. *Il teatro possibile. Stanislavskij e il Primo Studio del Teatro d'arte di Mosca*. Florence: La Casa Usher, 1989.

Pitches, Jonathan. *Science and the Stanislavsky Tradition of Acting*. London: Routledge, 2009.

Senelick, Laurence. 'Seduced and Abandoned. When Hollywood Wooed the Moscow Art Theatre', *Film History* 10, 4 (1998).

Senelick, Laurence. 'Stanislavsky's Second Thoughts on *The Seagull*', *New Theatre Quarterly* 20, 2 (May 2004).

Smeliansky, Anatoly. *Mikhail Bulgakov v Khudozhestvennom teatre*. Moscow: Iskusstvo, 1989. [Eng. trans. Arch Tait as *Is Comrade Bulgakov Dead? Mikhail Bulgakov at the Moscow Art Theatre*. (London: Routledge, 1993).]

Smeliansky, Anatoly. 'Stanislavsky and the Modern Russian Theatre', *Theater Three* 10/11 (1992).

Tulane Drama Review 9, nos. 1 and 2 (Fall and Winter 1964). Stanislavsky issues. [Repub. as *Stanislavsky and America*, ed. Erika Munk.(Greenwich, Conn., US: Fawcett, 1967).]

Whyman, Rose. *The Stanislavsky System of Acting: Legacy and Influence in Modern Performance*. Cambridge, UK: Cambridge University Press, 2008.

World Theatre 8, no. 1 (Spring 1959). The actor and Stanislavski issue.

World Theatre 12, no.2 (1963). Stanislavski issue.

Russian Works on the Moscow Art Theatre

Bertonson, Sergey. *Vokrug isskustva*. Hollywood: The author, 1957.

Bokshanskaya, Olga. *Pisma O. S. Bokshanskoy Vl. I. Nemirovichu-Danchenko 1922-42*. 2 vols. Moscow: Izd. Moskovsky Khudozhestvenny Teatr, 2005.

Efros, N. *Moskovsky Khudozhestvenny Teatr 1898-1926*. Moscow and Petersburg: Gos. Izd., 1924.

Khudozhestvenny teatr. Tvorcheskie ponedelniki i drugie dokumenty 1916-1919. Moscow: Izd. Moskovsky Khudozhestvenny Teatr, 2006.

Leonidov, L. D. *Rampa i zhizn. Vospominaniya i vstrechi*. Paris: Russkoe Teatralnoe Izd. Za-granitsy, 1955.

Markov, P. A. *V Khudozhestvennom teatre. Kniga zavlita*. Moscow: Vserossiiskoe Teatralnoe Obshchestvo, 1976.

Moskovsky Khudozhestvenny Teatr: istorichesky ocherk zhizni i deyatelnosti. 2 vols. Moscow: Rampa i zhizn, 1913.

Moskovsky Khudozhestvenny Teatr v russkoy teatralnoy kritike 1898-1943. Ed. Yu. M. Vinogradskaya, O. A. Radishcheva and E. A. Shingareva. 4 vols. Moscow: 'Aktyor. Rezhissyor. Teatr', 2005-10.

Nemirovich-Danchenko, V. I. *Tvorcheskie nasledie. Pisma. Iz proshlogo.* 4 vols. Moscow: Moskovsky Khudozhestvenny Teatr, 2003. [Eng. trans. of *Iz proshlogo* as *My Life in the Russian Theatre*, trans. J. Cournos, London: Geoffrey Bles, 1937.]

Nemirovich-Danchenko, V. I. *Rozhdenie teatra. Vospominaniya, stati, zametki, pisma.* Moscow: Pravda, 1989.

Nemirovich-Danchenko, V. I. *Tvorchestvo aktyora. Khrestomatiya,* ed. V. Ya. Vilenkin. Moscow: Iskusstvo, 1973.

Orlov, Yu. M. *Moskovsky Khudozhestvenny Teatr 1890-1917gg. Tvorchestvo, organizatsiya, ekonomika.* Moscow: GITIS, 2011.

Polkanova, Mariya, ed. *I vnov o Khudozhestvennom. MKhAT v vospominaniyakh i zapisuakh 1901-1920.* Moscow: Avantitul, 2004.

Rogachesky, M. L. and G. P. Mironova, eds. *MKhT v sovetskuyu epokhu. Materialy I dokumenty.* 2nd ed. Enlarged. Moscow: Iskusstvo, 1974.

Shverubovich, V. *O starom Khudozhestvennom teatre.* Moscow: Iskusstvo, 1990.

Smelyansky, Anatoly, ed. *Moskovsky Khudozhestvenny Teatr. 100 Let.* 2 vols. Moscow: Moskovsky Khudozhestvenny Teatr, 1998.

Sobolyov, Yury. *V. I. Nemirovich-Danchenko.* Petersburg: Solntse Rossii, 1918.

Solovyova, Inna. *Khudozhestvenny Teatr. Zhizn i priklyuchenniya idei.* Moscow: Izd. Moskovsky Khudozhestvenny Teatr, 2007.

Yezhegodniki Moskovskogo Khudozhestvennogo teatra. 1943-52. Moscow: Iskusstvo, 1945-56.

Works in Other Languages on the Moscow Art Theatre

Amiard-Chevrel, Claudine. *Le Théâtre artistique de Moscou (1898-1917).* Paris: CNRS, 1979.

Autant-Mathieu, Marie-Christine, ed. *Le Théâtre d'art de Moscou: Ramifications, voyages.* Paris: CNRS, 2005.

Benedetti, Jean Norman, ed. and trans. *The Moscow Art Theatre Letters.* London: Routledge, 1991.

Clark, Barrett H. 'The Moscow Art Theatre in Berlin', *Drama* (Jan. 1923).

Clowes, Edith W. 'Social Discourse in the Moscow Art Theater', in *Between Tsar and People: Educated Society and the Quest for Public Identity in Late Imperial Russia,* ed. E. W. Clowes, S. D. Kassow and J. L. West. Princeton, N.J., US: Princeton University Press, 1991.

Fovitsky, A. L. *The Moscow Art Theatre and its Distinguishing Characteristics.* New York: A. Chernoff, 1923.

Sayler, Oliver M. 'Dictatorship for the Moscow Art Theatre', *Theatre Arts Monthly* (Feb. 1926).

Sayler, Oliver M. *Inside the Moscow Art Theatre.* New York: Brentano's, 1925.

Worrall, Nick. *The Moscow Art Theatre.* London: Routledge, 1998.

INDEX

Page numbers in bold-face indicate a letter to the individual.